# The World Wide Web of Work

WORK AROUND THE WORLD: STUDIES IN GLOBAL LABOUR HISTORY

*Series Editors*
KARIN HOFMEESTER (IISH and University of Antwerp)
and ULBE BOSMA (IISH and Vrije Universiteit Amsterdam)

*Executive Editor*
AAD BLOK (IISH)

Over the past six hundred years an increasingly connected and competitive global economy has had tremendous consequences for how people have made a living. It has brought unprecedented opportunities for many, but also massive dispossession of livelihoods and natural habitats to this very day. People have moved towards agricultural frontiers and industrial centres in growing numbers and over increasing distances for work. Slavery and other coerced labour regimes have shaped persistent social inequalities, racial discrimination and exclusion. Confronted with exploitation, disenfranchisement, gender inequalities, racism and xenophobia, workers have tried to improve their position either individually or collectively.

Drawing on core research at the International Institute of Social History in Amsterdam, this series explores the connectivity between changes in work and shifting labour relations, evolving social and economic inequalities that result from or are connected to these changes, and individual as well as collective responses to these inequalities. Situating these historical dynamics within the context of an unfolding global economy that externalizes social and environmental costs, the series aims for global comparisons across time, space and scale to bring out how evolving social inequalities are connected to the development of work and labour relations, and how these histories may help to understand the causes of inequalities in the present. By combining broad diachronic, transnational and transcontinental comparisons, synthetic overviews and exemplary case studies, the series offers a conversant global perspective on how work and the social and economic relations and contexts in which it is performed, has shaped and defined our world.

*Series advisers*
Carlos Illades Aguiar, Universidad Autónoma Metropolitana, Mexico City, Mexico
Görkem Akgöz, Humboldt Universität, Berlin, Germany
Asef Bayat, University of Illinois at Urbana Champaign, Chicago, USA
Akua Opokua Britwum, University of Cape Coast, Ghana
Paulo Drinot, UCL, UK
Omar Gueye, Université Cheikh Anta Diop de Dakar (UCAD), Dakar, Senegal
Peyman Jafari, Princeton University and IISH, Amsterdam, The Netherlands
Marcel van der Linden, IISH, Amsterdam, The Netherlands
Leo Lucassen, IISH, Amsterdam and Leiden University, The Netherlands
Christine Moll-Murata, Ruhr-Universität Bochum, Germany
Samita Sen, University of Cambridge, Cambridge, UK
Paulo Cruz Terra, Universidade Federal Fluminense, Niterói, Rio de Janeiro, Brazil

# The World Wide Web of Work
*A history in the making*

Marcel van der Linden

First published in 2023 by
UCL Press
University College London
Gower Street
London WC1E 6BT

Available to download free: www.uclpress.co.uk

Text © Marcel van der Linden, 2023
Images © Copyright holders named in captions, 2023

The author has asserted his rights under the Copyright, Designs and Patents Act 1988 to be identified as the author of this work.

A CIP catalogue record for this book is available from The British Library.

Any third-party material in this book is not covered by the book's Creative Commons licence. Details of the copyright ownership and permitted use of third-party material is given in the image (or extract) credit lines. If you would like to reuse any third-party material not covered by the book's Creative Commons licence, you will need to obtain permission directly from the copyright owner.

This book is published under a Creative Commons Attribution-Non-Commercial 4.0 International licence (CC BY-NC 4.0), https://creativecommons.org/licenses/by-nc/4.0/. This licence allows you to share and adapt the work for non-commercial use providing attribution is made to the author and publisher (but not in any way that suggests that they endorse you or your use of the work) and any changes are indicated. Attribution should include the following information:

Van der Linden, M. 2023. *The World Wide Web of Work: A history in the making*. London: UCL Press. https://doi.org/10.14324/111.9781800084551

Further details about Creative Commons licences are available at
https://creativecommons.org/licenses/

ISBN: 978-1-80008-457-5 (Hbk)
ISBN: 978-1-80008-456-8 (Pbk)
ISBN: 978-1-80008-455-1 (PDF)
ISBN: 978-1-80008-458-2 (ePub)
DOI: https://doi.org/10.14324/111.9781800084551

*I dedicate this book to Alice Mul. Although she sometimes feels I devote too much time to scholarship, I could not have written these chapters without her.*

# Contents

*List of figures*   ix
*List of tables*   xii
*Provenance of the texts*   xiv
*Foreword, by Sven Beckert*   xvii
*Acknowledgements*   xxi

Introduction   1

**Part I: Challenges**   19

1. Tree bark mysteries: or the invisible workers   21
2. Caribbean radicals, a new Italian saint, and a feminist challenge   30
3. Six insights from Gujarat   43

**Part II: Concepts**   55

4. Capitalism   57
5. Workers   70
6. Coerced labour   84
7. Household strategies   111
8. Labour markets   125

**Part III: Connections**   149

9. Global cash-crop transfers, ecology, and labour   151
10. Slavery and convict labour: training-grounds for modern labour management   174

11. The abolition of the slave trade and slavery: intended and
    unintended consequences ... 189

12. The ILO, 1919–2019: an appraisal ... 217

13. How some workers benefit from the exploitation
    of other workers ... 243

**Part IV: Conflicts** ... 257

14. Walking fish: how conservative behaviour generates
    and processes radical change ... 259

15. Mass exits: who, why, how? ... 269

16. Workers and revolutions: a historical paradox ... 283

17. 1968: the enigma of simultaneity ... 306

Epilogue: global labour history and the crisis of workers'
movements ... 315

*References* ... 328
*Index* ... 380

# List of figures

| | | |
|---|---|---|
| 1.1 | The gathering and drying of *Cinchona* bark in a Peruvian forest. Wellcome Collection. https://wellcomecollection.org/works/werf33s3. | 22 |
| 1.2 | Gathering *Cinchona* bark. Date unknown. Wellcome Collection. https://wellcomecollection.org/works/m6bwbxes. | 27 |
| 2.1 | An image of San Precario carried at a demonstration in Milan on Mayday, 2011. © Samuele Ghilardi. | 32 |
| 5.1 | 'The Destruction of Roehampton Estate in the Parish of St. James's in January 1832'. Wikimedia Commons. https://bit.ly/3ymJstb. | 81 |
| 6.1 | Forms of *entry* into a coerced labour relationship. Source: Author. | 89 |
| 6.2 | 'Gang of captives met at Mbame's on their way to Tette'. Wellcome Collection. https://wellcomecollection.org/works/u3whmqgk/items. | 91 |
| 6.3 | Koreans forced to labour at a mine in Hokkaido, Japan, during World War II. Published courtesy of the National Memorial Museum of Forced Mobilization under Japanese Occupation, under the Korea Open Government License Type 4 (equivalent to CC BY-NC-ND). | 93 |
| 6.4 | Forms of labour *extraction*. Source: Author. | 97 |
| 6.5 | Forms of labour relationship termination (*exit*). Source: Author. | 102 |
| 8.1 | Italian immigrants posing in the central courtyard of the Hospedaria dos Immigrantes, São Paolo, c. 1890. Photographer: Guilherme Gaensly (1843–1928). https://bit.ly/3yn4qrE. | 131 |
| 8.2 | Estimated number of enslaved people who made the Atlantic crossing between 1501 and 1875. Source: http://www.slavevoyages.org/assessment/estimates. | 137 |
| 8.3 | Haddington Hiring Fair, early-1900s. Published courtesy of the John Gray Centre Library, Museum & Archive. | 140 |

| | | |
|---|---|---|
| 9.1 | Pepper harvest in Coilum, Southern India. © Archives Charmet / Bridgeman Images. | 153 |
| 9.2 | 'Triangulation' of agrarian production. Source: Author. | 156 |
| 9.3 | Workers in front of a greenhouse at the Botanical Garden in Bogor (Buitenzorg). https://bit.ly/3CDLEPo. | 159 |
| 9.4 | 'Planting the sugar-cane', a depiction of a large-scale sugarcane plantation in Haiti, c. 1820. British Library, public domain, https://www.bl.uk/collection-items/cutting-the-sugar-cane-antigua. | 164 |
| 10.1 | 'Prospect of the European Factorys, at Xavier or Sabee'. Engraving by Nathaniel Parr in *A New and General Collection of Voyages* by Thomas Astley. London, 1746, vol. 3, p. 64. | 176 |
| 10.2 | 'Nègres au Travail'. Men and women in a field gang at work, guarded by overseers. Source: Alcide Dessalines d'Orbigny, *Voyage pittoresque dans les deux Amériques* (Paris, 1836), facing p. 22, fig. 4. http://www.slaveryimages.org/s/slaveryimages/item/1148. | 179 |
| 11.1 | Sailor removing the manacle from a newly freed slave. Published courtesy of the National Museum of the Royal Navy, Portsmouth, UK. | 199 |
| 11.2 | 'Importing Chinese labourers to work in the gold mines of South Africa in 1904'. © Archives Charmet/Bridgeman Images. | 207 |
| 11.3 | 'The chain gang, Thomasville, Georgia'. Black convicts forced to work, c. 1884–91. Photograph by Joseph John Kirkbride. Library of Congress, LC-USZ6-1848. https://www.loc.gov/item/00652806/. | 208 |
| 12.1 | French socialist reformer Albert Thomas (1878–1932), 1910. https://commons.wikimedia.org/wiki/File:Albert_Thomas_LCCN2014700210.tif. | 220 |
| 14.1 | Postcard commemorating the discovery of the coelacanth by Marjorie Courtenay-Latimer in December 1938. South African Institute for Aquatic Biology, public domain, https://bit.ly/3ryaQR9. | 260 |
| 14.2 | 'Duck-billed platypus', engraving, 1809. George Shaw (1751–1813). New York Public Library, public domain, https://on.nypl.org/3EkUrqI. | 265 |
| 15.1 | Brass and steel instrument used for tattooing the initial 'D' for 'deserter' on the face or armpit, c. 1850. © National Army Museum/Bridgeman Images. | 277 |

| | | |
|---|---|---|
| 15.2 | Maroon village by the Cottica river near Moengo, Suriname. Photograph: C. R. Singh. Courtesy of Allard Pierson, Universiteit van Amsterdam (ref. VAR0266). | 279 |
| 16.1 | Late handcrafted Jingdezhen porcelain production. Photographer: Thomas M. Mueller © Shirley Maloney Mueller/Thomas M. Mueller, with permission. | 286 |
| 16.2 | The 'transition dip'. Source: Przeworski, *Capitalism and Social Democracy*, p. 177. | 300 |
| 17.1 | M8 Greyhounds (armoured vehicles) at the Zócalo (main square) of Mexico City, 28 August 1968. Photographer: Cel·lí. Public domain, https://bit.ly/3rDT8vz. | 307 |

# List of tables

| | | |
|---|---|---|
| 8.1 | Four types of labour-power exchange (examples). Source: Author. | 129 |
| 9.1 | The Columbian and Magellan exchanges of crop species. Sources: Wouter van der Weijden, Rob Leewis and Pieter Bol, *Biological Globalisation: Bio-Invasions and Their Impacts on Nature, the Economy and Public Health* (Utrecht: KNNV Publishing, 2007), p. 26; Stanley B. Alpern, 'The European Introduction of Crops into West Africa in Precolonial Times', *History in Africa*, 19 (1992), pp. 13–43, at 24–31. | 154 |
| 9.2 | Types of (sub)tropical cash crops. Source: Author. | 157 |
| 9.3 | Some botanical gardens that played a role in long-distance plant transfer, sixteenth–nineteenth centuries. Source: Author. | 160 |
| 9.4 | Development of agricultural productivity on a world scale. Source: www.fao.org/faostat/. | 169 |
| 11.1 | Slave exports from Africa, 1400–1900. Sources: for 1400–1900: Nunn, 'Long-term effects', Table II; for 1800–1900: Lovejoy, *Transformations in Slavery*, Table 7.1. | 195 |
| 11.2 | Major colonies importing Indian indentured labour, 1834–1921. Source: Lal, *Girmitiyas*. | 205 |
| 12.1 | Adoption of ILO Conventions by decade, 1919–2019. Source: ILO normlex. | 235 |
| 17.1 | Average per capita gross national product in different world regions (in international dollars, 1990) for a total of 56 countries, 1950–73. Source: Maddison, *Monitoring the World Economy*, pp. 23–4. | 308 |
| 17.2 | Average participation of relevant age groups in primary, secondary, and tertiary education, 1950–70. Source: Meyer et al., 'World Educational Revolution', p. 244. | 309 |

| | | |
|---|---|---|
| 17.3 | Formal independence of colonies, 1946–70. Source: Abernethy, *Dynamics of Global Dominance*, pp. 140–1. | 310 |
| 18.1 | Average parliamentary electoral results of Social Democratic and Labour Parties, 1920–2019. Source: Author. | 318 |

# Provenance of the texts

Chapter 1 was originally published as 'Geheimgeschichten der Baumrinde: Ein Plädoyer gegen die Verdrängung von Arbeitsprozessen aus der Geschichte'. In *Solidargemeinschaft und Erinnerungskultur im 20. Jahrhundert. Beiträge zu Gewerkschaften, Nationalsozialismus und Geschichtspolitik*, edited by Ursula Bitzegeio, Anja Kruke, and Meik Woyke, 119–26. Bonn: J. H. W. Dietz Nachf., 2009.

Chapter 2 was originally published in *NLI Research Study* 125/2017, V. V. Giri National Labour Institute, Noida, India.

Chapter 3 is an adaptation of 'Refuting labour history's occidentalism'. In *Work and Social Change in Asia: Essays in honour of Jan Breman*, edited by Arvind N. Das and Marcel van der Linden, 249–61. New Delhi: Manohar, 2002.

Chapter 4: an earlier version was originally published as 'Final thoughts'. In *Capitalism: The reemergence of a historical concept*, edited by Jürgen Kocka and Marcel van der Linden, 251–66. London: Bloomsbury Academic, 2016. Reproduced by courtesy of Bloomsbury Academic.

Chapter 5 was originally published as 'Who is the working class? Wage earners and other labourers'. In *Workers and Labour in a Globalised Capitalism: Contemporary themes and theoretical issues*, edited by Maurizio Atzeni, 70–84. Houndmills: Palgrave Macmillan, 2014. Reproduced by permission of Palgrave Macmillan.

Chapter 6 is a part of 'Dissecting coerced labor', originally published in *On Coerced Labor: Work and compulsion after chattel slavery*, edited by Marcel van der Linden and Magaly Rodríguez García, 293–322. Leiden and Boston: Brill, 2016. Reproduced by permission of Koninklijke Brill N. V.

Chapter 7 is a revised combination of 'Introduction' and 'Conclusion'. In *Rebellious Families: Household strategies and collective action in the nineteenth and twentieth centuries*, edited by Jan Kok, 1–23 and 230–42.

Oxford and New York: Berghahn, 2002. Reproduced by permission of Berghahn Books.

Chapter 8 was originally published in *In Search of the Global Labour Market*, edited by Ursula Mense-Petermann, Thomas Welskopp and Anna Zarieva, 18–49. Leiden and Boston: Brill, 2022. Reproduced by permission of Koninklijke Brill N. V.

Chapter 9 is a much-abbreviated version of 'Globalization's agricultural roots: Some final considerations'. In *Embedding Agricultural Commodities: Using historical evidence, 1840s–1940s*, edited by Willem van Schendel, 146–89. London: Routledge, 2016. Reproduced by permission of Taylor & Francis Group.

Chapter 10: an earlier version appeared as 'Unfree labour: A training ground for modern labour management'. In *NLI Research Study* 125/2017, V. V. Giri National Labour Institute, Noida, India. An even earlier version was published in *Labor History* 51 (2010): 509–22.

Chapter 11 is a heavily abbreviated version of 'Introduction'. In *Humanitarian Intervention and Changing Labor Relations: The long-term consequences of the abolition of the slave trade*, edited by Marcel van der Linden, 1–54. Leiden and Boston: Brill, 2011. Reproduced by permission of Koninklijke Brill N. V.

Chapter 12 was originally published in *Labor: Studies in working-class history* 16 (2019): 11–41. Copyright 2019, Labor and Working-Class History Association. All rights reserved. Reproduced by permission of Duke University Press.

Chapter 13 appeared originally in *REVLATT: Revista Latinoamericana de Trabajo y Trabajadores* 1 (November 2020–April 2021): 223–39.

Chapter 14 is an adaptation of my valedictory lecture, given at the University of Amsterdam, 27 October 2017. An earlier version was published in the International Social History Association's *Newsletter*, December 2017, 9–14.

Chapter 15 was originally published in *Desertion in the Early Modern World: A comparative history*, edited by Jeannette Kamp and Matthias van Rossum, 31–45. London: Bloomsbury Academic, 2016. Reproduced by permission of Bloomsbury Academic.

Chapter 16 was originally published in *Worlds of Labour Turned Upside Down: Revolutions and labour relations in global historical perspective*, edited by Pepijn Brandon, Peyman Jafari and Stefan Müller, 19–49. Leiden and Boston: Brill, 2020. Reproduced by permission of Koninklijke Brill N. V.

Chapter 17 was originally published as '1968: Das Rätsel der Gleichzeitigkeit'. In *Weltwende 1968? Ein Jahr aus globalgeschichtlicher Perspektive*, edited by David Mayer and Jens Kastner, 23–34. Vienna: Mandelbaum, 2008.

The Epilogue integrates parts of 'Why the global labor movement is in crisis', *Journal of Labor and Society* 24 (2021): 375–400. Reproduced by permission of Koninklijke Brill N. V., Leiden.

# Foreword

In 1935, when German poet and playwright Bertolt Brecht wrote his poem 'Questions from a Worker who Reads', he reminded his audience of all the enormous labour that had gone into making the world we inhabit. He insisted that we remember not just the rulers, architects, bureaucrats, and rich people whose names are attached to the great works, monuments, and events of history, but also the 'hewers of wood and the drawers of water' – the millions of women, men, and children who spent their lives labouring under the direction of others.

This book is entitled *The World Wide Web of Work: A history in the making*, but another possible title for this academic pendant to Brecht would be 'Questions from a Scholar who Reads very Widely'. Probing received wisdom and not shying away from pointing out the limitations of some of the most revered social scientists of the past two centuries, Marcel van der Linden's undogmatic foray into global labour history reminds us that, to understand the history of labour, we need to look not just at cities but also at the countryside; not just at wage work but also at slavery, indentured servitude, and sharecropping; not just at formally commodified labour but also at unpaid subsistence labour. He looks at both men and women, at the Global North and the Global South. His essays are a departure for labour history because of their scope – both vis-à-vis the globe and also how they draw on the insights of multiple academic disciplines – and because of their subtle integration into the recent endeavour of rewriting the history of capitalism. Together, these essays on the global history of labour across the past two centuries offer nothing less than a powerful rethinking of modern history.

The book offers its readers a tapestry of mostly short essays, each one intellectually unique and powerful. Like the details in a tapestry, each essay has its own distinct shape, colour, and flavour, dealing with distinct questions, time periods, and regions of the world. But it is when they are considered as an interwoven whole that the true import of the book emerges: collectively, the essays produce an entirely new logic and coherence. Van der Linden evokes a world of labour that is, at once, familiar and strange, connected and diverse, propelled by large structural changes and by individual actors. Raising new questions and offering new answers, he leaves the reader with a sharp sense that this cosmopolitan and undogmatic inquiry is exactly what is needed to rejuvenate the academic field of labour history and reorient our thinking about global capitalism.

In some ways, the primary rationale for this journey into the history of global labour comes at the end of the volume, when Van der Linden argues that a great cycle in that history has recently ended – the period from about the mid-eighteenth century to the 1980s, when widespread commodified labour (a historical anomaly) emerged, workers organized collectively, mobilized in unions, political parties, and (infrequently) revolutions, and put their stamp on modern capitalism. This cycle ended in a whirlwind of neoliberal ascendancy, financialization, and the reemergence of merchant capital as well as the ideological and material incorporation of workers (in some parts of the world) into this recast capitalism. Van der Linden invites us to look back over its 200-year-long history. Only now, when we have some historical distance from the incredible diversity of patterns, movements, and politics that propelled global labour under this moment of capitalism's development, can we understand this global moment as a whole. One of the striking intuitions of the book is that this moment has clearly ended and that, 40 years out, we can see it with new clarity in the rear-view mirror.

Van der Linden, the world's leading labour historian, rethinks the global working class from the ground up – dealing with the nitty-gritty details of proletarianization, labour market structures, and collective action, as well as the field's biggest questions such as the definition of labour under capitalism and labour's role in revolutions. His working class is not predominantly composed of the skilled, male industrial wage workers of the first and second Industrial Revolutions so familiar from most labour history. Instead, it includes enslaved workers on Barbados, indentured servants on Mauritius, precariously employed Italian wage workers of the early twenty-first century, and women performing reproductive labour.

One of the book's major contributions is its ability to identify key questions we need to ask. How can we think on the broadest possible conceptual canvas about different kinds of coerced labour? What is the relationship between the material integration of workers in the welfare states of the Global North and the hyper-exploitation of workers in the Global South? What was the role of slavery and convict labour in the arrival of modern labour management? How should we think about the political in labour's history, from eighteenth-century abolitionism to the twentieth-century International Labour Organization (ILO)? How can conservative actions produce revolutionary outcomes? Why did social upheaval, often led by students, unfold globally in 1968?

Despite their striking diversity, the essays have a common approach. They emphasize the need to define causal mechanisms instead of building increasingly general theories; and each is framed by a clearly articulated question. They are often self-consciously provisional, tracing the author's thought processes along with the answers he has come to, thus far. But this reflexive approach does not keep van der Linden from making big arguments and challenging some of the holy cows of the social sciences. He reproaches economists and sociologists for their ahistorical understanding of labour markets. He takes philosopher Michel Foucault to task for his insufficient attention to the slave plantation as a source of the 'disciplinary revolution' he identified: '[A] blind spot can remain undetected for a long time', notes van der Linden in a characteristic understatement. Two social scientists whom van der Linden clearly admires and whose work deeply influences many of his questions – Karl Marx and Friedrich Engels – also come in for serious criticism. Their view of working-class formation: wrong. Their view of the source of value under capitalism: wrong. Their view of the non-European world: wrong. Of revolution: wrong. As van der Linden puts empirical historical analysis in conversation with social theory, it becomes possible to see that events often unfolded quite differently than many great theorists conceptualized. Perhaps this is unsurprising, since the world has changed a great deal since the mid-nineteenth century; but, considering the staying power of some of these ideas, it is important to note.

Van der Linden combines an expansive command of history and the ability to traverse space and time (including into prehistory) with a modesty that enables him to acknowledge the limits of what we know, the hurdles we still face in understanding these questions, and the need for new, mass-scale research programmes to help us arrive at firmer answers. The book gains its particular power from his deep sympathy for the concerns of labour, as well as the theories, politics, movements, parties, and revolutions that emerged from the world's working class. Considering all van der Linden has to say about the crisis of contemporary labour, it may surprise some that he ends on an optimistic note for labour, with the hope of a 'second great cycle'. That hope, for him, rests on our ability to come to terms with labour's first great cycle. As van der Linden is the first to say, the new global labour history is still under construction. Like a great architect who sketches a first draft of a new building on a restaurant napkin, van der Linden provides an agenda for a vast (and vastly important) field. Let's get going!

Sven Beckert
Laird Bell Professor of History
Harvard University

# Acknowledgements

The chapters in this collection are the result of many discussions. Over time, countless friends and colleagues have assisted me by offering advice and critique. I am especially grateful to Ravi Ahuja, Kate Alexander, Eric Arnesen, Patrik Aspers, Touraj Atabaki, Marcelo Badaró Mattos, Amiya Kumar Bagchi, Jairus Banaji, Peter-Paul Bänziger, Rossana Barragán, Sven Beckert, Hans de Beer, Rana Behal, Greg Benton, Stefan Berger, Bhaswathi Bhattacharya, the late Sabyasachi Bhattacharya, Andreas Bieler, the late Philip Bonner, Eileen Boris, Ulbe Bosma, Pepijn Brandon, Jan Breman, Sidney Chalhoub, Tamira Combrink, Zak Cope, Fred Cooper, Christoph Dejung, Angelika Ebbinghaus, Andreas Eckert, Babacar Fall, Sara Faris, Leon Fink, Paulo Fontes, Heide Gerstenberger, Rebecca Gumbrell-McCormick, Dorothea Hoehtker, Dirk Hoerder, Karin Hofmeester, Peyman Jafari, Chitra Joshi, Naila Kabeer, Jeannette Kamp, K. P. Kannan, Amarjit Kaur, Joost Kircz, Knut Kjeldstadli, Jürgen Kocka, Andrea Komlosy, Sandrine Kott, Michael Krätke, Thomas Kuczynski, Rina Lis, the late Alf Lüdtke, Jan Lucassen, Jiahong Ma, Daniel Maul, Charles Mayer, David Mayer, Nicole Mayer-Ahuja, Prabhu Mohapatra, David Motadel, Ronaldo Munck, Elise van Nederveen Meerkerk, Silke Neunsinger, Bryan Palmer, Lucas Poy, Emmanuel Reynaud, Magaly Rodríguez García, Matthias van Rossum, Karl Heinz Roth, Joan Sangster, Ratna Saptari, Willem van Schendel, Christoph Scherrer, Jürgen Schmidt, Ben Selwyn, Steve Smith, Hugo Soly, Alessandro Stanziani, Shel Stromquist, Jean Stubbs, Jakob Tanner, Limin Teh, Göran Therborn, Peter Thomas, Reiner Tosstorff, Raquel Varela, Peter Wagner, the late Thomas Welskopp, Theresa Wobbe, Michael Zeuske, Bahru Zewde, Susan Zimmermann, and Erik-Jan Zürcher.

As always, I have benefited greatly from the inspiring intellectual environment at my base camp, the International Institute of Social History in Amsterdam. In addition, the many discussions at the research institute 're: work – IGK Work and Human Life Cycle in Global History' at Humboldt University in Berlin, the Zentrum für interdisziplinäre Forschung at

Bielefeld University, the project 'People, Plants and Work' funded by the Netherlands Organization for Scientific Research, Harvard's Weatherhead Initiative on Global History, and the International Panel on Social Progress have helped me immensely.

Any texts that I did not write in English have been translated from Dutch by Jurriaan Bendien, Chris Gordon, and Lee Mitzman. Jessica Eitelberg translated Chapters 1 and 17 from German. Lee Mitzman provided the linguistic finishing touches to the entire manuscript, in her consistent and meticulous fashion. Any quotations from non-English sources are my own unless otherwise stated in the Notes and References. Aad Blok, Ulbe Bosma, Karin Hofmeester, Leo Lucassen, Jacqueline Rutte, and Marie-José Spreeuwenberg made the Open Access publication of this book possible. And Pat Gordon-Smith at UCL Press helped me enormously with the preparation of the manuscript. I am grateful to all of them.

# Introduction

Global labour history is a field of research that has rapidly gained ground since the early 2000s. While scholars were already venturing there in the 1980s and 1990s, the true breakthrough came at the turn of the new millennium.[1] The new approach has attracted a growing group of adherents on different continents in the Global South and Global North alike. Young scholars, in particular, derive inspiration from the broad perspective offered by this field and its effort to perceive connections between trends everywhere in the world, over the centuries, in matters related to work, workers, and labour relations, incorporating slaves, indentured labourers, and sharecroppers, as well as housewives and domestic servants.

## Growing interest

The increased interest in global approaches in labour history manifests in many ways. A few examples may illustrate this trend.[2] First, more and more journals and monograph series explicitly highlight 'global labour history'. The *International Review of Social History* and *International Labor and Working Class History* were the first journals to venture into this arena. Others soon followed, as exemplified in 2003, when the authoritative New York-based journal *Labor History* (published since 1960) became entangled in a dispute with the publisher. Leon Fink, then editor, resigned together with over 40 people associated with the journal and started a new journal, which from the outset was affiliated with the United States' (US) Labor and Working-Class History Association.[3] The old journal continued under its new editor, Craig Phelan. Remarkably, both journals immediately broadened their scope and no longer focused exclusively on US labour history. Fink's periodical was renamed *Labor: Studies in Working-Class History of the Americas*, indicating that Canada and Latin America would be addressed as well. A few years later, the subtitle was shortened to *Studies in Working-Class History*, so that, henceforth, the entire world might be covered. From the start, Phelan's *Labor History* aimed for a 'greater international scope', with '[c]utting edge historical articles on labor in Europe, Africa, Asia and Latin America'.[4] Several monograph series now focus on global labour history as well: *Studies in Global Social History* (Leiden: Brill, since 2008); *Work in Global and Historical Perspective* (Berlin: Walter de Gruyter, since 2016); and the present series *Work Around the World*, published by UCL Press.

At the same time, transnational and transcontinental networks of labour historians expanded, promoting the development and rise of comparative and global studies. In 2013, in Amsterdam, the European Labour History Network was founded and has organized biannual conferences (2015 in Turin, 2017 in Paris, 2019 in Amsterdam, and Vienna in 2021). In 2015, in Barcelona, the Global Labour History Network came about and, to date, has organized conferences in India (Noida, 2017), Sweden (Stockholm, 2020), and Senegal (Saint-Louis, 2022). In 2017, in La Paz, the REDLATT network (Red Latinoamericana y del Caribe de Trabajo y Trabajador@s) was founded, organizing a second conference in 2019 and launching its own journal, *REVLATT* (*Revista Latinoamericana de Trabajo y Trabajadores*). In addition, the International Association Strikes and Social Conflicts was founded in 2011 and also organizes conferences (Lisbon, 2011; Dijon, 2013; Barcelona, 2015; São Paulo, 2018; and Rotterdam, 2022) and publishes a journal, *Workers of the World*.

Initially, the International Institute of Social History (IISH) in Amsterdam was the only academic centre for global labour history, but other centres have now entered this field. The Berlin-based international research institute 're: work – Work and Human Life Cycle in Global History', funded by the German Ministry of Education and Research, has been immensely important. Since 2009, under the aegis of the Africanist Andreas Eckert, ten to fifteen researchers from different academic disciplines and nationalities have worked together there every year. Unfortunately, this initiative has now been concluded. In 2017, in Germany, thanks to the initiative of the Islamologist Stephan Conermann, the Bonn Center for Dependency and Slavery Studies was established, where a large group of researchers examines 'asymmetrical dependencies in pre-modern societies'. In addition, ever more university centres, though not focused entirely on global labour history, address the field extensively, such as the Weatherhead Initiative on Global History (Harvard University), the World History Center (University of Pittsburgh), and the Commodities of Empire project (University of London).[5] And adjacent disciplines are following the same course, for example by developing 'global labour studies' and a 'global anthropology of labour'.[6]

## Global labour history

Despite its growing popularity, however, the concept of global labour history remains somewhat vague and lacks a clear and convincing definition. Perhaps, practically, this omission was inevitable. After all, as Arthur Schopenhauer observed, poets do not write aesthetics before they compose poetry. Now that the practice of global labour history has begun to crystallize, defining the object of study more precisely seems like a good idea.

The first question that comes to mind is: what is labour history? The term 'labour history' has always had a dual meaning. Strictly speaking, the concept refers to the history of labour movements: trade unions, cooperatives, strikes, workers' parties, and so on. More broadly interpreted, the concept also refers to the history of the working classes, referring, for instance, to the development of labour relations, family life, or mentalities. This ambiguity seems characteristic of the term in English. In most other languages, labour-movement history and working-class history cannot be summed up in a single term.

'Broad' labour history is older than 'narrow' labour history. The former could be written as soon as capitalist development had advanced to a certain point, especially in Western Europe, and the need arose to situate historically the corresponding social changes, in general, and the 'social question', in particular.[7] Projects along these lines were undertaken as early as in the aftermath of the 1848 revolutions. 'Labour' tended to be perceived very broadly. For example, Emile Levasseur (1828–1911) – a trailblazer who, in the late 1850s and 1860s, published a four-volume study of French labour history since Julius Caesar – defined the 'working classes' as 'all those who earned their living in and from industry, from simple apprentices to great merchants'.[8]

'Narrow' labour history began to develop only in the 1870s, with political as well as theoretical factors contributing to its rise. Politically, it was significant that labour movements began to be visible on a national scale from the late 1860s onward. The British Trades Union Congress was established in 1868 and, in the following decades, national trade union federations were founded in virtually the whole North Atlantic region, including the Canadian Trades and Labour Congress and the American Federation of Labor in 1886. In this same period, the rise of working-class parties began. These developments made clear to everyone that labour movements had come to stay, while, simultaneously, a theoretical obstacle – the doctrine of the 'wage fund' – was also removed. According to this theory, there exists a 'natural wage' that collective action is incapable of influencing. By about 1870, the wage-fund theory had begun to lose its credibility and, within a few years, many intellectuals in Europe and North America had changed their standpoint. Evidently, the consolidation of the British union movement played a role in this shift.

This combination of political and theoretical impulses was sufficient reason for a number of scholars to concern themselves with labour-movement history. These labour historians generally belonged to the political Left; most of them were socialists or socially conscious liberals. Epoch-making was the work of the German economist Lujo Brentano (1844–1931), who published *On the History and Development of Gilds, and the Origin of Trade Unions* in 1870. A few years later, the US economist Richard T. Ely (1854–1943) followed with *The Labor Movement in America*, published in 1886.[9] In the 1870s–80s, the foundations were thus laid for both broad and narrow labour history.

At first, the two were distinguished from one another. Narrow labour history was mainly, albeit never exclusively, institutional and focused primarily on the description of organizational developments, political debates, leaders, and strikes. It was represented by Sidney and Beatrice Webb, the Wisconsin School of John Commons and others, and also by Marxists like Philip Foner. Some exceptions appeared early on – for example, in Britain, John and Barbara Hammond, with their magnificent trilogy *The Village Labourer* (1911), *The Town Labourer* (1917), and *The Skilled Labourer* (1920).[10] But the genuine rapprochement of broad and narrow labour history began only in the 1950s and 60s, when workers' struggles were contextualized more frequently. As Eric Hobsbawm put it, the 'new' approach accentuated 'the working classes as such … and the economic and technical conditions that allowed labour movements to be effective, or which prevented them from being effective'.[11] The seminal book that marked this turning point was E. P. Thompson's *The Making of the English Working Class* (1963).[12] During the years that followed, the discipline underwent dramatic renewal. Not solely labour processes and everyday culture, but gender, ethnicity, race, and age also finally gained the attention they deserved, along with household structures, sexuality, and informal politics.

Despite its ground-breaking achievement, *The Making of the English Working Class* embodied a certain continuity with earlier labour history. The field as a whole was characterized from the beginning by a combination of methodological nationalism and Eurocentrism. Methodological nationalism links society and the state together and, therefore, considers the different nation-states as 'Leibnizean monads' for historical research. Eurocentrism is the mental ordering of the world from the standpoint of the North Atlantic region: thus, the 'modern' period begins in Europe and North America, and extends step-by-step to the rest of the world. And the temporality of this 'core region' determines the periodization of developments in the rest of the world. Hence, historians reconstructed the history of the working classes and workers' movements in France, Britain, the US, and so on as separate developments. To the extent that they paid attention to the social classes and movements in Latin America, Africa, or Asia, these were interpreted according to North Atlantic schemes.

That is not to say that labour historians did not look beyond national borders. Of course they did, and from early on, but the approach nevertheless remained monadological: the 'civilized' European world was regarded as consisting of peoples who all developed in the same direction, albeit each in its own tempo. One nation was regarded as more advanced than another, and that is why the more 'backward' nations could see their future more or less reflected in the leading ones.

It is only in the last few decades that the Eurocentric monadology as a whole has been questioned. This second turning point appears to be related to a series of changes that occurred since World War II or started even earlier, namely: decolonization, which gave rise to many new independent countries, especially in Africa and Asia, that began to investigate their own social histories; the development of notions related to imagined transcontinental communities, such as Pan-Africanism; the 'discovery' of border cultures and transcultural migrant communities; and the detection of transnational cycles of protests and strikes.

The next question is: what is global? Opinions vary, but I consider global labour history to be a distinctive 'field of research', just like art history or linguistics. Within that research area, different theories can be constructed and tested, whether inspired by Karl Marx, Max Weber, or other thinkers. By implication, global labour history is not a 'theory' in its own right and is therefore not an alternative to Immanuel Wallerstein's world-systems theory or any other interpretations of the capitalist world order. That said, the question, by its nature, suggests how we should define the dimensions and boundaries of this area of inquiry.

Since the 1980s, historians have had cause to relativize the boundaries of the nation-state. At first, they made attempts to criticize this fixation implicitly. In the Global South, historians had previously concluded that writing the labour history of a country as if it were a self-contained unit was impossible. How could the working-class history of, say, Vietnam, Nigeria, or Indonesia be reconstructed, without continuously considering the connections with their colonial motherlands France, Britain, and the Netherlands? Moreover, how could the history of wage-earners in these countries be written without an eye for the history of other labour relations, such as slavery (and the slave trade) or exploitation of contract labourers ('coolies')?

Global labour history involves attempting to accommodate these objections by devising a new approach. But: what is global history? In my view, *global history is primarily concerned with describing and explaining the intensifying (or weakening) connections (interactions, influences, transfers) between different world regions, as well as the economic, political, social, and cultural networks, institutions, and media that have played a role*. This historiography extends well beyond the historiography of globalization alone, unless we define globalization very broadly. Comparative studies, exploring the causes and consequences of combined and uneven differential developments, are an integral part of global labour history.

The adjective 'global' has the disadvantage of potentially conveying the impression that only 'Big History' is included – the 'great divergence' between China and Europe, for example, or the connection between world wars and hegemonies. But global history need not be exclusively large-scale and may include micro-history as well. Writing a global history of a small village, a work site, or a family is quite feasible. The important consideration is to follow the traces that are of interest to us, wherever they may lead: across political and geographic frontiers, timeframes, territories, and disciplinary boundaries. Migration patterns, mass media, world markets, corporations, religious hierarchies, climate changes, wars, and so on, can all constitute bridges to a wider world. Sometimes, we will discover the interconnections and explanations within reasonable proximity, and sometimes we will have to travel further afield.

Obviously, some groups lived in relative isolation and were connected with others, at best, via sporadic long-distance trade. Though global history is not a 'history of everything', such groups are also part of the field of inquiry, inasmuch as the interactions and transfers that did not eventuate are also of interest. Distilling the big picture into small details (and, conversely, discovering micro-realities in macro-processes) is what matters! Global history is therefore primarily about perspective. Researchers should be bold in their inquiry and dare to venture outside their own familiar terrain.

## First research results

The impact of global labour history is clear, in the first place, from scholars' scrutiny of ever more forms of commodified labour. In addition to wage labour and slavery, other subjects – convict labourers, debt peons, indigenous labour, and colonial forced labour – are now also of considerable interest.[13] Hitherto largely neglected occupations, such as those of domestic servants and mail runners, are being explored in the literature.[14] Interest in indigenous labour in 'settler colonies' is gradually rising as well,[15] while studies of the working classes in 'socialist' Central and Eastern Europe and the former Soviet Union are also getting under way.[16]

The number of internationally comparative studies extending their scope beyond the wealthy countries has increased rapidly in recent years. Occupational groups and other segments of the working class remain obvious subjects of comparative analyses. Following the early consideration for coal miners, there have since been large-scale studies dealing with longshoremen, sailors, textile workers, brickmakers, soldiers, prostitutes, shipbuilders, domestic and caregiving workers, and child labourers.[17] And, increasingly, workers' resistance and organizations are depicted in a global context. Runaways, anarchist and syndicalist movements, revolutionary Pan-Africanism, and municipal socialism have inspired additional reflections.[18] A longstanding problem in this respect is that many comparative studies still merely convey contrasts between individual cases. In the end, however, as Neville Kirk has noted, the objective is 'to tease out and explain cross-national similarities and differences rather than simply present a number of additive or parallel national case studies in which the explicit process of comparison is left largely to the wit of the reader'.[19]

At the moment, far fewer studies are aimed at identifying connections between developments in different parts of the world. In his innovative monograph, Jefferson Cowie revealed how, over the course of the twentieth century, in its search for cheap and compliant workers, the former Radio Corporation of America relocated its production from Bloomington, Indiana, to Ciudad Juárez, Mexico. A similar process is described in a study by Aviva Chomsky, who traces the path of the textile industry from New England, first to the US South and then to Puerto Rico, Japan, Mexico, Central America, the Caribbean, and Colombia. Chomsky sees the flight of metropolitan capital to low-wage countries as mirroring the recruitment of cheap foreign labour in metropolitan locations. Elsewhere, in the pioneering book *The Many-Headed Hydra*, Peter Linebaugh and Marcus Rediker convincingly demonstrate that, in the eighteenth century, wage workers and slaves sometimes joined forces to resist intolerable working relationships.[20] The rapidly burgeoning oeuvre of Alessandro Stanziani merits special mention. Originally a

Russian historian, he has vastly expanded the geographic scope of his work and is now interested mainly in contrasts and linkages between forms of bonded labour in different parts of the world.[21]

Still more fascinating perspectives have emerged. Commodity chains (supply chains), for example, are series of production processes connecting miners and agriculturalists with the final producers and consumers of a commodity via various intermediate steps. Commodity chains therefore connect workers all over the world. Karin Hofmeester has illustrated this with the example of diamonds that were mined in South Africa, Brazil, and elsewhere and ultimately underwent their final processing in Surat, Tel Aviv, or Antwerp. Sven Beckert's major study of cotton production is another fascinating example of how such chains operate.[22] And, in an intriguing approach, Elise van Nederveen Meerkerk shows how colonial entanglements simultaneously influenced women's economic role in both Java and the Netherlands.[23]

The global history of forced and 'free' migratory labour has made a quantum leap, as the relative bias towards the Atlantic region has started to make way for a truly global approach.[24] Adam McKeown, who died prematurely, revealed in his groundbreaking work that Asian migration in the nineteenth century was comparable in size to the Atlantic migrations.[25] Like McKeown, Ulbe Bosma does not primarily consider the regions where migrants arrive but the regions from whence they have come. The explanation he offers as to how the Philippines and Indonesia became mass exporters of labour will certainly give rise to additional discussion.[26] In their inspiring joint work, Jan and Leo Lucassen have sought to develop a universal method for quantifying and qualifying cross-cultural migrations for the period 1500–2000, to enable researchers to visualize and explain regional differences.[27]

By the nineteenth century, institutional aspects of labour movements were, of course, addressed by labour historians, although this aspect is now covered from a global as well as, more frequently, from a social and economic perspective. Important studies have been published on the First International (1864–76), consumer cooperatives, and trade unions.[28] In addition, the ILO has recruited far more researchers since the start of the twenty-first century.[29]

Initial compendiums have appeared as well. In 2006, Jan Lucassen published his vast collection of essays on *Global Labour History*, highlighting a worldwide inventory of relevant historical research. The *Handbook* that Karin Hofmeester and I edited elaborated on this first collection; our book is focused more on types of work, labour relations, work incentives, and workers' organization and resistance.[30] In her inspiring interpretative essay, Andrea Komlosy addressed the coexistence and interaction of multiple forms of labour (paid/unpaid, free/unfree, etc.) during the previous millennium, from a gender perspective.[31] Jan Lucassen wrote a still more ambitious book: a 'concise' history of work since Ancient Mesopotamia.[32] And the publication of *General Labour History of Africa*, coordinated by Stefano Bellucci and Andreas Eckert, is especially significant.[33] Their impressive collection of essays covers the period from around 1900. Volumes on earlier African labour history are in preparation.

## Building datasets

A striking number of initiatives seek to construct global datasets. In some cases, such projects can build on the work of the ILO, which, since the 1920s, has gathered statistical data not only about the composition and development of the world's labour force, occupational health and safety, social security and working hours, among other variables, but also about international labour standards as well as national labour and social security laws.[34] One of the early efforts in this direction was the global database on labour unrest that, inspired by Immanuel Wallerstein's world-systems theory, was built entirely manually at the Fernand Braudel Center in Binghamton in the 1980s.[35] Since the invention of computerized data-mining techniques, more extensive and more accurate datasets about strikes can be compiled.[36]

Clio Infra, a set of interconnected databases that has evolved since 2010 under the aegis of Jan Luiten van Zanden, is immensely useful. These datasets provide information about the long-term development of worldwide economic growth and inequality over the past five centuries.[37] Patrick Manning's Collaborative for World-Historical Information at the University of Pittsburgh has, since 2011, developed a global archive enabling global historical analysis, overlapping with Clio Infra in some respects.[38] While neither focuses exclusively on labour, both contain a wealth of information on the subject.

Deriving directly from global labour history, the Global Collaboratory on the History of Labour Relations, 1500–2000, is an initiative by IISH staff member Jan Lucassen. Karin Hofmeester, the central coordinator, described the course of the project as follows:

> The first phase of this project (2007–2012) involved data mining. A large group of international scholars met during workshops,

worked together online, and developed a large number of datasets containing data on the occurrence of all types of labour relations in all parts of the world during five cross sections in time: 1500, 1650, 1800, 1900 (and, for Africa, 1950 too), and 2000, thereby also developing a new taxonomy of labour relations based on a shared set of definitions. The second phase of the project sets out in search of explanations for shifts in labour relations as well as for the possible patterns observed therein. We look for causes and consequences of shifts in labour relations by looking in depth at possible explanatory factors, such as the role of the state; demography and family patterns; the role of economic institutions; and mechanisms that determine shifts in and out of self-employment.[39]

In the meantime, the collaboratory has resulted in a considerable number of publications.[40]

Overall, an impressive wealth of data has been collected about the development of transnational and transcontinental labour markets. Emory University is the repository of a huge multisource dataset of transatlantic slave voyages, which it has been building since the 1990s. This resource now features information about 36,000 individual slaving expeditions between 1514 and 1866.[41] In Amsterdam, a dataset concerning the Asian slave trade, including East, Southeast and South Asia as well as East Africa, has also been in progress since 2016.[42] Datasets on indentured labourers are comparatively less advanced. Exceptions include the particularly detailed datasets about the Chinese, South-Asian, and Javanese contract workers transported to Suriname between 1858 and 1930.[43] Material on the migration of 'free' labour migrants abounds and is collected by bodies such as the United Nations (the International Organization for Migration and the ILO).[44]

## This book

The expansion of the field renders critical introspection desirable, as historical scholarship comprises both meaningful silences and misleading conceptualizations. Part I (Chapters 1–3 of this collection) addresses this issue, referring to important challenges – aspects that have thus far received insufficient consideration in historical research. Neglect of labour processes (Chapter 1) is crucial in this respect. The production processes of cinnamon and quinine illustrate how and why many types of work have thus far been shrouded in silence or concealed by myths, when, in fact, we need serious research on the trials and tribulations of the workers involved.

In addition to labour processes, certain labour relations have tended to be disregarded because they did not qualify as 'wage labour'. Chapter 2 elaborates on various examples: chattel slaves, who were often severely exploited and were expected to generate an enormous profit for their owners but, in most cases, have not been regarded by labour historians (even to this day) as pertaining to their field, because they were not employed as wage workers; precarious labourers who changed employer frequently and did not have straightforward employment contracts; and housewives who ostensibly 'did not work', simply because they did not receive wages for the long hours they laboured. Regarding the omission of such groups, I argue that we need a new, far broader, definition of the 'working class': labour history is not solely the history of so-called 'free' wage-earners but also that of slaves and other unfree workers and of unpaid subsistence-labourers, especially housewives. The task of global labour history is therefore to integrate an international multiverse of class forces in one totalizing analysis. If we take on this task, in my view, we will also need to reinterpret the history of the last few centuries – possibly revealing, for example, that England was *not* the cradle of industrial capitalism (compare Chapters 2 and 10).

An additional complication is that, when historians *do* consider labour processes, they often base their approach on assumptions that, upon closer consideration, prove untenable. Ethnography offers many valuable lessons for overcoming such biases. In Chapter 3, based on Jan Breman's studies of the labouring poor in the Indian state of Gujarat since the early 1960s, we see which methodological lessons may be learned from anthropological fieldwork. Rather than focusing on individual workers, for example, we need to situate them in their family and kinship networks. We also need to transcend the 'urban' versus 'rural' dichotomy – the reality consists of too many connections and hybrids between both sectors.

Building on these considerations, the core concepts of global labour history undergo critical analysis in Part II (Chapters 4–8). Exactly what do we mean by 'capitalism' and 'workers', and how can we refine concepts such as 'coerced labour', 'household strategies', and 'labour markets' to enable subtle analyses? In Chapter 4, I propose – elaborating on my book *Workers of the World* – that we regard capitalism not as a state but as a process, in which commodified labour-power uses commodified raw materials and commodified means to produce commodified goods and services. All inputs and outputs therefore qualify as commodities, which means that they are turned into objects that have both a use-value and an exchange-value. In other words, both meet the needs of particular consumers (individuals, enterprises, institutions) and can be traded in defined proportions for other commodities. Such 'production of commodities by means of commodities' never encompasses the complete reality because commodified labour-power is perpetuated by non-commodified subsistence labour (work performed by housewives and other unpaid individuals) and because a share of the inputs derives from non-commodified gifts of nature (air, water, and so on).

Commodified labour-power does not solely comprise 'free' wage labourers, about whom Marx noted ironically that, as free individuals, they can dispose of their labour-power as their own commodity and have no other commodities for sale. In Chapter 5, I argue that commodification of labour-power has many manifestations, including chattel slavery, sharecropping, or debt peonage. 'Free' wage labourers are no different from other labourers in being unfree from coercion. Nearly all people whose labour-power is commodified experience coercion. In the case of 'free' wage labourers, however, such coercion arises primarily from economic balances of power (which are, of course, based indirectly on physical coercion – that is, property relations), while slaves, debt peons, and others experience *direct* physical coercion. The term 'free' wage labour is misleading in that sense. With this in mind, in Chapter 6, I attempt to dissect all the different types of coerced labour. I identify three essential aspects (entry into the labour relation; extraction of labour during the labour relation; and exit from the labour relation) and, in the process, endeavour to establish the foundation for a new typology that is considerably more detailed than the customary one.

Most, although by no means all, labourers live in households. Yet, labour historians have long treated the working classes as coalitions of isolated individuals. That was true as far back as Karl Marx, who referred to 'the dot-like isolation' (*Punktualität*) of the 'free worker'.[45] The same assumption prevails among modern theorists of 'rational choice', 'resource mobilization', and so on. Of course, all these scholars *know* that most people belong to families or other small-scale communities and that they are members of a wide range of social networks (such as neighbourhoods or religious communities), but these same scholars scarcely consider this fact in their class analyses. Feminist historiography has made it absolutely clear that this is no longer acceptable. In Chapter 7, I attempt to apply the feminist approach to the world's working class. In doing so, I focus mainly on the strategies of subaltern households – that is, the different (combinations of) resources they use to try to survive in relative autonomy, security, and dignity. In Chapter 8, I address the long-term development of labour markets – concrete or virtual markets where, among others, wage workers and slaves are traded. Wage workers were long tasked (though not exclusively) with temporary duties, while slaves were assigned long-term activities. Only in the nineteenth century did slavery become far less prevalent and were wage workers increasingly assigned permanent activities – a transition that coincided with progressive segmentation of labour markets and, recently, with growing re-casualization.

In Part III (Chapters 9–13), I explore several connections between labourers in different parts of the world. In Chapter 9, I introduce two aspects I have neglected all too often in the past: agriculture and ecology. I base my research on the observation that 'globalization' – the transfer of production sites from one part of the world to another – originated in agriculture and was only later introduced in industrial settings. I analyse long-distance cash–crop transfer as a process composed of managerial, intellectual, and manual labour that may be thoroughly understood only through a combination of business, ecological, and labour history. Chapter 10 aligns with this to some extent. Reinterpreting the early history of labour management, I note the importance of physically coerced labour as an opportunity to test 'modern' forms of labour management. The seventeenth-century sugar plantations in the Caribbean were 'factories in the field', where synchronized gang labour and forms of proto-Taylorism could be tried. The first detailed job descriptions were compiled for early-nineteenth-century convict labour in Australia, a century before Frank and Lillian Gilbreth did likewise for 'free' workers. Knowledge obtained from such experiments was propagated worldwide at the time.

In 1807, the royal assent to the British Act for the Abolition of the Slave Trade augured a new era in the international structure of labour relations, rendering the entire Atlantic slave trade illegal for British subjects. In subsequent decades, the British authorities attempted to convince other European slave-trading nations to prohibit such trade as well – followed by an international campaign to abolish slavery. Chapter 11 reconstructs several important aspects of these crucial developments and reveals that the gradual reduction of chattel slavery usually resulted not in 'free' wage labour but in other labour relations that relied on physical coercion.

Upon the establishment of the ILO in 1919, the quest for global regulation of labour relations became supra-national. In Chapter 12, I offer a critical appraisal of ILO activities to date. I argue that the ILO has certainly achieved positive effects for some workers on different continents but that it is increasingly likely to be reduced to an information and advice service. Chapter 13 poses a problem that, to this day, is all too often regarded as taboo: the question of whether workers in wealthy countries benefit from the exploitation of those in poor countries. Such relational inequality could have vast social, economic, and political implications.

Part IV (Chapters 14–17) focuses on conflicts and addresses different aspects of resistance and acquiescence. In Chapter 14, I take inspiration from 'Romer's Rule' (from palaeontology) to reveal how attempting to maintain a traditional way of life may instigate – usually unintended – radical changes. That is probably one of the reasons why workers' collective actions may have unanticipated consequences. In Chapter 15, I examine one of the most important forms of labour resistance: massive flight from the place where exploitation and oppression are occurring. I consider three aspects: which groups fled? What were the issues and triggers that led them to take such action? And how did they organize their escape?

In Chapter 16, I discuss what I call the Marx–Hess–Engels hypothesis, according to which the rise of capitalism leads to continuous expansion of the working class, such that labour would become ever more important in future revolutions, which would soon result in the subversion of capitalist relations. This idea appears to have been refuted, because the revolutions of the twentieth century all took place in pre-industrial or industrializing countries and never in fully developed capitalist societies. Workers have, however, often been crucial in early capitalist transitions. I suggest a few explanations for their importance. The situation that many believe best approximated a revolution in highly advanced capitalism was the Paris uprising in May and June 1968. 'Paris', however, did not occur in isolation. In Chapter 17, I question why uprisings coincided in many other places in the world at about the same time. I focus mainly on five aspects: relatively synchronized economic circumstances; the expansion of mass education; decolonization; inspiring 'external' events (the impact of the Cuban Revolution, etc.); and mutual learning experiences.

The Epilogue considers the present crisis in the world labour movement. Cooperatives, trade unions, and workers' parties are in general decline almost everywhere. I argue that a global labour history perspective may help explain this downward cycle. Factors that may come into play include underemployment in the Global South and the powerful rise of merchant capital in all its manifestations. Both aspects are probably best understood through worldwide diachronic comparisons.

Past and present alike render it highly challenging to deepen the global history of labour.

Although this book thus addresses a great many subjects, it raises only a few aspects of the vast field that global labour history covers. Moreover, much of what I share is tentative and exploratory. All scholarly assertions are provisional, and this certainly holds true in this work. As Friedrich Nietzsche wrote in his *Genealogy of Morals*: 'There is *only* a perspective seeing, *only* a perspective "knowing"; and the *more* affects we allow to speak about one thing, the *more* eyes, different eyes, we can use to observe one thing, the more complete will our "concept" of this thing, our "objectivity", be'.[46]

## Notes

1  The term 'global labour history' was introduced in 1999 in van der Linden & Lucassen, *Prolegomena*, and was elaborated in my *Workers of the World* of 2008. The present book is a sequel to *Workers of the World*.
2  For more details, see Lucassen, *Global Labour History*; Eckert, *Global Histories of Work*; Hofmeester & van der Linden, *Handbook Global History of Work*; van der Linden, *Global History of Work*.
3  Smallwood & Glenn, 'Editor of "Labor History" quits'.
4  Phelan, 'Editorial introduction', 4.
5  Weatherhead Initiative on Global History; World History Center; Commodities of Empire project.
6  For example, Taylor & Rioux, *Global Labour Studies*; Munck, *Rethinking Global Labour*; Kasmir & Carbonella, *Blood and Fire*. In 2017, the journal *Dialectical Anthropology* opened the forum series 'Workers of the World!'.
7  Breman et al., *The Social Question in the Twenty-First Century*.
8  Levasseur, *Histoire des classes ouvrières*, I, III.
9  Brentano, *On the History and Development of Gilds*; Ely, *Labor Movement in America*.
10  Hammond & Hammond, *The Village Labourer*; *The Town Labourer*; *The Skilled Labourer*.
11  Hobsbawm, *Labouring Men*, 4.
12  Thompson, *The Making of the English Working Class*.
13  For example, DeVito & Lichtenstein, *Global Convict Labor*; Anderson, *Global History of Convicts and Penal Colonies*; van der Linden & Rodríguez García, *On Coerced Labor*; Barragán, *Potosí Global*; Seibert, *In die globale Wirtschaft gezwungen*; Breman, *Mobilizing Labour*. For an impressive synthesis of the many studies on slavery, see Zeuske's monumental *Handbuch Geschichte der Sklaverei*. This book merits translation into English.
14  For example, Sinha, Varma & Jha, *Servants' Pasts*; Sinha & Varma, *Servants' Pasts*; Martínez, et al., *Colonialism and Male Domestic Service*; Joshi, 'Dak roads, Dak runners'.
15  Mysyk, 'Land, labor, and indigenous response'; Parnaby, 'Indigenous labor'; Riseman, 'Australian [mis]treatment of indigenous labour'; Weinberg & Mercollí, 'Sweet death'; Barragán, 'Trabajo forzado, indígena, femenino'; Martinez & Vickers, *Pearl Frontier*.
16  For example, *Sozialgeschichtliche Kommunismusforschung*; Hübner & Tenfelde, *Arbeiter in der SBZ-DDR*; Hübner, Klessmann & Tenfelde, *Arbeiter im Staatssozialismus*; Filtzer et al., *Dream Deferred*; Bartha, *Alienating Labour*; Cucu, *Planning Labour*; Siefert, *Labor in State Socialist Europe*. Major studies already existed on the Soviet Union; Donald Filtzer's four books on *Soviet Workers* are especially worth noting.
17  Feldman & Tenfelde, *Workers, Owners and Politics*; Gier & Mercier, *Mining Women*; Davies et al., *Dock Workers*; Fink, *Sweatshops at Sea*; Heerma van Voss, Hiemstra-Kuperus & Van Nederveen Meerkerk, *Ashgate Companion*; Beckert, *Empire of Cotton*; Kessler & Lucassen,

'Labour relations, efficiency and the great divergence'; Zürcher, *Fighting for a Living*; Haymond, *Soldiers*; Rodríguez García, Heerma van Voss & van Nederveen Meerkerk, *Selling Sex in the City*; Varela, Murphy & van der Linden, *Shipbuilding and Ship Repair Workers*; Hoerder, van Nederveen Meerkerk & Neunsinger, *Towards a Global History of Domestic and Caregiving Workers*; Lieten & van Nederveen Meerkerk, *Child Labour's Global Past*. See also Freeman, *Behemoth*.

18  Silver, *Forces of Labor*; Rediker, Chakraborty & van Rossum, *Global History of Runaways*; van der Walt & Hirsch, *Anarchism and Syndicalism*; Weiss, *Framing a Radical African Atlantic*; Slucki, *The International Jewish Labor Bund*; Shelton Stromquist, *Democratizing Cities*.
19  Kirk, 'Transnational labor history', 21.
20  Cowie, *Capital Moves*; Chomsky, *Linked Labor Histories*; Linebaugh & Rediker, *Many-Headed Hydra*. Compare also Fink, *Maya of Morganton*.
21  Stanziani, *Le travail contraint*; *Bâtisseurs d'empires*; *Labour, Coercion, and Economic Growth*; and *Bondage*.
22  Hofmeester, 'Diamonds from mine to finger'; Beckert, *Empire of Cotton*. See also Komlosy & Musić, *Commodity Chains and Labor Relations*.
23  Van Nederveen Meerkerk, *Women, Work and Colonialism*.
24  Hoerder, *Cultures in Contact*; McKeown, *Melancholy Order*; Lucassen, Lucassen & Manning, *Migration History in World History*; Gabaccia & Hoerder, *Connecting Seas and Connected Ocean Rims*; Bosma, Kessler & Lucassen, *Migration and Membership Regimes*; Hoerder & Kaur, *Proletarian and Gendered Mass Migrations*.
25  McKeown, 'Global migration, 1846–1940'; McKeown, 'World migration'.
26  Bosma, *Making of a Periphery*.
27  The foundational text is Lucassen & Lucassen, 'Mobility transition revisited'. But, see also Lucassen & Lucassen, *Globalising Migration History*.
28  Bensimon, Deluermoz & Moisand, 'Arise Ye Wretched of the Earth'; Hilson, Neunsinger & Patmore, *Global History of Consumer Co-operation*; Phelan, *Trade Unionism since 1945*; van der Linden, *International Confederation of Free Trade Unions*; Van Goethem, *Amsterdam International*; Rodríguez García, *Liberal Workers of the World, Unite?*; Waters & Van Goethem, *American Labor's Global Ambassadors*; Carew, *American Labour's Cold War Abroad*.
29  See the references in Chapter 12 and in Maul, *International Labour Organization*.
30  Lucassen, *Global Labour History*; Hofmeester & van der Linden, *Handbook Global History of Work*.
31  Komlosy, *Work: The Last 1,000 Years*.
32  Lucassen, *The Story of Work*.
33  Bellucci & Eckert, *General Labour History of Africa*. See also Fall, *Le travail au Sénégal au XXe siècle*.
34  ILOSTAT; NORMLEX.
35  See the update in Silver, Arrighi & Dubofsky, 'Labor unrest'. This database provided the foundation for Silver's path-breaking *Forces of Labor*, relating the rise of labour movements to capital mobility, product cycles, and world politics.
36  Sjaak van der Velden has done pioneering work in this field. See his *Striking Numbers*, and 'Strikes, lockouts, and informal resistance'. For the datasets, see Global Hub Labour Conflicts.
37  Clio-Infra. Partly based on Clio Infra is Van Zanden et al., *How Was Life?*
38  CHIA.
39  Hofmeester, 'Labour relations: Introductory remarks', 317. The datasets can be found on the History of Labour Relations website.
40  Major publications include: Hofmeester & Moll-Murata, *Joy and Pain of Work*; Mattos, *Relações laborais em Portugal e no mundo lusófono*; Hofmeester, Lucassen & Ribeiro da Silva, 'Labour Relations in Sub-Saharan Africa'; Hofmeester, Kessler & Moll-Murata, *Conquerors, Employers and Arbiters*; Mattos, Terra & Varela, *Historia das relações de trabalho*; Hofmeester & van Nederveen-Meerkerk, 'Family, demography and labour relations'; Hofmeester & de Zwart, *Colonialism*; Hofmeester & Lucassen, 'Shifting labor relations'.
41  See the SlaveVoyages website. The background of the project is addressed in an interview with the *spiritus rector* David Eltis by Leonardo Marques, 'Digital history of the transatlantic slave trade'.
42  ESTA: Exploring Slave Trade in Asia: Towards an Indian Ocean and maritime Asia slave trade database.

43 These datasets have been assembled thanks to the initiative of the private company Amrit Consultancy (Sitla Bonoo and Sandew Hira). They are managed by the National Archive in The Hague. See Chinese contractarbeiders in Suriname 1858–1874; Hindostanen in Suriname; Javaanse contractarbeiders in Suriname 1890–1930 (in Dutch only).
44 Migration Data Portal; ILOSTAT.
45 Marx, *Grundrisse*, 485.
46 Nietzsche, *On the Genealogy of Morals*, 119.

# Part I
**Challenges**

# 1
# Tree bark mysteries: or the invisible workers

## Cinnamon birds

Cinnamon is the dried bark of the tall *Cinnamomum (Lauraceae)* tree, which originally mainly grew on the island of Ceylon. The Arab merchants that brought the cinnamon sticks (dried bark in the form of a quill) to North Africa and the Middle East more than two thousand years ago protected their trade monopoly by obscuring the origin of their goods as much as possible. They claimed not to know where the sticks came from. However, they could describe how these were 'harvested'. In his *Histories*, Herodotus recounted:

> Great birds, they say, bring the sticks which we Greeks, taking the word from the Phoenicians, call cinnamon, and carry them up into the air to make their nests. These are fastened with a sort of mud to a sheer face of rock, where no foot of man is able to climb. So the Arabians, to get the cinnamon, use the following artifice. They cut all the oxen and asses and beasts of burden that die in their land into large pieces, which they carry with them into those regions and place near the nests: then they withdraw to a distance, and the old birds, swooping down, seize the pieces of meat and fly with them up to their nests; which, not being able to support the weight, break off and fall to the ground. Hereupon the Arabians return and collect the cinnamon, which is afterwards carried from Arabia into other countries.[1]

Recounting such exciting tales, the merchants effectively constructed an information blockade. Cinnamon sticks, they claimed, do not fall from heaven like Manna but are retrieved only through heroic endeavour.

The exotic masking of the actual labour process not only led to cinnamon being perceived as a very special pleasure but also justified its high price.

## Heroes, geniuses, and explorers

In the modern era, a further valuable product derived from dried and ground bark was discovered: quinine. Heroic stories were also told about this commodity. This time, however, the heroes were brilliant scientists and brave explorers. The predominant story of quinine is more or less as follows:[2] In c. 1630, Jesuits in Lima discovered that a remedy against malaria could be produced using the bark of the *Cinchona* tree (later named by Linnaeus) (Figure 1.1). The effectiveness of quinine was confirmed shortly thereafter when it saved the life of the Countess of Chinchón, the wife of the Spanish Viceroy of Peru.[3] As early as 1677, quinine was documented in the official British Dispensatory and thereby recognized as a drug that had valid medicinal properties. Thereafter, the demand for quinine grew slowly at first and then more rapidly. As the public authorities and the local merchants wastefully exploited the *Cinchona* trees, the danger of extinction continuously grew, starting in the

**Figure 1.1** The gathering and drying of *Cinchona* bark in a Peruvian forest. Wood engraving by C. Leplante, c. 1867, after Adrienne Faguet, active 1827–46. Wellcome Collection. https://wellcomecollection.org/works/werf33s3.

second half of the eighteenth century. The colonial powers of England, France, and the Netherlands were particularly concerned about this threat, as quinine was, by then, recognized as indispensable for Europeans who wanted to survive in the malaria-plagued tropics. Establishing *Cinchona* plantations in the South American highlands was deemed impossible – not solely because of the difficult terrain but also because of the many wars between the newly-founded states of Bolivia, Ecuador, and Peru.

European spies were sent to the Andes to retrieve specimens and seeds from this highly-prized tree. The first to successfully smuggle the seeds of *Cinchona calisaya* from Bolivia to Paris in the 1840s was the British–French botanist Hugh Weddell. Some of the seeds germinated in the Jardin des Plantes in Paris, and others in the gardens of the London Horticultural Society. Attempts to plant *Cinchona* in Algeria and Java, based on this genetic foundation, proved unsuccessful. It was only between 1852 and 1854, when the botanist Julius C. Hasskarl (who had been commissioned by the Dutch king and was carrying out an expedition under a false name) managed to bring thousands of seeds from a variety of *Cinchona* tree to the Dutch East Indies, that the systematic cultivation of the species became possible. Plantations were not only established in Java but also in British India.[4] The British attempts, however, were far less successful than the Dutch ones, and, towards the end of the nineteenth century, around 95 per cent of quinine was produced in Java. By creating cartels, the Dutch could hold on to this ruling position until the Japanese conquered Java in 1942. From then on, no more quinine was sold to the allies. Starting in 1942, then, under tremendous time pressure, the US attempted to create artificial quinine – a milestone achieved in 1944 by the young chemists William Doering and Robert Woodward, who worked for the Polaroid company.[5] At approximately the same time, *Cinchona* plantations were established in Latin America.[6]

In this standard history, everything evolves around the Peruvian Jesuit explorers, the Countess of Chinchón, the biologists Weddell and Hasskarl, and the chemists Doering and Woodward. But behind these heroes, of course, there were countless people involved: those who chopped down the trees and peeled off the bark in the South American mountains and those who worked on the Javanese plantations. The fact that historians hardly mention these figures in the background is not unusual: that is how it has always been, and the rise of social history has done little to change it. In this context, I am not primarily interested in the sheer fact that working conditions are often neglected by historians (incidentally, also by most social historians!)[7] but, rather, in the different forms this neglect takes.

## Andean labour

One form of neglect can be found in the example of the Andes, where labour processes and conditions have repeatedly been described by contemporaries. For example, in around 1800, writing of his travels there, Alexander von Humboldt devoted a number of pages to such topics. Among other features, he described forced *repartimiento* (tribute labour) in Ibagué in present-day Colombia:

> One divides the royal harvest between the 50 peones of the royal society by forcing each individual to supply one to one and a half to two arrobas of cinchona bark and giving him the pay in advance. The royal overseers and botanists then have to make sure that the peon fulfills his duty. Aside from the peones, there are agricultural workers who harvest on their own account and supply the king. Two arrobas is the maximum that one forces a worker to supply. That seems to be very little, when one considers that an efficient peon, who finds a nice tree, can peel half or three quarters of an arroba on one single day. But in the current situation [the dying-out of the *Cinchona* trees] everything is difficult. A peon needs almost two months to retrieve two arrobas, because his domestic affairs, his obligations toward the masters of the haciendas (many are serfs) force him to go home many times in between.[8]

The description by the French–British botanist and physician Hugh Weddell following his expedition from 1843 to 1845 was much more detailed.[9] He recounted that cutters of the *Cinchona* bark – *cascarillos* – usually worked for a merchant or small company and were sent into the woods with a *mayordomo* (representative). The *mayordomo* led the expedition, took possession of the bark brought from different parts of the woods, analysed it, and distributed provisions. Weddell specified how the *cascarillos* identified the suitable *Cinchona* trees; what their camps looked like; and how they extracted and dried the bark. He also described in blunt terms how precarious and miserable the working conditions of the *cascarillos* were. Often, they could find no suitable trees:

> Then he returns to the camp with empty hands and without any provisions left. And, often, when he sees signs of the tree on the side of the hill, he is separated from it by a river or an abyss. Then days can go by before he reaches the object that he has never taken his eye off.[10]

And when he had collected enough bark, the hardest work of all began:

> He still has to bring what he has collected to the camp. He has to walk back to the camp with a heavy load on his shoulders, taking the same path that he had difficulties advancing on already. This part of the process of collecting bark is so strenuous that it is hard to imagine. I saw more than one region in which the cinchona bark had to be carried for fourteen to twenty days in this way, before leaving the woods in which it is created. When one considers the price one pays for doing so, one can hardly understand how there can be such unhappy people who stoop to such badly rewarded work.[11]

The pharmaceutical entrepreneur Henry Wellcome, who travelled the 'Cinchona region' in 1879, added a further gruesome detail. He recounted the following tale regarding the transportation of the bark from the woods to the coast:

> The Indians, in carrying bark, bear the main weight of burden upon their heads, by placing over the forehead a strip of rawhide to which are attached cords of the same material lashed to the bale; they stoop forward to maintain their equilibrium, and use long Alpine sticks to steady and aid them in ascending or descending dangerous cliffs. The skeletons of hundreds of wretched peons can be seen in the far depths of the chasms below some of the older trails, bleaching beneath the tropical sun, their earthly toils ended by a misstep on the verge of one or the other frightful precipice; now and then ghastly human skulls are seen placed in niches or crevices in the projecting rocks of the mountainsides along the narrow passage, suggestive of lurking dangers.[12]

A cynical fact added by Wellcome was that a large percentage of the malnourished indigenous (up to a quarter of all workers) died of malaria during the harvest while carrying the very medicine that could treat their illness.

The reports by Humboldt, Weddell, and Wellcome are fragmented. They do not tell us how the indigenous were recruited, why they accepted their working conditions, whether they performed acts of resistance, what happened in the villages they came from during the *Cinchona* season, whether the women and children tilled the fields, and so forth. Nevertheless, we do receive quite detailed information about labour processes and conditions. What is all the more curious is that later historians almost never used this information.

### Javanese labour

Another form of labour displacement came into play as soon as the quinine production was transferred to Asia, especially to Java. It is noteworthy that not only the historians from the twentieth and twenty-first centuries but also those who had already observed the situation in the nineteenth century hardly paid any attention to the working conditions there. Although a whole array of manuals and practical instructions discuss exactly what needs to be done in order for *Cinchona* to grow or how to harvest and dry the bark, there is hardly any information regarding the workers in these texts. We learn that the trees are 'planted' and 'cleared', but who carries out these tasks and under which conditions remains unknown.[13]

We not only find this oversight in older publications but even in texts from the end of the Dutch colonial period and thereafter. In 1945, a compendium was published that outlined the quinine production in Java and provided precise descriptions of the actions that needed to take place on a plantation. Yet, while the actions of the planters are described in active terms ('The grower must provide himself with adequately shaded seed beds'), in contrast, the actions of the workers are rendered invisible by the use of passive language ('The trees … are cut up' and the bark 'is then put in the sun').[14] Only the photographs and their captions demonstrate the concrete work processes on the plantations. They also indicate that a lot of the work (such as the selection of the seeds or the refinement with the use of grafts in the nursery) was carried out by women (Figure 1.2). To my knowledge, later historians never attempted to lift the veil of secrecy.

## Variations of labour displacement

Aside from the falsifying, prescientific historiography practised by Herodotus, there are therefore at least two other forms of historical labour displacement: either concrete testimonies from the given period are overlooked, or the fact that such testimonies do not exist goes unquestioned. Thereby, a dual problem arises. First, why were the South American labour conditions described concisely and with empathy, while the Javanese conditions were mostly stated as a matter

Figure 1.2 Gathering *Cinchona* bark. Date unknown. Wellcome Collection. https://wellcomecollection.org/works/m6bwbxes.

of fact and accepted without question? Second, why were historians generally interested in neither the South American nor the Javanese workers?

The first question is perhaps simpler to answer than the second. In South America, the European observers found themselves confronted with feudal and barbaric misery. The indigenous worked under conditions that one could characterize as formal subsumption: the world market penetrated the feudal economy without fundamentally changing the labour processes. As Marx observed: 'Without revolutionizing the mode of production, it simply worsens the conditions of the direct producers, transforms them into mere wage-labourers and proletarians under worse conditions than those directly subsumed by capital, appropriating their surplus labour on the basis of the old mode of production'.[15] Because they were so 'backward', such working conditions gave cause for indignation – especially at a time when North Atlantic debates raged about the immorality of forced labour and slavery.[16] The Javanese production of quinine, on the other hand, was organized according to the most modern standards for capitalist plantations. The working conditions seemed progressive, and questioning them would have been tantamount to voicing radical criticism of the system.[17]

The prevailing indifference of many historians towards labour relations remains hard to understand. Especially, of course, when, as in the case of the South American production of quinine, documentation is readily available – in some cases even without archival research. Since the 1960s, social history has made much progress around the world, especially in the wealthy countries of the North Atlantic but also, to a lesser extent, in the so-called Global South. We can only attempt to expand these tendencies and thereby connect the macro-history with the lived experiences of millions and millions of subsistence peasants, serfs, slaves, and 'lumpenproletarians'. But, to do this, we must push aside all the 'guardians' that block labour's access to 'the parlor, which consciousness occupies'.[18]

## Notes

1   Herodotus, *History*, 144–5.
2   Headrick, *Tools of Empire*; see also Lee, 'Plants against malaria'.
3   For a long time, it was wrongfully claimed that the countess personally brought quinine to Europe. For this reason, Linnaeus suggested the term *Chinchona*, in which he integrated a spelling mistake that has since been canonized. For a demythologization of this episode, see Haggis, 'Fundamental errors'.
4   Regarding the transfer of the *Cinchona* tree to British and Dutch India, see Brockway, *Science and Colonial Expansion*, and Williams, 'Clemens Robert Markham'. Regarding the further development in British India, see NN, 'Manufacture of quinine in India' and NN, 'Cinchona cultivation in India'.
5   NN, 'Quinine synthesized'.
6   Fosberg, 'Cinchona plantation in the New World'; Popenoe, 'Cinchona cultivation in Guatemala'.
7   The way that social history relates to the study of working conditions deserves a separate analysis. The overwhelming majority of social historical investigations look at the prior conditions, the effects, and protests against specific types of labour and working conditions. However, it neglects to look at types of labour and working conditions as such. Of course, there have always been exceptions confirming this rule.
8   Humboldt, *Reise auf dem Río Magdalena*, 129. An *arroba* is an old Spanish unit of weight (usually 11.5 kg).
9   Weddell, *Histoire naturelle de Quinquinas*.
10  Weddell, *Histoire naturelle de Quinquinas*, 12.
11  Weddell, *Histoire naturelle de Quinquinas*, 15. Weddell's complaint was almost literally repeated in a Dutch study from 1855, in which the Cascarilleros were described as 'poor' and 'unhappy' and the author complained: 'one can only wonder why people are found that want to carry out such badly rewarded work'. De Vriese, *Kina-boom uit Zuid-Amerika*, 31, note 33.
12  Wellcome, 'Cinchona forests of South America'.
13  Berkhout, 'Rentabiliteit van eene kina-onderneming'.
14  Taylor, *Cinchona in Java*, 68, 72.
15  Marx, *Capital*, III, 453. Similar things can be noticed when it comes to another bark product, namely rubber (*hevea brasiliensis*). In this case, work was also organized in accordance with the principles of formal subsumption (in the Brazilian rainforest); and later, in other parts of the world (Ceylon, Malaya, Sumatra, etc.), it was organized based on real subsumption. Regarding the Brazilian production conditions, see Weinstein, 'Persistence of pre-capitalist relations of production'.

16  Regarding the complicated relationship between abolitionism and white consciousness of indigenous oppression, see Bolt, 'Anti-slavery origins'.
17  Eduard Douwes Dekker (Multatuli) voiced a fundamental critique of colonial agriculture in his novel *Max Havelaar* of 1860. But this book refers to the Javanese coffee production in the so-called Cultivation System (*cultuurstelsel*) that was in place until 1870 and embodied a variation of formal subsumption. A critique of modern plantation production that was published later on can, however, be found in Szekely-Lulofs, *Rubber*.
18  Freud, *General Introduction to Psychoanalysis*, 256.

# 2
# Caribbean radicals, a new Italian saint, and a feminist challenge

What is global labour history? To explain what I mean when I use this term, I would like to share four short historical vignettes. They are stories taken from very different situations in different places in the world, but, as I will try to show, there is a connection between them anyhow.

## Slaves and capitalism

In September 1938, a doctoral dissertation was defended at the Faculty of Modern History of Oxford University, entitled 'The Economic Aspect of the Abolition of the British West Indian Slave Trade and Slavery'. Six years later, this thesis was also published as a book, *Capitalism and Slavery*. The author, Eric Williams, would later become Prime Minister of Trinidad and Tobago. In *Capitalism and Slavery*, Williams referred to another milestone work published in 1938 by his countryman and one-time school teacher C. L. R. James: *The Black Jacobins: Toussaint L'Ouverture and the San Domingo Revolution*.[1]

In 1932, both James and Williams had migrated from Trinidad to Britain – James went to work as a writer and journalist, while Williams studied at Oxford. Later, from 1958 to 1960, the two worked together once again. When Williams became prime minister of Trinidad and led the country to independence, James supported him for some time, among other things as chief editor of the newspaper *The Nation*.

But Williams and James held very different political views, and their collaboration did not last. After a short while, they went their separate ways again.[2] James then increasingly developed into a champion of total democracy and interpreted Lenin's idea that 'every cook can govern' literally, while Williams sought a rapprochement with the US and, in the end, banned not only the distribution of the older publications by C. L. R. James but also his own early writings! Whatever their later political differences, though, it remains true that, in 1938, both men shared the same historical perspective. James argued that the British campaign to abolish slavery and the slave trade should be explained with reference to: 1) the dwindling profitability of sugar production in the British territories of the Caribbean; 2) the greater opportunities after the Battle of Plassey to produce more cheaply in British India than in the Caribbean; and 3) the British desire to wipe out their French competitors. The argument in Williams's doctoral thesis was similar in some important respects. In the book version of *Capitalism and Slavery*, Williams explicitly acknowledged that James had expressed 'clearly and concisely and, as far as I know, for the first time in English' the thesis that he – Williams – had subsequently advanced in his own work.[3]

There has been controversy about the precise extent to which the arguments of James and Williams differed or converged. Whatever position we might take on this issue, both authors endorsed the same basic idea. Both of them argued, explicitly or implicitly, that chattel slavery in the Caribbean was an important element in the growth of capitalism in Western Europe. The tropical plantations, with their perverse system of exploitation and oppression, the capitalist putting-out systems (cottage industries), and emerging factories formed *one transcontinental circuit*. Without saying as much, and possibly without fully realizing it, James and Williams had therefore abandoned the theory of Karl Marx. Marx had always assumed that the 'doubly free' wage-earner constitutes the real and privileged basis of capitalist production, or, in other words, that labour-power can be commodified in only *one* way that is 'truly' capitalist – namely, through free wage labour, in which the worker 'as a free individual can dispose of his labour-power as his own commodity' and 'has no other commodity for sale'.[4] Marx had emphasized that 'labour-power can appear upon the market as a commodity only if, and so far as, its possessor, the individual whose labour-power it is, offers it for sale, or sells it, as a commodity'.[5] Max Weber, the intelligent anti-Marx bourgeois, shared this opinion. Weber believed that labour that 'in formal terms is purely voluntary' was typical for capitalism.[6] In 1926, another kindred spirit, the conservative German sociologist Götz Briefs, defined the wage labourer as 'personally free' and with 'no property', living in 'economic circumstances in which means of subsistence can be obtained only through economic returns'.[7]

Contrary to Marx, Weber, and other classical theorists, James and Williams considered chattel slaves to be an integral element of capitalism. Thus, wage workers and chattel slaves both embodied a form of capitalist labour. This implicates, however, that there exists a large class of people within capitalism, whose labour-power is commodified in various *different* ways. In his *Grundrisse*, Marx declared that slavery is 'an anomaly opposite the bourgeois system itself', which is 'possible at individual points within the bourgeois system of production' but 'only because it does not exist at other points'.[8] The James/Williams approach goes much further: slavery is not a capitalist 'anomaly'. It is part of capitalist *normality*. The world's working class is, in reality, a variegated group, including chattel slaves, share-croppers, small artisans, and wage-earners. I think that it is the historical dynamics of this global 'multitude' that labour historians should try to understand.

## San Precario

Let me now take a leap through time. On 29 February 2004, Italy witnessed the ironic creation of a new saint by the Chainworkers of Milan (an anarcho-syndicalist collective seeking to subvert commercial advertising): San Precario, the patron saint of casual, temporary, freelance, and intermittent workers (Figure 2.1). San Precario was initially envisaged as a man but has since evolved into a rather androgynous being. He or she can appear anywhere and everywhere: on streets and in public squares but also in

**Figure 2.1** An image of San Precario carried at a demonstration in Milan on Mayday, 2011. © Samuele Ghilardi.

McDonald's outlets, supermarkets, or bookstores.[9] Prayers are even directed at the new saint, such as:

> Oh, Saint Precarious,
> protector of us all, precarious of the earth,
> Give us paid maternity leave,
> Protect chain store workers, call center angels,
> and all flexible employees, hanging by a thread.
>
> Give us paid leave, and pension contributions,
> income and free services,
> keep them from being fired.
>
> Saint Precarious, defend us from the bottom of the network,
> pray for us temporary and cognitive workers,
> Extend to all the others our humble supplication.
>
> Remember those souls whose contract is coming to an end,
> tortured by the pagan divinities:
> the Free Market and Flexibility,
> those wandering uncertain, without a future nor a home,
> with no pension nor dignity.
> Grant hope to undocumented workers,
> and bestow upon them joy and glory,
> Until the end of time.[10]

The arrival of Saint Precarious draws attention to a problem of burning actuality: the continued increase in the numbers of highly vulnerable employees who must live and work without any security or predictability, in irregular jobs.

Usually, we regard this troubling development through North-Atlantic eyes and take a short-term perspective. We are used to assuming a Standard Employment Relationship as the ruling norm for working life. Standard Employment is a form of wage labour defined by:

- continuity and stability of employment
- a full-time position with one employer, located only at the employer's place of business
- an income that enables an employee to support at least a small family (the wage-earner, a non-employed spouse, and one or two children) without falling below a basic standard of living

- legally stipulated rights to protection and participation/codetermination at work
- and social insurance benefits, often related to longevity of employment and the level of previously earned income.

In assuming all this, we ignore two things. First, we ignore that, even in the advanced capitalist countries, a Standard Employment arrangement is a relatively recent phenomenon. Insofar as wage labour existed throughout the history of civil society, it was actually, for the most part, casual labour. In ancient Greece, for example, there already existed landless labourers (*thètes*) hired-in for all kinds of casual work. They had a very low social status. Since they did not belong anywhere (that is, they were not included in an *oikos*, a patriarchal social unit with mutual obligations and a degree of social solidarity), the status of *thètes* was even lower than that of domestic slaves.

Throughout history, pure wage-labourers were regarded as extremely disadvantaged. In the *Cahiers de doléances* (petitions written during the French Revolution), the situation of the day-labourer (*journalier*) was usually defined as 'a kind of hell into which peasants may fall if things are not bettered'.[11] And, in post-medieval England, workers who were fully dependent on wages were assumed to be paupers; 'only the weakest' would, according to Christopher Hill, accept this status.[12]

Only the highest strata of the working class could escape from the existential insecurity just described. Unsurprisingly, it was therefore in the circles of nineteenth-century skilled labourers that the ideal of the 'male breadwinner' (or the 'family wage') became popular – the notion that the wage of the husband should be sufficient to support a wife and small children. Already before 1939, but especially after World War II, when capitalist economies experienced unprecedented growth and the expansion of social security became possible, a large tranche of the working classes in Western Europe, North America, Australasia, and Japan obtained a Standard Employment Relationship. This was partly a knock-on effect of the recognition by large corporations that the creation of stable labour relations required 'making long-term investments in employee good will' and giving up 'short-run output and efficiency in favor of long-run stability and predictability'.[13] This labour relationship was normally understood in a gendered way and went hand-in-hand with the increasing acceptance of the male-breadwinner model.[14] And so a gendered division of labour began to emerge: Standard Employment mainly concerned men, while, in other kinds of labour relationship, women were over-represented. Even more so than in the past, precarious labour became a female occupation.

Over the course of the twentieth century, and especially since the 1940s, the number of unemployed and underemployed in the Global South grew by leaps and bounds. In the late 1990s, the economic historian Paul Bairoch estimated that, in Latin America, Africa, and Asia, 'total inactivity' was 'in the order of 30–40% of potential working man-hours' – a situation without historical precedent, 'except perhaps in the case of ancient Rome'.[15] In Europe, North America, and Japan, the average level of unemployment has, for a long time, been significantly lower. Moreover, it has been determined mainly by the economic conjuncture and is therefore cyclical, while 'over-unemployment' in 'de Global South' (this term is used by Bairoch) has a structural character.

In 1969, the Argentinian economist José Nun had already argued that Marx's three modalities of the relative surplus population (latent, stagnant, and floating) were not sufficient to fully explain underemployment in the Global South.[16] More specifically, Nun questioned what he called 'leftist hyperfunctionalism', endeavouring to show that:

> ... in many places a surplus population was growing that in the best of cases was simply irrelevant to the hegemonic sector of the economy and in the worst of cases endangered its stability. This presented the established order with the political problem of managing such nonfunctional surpluses to prevent them from becoming dysfunctional.[17]

Nun called the excluded poor the 'marginal mass'. The Peruvian sociologist Aníbal Quijano soon extended and refined this assessment. Quijano argued that the tens of millions of permanently 'marginalized' workers in the Global South could no longer be regarded as a 'reserve army of labour' in the Marxian sense because their social condition was not temporary, and because they formed no 'mass of human material always ready for exploitation', since their abilities were simply incompatible with the requirements of capitalist industry.[18]

In the Global North, the Standard Employment Relationship is now being broken down – gradually and rather consistently. The balance of power has shifted even further in favour of employers. And, in the OECD countries, the relative proportion of precarious workers has steadily increased, simultaneously, since the 1980s. A 2004 report by the European Commission already concluded that 'in most countries precarious employment has increased over the last two decades'.[19] The same trend can be observed in the US and Canada.[20]

So, Standard Employment is becoming scarcer in the advanced capitalist countries, and it seems to be even more a male privilege now than before.[21] As a corollary, the labour relations of rich countries are beginning to look much more like those of poor countries. Precarization is a global trend and is on the rise almost everywhere. The fierce and increasingly global competition between capitals now has a clear downward 'equalizing' effect on the quality of life and work in the more developed parts of global capitalism.

Nevertheless, we should keep in mind that, when considered globally and historically, there are different kinds of precarization. I believe there are at least three basic variants:

- Before the arrival of Standard Employment, precarious labour in advanced capitalism was restricted to specific, limited sectors of national economies and had a mainly temporary and conjunctural character.
- Precarious labour in contemporary advanced capitalism has spread to all sectors and is now less conjunctural and more an effect of international competition. But it combines with some labour protection – by means of all kinds of laws and welfare-state regulations established from the 1940s to the 1970s, which still remain in force, even if they are being whittled away.
- Precarious labour in the Global South has spread to almost all sectors, is especially structural in nature, and is – to an important degree – an effect of international competition. This variant involves a far greater number of people and offers much less formal protection than that given to precarious labour in the Global North. In addition – and partly as a consequence of this difference – the income gap between precarious workers in the North vs. the South remains gigantic.

San Precario teaches us that wage labour occurs in many variations, and that insecurity and precariousness are historically normal in capitalist production. The 'social' phase of capitalism was a rather brief one, and it involved only a relatively small geographic area, in global terms.

## Household labour

More than a century ago, Rosa Luxemburg observed that female domestic labour may, indeed, be 'a gigantic accomplishment of self-sacrifice and effort', but, for capitalism, it is 'mere air'. This is because, she argues, 'as long as the domination of capital and the wage system lasts – only work that creates surplus value and generates capitalist profit is considered to be productive'. From this point of view, 'the dancer in the music hall, whose boss pockets profit generated by her legs, is a productive worker, whereas all the toil of the wives and mothers of the proletariat within the four walls of home is considered to be unproductive activity'.[22] It was almost a century before such observations led to a political economy of household labour. Margaret Benston was a pioneer in that area. She set the stage for it in 1969, when, in an article published in *Monthly Review*, she highlighted the importance of 'household labor, including child care'.[23]

Benston linked the fact that such labour by housewives was unpaid (and, therefore, 'valueless') to its utter lack of prestige: 'In structural terms, the closest thing to the condition of women is the condition of others who are or were also outside of commodity production, i.e., serfs and peasants'. In the 1970s, a very extensive and sophisticated international debate took place about the political economy of domestic labour, which simmered on well into the 1980s. One of the things this debate clarified was that subsistence production is omnipresent. As the so-called Bielefeld School in development studies argued, subsistence labour is a 'condition and part of all social production (and [is] therefore inherently social in its own right), it [is] also a precondition for perpetuating all forms of commodity production and wage labour, even the most sophisticated ones'.[24] While some households do not perform subsistence labour, they are exceptional and far from poor. The only proletarian reproducing without performing subsistence labour is:

> ... the 'yuppie' (Young Urban Professional) who, as a leading (probably male) executive climbing the hierarchical ladder of the multi-national company he works for, orders a sandwich for lunch, and in the evening meets his 'yuppie-wife' (who is likely to be a professor or a stockbroker) over dinner in a restaurant, while at the couple's rented apartment the maid is doing the household chores.[25]

This thought was developed further by C. L. R. James's wife Selma Deitch (b. 1930), an independent radical thinker who, in 1972 – together with Mariarosa Dalla Costa – published the classic book *The Power of Women and the Subversion of the Community*, which spelt out how 'women's unwaged housework and other caring work outside of the market produces the whole working class'.[26] Selma James (as she is generally known) coordinated the International Women Count Network, which won the United Nations decision in persuading governments to measure and value unwaged work in their national statistics.[27] Since 1972, she also played a leading role in the International Wages for Housework Campaign. Consistent with this, Selma James has long argued for a Global Women's Strike, directed at the abolition of military budgets and the investment of the capital thus released in human carework.

Whether or not we agree with the demand for wages in respect of housework, today, it can no longer be claimed that class relationships can be understood without including the ever-present subsistence labour that is being carried out alongside paid labour.

## Global connections

Selma James thinks globally, and the same can be said of two other personalities I would like to involve here. Like C. L. R. James, they both grew up in Trinidad, at roughly the same time. The first is Oliver Cromwell Cox (1901–74), a brilliant economist and sociologist, who not only developed his own account of world-systems theory ten years before Immanuel Wallerstein but who also – based on his global perspective – defended the following thesis as early as 1959: 'It should not be forgotten that, above all else, the slave was a worker whose labour was exploited in production for profit in a capitalist market. It is this fundamental fact which identifies the Negro problem in the US with the problem of all workers regardless of color'.[28] In this way, Cox formulated an essential aspect of international solidarity. The same brand of solidarity was put into practice by Malcolm Nurse (1903–59), alias George Padmore, a childhood friend of C. L. R. James.[29]

In the early 1930s, Padmore played a key role in the attempts of the Communist International to organize black workers. He was the main founder of the International Trade Union Committee of Negro Workers in 1930 and of the newspaper *Negro Worker*. In 1934, he was expelled from the communist movement but, within months, had established the International African Service Bureau with C. L. R. James, which became a meeting point for Caribbean and African anti-colonial intellectuals.

## Implications

Let me now draw some general implications from the four vignettes I have sketched here. If we think through the arguments of the Caribbean radicals, the Italian followers of San Precario, and feminists like Margaret Benston, Selma James, and others, then we arrive at far-reaching conclusions. The history of capitalist labour must encompass all forms of physically or economically coerced commodification of labour-power: wage labourers, slaves, sharecroppers, convict labourers, and so on, *plus* all labour that creates such commodified labour or regenerates it – that is, parental labour, household labour, care labour, and subsistence labour. And if we are seeking to take all these different forms of labour into account, then we should use households as the basic unit of analysis rather than individuals, because, as Jean Quataert noted, doing so enables us to keep 'in focus at all times the lives of both men and women, young and old, and the variety of paid and unpaid work necessary to maintain the unit'.[30] Moreover, we must constantly keep in mind that all people are influenced by a large number of factors such as class, gender, race, and age, which should always be analysed, as far as possible, as intersecting – that is, in their mutual coherence and interaction.[31]

These are very fundamental assumptions. If they are correct, then our picture of history must change drastically. To begin with, we will have to reconsider our concept of capitalism. Traditionally, Marxists and non-Marxists alike believed that the rise of capitalism necessarily goes hand in hand with the diffusion of 'free' wage labour, as we have seen. But, if capitalism does not have any structural preference for free wage labour, then it can also have occurred in situations where hardly any wage labour was performed but (for example) where chattel slavery prevailed. If we no longer define capitalism in terms of a contradiction between wage labour and capital but in terms of the *commodity form* of labour-power and other elements of the production process, then it makes sense to define capitalism as a circuit of transactions and work processes in which, tendentially, 'production of commodities by means of commodities' occurs (to borrow Piero Sraffa's famous expression). This ever-widening circuit of commodity production and distribution, where not just labour products but also means of production and labour itself acquire the status of commodities, is what I would call capitalism. This definition deviates somewhat from Marx's but it is also consistent with Marx, in that he regarded the capitalist mode of production as 'generalized' or 'universalized' commodity production.[32] It does differ, however, from definitions that view capitalism simply as 'production for the market' and disregard the specific labour relations involved in production. Hence, it differs from the description we encounter in the writings of Immanuel Wallerstein and his school.[33]

On the basis of my revised definition of capitalism, I think we might well conclude that the first fully capitalist society was not eighteenth-century England, but … Barbados, the small (430 km$^2$) Caribbean island that was probably the most prosperous slaveholding society in the seventeenth century. Colonization was started there in 1627 by Sir William Courten and Associates, a London merchant-adventurer company. The company's investments were originally in the cultivation of tobacco, subsequently in cotton and indigo production, and finally, roughly from 1643, in growing sugarcane. By 1680, the sugar industry covered 80 per cent of the island's arable land, employed 90 per cent of its labour force, and accounted for about 90 per cent of its export earnings. The so-called 'Sugar Revolution' dominated agricultural development in the English West Indies for several centuries.[34] The point is that the production and consumption process in Barbados was almost entirely commodified: the workers (chattel slaves) were commodities, their food was mainly purchased from other islands, their means of production (such as sugar mills) were manufactured commercially, and their labour product (cane sugar) was sold on the world market. There have been few countries ever since whose every aspect of economic life was so strongly commodified. According to Sheridan (1970), in 1672, Francis Willoughby, Governor of Barbados, estimated that the island 'did not furnish of its own growth "one quarter Victualls sufficient for its Inhabitants nor any other necessaries for Planting …"'.[35] It was, in that sense, a truly capitalist country, albeit a very small one. And it could, of course, only exist thanks to its integration within a wider colonial empire.

Thus, from now on, it is no longer so certain that England was the birthplace of modern industrial capitalism. If we adopt a non-Eurocentric perspective, we gain three insights: 1) important developments in the history of employment began much earlier than previously thought; 2) they began with unfree workers and not with free workers; and 3) they began not in the US or in Europe but in the Global South. With great sagacity, C. L. R. James, Eric Williams, George Padmore, and Oliver Cox already paved the way for these insights.

But there is more. Wage labour, as such, is – as the creators of San Precario have highlighted – very much a multifaceted phenomenon. Insecurity and lack of protection are the historical norm under capitalism, and the Standard Employment Relationship is really only a 'blip' on the movie screen of world history. The feminist discussion has clarified that capitalism cannot exist without subsistence labour – which is often called 'reproductive labour' although that term is a poor choice, since reproduction is production just like all its other forms.

The outsider-perspective of black people, women, and precarious workers draws attention to aspects of working life that traditional labour history has previously neglected.

## Notes

1. Williams, *Capitalism and Slavery*; James, *Black Jacobins*.
2. A standard work is Oxaal, *Black Intellectuals Come to Power*.
3. The addition 'in English' is relevant, because a similar idea had been articulated before by the German Franz Hochstetter, 'Die wirtschaftlichen und politischen Motive'. Hochstetter (1880–1948) unfortunately became a Nazi in later life.
4. Marx, *Capital*, I, 272.
5. Marx, *Capital*, I, 272.
6. Weber, *Economy and Society*, I, 165.
7. Briefs, 'Das gewerbliche Proletariat', 149.
8. Marx, *Grundrisse*, 464.
9. Tarì & Vanni, 'On the life and deeds of San Precario'.
10. Architecture Lobby.
11. Clapham, *Concise Economic History*, 212.
12. Hill, 'Pottage for freeborn Englishmen', 339.
13. Jacoby, *Employing Bureaucracy*, 281.
14. See, among others, Janssens, *Rise and Decline*; Pfau-Effinger, 'Socio-historical paths'; Osawa, 'Vicious cycle'.
15. Bairoch, *Victoires et déboires III*, 778.
16. Nun, 'Sobrepopulación relativa'.
17. Nun, 'End of work', 12.
18. Quijano Obregón, 'Marginal pole of the economy'.
19. European Commission, *Precarious Employment in Europe*, 58–9.
20. Tremblay, 'From casual work to economic security', 121.
21. One pioneering study was that of Benería, 'Shifting the risk'; and an international comparative perspective is offered by Vosko, MacDonald & Campbell, *Gender and the Contours*.
22. Luxemburg, 'Frauenwahlrecht und Klassenkampf', 9.
23. Benston, 'Political economy of women's liberation', 15–16.
24. Schiel & Stauth, 'Unterentwicklung und Subsistenzproduktion', 134.
25. Evers, 'Schattenwirtschaft', 360.
26. http://globalwomenstrike.net. For the historical context, see Bracke, 'Between the transnational and the local'.
27. Fourth World Conference on Women, Beijing, 1995. For more on Selma James, see *Sex, Race and Class*.
28. Cox, *Caste, Class, and Race*, xxxii.
29. James wrote about him: 'we were boys together, and used to bathe in the Arima River, underneath the ice factory'. James, *Spheres of Existence*, 238.
30. Quataert, 'Combining agrarian and industrial livelihood', 158. On this problematic, see also Chapter 7 in this volume.
31. See also Chapter 5.
32. Marx describes capitalist society as 'a society where the commodity-form is the universal form of the product of labour, hence the dominant social relation is the relation between men as possessors of commodities' (*Capital*, I, 152). He argues that 'The capitalist epoch is ... characterized by the fact that labour-power, in the eyes of the worker himself, takes on the form of a commodity which is his property; his labour consequently takes on the form of wage-labour. On the other hand, it is only from this moment that the commodity-form of the products of labour becomes universal' (*Capital*, I, 274 note). Thus, '... from the moment there is a free sale, by the worker himself, of labour power as a commodity ... from then onwards ... commodity production is generalized and becomes the typical form of production' (*Capital*, I, 733).

33 '[The large agricultural units in ancient Greece] were run mostly on capitalistic lines; their products, that is to say, were chiefly sold in the market, not consumed by the producers.' Rostovtzeff, *Social and Economic History*, I, 100–1. Compare Chapter 4 in this volume.
34 Beckles & Downes, 'Economics of transition', 226.
35 Cited in Sheridan, *Development of Plantations*, 28.

# 3
# Six insights from Gujarat

> I use the term 'occidentalism' when the horizon of the social and cultural sciences extends no further than the frontiers of researchers' own type of society, and their interest in the rest of the world remains limited to the 'centre's' impact on the 'periphery'.
> Jan Breman, 'Over oriëntalistiek en occidentalistiek'[1]

Jan Breman (b. 1936) is one of the most important social scientists focusing on the labouring poor in South and South East Asia. His painstaking micro-level studies combine 'closely specified accounts of the real conditions in which people live and work with analysis of the structural forces that shape their trajectories'.[2] What can labour historians learn from his approach? For a start, we must note that Breman has no explicit macro-theory. Although much of his work deals with exploitation and class contradictions, he is not a Marxist. Nor, even though he often cites Max Weber approvingly, is he a pure Weberian. Bremen does not like abstract discussions. He wants, first of all, to build up 'an empirical basis', since, without a foundation of this kind, theorizing often loses touch with its object. He has observed, for example, that 'reports which are based on factual research are often particularly critical of conceptualisation'.[3] On the great debate over the dominant mode of production in Indian agriculture, he has noted critically that it 'broke down in extremely mechanistic schemas and abstract argumentation, which on closer inspection had a mystifying rather than an enlightening effect on everyday praxis'.[4]

A multifaceted, detailed reconstruction of causal mechanisms is more important to Breman than theoretical purity, as his conceptual framework shows. He uses a vocabulary in which Weberian, Marxist, and other influences are intermingled. He speaks regularly of the 'proletariat', for example, but the term denotes for him all those who do not possess any means of production of their own, regardless of what relations of production they may be enmeshed in. Breman is thus referring to a 'negatively privileged property class', the same class to which Max Weber consigned unfree workers, the declassed (*proletarii* in the sense of European antiquity), debt peons, and 'the paupers'.[5] This is thus a far broader concept than that of Marx, who reduced the proletariat to 'doubly free' wage workers.[6]

Breman's conception of capitalism seems more reminiscent of Adam Smith's than Karl Marx's because it is based, above all, on trade-based divisions of labour and the effort to accumulate money.[7] Often, Breman uses words that have several different meanings, and only the context makes it possible to know what he means by them. The concept 'mode of production', for example, sometimes refers in his work to production processes, and sometimes to an economic system.[8] Scholars who fail to appreciate Breman's layered deployment of concepts can easily fall into mistaken interpretations.[9]

Thanks to his empiricism, Breman often prefers to speak in terms of continuums instead of polarities. He mentions a continuum from free to unfree labour; he observes that 'an economic continuum has been established between town and country'.[10] And, since the richness of empirical data always takes pride of place for Breman, he has been able to interpret the same empirical phenomenon (such as bonded labour in the form of *halipratha*) in different ways over the years without finding this problematic.

Like Max Weber, Jan Breman seems to assume that 'the number and nature of causes that have determined any one specific event … are always infinite'.[11] But, while Weber's standpoint is that we can create order in 'this chaos' only because our culturally determined opinions always lead us to attribute 'importance and meaning' to only 'part of individual reality',[12] all such epistemological relativism is alien to Breman. He is driven by the fact that we live in a world that is 'weighed down as never before by the realisation of a frightful lack of distributive justice'.[13] On the one hand, he therefore orders reality on the basis of his own powerful moral and political commitment; but, on the other, he also strives to arrive at as complete a picture of causal configurations as possible. He sides with the labouring poor but, in the quest for this completeness, engages with managers, big landowners, and other authorities as well.

Marxists have maintained, not without good reason, that the 'deeper' logic of development and its dynamic contradictions can never be unearthed with this kind of empirical approach. But Breman's method also has a demonstrable, compensatory advantage. The truth is that many Marxists believe they already know the 'essence' of social developments.

For this reason, they think that it suffices simply to subsume new facts into an old theory. Breman's brand of empiricism is much more open to unexpected or unknown phenomena. It is precisely this absence of preconceptions that makes Breman's scholarly writings so innovative. Here, I would like to illustrate this quality by looking at one limited aspect of Breman's research.

Breman's academic writings are usually pigeonholed as belonging to rural sociology or development studies. But they also constitute a contribution to labour history, the history of the working classes in the broad sense of the word. Breman's contributions to this field can be divided into two parts. First, there are his explicit historical studies, such as his history of bonded labour in precolonial and colonial Gujarat or his study of colonial labour policies in the Dutch East Indies and the Belgian Congo.[14] Second, while several of his contributions were written separately, each providing a contemporary analysis, in combination, they form a longitudinal series. This is true, in particular, of his many studies (from the 1960s to the present) on labour relations in Gujarat, which, when read successively, afford some marvellous insights into middle-term regional development.[15]

Until now, historians have scarcely taken any notice of all these publications, which, from their point of view, fall too far outside the mainstream. Not only is Breman not an 'official' historian himself, but also – and this is probably more important – his approach diverges considerably from what, until recently, was the norm among labour historians. For a long time, historians of the working classes have not only occupied themselves almost exclusively with a small part of the world – the advanced capitalist countries and Eastern Europe/Russia – but they have also conceived the object of their study in a very narrow and ultimately Eurocentric way. A number of remarkable preconceptions can be identified in the enormous stream of publications that have appeared since the discipline's first days in the 1860s. The typical worker to which the traditional labour historians devoted their attention was a 'doubly free' individual (in the Marxian sense), usually male, employed in the transport sector (docks or railways), mines, industry, or large-scale agriculture. His (or sometimes her) family seemed to have, above all, a consumptive or reproductive function: wages were spent on it and children were raised within it. Protests were taken seriously mainly when they took the form of strikes, trade unions, or left-wing political parties.

When, from the 1950s onward, more scholarly contributions began appearing on the labour history of colonies or former colonies, they initially made the same Eurocentric assumptions. They, too, focused on mineworkers, dockers, plantation workers, and the like, and neglected families and the work that took place within them. They, too, mainly sought out strikes, trade unions, and political parties. Naturally, historians' political leanings could differ greatly. J. Norman Parmer's thorough *Colonial Labor Policy and Administration* (1960), for instance, which deals with the rubber plantation industry in Malaya during the last decades before World War II, looked at workers through the eyes of entrepreneurs and authorities. Jean Chesneaux's *Le mouvement ouvrier en Chine de 1919 à 1927* (1962) was written from an official Communist standpoint; while Guillermo Lora's *Historia del movimiento obrero boliviano* (1967–70) was a Trotskyist work.[16]

Later attempts often tried to develop a less Eurocentric approach. Pathbreaking works include Charles van Onselen's *Chibaro* (London, 1976) on mine labour in Southern Rhodesia, and Ranajit Das Gupta's *Labour and Working Class in Eastern India* (Calcutta, 1994) on plantation workers, miners and textile workers in Assam, Bengal and elsewhere. These new developments have been covered over the years by a series of collections of essays.[17]

I am convinced that Breman's work can make an important contribution to the ongoing reorientation of labour history. And, while it may sound paradoxical, I think that his *explicitly* historical writings – though very valuable in themselves – are less important in this respect than his sociological studies of South Gujarat since the early 1960s. For, while the explicitly historical studies, particularly those about the Netherlands Indies, investigate fields that other authors have also written about, the results of Breman's Indian fieldwork are exceptionally innovative – ground-breaking in the true sense of the word. It is precisely the studies that were not intended as contributions to the historiography that can draw labour historians' attention to biases that they need to overcome if they are to understand the logic of developments in underdeveloped and newly industrializing capitalism. Let me give a capsule description of several 'lessons' that we labour historians can learn from Breman's Indian writings. These are not so much immutable rules as methodological hints.

It all began in the early 1960s when Breman decided to study the 'vast agrarian proletariat of tribal origin' in South Gujarat.[18] That was a remarkable decision, for (as Breman himself noted): 'In those years rural studies tended to neglect agricultural labour'.[19] Those were the years in which scholarly interest in the subject began to germinate, as could be discerned in the pioneering work of Daniel and Alice Thorner and Dharma Kumar.[20] Through these studies and his own fieldwork, Breman quickly discovered that the social reality in South Gujarat was far more complex than the textbooks had led him to suppose. Landless agricultural labourers were not a product of colonialism but had existed in great numbers as early as the beginning of the nineteenth century. Not only was the waged labour force in the countryside thus far older than was usually assumed but there had also always been a 'multiplicity' of relations of dependency and exploitation.[21] Up until the mid-twentieth century, the landless rural population had, to a great extent, been part of a pluriform unfree labour system in which people often remained bound by debt to a landlord for generations, in a relationship of bondage and patronage.

These forms of attached labour began to be worn away in the late colonial period. The 'unfreedom' gradually disappeared, meaning that the landless could decide for themselves whom they would hire their labour-power to – but, at the same time, they lost the 'basic subsistence security' that the patronage system had previously provided. 'The disappearance of the elements of patronage which had helped to conceal the earlier abundant supply of rural labour put an end to the state of unfreedom in which this class used to live, but not to the stark poverty that accompanied it'.[22] In recent decades, Breman has spent most of his intellectual energy on analysing the fate of the agrarian lower strata that have been 'freed' through this process. Because these strata seemed to be geographically mobile in their search for work and were also moving to the cities, Breman soon broadened his field of research towards rural *and urban* underclasses. Over the last half century he has developed six insights that I would like to mention explicitly because they can also be very useful in other times and places to people studying the development of labour relations.

*First insight: focus on households, not individuals*. While most class analyses (including Marxist ones) take individuals as their starting point, Breman came to believe that it was better to use households as his units of analysis. In so doing he was, perhaps unconsciously, following Joseph Schumpeter's old suggestion: 'The family, not the physical person, is the true unit of class and class theory'.[23] By a quite different route from that of the Austrian economist, Breman had arrived at the conclusion that households of the lower strata are budget-pooling institutions, in which the incomes of several different people are aggregated:

> Only by looking at the household, in which many if not all of its members are involved or do want to be involved either partly or completely in the labour system, can we begin to understand the relative elasticity with which they are able to counter unemployment,

severe fluctuations in income, and other similar vicissitudes. It also explains that mood of resignation, so striking to an outsider, with which they abandon the chance of a position, when the opportunity of a job is foregone for seemingly irrational reasons.[24]

Once one takes households rather than individuals as the starting point, then all sorts of all-too-simple dichotomies can be seen in proportion. For, in one family, people with varied and shifting socioeconomic positions can live together and support each other.[25]

*Second insight: the working class is much larger than the labour elite.* Breman's focus on broad layers of 'wage hunters and gatherers' in all their variety also led him to look differently at the 'pure' working class, employed mainly in the formal sector, than was usual among left-wing, critical scholars. Breman observed that not only was the classic proletariat (in the European and North American sense) not very numerous in underdeveloped capitalism but that, moreover, it did not constitute the vanguard of class struggle. In itself, this observation was, of course, far from new. Ever since the early 1960s, a Third Worldist current had existed that asserted just the opposite, that the so-called 'real' working class was inclined towards conservatism. The best-known advocate of this position was Frantz Fanon. In his *The Wretched of the Earth*, he wrote: 'In the colonial countries the working class has everything to lose … It is [working class people] … who because of the privileged place which they hold in the colonial system constitute also the "bourgeois" fraction of the colonized people'.[26] Fanon counterposed to these workers the peasants and lumpenproletariat, 'that horde of starving men, uprooted from their tribe and from their clan', to which 'the pimps, the hooligans, the unemployed and the petty criminals' belonged. Fanon saw the lumpenproletariat as the real vanguard: 'This *lumpen-proletariat* is like a horde of rats; you may kick them and throw stones at them, but despite your efforts they'll go on gnawing at the roots of the tree'.[27]

Jan Breman follows Fanon, in the sense that he, too, has little confidence in the minority of workers who are 'employed on the basis of regular employment and standardised working conditions and are thus able to lead a relatively secure existence'. But he warns against overestimating the homogeneity of this 'elite',[28] given, among other factors, 'the differences between salaried employees of major enterprises and government institutions on the one hand, and skilled blue collar workers on the other'.[29] Various 'ranks and categories' exist within the labour elite – a fact that becomes apparent in several circumstances, including in 'the numerous trade unions which, instead of defending class interests, seem to be more concerned with sectoral interest on the basis of status differences. A common front is only seen as regards the defence of these protected forms of labour'.[30] At the same time, Breman never placed his hopes in the lumpenproletariat because his class analysis was much subtler than Fanon's.[31]

*Third insight: the labouring poor consist of several sub-classes.* Unlike Fanon, Breman does not think there is only *one* alternative to the labour aristocracy. Beneath the top layer of privileged workers, Breman distinguishes three more 'classes' within the 'working population'.[32] First, there is the 'petty bourgeoisie', which includes 'owners of small-scale enterprises, certain categories of one-man firms such as self-employed craftsmen, retail traders, shopkeepers, and those who earn their daily bread by economic brokerage, such as moneylenders, labour recruiters, contractors of piece-work or house industry, rent collectors, etc.'. This is the group that corresponds more or less to what Sol Tax once called the 'penny capitalists'.[33] Second, there is the 'sub-proletariat', the largest segment of the working population, which includes 'ambulent craftsmen who each morning tender their labour and (paltry) tools in the urban marketplace, the houseworkers, street-vendors, and a long list of others, including the inevitable shoeshine'. This segment also includes 'casual and unskilled labourers' and workers 'employed by small-scale workshops and [the] labour reserve of large enterprises'. The third and final group is the lumpenproletariat, which Breman defines as 'the urban residue with criminal tendencies' – the group of declassed people 'who have broken all ties with their original environment, who have nowhere to live, and who have no proper or regular contact with others in their immediate surroundings'. Having fallen into a state of pauperization, 'they form a beaten and apathetic muster of lone men, women with children, children without parents, the maimed and the aged. Prepared to do anything that will earn them a penny, the majority roam the streets begging, collecting old paper and bottles, and scavenging through the city's garbage for anything edible or usable'. Any 'rigid and static classification' must be rejected.[34]

*Fourth insight: complicate the informal sector.* The transitions between the different segments of the labouring poor are fluid and vague. A substantial proportion of the labouring poor is counted as part of the 'informal sector' but Breman has serious doubts about this concept.[35] Many writers think of the informal sector as a relatively homogeneous group of urban self-employed people, while the reality is much more complicated than that. First of all, the informal sector is socially much more differentiated than is often supposed. Besides self-employment, there is also, for example, casual labour as well. In reality, the informal sector includes most of the aforementioned three sectors 'under' the labour elite. And it is exceptionally difficult – if not impossible – to split the informal sector analytically into different elements: 'The specific structure of the informal sector – dominated by exchangeability and discontinuity and knowing only a very slim margin between employment and unemployment – makes categorisation according to the standard concepts and problems defined in terms of the formal sector a rather dubious affair'.[36]

*Fifth insight: complicate the urban–rural dichotomy*. An additional wrinkle is that the informal sector is far from an exclusively urban phenomenon. When the formal–informal distinction is restricted to urban labour, the concept 'loses some of its practical and policy relevance'.[37] The enormous geographical mobility of the labour force means that 'town and country cannot be regarded as separate economic sectors'.[38] More generally, there are too many stereotypes in the literature, as if all migration occurred from the country to the city or as if non-agrarian activities existed only in cities. This kind of sharp counterposition between rural and urban areas does not correspond to reality. In many respects, it makes more sense to see a gradual transition, a continuum. First, many extractive and industrial activities take place in rural areas. Plantations are a major example of this. Second, there is considerable geographical mobility *within* rural areas in the form of a seasonal movement of labour.[39] Third, the move from country to town is often temporary: 'Large groups of seasonal migrants wander wretchedly to and fro between town and country, recruited or rejected as need arises'.[40] And, fourth, there is also movement from city to countryside: 'In the harvest season in particular, farmers from distant neighbourhoods will travel by tractor to [daily labour] markets in Valsad and Bardoli, for instance, to hire gangs of workers to harvest their crops'.[41]

*Sixth insight: complicate migration processes*. It is often assumed that people are either sedentary (and thus work where they live) or they migrate over great distances. Breman shows, however, that there are all sorts of intermediary forms. Even in South Gujarat, 'the predominant pattern of labour mobility is not migration but circulation'.[42] Breman distinguishes among several variants. The first one, of course, is daily commuting by workers in the formal as well as the informal sector, 'with a fixed workplace to which they travel daily', and by casual labourers who, in 'the course of a few weeks or even days ... will visit numerous locations, situated near or further away from the village, to perform the same or even different work each time: as helper in the building trade, loader-unloader on a lorry, navvy or road worker, or as agricultural day labourer'.[43]

In the second variant, there is seasonal work, which 'started in the first half of the twentieth century'.[44] As early as the 1920s, the Halpatis who worked as *halis* (bonded servants) took part in seasonal migration. 'By giving them permission to do so, the landed gentry avoided being held responsible for their livelihood in the slack season'.[45] These migratory processes cannot all be simply reduced to push- and pull-factors. Migration, above all circular migration, does not take place primarily because of a labour shortage in one spot and a labour surplus in another. On the contrary, sometimes workers go from A to B to work when, at the very same moment, there are workers from B doing the same work in A. What is most important in such cases is the power of the employer. Not only can workers 'from the outside world' be more easily let-go at the employer's convenience, but outsiders are also far easier to control: 'Labourers coming from elsewhere are often not familiar with the local customs and language; in the most literal of senses, they do not know their way around within the milieu in which they find themselves, and are defenceless in the face of the power exercised over them at the work site, which was usually also the place where they took up residence'.[46] This powerlessness is often strengthened because the employer makes sure his labour force is made up of people with varied ethnic and geographical origins.

With these six insights, Breman has provided building blocks for a truly global, non-Eurocentric labour history. His approach demonstrates that we should re-examine all the schemas we were educated in on their merits. Why, for example, do we still take the formal sector as our starting point and consider the informal sector as a deviation from this norm? Shouldn't we turn the questions around? If the majority of the wage-earning labour force is involved in informal labour relations, isn't the conclusion obvious that 'more than the persistence of the informal sector economy, the emergence of the formal sector employment needs explanation'?[47] In short, Breman's writings constitute a great intellectual challenge. Since Breman himself does not theorize much but has always stayed quite close to his empirical data, theoretically-minded people who seek to derive further interpretation of his research findings have a considerable amount of work ahead of them.

# Notes

1. Breman, 'Over oriëntalistiek en occidentalistiek', 504.
2. Benanav, 'Landscapes of labour', 222.
3. Breman, *Wage Hunters and Gatherers*, 7.
4. Breman, *Wage Hunters and Gatherers*, 375.
5. Weber, *Economy and* Society, I, 303. Compare Breman, *Of Peasants, Migrants and Paupers*, 66–74.
6. '[T]his worker must be free in the double sense that as a free individual he can dispose of his labour-power as his own commodity, and that, on the other hand, he has no other commodity for sale'. Karl Marx, *Capital,* I, 272.
7. Smith, *Wealth of Nations*, Books I–III.
8. Breman speaks, for example, about 'a more aggregate mode of production' and about the plantation industry as 'a mode of capitalist production'. Breman, *Taming the Coolie Beast*, 23 and Chapter III.
9. An example of a mistaken interpretation can be found in Brass, 'Immobilised workers, footloose theory'. Brass argues in this article, among other things, that Breman misunderstands 'Marxist theory in general, and in particular those concepts (proletarianisation, deproletarianisation, repeasantisation) which are crucial to a Marxist analysis of agrarian change and the role in this of unfree labour' (339). The author fails to see that Breman, despite his Marxist-sounding terminology, is, in fact, an eclectic thinker with neo-Weberian leanings.
10. Breman, Das & Agarwal, *Down and Out*, 33.
11. Weber, '"Objektivität"', 177–8.
12. Weber, '"Objektivität"'. See the critical analysis in Lefèvre, *Zum historischen Charakter*.
13. Breman, 'De strijd voor maatschappelijke gelijkheid', 408.
14. Breman, *Patronage and Exploitation*; 'Village on Java'; *Taming the Coolie Beast*; 'Primitive racism'; *Mobilizing Labour*.
15. See, above all, the trilogy: Breman, *Patronage and Exploitation*; *Of Peasants, Migrants and Paupers*; *Footloose Labour*.
16. Parmer, *Colonial Labor Policy*; Chesneaux, *Le mouvement ouvrier en Chine*; Lora, *Historia del movimiento obrero boliviano*.
17. Sandbrook & Cohen, *Development of an African Working Class*; Gutkind, Cohen & Copans, *African Labor History*; Cohen, Gutkind & Brazier, *Peasants and Proletarians*; Munslow & Finch, *Proletarianisation in the Third World*; Agier, Copans & Morice, *Classes ouvrières d'Afrique noire*; Amin & van der Linden, 'Peripheral' Labour?'; Bellucci & Eckert, *General Labour History of Africa*.
18. Breman, *Beyond Patronage*, vi.
19. Breman, *Beyond Patronage*.
20. Thorner & Thorner, *Land and Labour in India*; Kumar, *Land and Caste in South India*.
21. Breman, *Patronage and Exploitation*, 8.
22. Breman, *Beyond Patronage*, 264.
23. Schumpeter, *Imperialism and Social Classes*, 148.
24. Breman, *Wage Hunters*, 60–1.
25. This does not imply that the household-family is necessarily a picture of peace and harmony. On the contrary, members do not necessarily work for the common good of the household; they may be driven by selfish motives. Conflicts of interest are also possible, as well as oppression and resistance to it. See Chapter 7.
26. Fanon, *Wretched of the Earth*, 86.
27. Fanon, *Wretched of the Earth*, 103.
28. Breman, *Wage Hunters*, 29.
29. Breman, *Wage Hunters*, 35.
30. Breman, *Wage Hunters*.
31. Breman presumably agrees with Peter Worsley's rejection of Fanon's 'assertion that the employed are always "privileged", since the mass of unskilled labourers in the towns are hardly living high on the hog, and since the employed poor, too, are "sub-proletarian" in living standards and pursue "informal" income-opportunities (so that [there] is no clear border-line between "proletariat" and "sub-proletariat")'. Worsley, 'Fanon and the "Lumpenproletariat"', 225.
32. For what follows, see Breman, *Wage Hunters*, 30–2.
33. Tax, *Penny Capitalism*.

34 Breman, *Wage Hunters*, 33.
35 See Breman's essay 'Dualistic labour system? A critique of the "informal sector" concept'. In Breman, *Wage Hunters*, 3–45.
36 Breman, *Wage Hunters*, 61.
37 Breman, *Footloose Labour*, 3; Breman refers to Jaganathan, *Informal Markets*.
38 Breman, *Wage Hunters*, 50.
39 For example, Breman, *Wage Hunters*, 182–8.
40 Breman, *Wage Hunters*, 9.
41 Breman, *Footloose Labour*, 47.
42 Breman, *Footloose Labour*, 33.
43 Breman, *Footloose Labour*, 35.
44 Breman, *Footloose Labour*, 44.
45 Breman, *Footloose Labour*. Breman refers to Mukhtyar, *Life and Labour*.
46 Breman, *Labour Migration*, 18–19.
47 Breman, *Footloose Labour*, 5. A similar point is made in Wallerstein, *Historical Capitalism*.

# Part II
# Concepts

# 4
# Capitalism

Capitalism remains a controversial idea. When, at the end of the nineteenth century, it became a widely used expression in the academic world, this led almost straight away to various terminological controversies and confusions. In 1918, the German economist Richard Passow remarked tellingly: 'It is always when clear concepts are missing, that this word makes its timely appearance'.[1]

When R. H. Tawney published his book *Religion and the Rise of Capitalism* in 1922, one reviewer commented that the term 'capitalism' was a political catchphrase that did not belong in a serious historical study. Tawney replied as follows:

> Obviously, the word 'Capitalism', like 'Feudalism' and 'Mercantilism', is open to misuse … But, after more than half a century of work on the subject by scholars of half a dozen different nationalities and of every variety of political opinion, to deny that the phenomenon exists; or to suggest that, if it does exist, it is unique among human institutions, in having, like Melchizedek, existed from eternity; or to imply that, if it had a history, propriety forbids that history to be disinterred, is to run willfully in blinkers. Verbal controversies are profitless; if an author discovers a more suitable term, by all means let him use it. He is unlikely, however, to make much of the history of Europe during the last three centuries, if, in addition to eschewing the word, he ignores the fact.[2]

Despite repeated attempts to abolish it, then, the concept of capitalism persisted. The reason for its staying power is that it refers to a pattern of qualitatively novel experiences in social life. These new experiences stand in clear contrast with preceding societies, which were mainly oriented towards the utility of resources: their economic activities served to acquire specific goods and services, such as foodstuffs, clothing, weapons, ornaments, servants, and soldiers. Economic activities were oriented to subsistence, or, additionally, to the production of a surplus that enabled an intellectual and artistic *praxis* by an elite (such as in ancient Greece) or conspicuous consumption, warfare, and empire-building. We can find examples of this utility-orientation everywhere around the world, among hunter-gatherers, small peasants, and patriarchal households.[3]

Of course, trade also existed in use-oriented societies – for example, because the surplus owned by *A* could be exchanged for a different surplus owned by *B*. Transactions could even occur across great distances and via intermediaries. Usually, though, they played a subordinate role within these societies themselves. Most of the transactions occurred in markets, which were held daily or almost daily, although many ancient societies also featured larger markets occurring less frequently. Such large markets were usually special events. They were more than simply an opportunity to trade goods; they also involved the expression of desires and their satisfaction, a wish to access foreign domains, a discovery of the unknown and the exotic, and so forth. As such, they often had a festive atmosphere. Among the Aztecs, the largest market was the *macuiltianquiztli* in Tlatelolco, a neighbourhood in Tenochtitlan (Mexico). Here, more than 100,000 people assembled once every 20 days, combining trade with religious festivities. In eighteenth-century Egypt, large religious and commercial festivals were held along with smaller markets, to celebrate deities. In these festivals, merchants could reach more customers, and the local peasants could inspect goods that were not available at ordinary *suqs*. In pre-revolutionary China, annual fairs were usually combined with the feast day of the local temple's principal deity. In the European languages, words such as *feriae*, *foire*, *fair*, and *Fest* refer to the common root of market and feast, exchange and pleasure.[4]

As soon as traders had become a separate occupational group, we also witness the emergence of another orientation, focused less on considerations of utility than on making money. It gives rise to the idea of *abstract accumulation* – that is, accumulation that is not aimed at realizing a specific kind of lifestyle but that becomes a goal, in and of itself. *Oikonomia* ('housekeeping' in the Ancient Greek sense) is replaced by *pleonexia* (self-enrichment) – a goal that acquires an independent existence vis-à-vis its social and moral context. Already in the fourteenth century, Ibn Khaldûn noted that trade means 'buying goods at a low price and selling them at a high price, whether these goods consist of slaves, grain, animals, weapons, or clothing material'. He added:

> ... honest (traders) are few. It is unavoidable that there should be cheating, tampering with the merchandise which may ruin it, and delay in payment which may ruin the profit, since (such delay) while it lasts prevents any activity that could bring profit. There will also be non-acknowledgement or denial of obligations, which may prove destructive of one's capital unless (the obligation) has been stated in writing and properly witnessed.[5]

When this attitude of merciless accumulation gains influence in areas that were previously only use-oriented, the distinction between the two is recognized by more and more people. In Europe, for example, 'true friendship' begins to mean that there is a relationship between people that exists beyond the logic of commodification, beyond calculated self-interest.[6] A friend can make sacrifices and can set his or her self-interest aside to support a companion. This 'anti-commercial' notion of friendship spread through Europe in the eighteenth century and, from there, to other parts of the world. It involves an ideology that became highly influential and durable precisely because it developed in response to the realities of commercial self-interest.

In 1840, Thomas Carlyle summed up the trend in an exaggeration: 'Cash Payment', he asserted, had 'grown to be the universal sole nexus of man to man!'.[7] A few years later, this idea of a *cash nexus* appears again in Marx and Engels's *Manifesto of the Communist Party*, according to which the bourgeoisie 'has pitilessly torn asunder the motley feudal ties that bound man to his "natural superiors"' and has left remaining no other nexus between man and man than naked self-interest and callous 'cash payment'.[8] More theorizing along these lines occurred in the 1860s and 1870s, when the emerging discipline of anthropology led to evolutionist reflections by scholars about 'then' and 'now' – where 'then' referred to the 'primitive' societies, about which more became known through the explorations of colonists. Sir Henry Maine wrote in his book *Ancient Law*:

> The movement of the progressive societies has been uniform in one respect. Through all its course it has been distinguished by the gradual dissolution of family dependency and the growth of individual obligation in its place. The individual is steadily substituted for the Family, as the unit of which civil laws take account ... Nor is it difficult to see what is the tie between man and man which replaces by degrees those forms of reciprocity in rights and duties which have their origin in the Family. It is Contract. Starting, as from one terminus of history, from a condition of society

in which all the relations of Persons are summed up in the relations of Family, we seem to have steadily moved towards a phase of social order in which all these relations arise from the free agreement of individuals.[9]

Subsequently, Ferdinand Tönnies published his work *Gemeinschaft und Gesellschaft*, in which he distinguished two kinds of societies: those based on non-contractual solidarity and those held together only by the influence of the state. Emile Durkheim criticized the implicit conservatism of Tönnies (as well as Comte and Spencer), replying that 'I believe that the life of the great social agglomerations is just as natural as that of small aggregates. It is neither less organic nor less internal'. Although it is 'certainly distinct', he argued, there is 'no difference in nature'.[10] In his book *De la division du travail* (1893), Durkheim elaborated his thesis: while, in traditional ('mechanical') society, social cohesion was accomplished by the *conscience commune*, modern ('organic') society is held together by the division of labour – primarily, that is, by occupational specialization. The second form of society had proved historically superior to the first.[11]

The new individualized and businesslike relationships pervaded daily life in many different ways. One symptom of this phenomenon was an increasing awareness of time. In the 1880s, the philosopher Friedrich Nietzsche observed in his *Gay Science*:

> One is now ashamed of repose: even long reflection almost causes remorse of conscience. Thinking is done with a stop-watch, as dining is done with the eyes fixed on the financial newspaper; we live like men who are continually 'afraid of letting opportunities slip' … – one has no longer either time nor energy for ceremonies, for roundabout courtesies, for any *esprit* in conversation, or for any *otium* whatever. For life in the hunt for gain continually compels a person to consume his intellect, even to exhaustion, in constant dissimulation, overreaching, or forestalling; the real virtue nowadays is to do something in a shorter time than another person.[12]

A tendency to 'measure' more and more things (pantometry)[13] was also evident in the education system, where pupils were encouraged to compete with each other, and where their performance was judged in terms of linear criteria such as grades. In the early-twentieth century, Werner Sombart used the 'taxametrization' of coaches as an example to describe a trend towards formalization:

> [T]he old relationship between coachman and customer is of a very personal character: the conditions under which the journey is undertaken are fixed in a personal talk on a case by case basis; at the time of payment, the personal character of the relationship is most clearly expressed by the variation in charges. If however a taxameter is affixed to the carriage, then all the personal, individual or coincidental aspects in the relationship between coachman and passenger are annulled; the latter just mutely pays the amount shown by the meter.[14]

Taxametrization was Sombart's metaphor for expressing the *general* depersonalization occurring, which he noticed in many different areas of life, including catering and hotel accommodation, written correspondence, street numbering, and the transition to stable feeding.

It is against this backdrop that the ascent of the concept of capitalism began. The term expresses that the *concrete* aim to procure useful things is subordinated to the *abstract* aim to make money and realize profits. And it is precisely this experiential context that can explain the stubborn persistence of the concept – despite repeated attempts to banish it from public and scientific discourse. As soon as we attempt to ban the notion, it returns in another guise, whether as commodification, commercialization, money-making, or market-orientation, among other concepts. In his book *The Wheels of Commerce*, Fernand Braudel wrote on the notion of 'capitalism':

> Personally, after a long struggle, I gave up trying to get rid of this troublesome intruder. I decided in the end that there was nothing to be gained by throwing out along with the word the controversies it arouses, which have some pertinence to the present-day world ... [If] capitalism is thrown out of the door, it comes in through the window.[15]

## Definitions

Although 'capitalism' refers to real experiences, there is certainly no unanimity about its definition. Initially, historians tended towards a broad description. Some, like Norman Gras, even thought that capitalism could be found in every civilization; it meant nothing more than saving, planning, and cultivating 'nature's products (berries, nuts, timber, animals) ... for future use'.[16] A century ago, the medievalist Henri Pirenne believed that capitalism was at least a thousand years old. And, According to the historian Michael Rostovtzeff, capitalism had existed in European antiquity, since it concerned the production of goods that 'were chiefly sold in the market, not consumed by the producers'.[17]

Nowadays, two interpretations seem to predominate that are often at loggerheads with each other. One interpretation goes back to Adam Smith and is defended by Immanuel Wallerstein, among others. It says that capitalism exists wherever there is 'a system of production for sale in a market for profit and appropriation of this profit on the basis of individual or collective ownership'.[18] According to this approach, it does not matter what the social relations *within* the production system look like (whether there is serfdom or wage labour, for instance); all that matters is a type of economic behaviour that is oriented towards market sales and profit-making. The other interpretation has its source in the Marxian tradition, defining capitalism (or the capitalist mode of production) as generalized commodity production. This interpretation means that capitalism exists when not only the outputs (goods and services) created by the production system take the form of commodities but also all the *inputs* of that system – including labour, resources, and means of production – are purchased as commodities.[19]

It is true that intermediate definitions between the two also exist. Max Weber, for example, was closer to the Smithians than to the Marxists, but he nevertheless built a bridge between the two approaches. He distinguished between a 'pre-rationalist capitalism' (of which there were supposedly examples across the last four millennia in China and India, as well as in the European antiquity and middle ages) and a 'rationalist capitalism' (which flourished in the West and was characterized by 'rational capitalist firms' with their own fixed capital, free labour, rational division of labour, and competitive economic behaviour).[20] This second variant strongly resembles Marx's capitalism.

Capitalism can be seen as the competitive accumulation of capital based on commodification.[21] It involves a progressive circulation of commodity production and distribution, such that not only labour products but also means of production and labour capacity acquire the status of commodities. The commodification of human labour capacity does not necessarily have to take the form of wage labour (as both Marx and Weber believed) but can also be based on physical coercion, as is the case with indentured labour or chattel slavery.[22] Nevertheless, it remains true that capitalism's 'single most important innovation is the vast expansion of wage labor' – as Sven Beckert has observed.[23]

Essential for capitalism, however defined, is the transformation of outputs (labour products) and inputs of labour processes (human labour capacity, raw materials, means of production) into commodities – into goods and services that have both a use-value and an exchange-value. That is, the goods and services both meet the needs of particular consumers (individuals, enterprises, institutions) and can also be traded in fixed proportions for other commodities. Capitalism cannot exist without commodity production and commodity trade. Yet, commodities are not a 'stand-alone' phenomenon: their existence presupposes the presence of at least three other phenomena: property rights, money, and competition.

*Property rights*: Commodities can be bought and sold only by their owners (or the legal representatives of those owners). Commodities therefore assume property rights – bundles of enforceable claims.[24] Each property right is backed with the threat of public enforcement via some kind of sanction – and, as a last resort, physical coercion.

*Money*: Commodities are bought and sold for money, a general equivalent (and a special kind of commodity) with which the price of diverse goods and services can be reckoned. Money (which originally may have had a religious and cultic function)[25] can become a fetish because, in capitalism, it appears that everything revolves around it (abstract wealth) as a means of acquiring every possible kind of goods and services. Money makes financial credit possible, and therefore also an independent currency trade and a finance industry. 'Credit creation' is, as Harold James has observed, 'the driving force of the modern monetary economy'.[26]

*Competition*: As such, competition is obviously not unique to capitalism. Chiefdoms and states also compete with each other. But the nature of competition in the field of commodity production and trade is specific. 'The basic law of capitalist competition' is not mainly about territory or political power but, as Marx emphasized,[27] about realizing profit from the production and sale of commodities – in which control over territories and political power can, of course, be a very useful aid. The biggest profit rate is naturally reached when there are no rivals in the market. As Immanuel Wallerstein says: 'If there is a monopoly, the seller can demand any price, as long as he or she does not go beyond what the elasticity of demand permits'.[28] That is why competition constantly involves attempts to negate it – a tendency that Norbert Elias calls the *monopoly mechanism*.[29]

These aspects make it clear that the history of capitalism cannot be written without systematic attention to rules, laws, and politics. Furthermore, a history of capitalism is inconceivable without a parallel, integrated history of nation-states, national banks, government debt, and labour relations. Every manifestation of capitalism requires institutions that regulate markets, the circulation of money, and forms of employment. Capitalism is not just an economic system; the discontinuous yet still progressing commodification process influences every sphere of life, from ecology and agriculture, via kinship and family life, to war-making.

The regulated combination of commodification with property rights, money, and competition makes capitalism an ever-restless and enormously dynamic system. Almost two centuries ago, John Ramsay McCulloch remarked: 'There are no limits to the passion for accumulation',[30] while a 1952 study commissioned by the American Economic Association made an equally striking observation about this perpetual striving:

> [In capitalism], real assets and consumables, in bulk, if not in composition, are valued not for themselves but for their monetary equivalent. All things are thought of as exchangeable and saleable, and therefore as convertible into money, the universal solvent. The money measure of goods becomes the *real* expression of their value. Goods are money, and, from the viewpoint of capitalist motivation, it is from this equivalence that they derive their worth ... Thus the energy and ability which, in some societies, are directed toward religion, politics, art, or war are, in the developed capitalist milieu, channeled into business.[31]

Greed can certainly play a role in this incessant process of accumulation but it is not an absolute requirement. Other motives, such as frugality and ambition, can be just as important, as Max Weber already knew.[32]

## Periods and types

A broad definition of capitalism will inevitably lead to a different historical periodization than a narrow one. According to some Smithians, capitalism has already existed for more than two thousand years. According to most Marxian scholars, however, we should date the beginning of capitalism to the eighteenth century because, at that time, a lot of wage labour and manufactories first emerged in Western Europe. Depending on the definition applied, further periodizations are possible. Such attempts are certainly useful and they have a lengthy history.[33] They enable us to order the historical material and put it into perspective. At the same time, however, this obviously also carries a risk of over-systematization, whereby turning points are exaggerated and continuities overlooked. Every attempt to periodize a phenomenon necessarily assumes that its development contains both continuities and discontinuities. If nothing changed over the course of time, a periodization would not make any sense. Inversely, if everything changed *all* the time, purely by accident, no periodization would be possible. Periodizing assumes the simultaneity of relative continuity and relative discontinuity. The former implies not that there is a constant recurrence of events but, rather, that, even when major changes occur, a definite structural coherence remains discernable. Inversely, relative discontinuity means not that arbitrary changes occur but that a disturbance of the existing relationships occurs according to some kind of identifiable logic.[34]

Naturally, various periodizations can be applied side-by-side. Fluctuations in economic growth, demography, technology, consumer behaviour, trade union structures, ecological frontiers, or cultural value systems can all have divergent temporalities.[35] Changes within capitalism, moreover, do not occur everywhere at the same time: sometimes, they generalize over the course of time and, in the process, often change their form; sometimes, they occur unevenly and in combination with other shifts. That is one reason why it is almost impossible to mark off the precise 'beginning' and 'end' of a period. Periodizations 'seldom fit neatly and exactly; historical events resist periodization into watertight compartments'.[36] It seems wise to allow for the possibility of transition periods, in which the old and the new co-exist with each other.

Even more important, it seems to me, is a thesis defended by Andrea Komlosy: we should not take as a point of departure the stages of development in separate regions and states but, instead, focus on the connections *between* regions and states.[37] Taking this approach, it also becomes possible to understand cultural, economic, and political transfers between different parts of the world, which often result in combined and uneven developments, in which 'innovations' in one place are combined with 'regressions' in other places. The transatlantic slave trade offers a good example: already in the seventeenth century it rendered highly modern and profitable plantations possible in the Caribbean, yet, simultaneously, promoted impoverishment in parts of Africa. There are nevertheless also moments that hit different parts of the world almost simultaneously, although they have different levels of impact in separate regions. Global economic crises (1857–9, 1873–9, 1929–33, 1966–7, and 2007–8) are examples of such moments.[38]

The issue of periodization is bound up with the issue of typologies. Wallerstein is obviously right when he claims that, on a world level, there is only one kind of capitalism, a 'singular structure', but that does not preclude that highly diverse variants of capitalism have emerged within the world system. One does not have to agree with the whole analysis of Gøsta Esping-Anderson's *The Three Worlds of Welfare Capitalism* (1990) or Michel Albert's *Capitalisme contre capitalisme* (1991) to realize that capitalism knows many different guises. Some variants occur quite regularly in the historical literature. One of them is 'merchant capitalism' – a somewhat undertheorized concept that refers to an early form of capitalism (occurring in North Africa and the Middle East since the ninth century, and in Europe since the twelfth century) in which industry and finance capital played a subordinate role.[39]

Another variant is 'organized capitalism' – a concept that goes back to the Austro-Marxist Rudolf Hilferding. Hilferding claimed that, since about 1915, European capitalism had begun to exhibit some of the characteristics of a planned economy through cartelization and, therefore, could be fundamentally reformed through state intervention. This idea was introduced into the historical literature in the 1970s, although, soon enough, 'the end of organized capitalism' was diagnosed as well.[40] One can also distinguish between different business models, which appear in changing combinations. Patrick Fridenson has identified four types of capitalist business trajectories, varying from small enterprises to large corporations. These different modes of business are generally characterized by more or less strong entrepreneurial family ties and diverse systems of finance, with different forms of liability, but also by different locations in global commodity chains, local labour relations, and workers' household economies.[41]

A drawback of many typologies and periodizations of capitalism is that they are based on the histories of the old core regions in the world-system: Western Europe, North America, and Japan.

## Patterns and trends

Many authors have attempted to discover general tendencies in capitalist development. About some trends there is a fairly broad consensus – for example, the constantly interrupted but steadily progressing concentration and centralization of capital since the nineteenth century, or the likewise discontinuous but nevertheless progressing internationalization (globalization) of production and distribution. The surge in importance of the sphere of consumption and of the financial sector is generally accepted. Other trends are more controversial: is there, in reality, a tendential fall in the average rate of profit, as various classical economists have argued? And is the rate of return on capital in the long term really larger than the rate of growth, as Thomas Piketty claims?[42] Does the gap between rich and poor countries really continue to grow wider?

At the same time, the development of capitalism is clearly uneven, both on a world scale and within different regions. Precisely by viewing the world as a unitary but differentiated whole, it becomes possible to contextualize developments in the historical core zones of capitalism much better. Consider, for example, the welfare states that emerged in a limited number of countries after World War II. Already in the late 1960s, the political economist Ernest Mandel was arguing that welfare states with mass consumption minimally require a high level of industrialization and aggregate wealth, combined with a steady rhythm of expansion. That would exclude 'three-quarters of the countries of the world from all chance of success in such experiments. At most, these can find a momentary success in about twenty countries (the US, Canada, Australia, New Zealand, Japan, and Western Europe), which account for less than 20 per cent of the world's population'.[43] Welfare states would therefore necessarily be 'temporary'. Current trends do not seem to contradict this hypothesis. In advanced capitalist countries, social security provisions are being gradually reduced, while precarious and unstable jobs are on the rise.

One final crucial question is this: if capitalism is a historical phenomenon, which has conquered the world since the seventeenth or eighteenth century, will it also reach an endpoint? Marxists, in particular, have often claimed that capitalism is doomed in the long run; some even believed that the timing of the end could be calculated.[44] But Youssef Cassis has rightly pointed out that 'capitalism has never *really* been threatened by collapse during an economic crisis in the last 150 years'.[45] So far, the system has recovered after each crisis, often instituting reforms intended to prevent a repetition of any collapse.[46] Still, there is a definite scholarly undercurrent that believes that the growth possibilities for capitalism are reducing, because 'On the three frontiers of commodification—labour, nature and money—regulatory institutions restraining the advance of capitalism for its own good have collapsed, and after the final victory of capitalism over its enemies no political agency capable of rebuilding them is in sight'.[47]

\*\*\*

Concepts reveal, in Hegel's words, 'that which is genuinely permanent and substantial in the complexity and contingency of appearance and fleeting manifestation'.[48] Concepts, as such, cannot explain reality, but they can act as building-blocks for such an explanation. A scientific concept is most useful if it contributes to the building of theories that can explain a significant part of reality; has a meaning that is entirely clear to all participants in the research; and is not changed over time by stealth (that is, without the change being mentioned explicitly). I believe capitalism can be such a concept. The notion of 'capitalism' is 'something that historians need in our toolkit', as Gareth Austin has said;[49] it allows us to comprehend the interconnectedness of many diverse aspects and processes in world society.

## Notes

1. Passow, *'Kapitalismus'*, 1.
2. Tawney, 'Preface to 1937', vii–viii.
3. See, for example, Sahlins, *Stone Age Economics*; Scott, *Moral Economy of the Peasant*.
4. Thiemer-Sachse, 'Marktwesen und Fernhandel', 245–6; Larson, 'Rural marketing system', 504; Skinner, 'Marketing and social structure', 38; Kurnitzky, *Der heilige Markt*, 18.
5. Ibn Khaldûn, *Muqaddimah*, II, 336 and 342.
6. Silver, 'Friendship in commercial society'.
7. Carlyle, *Chartism*, 58.
8. Marx & Engels, 'Manifesto', 70.
9. Maine, *Ancient Law*, 163. Maine sums it up as a movement 'from status to contract' (165).
10. Durkheim, review of *Gemeinschaft und Gesellschaft*, 421.
11. Durkheim, *De la division de travail*.
12. Levy, *Complete Works of Friedrich Nietzsche*, Vol. 10, 254–5 (§ 329).
13. Crosby, *Measure of Reality*.
14. Sombart, *Der moderne Kapitalismus*, II/1, 1078.
15. Braudel, *Civilization and Capitalism*, II, 231.
16. Gras, 'What is capitalism …?', 83.
17. Pirenne, 'The stages in the social history of capitalism'; Rostovtzeff, *Social and Economic History*, I, 100–1.
18. Wallerstein, 'Dependence in an interdependent world', 1.
19. See, for example, Brenner, 'Origins of capitalist development'.
20. Weber, 'Parlament und Regierung', 453; Weber, *Die protestantische Ethik*, 34; Weber, *Economy and Society*, I, 165.
21. See also Kocka, *Capitalism*, 21–4.
22. For a more elaborate argument, see my book *Workers of the World*.
23. Beckert, 'The new history of capitalism', 239.
24. Hohfeld, *Fundamental Legal Conceptions*. Modern legal theory breaks property rights into the following rights and duties: '(i) the right to possess, (ii) the right to use, (iii) the right to manage, (iv) the right to the income of the object, (v) the right to the capital, (vi) the right to security, (vii) the right of transmissibility, (viii) the right of absence of term, (ix) the duty to prevent harmful use, (x) liability to execution, and (xi) the incident of residuarity'. For full ownership in an object, a proprietor must hold most (but not necessarily all) of these elements regarding that object. See Honoré's classical essay 'Ownership'.
25. Laum, *Heiliges Geld*, esp. 126–57; Benveniste, *Vocabulaire des institutions indo-européennes*, I, 132–3; Servet, *Nomismata*.
26. James, 'Finance capitalism', 139.

27  Marx, *Capital*, III, 127.
28  Wallerstein, 'Capitalism', 192.
29  Elias, *Civilizing Process*.
30  McCulloch, *Principles of Political Economy*, 178.
31  Abramovitz, 'Economics of growth', 159–60.
32  Greed can, of course, be found in all kinds of societies in which money is used, even if only very limited commodity trade occurs. The record of an early-nineteenth-century talk by William Mariner (a young Englishman) with Finow (the chief of the Pacific island of Tonga) is insightful. Mariner tried to explain the meaning of money to Finow. After the basic idea had been clarified, Finow responded as follows: '"If", said he, "it were made of iron, and could be converted into knives, axes, and chisels, there would be some sense in placing a value on it; but as it was, he saw none: if a man", he added, "has more yams than he wants, let him exchange some of them away for pork or gnatoo; certainly money was much handier, and more convenient, but then as it would not spoil by being kept, people will store it up, instead of sharing it out, as a chief ought to do, and thus become selfish; whereas, if provision was the principal property of a man, and it ought to be, as being the most useful and the most necessary, he could not store it up, for it would spoil, and so he would be obliged either to exchange it away for something else useful, or share it out to his neighbours, and inferior chiefs and dependants, for nothing." He concluded by saying, "I understand now very well what it is that makes the Papalangis [i.e. Europeans] so selfish; – it is this money!"'. Martin, *Account of the Natives*, I, 263–4.
33  See the concise reconstruction in Green, 'Periodization', 16–29.
34  Jessop, 'What follows Fordism?'.
35  See, for example, Duby, 'L'histoire des systèmes de valeurs'; Hugill, *World Trade since 1431*; Stearns, 'Stages of consumerism'; van der Linden, *Workers of the World*, ch. 12; Barbier, *Scarcity and Frontiers*. A theoretical exploration can be found in Jordheim, 'Against periodization'.
36  Cameron, 'Periodization of Chinese history', 177.
37  Komlosy, 'Work and labour relations'.
38  Consider, in this context, the numerous theories of 'long waves' of economic growth, whose turning points would, according to many, coincide with such large crises. The challenge here is that the reality of long waves is difficult to prove empirically, precisely because of their relatively long duration. When, in the 1920s, Nikolai Kondratieff presented his theory of long cycles lasting about 45 to 60 years, only two of these cycles had already occurred according to his own testimony (i.e., circa 1790–1844/51, with a turning point around 1810/17, and 1844/51–1890–6, with a turning point around 1870/75). A third cycle would, according to Kondratieff, hypothetically have its turning point in 1914/20. Yet, such long-term fluctuations could, of course, also be the effect of contingent influences. The regularity in the rises and falls of prices and interest rates that Kondratieff postulated was still very much a speculation, not a scientific certainty. Now that we are nearly a century ahead in time, there seems to be more evidence for the existence of long waves. Empirical substantiation of the waves nevertheless still remains rather controversial, and there is no clarity about the causal mechanisms involved. See Kondratieff, 'Die langen Wellen der Konjunktur'.
39  See, for example, Genovese & Fox Genovese, *Fruits of Merchant Capital*; Miller, *Way of Death*; van Zanden, *Rise and Decline of Holland's Economy*; Day, *Money and Finance*; Banaji, *Brief History of Commercial Capitalism*.
40  Very important was Winkler, *Organisierter Kapitalismus*. See also Offe, *Disorganized Capitalism*, and Lash & Urry, *End of Organized Capitalism*.
41  Fridenson, 'Is there a return of capitalism in business history?'.
42  Piketty, *Capital in the Twenty-First Century*.
43  Mandel, 'Introduction', 21–2.
44  Grossmann, *Akkumulations- und Zusammenbruchsgesetz*.
45  Cassis, 'Economic and financial crises'.
46  Cassis, 'Economic and financial crises'.
47  Streeck, 'How will capitalism end?', 64.
48  Hegel, 'Vorrede zur zweiten Ausgabe', *Wissenschaft der Logik*, § 23.
49  Austin, 'Return of capitalism as a concept'.

# 5
# Workers

The concept of the 'working class' emerged towards the end of the eighteenth century, and was at first used especially in the plural form. The 'working classes' comprised all those people employed to work for wages in manual occupations. The term probably came into use when, due to the rise of manufactories and factories, new groups of wage-earners became visible, who could be counted neither among domestic servants nor among day-labourers or journeymen.

The precise meaning of the term 'working class' is disputed. While some emphasize manual labour, broader interpretations are also advanced. Not infrequently, lower-level white-collar employees are included in the working class, and sometimes the position is defended that *all* wage-earners belong to the working class, except for higher managers. Nevertheless, all definitions of the working class that are used today have three aspects in common. First, they assume that members of the working class share at least one characteristic – namely, that they are *dependent on a wage* for their survival, while other sources of income are either lacking or much less important. Second, they involve the (often implicit) assumption that workers are part of *families* whose members, in principle, also belong to the working class. Sometimes, it is assumed that there is a male breadwinner who earns the income of the whole household, while other members of the family perform (at most) subsistence labour; other times, the possibility that other family members can also contribute to the household income is recognized. Third, all definitions assume that the working class is counterposed to *other social classes* – in particular, the employers ('capitalists'), the self-employed, the unfree, and so-called 'lumpenproletarians' (beggars, thieves, prostitutes, and such like).

All these descriptions emphasize structural, social-economic characteristics. But the working class also has a subjective side, as manifested by its culture, mentality, and collective action. Accordingly, the influential British historian E. P. Thompson considered 'class' to be an outcome of experience, emerging out of those socio-economic characteristics. 'Class', he argued, 'happens when some men, as a result of common experiences (inherited or shared), feel and articulate the identity of their interests as between themselves, and as against other men whose interests are different from (and usually opposed to) theirs'.[1] The ways in which class 'happens' can diverge strongly and are unpredictable: 'We can see a *logic* in the responses of similar occupational groups undergoing similar experiences, but we cannot predicate any *law*. Consciousness of class arises in the same way in different times and places, but never in just the same way'.[2]

## Formation

In the early twenty-first century, wage labour has probably become the second-most prevalent form of work after domestic subsistence labour. But wage labour is not a phenomenon of recent vintage. Wage labour has been performed more or less sporadically for thousands of years. Originally, it concerned work activities of a non-permanent nature, such as the work of itinerant artisans, the service of military recruits, or help with the harvest.

What is special about modern wage-labour is not only that it has become a socially dominant phenomenon but also that a relatively large tranche of wage workers have longer-term jobs that often last for years, or sometimes even a lifetime. This historical shift occurred gradually (albeit more rapidly from the fifteenth century), beginning in the North Atlantic region and then spreading to other parts of the world. Among the underlying causes of this development were the rise of capitalist production and distribution, increasing state apparatuses that intervened more powerfully in economic and social life, and population growth. These processes contributed to the emergence of regional, national, and international labour markets, and new forms of social inequality (see Chapter 8).

Such trends did not always lead to a growing number of wage workers (in the seventeenth and eighteenth centuries, they were accompanied by an intensification of slavery); but, in the long term, they meant that more and more families depended on a wage for their survival. This 'proletarianization' rendered a growing part of the world population dependent on one kind of income and, therefore, socially vulnerable:

> The opportunities or risks for such workers are determined by markets and market changes. They do not possess the tools they use, the raw materials they process, or the products they produce. Their work is determined by those who possess all of this in the form of capital and who, on this basis, employ and direct them (often through managers, supervisors, or other types of middlemen). The relation between wage workers and employers is based on a contract of exchange (work for wages), terminable by both sides, and not by extra-economic compulsion or tradition.[3]

Parts of the large group of wage workers so emerging develop collective identities, based on shared interests, experiences, opinions, fears, and expectations. They articulate these collective identities in all kinds of ways, through sociability, religious rituals, or organizations for mutual aid. Not infrequently, the new identity is also the expression of a nascent class-awareness, based on the consciousness that the interests of workers are different from, and often counterposed to, those of the employers. Whether such consciousness emerges, and what exact forms it will have, always depends on the circumstances and cannot be predicted in advance.

In some circumstances, class awareness becomes more militant because groups of workers try to defend their perceived common interests against the state or the employers, through economic or political action. In support of this struggle for their interests, they can form diverse kinds of organizations, such as trade unions, political parties, or sometimes even paramilitary units. Here, again, it is true that this can happen in all manner of ways, and that the content of a conflict of interest can present great variations. Only rarely do such interest groups strive to unite all workers; more often, they exclude segments of the class due to reasons of gender, ethnicity, nationality, education, and so on.

## 'Peripheral' working classes

In recent decades, more and more voices argue that the foregoing interpretation of 'working class' is too restrictive. The distinctions between 'classical' wage-earners and some other subordinate groups are very subtle indeed. There are all kinds of forms of 'hidden' wage labour, such as sharecropping, where a peasant family supplies labour and the landowner supplies the land and means of production, while the revenues are shared between them according to some formula. Or there are self-employed workers, who are formally employers without staff but, in reality, are often dependent on one specific client who is therefore their *de facto* employer. This relativization of the boundaries of the working class has recently motivated historians to redefine it, such that slaves and other unfree workers can also be included, just like ostensibly 'independent' self-employed operators.[4]

Historians Peter Linebaugh and Marcus Rediker, for example, revealed how, in the early-modern North Atlantic region, a multiform proletariat of 'hewers of wood and drawers of water' developed, with various sites of struggle, 'the commons, the plantation, the ship, and the factory'.[5] According to Linebaugh and Rediker, it is likely that slaves from Africa, indentured labourers from Europe, native Americans, and 'free' wage-earners and artisans constituted a complex but also socially and culturally interconnected amorphous 'multitude', which was regarded as one whole (a 'many-headed Hydra') by those in power. Linebaugh and Rediker referred to the 1791 rebellion of Haitian slaves as 'the first successful workers' revolt in modern history'. They suggested that this revolution later contributed to the segmentation of that rebellious 'multitude': 'What was left behind was national and partial: the English working class, the black Haitian, the Irish diaspora.' The narrow nineteenth-century concept of the proletariat we find in Marx and others was, they suggest, a result of this segmentation

We have to rethink the traditional notion of the working class. On the one hand, the experience of the *contemporary* Global South tells us that the distinctions between 'classical' wage-earners and some other subordinate groups are vague indeed. 'Pure' wage workers have been a minority in the labour force of many countries in the Global South; there, the process of class formation was never completed. Most of these wage-earners do not freely dispose of their own labour-power – for example, because they are tied down by debt – or they do not have any formal (legally recognized) contractual relationship with their employers. In addition, wage labour in the South is carried out by households and families whose survival very often remains partly dependent on subsistence labour as well – performed especially, but not exclusively, by women – and on independent production of commodities for the market, for instance.

The economic roles that different family members take on are often not fixed and permanent but, rather, signify a transient social relationship, one that can be replaced rather quickly by other sources of income.

That is one reason why the dividing line between workers and so-called lumpenproletarians is not always easy to draw. Referring to Africa, Vic Allen concluded some fifty years ago that '[i]n societies in which bare subsistence is the norm for a high proportion of all the working class, and where men, women, and children are compelled to seek alternative means of subsistence, as distinct from their traditional ones, the *lumpenproletariat* is barely distinguishable from much of the rest of the working class'.[6]

On the other hand, *historical* studies reveal that, in the past, the dividing line between chattel slaves, serfs, and other unfree subalterns (taken together) and 'free' wage-earners was rather vague, at best. On the African east coast in around 1900, for example, there lived quite a number of slaves who:

> ... worked as self-employed artisans or skilled workers, some of whom had previously worked as day labourers but had learnt a more lucrative trade ... These self-employed slaves ... were respected for their knowledge and thus commanded exceedingly high prices in the market, but they were rarely for sale. With almost the same status as freed slaves, a number of them actually owned small garden plots, and occasionally even slaves.[7]

Brazilian historians, especially, have pointed to the fluid dividing line between 'free' wage labour and chattel slavery, for example in the case of the *ganhadores* (slaves-for-hire), who earned their own wages, a proportion of which they had to hand over to their owners.[8] In South Asia, other ambivalences occur, for example in the case of 'coolies' or indentured labourers who were employed in South Asia itself but also in the Caribbean, Malaya, Natal, Fiji, and elsewhere. Their situation is sometimes described as a 'new form of slavery' but, at other times, as 'nearly free' wage labour.[9] In Australia, after lengthy hesitations, labour historians no longer have any difficulty describing the numerous convict labourers originally settling in the country as 'working class' in the broad sense of the word, even though these workers performed forced labour.[10] And, for Europe, the research of recent decades reveals that many so-called 'free' workers were really *bonded* labourers, far into the nineteenth century. Master-and-servant laws, apprenticeship arrangements, and so forth, ensured that workers were tied to their employers, and had significantly fewer legal rights than the literature previously suggested.[11]

But developing a broad and inclusive notion of the working class is not enough. We will also have to recognize that the working class is extremely heterogeneous and complex on all levels. If we leave the single-axis framework of the white, male industrial worker behind, a multi-dimensional picture emerges of interacting factors that, in concert, keep people in subordinate social positions in different ways. In a famous article, the jurist Kimberlé Crenshaw explained this idea with an analogy: 'traffic in an intersection, coming and going in all four directions. Discrimination, like traffic through an intersection, may flow in one direction, and it may flow in another. If an accident happens in an intersection, it can be caused by cars traveling from any number of directions and, sometimes, from all of them'. Similarly, a black woman can be harmed in several ways at the same time.[12]

Applying the idea is difficult,[13] for two main reasons. First, we are confronted with what the Australian feminist historian Ann Curthoys identified as the indeterminacy involving the relationship between class, gender, ethnicity, religion, and other multiple aspects of historical analysis. Curthoys pointed out how complicated it is to work simultaneously with concepts such as gender, ethnicity (or race), and class – in her terms, the 'three-body problem':

> Trying to keep just two of these concepts in play has proved extremely difficult ... But if keeping two such concepts in play is hard enough, look what happens when the third concept, be it ethnicity or class or sex, is brought seriously into play. The system, the analysis, becomes too complex to handle.[14]

Second, there is the question of the cohesion between different social categories. There are two options. Either we assume that the categories are 'structurally distinct, only to then equitably "intersect" or "entangle" each other', and then we find ourselves 'under the obligation to provide a theoretical framework for (and a sociohistorical account of) how exactly such evenly distributed "intersections" or "entanglements" take place'.[15] Or we assume that the different social categories are not only interdependent but are also part of ever-changing hierarchies. In that case, as Kelvin Santiago-Valles points out: 'The challenge remains for us to address and further research the structurally asymmetrical and variable articulation of the seemingly distinct aspects of social stratification as world-historical processes and shifting lived experiences – individually and collectively, locally and globally'.[16]

However, these difficulties, of course, do not diminish the heuristic value of the intersectionality idea.

## Critiquing the classics

Whatever the methodological problems, we obviously need to rethink the complex connection between wage labour and capitalism. In my view, Marx's distinction between chattel slave and 'free' wage-earner was incorrect. Marx engaged with issues relating to slave labour in many passages of his work. He was more aware of the contrast between 'free' wage labour and slavery than most twenty-first-century scholars. As an expert on European antiquity (on which he wrote his PhD thesis) and as a contemporary to the American Civil War, Marx was very conscious of the slavery problem.[17] The first volume of *Capital* was published two years after the abolition of slavery in the US (in 1865) and 21 years before abolition was officially proclaimed in Brazil. Marx considered slavery a historically backward mode of exploitation that would soon be a thing of the past, as 'free' wage labour embodied the capitalist future. He compared the two forms of labour in several of his writings. He certainly saw similarities between them – both produced a surplus product and 'the wage-labourer, just like the slave, must have a master to make him work and govern him'.[18] At the same time, Marx distinguished some differences that overshadowed all the common experiences these two collectives shared. Let me offer some brief critical comments on them and indicate some doubts.

First, wage workers dispose of labour capacity – viz. 'the aggregate of those mental and physical capabilities existing in the physical form, the living personality, of a human being, capabilities which he sets in motion whenever he produces a use-value of any kind'[19] – and this labour capacity is the source of value. The capitalist purchases this labour capacity as a commodity because he expects it to provide him with a 'specific service', namely, the creation of 'more value than it has itself'.[20] The same is not true of the slave's labour capacity. The slaveholder 'has paid cash for his slaves', and so 'the product of their labour represents the interest on the capital invested in their purchase'.[21] But, since interest is nothing but a form of surplus value, according to Marx,[22] it would seem that slaves would have to produce surplus value. And it is a fact that the sugar plantations on which slave labour was employed yielded considerable profits because the commodity of sugar embodied more value than the capital invested by the plantation owner (ground rent, amortization of the slaves, amortization of the sugarcane press, and so forth). So is it really the case that only the wage worker produces the equivalent of his/her own value plus 'an excess, a surplus-value'?[23] Or is the slave a 'source of value' as well?

Second, Marx states that the wage labourer 'must be the free proprietor of his own labour-capacity, hence of his person'.[24] The future wage worker and the money owner 'meet in the market, and enter into relations with each other on a footing of equality as owners of commodities, with the sole difference that one is a buyer, the other a seller; both are therefore equal in the eyes of the law'.[25] In other words: labour-power should be offered for sale by the person who is the carrier and possessor of this labour-power; and the person who sells the labour-power offers it exclusively. Why should that be so? Why can the labour-power not be sold by someone other than the carrier (as, for example, in the case of children who are made to perform wage labour in a factory by their parents or guardians)? Why can the person who offers (his or her own, or someone else's) labour-power for sale not sell it conditionally, together with means of production? And why can someone who does not own his own labour-power nevertheless sell it (as in the case of rented slaves, whose owners provide them to someone else for a fee)?[26]

Third, the wage worker embodies variable capital:

> It both reproduces the equivalent of its own value and produces an excess, a surplus value, which may itself vary, and be more or less according to circumstances. This part of capital is continually being transformed from a constant into a variable magnitude. I therefore call it the variable part of capital or, more briefly, variable capital.[27]

Further, Marx argues:

> It is only because labour is presupposed in the form of wage-labour, and the means of production in the form of capital (i.e. only as a result of this specific form of these two essential agents of production), that one part of the value (product) presents itself as surplus-value and this surplus-value presents itself as profit (rent), the gains of the capitalist, as additional available wealth belonging to him.[28]

To Marx, the slave is part of fixed capital and therefore no different, economically, from livestock or machinery: 'The slave-owner buys his worker in the same way as he buys his horse'.[29] The slave's capital value is his purchasing price, and this capital value has to be amortized over time, just as with livestock or machinery.[30] But how justified is Marx in defining only wage labour as variable capital, on the grounds that 'this part of capital' can 'be more or less'?[31] Is the same not true of commodity-producing slave labour?

Fourth, when the wage worker produces a commodity, this commodity is 'a unity formed of use-value and value', and, hence, 'the process of production must be a unity, composed of the labour process and the process of creating value [*Wertbildungsprozess*]'.³² There can be no doubt that slaves producing cane sugar, tobacco, or indigo are producing commodities, just like wage workers. But, if this is the case, then slaves also produce value. Marx denies this, since he considers slaves part of constant capital and holds that only variable capital creates value.

Fifth, the wage worker always divests himself of his labour-power 'for a limited period only, for if he were to sell it in a lump, once and for all, he would be selling himself, converting himself from a free man into a slave, from an owner of a commodity into a commodity'.³³ Normally, one would refer to such a transaction (the 'sale' of a commodity in instalments, without any change of owner) as a lease and not as a sale – an obvious idea that was already formulated by others before.³⁴ The distinction between a lease and a sale may appear insignificant but it is not. 'When a sales contract is closed, the substance of the commodity becomes the property of the other party, whereas when a lease contract is closed, the other party merely purchases the right to use the commodity; the seller only makes his commodity available temporarily, without relinquishing ownership of it', as Franz Oppenheimer has rightly noted.³⁵ When *A* sells *B* a commodity, *B* becomes the owner in lieu of *A*. But when *A* leases *B* a commodity, *A* remains the owner and *B* merely receives the right to use the commodity for a fixed term. The 'substance' of the commodity remains with *A*, whereas *B* receives its 'use and enjoyment'.³⁶ Thus, if wage labour is the leasing of labour-power, the difference between a wage worker and a slave does not lie in the 'definite period of time'³⁷ during which labour-power is made available but in the fact that, in one case, labour-power is *leased*, while, in the other, it is *sold*. Why do we not find this consideration in Marx? Presumably, because it shows the process of value-creation in a different light. The substance of the value of labour-power is retained by the worker rather than being yielded to the capitalist.³⁸ Thus, if wage labour were a lease-type relationship as well, it could not create surplus value.

Sixth, according to Marx, the rate of profit tends to decline because the social productivity of labour increases constantly:

> Since the mass of living labour applied continuously declines in relation to the mass of objectified labour that sets it in motion, i.e. the productively consumed means of production, the part of this living labour that is unpaid and objectified in surplus-value must also stand in an ever-decreasing ratio to the value of the total capital applied.³⁹

The endpoint of this tendency would, of course, be a situation in which variable capital has been reduced to zero and total capital consists exclusively of constant capital. In such a situation, the collapse of capitalism would be a fact. But the odd thing is that there already existed such a terminal phase prior to the Industrial Revolution – on the plantations of the seventeenth and eighteenth centuries. These plantations employed slave labour; so, according to Marx's premises, total capital consisted exclusively of constant capital. How are we to account for the economic dynamism of the plantations on this basis?

The example of slave labour shows that Marx did not provide a consistent justification for the privileged position productive wage labour is given within his theory of value. There is much to suggest that slaves and wage workers are structurally more similar than Marx and traditional Marxism suspected. The historical reality of capitalism has featured many hybrid and transitional forms between slavery and 'free' wage labour. Moreover, slaves and wage workers have repeatedly performed the same work in the same business enterprise.[40] It is true, of course, that the slave's labour capacity is the permanent property of the capitalist, whereas the wage worker only makes his labour capacity available to the capitalist for a limited time, even if he does so repeatedly. It remains unclear, however, why slaves should create no surplus value while wage workers do. The time has come to expand the theory of value in such a way as to recognize the productive labour of slaves and other unfree workers as an essential component of the capitalist economy.

## A new concept

The implications are far-reaching. Apparently, there is a large class of people within capitalism whose labour-power is commodified in various ways. I would like to call this class the *extended working class*. (In my earlier book, *Workers of the World*, I used the term 'subaltern workers' but this proved to be confusing.) Its members make up a very varied group: it includes chattel slaves, sharecroppers, small artisans, and wage-earners. It is the historical dynamics of this 'multitude' that we should try to understand. We have to consider that, in capitalism, there *always* existed, and probably will continue to exist, several forms of commodified labour subsisting side-by-side.

In its long developmental trajectory, capitalism utilized many kinds of work relationships, some mainly based on economic compulsion and others with a strong non-economic component. Millions of slaves were brought by force from Africa to the Caribbean, to Brazil, and to the southern states of the US. Contract workers from India and China were shipped off to toil in South Africa, Malaysia, or South America. 'Free' migrant workers left Europe for the New World, for Australia, or the colonies. And, today, sharecroppers produce an important portion of world agricultural output. These and other work-relationships are synchronous, even if there seems to be a secular trend towards 'free wage labour'. Slavery still exists and sharecropping is enjoying a comeback in some regions. Within certain cultural and legal limits, capitalists could (and can) choose whatever form of commodified labour they see fit in a given historical context: one variant seems most profitable today, another tomorrow. If this argument is correct, then it behoves us to conceptualize the wage-earning class as one (important) kind of commodified labour among others. Consequently, so-called 'free' labour cannot be seen as the only form of exploitation suitable for modern capitalism but as one alternative among several (see Chapter 2).

Such a reconceptualization and broadening of the notion of the working-class will help us to better understand the many forms of resistance that have been used by workers over time. The classical approach suggests, for example, that strikes are a form of collective action that is associated especially with free wage labourers. But, if we look at the ways in which protest is expressed and pressure is exerted by the different groups of workers (including slaves, the self-employed, the lumpenproletarians, and the 'free' wage labourers), these appear to overlap considerably.[41] In the past, all kinds of subaltern workers went on strike. The sharecropping silver miners in Chihuahua protested as early as the 1730s against the termination of their work contracts by the mine owners. They entrenched themselves in the nearby hills, where:

> ... they built a makeshift stone parapet, unfurled a banner proclaiming their defiance, and vowed to storm the villa of San Felipe, kill [the mine owner] San Juan y Santa Cruz, and burn his house to the ground. For the next several weeks they refused to budge from their mountain redoubt, where they passed time by composing and singing songs of protest.[42]

The miners returned only after mediation by a priest, sent by the bishop. Slaves regularly went on strike, too. Serfs in Russia refused 'to recognize their owner's authority over them'; they stopped working for him and decided 'to go on strike'.[43] On plantations in the British

Caribbean in the early-nineteenth century, there were also walkouts by slaves:

> The rebellions in Demerara in 1829 and Jamaica in 1831 both began as versions of the modern work strike, coupled with other acts of defiance, but not with killing. Only when the local militia retaliated with force, assuming that this was another armed uprising, did such an occurrence actually take place.[44] [See Figure 5.1.]

The broadened concept of the working class that I propose will enable us to rethink the strike phenomenon. By including slaves and indentured labourers, it becomes possible to see that the strike is a very important, but also specific, form of the collective refusal to work. So-called unfree workers have used other forms of collective refusal that deserve to be integrated into our analysis. We all know of the maroons, the slaves who fled the plantations in North America as well as the Caribbean and South America. But this kind of resistance is not confined to the New World. On the mainland coast of Tanganyika in 1873, plantation slaves fled in huge numbers and founded the village of Makorora, 'hidden in a thicket of thorny bushes' and with 'heavy fortifications'.[45]

**Figure 5.1** 'The Destruction of Roehampton Estate in the Parish of St. James's in January 1832. The property of J. Baillie Esq.' Lithograph, Adolphe Duperly, Jamaica 1833. Wikimedia Commons. https://bit.ly/3ymJstb.

Seen against this backdrop, the strikes of so-called free wage-earners constitute just *one* form of collective resistance against the exploitation of commodified labour. And we should also acknowledge that, conversely, free wage labourers have often employed methods of struggle that are usually associated with other groups of subaltern workers, such as lynching, rioting, arson, and bombing.

By broadening our perspective on commodified labour under capitalism, we will be better placed to write the history of all those anonymous individuals and families who, as the playwright and poet Bertolt Brecht, wrote, 'built Thebes of the seven gates' and so often 'cooked the feast for the victors'.[46]

## Notes

1. Thompson, *Making of the English Working Class*, 8–9.
2. Thompson, *Making of the English Working Class*, 9.
3. Kocka, 'Problems of working class formation', 282.
4. van der Linden, *Workers of the World*.
5. Linebaugh & Rediker, *Many-Headed Hydra* (and the rest of this paragraph); see also Linebaugh, *London Hanged*, 348–56, 415–16; and Sarkar, *Writing Social History*, 66.
6. Allen, 'Meaning of the working class', 188.
7. Deutsch, *Emancipation without Abolition*, 71–2.
8. Groundbreaking was the article by Lara, 'Escravidão, cidadania e história do trabalho'; see also the important case study by Reis, '"The Revolution of the Ganhadores"'.
9. Tinker, *New System of Slavery*.
10. An excellent overview is provided by Roberts, 'The "knotted hands that set us high"'.
11. Comparative perspectives are offered in Steinfeld, *Invention of Free Labor*; Hay & Craven, *Masters, Servants, and Magistrates*; Stanziani, *Le travail constraint*; Keiser, *Vertragszwang und Vertragsfreiheit*.
12. Crenshaw, 'Demarginalizing the intersection of race and sex', 149.
13. For example, compare the complex considerations in Ehrenreich, 'Subordination and symbiosis'.
14. Curthoys, 'The three body problem', 15. On later debates, see Cole, 'Twenty years on'.
15. Santiago-Valles, 'Coercion and concrete labor', 25–6.
16. Santiago-Valles, 'Coercion and concrete labor', 25–6.
17. Backhaus, *Marx, Engels und die Sklaverei*; De Sainte Croix, 'Karl Marx'; Lekas, *Marx on Classical Antiquity*; Reichardt, 'Marx'.
18. Marx, *Capital*, III, 510.
19. Marx, *Capital*, I, 270.
20. Marx, *Capital*, I, 301.
21. Marx, *Capital*, III, 762.
22. 'Rent, interest, and industrial profit are only different names for different parts of the surplus value of the commodity, or the unpaid labour enclosed in it, and they are equally derived from this source and from this source alone.' Karl Marx, *Value, Price and Profit*, MECW, Vol. 20, 133.
23. Marx, *Capital*, I, 317.
24. Marx, *Capital*, I, 271.
25. Marx, *Capital*, I, 271.
26. Marx was quite aware of this practice of renting slaves but he drew no theoretical conclusions from it. See, for example, Marx, *Capital*, III, 597: 'Under the slave system the worker does have a capital value, namely his purchase price. And if he is hired out, the hirer must first pay the interest on this purchase price and on top of this replace the capital's annual depreciation.'
27. Marx, *Capital*, I, 317.

28 Marx, *Capital*, III, 1021. This is why surplus labour appears in two very different forms in these two cases. In the case of wage labour, the wage form eradicates 'every trace of the division of the working day into necessary labour and surplus labour, into paid labour and unpaid labour'. Marx, *Capital*, I, 680. By contrast, in the case of slave labour, 'even the part of the working day in which the slave is only replacing the value of his own means of subsistence, in which he therefore actually works for himself alone, appears as labour for his master. All his labour appears as unpaid labour'. Marx, *Capital*, I, 680.
29 Marx, *Capital*, I, 377; the *Grundrisse* contain a similar passage: Marx, *Grundrisse*, 489–90.
30 Marx, *Capital*, III, 597.
31 Marx, *Capital*, I, 317.
32 Marx, *Capital*, I, 293.
33 Marx, *Capital*, I, 271.
34 Marx himself referred repeatedly to the analogy between rent and wage labour. He did so most extensively in the *Theories of Surplus Value*, where he writes that the worker is paid for his commodity (his labour capacity) only after he has finished working: 'It can also be seen that here it is the worker, not the capitalist, who does the advancing, just as in the case of the renting of a house, it is not the tenant but the landlord who advances use-value.' *MECW*, Vol. 32, 302; see also Marx, *Capital*, I, 279: 'The price of the labour-power is fixed by the contract, although it is not realized till later, like the rent of a house.' On this, see also Kuczynski, 'What is sold on the labour market?'.
35 Oppenheimer, *Die soziale Frage und der Sozialismus*, 120.
36 Contrary to what Oppenheimer believed – 'only the labor capacity that is intended for sale (e.g. that of the work ox, the slave) is a commodity, not that intended merely for lease' (*Die soziale Frage und der Sozialismus*, 121) – a lease contract also operates according to the logic of the commodity; this is precisely why the leasing fee depends on the value of the leased commodity.
37 Marx, *Capital*, I, 271.
38 Engels held that lease transactions are 'only a transfer of already *existing*, previously *produced* value, and the total sum of values possessed by the landlord and the tenant *together* remains the same after as it was before'. Engels, 'The housing question', *MECW*, Vol. 23, 320.
39 Marx, *Capital*, III, 319.
40 For example, on the coffee plantations around São Paulo, or in a chemical factory in Baltimore. Hall & Stolcke, 'Introduction of free labour'; Whitman, 'Industrial slavery'.
41 I am borrowing here two paragraphs from my *Workers of the World*, 31, 175–7.
42 Martin, *Governance and Society in Colonial Mexico*, 51.
43 Kolchin, *Unfree Labor*, 258.
44 Craton, *Testing the Chains*, 301; Schuler, 'Akan slave rebellions', 382–3.
45 Popovic, 'al-Mukhtara'; Glassman, 'Bondsman's new clothes', 308.
46 Bertolt Brecht, 'Fragen eines lesenden Arbeiters' (Questions from a Worker who Reads).

# 6
# Coerced labour

> Science may indeed purchase its exactness at the price of schematization. But the remedy in this case is to confront it with an integral experience.
>
> Maurice Merleau-Ponty, *Signes*[1]

There is wide disagreement about the concepts needed to analyse coerced labour. Contemporary Brazilian legislation regards as 'modern slavery' what others would regard as 'forced labour'. Since very early on, the definitions of slavery and other forms of coerced labour adopted by international organizations have been at odds with one another. The confusion dates from the 1920s at the latest. Article 1 of the 1926 League of Nations Slavery Convention defined slavery in legal terms: 'the status or condition of a person over whom any or all of the powers attaching to the right of ownership are exercised'. Article 2.1 of the ILO's Convention Concerning Forced or Compulsory Labour of 1930 (No. 29), however, does *not* presume the existence of a legal basis: indeed, 'all work or service that is exacted from any person under the menace of any penalty and for which the said person has not offered himself or herself voluntarily' is regarded as forced or compulsory labour.[2]

Not only have the standard definitions been inconsistent for so long, but they are also generally vague. That vagueness began with the League of Nations. What does the League mean when it talks about 'any or all of the powers attaching to the right of ownership'? Modern legal theory distinguishes at least 11 such 'powers', including the duty to prevent harmful use. The UN Convention of 7 September 1956 refers to 'slavery, the slave trade, and institutions and practices similar to slavery'.[3] But what does 'similar to slavery' mean?

Today's non-governmental organizations (NGOs) have done nothing to lessen the confusion. The Walk Free Foundation defines 'modern slavery' as 'one person possessing or controlling another person in such a way as to significantly deprive that person of their individual liberty, with the intention of exploiting that person through their use, management, profit, transfer or disposal'.[4] Applying this definition, in its 2014 report, the Foundation estimates that 35.8 million people are 'living in some form of modern slavery globally'. Other NGOs arrive at differing conclusions. Anti-Slavery International (ASI) takes the following view:

> Someone is in slavery if they are: forced to work – through mental or physical threat; owned or controlled by an 'employer', usually through mental or physical abuse or the threat of abuse; dehumanised, treated as a commodity or bought and sold as 'property'; physically constrained or has restrictions placed on his/her freedom of movement.[5]

Based on this definition, ASI estimates that 21 million people are 'in a form of slavery', drawing on an estimate published by the ILO in Geneva. To advance the academic debate on this question, it would seem advisable not to remain focused on discussions about general but inevitably contentious terms such as 'slavery', but to go beyond that and to analyse as precisely as possible all forms of coerced labour – of which 'slavery' is but one example. Probably only then will we be able to identify clearly the differences and similarities between various forms of exploitation and repression. This might make it easier to understand the causalities and to develop effective policies. The present chapter makes a preliminary attempt at such an analysis.

## Conceptual clarifications

If we are to discuss the phenomenon of coerced labour, we also need to know what non-coerced labour entails. An example might help. On 21 November 1857, a Caribbean planter complained about his unhappy fate in London's *The Times* newspaper. The abolition of slavery in the 1830s had resulted in an acute shortage of labourers willing to work on the plantations, since the former slaves refused to accept such a dependent labour relationship any longer:

> The freed West India negro slave will not till the soil for wages; the free son of the ex-slave is as obstinate as his sire. He will cultivate lands which he has not bought for his own yams, mangoes, and potatoes. These satisfy his wants; he does not care for yours. Cotton

and sugar and coffee and tobacco – he cares little enough for them. And what matters it to him that the Englishman has sunk his thousands and tens of thousands on mills, machinery, and plant, which now totter on the languishing estate that for years has only returned beggary and debts? He eats his yams, and sniggers at 'Buckra' [the white man].[6]

Marx commented on this sort of lamentation by planters when he observed that the former slaves had become 'self-sustaining peasants for their own consumption'; for them, 'capital does not exist as capital, because autonomous wealth as such can exist only on the basis of *direct* forced labour, slavery, or *indirect* forced labour, *wage labour*'.[7] In other words, the slaves who had been able to cast off their chains completely and who now produced only for themselves were *free* labourers, while slaves and wage labourers *both* performed forced labour. Or, in modern microeconomic terms: anyone who works as an agent for a principal is unfree.[8]

Marx's view placed him in a long tradition. In his *Politeia*, Aristotle argued that the actions of a man who 'does or learns anything for his own sake or for the sake of his friends, or with a view to excellence, ... will not appear illiberal [unfree]; but if done for the sake of others, the very same action will be thought menial and servile'.[9] Based on that argument, wage labour in Ancient Greece was frequently considered unfree labour, which is why slaves (*douloi*) and wage labourers (*thètes*) were often regarded as belonging to the same group.[10] The distinction between non-coerced and coerced labour mirrored, then, the distinction between labour for oneself and labour for others. Moses Finley described this distinction thus:

> 'Oneself' is to be understood not in a narrow individualistic sense but as embracing the family, nuclear or extended as the case may be in any particular society ... Nor is interfamily cooperative activity, as during harvest periods. 'Labour for others' implies not only that others take some of the fruits but also that they customarily control, in direct ways, the work that is done and the manner of its doing, whether in person or through agents and managers.[11]

Aristotle implicitly presumed that *all* members of the *oikos* (the household as a patriarchal community) performed 'free labour'; but, from a feminist perspective, such a view is untenable of course. The male head-of-household does, indeed, work for his family without having to submit to others. But women, children, and servants working under his authority are *not* free; they, too, work and are subject to the authority of another – in this case, the patriarch.[12] Whatever the case, the work of the patriarch is free, since it is autonomous, while 'labour for others' represents a heteronomous activity that I will regard here as coerced labour. If free workers were to support one another mutually – by rotating labour, for example – that, too, would be free labour.

What does coercion mean in this context, though? To answer this question, we must first briefly discuss 'coercion' as an abstract concept. Every coercive act represents a relationship between two actors and two behaviours. There is a *coercer* who attempts, by means of a *coercive act*, to induce a *recipient of coercion* (the victim) to perform a *compliant response*.[13] The coercer might be a person but it could equally be an organization or institution, or even a social structure. The coercive act can take two forms: constrained choice and physical compulsion. *Constrained choice* is when the coercer threatens the victim along the lines of 'if you do (not do) X or Y, then harm will be inflicted on you'. The victim is effectively being ordered by the coercer to do (or not do) something. Sometimes the threat is multiconditional; in that case, the victim has two or more 'permitted' choices ('you may do A or B, but not C'). Sometimes, the threat is biconditional, in which case the victim is permitted just one choice. The coercer threatens that the victim will be harmed if s/he fails to accede to what the coercer demands. This harm *can* be inflicted by the coercer (if, for instance, an attacker threatens: 'your money or your life') but that is by no means necessary. A statement along the lines of 'If you violate this commandment, you will go to hell' is also a threat. In constrained choice, the coercer aims to induce the recipient of coercion to respond compliantly; this might take the form of an action or an omission. Action, here, means purposeful behaviour or a failure to perform an action that one has the ability and the opportunity to perform.[14] In the case of *physical compulsion*, the coercer uses force to restrict the spatial freedom of movement of the victim without the latter being able to do anything to resist. Examples include slave raiding and confinement in a labour camp. In the case of physical compulsion, victims have no choice; in the case of constrained choice, they have one or more choices.[15]

Sometimes, forms of coercion completely coalesce; then they can be said to form intrinsic combinations. Torture as a means of forcing a confession from someone is an example of an intrinsic combination, with physical compulsion and threat (constrained choice) forming a whole. In the case of other coercive acts, forms of coercion are employed as two distinct, but closely related, methods.

The victim can respond to the coercive act in various ways, of course: he or she can obey, refuse to obey, partly obey, or just pretend to obey. The first two options are unambiguous; the last two are ambiguous. Hidden forms of disobedience can be both frequent and take a number of different forms.[16]

## The three moments of coerced labour

In analytical terms, all forms of coerced labour are characterized by three 'moments': the individual's *entry* into the labour relationship; the period during which they work – when their labour is *extracted* from them; and their *exit* from the labour relationship. These three moments are interrelated, of course – a point to which I will return later.

### Entry

Why do workers enter into a coerced labour relationship? There are, I would argue, ten varying reasons, of which only one is actually voluntary (Figure 6.1).

1) When the worker is *sold*, the worker becomes the property of one or more individuals or of an organization, such as a company or a state, and is subsequently sold-on to another person or organization for the purpose of performing work.
2) *Hiring-out* occurs when a person, although the property of an owner, has to work for someone else, an employer. A Brazilian study of these slaves-for-hire (so-called *ganhadores*) in the nineteenth century says:

    > The *ganhadores* moved about freely in the streets looking for work. It was a common, although not general, practice for slave owners to permit their slaves to live outside the master's home in rented rooms, sometimes with former slaves as their landlords. They only returned to the master's house to 'pay for the week', that is, to pay the weekly (and sometimes daily) sum agreed upon with their masters. They were able to keep whatever exceeded that amount.[17]

    In the eighteenth and nineteenth centuries, such slaves-for-hire could be found in various parts of the Americas and Africa.
3) *Self-sale*. Sometimes, workers feel compelled to sell themselves to an employer for a number of years or the rest of their lives because, for example, they would otherwise be unable to pay off their debts or

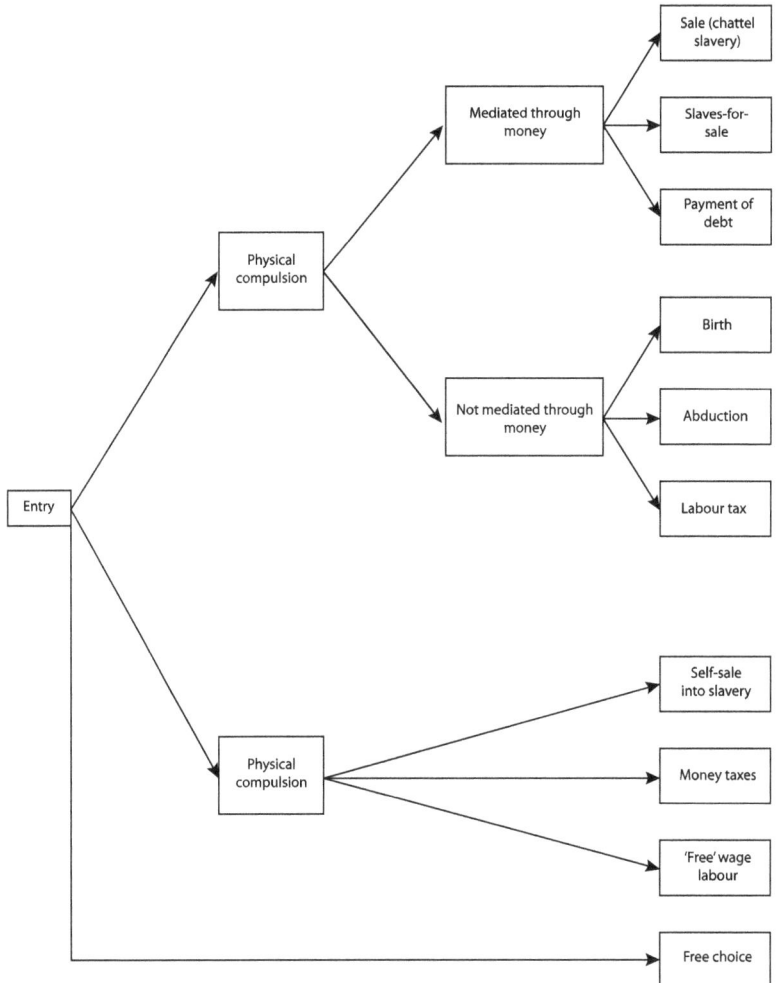

**Figure 6.1** Forms of *entry* into a coerced labour relationship.
Source: Author.

they would starve. This is self-sale, with the worker opting to become a slave. Self-sale is an ancient phenomenon, mentioned even in the *Code of Hammurabi* (c. 1780 BCE), and it inspired theoretical reflections on the part of Locke, Montesquieu, and Rousseau.[18] As Patterson observes:

> Poverty was, of course, one of the main reasons for self-sale, and ... in several advanced societies such as China and Japan it was at times a major source of slaves. In Russia between the

COERCED LABOUR

seventeenth and nineteenth centuries self-sale as a result of poverty was the most important reason for enslavement among the mass of domestic slaves ... Yet there were reasons other than poverty why persons sold themselves. Sometimes it was because of political rather than economic security. Strangers who found themselves cut off from their kinsmen in tribal societies often sought self-sale into slavery as the only path to survival ... Another cause of self-enslavement was the sale of self and relatives in order to escape either military services or prohibitive taxes – whether in cash, kind, or corvée labor.[19]

4) *Debt* can induce people to work for others. Tom Brass has distinguished two ways in which debt bondage can be created. The first is 'voluntary' indebtedness and it occurs:

> ... when an individual voluntarily seeks a loan which he or she is unable to repay subsequently. Thus loans taken for non-recurrent items of expenditure, such as the purchase of medicines for illness, the finance of important life cycle ceremonies (such as marriage or death rites) may result in the labour-power of the debtor being acquired by the creditor. Because the advance is requested, this form lacks the coercive appearance of bonded labour: the worker becomes indebted and exits from the free labour market 'voluntarily'.[20]

The second is 'involuntary':

> ... a loan is neither sought nor is the necessity for doing so present initially. Indebtedness is involuntary, and furthermore appears as such. It follows from a situation in which payment due a worker at the end of his contract is withheld by the creditor-employer precisely in order to retain his services, the resulting period of unpaid labour (engineered by the creditor-employer) necessitating recourse to subsistence loans on the part of the worker. Though different in appearance, both these forms are in substance the same, and initiate the cycle of debt-servicing labour obligations which constitutes bondage.[21]

5) *Birth*. The principle that the child of a slave is also a slave is of ancient origin. We find it in pre-Columbian America, for example, and it has persisted ever since.[22] Slaveholders sometimes exploited this principle to engage in conscious slave-breeding, as was the case in Ethiopia, as late as the end of the 1920s, when the price of slaves

had risen to incredible levels owing to decreasing supplies.²³ The journal of the ILO remarked at the time:

> In fact, just as livestock is placed in favourable conditions for breeding, so a male may be assigned to a female slave in order that their offspring may add to their owner's property ... The owner has theoretically the right to dispose of the child from the moment of its birth; he can take the baby from the breast and sell it. As a matter of fact, it is clear that the owner's interest demands that the new-born child should live under the best possible conditions, so that he may be a fine specimen if sold young or that he may develop normally and become a vigorous worker. These two reasons usually prevail to prevent the child being taken from his mother until he is weaned.²⁴

6) *Abduction*. An armed group captures one or more individuals (Figure 6.2) and puts them to work or sells them for the purpose of having them work for others (which brings us back to the first variant). For example, a French traveller writing at the

**Figure 6.2** 'Gang of captives met at Mbame's on their way to Tette'. Men, women and child slaves near Tete, Mozambique, are forced to walk through the fields fettered at the neck and wrists. Wood engraving by J. W. Whymper after J. B. Zwecker, 1865. Wellcome Collection. https://wellcomecollection.org/works/u3whmqgk/items.

end of the nineteenth century about the Mossi people in Africa reported that:

> From time to time, his cavalrymen storm the outskirts of some Gurunsi or Kipirsi village, taking by surprise and seizing the inhabitants who are farming or collecting firewood. His people also lie separately in ambush on the roads and capture anyone who comes within their reach ... During my second stay in Banéma, Boukary, knowing my horror of plunder and slavery and fearing to displease me, sent out two expeditions at night without telling me: one into the west towards Nabouli, the other into the south towards Baouér'a. At ten o'clock the next morning, the sound of gunfire announced the cavalrymen's return. Soon afterwards, a row of male and female slaves appeared, tied one behind the other with a rope around their necks. The expedition to Nabouli brought back seventeen slaves, that to Baouér'a, only five, as well as a donkey loaded with salt and a little cotton fabric. Upon the arrival of these unfortunates, we let them drink, and used mallets to remove the copper rings and hoops they wore around their arms and legs.[25]

The adult men and women were sold, but:

> ... the little children, boys and girls, were divided up between the warriors, who took charge of them. Until further notice, these children will serve the warriors as their grooms; those who are deemed capable of later service and who prove themselves obedient will be kept on. The others will be sold off at the first opportunity. The girls are married off to those warriors who have distinguished themselves.[26]

It is important to note that abduction can also be state-supervised, as in the case of Korean forced labourers who, during World War II, were 'conscripted' by the Japanese Government – a euphemism for 'abducted' (Figure 6.3).

7) *Kinship and community pressure* refers to cases where workers felt obliged to work because their family or the head of the community (the village chief, for example) wanted them to. In early-twentieth-century French West Africa, the colonial administration obliged villages to supply contingents of labourers, to build railways, for example:

> To that end, the indigenous communities (e.g. families, ethnic groups and villages) are expected to give up the labourers required. Following their recruitment, the chief of the province

**Figure 6.3** Koreans forced to labour at a mine in Hokkaido, Japan, during World War II. Published courtesy of the National Memorial Museum of Forced Mobilization under Japanese Occupation, under the Korea Open Government License Type 4 (equivalent to CC BY-NC-ND).

> chooses from his advisers and/or friends a person responsible for breaking down the contingent into three crews, appointing a leader and taking the entire workforce to the sites. He must remain there to ensure that labourers who are ill, who have deserted or who are otherwise unavailable for work are replaced, to provide information on the men mobilised and, if necessary, to receive complaints. The men are scheduled to set out for the sites after the harvest – starting from 1 November. Labourers are enlisted to work from 1 November to 1 May ... [27]

8) *Monetary taxes* were levied, especially by the colonial authorities, to induce people to engage in wage labour – because it was only through wage labour (or the production of cash crops for the market) that they could earn the cash they were required to pay to the state. Two managers at a commercial company in Congo wrote about this on the eve of World War I:

> The goal of the tax system is not only to reimburse the government in some measure for the cost of occupying all the territories, and of providing protection for the native population.

> Taxes also have a higher purpose, which is to accustom the Negroes to work ... The native from the Upper Congo region has not yet reached that stage of evolution where he would increase his comfort by trade and work, and for this reason the tax system will continue to provide for a long time the main incentive to work.[28]

Sometimes, taxes were levied not in a monetary form but in the form of labour – what the French colonial authorities termed *prestation*. The link with kinship and community pressure (variant 7) is seamless, since the *prestation* usually had to be paid by the community.

9) *'Free' wage labour*. In theory, under capitalism, there are multiple alternatives to wage labour for the individual 'free' wage-earner;[29] he or she 'can go on the dole, or beg, or simply make no provision ... and trust to fortune'.[30] They can also become self-employed, set up a workers' cooperative, or become a capitalist employer. Many of these variants make it possible to acquire the money required to purchase or rent the consumer goods necessary for one's own household (a home, clothing, food, and so on). But, for most wage-earners, these alternatives are neither reasonable nor acceptable. As individuals, they often do not feel attracted by the alternatives because these are regarded as ignominious (begging) or difficult to realize (setting up their own business).[31] Moreover, there is also a collective unfreedom: the number of workers who manage to escape from wage labour by becoming employers is, by definition, limited: their freedom to escape is 'contingent on the others not exercising their similarly contingent freedom': 'although most proletarians are free to escape the proletariat, and, indeed, even if everyone is, the proletariat is collectively unfree, an imprisoned class'.[32] Seen in this way, wage labour thus is a clear case of constrained choice.

10) *Free choice*. Finally, there are, of course, also those not forced by material necessity but who nonetheless enter into a heteronomous labour relationship. They include subsistence peasants who accept wage labour temporarily to acquire 'extras' (luxury items, for instance) with the money they have earned, and also wealthy individuals who accept an employment position to ensure they are usefully occupied.[33]

Two caveats should be made concerning this classification. First, the distinction between these variants (and especially the first nine) is not always as clear-cut as it might seem. Take contemporary Brazil, for instance:

> Victims are recruited in poor regions of Brazil by labor contractors, who promise good jobs and transport voluntary workers in buses over long distances. Upon arrival, workers are surprised to find that the reality differs from the promises. Workers are informed that they already have a debt for the cost of transportation and for the food they received. They are told that they will be charged for the tools, boots, hats, and clothes that are necessary to carry out the job, as well as for the rental of their beds. The cost of their food is also retained from their salaries. Workers who complain are told that they cannot leave until they have paid their debt. Those who still do not submit are retained by violence.[34]

In this case, the workers are victims of both abduction and debt peonage. And what about the following case, from the US? In 1908, thus long after slavery had been officially abolished, the sheriff of Shelby County, Alabama, arrested a young African-American man, Green Cottenham, for 'vagrancy'. Cottenham, a 22-year-old descendant of former slaves, was sentenced to 30 days' hard labour:

> Unable to pay the array of fees assessed on every prisoner – fees to the sheriff, the deputy, the court clerk, the witnesses – Cottenham's sentence was extended to nearly a year of hard labor. The next day, Cottenham … was sold. Under a standing arrangement between the county and a vast subsidiary of the industrial titan of the North – U.S. Steel Corporation – the sheriff turned the young man over to the company for the duration of his sentence. In return, the subsidiary, Tennessee Coal, Iron & Railroad Company, gave the county $12 a month to pay off Cottenham's fine and fees. What the company's managers did with Cottenham, and thousands of other black men they purchased from sheriffs across Alabama, was entirely up to them. A few hours later, the company plunged Cottenham into the darkness of a mine called Slope No. 12 – one shaft in a vast subterranean labyrinth on the edge of Birmingham known as the Pratt Mines.[35]

Here, a relatively small debt was vastly inflated, after which the convict could be leased for a limited period as a slave. This particular case combined debt bondage with slave-for-hire. There are, in short, many combinations and hybrid forms.

A second point is that the coercion might be indirect: the coercer can compel the victim to work through intermediaries. The relationship between debt peon and employer can be indirect because, for example, intermediaries – perhaps multiple – are involved:

> Employers provide a sum of money to these intermediaries who, in turn, use this money to provide wage advances to workers. In some instances the chain of intermediaries can be relatively long. In [contemporary] Peru, for example, it was observed that some employers pay an advance to so-called *habilitadores*, who then make smaller advances to local *patrones* (bosses), who in turn recruit workers through wage advances.[36]

Intermediaries (so-called jobbers, sirdars, and so on) were often used to recruit wage labourers and indentured labourers. This was the case in China's coalmines in the early decades of the twentieth century but also, for example, in the Indian textile industry and in Russian agriculture.[37]

In short, my classification is more indicative than complete, and it is embedded in more complex hierarchical relationships.[38]

### *Labour extraction*

Once an employer has a worker at his disposal, he must induce that worker to translate his capacity to labour (labour-power) into actual work. The question then arises: why do workers do this – why do they work? The fact that workers are present and available at a worksite says little about the effort they put in for their employer.[39] Individuals cannot be forced to work by dint of physical compulsion alone. Physical compulsion restricts the victim's freedom of movement, but the actions that the victim can (or is required to) perform within the limited scope for movement available to him or her require a degree of cooperation on the part of that same victim. As Barrington Moore has rightly noted, even in Nazi concentration camps, the SS guards 'needed some minimal cooperation from the prisoners in order to carry out the day's routine of getting them to the dormitories, feeding them, and making them work'.[40] Physically incarcerating workers therefore provides no guarantee that they will actually work. And using force to compel a victim to do something is not only very labour-intensive – owing to the need to deploy a permanent means of coercion directed at that individual – it is also extremely ineffective. I do not mean that force cannot play a role within a labour relationship, but that force (or the omnipresent potential for it) operates as part of a conditional threat: if you don't work hard/well enough, you will be physically punished.[41] Physical compulsion would *seem* to be one component of constrained choice.

Whether workers work hard and well will always depend on a combination of three factors: compensation, conditional force (coercion), and commitment. Together, these explain the degree to which workers are motivated to work in accordance with the standards set by the employer (Figure 6.4).[42]

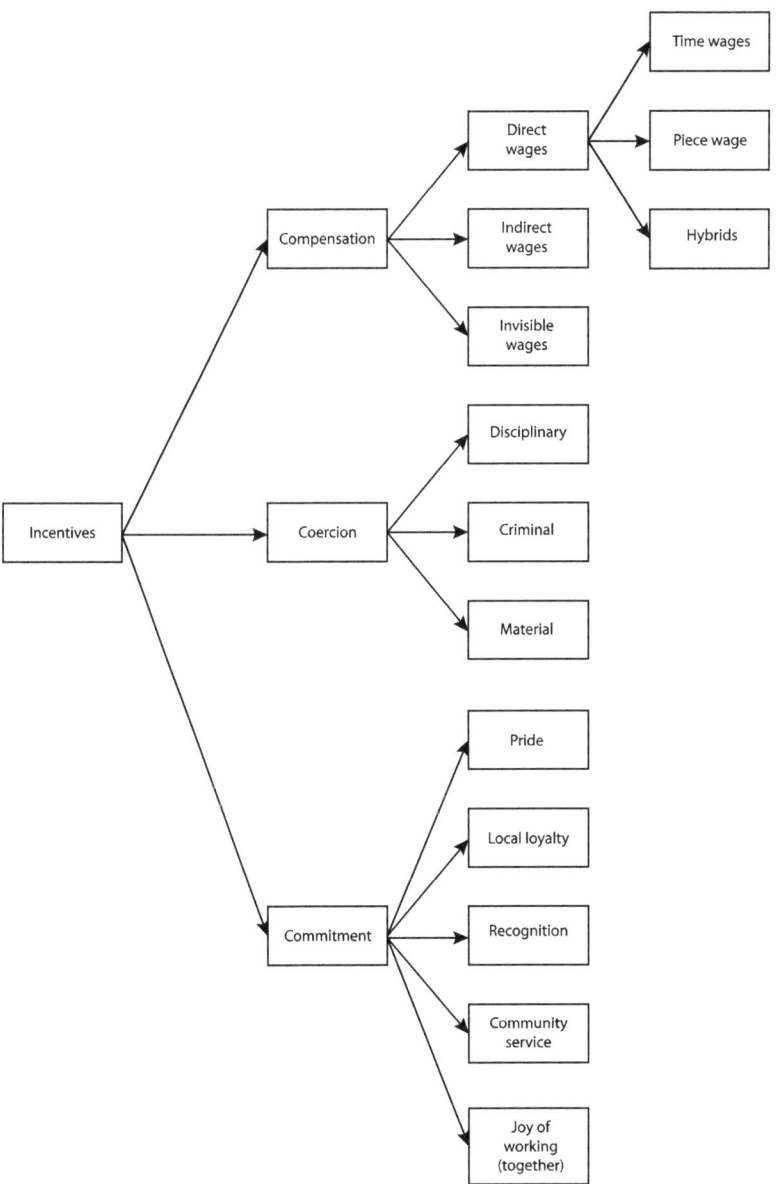

**Figure 6.4** Forms of labour *extraction*. Source: Author.

1) *Compensation*, or the offer of contingent rewards such as wages and other benefits, can be divided into three categories.

   First, *direct wages*, that is, money wages. These can be further subdivided into a) compensation for the *time* people work (time rates);[43] b) compensation for the *results* of people's work (piece rates: payment for each item produced; commission (for salespeople), whereby workers receive a fraction of the value of the items they sell; gainsharing: group incentives that are partially tied to gains in group productivity, reductions in cost, increases in product quality, or other measures of group success; profit-sharing and bonus plans (which link wages to the enterprise's profits); and c) combinations of time-based and result-based wages (hybrids).

   Second, *indirect wages*, such as perquisites, insurance arrangements, holiday pay, and services.[44]

   Third, *invisible wages* – the non-contractual appropriation by employees of enterprise goods and services. This category covers a range of wage forms, including open and legal perks, semi-legal pilfering, and outright theft.[45]

2) *Coercion*, or the conditional threat of inflicting harm, comprises disciplinary rules and their sanctioning. Coercion can be applied to enforce discipline but can hardly be used as a punishment to make people more creative. Three areas in which coercion may be applied can be distinguished: a) the area of *disciplinary liability*, in other words the breaking of factory rules. Punishment may include reprimands, demotion (transfer to other, lower-paid, work for a certain period) or dismissal; b) the area of *criminal liability*, or violating the criminal law, with corresponding punishments; and c) the area of *material liability*.[46] Punishment may include restitution in cash or kind to the enterprise for damage to its property resulting from an infringement of labour discipline.

3) *Commitment*, or the invocation of loyalty, comprises incentives based on five main motives: a) professional pride (craftsmanship); b) loyalties to a local community; c) loyalties to a wider community; d) desire for public recognition and appreciation; and e) the joy of working as such and/or with co-workers. These motives are closely linked to the cultural context. What the English observer Geoffrey Russell Barker wrote in the 1950s is illustrative in this respect:

   > The stimuli most widely used in the USSR, for example, would generally prove useless or worse in our [English] conditions. The honours awarded to categories of people regarded as socially

valuable in the way of uniforms, medals, decorations and badges would provoke not competition for them, as visible tokens of high status, but embarrassment and possibly even contempt. In this respect, the USSR was probably fortunately placed in having (a) a tradition upon which it was easy to build, and (b) in starting from a cultural level which largely reflected pre-capitalist conditions, in which awareness of the 'cash nexus' was not very fully developed – at any rate not so fully developed as to make it very difficult to persuade workers to accept such symbols of status as being equal or of comparable value to higher wages.[47]

The relative weight of these three motives, which varies over time and from job to job, defines the systems of work rules. These systems are always the result of 'negotiation' between employers and workers; and they determine more or less what constitutes proper or improper behaviour among workers and what behaviour can be punished or rewarded. Punishments and rewards can be discretionary (applied as the employer sees fit) or they may be bound by formal and informal rules.[48]

Regardless of the rules, there is always a lot of scope for manoeuvre among employers or their managers/overseers, if only because it is they who decide whether an employee's behaviour is correct and which incentives should be applied. Historically, workers have generally been in favour of restricting management's discretionary power as much as possible and expanding the domain of rules and meta-rules (rules about the making of rules).[49] The American sociologist Philip Selznick has written about the transition from a so-called prerogative contract – according to which management can deploy hired labour-power at its discretion – to a constitutive contract that sets out procedures and regulations for the utilization of labour-power.[50] This transition might reflect the enhanced power of workers at the worksite as well as the influence of external authorities, such as the state. In the case of a highly developed constitutive contract, the rule system becomes relatively autonomous, 'because it ensures the reproduction of relations in production by protecting management from itself, from its tendency towards arbitrary interventions that would undermine the consent produced at the point of production'.[51]

*Exit*

In what circumstances may the worker terminate his labour relationship? I distinguish seven important variants here.

1) *Exit forced by employer.* In some cases, employers wanted to shed their workers, by dismissal or deception, for example:

> Vessels with lengthy voyages typically had multiple stops, usually picking up a cargo in one and selling it at the next. The wait for more freight to come along could last for months. During this downtime the crewmen dared not leave because they would not receive their earned wages until reaching the agreed-upon final port of call. Those who did so lost all their pay. By law a [US] captain had to feed and provision his crew during such lulls, but if he chased them off, he kept their wages for himself. This prompted many unscrupulous masters to make their men's lives hell in an effort to entice them to desert. If successful, captains contracted a crimp [labour recruiter] for replacements when they needed to sail, then repeated the process in the next port.[52]

This was the case, too, with slaves who were dismissed because they were old or sick.

2) *Exit forced by another power.* British campaigns to abolish the slave trade (since 1807) and slavery (since 1834) changed labour relations throughout the world.[53] This was similarly true of the conventions adopted since 1919 by the ILO. The victory of the Northern states against the Confederacy in the American Civil War triggered important shifts, too, however, as did the emancipation of the serfs in the Habsburg Empire and Russia.

3) *Impeded (no way out)*, temporarily or permanently. Permanent impediments to leaving can be seen in traditional forms of slavery but also in the case of certain forms of debt peonage. Jan Breman reported the following in relation to poor peasants in Gujarat in the 1960s, who had become bonded labourers (*hali*):

> Because the hali's low income did not extend to celebrations in the household, like births and marriages, or setbacks, such as illness or death, the debt grew larger rather than smaller. This cumulative shortfall in income forced the labourer to remain attached to the master, and because it was impossible to end the relationship ... the contract took on the characteristics of servitude. After a lifetime's work, the hali was just as poor as when he entered the master's service.[54]

Temporary impediments characterize seasonally related debt bondage, for example. Jan Breman writes that cane cutters and brickmakers in contemporary Gujarat could be bonded by payment of an advance:

> ... for the season's duration, a period ranging from six to eight months. Payment of an advance is intended to force them to move and to prevent them from withdrawing prematurely from their contracts. To ensure immobilization of the floating workforce for the duration of the production process, payment of the wage is deferred until the season ends ... The new regime of bondage differs from the traditional one in terms of the short duration of the agreement (often no longer than one season), its more specific character (labour instead of a beck-and-call relationship) and finally, its easier termination or evasion (even without repayment of the debt).[55]

The techniques employers used to bind relatively freer workers to them were many, varying from workbooks (*livrets d'ouvriers*) to company housing. A workbook was a compulsory record that each worker had to hand over to their employer. As they could only leave that employment upon return of the workbook, duly signed by the employer, this restricted their free movement.

4) *Exit despite impediment*. If employers attempt to retain their workers against their will, those workers can decide to run away, as tens of thousands of slaves and convict labourers have done over the centuries, or desert, as sailors sometimes did.[56] Mass protests such as those culminating in the revolution on Saint-Domingue (1791–1804) could also terminate certain exploitative labour relations.

5) *Conditional exit*. Often, the exit is conditional, with workers having to meet certain obligations before being permitted to leave. Examples include indentured labourers, who were first required to complete the duration of their initial contract, and slaves striving to purchase their freedom (manumission) and who had to save their own price before they could be manumitted. Conditional exit applies, too, to 'free' wage labourers whose contracts include a period of notice.

6) *Unconditional exit*. Some groups of workers can leave at any moment they choose; these include casual labourers hired for perhaps just a few hours.

7) *Death* is, of course, the ultimate and irrevocable termination of a labour relationship.

Figure 6.5 captures all of these forms of exit.

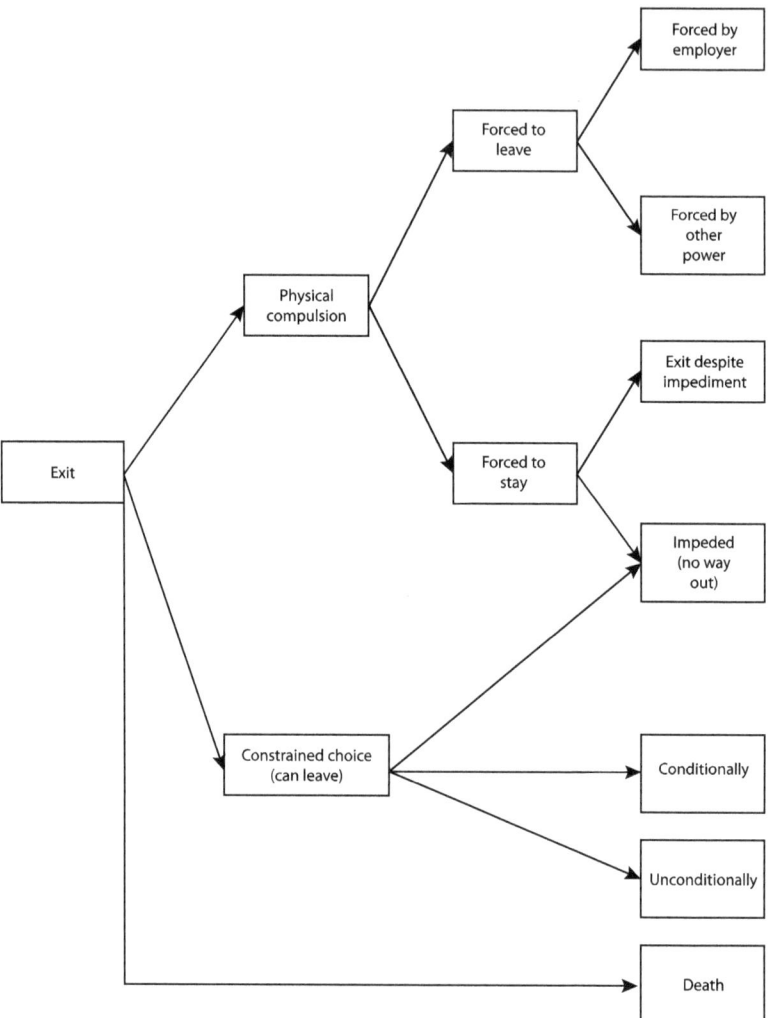

**Figure 6.5** Forms of labour relationship termination (*exit*). Source: Author.

## Combination of the three elements

The three 'moments' that characterize coerced labour (entry, labour extraction, and exit) all affect, and are affected by, each other. How a worker enters into a labour relationship influences how s/he has to work and the scope for exiting the labour relationship. A worker physically compelled to enter into a labour relationship will most likely also be subject to physical force for the duration of that relationship. These elements are thus inseparable but their permutations and intersections can be distinguished. In purely abstract terms, at least 770 combinations are possible (10 × 11 × 7) (see Figures 6.1, 6.4, and 6.5) but, in practice, not all variants are found.

The imprecise nature of our standard classifications is evident from the fact that, often, multiple combinations of the three elements are given the same label. In the case of chattel slaves, for example, four forms of entry are possible (sale, birth, abduction, or self-sale); labour extraction tends to be the result of coercion and compensation, and seldom of commitment; and the labour relationship can be exited in all of the six variants indicated earlier. That is, owners can compel slaves to leave or they can be forced to free them by another entity (an abolitionist state, for example) but they can also free them unconditionally; slaves can run away or mutiny; they can purchase their own freedom; or they can remain as slaves.

*Debt peons* enter into a labour relationship to pay off a debt or because they have been abducted; the main incentives inducing them to work are, as in the case of chattel slaves, coercion and compensation (seldom commitment); and they may not leave, or only under certain conditions, unless they run away or their debt is remitted.

*'Free' wage labourers* enter into a labour relationship on their own initiative; they are induced to do so primarily through compensation and commitment; they can leave their employer conditionally or unconditionally; or they can remain.

All of this suggests that we need more refined categories if we are to characterize individual forms of labour relationship.

## Multicausality

Of course, the approach sketched above is still rudimentary and can certainly be refined. Nonetheless, it shows that coerced labour is a more complex phenomenon than is often thought. But there is a second limitation to my argument: it is constructed at the level of the individual and disregards all broader structural and cultural factors. This might be taken to imply a tendency towards methodological individualism on my part but that is not the case.[57] Though I am of the opinion that individuals and their micro-situations should be given priority over both the political and humanitarian points of view, that does not constitute individualism. As Alex Callinicos remarked: 'To say this is to make no real concession to individualism, since the bases of collective action comprise not just agents but the structures from which they derive their power to realize their ends'.[58] A necessary next stage in the analysis is therefore to introduce structures, as being 'both the ever present *condition* (material cause) and the continually reproduced *outcome* of human agency'.[59]

By integrating structures and their transformation into the analysis, the foundation is laid for a historical *explanation* of various possible forms of entry, extraction, and exit. So far, the debate has been characterized largely by two weaknesses. First, one often sees very different types of coerced labour being treated as if there were no distinction between them. Take, for example, Evsey Domar's famous essay 'The causes of slavery and serfdom', in which the author presupposes that serfdom and slavery have the same origins,[60] even though the possibility cannot be ruled out – indeed, it is very likely – that 'one institution has often been made possible by the very same set of factors that made the other impossible, because of what the two institutions do not have in common'.[61] Of course, refining the analysis in the way I propose above makes everything even more complex, for it now becomes possible to distinguish between a large number of variations whose causal configurations are congruent to a greater or lesser extent.[62] I suspect that, for the development of a more sophisticated typology, entry and exit will prove to be of crucial importance, while the way in which labour is extracted in the intervening period is of secondary importance and largely derived from those two elements. Of overriding importance is how labourers are recruited and under what conditions they can subsequently leave.

Second, there is a persistent tendency to apply monocausal thinking, going back as far as Adam Smith, who could explain slavery only in psychological terms:

> The pride of man makes him love to domineer, and nothing mortifies him so much as to be obliged to condescend to persuade his inferiors. Wherever the law allows it, and the nature of the work can afford it, therefore, he will generally prefer the service of slaves to that of freemen.[63]

Ever since Edward Gibbon Wakefield, economistic explanations have been fashionable, and, even today, new variants are regularly adduced.[64] In such analyses, neither resistance on the part of labour nor the political, legal, or cultural environments play roles of any significance. Under the influence of the institutionalist turn seen especially among economic historians in recent decades, some authors have become aware of this limitation. In an article on labour coercion, Daron Acemoglu and

Alexander Wolitzky concluded their pure neoclassical thesis by observing that 'in many instances, coercion comes to an end, or is significantly curtailed, when political forces induce a change in the institutional environment'.[65] What we now need to do, though, is to 'endogenize' 'political forces' and other non-economic influences, to fully integrate them into the analysis, just as Folke Dovring, Stanley Engerman, and Orlando Patterson advocated in the 1960s and 70s.[66] Almost 20 years ago, in their study of the relationship between child labour and debt bondage, Arnab Basu and Nancy Chau took a further step and argued that child labour was caused, in part, because peasant households were unable to 'collectively bargain and coordinate child labor supply'.[67] As a result 'basic labor rights such as freedom of association, and the right to organize, complement efforts to eradicate forced and bonded child labor'. Such a broadening of the horizon is of great significance.

Even if much of the current theoretical literature is simplistic, monocausal, and economistic, that does not, of course, invalidate its usefulness for further theoretical development. The countless studies by development economists and others include not only a great deal of factual material; they also reveal patterns that, though often remaining historically decontextualized, are nonetheless of heuristic value. The following lists a number of factors, without aiming to be exhaustive:

- *Seasonal variations*. Some labour relations, such as in agriculture, are affected by seasonal factors, irrespective of the state of supply and demand. Others are affected by a seasonally variable supply of raw materials (industries that use or transport agricultural products as raw materials, for example). Certain other labour relations are affected by the seasonal variations in the demand for goods produced and services provided.[68] Periodic fluctuations in the deployment of labour can lead to a two-tier system, in which the employer attempts to oblige some labourers to work for him relatively permanently (for example, through indebtedness or by providing a homestead) while others are employed on a casual basis. However, there are, of course, examples where the employer used only permanent labourers but paid them very low wages or no wages at all (as in the case of chattel slaves), ensuring labour costs remained low even during slack seasons.
- *Labour supply*. Nieboer and Domar's conception of a positive relationship between labour scarcity and bonded labour, under their hypothesis that abundant labour supply is a condition of 'free' labour, has proved untenable as a general hypothesis.[69] Nonetheless,

their proposed understanding continues to play a role in the literature because, under extremely specific conditions, it might be valid – although research has so far failed to delineate those conditions sufficiently.[70]

- *Credit facilities*. Employers as well as workers sometimes need credit to bridge periods of more modest income or greater expenditure. In the case of employers, that might, for example, mean their combining wage-earners with rent tenants, to some extent.[71] Workers lacking access to cheap credit from banks are obliged to pay usurious rates of interest, which render them dependent on the creditor – in many cases, their employer.[72]
- *Supervision*. 'With agricultural development, as the hired labor force grows in size, the landlord finds it useful to mobilize the services of his attached laborer in overseeing the work of casual laborers and reporting on cases of delinquency or rebelliousness. In general, the two-tiered labor system on a farm is an important check on the development of class solidarity of farm workers'.[73]

In addition to these factors, there is also a wide range of extra-economic considerations that might play a role, such as:

- *Resistance*. There is a continuous latent struggle between employers and workers regarding the latter's autonomy. Depending on power relations, there is an endlessly shifting 'frontier of control'[74] that defines what workers may and may not do. Sometimes, that latent struggle is transformed into open conflict, the most dramatic example being the slave revolt on Saint-Domingue in 1791, which culminated in the abolition of slavery.
- *Ideologies*. Racist or sexist belief systems used by employers – or some of the working class – to legitimize the exploitation of certain groups of labourers; and humanitarian belief systems that condemn such exploitation.
- *National legislation* prohibiting certain forms of coerced labour (slavery) or actually promoting them (convict labour).
- *International pressure*, such as the abolitionist movement, which, starting with Great Britain, succeeded in securing the abolition of the slave trade and slavery in more and more parts of the world in the nineteenth century, leading to the introduction of other forms of coerced labour, such as indentured labour, *engagés*, sharecropping, and debt bondage. There is also the influence of the ILO, which attempts, through its conventions, to ban certain forms of labour.

- *Wars*. During armed conflicts, one often sees major changes in employment systems. The relative autonomy of workers is generally restricted; women who had previously performed largely subsistence labour might be mobilized for wage labour in industry, for example.

All these factors together – and many more – form the causal configurations that give rise to systems of labour relations, which then begin to develop their own dynamics. Stanley Engerman, for example, noted that we should distinguish between those features that lead to the imposition of a slave system and those that make for its continuation:

> Although the inauguration of the system might be due to seemingly minor and accidental factors, once created the slaveowning class has an incentive to avoid capital losses by perpetuating the system. The initial rents upon imposing the system would not go to the slaveowners, the actual allocation of rents divided between owners and enslavers dependent upon the accuracy of forecasts as to the future course of the system, but the attempt to avoid a once-for-all capital loss from uncompensated emancipation has generated the political, social, and economic problems found in abolition discussions. 'Buying in' to the system need not provide more than normal profits; that, however, does not mean that slaveowners will easily accept its demise.[75]

## A final remark

It is obvious that, *within* their unfreedom, workers may have very different degrees of autonomy. Chattel slaves who are limitlessly exploited and whose owners, when purchasing them, will already have factored-in a seven-year period of amortization, have scarcely any room for manoeuvre during their lifetime. In contrast, wage labourers who have acquired many rights, who can switch regularly from one employer to another, supported by powerful trade unions, and who are in a position to negotiate their terms of employment are much more autonomous. For workers, the type of labour relationship in which they work makes a lot of difference.

## Notes

1  Merleau-Ponty, *Signes*, 128.
2  Lachs, 'Slavery'.
3  Supplementary Convention on the Abolition of Slavery, the Slave Trade, and Institutions and Practices Similar to Slavery, 3.

4   Walk Free Foundation, *Global Slavery Index 2014*, 8.
5   Anti-Slavery International, 'What is modern slavery?'.
6   Expertus, 'Negroes and the slave trade'.
7   Marx, *Grundrisse*, 326.
8   'The principal-agent literature is concerned with how one individual, the principal (say an employer), can design a compensation system (a contract) which motivates another individual, his agent (say the employee), to act in the principal's interest.' Stiglitz, 'Principal and agent (II)', 966.
9   Aristotle, *Politeia*, 1337b17–21. Translation taken from the New Oxford edition.
10  Examples in Zelnick-Abramovitz, *Not Wholly Free*, 34–5.
11  Finley, *Ancient Slavery and Modern Ideology*, 67.
12  Finley himself did not share this view. He argued that 'the work of the women and children within the family, no matter how authoritarian and patriarchal its structure, is not subsumed under [the] category of labour for others (though I am aware that I face objections from several directions when I say that)'. See *Ancient Slavery and Modern Ideology*, 67.
13  Gorr, 'Toward a theory of coercion', 384–5.
14  Gorr, 'Toward a theory of coercion', 385.
15  Physical compulsion is sometimes also termed 'occurrent coercion', and conditional threats 'dispositional coercion'. See Bayles, 'Concept of coercion', 17. Unconditional threats exist alongside conditional threats, as when someone says 'I will kill you', without the person threatened being in a position to exert an influence on the person making the threat. For an interesting sociological analysis of threats, see Paris and Sofsky, 'Drohungen'.
16  See, for example, Cohen, 'Resistance'; Scott, *Weapons of the Weak*; Ihonvbere, 'Resistance'; Gutmann, 'Rituals of resistance'.
17  Reis, '"Revolution of the *Ganhadores*"', 359.
18  Article 117 of the *Code of Hammurabi* stated: 'If any one fail to meet a claim for debt, and sell himself, his wife, his son, and daughter for money or give them away to forced labor: they shall work for three years in the house of the man who bought them, or the proprietor, and in the fourth year they shall be set free.' Hammurabi, 15. See also Dorn, 'Selbstverknechtung'.
19  Patterson, *Slavery and Social Death*, 130. See also Hellie, *Slavery in Russia*; Testart, *L'esclave, la dette et le pouvoir*; and Engerman, 'Slavery, freedom, and Sen', esp. 94–100.
20  Brass, *Towards a Comparative Political Economy*, 11–12.
21  Brass, *Towards a Comparative Political Economy*, 11–12. For a slightly different view, see Rao, 'Agrarian power and unfree labour'.
22  See, for example, MacLeod, 'Some aspects of primitive chattel slavery'; Watson, 'Chattel slavery'; Mitchell, 'American origins'; Card, 'Genocide and social death'.
23  Edwards, 'Slavery'.
24  Griaule, 'Labour in Abyssinia', 194.
25  Binger, *Du Niger au Golfe du Guinée*, 470–3.
26  Binger, *Du Niger au Golfe du Guinée*, 470–3.
27  Fall, *Le travail forcé*, 108. For similar recruitment practices in British Africa, see Mason, 'Working on the railway', and Cooper, *From Slaves to Squatters*, 92–104.
28  Quoted in: Peemans, 'Capital accumulation', 175. For other cases, see, for example, Ford, 'Political economy of taxation'; Gardner, *Taxing Colonial Africa*.
29  Cohen, 'Structure of proletarian unfreedom', 3.
30  Elster, *Making Sense of Marx*, 213.
31  When the US social scientist E. Wight Bakke lived in the working-class neighbourhood of Greenwich (London) in the early 1930s, he observed an 'unwillingness to launch out into some sort of independent enterprise'. He explained this by 'the inability of one who has been born and bred in the tradition of a wage-earner to visualize himself as an independent worker, his own boss'. This 'lack of imagination' resulted from the wage-earner's work socialization: 'The work routine, the regularity and simplicity of the routine outside working hours, the plodding necessities of the household economy – all of these enforce a discipline which trains for stability as a wage-earner but not for the independence and adaptability and personality necessary for success in an independent enterprise.' Bakke, *The Unemployed Man*, 126–7.
32  Cohen, 'Structure of proletarian unfreedom', 11–12.
33  Berger, 'Warum arbeiten die Arbeiter?'.
34  Sakamoto, '"Slave labor" in Brazil', 15.
35  Blackmon, *Slavery by Another Name*, 1–2.

36  Bedoya, Bedoya & Belser, 'Debt bondage', 41.
37  See, for example, A Mining Expert, 'The contract system in Chinese mining'; Wright, '"A method of evading management"'; Chandavarkar, 'Decline and fall of the jobber system'.
38  Marradi, 'Classification, typology, taxonomy'.
39  There is a fundamental asymmetry here between 'employer' and 'worker' (where 'worker' can also be a slave). In the transaction, the worker who hires himself or herself out or the slave who is sold (regardless of whether the worker himself is a party to the contract [the 'free' wage labourer] or not [the slave]) merely represents labour power (labour capacity). Once the transaction has been effected, however, this potential energy still needs to be translated into work (labour). It is not until the actual labour process has commenced that work is extracted from the labour power. In relation to the example of wage labour, Herbert Simon once explained this distinction by comparing an employment contract with a standard sales contract: 'We will say that W [the worker] enters into an employment contract with B [the boss] when the former agrees to accept the authority of the latter and the latter agrees to pay the former a stated wage (w). This contract differs fundamentally from a sales contract – the kind of contract that is assumed in ordinary formulations of price theory. In the sales contract each party promises a specific consideration in return for the consideration promised by the other. The buyer (like B) promises to pay a stated sum of money; but the seller (unlike W) promises in return a specified quantity of a completely specified commodity. Moreover, the seller is not interested in the way in which his commodity is used once it is sold, while the worker *is* interested in what the entrepreneur will want him to do (what x [element of the set of possible behavior patterns] will be chosen by B).' Simon, 'Formal theory of the employment relationship', 294.
40  Moore, Jr., *Injustice*, 65.
41  Nor should we lose sight of the fact that unfreedom can lead to 'unfunctional' violence, such as the rape of female workers by those 'higher up'.
42  Tilly & Tilly, *Work Under Capitalism*.
43  This is most common in the West: in 1991, 86 per cent of US employees were paid either by the hour or by the month. See Ehrenberg & Smith, *Modern Labor Economics*, 412.
44  'Inasmuch as these are generally made uniformly available to all employees at a given job level, regardless of performance, they are really not motivating rewards. However, where indirect compensation is controllable by management and is used to reward performance, then it clearly needs to be considered as a motivating reward.' Robbins, *Organizational Behavior*, 660.
45  Ditton, 'Perks, pilferage, and the fiddle'.
46  Barker, *Some Problems of Incentives*, 98–9.
47  Barker, *Some Problems of Incentives*, 113–14.
48  It might be useful to distinguish between (a) the *making* of the rules; (b) the *monitoring* of the personnel's obeying of these rules; and (c) the punishing or rewarding of personnel (not) obeying these rules (*incentives*).
49  In *Employing Bureaucracy*, Jacoby has argued that trade-union opposition to managerial discretionary power has furthered the bureaucratization of American industrial firms.
50  Selznick, *Law, Society and Industrial Justice*, 135–7, 151–4.
51  Burawoy, *Manufacturing Consent*, 117.
52  Strecker, *Shanghaiing Sailors*, 5.
53  This is covered more extensively in van der Linden, *Humanitarian Intervention*.
54  Breman, *Labour Bondage in West India*, 36.
55  Breman, 'Study of industrial labour in post-colonial India', 421–2. See also Bedoya, Bedoya & Belser, 'Debt bondage', 46.
56  On this, see Chapter 15.
57  On this, see van der Linden, 'Old workers' movements'.
58  Callinicos, *Making History*, 134.
59  Bhaskar, *Possibility of Naturalism*, 43.
60  Domar, 'Causes of slavery and serfdom'.
61  Patterson, 'Structural origins of slavery', 17.
62  For my interpretation of the concept 'causal configuration', see van der Linden, *Transnational Labour History*.
63  Smith, *Wealth of Nations*, Books I–III, 489.
64  Wakefield, *View of the Art of Colonization*.
65  Acemoglu & Wolitzky, 'The economics of labor coercion', 588.

66 Dovring, 'Bondage, tenure and progress'; Engerman, 'Some considerations', 59; Patterson, 'Structural origins of slavery'.
67 Basu & Chau, 'Exploitation of child labor', 229 and 233.
68 Jones, *Outcast London*, 33–51; Kuznets, *Seasonal Variations*.
69 For example, Siegel, 'Some methodological considerations'; Engerman, 'Some considerations'; Patterson, 'Structural origins of slavery'; Vries, *Escaping Poverty*, 190–2.
70 For one preliminary attempt, see Green, 'Economics of slavery'.
71 Harris, 'Circuit of capital'.
72 See, for example, Knight, 'Debt bondage in Latin America'; Moulier Boutang, *De l'esclavage au salariat*. For a seldom-studied variant of bondage in which the employer obstructs the migration of workers by making payments in kind, see Friebel & Guriev, 'Attaching workers'.
73 Bardhan, 'Labor-tying', 507.
74 See Goodrich, *The Frontier of Control*.
75 Engerman, 'Some considerations', 60.

# 7
# Household strategies

Traditionally, the vast majority of workers lived in families and households. There were, however, significant exceptions to this general rule, including chattel slaves who lived alone, without family, in slave quarters. Ordinarily, only a limited share of all slaves had to endure such coerced individualization. But slaves who managed to form intimate ties often faced serious challenges as well, as slave narratives from the US clearly reveal. In the 1930s, the ex-slave Samuel Boulvware remembered that his father came to see the family even though he faced punishment for doing so:

> My daddy was a slave on Reuban Bouwave's plantation, 'bout two miles from Marster Hunter's place. He would git a pass to come to see mammy once every week. If he come more than dat he would have to skeedaddle through de woods and fields from de patrollers. If they ketched him widout a pass, he was sho' in for a skin cracklin' whippin. He knowed all dat but he would slip to see mammy anyhow, whippin' or not.[1]

Establishing meaningful domestic and kin arrangements was, of course, exceptionally difficult under such repressive conditions. But many enslaved people had strong adaptive capacities, and enduring marriages were not unusual. Still, there was always a serious threat that family members would be separated by sale.[2] Everything I write here about household strategies relates only to workers who, regardless of their circumstances, were at any rate sufficiently autonomous to set up a fairly enduring private sphere.

## Principles

Let me describe the central concepts involved in more detail. By *families*, I mean the small social units based on marriage or descent from common ancestors ('lineage'). These should be distinguished from *households*. This second concept is rather ambiguous and has been subject to extensive terminological debates.[3] To avoid a digression into this issue, I will use the description in McGuire et al., which states that households are 'those sets of relationships, historically variable yet relatively constant, that have as one of their principal features the sharing of sustenance gained from the widest possible variety of sources'.[4] This description is loose enough to cover a variety of situations. It stresses the budget-pooling aspect of households, an approach that serves my purpose. The following reservations apply to using the designation 'household':

- Households do not necessarily consist of two or three generations of one family. They may include several families, other types of biological kinship (such as siblings), or members not related by blood or marriage.
- Households do not necessarily entail co-habitation, even according to Donald Bender's definition, which calls for 'a proximity in sleeping arrangements and a sentiment similar to that expressed in our folk concept of home'.[5] For example, at least one member in a household of seasonal migrants is likely to live elsewhere for months at a time and can nevertheless contribute substantially to the household budget.[6]
- This focus on economic aspects should not diminish the role of households as culturally significant units shaped by symbolic processes.[7]
- Rather than being predetermined, the composition of households is a product of negotiations. The composition of a household may be affected by income, marriage prospects for men and women, employment opportunities, arrangements for the care of elderly parents, and governmental factors such as legislation and taxation.[8]
- Households should not be considered anthropomorphic entities through being designated as products of collective will. Members do not necessarily work for the common good of the household; on the contrary, they may be driven by selfish motives. Conflicts of interest are also possible, as well as oppression and resistance against oppression.[9] Both dependency and authority may vary according to the member of the household. Laslett pointed out that infants and children have the greatest stake in the household's survival, 'since their life chances depend almost wholly on its existence and persistence, on their being accepted and retained as members. But children also have the least power to affect the

household's decisions and none whatever to carry them out'.[10] This statement about influencing household decisions implies that, while we should not arbitrarily ascribe a collective will to households, members nevertheless try to find (a variety of) ways to control their fate, whenever possible. To this end, they negotiate to devise a strategy for generating and allocating the common budget.

In everyday language, hardly any distinction is made between families and households. There is much to be said for this, since households are generally based on marriage and/or real or fictive kinship. But it is nonetheless useful to make an analytical distinction between the two concepts. There are enough examples of non-kin-related household members, and kinship can extend beyond purely the household, as is shown by the case of male labourers working in the agricultural industry in Madagascar who are members of more than one family at the same time.[11]

The third central concept is that of *household strategies*. This is a somewhat controversial notion. Some scholars argue that the term 'strategy' implies the existence of a 'master plan' that households and families use to ensure their survival. Of course, this is not the case. In fact, the 'strategy' that is to be adopted is a matter for continual negotiation between household members, and, occasionally the plans of some members are even opposed by others in no uncertain terms. We may consider alternatives ('coping methods', for example) but they are not really much of an improvement. Furthermore, the concept of 'household (or family) strategies' is now fairly well established in the academic literature, and so it seems wise to retain it.

By 'strategies' I mean here the (one-off or repetitive) coordinated use of resources to achieve a particular purpose.[12] Within each strategy, one can therefore make a distinction between the following: (i) the resources mobilized, such as time, money, land, means of communication, and networks used to achieve that purpose; (ii) the purpose of the strategy – what the actors wish to achieve; and (iii) *how* the resources are *combined* to achieve that purpose (who decides, who carries the action out, what resources are to be used, and how). We must be wary, though, of tautologies; not all actions carried out by household members are household strategies. Only those intended to contribute directly to the welfare of the household can be considered as such.[13]

The fourth and final concept I wish to note here is *collective action*. Collective action can be defined as the more or less coordinated action by a group of people to achieve a particular purpose that none of them acting on their own, with the resources at their disposal, could achieve in the same space of time. This definition is exceptionally wide, since it also includes the participation of a team in a football tournament. Not all forms of collective action are intended to promote the interests of households, by any means. Here, I am talking about collective actions that are primarily socio-economic in nature and vary from food riots and wildcat strikes, through mutual aid societies and producer or consumer cooperatives, to trade unions and political parties.

In this context, the reference to 'more or less coordinated actions' of a group of workers is not intended to suggest the existence of a formal organization. It could just as easily be an extremely short-lived ad-hoc coalition formed specifically for that one action, which collapses once that action has been carried out. The difference between formal and informal organizations is sometimes vague. Moreover, a collective action does not necessarily need to have the character of a protest. There are many types of collective action that are not regarded as protests either by the workers involved or the authorities.[14] Whether an action entails a violation of existing rules is determined solely by the specific historical context. The authorities repeatedly redefine these rules (partly in response to the pressure of collective action), and so actions that, at one moment, constitute a serious breach of the law might, at some other time, be completely legal.

Individual workers and their families always combine a number of activities to be able to cope with problems related to waged labour. Not only does a great deal of subsistence labour take place every day in every family (especially, but not exclusively performed by women),[15] but there are usually also several forms of activities remunerated with money. The social budget-pooling function of households entails income and expenditure, and this process need not be exclusively monetary: it may also consist of goods and services.

The pattern of *expenditure* in independent households is composed of at least five types of expenses:[16]

- support of household members involved in productive labour
- support of these same individuals during periods of disability or unemployment
- support of older household members who used to be involved in productive labour
- support of younger household members not yet involved in productive labour
- the means to make payments to third parties (such as taxes, duties, and repayment of debts).

This list includes the possibility of economies of scale arising from the common use of certain goods. (To give a modern example: whether a household consists of two people or five, one vacuum cleaner will suffice.) The income of independent households is derived from at least seven sources:[17]

- means obtained through labour remunerated in wages or in kind
- means obtained through non-commercial labour (directly consumable goods), including homemade clothing, raising domestic animals such as pigs and poultry,[18] and collecting rubbish for direct reuse[19]
- means obtained through petty commodity production or petty commerce, including manufacturing cottage-industry textiles, raising livestock for sale, peddling,[20] and professional scavenging[21]
- means derived from providing resources such as land, tools for labour, accommodation, and money. These means may include income received from renting-out beds or rooms[22]
- means obtained through transfer payments, received without immediate reciprocal exchange of labour or commodities, including support from friends and acquaintances in times of need, charity, and social benefits
- means that result from theft, including both conventional methods of stealing and pilfering at the workplace[23]
- means obtained through credit, including billing in instalments, deferred payments, or pawning personal property.[24]

*Wage-earning households* are those in which the first-mentioned source of income (remunerated labour) prevails in importance. This statement does *not* exclude the role of other sources of income. On the contrary, wage-earning households usually rely on a variety of sources of income; virtually all members generate an income; and individual members (especially over the course of their entire lives) tend to provide income from numerous sources. While these observations do not imply the absence of a clear correlation between age and gender, on the one hand, and revenue-producing activities, on the other, it is likely that the degree of correlation varies according to the source of income.[25]

The various reproductive activities of the household have a gendered nature. Some are typically 'male', some typically 'female', and these gendered definitions may be flexible, depending on the circumstances. There are many examples of gender transgressions, with men doing 'women's work' and vice versa.[26] The management of the household is a distinct type of work and is normally done by a woman. As far as I am aware, there is no satisfactory comparative historical analysis of this management.[27]

## A range of strategies

What are the potential strategies for survival and improvement available to a working-class household? Let's begin with the means for self-improvement at the disposal of *separate* households. First, they might move to another neighbourhood, city, or country in the hope of finding more satisfactory conditions. Millions have already chosen this option.[28] Second, they can take advantage of better times to take precautionary measures for the hard times that lie ahead. These measures may include saving money[29] or purchasing a house.[30] Third, households may reduce expenses through measures such as living (even more) frugally, opting to not pay their debts, and expelling non-productive members.[31] Fourth, they can change how they obtain their income, for example by seeking other work or through diversification or curtailment of their sources of income.

In addition to measures taken by households to improve their living conditions by themselves, there are several strategies involving help from outside sources. As a first strategy, households may appeal to *relatives*. Many authors have indicated the value of kinship for households. Tamara Hareven wrote that, to many American immigrants and urban workers, kin were:

> … the main, if not the only, source of assistance and survival. In the absence of public welfare agencies and social security, kin were the exclusive source of social insurance. Kin assistance was crucial in handling personal and family crises (such as child-bearing, illness, and death), and in coping with the insecurities imposed by the industrial system (such as unemployment, accidents, and strikes).

Furthermore, Hareven continued:

> Strategies for kin assistance required both short-term and long-term investments over the life-course. Short-term investments entailed assistance in the workplace, in housing, in loaning money or tools, and trading skills, goods, or services. Among the long-term investments, the most pervasive exchange was that between parents and children—old-age support in return for child-rearing.[32]

Kinship relations *outside* one's immediate surroundings often proved especially important. One interesting method of distributing the risks involves mutual assistance between rural/agrarian and urban relatives. Heidi Rosenbaum described an example of this system when she mentioned the importance 'of family support from relatives in the countryside' for workers in Linden (Germany) in the early-twentieth century.[33] Jean Peterson showed how the reverse currently holds true for Philippine peasantry, writing that 'some families explicitly plan to establish some siblings … as wage-earners in the city' to generate revenue in cases of crop failure or poor harvests.[34]

A second source of relief lies in *personal communities*. These communities consist of informal networks based on companionship, emotional aid, and small acts of service in daily life. While the networks may be locally based (neighbourhoods), this restriction is not essential to their operation. Personal communities also include kinship networks and require the same investment as strategies for short-term kin assistance (relatively small-scale and readily available skills and services).[35] Personal communities have always been gendered, although their focus varies depending on the historical context, the place, and the culture.[36] There is often a fluid boundary between blood relatives and personal communities, as proved by frequent transformations of friendships into fictitious kinship relations, such as with the Latin American *compadrazgo* (fictitious parenthood usually involving the relationship between the parents and godparents to a child)[37] and the selection of *Taufpaten* (godparents) among the nineteenth-century German working class.[38]

Acceptance of *patronage* is a third strategy. Whereas the first two forms of social insurance are generally horizontal (because the actors pertained to similar social classes), this configuration is clearly vertical. As Y. Michal Bodemann wrote, it involves 'a form of class rule and class struggle and at the same time its concealment'.[39] Weak subalterns seek protection from higher-status more powerful individuals who help them in emergencies in return for material or other types of services. This relationship is not merely economic but sociocultural as well, as patrons receive their clients' loyalty and esteem in return for their protection and help. Forms of patronage may vary from political clientelism to patriarchal enterprise.[40]

The fourth and final strategy is that of *collective action* to bring about overall improvement in the conditions of (segments of) the working class. Obviously, the amount of personal freedom that workers happen to have strongly influences their ability to organize. Plantation slaves and other groups of physically coerced workers will often find it impossible to build elaborate, durable organizational structures of their own. They may choose to run away (see Chapter 15) or to use 'hidden' forms of resistance (arson, poisoning, and so on). Workers with some autonomy may initiate mutual-aid societies, consumer cooperatives, trade unions, or even political parties.

At least eight ways thus exist for households to improve their circumstances, whether they do so autonomously or with outside help. *How* households devise their strategy is crucial. Several factors need to be considered. The preceding description is *taxonomic* in that it covers opportunities that *may* arise over time. The various options are actually limited to specific historical contexts. Paternalism, for example, is less common in highly developed industrial societies than in less developed ones.[41] Each situation will therefore present fewer opportunities, overall, than those described here. On the other hand, each strategy consists of several options: those who wish to join social movement organizations can sometimes choose from a wide range of possibilities. It is also possible (and even common) to employ several strategies at once. Furthermore, the strategies described here are interrelated and can alternatively undermine or reinforce one another. Frequent geographical mobility can work against the establishment of powerful unions, in some cases, whereas it might actually form the basis for organizations in other cases.[42] Strategies may even intermingle. Extremely close non-kin relationships can, for example, be transformed into fictitious kinship relations.[43] Alternatively, kinship and personal communities may provide a valuable basis for a social movement organization.[44]

## Final observations

Working-class families usually prefer not to make themselves dependent on a single household strategy. They tend to prefer a combination of different strategies – a *strategic repertoire*, if you like. Essentially, then, the issue is how families develop this repertoire, in response to changes in the environment in which they live and work. The answer cannot be found simply by studying the families themselves. Obviously, labour relations and the social networks of the various family members also play an important role, as does the extent to which the institutional environment facilitates or impedes the various components of a strategic repertoire.

Naturally, when a repertoire is being compiled, the relative advantages and disadvantages of individual strategies will be assessed and compared. Two sorts of considerations play a role in this process:

- Instrumental considerations: Which combination involves the fewest risks, offers the greatest gains, or involves the least effort?
- Normative considerations: Which combination is the most dignified, pleasant, and justified?

Both sorts of considerations are closely related, and their mutual boundaries are sometimes vague. For example, a strategy might be considered dignified either because it is hazardous or, depending on the circumstances, because it is not. The arguments for or against adopting a certain combination of strategies might be mutually inconsistent. There are so many potential considerations and it is impossible to predict what the outcome will be. Naturally, not everyone takes the same factors into account. This is true both of individual family members and of a family as a whole. Every judgement about the reasons for adopting a certain repertoire must thus take account of the fact that it involves contingent processes.

A number of factors seem to play a role in reconstructing strategic household repertoires. First, cost–benefit analyses have their place in the selection of household strategies. Such analyses are often much more complex than they initially seem. Using a rational-choice approach, Debra Friedman, for example, has devised a quasi-mathematical formula to ascertain the influences contributing to a worker's decision to join a strike. Her list includes no fewer than ten factors.[45] In her analysis, she shows clearly that – in terms of the rational-choice approach – a *host* of cost–benefit analyses have to be made simultaneously.

One wonders whether, in practice, individuals actually weigh up the advantages and disadvantages of their potential strategies in this way. I suspect the 'cost–benefit analysis' carried out by each individual can become so complex that people are likely to take it less seriously than many theorists presume; in such cases, people rely on more practical formulas, *algorithms of everyday life*. The decision regarding whether or not to join a strike might also often be based on such abridged reasoning.[46]

Second, *contra* Friedman and others, decisions are not always 'rational', even though it remains unclear what 'rationality' means precisely in this context. Choices are also shaped by 'habit, impulse, dispositions, emotions, and desires, many of which are not notably rational'.[47] Not only might household members seriously differ from one another in their opinions regarding the composition of a strategic repertoire, but they might also have doubts and defer decisions longer than would be 'necessary' in rational terms, due to the affective forces influencing those decisions. In relation to a strike among textile workers in Manchester (New Hampshire), Tamara Hareven observed the following: 'Whether or not to strike divided some families and caused conflicts that took years to overcome. Some relatives, in fact, have not spoken to each other since their split over the strike of 1922'.[48]

Third, some of the household methods that appear to be rational are not actually included in a strategic repertoire because they are 'inconceivable' strategies for the household in question and, thus, excluded by definition from the cost–benefit analysis. There are a number of reasons for this. For a start, the general material situation of a family should be taken into account. Do families succeed only in surviving from day to day or do they have sufficient scope to plan their lives to some extent? Maurice Merleau-Ponty has wondered 'why a return of prosperity frequently brings with it a more radical mood among the masses. It is because the easing of living conditions makes a fresh structure of social space possible: the horizon is not restricted to the most immediate concerns, there is economic play and room for a new project in relation to living'.[49] A working-class family on the edge of subsistence is, in the words of Ditmar Brock, 'a sort of emergency organization for mutual assistance (*Notgemeinschaft*)', whose survival depends more on their skill in improvising than their ability to plan long-term. Such a situation 'permits only *the short-term, situative realization of needs*'.[50]

Only with the development of more material 'opportunities' does participation in longer-term activities (trade-union membership, for instance) become possible. Pierre Bourdieu goes a step further and suggests that even people with extremely limited material opportunities make 'plans' but these 'plans' tend to resemble daydreams rather than projects rooted in the present: 'It is not surprising to find that aspirations tend to become more realistic, more strictly tailored to real possibilities, in proportion as the real possibilities become greater'.[51] It is therefore conceivable that strategies that require sacrifices today, to effect possible improvements in the more distant future, will find support among working-class families only where there is some material 'manoeuvring space'. In addition, much like theatrical repertoires, strategic repertoires are also path-dependent. The 'players' have a limited number of pieces in their repertoire, and, if these are insufficient, a learning process is necessary before a new repertoire becomes available.[52] In this way, the composition of the old repertoire influences the composition of the new one.

Some household strategies are not included in a repertoire because they are culturally unacceptable and contravene norms of decency and justice. A simple example will suffice to illustrate this. When beef and pork became far too expensive for many Berlin working-class families, in 1848 the city authorities attempted to persuade them to eat horsemeat instead. This led to food riots. Although a 'rational' analysis would show that horsemeat is every bit as healthy and nourishing as beef or pork, Berlin's working-class families regarded eating horsemeat as degrading.[53]

Fourth, weighing up the pros and cons of certain household strategies to which family members had access is also important. The 'newer' and less familiar the household strategy, the greater the reluctance to employ it. This reluctance can be overcome if people become aware that others have used the method successfully. Related to this is the perception of risks. Risks associated with strategies are social constructs, not 'objective facts'; and the perception of those risks is extremely susceptible to social pressures and rhetorics.[54] People rate a risk as being lesser when an influential person from their immediate environment does the same, since trust is crucial for everyone who has to operate in situations about which they have insufficient information.[55]

The study of household strategies enables us to '[keep] in focus at all times the lives of both men and women, young and old, and the variety of paid and unpaid work necessary to maintain the unit'.[56] I do not wish to suggest, though, that the household-perspective might be a panacea for all the analytical problems of global labour history. There is no such perspective. Analytical progress is more likely to be achieved by a *combination* of different perspectives, those of households, of other social networks, of labour relations, but also of the public authorities and employers. The 'history from below' must be completed with a 'history from above', since, as Perry Anderson once remarked, without the latter the former becomes 'one-sided (if the better side)'.[57] Moreover, each of the multiple perspectives requires an understanding of a wide variety of cultural, social, economic, and political aspects.

## Notes

1 Crawford, 'Slave family', 334.
2 Gutman (*Black Family*, 129), in some cases, even speaks of 'a cycle of family destruction, construction, and dispersal'.
3 It is difficult to provide a generally valid definition of households. Attempts to find 'a precise, reduced definition' have been unsuccessful, as households are 'inherently complex, multifunctional institutions imbued with a diverse array of cultural principles and meanings'. See Yaganisako, 'Family and household', 200.

4   McGuire, Smith & Martin, 'Patterns of household structures', 76.
5   Bender, 'Refinement of the concept of household', 498.
6   In the absence of co-residence, it is possible to form what I will call secondary households. Examples of secondary households include the Canadian bushworker camps in Radforth's *Bushworkers and Bosses*, ch. 5, and the travelling groups of German brickmakers in Lourens and Lucassen, *Arbeitswanderung und berufliche Spezialisierung*, 73–86.
7   Yaganisako, 'Explicating residence', 330.
8   Yaganisako, 'Family and household', 167–75; Maume & Dunaway, 'Determinants'; Mitterauer, 'Faktoren des Wandels'.
9   Bruce, 'Homes divided'; Wolf, 'Daughters'; Diane Wong ('Limits of using the household', 57) distinguishes two levels of inner-household struggle, regarding: (i) who is to control child labour, and (ii) who is allowed to reproduce, that is 'to establish a family and a household'.
10  Laslett, 'Family as a knot', 370–1.
11  Rabeherifara, 'Réseaux sociaux et familiaux'. For Ghanaian examples of activities that cut across several households, see Woodford-Berger, 'Women in houses'; Sanjek, 'Organization of households'; Vellenga, 'Women, households, and food commodity chains'.
12  An example of a one-off strategy is the desertion of coerced labourers, about which Robin Cohen and others have written. Cohen, 'Resistance and hidden forms of consciousness'. See also Chapter 15 in this volume. Wage labour, on the other hand, is often a repetitive strategy.
13  Diane Wolf has criticized the concept of household strategies because of its alleged tautological character: 'A strategy is everything a household does, and everything a household does is a strategy.' Wolf, *Factory Daughters*, 20.
14  Some historians tend to interpret every form of workers' collective action as a protest, even when the workers involved did not. This seems to me 'one of the subtler forms of condescension in historical writing' about which John Stevenson has written. See his *Popular Disturbances*, 4.
15  Men often contribute too, of course. The subsistence labour of children has less often been studied. See, however, Davin, 'Working or helping?'; Papathanassiou, *Zwischen Arbeit, Spiel und Schule*, Chapters 5, 7, and 8.
16  This distribution is based, in part, on Claude Meillassoux's three categories of reproduction costs: 'The value of labour-power is derived from three factors: supporting workers during periods of employment (*retaining* the existing workforce), *maintaining* workers during periods of idleness (such as unemployment or illness), replacing workers by providing for their progeny (known as *reproduction*).' Meillassoux, *Femmes, Greniers & Capitaux*, 152.
17  Kathie Friedman listed the first five of these sources of income in 'Households as income-pooling units', 46.
18  Bradbury, 'Pigs, cows, and boarders'; Cabedoce, 'Jardins ouvriers et banlieue'.
19  See Barrett, *Work and Community*, 104.
20  Benson, *Penny Capitalists*; Jaumain, 'Contribution à l'histoire comparée'; Uselding, 'Peddling in the Antebellum Economy'.
21  Faure, 'Classe malpropre'; Birkbeck, 'Self-employed proletarians'; Furedy, 'Survival strategies'; Sicular, 'Pockets of peasants'; Tevera, 'Dump scavenging'.
22  Bradbury, 'Pigs, cows, and boarders'; Modell & Hareven, 'Urbanization'; Brüggemeier & Niethammer, 'Schlafgänger'; Ehmer, 'Wohnen ohne eigene Wohnung'; Hoover, 'Supplemental family income sources'.
23  See Mars, 'Dock pilferage' and Ditton, *Part-Time Crime*. Historical case studies include Grüttner, 'Working-class crime'; d'Sena, 'Perquisites'; Randall, 'Peculiar perquisites'; Green, 'Spelling'. William Freund reveals the possibility of a smooth transition to theft as a collective act in 'Theft and social protest'.
24  Perrot, *Ouvriers en grève*, I, 210–12; Tebbutt, *Making Ends Meet*; Johnson, *Saving and Spending*, ch. 6; Führer, 'Kreditinstitut der kleinen Leute'; Scott & Walker, 'Working-class household consumption smoothing'.
25  Smith & Wallerstein, 'Households', 11–12.
26  See, for example, Benson, 'Living on the margin', especially 233–4.
27  After studying these financial aspects in more detail, one might concur with Richard Wilk, who distinguishes three components of the household budget: (i) an 'obligated fund' for a specific purpose that is not open to negotiation; (ii) a 'personal fund' under the control of a single

person and not designed for a particular purpose; and (iii) an unobligated 'general fund' that is available for any number of uses in the future. Many or all members of the household can have a claim on general funds. Wilk, 'Inside the economic institution', 375–8. See also Acheson, 'Household organization'. One should be wary, though, of being too quick to generalize. For example, it is by no means the case that every household has an undivided obligated fund. We also know of cases of households in which the obligated fund comprises two elements: one managed by the woman and the other by the man. See, for example, Okeke, 'Female wage earners'; Elwert, 'Conflicts inside and outside'.

28  For interpretations of certain migration patterns from the perspective of the household, see, for example, Itzigsohn, 'Migrant remittances'; Howell, 'Household coping strategies'; De Haan, 'Migration as family strategy; Schüren, 'Reconceptualizing the post-peasantry'; Cohen, 'Migration'.
29  Schulz, '"Der konnte freilich ganz anders sparen als ich"'; De Belder, 'Het arbeiderssparen 1850–1890'; Johnson, *Saving and Spending*, ch. 4.
30  Barrett, *Work and Community in the Jungle*, 104–7.
31  Still useful in this context is Bosanquet, 'Burden of small debts', an article marred unfortunately by an anti-Semitic passage. Isabelle Devos describes how, in Belgium around 1900, parents invested less in their young daughters because they earned the least. This, combined with their heavy workload, led to girls dying young more often than boys. Devos, 'Te jong om te sterven'.
32  Hareven, 'Complex relationship'.
33  Rosenbaum, *Proletarische Familien*, 153.
34  Peterson, 'Interhousehold exchange', 136.
35  Wellman, Carrington & Hall, 'Networks', 163.
36  Compare personal communities in London between 1870 and 1914 in Ross, 'Survival networks' to those in Lebanon in the 1970s in Joseph, 'Working-class women's networks'. See also John, '"Kultur der Armut" in Wien'; Moch & Fuchs, 'Getting along'.
37  Mintz & Wolf, 'Analysis of ritual co-parenthood'.
38  Zwahr, *Konstituierung des Proletariats*, 163–89.
39  Bodemann, 'Relations of production', 215.
40  For a comprehensive analysis of industrial paternalism, see Sierra, *El obrero soñado*, 7–164. Important case studies are Joyce, *Work, Society and Politics*, and Steinberg, *Moral Communities*.
41  Robin Theobald and Michael A. Korovkin debate the historical conditions necessary for patronage in Theobald, 'The decline of patron–client relations'; Korovkin, 'Exploitation, cooperation, collusion'; Theobald, 'On the survival of patronage'.
42  Scott, *Glassworkers*, 68, 83–7; Southall, 'Mobility'.
43  The discussion of personal communities provided some examples of this transformation. It may also occur with patronage – patrons and patronesses can become godfathers or godmothers, respectively – or self-organizations. Emily Honig's example of female textile workers in Shanghai during the first half of the twentieth century illustrates this point: 'After working together for several years, six to ten women would formalize their relationship with one another by pledging sisterhood. Once they had formed a sisterhood, the members would call each other by kinship terms based on age: the oldest was "Big Sister", the next oldest "Second Sister", and so forth ... Often the sisterhoods functioned as an economic mutual aid society.' Honig, 'Burning incense', 700–1. Better known than this case of surrogate kinship among women are the countless fraternal organizations that have sprung up in workers' movements over time. For examples, see Clawson, *Constructing Brotherhood*.
44  See Zwahr, *Konstituierung des Proletariats*. Furthermore, Bert Altena convincingly argues that 'family acquaintance played an important part' in the formation of early working-class organizations. See Altena, 'The Dutch Social Democratic Workers' Party', 401.
45  Friedman, 'Why workers strike'.
46  I discuss this in more detail in 'Old labour movements'.
47  Roberts, *Logic of Historical Explanation*, 162. See also Jasper, 'Emotions of protest'.
48  Hareven, *Family Time and Industrial Time*, 114.
49  Merleau-Ponty, *Phenomenology of Perception*, 446.
50  Brock, *Der schwierige Weg in die Moderne*, 66, 77 (my emphasis).
51  Bourdieu, *Algeria 1960*, 51.

52 There is a clear parallel here with Charles Tilly's concept of 'repertoire of contention', which as such relates to the multitude of collective action methods. See, for example, Tilly, 'Getting it together'; Tilly & Tilly, *Class Conflict and Collective Action*, Introduction. An assessment and a historical criticism of Tilly's concept of repertoire can be found in Traugott, 'Barricades as repertoire'.
53 Gailus, *Straße und Brot*, 13–20.
54 Tierney, 'Toward a critical sociology of risk', especially 219–22 and 226. Extensive support for this argument can be found in Douglas & Wildawsky, *Risk and Culture*.
55 Preisendörfer, 'Vertrauen als soziologische Kategorie'. See also Gambetta, *Trust*.
56 Quataert, 'Combining agrarian and industrial livelihood', 158.
57 Anderson, *Lineages*, 11.

# 8
# Labour markets

## Introduction

About eighteen centuries ago, the New Testament was written. Its Gospel of Matthew (20: 1–2) narrates the parable of 'a householder who went out early in the morning to hire labourers for his vineyard' and who, 'after agreeing with the labourers for a denarius a day … sent them into his vineyard'. Much earlier, in ancient Athens, there was a space known as the *kolonos misthios*, probably at the western end of the agora, where those who wanted to hire themselves out as land labourers offered their services daily.[1] Indeed, in the ancient city of Rome, a large part of the male population – perhaps even the majority – had to rely on casual wage labour as dockers, porters, storemen, and construction workers.[2] As Peter Temin explains:

> Since the demand for labour fluctuated, workers must have been hired for varying lengths of time, from a day to weeks or even months, while some people were probably hired for the completion of a particular task … Casual labour is inherently unstable and this led to many in Rome living correspondingly unstable lives. Competition for jobs also likely kept wages low, resulting in widespread structural poverty in the city.[3]

Moreover, Temin continues, wage dispersion in the early Roman Empire was 'indistinguishable from that in preindustrial Europe', and Roman labour contracts were 'distinctly modern'.[4] Everything indicates that spot markets for casual labour have existed for thousands of years and are, therefore, much older than capitalism. Jan Lucassen assumes that markets for wage labour emerged in the Middle East 'between 2000 and 1000 BCE, when officials organizing work for temples turned into subcontractors'.⁵ Meanwhile, labour markets have, as we know, become much more general, more extensive, and often more abstract. How did this transition come about? How did labour markets evolve from local to global? Allow me to offer a few preliminary thoughts on these questions.

My approach differs both from mainstream labour economics and mainstream labour sociology. Most labour economists nowadays deliberately ignore history. One major textbook declares, for example:

> The field of labor economics has long been recognized as an important area of study. But the content or subject matter of the field has changed dramatically in the past few decades. If you were to go to the library and examine a labor text published 30 or 35 years ago, you would find its orientation highly descriptive and historical ... To be sure, labor markets and unemployment were accorded some attention, but the analysis was typically minimal and superficial. This state of affairs has changed significantly in recent decades. Economists have achieved important analytic breakthroughs in studying labor markets and labor problems. As a result, economic analysis has crowded out historical, institutional, legal, and anecdotal material. Labor economics increasingly has become applied micro and macro theory.⁶

The implication is, of course, that applied economic micro and macro theory must necessarily be ahistorical. Labour sociologists are often less dogmatic than most labour economists. In a recent important contribution to the field, Bengt Furåker rightly argues that 'labor markets are not only associated with capitalism, although we have a tendency to think of them in that way'; they also existed in 'pre-capitalist and state socialist nations'.⁷ But Furåker nevertheless limits labour markets to markets for free wage labour:

> [T]he labor market is a system for hiring labor power. I prefer the terms 'hiring' and 'hiring out' instead of 'buying' and 'selling', simply because I find the former more adequate to describe the characteristics of modern labor markets. A table or a chair can be bought and sold once and for all, which means that these objects cease to belong to their previous owner. Labor power is, however, different in this respect; it is not turned over to the employer but only for a limited period of time ... If, in the labor market, labor power is not the property of its bearer, slavery is the proper notion.⁸

*Contra* the majority of labour economists and sociologists, I will argue that we can best understand the development of labour markets if we use a historical approach and do not limit ourselves to 'free' wage labour but also include physically coerced labour (chattel slavery, etc.). First, I will attempt to clarify some of the relevant concepts, and then I will outline a few major trends from antiquity until the present.

## Concepts

Obviously, a labour market is a type of market. And a market is an actual (physical, concrete) or nominal (virtual) place where commodities are exchanged – that is, sold or hired-out for money or a money equivalent. Let us first take a closer look at the most important components of this general definition.

To begin with, what are commodities, and what is exchange? *Commodities* are, as Adam Smith already knew, 'objects' that combine 'value in use' (their utility) with 'value in exchange' (their price).[9] An object that has no utility for anyone cannot be a commodity, and nor can an object that has no price. Karl Marx reintroduced this definition in the first chapter of *Capital*, giving it his own particular theoretical twist.

Commodities may be *real* or *fictitious*. In other words, not only objects intentionally produced for sale (cars, houses, or shoes, for instance) can be exchanged on markets; objects that are 'just there' as gifts of nature can also become commodities (for example, the Amazonian rainforest, sandy beaches, or ivory).

*Exchange* – the act of reciprocal giving and receiving – in markets is always the exchange of money (or a good in-kind as a general equivalent) in return for property rights over an object or service. Property rights are bundles of enforceable claims. Property rights therefore presuppose the existence of a public authority with coercive power. Modern legal theory breaks property rights into the following rights and duties:

> (i) the right to possess, (ii) the right to use, (iii) the right to manage, (iv) the right to the income of the object, (v) the right to the capital, (vi) the right to security, (vii) the right of transmissibility, (viii) the right of absence of term, (ix) the duty to prevent harmful use, (x) liability to execution, and (xi) the incident of residuarity.[10]

For full ownership of an object, a proprietor must have most (but not necessarily all) of these elements regarding that object. There is no consensus on the question of which, if any, of these rights and duties are essential for property to exist.

Exchange can be temporary or permanent. Hiring is a temporary exchange, while a sale is a permanent exchange – a transaction in which the original owner/proprietor of the commodity is replaced by another owner/proprietor in exchange for money. And the property rights connected with the commodity are automatically transferred from one person/institution/organization to another. Hiring is a transaction in which the original owner/proprietor remains the owner/proprietor but another party can – in exchange for money – use the commodity for a certain period of time. An exchange may take place under competitive or non-competitive circumstances. There is no competition if there is only one supplier and one buyer/renter, or if the conditions of trade between suppliers and buyers/renters (in particular, prices and other aspects of commercial transactions) are heavily regulated, frequently by a public authority. There is competition if at least two suppliers or buyers/renters are haggling or bidding against each other.[11]

If we turn to labour markets now, two additional questions arise: what is exchanged and who is exchanging? The term 'labour market' is a misnomer. *No labour is ever exchanged in labour markets*. What is sold or hired-out is the human capacity to labour (labour-power), not the labour itself. The old Aristotelian distinction between *dunamis* (potentiality) and *energeia* (actuality) is of crucial importance here. 'The purchaser of labour-power consumes it by setting the seller of it to work. By working, the latter becomes in actuality what previously he only was potentially, namely labour-power in action, a worker'.[12]

Who is exchanging the labour-power? When we speak of labour markets, we usually think of contemporary exchanges in which free workers, mostly driven by economic necessity, hire themselves out to employers in exchange for a monetary wage. The aforementioned examples from antiquity all involve such 'voluntary' transactions. The implicit assumption of the present-day notion of labour markets is that the workers have to offer their labour-power *themselves*. Only if the carrier of the labour-power is also the possessor of the labour-power is 'the polarization of the commodity-market' possible, according to Marx.[13] This is a highly questionable view. Why can't labour-power be sold by somebody *other* than the carrier? Is a slave market not a market where labour-power is sold?

**Table 8.1** Four types of labour-power exchange (examples).

|  | Lease | Sale |
|---|---|---|
| Carrier of labour power is possessor of labour power | 'Free' wage labour<br>Sharecropping | Self-sale[i]<br>Sale of debt peon |
| Carrier of labour power is not possessor of labour power | Slave for hire<br>Child labourer | Chattel slave |

Source: Author.

[i] Self-sale is an ancient phenomenon, even mentioned in the *Code of Hammurabi* (c. 1780 BCE). Hammurabi's case probably does not fit our definition of a market since it seems to have been a transaction between one seller and one buyer. Market-conform self-sales can be found in more recent centuries. See, for example, Patterson, *Slavery and Social Death*, 130; Hellie, *Slavery in Russia*; Testart, *L'esclave, la dette et le pouvoir*; Engerman, 'Slavery, freedom, and Sen', 94–100; and Dorn, 'Selbstverknechtung'.

In labour markets, the distinction between possessor and commodity may become blurred. For example, the possessor can become the commodity to be sold or hired-out. The wage-earner who offers his/her labour capacity for hire for, say, a month, is turning his/her own self into a commodity. But the enslaved person, who is sold or hired-out by his or her proprietor, is also a commodity. Both slave markets and 'free' labour markets meet the definition of a market. In both cases, there is a social structure for exchange of rights, which enables people, firms, and products to be evaluated and priced. In both cases, the actors are independent. This is not to deny, of course, that there are fundamental differences between the two types of markets.

Simply by making the distinction between a 'carrier' and a 'possessor' of labour-power, we can already distinguish four different types of labour-market exchange, namely: markets in which the carrier of labour-power is also its possessor and markets in which it is not; and, in both cases, markets where the carrier's labour-power can be offered by the carrier him- or herself or where it is offered by another person (Table 8.1).

## Early labour markets

Up until the nineteenth century, most of humanity performed subsistence labour. In other words, people worked to provide for their own immediate consumption needs. This was particularly true for the main economic sector, agriculture. As Chris Wickham wrote:

> In human history, most cultivators have been peasants, who work the land autonomously, in family groups … Peasant families control a given set of lands at any one time, cultivate it, rely on its produce to survive, and also give a part of the produce to a landlord if they have one, and/or to the state if it exists.[14]

For instance, discussing South China, Evelyn Sakakida Rawski observed:

> For at least the last millennium, Chinese agriculture has been dominated by a large number of free, small-scale farmers, working under a system of private landownership. A Chinese peasant, if he did not own his land, aspired to eventually do so. Both tenants and landowning farmers were free to decide what to grow on their plots and to dispose of their own produce.[15]

Consequently, for a very long time, labour-power commodification accounted for only a small section of the world's labour force. Take wage labour, for instance. There were, in fact, at least four basic forms of early wage labour: casual labour, particularly in agriculture (such as harvesting) but also in building, lumbering, and so on; artisanal labour – skilled work carried out from time to time but not continuously (such as metalwork or carpentry); military service, with mercenaries constituting the first large group of wage-earners; and artisans' apprenticeships – wage labourers who had to learn specific skills. All these have one thing in common: 'free' wage labour was used, in particular, when the activities were of a temporary nature. This could mean temporary either in the sense of being seasonal or work carried out at a certain stage of the worker's life (in the case of apprentices).[16] Wage labour was frequently a side-activity for peasants and artisans who also had other sources of 'income' such as subsistence labour or petty commodity production.

Conversely, slave labour was appropriate for activities carried out continuously. Slavery of shepherds was, for instance, the first form of economically significant slavery in ancient Greece:

> In contrast to arable farming and horticulture, [livestock farming] was an area of economic activity in which the amount of labor required remained relatively constant. This created the demand, and favoured the deployment of a constant number of workers.

'Serfs', but also slaves certainly fitted better into this regime than impoverished free migrants, who in all probability would only consent to contract out their services for a limited period.[17]

Enslaved and wage labourers often – but not always – did the same type of work. In Babylonia and Assyria, 'free workers and slaves worked shoulder to shoulder in royal factories, in temple establishments, and in private industries'.[18] In ancient Rome:

> ... slaves were interchangeable with free wage laborers in many situations ... Roman slaves appear to be like long-term employees. The analysis of slave motivation and the wide distribution of slave occupations suggest that slaves were part of an integrated labor force in the early Roman Empire.[19]

Once Brazil had abolished the slave trade in 1850, the coffee planters in the São Paulo region recruited Italian immigrants who worked in the fields side-by-side with Afro-Brazilian slaves (Figure 8.1).[20] In North America, there were also frequently mixed labour forces.[21] At the waterfront of mid-eighteenth-century New York, '[s]laves toiled alongside

**Figure 8.1** Italian immigrants posing in the central courtyard of the Hospedaria dos Immigrantes, São Paulo, c. 1890. Photographer: Guilherme Gaensly (1843–1928). https://bit.ly/3yn4qrE.

unskilled white workers as teamsters, wagoners, dockers, stockmen, ropewalkers, and cartmen'.[22] Moreover, a study of two nineteenth-century ironworks in New Jersey and Virginia concluded:

> Both slavery and free labor met the demands of entrepreneurs for flexibility. In a rural industrial setting, the methods by which proprietors attempted to create a disciplined labor force, whether slave or free, had much in common, particularly how they dealt with tradesmen. Both labor systems required ironmasters to strike a careful balance between encouragement and coercion, although slavery allowed for a wider range of options, especially punitive measures.[23]

Even so, the labour markets for slaves and wage labourers were, to the best of my knowledge, always physically separate. Apparently, the difference between the two forms of exchange was too great to allow for their integration.

Slave markets can take different shapes. For the Roman Empire, William Harris distinguishes four settings in which slave sales took place: small-scale 'everyday' transactions; opportunistic markets of, for example, slave traders following the Roman army to buy captured enemy soldiers; periodic markets in small locations; and large-scale trade in bigger cities, with Rome as the main trade centre.[24] Slave markets could also become extensive. The Greek geographer Strabo, who lived in the first century AD, reported on the tiny island of Delos (3.43 km$^2$), stating that it 'could both admit and send away ten thousand slaves on the same day; whence arose the proverb, "Merchant, sail in, unload your ship, everything has been sold"'.[25] Little is known about the slave trade between Japan, China, and Korea in the sixteenth and seventeenth centuries.

In pre-capitalist times, wage labourers were never, as far as I have been able to determine, traded in large markets. But there was at least one exception: mercenaries. In China, military labour markets predate the emergence of the first imperial dynasty, the Qin, in 221 BCE.[26] As far as Western Europe is concerned, Erica Schoenberger ascertained:

> Beginning in the tenth and developing through the twelfth centuries, then, the market for mercenaries was perhaps one of the better-developed branches of international trade. It was not a huge market; a mercenary army was rather more likely to run into the four digits than five. But they could be kept in the field for a long time and then dismissed ... when they were no longer needed.[27]

Labour markets could cover long distances. The Roman Empire sent British military units all the way to the Dacia region (contemporary Romania) during the first and second centuries CE.[28] The African slaves from the Swahili coast (the *Zanj*) who were forced to work in the salt marshes in south Iraq are well-known.[29] Non-military wage labourers were hired long-distance mainly if they had special skills. We know, for example, that, in fourteenth- and fifteenth-century Anatolia, tile makers from Transoxiania (modern-day Uzbekistan, Tajikistan, and parts of Kyrgyzstan and Kazakhstan) were recruited thanks to their mastery of the unique blackline technique.[30] And, in the sixteenth century, German silver miners worked not only in the south of France, Southeast Europe, and Spain but also in Saint-Domingue (Haiti) and Venezuela.[31] It seems logical that the size of such labour markets remained limited.

On a global scale, labour markets for slaves remained of minor importance until the eighteenth century. In China, for instance, slavery was rare: 'there is little evidence that slaves formed a large part of the whole population at any time'.[32] In other parts of Asia, slavery remained a marginal phenomenon, too: 'Although slavery existed in Mughal India [1526–1858], it was almost universally domestic slavery'.[33] 'Agrarian slavery and serfdom were rare in India'.[34] In Tokugawa Japan (1600–1867), slaves were 'primarily criminals and prisoners'.[35] In the Ottoman Empire, '[m]arkets for slaves existed until the second half of the nineteenth century but most of the limited numbers of slaves were employed as domestic labour. Slave labour was virtually non-existent in agriculture, trade and manufacturing'.[36]

For a long time, free wage labour remained rare, too. In China, '[n]either the Qing nor the Ming [penal] codes showed much concern with hired labour, although its existence is attested to'.[37] In nineteenth-century Southeast Asia, '[f]ree (wage) labour had probably always been available in small (sometimes no doubt very small) numbers, but during the early modern period various forms of dependent or bonded labour were predominant'.[38] Moreover, 'wage labour, whether semi-permanent or on a permanent basis, played an insignificant role in the economy. It occurred on an irregular basis in some larger centres in Java where, for instance, people did not have any association with land and sold their labour-power'.[39] In India, only a 'few examples of large-scale migration or circulation before the eighteenth century involved wage work in permanent sites that employed hundreds of people together, such as the mills, plantations, canals and railways of the nineteenth century'.[40] In the Ottoman Empire, 'farms using year-round wage labour or servile labour were exceptional'.[41] In Germany, around 1800, free wage labour was still a 'minority phenomenon'.[42]

There were, however, exceptions confirming this rule. In North Africa, in the fourth and fifth centuries, there were about 300,000–350,000 landless labourers:

> ... who moved on a seasonal basis from the North African towns and neighboring districts to areas where there was a high demand for [agricultural] labor ... Writing in the mid-fourth century, Optatus of Milevis claimed that North African urban areas and periodic fairs were the main pools from which laborers could be recruited.[43]

Arguably, perhaps, the social weight of wage-earners was greater in the Low Countries, where, during the fifteenth and sixteenth centuries:

> ... arrangements in the country between employers and laborers were market-driven and based on a cash wage, paid daily, weekly, or monthly. Labor contracts in these areas were mostly formal and short-term – verbal agreements for the day and written ones for the year.[44]

According to economic historian Jan de Vries, 'the [Dutch] labour market already in the early sixteenth century was large and largely free of feudal constraints ... Wage labour played a larger role here than in many other European countries three hundred years later'.[45] In the cities of Tokugawa Japan, free wage labour seems to have grown in importance, too.[46]

In cases in which households could not work autonomously but were physically forced to labour, coercion could take many different forms. The number of variations of coerced labour is dizzying. One of these many variations was *unfree* wage labour, that is, a labour relation in which the workers received wages but were tied to their employers through multiple obligations. Large numbers of unfree wage labourers could be found in South Asia and pre-industrial Europe. In Mughal India, landless agricultural workers constituted between one-sixth and one-fifth of the rural population, belonging to 'the menial castes, compelled to serve the interests alike of peasants and of superior cultivators, and forming a vast rural semi-proletariat, maintained entirely through non-economic compulsions'.[47]

For Europe, Charles Tilly has estimated that, in 1500, about 30 per cent of the entire labour force consisted of proletarians, and, in 1900, almost 44 per cent.[48] In so far as they were not casual labourers (either fully proletarianized or peasant workers whose households combined several sources of income), the majority were probably bonded wage labourers who were not allowed to hire-out their labour-power to an employer of their choice on their own initiative.

Moreover, research in recent years has revealed that many so-called free workers were really *bonded* labourers, far into the nineteenth century. Master and Servant laws, apprenticeship arrangements, and so on, ensured that workers were tied to their employers and had significantly fewer legal rights than the literature previously suggested. In this context, there has, indeed, been mention of 'industrial serfdom'.[49] The legal historian Thorsten Keiser has even argued that, in nineteenth-century Germany, 'multiple bonds existed for factory workers and craftsmen as well. For adult industrial workers, these bonds were completely removed only around 1900, and for domestic servants [*Gesinde*] and agricultural labourers, not until 1918'.[50]

## The rise of transcontinental labour markets

From the fifteenth century onward, labour relations began to change fundamentally on a global scale. This change was gradual and uneven. The rise of colonialism was crucial. Colonialism, says Jürgen Osterhammel, is 'a relationship of domination between an indigenous (or forcibly imported) majority and a minority of foreign invaders'.[51] Such an asymmetric relationship has two salient features. Colonial rulers make most decisions of consequence for the lives of the colonized people 'in pursuit of interests that are often defined in a distant metropolis'. And, in making and implementing these decisions, the rulers assume that they are superior to the colonial subjects and that they therefore have a 'mandate to rule'. Colonialism is far older than capitalism and may arise from many different motives: in addition to purely economic ones, the drivers may be religious, political, demographic, or military. Early examples include the American Pre-Columbian empires or Han China (202 BCE–220 CE), which subdued parts of Korea, Vietnam, and Central Asia. The powers carrying out colonial projects have therefore certainly not been exclusively European or North American. The clearest recent example that illustrates this is Japan, which controlled a vast colonial territory between 1895 and 1945.

During the first four centuries, expansion to other continents was, however, mostly European in nature and impelled by two types of social forces: on the one hand, absolutist regimes in Spain, Portugal, and (to a somewhat lesser extent) France; and, on the other hand, merchant capitalists from the Netherlands and England. The first form of expansion was driven by the quest of monarchs and their aristocratic entourage to increase their wealth, and merchants were secondary and subordinate. The second type of expansion was the exact opposite: merchants took the initiative and the state facilitated the process. This second form became dominant after about 1800.

With the rise of colonialism, we see – despite the dominance of non-commodified labour – the rapid growth of three types of transcontinental labour markets: indentured service, chattel slavery, and wage labour. The earliest important type was indentured labour. In this form of contract labour, an intermediary (perhaps paid by the employer) covers the cost of a worker's journey to a distant country. In return, the worker agrees to remain in the service of an employer at his/her assigned destination for a certain number of years (perhaps three, five, or ten). Throughout this period, the worker is entirely subject to the authority of that employer and is not allowed to switch jobs. Workers violating the rules are treated as criminals and face possible incarceration. Although indentured labourers often accepted contracts 'voluntarily' (albeit compelled by material need), in many cases, their fate was regarded as simply a new state of slavery.[52] In particular, the English colonies in North America initially employed indentured servants. Precise numbers are not available, but '[a]n estimated 70 per cent of white migrants to England's American colonies in the seventeenth century were bound in indentured servitude as servants in agriculture or other employments, particularly in the staple-exporting colonies'.[53]

Over the course of the seventeenth and eighteenth centuries, colonists resorted less and less to indentured servants, who were increasingly replaced by African chattel slaves. There has been debate on the reasons for this. Here, it should be sufficient to say that slavery took the place of white servitude in two steps. First, slaves replaced indentured servants in 'the unskilled field labour of staple-crop cultivation';[54] and, when slaves had been trained to perform skilled jobs, 'this ultimately led planters to cease importing servants altogether'. The African continent became the main supplier of enslaved labourers not only in the Americas but also in the Middle East and South Asia. Between 1400 and 1900, some 10.3 million Africans were deported to the Americas. Moreover, 3.1 million Africans became victims of the trans-Saharan trade, while 1.3 million were shipped across the Red Sea, and just under a million across the Indian Ocean.[55]

The transatlantic slave trade peaked somewhere between 1750 and 1825. Over the following decades, the number of victims declined, thanks to the British abolitionist campaign that increasingly resonated with other European potentates. In all likelihood, the transcontinental labour

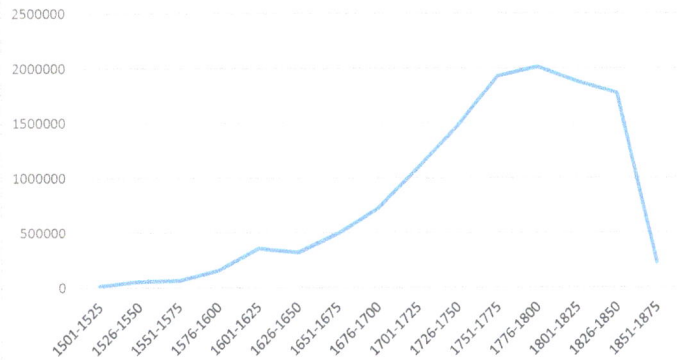

**Figure 8.2** Estimated number of enslaved people who made the Atlantic crossing between 1501 and 1875. Source: http://www.slavevoyages.org/assessment/estimates.

market for chattel slaves was the most deadly labour market in history. The numbers of slaves embarking on ships differed vastly from the numbers disembarking, hinting at the scale on which enslaved Africans perished *during* the voyage to the Americas – be it from disease, abuse, murder, or suicide. Canadian historian David Eltis and his team gathered data on over 35,000 slave voyages, arriving at the conclusion that, in the period 1501–1866 one-seventh (14.5 per cent) of the slaves who embarked 'disappeared' (Figure 8.2).

When the slave trade began to decline numerically in the nineteenth century, employers in subtropical and tropical countries resorted to indenture once again. The immediate reason was the shortage of labour on sugar plantations following the abolition of slavery in the British Empire in 1834. Ex-slaves were reluctant to voluntarily engage in plantation labour, and this resulted in the search for other sources of labour. Many planters in the West Indies 'initially turned their attention to Europe and Africa. Between 1834 and 1837, some 3000 English, 1000 Scottish and German, and 100 Irish labourers were introduced into Jamaica, with smaller numbers going to St. Lucia, on three- to five-year contracts'.[56] When these and other experiments failed, attention shifted towards Asia.

South Asians and the Chinese, in particular, as well as the Javanese, became important in this practice. It has been estimated that, between 1801 and 1925, 'about three million contract labourers were shipped out of China'.[57] A total of around 1.5 million indentured Indians emigrated to overseas destinations between 1834 and 1916.[58] *Within* countries, indenture became more common as well. When, for example, in around 1840, tea plantations were established in Assam, hundreds of thousands of indentured labourers were recruited in other parts of British India.[59] Indentured migrations gradually diminished in the early decades of the twentieth century. By then, however, other migration flows were in progress. In the century from 1840 to 1940, three new migration systems emerged – from North Asia, from Southeast Asia, and across the Atlantic Ocean – and, in each of them, 50 to 60 million people were relocated.[60] Migrants in these systems usually left not because of physical coercion but out of economic necessity, although some were kidnapped (shanghaied) and shipped out against their will.

The advance of global markets for free wage labour was, from a historical point of view, the result of a very long struggle between different systems of labour mobilization and various types of labour markets. Only the (partial) demise of the trade in slaves and indentured labourers made room for free labour markets. Nevertheless, we should not forget that some long-distance labour markets existed before the breakthrough of global markets. As mentioned earlier, there were the mercenaries, the Timurid tile makers in Anatolia, and the German silver miners in Saint-Domingue and Venezuela.

Zooming-in on the markets for free wage labour, we see two important trends. First, labour markets for non-casual workers gained ground, particularly in the agricultural sector. In China, during the early- and mid-Qing Dynasty, the majority of labourers were still hired on a short-term basis, although longer contracts also existed. It was often the case that two labourers were hired for the year, and three to five for the busy sowing and harvesting seasons. There had long been a labour market in the Chinese countryside and there are records of 'hiring markets' (*gongfushi* or *renshi*) existing in Kaiyuan in Fengtian, Linxian in Henan, Yanggao *xian* in Shanxi, Xinhui in Guangdong, and Shandong.[61]

In British India:

> … [p]ermanent sites of hiring began to emerge from the eighteenth century, to receive migrant workers. Indigo factories of Bengal in the 1830s and 1840s, coal mines of Chota Nagpur and tea plantations of Assam somewhat later recruited workers who came from villages hundreds of miles away. From the end of the century, industrial cities recruited workers from longer distances and different regions.[62]

In Southeast Asia:

> ... locally from the late eighteenth century, and across the region during much of the nineteenth, corvée obligations and fully fledged slavery were being increasingly abolished, while free wage labour took their place. This development was linked to three factors – population growth (which led to falling man–land ratios and therefore to cheaper labour), the continuing growth of international trade and measures taken by the colonial rulers.[63]

In the late-eighteenth century, William Marshall wrote about the annual hiring fair for farm labourers in Polesworth in the English West Midlands:

> The number of servants collected together, in the 'statute yard', has been estimated at two to three thousand. A number, however, which is the less extraordinary, as Polesworth being the only place, in this district, and this the only day, farm servants, for several miles round, consider themselves as liberated from servitude, on this day ...[64]

A hundred years later, Peter Ditchfield pointed out that, in Yorkshire and Derbyshire, 'statute fairs' used to be very common. (For an early-twentieth-century example of a hiring fair, see Figure 8.3):

> The servants used to stand in rows, the males together and the females together, and masters and mistresses walked down the lines and selected those whom they considered suitable. The custom seemed to savour of slave-dealing, and the mingling of so many youths and maidens in a strange town without guardianship was not conducive to good morals.[65]

The tendential decasualization of wage labour meant that long-term employment was no longer the 'privilege' of enslaved workers but increasingly extended to wage-earners. Why was this so? From an economic point of view, two factors deserve attention. The first (microeconomic) factor was already identified several decades ago by John Hicks: the more that free wage labour becomes a general phenomenon, unfree labour becomes more expensive because 'they are competing sources: when both are used the availability of one affects the value (wage or capital value) of the other'.[66] After all, the maintenance cost of a slave increases as the supply of slaves declines, while, conversely, an increase in the number of wage labourers makes this form of labour cheaper. The second factor is

**Figure 8.3** Haddington Hiring Fair, early-1900s. At a time when holidays were few and far between, the Hiring Fair offered a day out and a social occasion that people looked forward to. Employers would move among the workers discussing terms and experience. In this photograph, workers can be distinguished from employers by their headwear; the farm workers are wearing flat caps or bonnets while the hiring farmers sport bowlers and top hats. Published courtesy of the John Gray Centre Library, Museum & Archive.

macroeconomic: slaves have (almost) no purchasing power but wage-earners do. Twentieth-century capitalism based on mass consumption was only possible thanks to the growing buying power of the working classes in the metropoles. In fact, wage labour in the metropoles was, from this point of view, a *conditio sine qua non* for advanced capitalist prosperity.

A second trend was also of crucial importance: the integration of local labour markets. Apart from markets for mercenaries, free labour markets were mostly local. To borrow a metaphor from the economist Arthur MacEwan, they were 'like clearings in a forest, surrounded by a different and often hostile environment of other forms of socio-economic organization'.[67] As the clearings expanded and international trade increased, a network of long-distance connections between the separate clearings began to grow. Initially, this network concerned transport and the transfer of artisanal expertise but, gradually, it entered agriculture and manufacturing.

From the seventeenth century onward, the relative weight of transcontinental free labour markets grew. This was most clearly evident in the transport sector. One example is the Dutch East India Company, which, during its years of operation (1602–1795), 'may have sent over 900,000 or nearly a million individuals to the East'.[68] In addition, the organization recruited numerous free wage labourers (and slaves) as sailors in Asia, in particular for intra-Asian trade. More generally, according to historian Matthias van Rossum, there was a clear long-term trend in Asiatic maritime labour markets:

> The labour markets in Europe and Asia became increasingly entangled from 1500 onwards. This happened in partly overlapping stages: from almost entirely separated labour markets in maritime Europe and maritime Asia (before 1500); increasing connections between Asian and European maritime labour markets through intensified intra-Asiatic shipping (1500–1750); increasing integration in intercontinental shipping between Asia and Europe, including the recruitment of Asian sailors (1700–1800); increased and accelerated internationalization of recruitment of maritime labour in shipping in Asia (from the late eighteenth century onwards) and in intercontinental shipping (from the 1830s onwards); and finally, near-complete integration of European and Asian maritime labour markets, and the movement and settlement of Asian and European sailors in both Asia and Europe (1870 onwards).[69]

During the eighteenth and nineteenth centuries, members of other occupational groups began to cross the oceans in search of work. Sometimes, they kept in touch with their former colleagues in the sending country for a long time. J. T. Cumbler studied the mid-nineteenth-century migration of English and Irish textile workers from Lancashire (England) to Fall River, Massachusetts:

> Lancashire's leading working-class newspaper during the late nineteenth century was the *Cotton Factory Times*. This weekly circulated widely among Lancashire textile workers and was used by workers on both sides of the Atlantic for information concerning the state of the trade, the cost of cotton in New York and New Orleans, wage rates in various sectors of the shire, strikes and union business, as well as political and social news of interest to the working class.[70]

And there have been more examples: the skilled Scottish jute workers who, from the 1850s, relocated to Bengal and helped operate new jute factories there; the Belgian and English window-glass makers who, in the 1870s and 80s, migrated to the US; or the Italian workers (*golondrinas*) who seasonally helped with the harvests in Argentina.

The growth and geographical expansion of labour markets were often accompanied by the increasing influence of intermediaries These might be individuals (variously called crimp, jobber, *kangani*, *sirdar*, or *baogongtou*), trade unions, commercial firms (temping agencies), or public institutions (labour exchanges). Intermediaries tended to appear wherever 'work must be done at many different locations, especially with heavy seasonal demand' or where the potential labour force was very heterogeneous, as was the case in large and international ports.[71] In fact, these intermediaries have a very long history; they seem to have frequently played a role in ancient Rome, particularly in the transport sector.[72] Labour intermediaries reduced the transaction costs involved in labour recruitment. They always did at least one of three things: they recruited potential labourers in places outside the potential employer's information system (if labourers could be found in a huge urban labour pool or in remote places); they preselected potential labourers and thus reduced the employer's risk of hiring a man or woman unfit for the job; and they acted as interpreters in case of communication problems of a linguistic or other nature.

## Segmentation, integration, and expansion

It is well known that labour markets under capitalism are segmented in multiple ways. In 1874, economist John E. Cairnes noted:

> What we find, in effect, is not a whole population competing indiscriminately for all occupations, but a series of industrial layers, superposed on one another, within each of which the various candidates for employment possess a real and effective power of selection, while those occupying the several strata are, for all purposes of effective competition, practically isolated from each other.[73]

However, the history of labour-market segmentation goes back much further. We have seen that the markets for slaves and wage labourers have always been separate. Moreover, other forms of segmentation have a long history, too. Gender divisions are very old, and have always had an impact on all labour relations. A study of *famuli* (unfree wage labourers) on English estates in the thirteenth century reveals, for example:

> ... first, that sex was a major criterion in determining access to most positions; secondly, that there were far fewer opportunities for gainful employment open to women and girls; thirdly, that the *range* of jobs open to women was more restricted than that available to men; fourthly, that most women were recruited to service positions of an unspecified nature (e.g. 'one woman-servant'), whereas adult males were usually employed in a specialist function; and finally, that there was a tendency for some women to be employed in personal services. It is among the permanent *famuli*, the unfree wage-labourers, that we find the first clear signs of occupational specialization and discrimination between the sexes that later came to typify free wage-labour under capitalism.[74]

A third very old partition, mentioned earlier, is that separating casual from permanent labour, although the boundary between the two segments has not necessarily been impermeable. In China during the Qing period, day labourers 'were not fundamentally different from labourers hired by the year; indeed if there was sufficient demand they too could become *changgong*'.[75] Under capitalism, all these segmentations were maintained and sometimes amplified. For example, there are indications that, in Europe, female wage labour under pre-capitalist conditions was relatively extensive, then became much reduced, and increased again during the 'Industrial Revolution' of the eighteenth and nineteenth centuries.[76]

The arrival of the 'modern' times of capitalism, colonialism, and nation-state-building brought about at least one additional dividing line: the separation of workers according to their nationalities. Referring to Europe, Stephan Epstein argued that:

> ... political integration rather than technical change was the principal driver of market integration after the Black Death. Political integration increased domestic stability, which was the precondition for trade; it established a quasi-customs union between formerly 'foreign' markets and reduced the incidence of local tariffs; it enabled weaker rural communities to establish markets and fairs against urban opposition; it stimulated the rationalization of road networks; and it improved market coordination. Each one of these developments was a result of political bargains, and political structures were therefore decisive for the speed and character of integration.[77]

The national integration of labour markets occurred gradually. For some time, internal national markets remained 'simply a loose collection of separate municipal markets'.[78] And the national borders often remained permeable for long periods. Moreover, the growth in economic inequality between different parts of the world during the nineteenth and twentieth centuries led to a prosperity gap between the Global South and North. In general, it can be observed that 'the more advanced a country is economically, the higher-priced will be its indigenous labor force'.[79] This situation, in combination with a growing labour reserve in the South, caused massive migration to the North. In the North, as a result, competition developed between the higher-priced workers of Northern origin and the lower-priced workers from the South.

All other things being equal, employers will gravitate towards the 'cheap' workers since this will deliver higher profits. The higher-priced workers will oppose this. They may block immigration of 'cheap' workers (for example, the White Australia policy or the exclusion of Chinese immigrants in California); they may lock 'cheap' workers into certain low-wage sectors of the economy; or they may equalize wage levels by raising the wages of the lower-paid workers. The first two options are usually accompanied by racist and xenophobic campaigns. Employers, in turn, can of course react to such strategies by moving their enterprises partially or entirely to runaway shops in the South.

Split labour markets received a further boost due to the rise of Northern welfare state arrangements. From the end of the nineteenth century, states in advanced capitalist countries took various steps to improve social security, such as introducing protective labour legislation and obligatory insurance, regulating working hours, and so forth. These measures required costly investments that stimulated 'social protectionism' against foreign workers; newcomers had to be excluded from expensive social arrangements because they had not yet contributed – or not contributed enough – to financing them.

Through capitalist colonialism, this splitting of labour markets began to extend beyond the territories of separate metropolitan nation-states. Matthias van Rossum writes about the maritime labour markets in Asia:

> In the eighteenth century, Asian sailors seem to have had a relatively good bargaining position, apparently better than that of European sailors. From the early nineteenth century onwards, increased European colonial interference in Asian societies – and especially in Asian labour markets – resulted in changing recruitment patterns, the

breakdown of the negotiating positions, and the lowering of wages and working conditions for Asian sailors. Undermining the position of Asian sailors, colonial reforms advanced the position of employers and intermediaries, and increased their control over the Asian workforce ... Colonialism, in that respect, was not only an important factor in the increasing integration of labour markets, but at the same time in the increasing segmentation of these labour markets.[80]

The demise of colonialism and the new international division of labour that has spread across the globe since the 1960s have fundamentally changed labour markets. For a start, we have to take note of a massive return of casual labour markets, both in the industrializing Global South *and* in the Global North. During the twentieth century, in the South, the number of unemployed and underemployed grew by leaps and bounds, particularly from the 1940s. For the poor, begging, prostitution, crime, and casual labour were often the only options.[81]

In the Global North, the standard employment relationship is gradually becoming rarer as well. In his 2009 Presidential Address for the American Sociological Association, Arne Kalleberg summarized the causes as follows:

> The process that came to be known as neoliberal globalization intensified economic integration, increased the amount of competition faced by companies, provided greater opportunities to outsource work to low-wage countries, and opened up new labor pools through immigration. Technological advances both forced companies to become more competitive globally and made it possible for them to do so ... Unions continued to decline, weakening a traditional source of institutional protections for workers and severing the postwar business-labor social contract. Government regulations that set minimum acceptable standards in the labor market eroded, as did rules that governed competition in product markets.[82]

Overall, the balance of power has shifted in favour of employers, while, in OECD countries, the relative proportion of precarious workers has steadily increased. A 2004 European Union report concluded that 'in most countries precarious employment has increased over the last two decades'.[83] The same applies to the US and Canada.[84]

Consequently, labour relations in wealthy countries are beginning to look more like those in poor countries – precarization has become a global trend. The current demolition of 'social capitalism' confirms an insight into long-term developments that István Mészáros outlined as follows:

> The objective reality of *different rates of exploitation* — both within a given country and in the world system of monopoly capital — is as unquestionable as are the objective differences in the *rates of profit* at any particular time ... All the same, the reality of the different rates of exploitation and profit does not alter the fundamental law itself: i.e. the growing *equalization* of the differential rates of exploitation as the *global trend* of development of world capital.[85]

The fierce, increasingly global competition between capitals now has a clear downward 'equalizing' effect on the quality of life and work in the more developed parts of global capitalism.

## Coda

The long movement towards decasualized labour markets seems to have reached its end. Three important trends accompany the rise of transnational labour markets: precarization, integration, and fragmentation. These tendencies are not absolute; there has always been a segment of the labour force with long-term employment (either in the form of slavery or tenured wage labour), and this will probably never change completely. Wage differentials between different segments of the world's working class are still very considerable, both in terms of geography *and* gender and ethnicity.

Moreover, a historical perspective reveals that labour markets are consistently 'messy'. In empirical reality, employers persistently combine several methods of recruitment, sometimes seeking to tie workers down, and sometimes preferring loose connections. Naturally, there are patterns, but these patterns are usually far from law-like. As Sigmund Nosow said in the mid-twentieth century: 'Those working with labor market phenomena must ultimately face up to the problem that the deviations from the model of the economist are persistent, profound, and inexplicable through reference to this model'.[86] Labour markets are very rarely fully transparent, competition is never perfect, and stable equilibrium prices do not exist.

Labour markets are power structures determining barriers to entry, accessibility of information, transactions, and outcomes. They include all forms of labour-power commodification and cannot be studied in isolation but are historically-shaped exchange systems, path-dependent, embedded in a societal context, and – under capitalist conditions – linked to other economic subsystems, such as product markets and financial markets.[87] If labour economics and labour sociology were to incorporate these insights, an integrated historical social science of commodified labour-power would become possible.

## Notes

1. Fuks, 'κολωνος μισθιος'.
2. Brunt, *Italian Manpower*, 383.
3. Temin, *The Roman Market Economy*, 114.
4. Temin, *The Roman Market Economy*, 114.
5. Lucassen, 'Wage labour', 405.
6. McConnell, Brue & Macpherson, *Contemporary Labor Economics*, 3–4.
7. Furåker, *Sociological Perspectives*, 1–2.
8. Furåker, *Sociological Perspectives*, 17–18.
9. Smith, *Wealth of Nations*, Books I–III, 131–2.
10. Honoré, 'Ownership'.
11. Aspers, 'Markets, sociology of'; North, 'Markets and other allocative systems'. Many examples of regulated markets can be found in Medieval Europe. See, for example, Weber & Mayer-Maly, 'Studie'; Casson & Lee, 'Origin and development of markets'. Attempts to break through such regulations have been reconstructed in, for instance, Kaplan, 'Les corporations'.
12. Marx, *Capital*, I, 283.
13. Marx, *Capital*, I, 271, 874.
14. Wickham, *Framing the Early Middle Ages*, 260.
15. Rawski, *Agricultural Change*, 3.
16. van der Linden, *Workers of the World*, 42–5.
17. Audring, 'Zur sozialen Stellung der Hirten', 16.
18. Mendelsohn, 'Free artisans and slaves', 25.
19. Temin, *Roman Market Economy*, 130.
20. Hall & Stolcke, 'Introduction of free labour'.
21. Steffen, 'Pre-industrial iron worker'; Whitman, 'Industrial slavery at the margin'; Schechter, 'Free and slave labor'.
22. Rediker, *Between the Devil and the Deep Blue Sea*, 68.
23. Bezís-Selfa, 'A tale of two ironworks', 700.
24. Harris, 'Towards a study of the Roman slave trade', 125–6.
25. Strabo, *Geography of Strabo*, 329.
26. Lewis, *Sanctioned Violence in Early China*, 54–66.
27. Schoenberger, 'Origins of the market economy', 682.
28. Ivleva, 'Peasants into soldiers', 161.
29. Nöldeke, 'Servile war in the East'; Popovic, *Revolt of African Slaves in Iraq*.
30. Golombek, 'Timurid potters abroad'; Samkoff, 'From Central Asia to Anatolia'.
31. Probert, 'Bartolomé de Medina', 102; Laube, 'Zum Problem des Bündnisses', 88; Denzer, *Konquista der Augsburger Welser-Gesellschaft*, 79–81.
32. Pulleyblank, 'Origins and nature of chattel slavery', 220.
33. Habib, *Essays in Indian History*, 197.
34. Roy, 'Factor markets', 149.
35. Leupp, *Servants, Shophands, and Laborers*, 15.
36. Pamuk, 'Changes in factor markets', 123.
37. Moll-Murata, 'Work ethics and work valuations', 175.
38. Boomgaard, 'Labour, land, and capital markets', 59.
39. Kaur, *Wage Labour in Southeast Asia*, 21.
40. Roy, 'Factor markets', 147.

41  Pamuk, 'Changes in factor markets', 121.
42  Pierenkemper, 'Auf- und Ausbau eines "Normalarbeitsverhältnisses"', 84.
43  Tedesco, '"The missing factor"', 413–14.
44  van Bavel, 'Markets for land, labor, and capital', 525.
45  De Vries, 'Labour market', 56.
46  Leupp, *Servants, Shophands, and Laborers*, 123–54; Nagata, *Labour Contracts and Labor Relations*, 16; Mathias, 'Japan in the seventeenth century', 234–8.
47  Habib, *Essays in Indian History*, 197.
48  Tilly, 'Demographic origins of the European proletariat', 36.
49  Hay & Craven, *Masters, Servants, and Magistrates*; Stanziani, *Bondage*.
50  Keiser, *Vertragszwang und Vertragsfreiheit*, 404.
51  Osterhammel, *Colonialism*, 16–17 (and quotes in the rest of this paragraph).
52  Tinker, *New System of Slavery*.
53  Wareing, *Indentured Migration*, 39.
54  Galenson, *White Servitude in Colonial America*, 174.
55  Nunn, 'Long-term effects of Africa's slave trades', Table II; Lovejoy, *Transformations in Slavery*, Table 7.1.
56  Lal, 'The indenture system', 46.
57  Pan, 'Patterns of migration', 61.
58  Lal, *Girmitiyas*.
59  Behal, *One Hundred Years of Servitude*; Varma, 'Chargola exodus and collective action'.
60  McKeown, 'Global migration, 1846–1940'.
61  Shi & Zhuofen, 'Capitalism in agriculture', 144.
62  Roy, 'Factor markets', 150.
63  Boomgaard, 'Labour, land, and capital markets', 59–60.
64  Marshall, *Rural Economy of the Midland Counties*, 18.
65  Ditchfield, *Old English Customs*, 247.
66  Hicks, *Theory of Economic History*, 132.
67  MacEwan, 'What's "new" about the "new international economy"?', 115–16.
68  Lucassen, 'A multinational and its labor force', 17.
69  van Rossum, 'Changing tides', 260.
70  Cumbler, 'Transatlantic working-class institutions', 284.
71  Granovetter, *Getting a Job*, 122; van der Linden, 'Notes from an outsider'.
72  Mayer-Mali, *Locatio conductio*, 28.
73  Cairnes, *Some Leading Principles of Political Economy*, 66.
74  Middleton, 'Sexual division of labour in feudal England', 160.
75  *Changgong* were workers employed for ten months or a year. Shi & Zhuofen, 'Capitalism in agriculture', 144–5.
76  Humphries, 'Class struggle'; Middleton, 'Familiar fate of the *famulae*', 26–9.
77  Epstein, *Freedom and Growth*, 167.
78  Wood, 'From opportunity to imperative', 22.
79  Bonacich, 'Past, present, and future', 21.
80  van Rossum, 'Changing Tides', 260–1.
81  Compare Chapter 2.
82  Kalleberg, 'Precarious work, insecure workers'.
83  European Commission, *Precarious Employment in Europe*, 58–9.
84  Tremblay, 'From casual work to economic security', 121.
85  Mészáros, *Beyond Capital*, 891.
86  Nosow, 'Toward a theory of the labor market', 233.
87  Patnaik, 'Labour market under capitalism'.

# Part III
## Connections

# 9
# Global cash-crop transfers, ecology, and labour

> The great benefit resulting from colonies is the cultivation of staple commodities different from those of the mother-country.
> Arthur Young, *Political Essays*[1]

Our lives have become unimaginable without plants that at, one time, existed only in entirely different parts of the world. Rice, maize, potatoes, tomatoes, cassava, and countless other crops have spread all over the world and are important ingredients in the daily nutrition of hundreds of millions or even billions of people. Natural rubber enables car transport on all continents, and cotton and flax are indispensable in the textile industry.

Over the centuries, plants have travelled widely, frequently without any human intervention. Sweet potatoes, for example, appear to have originated in the Americas and were then transported to Africa, presumably by certain sea currents. Conversely, coconuts are thought to have reached South America from Africa in a similar way.[2] More recently, when plant transfers did come about through human intervention, this was often unintentional, for example because constructing canals and bridges removed longstanding distribution barriers or because species came along with human travellers, means of transportation, or plants and animals in transit. Seeds of several African crops, such as oil palms, are assumed to have been brought to the Americas this way, as a side-effect of the slave transports.[3]

In many cases, humans also *deliberately* transported plants from one area to the next, for example because of their value as food, medicine, or decoration, and frequently for a combination of these reasons. Strategic considerations sometimes came into play as well. Already around 2800 BCE, the Chinese Emperor Shen Nung dispatched collectors to remote areas to gather plants with medicinal or agrarian value.⁴ In the early centuries CE, sandalwood trees were transported from Indonesia to India, across about five thousand kilometres, where they were used to build Hindu temples, incense burners, and the stakes at which the Brahmans were burned.⁵

Europeans engaged in deliberate transfer early on as well, bringing plants back from Asia and Africa to Europe. Bitter oranges (*citrus aurantium*), citrons (*citrus medica*), and lemons (*citrus limon*) came from Asia and are known to have been cultivated in the Mediterranean since antiquity. Sugarcane, basil, muskmelons, and watermelons are believed to have arrived somewhat later from the East as well, while cress found its way to Europe from Africa and the Near East.⁶ Sugar beets (*beta vulgaris*) originated in the southern Himalayas and the Middle East but are thought to have arrived in Europe over two thousand years ago.⁷ During the early centuries of Islam, plant transfers appear to have increased, driven by initiatives among peasant growers and rulers who longed for these exotic crops in their botanical gardens.⁸ Such international transfers concerned mainly, though not exclusively, plants that were edible and could be stored for extended periods: cereals (rice, wheat, maize, rye, barley, oats, and millet) and leguminous plants containing protein (peas, beans, and lentils).⁹

On Khubilai Khan (r. 1260–94), the Mongolian founder of China's Yuan dynasty, we read:

> Near Canton in southern China, the Mongol authorities planted an orchard of eight hundred lemon trees imported from their territories in the Middle East. At Tabriz in Persia, the Mongols similarly planted groves of a different variety of lemon and other citrus trees imported in the opposite direction – from China to the Middle East. The Mongols transplanted an ever-expanding variety of peas, beans, grapes, lentils, nuts, carrots, turnips, melons, and diverse leaf vegetables, and in turn they developed new varieties and hybrids. In addition to food crops for humans and animals, Mongol authorities had a persistent interest in varieties of cotton and other crops for making textiles, as well as various materials for making rope, dyes, oils, ink, paper, and medicine.¹⁰

Some efforts to transfer plants were, of course, economically motivated. In the fifteenth century, for example, Japanese traders sold so much pepper in Korea that the Koreans thought it was a Japanese product. In the 1480s, King Songjong therefore repeatedly asked the Japanese

**Figure 9.1** Pepper harvest in Coilum, Southern India. Illustration from the *Livre des Merveilles du Monde*, c. 1410–12 (tempera on vellum). © Archives Charmet / Bridgeman Images.

envoys to provide him with pepper-plant seed, so that the crop might be grown in Korea.[11] Black pepper (*piper nigrum*) came from southwest India (Malabar) (Figure 9.1) and was subsequently, also in the fifteenth century, transferred to Sumatra to meet the immense Chinese demand.[12]

After 1500, and especially from 1600, the volume of long-distance plant transfers increased rapidly. The 'discovery' of the Americas and the circumnavigation of Africa greatly facilitated the transportation of crops from one continent to another. Both planned and unintentional transcontinental transfers of plants between the 'Old' and the 'New' worlds started with the Columbian Exchange, the exchange of crops between Europe and the Americas. The Magellan Exchange – the exchange of crops between the Americas and Asia – soon followed.[13] Table 9.1 depicts these events.

Crops were deliberately distributed as commodities, as diplomatic gifts, or as food products for settlers. In the sixteenth century, the Spanish and Portuguese brought important plants to China from the Americas, including the groundnut, which was cultivated around Shanghai from the 1530s; and the sweet potato, which was first mentioned in Yunnan in

Table 9.1  The Columbian and Magellan Exchanges of crop species.

| From Old to New World | | From New to Old World | |
|---|---|---|---|
| banana | olive | arrowroot | paprika |
| barley | onion | avocado | peanut |
| black pepper | pea | beans | pecan |
| buckwheat | peach | capsicum | pineapple |
| cabbage | pear | pepper | potato |
| citrus | rice | cashew nut | rubber |
| coconut | rye | cassava | squash |
| coffee | sorghum | chilli pepper | (incl. pumpkin) |
| eggplant | soy | kina (cinchona) | sunflower |
| (aubergine) | spelt | cocoa | sweet potato |
| garlic | sugar beet | cranberry | tobacco |
| lentils | sugarcane | guava | tomato |
| lettuce | turnip | maize (corn) | vanilla |
| nutmeg | wheat | okra | |
| oats | | papaya | |

Sources: Wouter van der Weijden, Rob Leewis & Pieter Bol, *Biological Globalisation: Bio-invasions and their impacts on nature, the economy and public health*. Utrecht: KNNV Publishing, 2007, 26; Stanley B. Alpern, 'The European introduction of crops into West Africa in precolonial times', *History in Africa* 19 (1992): 13–43, at 24–31.

1563 and gained popularity as a good alternative to the Chinese taro; and, in the seventeenth century, maize.[14] Products brought by the Portuguese from Brazil to South and Southeast Asia included cashew nuts, pineapples, sweet potatoes, cassava, groundnuts, and chilli pepper (*capsicum*). In Angola, they tried to cultivate the same food plants on small farms from around 1629.[15]

All these transfers had major consequences. In most parts of the world, patterns of consumption changed. Today, American chilli has become 'the world's most used spice',[16] hundreds of millions of people on all continents (still) smoke tobacco, and potatoes, maize, and rice have become staple foods way beyond their areas of origin. The textile industry relies heavily on cotton, and rubber tyres are a fundamental resource for transportation the world over. Demographic trends would have been entirely different as well, were it not for large-scale plant transfers. Africa, despite the export of countless slaves to other parts of the globe, experienced considerable population growth after 1600, thanks to the introduction of maize, which replaced the traditional sorghum, and cassava (manioc), which replaced the yam. The new crops enabled expansion to previously uninhabited areas.[17] In China, new crops led to 'a true agricultural revolution' and strong population growth in the eighteenth century.[18]

## The global triangle

Not only have intercontinental agricultural connections been long-standing, but we have also been aware of them for quite some time as well. When the German historian and playwright Friedrich Schiller was granted a Chair at the University of Jena in 1789, for example, he stated in his inaugural address that 'the most remote regions of the world contribute to our luxury'. After all, he continued, '[t]he clothes we wear, the spices in our food, and the price for which we buy them, many of our strongest medicines, and also many new tools of our destruction – do they not presuppose a Columbus who discovered America, a Vasco da Gama who circumnavigated the tip of Africa?'[19]

Nevertheless, it was quite some time before professional historians began to consider these global connections seriously in their research. And any interest taken in them was more likely to address their industrial and military than their botanical and agricultural elements. This may have been because, since the days of Marx, capitalism had been associated with factories and industries. The overwhelming majority of studies on the capitalist production system focus on urban merchant capital and its gradual transformation into manufacturing and later industrial production.

In recent decades, however, it has become increasingly clear that this interpretation of the past merits review. Renewed interest in rural cottage industries since the 1970s has enhanced this awareness. In his world-systems theory, Immanuel Wallerstein has considered agriculture at length and has demonstrated that agrarian cash crops were paramount in the rise of world capitalism. A cautious revaluation of agriculture is emerging in political economics as well. There is now a general awareness that the founders of this discipline formulated their ideas in an era that predates the first Industrial Revolution. William Petty devised his theories based on his experiences as an agrarian colonist in Ireland. Physiocrats such as François Quesnay and Turgot focused entirely on the agrarian sector. Even Adam Smith thought primarily in agrarian terms and argued: 'The capital … that is acquired to any country by commerce and manufactures is all a very precarious and uncertain possession till some part of it has been secured and realized in the cultivation and improvement of its lands'.[20]

The process of globalized production that has received so much attention in recent decades also derives largely from agriculture. The idea that production sites generating commodities for the global system may be transferred from one part of the world to another originated in agriculture and gained ground in the processing industries only later on.[21] Long-distance trade made traders and affluent consumers of luxury commodities (in areas with a temperate climate, especially in East Asia and Europe) aware that, in subtropical and tropical areas, crops were grown that also appealed greatly to consumers in the Global North as stimulants, as food products, or for the garment industry. All the spices from Southern India, Ceylon, and the Southeast-Asian archipelago were already renowned in China and Europe two millennia ago. When capitalist influences increased, traders and settlers attempted to control the production of these profitable tropical and subtropical crops. In this context, Europeans started attempting to transfer crops all over the world *within* the belt of tropical and subtropical areas, for example when expanding total production was certain to increase profits, or because a crop in a certain region was in danger of extinction due to overcropping. This led to a 'triangulation', in which the Global North organized transfer (or expansion) of agrarian production systems in the Global South (Figure 9.2).

This triangle expresses the balance of power in which states and companies from the Global North take decisions on work processes in the Global South that have ecological consequences.

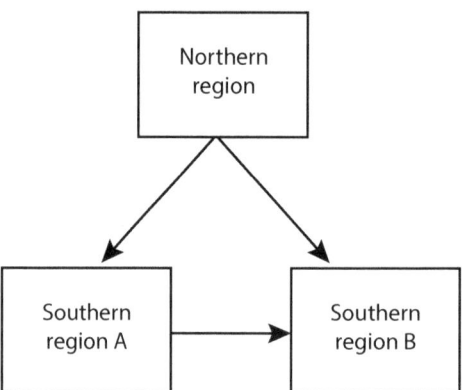

**Figure 9.2** 'Triangulation' of agrarian production. The 'North' controls different parts of the 'South' and moves crops from one region to another. Source: Author.

## Cash-crop trajectories

Crops are difficult to classify by typology from the perspective of human consumption because they may serve multiple purposes. Many spices were used both as flavourings in food preparation and for medicinal purposes, at times obscuring the distinction between 'medicinal' and 'culinary' use. In ancient and medieval India, pepper was believed 'to warm the stomach and liver, combat flatulence, purify the brain when used as a sternutator, and stimulate erections'.[22] Even sugarcane was long regarded as a medicine. In 1572, Ortelius wrote in his *Théâtre de l'Universe*: 'Whereas before, sugar was only obtainable in the shops of apothecaries, who kept it exclusively for invalids, people devour it out of gluttony … What used to be a medicine is nowadays eaten as a food'.[23] Clusters of crops are therefore identifiable based on their use but these clusters inevitably overlap (Table 9.2).

Cash-crop trajectories have varied considerably over the centuries. Indigo was once in great demand but has been replaced almost entirely by artificial dyes for over a century. Coffee, on the other hand, has now become the strongest revenue-generating primary commodity worldwide, after crude oil. Some crops are labour-intensive, while others require little work. Some crops tend to be grown on large plantations, others on small plots of land. Many contingent factors helped to shape the global trajectories of cash crops: the great slave rebellion of Saint-Domingue (present-day Haiti) and the abolition of slavery by the British Empire

Table 9.2 Types of (sub)tropical cash crops.

| Crop type | Examples |
| --- | --- |
| 1) Staple foods | Rice, maize, potatoes, cassava |
| 2) Flavourings | Pepper (*capsicum*), cinnamon, cloves, nutmeg, mace, sugarcane |
| 3) Stimulants | Tea, coffee, cocoa, tobacco, cocaine, opium |
| 4) Fragrants | Sandalwood, camphor, myrrh |
| 5) Medicines | *Cinchona* (quinine) |
| 6) Fruits | Bananas, oranges, mangos, lemons |
| 7) Construction materials | Bamboo, teak, brazilwood |
| 8) Industrial raw materials | Cotton, jute, indigo, rubber |

Source: Author.

moved many Caribbean planters to South Asia (Chapter 10). Wars and the resultant power shifts, scientific discoveries, consumer preferences, and so on, played major roles too. Nevertheless, it is possible to discern a certain logic in developments – a logic that is not deterministic but, rather, reveals historical tendencies and opportunities. The process of long-distance cash-crop transfer is a composite labour process that combines managerial, intellectual, and manual efforts. It *always* consists of four necessary steps: 1) the acquisition of seeds or seedlings; 2) the transfer of these seeds and seedlings to new locations in the South; 3) the growing and harvesting of the crops; 4) the transportation and sale of these crops to the North. Let us now examine each of these steps in turn.

## Acquisition of seeds and seedlings

Whoever wants to relocate crops needs first to acquire seeds or seedlings. Within the boundaries of colonial empires, this was often quite simple, provided that the would-be planters acted in accordance with the local authorities in the crop's area of origin. Things became more problematic if the authorities were opposed to a transfer, for example because this could harm national export. In such scenarios, transfer then became an illegal act. There have been many such illicit operations. A well-known example is that of the Englishman Henry A. Wickham, who, in 1876, with the help of native locals, gathered seeds from the rubber tree *hevea brasiliensis* along the Tapajoz River in Brazil: 'Working with as many Tüpayo Indians as I could get together at short notice, I daily ranged the forest, and packed on our backs in Indian pannier baskets as heavy loads of seed as we could march down under'.[24] Wickham and his helpers managed to transport the delicate loot across many hundreds of kilometres to Belem. The crew of the *Amazonas* then shipped the cargo to the Royal Botanic Gardens at Kew, England. There, botanists and gardeners cultivated the small sample of the seeds that had survived the journey. Next, sailors transferred about two thousand seedlings to botanical gardens in Ceylon, Malaya, and Java (Figure 9.3).[25]

Transport was made easier by intermediate stops so that the seeds and seedlings could recover from the hardships of travel and could later continue their journey in a better condition. The 'intermediate stops' were – as in the case of Henry Wickham's *hevea* seeds – hosted by botanical gardens. These had a very long history, stretching back to antiquity, the

**Figure 9.3** Workers in front of a greenhouse at the Botanical Garden in Bogor (Buitenzorg). The Garden was officially established by the Dutch East Indies Government on 17 May 1817. It played a major role in the introduction of *Cinchona* trees to Java in 1854, which would ultimately make the island the largest producer of quinine bark for malaria treatment. https://bit.ly/3CDLEPo.

early Islamic states, and the Aztec Empire. The first botanical gardens in Europe were probably established in Italy: in Pisa (1543), Padua (1545), Florence (1550), and Bologna (1568). These gardens were primarily meant to train students and not for the transfer of plants.

Since the eighteenth century, botanical gardens have gained economic significance. The less improvised cash-crop transfers became, the more importance systematically organized and well-documented institutions with practical knowhow acquired. The botanical gardens thus developed into scientific plant-transfer nodes,[26] and it was not long before colonial powers founded the first gardens in tropical regions as bridgeheads for biological imperialism (Table 9.3).

Soon, the different botanical gardens formed a global network and exchanged data. An important resource was the so-called *Index semina* (or *Index seminum*), a catalogue of seeds regularly published since the eighteenth century.[27]

Table 9.3  Some botanical gardens that played a role in long-distance plant transfer, sixteenth–nineteenth centuries (year of foundation in brackets).

|  | **British Empire** | **Dutch Empire** | **French Empire** |
|---|---|---|---|
| Metropolitan | Royal Botanic Gardens (Kew, 1759) | Hortus botanicus, Leiden (1590) | Jardin des plantes, Paris (1635) |
| Colonial | Kingstown, St. Vincent (1765) | Buitenzorg (Bogor, Java, 1817) | Pamplemousses, Mauritius (1770) |
|  | Howrah (near Calcutta), India (1787) |  |  |
|  | Port of Spain, Trinidad (1818) |  |  |
|  | Peradeniya, Ceylon (1821) |  |  |
|  | Singapore (1822/1859) |  |  |

Source: Author.

## Transfer of seeds and seedlings to new locations in the South

For centuries, long-distance transfer of seeds and plants by sea was particularly difficult: packaging methods were often imprecise and extended voyages very risky. Sarah Stetson described some of the problems as follows:

> Months might be spent in the painstaking gathering and careful preparation of specimens, which became a total loss in the course of the long sea voyage. The sailing ships which crossed the ocean were small affairs at best, dependent entirely upon wind and current for their speed; the length of the trip was a matter of weeks instead of days. Storms delayed the vessel until plants rotted and seeds lost their vitality; yet brisk winds and quiet sea might just as surely bring a ruined cargo to port, due to improper packing. It was an irregular traffic, with no tried and certain methods about it either in consignment or in transportation.[28]

Only after the so-called Wardian case was invented did the transfer of plants become less of an odyssey. In around 1829, Dr Nathaniel Ward (1791–1868) built a kind of proto-herbarium that considerably facilitated the safe transportation of plants. It was first tested in 1833, when Ward successfully had two cases of ferns and grasses transported to Australia, a journey that took months.[29] Over the following years, carriers used this case ever more frequently, thereby accelerating and increasing the number of transfers. Around the mid-nineteenth century, 'almost every domesticated plant had been transferred, at least experimentally, to every likely environment on earth'.[30]

## Growing and harvesting of the crops

Once seeds and seedlings have been safely transferred to a new environment, their commercial exploitation is supposed to follow. But, in many cases, such relocations failed. Indigo did not fare well in Senegal, nor did *Cinchona* in Algeria or the Ford Company's attempt to develop a rubber plantation in Brazil. The factors influencing success were numerous and were often interconnected. On the one hand, we have the elements affecting the prices received by the farmer for different products; these include commercial opportunities, transportation, and handling costs. On the other hand, we have the elements affecting the per-unit cost of producing different products: climate, soil, and topography all influence the yields and, hence, the cost; and the relative availability of labour-power will also lead to different costs. These factors, which determine price differences *and* cost differentials, will determine which products are most profitable.

Agricultural 'globalists' had to take into account a wide variety of aspects, including plant diseases, predators (insects and other pests), energy sources, water supply, labour recruitment, labour discipline, the relationship with financiers, transport facilities, the relationship with the local authorities, and market opportunities. Crop transfer, therefore, was a difficult and risky enterprise. Its history is often presented as a continuous success story but, in reality, failures have probably outnumbered successes by far. P. F. Knowles was justified in saying: 'Often in early stages of a crop's development the best area of production is not known, mistakes may occur through ignorance, or unanticipated pests may appear. Usually the average yield is very low'.[31] Arguably typical is the following observation from Carol MacLennan on the introduction of sugarcane in Hawai'i: 'Managers taught themselves how to organize a plantation and manufacture sugar (a delicate chemical process) by trial and error. Sugar mills broke down, burned down, and generally proved inadequate ... Often error led to business failure'.[32]

The historian of technology Nathan Rosenberg stated a truism when he wrote that 'there are many things that cannot be known in advance or deduced from some set of first principles'.[33] This fundamental uncertainty:

> ... has a very important implication: the [innovative] activity cannot be planned. No person, or group of persons, is clever enough to plan the outcome of the search process, in the sense of identifying a particular innovation target and moving in a predetermined way to its realization—as one might read a road map and plan the most efficient route to a historical monument.[34]

This is also the reason why pioneers are often 'punished'. Indeed, Karl Marx emphasized:

> ... [the] much greater costs that are always involved in an enterprise based on new inventions, compared with later establishments that rise up on its ruins, *ex suis ossibus*. The extent of this is so great that the pioneering entrepreneurs generally go bankrupt, and it is only their successors who flourish, thanks to their possession of cheaper buildings, machinery, etc. Thus it is generally the most worthless and wretched kind of money-capitalists that draw the greatest profit from all new developments of the universal labour of the human spirit and their social application by combined labour.[35]

As the knowledge of agricultural 'globalizers' increased over time, their mutual competition became more sophisticated. While, during the eighteenth century, former soldiers and other 'meritorious' Europeans were rewarded with a piece of land on which to build a farm or plantation, this became almost impossible at a later stage due to the enormous knowhow that had been accumulated in the meantime. In his manual on *Modern Coffee Production* (1956), A. E. Haarer cautioned, for instance:

> The time has long since passed when ex-soldier land settlement schemes are of any value. Nor is it wise for a banker, a stockbroker, or a lawyer to throw up his profession and start planting coffee ... Nowadays a farm requires a technically trained farmer, and an orchard needs a man who is trained in horticulture, though agriculture and horticulture are complementary. Money has been wasted and land misused far too often in the past by men who knew little about either of these trades.[36]

Let me highlight, then, three essential conditions for a successful agricultural enterprise in the tropics or subtropics, relating to ecology, business organization, and labour.

*Ecology*

Ecology is of great importance since plants do not grow everywhere but require specific surroundings. Coffee, for example, can be cultivated between 24° northern and 24° southern latitude, at an elevation of no more than 800 m, and at temperatures between 17 and 23 °C; rainy and dry seasons should alternate, while both extended droughts and long-lasting precipitation are harmful; the soil should be highly porous, with a stable structure and moisture permeability.[37] This already sounds quite constraining but many more aspects come into play, such as soil acidity, the need for shade or the need for plants *not* to be in the shade, etc. The spectrum of growth-promoting factors for individual plants is very broad. Nowadays, based on such parameters, we can more or less determine the potential growing areas for every cash crop – the regions where a given crop would theoretically prosper. Such *potential growing areas* tend to be considerably larger than the actual ones, both because many other factors may be relevant (such as wind, running water, etc.) and because of competition from other crops and land use.[38]

The parameters may be very specific. When clove trees were transferred from the Moluccas to the East African coast, the effort was only barely successful. After all, rainfall is far heavier on the Moluccas than in East Africa. On the island of Amboina (now Ambon), annual precipitation is about 1,360 mm, whereas on Zanzibar island it is approximately 600 mm and in Pemba 800 mm. In their new surroundings, clove trees had to subsist from an absolute minimum of moisture, which probably explains why the crop did better in Pemba than on Zanzibar.[39] Throughout history, European 'globalizer' agriculturalists have made countless unsuccessful trial-and-error attempts at growing plant crops outside their potential growth areas, eventually identifying the best locations.

*Business organization*

A second major factor in achieving a successful agricultural endeavour is business organization. In principle, it is possible to cultivate every crop with every type of business organization. But, clearly, there are elective affinities. Sugarcane, for instance, is preferably grown on large-scale plantations (Figure 9.4), while tobacco is often produced by small farmers. At least two factors create such affinities.

**Figure 9.4** 'Planting the sugar-cane', a depiction of a large-scale sugarcane plantation in Haiti, c. 1820. Artist: William Clark. British Library, public domain, https://www.bl.uk/collection-items/cutting-the-sugar-cane-antigua.

First, there is the crop's gestation period. Some crops bear fruit within a few months, others only after many years. The classical plantation crops are so-called perennials – that is, crops that, once planted, need several years before they can be first harvested (such as palm oil, rubber, or cacao). So-called annuals, on the other hand, yield a harvest after just one year. These include cotton, jute, tobacco, or groundnuts. The economic implications of this contrast are several. The production of annuals can be adjusted easily to changes in demand. Perennials, however, are less flexible. They will therefore be grown 'either as a secondary crop on a food farm, or by a large corporation which can afford to wait out the period between planting and production'.[40] Furthermore, 'the decisions to make extra plantings are taken five to ten years before the crops begin to bear, thus accounting for the violent fluctuations in supply'.[41]

Second, processing is also a major factor. After harvesting, green coffee beans can be stored for months and therefore do not need immediate roasting. In contrast, sugarcane has to be processed quickly to preserve the sucrose content. This calls for either large plantations with their own central mills or a cooperative sugar mill shared by a large number of smallholders. In both cases:

> ... the mill's profitability largely depended on the minimization of the average fixed costs of producing sugar. This, in turn, depended on the mill working continuously at full capacity during the harvesting season. Thus the provision of adequate supplies of cane and the coordination of the pace of harvesting, transport, and milling was of prime concern.[42]

The cooperative approach frequently led to higher transaction costs because the harvesting and milling had to be coordinated between numerous smallholders, and this increased the risks borne by the mill: 'It was in these ways that the capital requirements of crushing mills hindered the growth of the smallholding system in sugar cane farming'.[43]

The combination of these two influences goes some way towards explaining how agricultural enterprise was organized in separate places. Perennials and costly processing favoured large-scale businesses, while annuals and low processing costs favoured small-scale production. Small-scale production could be indirect or direct. In the first case, Northern entrepreneurs did no more than make (often coercive) deals with local Southern elites who then were supposed to deliver a certain amount of crops periodically by exploiting 'their' peasantry. In the second case, smallholder production was stimulated through economic incentives, money taxes, or taxes in-kind – such as under the Cultivation System in the Netherlands Indies during the nineteenth century.[44] The large-scale option would be for 'globalizers' to start their own farms and plantations. Generally, this choice was the least popular.[45]

### *Labour*

The third essential condition for these business ventures in the tropics or subtropics was the right labour, and here the requirements for crops diverge widely. Some crops, like cotton or tobacco, need substantial labour for short periods, while other crops have labour requirements that can be spread more evenly over the year.[46] And some plants do not need much labour at all. The coconut, for instance, was sometimes referred to as the 'lazy man's crop' for, 'once the tree is well started, the owner may, figuratively, recline under it the rest of his life with coconuts falling in his lap. The coconut palm has a very long productive life, with a maximum not clearly determined but appearing to approach one hundred years'.[47]

Labour demand for most crops fluctuates seasonally. Harvest-time is a busy period, and requires lots of workers, while fewer people are necessary during other times of year. Agriculturalists generally have two options to solve this problem. One option is to employ a small group of workers permanently and, in addition, hire large numbers of temporary workers for shorter periods. This is, for example, how it is done on the *fincas* or *cafetales* in the coffee region of La Guaca in Colombia:

> Because coffee beans must be picked at just the right time, before they become over-ripened, a relatively large and dependable labor force must be available. Coffee harvesting takes place twice a year in this highland temperate zone. The collection of coffee beans is tedious and exhausting work … Coffee harvesting is task labor and the pickers are paid according to the quantity collected each day … Because of the large numbers of people (whole families participate) involved in the harvest and the rapidity with which the bushes are cleared, there are only a few days when the picking is financially rewarding for the workers. Between the harvest seasons work is extremely scarce for the majority of the population, and there are about three months during the year (June–August) when there is no work on the coffee farms for most of the *campesinos*. Many Guaqueños supplement their low and sporadic wages with subsistence gardening or petty commodity production. They also hire themselves out as common day-laborers whenever the occasion may arise.[48]

The other option is to have *all* the work done by permanent workers, even if that leaves them idle for a part of each year. This option is only attractive for agriculturalists if they can keep the cost of these workers extremely low. Slaves on sugar plantations in the English West Indies were a case in point. They had only three tools – an axe, a hoe, and a bill hook – at their disposal:

> Men did the work of animals. Such tasks as planting and cultivating, performed on English and North American farms by horse-driven plows and harrows, were carried out in the Indies entirely by hand. Caribbean farm implements were few and simple … The reason for all [this inefficiency] was to keep the slaves busy year-round.[49]

### Transportation and sale to the North

Even if the crop yielded a good harvest, the product had yet to be shipped to distribution centres in the North, and by no means all crops were suited to this purpose. Whether long-distance transfers were commercially viable depended on which means of transport were available. If the transport had limited carrying capacity or if the transit would be slow and entailed serious risks, then only crops that could be well-preserved and had a high value–weight density, such as spices, were eligible to be transferred. As transport became faster, cheaper, and less risky, bulkier vegetable products entered the picture as well. And when, moreover, at the end of the nineteenth century, reliable refrigeration techniques became available, perishable goods, such as bananas and other fruit, could be transported across long distances as well.[50]

The transport revolution that dramatically changed the world market for cash crops from the late-nineteenth century onward was multi-faceted. In the shipping industry, the wooden ships that were still dominant around 1870 were rapidly replaced by larger, faster, and more reliable ships powered by steam engines.[51] The opening of the Suez Canal in 1871 and the Panama Canal in 1914 shortened sea routes from Asia and the Americas to Europe enormously. The construction of railways enabled huge advances in the tropics, where, in many regions, colonial authorities, assisted by willing investors, or multinationals, such as the United Fruit Company, established connections between plantations and harbours along the coast.[52]

In addition to the invention of refrigeration systems, the transportation of perishable items also benefited greatly from the introduction of canning techniques. Originally devised by Nicolas Appert in 1809 to supply Napoleon's troops across long distances, these techniques were subsequently perfected for increasingly broad application.[53] The success of the canning method is illustrated by developments on Hawai'i, where the number of cans of pineapple produced there increased from 1,893 in 1903 to 8,728,580 in 1925. In the 1920s, the island group became home to the largest fruit cannery in the world:

> It employs 2,000 persons and is filled with special machinery for economical, sanitary operation. Much of the machinery has been invented in Hawaii and is of special manufacture. The fruit is not touched by human hands during the process of canning. Tin cans are manufactured in a plant next door to the cannery and are brought on an endless belt for immediate use. Some 200,000,000 cans a year are made.[54]

Considering all these interconnected influences, the business of plant transfer was clearly an extremely complicated process, which, even today, we understand only partly. Towards the end of the nineteenth century, the possibilities for commercially attractive crop transfers were increasingly exhausted and most possible plant relocations had been tested in practice. The focus thus shifted from transfers of plants to refinement and genetic manipulation of seeds.[55] It was no longer *one* science (botany) that studied all plants but, rather, many sciences together focused on single plants:

> Instead of transferring plants from one area to another, scientists now manipulate familiar plants, adjusting their characteristics to human requirements and to specific environments. Geneticists have replaced the traditional domesticated plants with new and far more productive varieties, while soil scientists, agricultural chemists, plant pathologists, and entomologists have learned to improve the environment in which the plants can grow.[56]

A first symptom of this new trend was the founding of agricultural research stations. Building on the work of the pioneer of agricultural chemistry, Justus von Liebig (1803–73), Germany introduced such stations from 1861, and shortly thereafter began to export the practice to other countries.[57] In Brazil in 1885, for example, the German agronomist Franz Wilhelm Dafert founded an agricultural research station in the coffee region of Campinas.[58] The colonial empires followed suit. In British West Africa, eight stations were established between 1890 and 1909; in French Africa, similar stations were initiated almost simultaneously; while, in the Netherlands Indies, so-called *proefstations* (testing stations) were founded for sugarcane (1893), tobacco (1894), cacao (1901), and other crops.[59] The work of the research stations led to remarkable results, such as the introduction of nobilized sugarcane and hybrid maize in the 1920s.[60] Production per hectare of most crops rose, gradually at first and then explosively after World War II (Table 9.4).

One important driver of this growth was the strategy known as the Green Revolution, which changed much of agriculture in the Global South from the 1960s by introducing new crop varieties, irrigation, pesticides, and fertilizers. This postwar campaign, supported primarily by US institutions, was intended explicitly to avert a 'Red Revolution' by boosting agricultural technology in hungry countries around the world.[61] The effects were contradictory. On the one hand, significant productivity gains were realized.[62] On the other, the middle peasantries were the main beneficiaries, while the position of poor farmers worsened. There were

Table 9.4  Development of agricultural productivity on a world scale.

| Crop | 1961 | | | 2011 | | |
|---|---|---|---|---|---|---|
| | Area harvested (ha) | Production quantity (tonnes) | Tonnes per ha | Area harvested (ha) | Production quantity (tonnes) | Tonnes per ha |
| Cloves | 80,800 | 27,770 | 0.34 | 514,981 | 97,890 | 0.19 |
| Tobacco | 3,398,158 | 3,573,815 | 1.05 | 4,251,760 | 7,568,208 | 1.78 |
| Sugarcane | 8,911,877 | 447,977,518 | 50.27 | 25,436,924 | 1,794,359,190 | 70.54 |
| Coffee | 9,757,455 | 4,527,872 | 0.46 | 10,476,355 | 8,284,135 | 0.79 |
| Bananas | 2,021,093 | 21,493,119 | 10.63 | 5,157,466 | 106,541,709 | 20.66 |
| Natural rubber | 3,879,860 | 2,120,070 | 0.55 | 9,821,061 | 11,281,768 | 1.15 |

Source: Author, based on data drawn from the Food and Agriculture Organization. www.fao.org/faostat/.

also harmful environmental effects, such as greater water use, soil erosion, and chemical runoff.[63]

Coffee-producing farms, many of which had undergone dramatic changes in the last quarter of the previous century, aptly exemplify these ambiguities. Coffee plants were long grown in the shade of fruit and other trees, which were a natural habitat for insects and animals. Coffee farms were therefore forest-like agro-ecosystems, 'providing protection from soil erosion, favorable local temperature and humidity regimes, constant replenishment of the soil organic matter via leaf litter production, and home to an array of beneficial insects that can act to control potential economic pests without the use of toxic chemicals.[64] Moreover, the combination of trees and coffee plants enabled farmers to diversify production and, thus, derive additional income (from selling fruit or timber, for instance).

During the Green Revolution, international agencies and national governments propagated what was known as 'technification' – nowadays also called 'modernization' – which consisted of replacing traditional varieties of coffee (*típica*, *bourbón*) with varieties capable of growing without shade, enabling the density of coffee plants to be increased from 1,100–1,500 plants per hectare to 4,000–7,000 plants per hectare. The new-style coffee farms took on an 'industrial' look, with long rows of coffee plants in the sun, regularly sprayed with fertilizers and chemical pesticides. While coffee output has clearly increased, farmers have become more dependent on a single source of income than in the past, the eco-system has deteriorated, and bio-diversity has been reduced.

The globalized production and distribution of cash crops has not only changed our consumption habits; it has also drastically modified labour relations, landscapes, and ecologies. Agricultural output has dramatically increased and our daily menus have become much more variegated. But this progress has come at a high price. In the past, millions of slaves and other unfree workers were put to work on farms and plantations. And, with the coming of modern colonialism, peasants and farm labourers became, as Mike Davis convincingly argued, 'dramatically more pregnable to natural disaster after 1850 as their local economies were violently incorporated into the world market'.[65] Not only was traditional food security undermined by 'the forcible incorporation of smallholder production into commodity and financial circuits controlled from overseas'; but also, 'the integration of millions of tropical cultivators into the world market during the late nineteenth century was accompanied by a dramatic deterioration in their terms of trade'.[66]

However, not only the social but also the ecological consequences of agricultural globalization have been enormous. The expansion of coffee cultivation, for example, has often 'coincided with territorial expansion, the movement of settlers into frontier zones where tropical forests were destroyed, "new forests" of coffee and shade planted, towns established, roads and railroads built, regional identities forged'.[67] What is more:

> In periods of rising prices, cultivated acreage has frequently expanded in regions whose arid and erratic climate or steep slope make them unfit for permanent cultivation. Soil depletion has often occurred during and after a period of prosperity for certain cash crops (for example, wheat, cotton, tobacco, sugarcane, rubber) which expanded as monocultures or near-monocultures in areas suitable for permanent cultivation only under a diversified system of farming.[68]

The globalization of agriculture has thus been a profoundly ambivalent process of world-historical importance.

## Notes

1. Young, *Political Essays Concerning the Present State of the British Empire*, 274.
2. Grigg, *Agricultural Systems*, ch. 3; Sauer, *Historical Geography*, 37ff.; Brand, 'Origin and early distribution', 112–13.
3. Carney & Rosomoff, *In the Shadow of Slavery*.
4. Hill, 'History and functions', 185–6.
5. De Roever, *De jacht op sandelhout*, 44; Donkin, *Between East and West*, 16.
6. Wendt, 'Globalisierung von Pflanzen', 208, note.
7. Pruns, *Europäische Zuckerwirtschaft*, I, 50–6.
8. Watson, *Agricultural Innovation*, esp. 9–73.
9. The biologist Wes Jackson has noted: 'We seldom appreciate how narrow our food requirements really are. But of the 350,000 plant species worldwide, only two dozen are of particular importance to us for food. Of the top 18 sources, 14 come from but two flowering plant families, the grasses and legumes.' Jackson, 'Toward a unifying concept', 212.
10. Weatherford, *Genghis Khan*, 228.
11. Ts'ao, 'Pepper trade in East Asia', 242.
12. Jacobs, *Merchant in Asia*, 60.
13. On the Columbian Exchange, see Crosby, *Columbian Exchange*; Crosby, *Ecological Imperialism*; and Crosby, *Germs, Seeds, and Animals*. See also Richards, *Unending Frontier*. On the Magellan Exchange, see Gerber & Guang, *Agriculture and Rural Connections*.
14. Gernet, *Monde chinois*, 420.
15. Kapil & Bhatnagar, 'Portuguese contributions', 452; Rodrigues, 'Influence of Africa on Brazil', 63.
16. Wright, 'Medieval spice trade', 42.
17. Collins & Burns, *History of Sub-Saharan Africa*, 198–9.
18. Gernet, *Monde chinois*, 420–1.
19. Schiller, 'What is … universal history?', 253.
20. Smith, *Wealth of Nations*, Books I–III, 519.

21  Porcelain is probably the most significant exception to this rule. In the early-eighteenth century, the Chinese production process was 'reinvented' in Saxony and was subsequently disseminated across Europe and later to other parts of the world.
22  Jacobs, *Merchant in Asia*, 71.
23  Abraham Ortelius, *Théâtre de l'Universe contenant les cartes de tout le monde*, 2, quoted in Braudel, *Civilization and Capitalism*, I, 225.
24  Wickham, *On the Plantation*, 50.
25  Keong, *Western Rubber Planting Enterprise*, 4–7; Imle, 'Hevea rubber', 265; Dean, *Brazil and the Struggle for Rubber*, 11–22.
26  Ortmayr, 'Kulturpflanzen', 74.
27  Sometimes, scientific curiosity could hinder economic utility, as became clear in Calcutta's botanical garden during the early-nineteenth century: 'The Court of Directors were disturbed by the growing emphasis on science. Since the foundation of the Calcutta Garden they had never ceased to view it as a horticultural establishment, above all else designed to foster economic botany on the periphery. Its scientific function was limited to the domestication of profitable plants and the collection of samples which could be studied by scientists *in Europe*.' Vicziany, 'Imperialism, botany and statistics', 641–2.
28  Stetson, 'Traffic in seeds and plants', 47. Precisely because transfers entailed so many risks, their success was often attributable to coincidence and luck. Alexander von Humboldt reported about a black slave in New Spain, who, while preparing rice, 'had found three or four grains of wheat among the rice intended to feed the Spanish army: these grains appeared to have been planted before 1530 … Historical records mention a Spanish lady, Marie d'Escobar, the wife of Diego de Chaves, who was the first to bring some grains of wheat to the city of Lima, then known as Rimac. The product of harvests from which she obtained these grains was distributed for three years among the new settlers, so that each farmer received twenty or thirty grains'. Humboldt, *Essai politique*, III, 67–8. This was how wheat spread across South America. See also Robertson, 'Some notes on the transfer', 14.
29  Hershey, 'Doctor Ward's accidental terrarium'.
30  Headrick, 'Technological change', 61.
31  Knowles, 'New crop establishment', 267.
32  MacLennan, 'Foundations of sugar's power', 43, 53.
33  Rosenberg, 'Economic experiments', 182.
34  Rosenberg, 'Economic experiments', 186–7.
35  Marx, *Capital*, III, 199.
36  Haarer, *Modern Coffee Production*, 138.
37  Franke, *Nutzpflanzen*.
38  Jonasson, 'Potential areas of coffee-growing', 94. The Swedish geographer Jonasson was probably the first to examine this subject matter. See his study *Kaffet och kaffeländer*. He was driven by colonial and racist motivations and intended to indicate 'the regions within the tropics where possible future cultivation … might extend the settlement and successful permanent occupancy by the white race of certain favorable equatorial regions'. Jonasson, 'Natural conditions for coffee culture', 356. For considerable refinements of Jonasson's approach, see Chang, 'Potential photosynthesis'; Chang, 'Global distribution of net radiation'; Chang, 'Tropical agriculture'; Porter, 'Note on cotton and climate'.
39  Tidbury, *The Clove Tree*, 23–4.
40  Grigg, *Agricultural Systems*, 211.
41  Grigg, *Agricultural Systems*, 211.
42  Shlomowitz, 'Plantations and smallholdings', 7.
43  Shlomowitz, 'Plantations and smallholdings', 9.
44  Brown, *Economic Change*, 96–127; Bosma, 'The Cultivation System'.
45  'Plantations covered only 1.01 per cent of the cultivated area of British India in 1895.' Habib, *Indian Economy*, 78. One consideration may have been that '[f]amily labour does not require as much supervision as hired labour. This is partly because family members can be expected to share an emotional bond, and so to a great extent can trust one another not to shirk'. Dasgupta, *Inquiry into Well-Being*, 222.
46  Grigg, *Agricultural Systems*, 211–13.
47  Spencer & Horvath, 'How does an agricultural region originate?', 82.
48  James, 'Subsistence, survival and capitalist agriculture', 88–9.
49  Dunn, *Sugar and Slaves*, 198, 200.

50  Teuteberg, 'Geschichte der Kühlkost'.
51  For a quantitative overview of the changes between 1850 and 1950, see Woytinsky & Woytinsky, *World Commerce and Governments*, 433 (Table 154).
52  Lewis, 'Export stimulus', 18.
53  Bruegel, '"Un sacrifice de plus … "'; Bruegel, 'Du temps annuel au temps quotidien'; Graham, 'The French connection'.
54  Freeman, 'Economic geography', 268.
55  Perkins, *Agricultural Development in China*, 51.
56  Headrick, 'Technological change', 62.
57  Krohn & Schäfer. 'Ursprung und Struktur der Agrikulturchemie'; Finlay, 'German agricultural experiment stations'; Jas, *Au carrefour de la chimie et de l'agriculture*. On the worldwide spread of agricultural research, see Busch & Sachs, 'Agricultural sciences'.
58  Dean, 'Green wave of coffee'.
59  Yudelman, 'Transfer of agricultural techniques'; NN, 'Stations (proef-)'.
60  Headrick, 'Technological change', 62. Nobilization refers to a process of repeated crossbreeding to produce a particular desired trait.
61  The term 'Green Revolution' was coined by William Gaud, Director of the United States Agency for International Development. In 1968, he called the changes in agriculture 'a new revolution. It is not a violent Red Revolution like that of the Soviets, nor is it a White Revolution like that of the Shah of Iran. I call it the Green Revolution'. Gaud, 'The Green Revolution'.
62  See, for example, Evenson & Gollin, 'Assessing the impact of the Green Revolution'.
63  Pingali, 'Green Revolution'. Vandana Shiva therefore regards the Green Revolution mainly as a failure: 'It has led to reduced genetic diversity, increased vulnerability to pests, soil erosion, water shortages, reduced soil fertility, micronutrient deficiencies, soil contamination, reduced availability of nutritious food crops for the local population, the displacement of vast numbers of small farmers from their land, rural impoverishment and increased tensions and conflicts. The beneficiaries have been the agrochemical industry, large petrochemical companies, manufacturers of agricultural machinery, dam builders and large landowners. The "miracle" seeds of the Green Revolution have become mechanisms for breeding new pests and creating new diseases.' Shiva, 'Green Revolution in the Punjab'.
64  www.nrdc.org/health/farming/ccc/chap3.asp.
65  Davis, *Late Victorian Holocausts*, 288–90.
66  Davis, *Late Victorian Holocausts*, 288–90.
67  Roseberry, 'Introduction', 3.
68  Ciriacy-Wantrup, 'Resource conservation', 417.

# 10
# Slavery and convict labour: training-grounds for modern labour management

Besides, as the Master is placed so high above the Condition of the Journeyman, both their Conditions approach much nearer to that of a Planter and Slave in our *American* colonies than might be expected in such a country as *England* ... The Master ... is naturally tempted by his situation to be proud and over-bearing, to consider his people as the Scum of the Earth, whom he has a right to squeeze whenever he can; because they ought to be kept low, and not to rise up in Competition with their Superiors.

Josiah Tucker, *Instructions for Travellers*[1]

Many mechanical arts, indeed, require no capacity; they succeed best under a total suppression of sentiment and reason; and ignorance is the mother of industry as well as of superstition. Reflection and fancy are subject to err; but a habit of moving the hand, or the foot, is independent of either. Manufactures, accordingly, prosper most, where the mind is least consulted, and where the workshop may, without any great effort of imagination, be considered as an engine, the parts of which are men ... If the pretensions to equal justice and freedom should terminate in rendering every class equally servile and mercenary, we make a nation of helots, and have no free citizens.

Adam Ferguson, *An Essay*[2]

The overseer's book of penalties replaces the slave-driver's lash.

Karl Marx, *Capital*[3]

Working and living together in gangs of hundreds on the huge sugar-factories that covered the North Plain, they [the slaves on Saint-Domingue] were closer to a modern proletariat than any group of workers at the time.

C. L. R. James, *The Black Jacobins*[4]

## Introduction

Referring to the repetitive industrial task of shifting pig-iron ingots, Frederick Winslow Taylor famously wrote in 1911: 'This work is so crude and elementary in its nature that the writer firmly believes that it would be possible to train an intelligent gorilla so as to become a more efficient pig-iron handler than any man could be'.[5] Antonio Gramsci believed that Taylor was employing a metaphor here, 'to indicate how far one can go in a certain direction: in any physical work, no matter how mechanical and degraded, there is a minimum of technical skill, that is, a minimum of creative intellectual activity'.[6] But was the 'intelligent gorilla' really only a metaphor? One US agricultural historian noted: 'As early as 1820 an imaginative Louisiana planter imported a cargo of Brazilian monkeys with the hope of training them to pick cotton'.[7] (The experiment failed.)

The conceptualization of the worksite as 'an engine, the parts of which are men', where, according to Adam Ferguson, there is 'a total suppression of sentiment and reason'[8] is usually seen as a result of the first and second Industrial Revolutions in Western Europe and North America – in factories employing 'free' wage labourers. In this chapter, I contend that we need to fundamentally rethink the history of modern labour-management techniques in several ways. We have to step outside the traditional intellectual grid to take into consideration the Global South, non-industrial, and physically-coerced labour.

The colonies and unfree labour represent blindspots in management history; they are almost never part of the story that is told. This is not to deny that, during the last few decades, some very important work has been done in the field of management history and that we now understand many aspects of how employers have dealt with their employees much better than we used to. But, despite these significant achievements, the dominant narrative remains deeply Eurocentric.[9]

Mainstream historiographies usually start by saying that labour management has been around for thousands of years, and that large-scale projects like the construction of the Egyptian pyramids or China's Great Wall would not have been possible without the conscious coordination of labour processes. Modern labour management, however, began in the middle of the eighteenth century, with the birth of factories (Figure 10.1) and their capitalist logic: 'unlike the builders of pyramids', the new managers 'had not only to show absolute results in terms of certain products of their efforts, but to relate them to costs, and sell them competitively'.[10] Modern-age time discipline, technical training, and other innovations were the outcome. During the second half of the

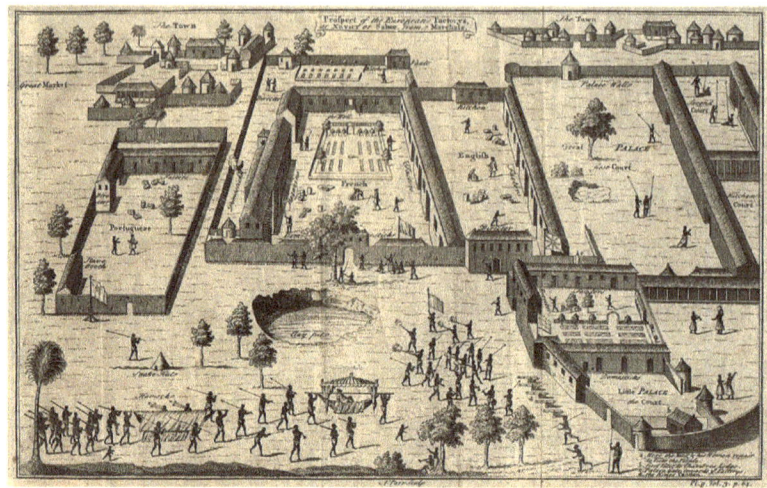

**Figure 10.1** 'Prospect of the European Factorys, at Xavier or Sabee' (European slave factories or compounds maintained by traders from four European nations on the Gulf of Guinea). Engraving by Nathaniel Parr, published in *A New General Collection of Voyages and Travels* by Thomas Astley. London, 1746, vol. 3, p. 64.

nineteenth century, further important changes took place, primarily in the US, resulting in the invention of Scientific Management and such like.

This narrow historiographical perspective broadened in the 1930s when critical criminologists began to pay attention to parallels between prisons and factories.[11] Building on this trend, Michel Foucault and others focused on the rise of disciplinary power in schools, psychiatric institutions, barracks, and factories, claiming that 'the technological mutations of the apparatus of production, the division of labour and the elaboration of the disciplinary techniques sustained an ensemble of very close relations. Each makes the other possible and necessary; each provides a model for the other'.[12] Studies began to explore the homologies between monastic, military, and industrial discipline.[13]

Despite such revisions and extensions, the approach to the history of labour management continued to be based on two hidden assumptions. On the one hand, the underlying model was deeply internalist: the developments in the North Atlantic region were explained through developments in the North Atlantic region; all the big innovations began in Britain, the US, France, or Germany. On the other hand, the emphasis was very much on 'free' wage labour. Few historians paid attention to unfree labour. Even Alfred Chandler, in his classical book of over

600 pages, *The Visible Hand*, devotes fewer than three pages to the slave plantation, arguing that, 'as the first salaried manager in the country, the plantation overseer was an important person in American economic history', though the plantation followed 'a traditional pattern' and 'had little impact on the evolution of the management of modern business enterprise'.[14]

Contrary to the mainstream, I want to suggest that: 1) important innovations were born outside the North Atlantic region (especially in the colonies), in attempts to control *unfree* workers; 2) that some of these innovations date from long before the first Industrial Revolution; and 3) that knowledge about such innovations travelled across all parts of the globe. What I have to say is tentative, though, and will need more research.[15]

## Real subsumption

The management techniques that I will be discussing in this chapter are all about what Marx called 'the real subsumption of labour under capital'. Somewhat simplifying, there are two possibilities. One is that capitalist entrepreneurs incorporate older (pre-capitalist) labour processes into their enterprises without changing the nature of those processes. In this case, technologically speaking, 'the *labour process* goes on as before, with the proviso that it is now *subordinated* to capital'.[16] This so-called *formal* subsumption of labour under capital alters, however, two aspects of the labour process: its endogenous power relations (a new 'relation of supremacy and subordination' is introduced); and the use of labour time: 'labour becomes far more continuous and intensive, and the conditions of labour are employed far more economically, since every effort is made to ensure that no more (or rather even less) *socially necessary* time is consumed in making the product'.[17] The *real* subsumption of labour under capital – the second possibility – begins once the entrepreneur starts to reshape the work process as such, by transforming 'the nature of the labour process and its actual conditions' and by introducing new methods of production, based on 'the direct application of science and technology'.[18]

This transition from formal to real subsumption changes labour relations fundamentally. Under formal subsumption, work remained volatile. There was, as Werner Sombart observed, little cooperative 'restraint, discipline, cogency', since effective coordination was absent and the 'personal lack of discipline of each separate worker' impacted on the collectivity. Production was also interrupted frequently for a number of other reasons: the workers' movement back and forth between agriculture and industry, the seasonal nature of many industrial activities, or stagnant markets.[19] Under real subsumption, the labour process becomes much more continuous, coordinated, and uniform.

There are at least two important aspects of real subsumption that deserve our attention: direct supervision and standardization. The best way to explain these aspects is to travel, first, to seventeenth-century Barbados and, second, to early-nineteenth-century Sydney, Australia.

## Direct supervision: seventeenth-century Barbados

When they started the colonization of the small Caribbean island of Barbados in the 1620s, the planters at first mainly used indentured labourers (servants) but, for economic reasons, they quickly shifted to the employment of African slaves. From the 1650s, unskilled labour was increasingly performed by slaves of African descent; later slaves took over skilled labour as well, and 'by 1690 servants had a monopoly of only the overseer functions, most carpenters, masons, sugar boilers, and bricklayers being black slaves'.[20]

On seventeenth-century Barbados, the optimum size for efficient sugar production was a plantation of about 200 acres, equipped with a hundred slaves.[21] This was quite a large kind of enterprise at the time. The sugar planter was simultaneously a farmer and a manufacturer:

> He had to feed, clothe, house, and supervise his labor force year-round. He needed one or two mills to extract juice from the harvested cane, a boiling house to clarify and evaporate the cane juice into sugar crystals, a curing house for drying the sugar and draining out the molasses, a distillery for converting the molasses into rum, and a storehouse in the nearest port for keeping his barreled sugar until it could be shipped to England. An operation of this size required a capital investment of thousands of pounds.[22]

The whole process of sugar production was both labour-intensive and also required, for biological and ecological reasons, careful planning and supervision. It was under these circumstances that modern labour management, based on the real subsumption of labour under capital, came to be: large numbers of recalcitrant labourers doing monotonous work and, by their very existence, threatening the tiny white European elite. If the planters wanted to survive, intensive supervision of the

**Figure 10.2** 'Nègres au Travail'. Men and women in a field gang at work, guarded by overseers. Source: Alcide Dessalines d'Orbigny, *Voyage pittoresque dans les deux Amériques* (Paris, 1836), facing p. 22, fig. 4. http://www.slaveryimages.org/s/slaveryimages/item/1148.

workforce was of the essence. As Robert Fogel observed, sugar plantations created industrial discipline (see Figure 10.2):

> … partly because sugar production lent itself to a minute division of labor, partly because of the invention of the gang system, which provided a powerful instrument for the supervision and control of labor, and partly because of the extraordinary degree of force that planters were allowed to bring to bear on enslaved black labor.[23]

In principle, there are two broad approaches to supervising workers: by overseeing the effort or overseeing the result. An example of overseeing the result is the so-called task system. Slaves were assigned a daily task, such as working a certain number of square-metres, and if that task had been correctly fulfilled, in the opinion of the overseer, the working day was deemed over. Overseeing results becomes easier the more workers work independently from each other. Conversely, the greater the interdependence of the tasks, the more difficult it becomes for the overseers to judge individual results. In overseeing the *effort*, the overseer ensures that the worker works hard enough. This type of oversight presupposes permanent control, and is easier the simpler the tasks to be fulfilled are. If additional qualifications and skills are necessary, it becomes more difficult for the overseer to estimate the intensity of labour.[24]

Overseers, or others contracted for this work, can punish or reward workers for their efforts. They have three basic means at their disposal: compulsion; material and immaterial rewards; and persuasion.[25] Compulsion includes threats (with or without the application of force), including incarceration, tormenting, mutilation, sale (of slaves), dismissal (of wage workers), or even death. Such negative sanctions may, indeed, lead the workers to work hard, but are not conducive to their working *well*. And negative sanctions encourage resistance and sabotage (which, in turn, are more effective the more complicated and skilled the labour process is). Compulsion is therefore most effective for very simple labour processes that are easy to oversee.[26]

The gang system was almost exclusively used for unskilled routine labour. That the gang system was very efficient has been confirmed by numerous scholars. But the experts disagree on the precise reasons for this efficiency: was it that the close supervision made the slaves less careless and hasty, thus improving the quality of their work? Was it the 'steady and intense rhythm of work' that it achieved? Or was it the effective utilization of slaves with different physical capabilities?[27] From a management perspective, the introduction of effort control was a major innovation. It robbed the individual workers of almost all autonomy and made domination at the worksite virtually absolute. Historically, totalizing control and unfree labour went hand-in-hand.[28]

From Barbados, the method of controlling labour directly through a gang system spread to other parts of the Caribbean and the US South.[29] It transformed work into a machine-like process. Frederick M. Olmstedt, an observer of slave plantations in the US South, wrote in 1861:

> [Slaves] are constantly and steadily driven up to their work, and the stupid, plodding, machine-like manner in which they labor, is painful to witness. This was especially the case with the hoe-gangs. One of them numbered nearly two hundred hands (for the force of two plantations was working together), moving across the field in parallel lines, with a considerable degree of precision. I repeatedly rode through the lines at a canter, with other horsemen, often coming upon them suddenly, without producing the smallest

change or interruption in the dogged action of the labourers, or causing one of them ... to lift an eye from the ground ... [The cruelty of slavery] was emphasized by a tall and powerful Negro who walked to and fro in the rear of the line, frequently cracking his whip, and calling out in the surliest manner, to one and another, 'Shove your hoe, there! Shove your hoe!'[30]

Peter Coclanis seems to be justified in saying that 'agricultural units organized under the gang system more closely resembled factories in the fields, and everything that this nineteenth-century metaphor connoted'.[31]

## Standardization: early-nineteenth-century Sydney

To understand the other key aspect of real subsumption, let us now travel to Sydney. After Britain lost its North American colonies in 1776, it needed a new outlet for its 'surplus' of prisoners. Australia, and in particular New South Wales, became the new 'open-air prison'. In around 1800, the area counted five thousand British residents, about a third of whom were convicts. The working day of the prisoners employed by the public authorities consisted of two parts. In the morning, they performed public labour and received public rations, and in the afternoon they worked on their own account so that they could pay for their housing and food. Discipline was enforced with physical punishment, such as whipping; the maximum number of lashes was five hundred.[32] After several rebellions of the prisoners and destabilizing intra-elite conflict, London sent over a new governor in 1810, Lachlan Macquarie.

As a military man, Macquarie was familiar with formal approaches to work regulation, and, in his attempt to reorganize the colony, he introduced advanced labour management techniques. His main initiatives were:

> ... improving convict supervision so as to tighten the span of supervisor control; reducing negative and increasing positive reward systems to improve convict motivation; rationally matching convict skills with convict employment; transforming work measurement into regular and detailed weekly reports; and in the construction of convict job descriptions.[33]

Macquarie's Regulations for the Police of Sydney (1811) contained the first detailed job descriptions outlining the tasks of individual police officers – the majority of whom were convicts! – and the structure of command. These job descriptions contributed to the systematic bureaucratization of labour processes. In June 1813, Macquarie designed job descriptions for the workers at the Government Stock (keepers of cattle) and 'was still writing and defining job instructions in his final year in 1821, when he wrote a small document of instructions for the Government Dock Yard'.[34]

These experiments in standardization are also remarkable because the mainstream management histories often tell us that the first systematic non-military job descriptions were attempted by Frank and Lilian Gilbreth, a whole century later.[35]

## Circulation of knowledge

Crucial labour-management techniques were thus invented under colonial, unfree circumstances, long before these methods were applied in Europe as well. Perhaps this, in itself, does not necessarily come as a surprise, because experiments with labourers are always easier when those labourers are extremely subjected. And the colonies had, of course, also been laboratories for other experiments:

> The first systematic inventory of population, livestock, crops and landholdings was conducted by Cromwell's adviser William Petty after the conquest of Ireland. Cadastral surveys were instituted as administrative routine by the British in India long before they came to Britain itself, where they threatened the monopoly on information enjoyed by local solicitors. It was in the colonies, too, that identity cards were first designed and issued; fingerprinting was first used in Bengal, to ensure that only certified pensioners were collecting their monthly remuneration, and collecting it only once. If these field trials were successful, the technique could be repackaged and exported back to the metropole.[36]

Several questions thus arise. Did the same techniques (direct supervision of unskilled labour, and standardization of work processes through detailed job descriptions) develop independently in Europe? Were these techniques transferred? Or was there a combination of these two possibilities? I suspect that all three variations are part of the story but, here, I would like to focus on the transfer of managerial techniques across continents, a very much understudied topic.

## The South–North transfer

As almost nothing is known about the South–North transfer of managerial techniques, we must mainly speculate. According to Robin Blackburn, the notion of the 'plant' (the industrial complex) is derived from the older notion of the 'plantation': 'By gathering the workers under one roof, and subordinating them to one discipline, the new industrial employers were able to garner the profits of industrial co-operation and invigilation – as it were adapting the plantation model (which is why people came to speak of steel "plants")'.[37]

It is not entirely certain that Blackburn is right. Chronologically, his hypothesis makes sense, however. 'Plantation' in the sense of a large estate where cotton, tobacco, or other cash crops are grown was first recorded in 1706 in Phillips' *Dictionary*. 'Plant' in the sense of a productive complex was mentioned for the first time in 1789.[38] But not all etymologists agree with Blackburn. Many of them seem to believe that 'plant' is not derived from 'plantation' but that both 'plant' *and* 'plantation' are derived from the verb 'planting', the activity of putting something in a place. The question of whether or not this interpretation is testimony to a Eurocentric bias needs to be investigated.

Similarly, Elizabeth Esch and David Roediger point out that:

> … the words 'overseer', naming the manager responsible for superintending and speeding up the labour of slaves, and 'supervisor', naming the manager performing the same roles in industry, have the same literal meaning. Similarly, the word 'factories' had named the West African staging areas gathering labouring bodies for the slave-trade, and then for the production of cotton, making possible the textile 'factories' of England and New England.[39]

More specific instances of circumstantial evidence come from the fact that the ties between the elites of the colonies and those of the metropoles were strong. Eric Williams, in his seminal *Capitalism and Slavery*, provides detailed evidence of the intimate connections between Caribbean planters and the British bourgeoisie and aristocracy. Williams not only gives numerous examples of absentee landlords living in great luxury in England but also points out that, every year, the planters in the British West Indies were sending back hundreds of children to be educated.[40] It is also likely that members of the West Indian and English elites discussed methods of agricultural management, which were so important in the eighteenth century,[41] and that some of the insights gained in these discussions spilled over into the ideas about factory management that were emerging at the end of that century. In this context, we should also not forget that the first British factories were often built in agricultural areas.

In addition, it was not unusual for enterprises in the South of the US, before the defeat of 1865 and the abolition of slavery, to employ slaves and free wage-earners side-by-side.[42] Transfer of labour-management techniques from unfree to free workers does not seem to be a far-fetched idea under such circumstances. And, more generally, the close-knit networks of US entrepreneurs in the nineteenth century must surely have stimulated the exchange of managerial ideas between slaveholders and managers of free labour.

## The South–South transfer

South–South transfer of managerial knowledge (regarding labour-related matters but also agricultural techniques) took place on a wide scale, both within and between colonial empires. Two mechanisms seem to have been of special importance,[43] starting with the migration of planters and managers. The slave revolution of Saint-Domingue in 1791–1804 triggered an exodus of experts to, *inter alia*, Bengal.[44] In particular, the abolition of slavery and the decline of the sugar plantations in the British West Indies in the 1830s and 1840s set in motion a chain of migratory movements of planters to other parts of the colonial world. The decline of the profitability of large-scale Caribbean agriculture stimulated a transfer to Asia:[45]

> Sometimes they [the planters] stayed in sugar; often they tried to change their luck by changing their product – and switched to coffee. Planters from the West Indies were employed in Natal and Ceylon. Some also went to Malaya, to the sugar and coffee estates of Province Wellesley; while the difficulties of coffee in the 1850s also caused some of the Ceylon planters to go to Malaya. When Fiji opened up in the 1870s, experienced sugar planters from Mauritius and Ceylon were attracted there (though many of the Fiji planters came from Queensland in Australia). When coffee-growing in Ceylon suffered the disastrous disease which ruined thousands of acres, most of the planters turned over to tea. A few joined the booming tea industry of Assam. Finally, at the beginning of the twentieth century, the rapid expansion of rubber-growing in Malaya started … The demand for managers and assistants attracted

hundreds of British, Dutch, French and Australian planters who had worked in the British sugar colonies, or on plantations in Java, or on the plantations of Queensland and the Pacific islands.[46]

Naturally, global circuits like these led to the transcontinental transfer of managerial knowledge. According to historian Patrick Peebles, 'the plantations of Ceylon were modeled directly on the slave plantations of the Caribbean'. Extracts from P. J. Laborie's handbook *Coffee Planter of Saint Domingo* (1798) were published in Ceylon in 1842, 'without even changing the word "Negro"'.[47]

The second important source of knowledge-transfer was that of expert committees travelling back and forth between colonies, studying planting methods, workers' housing, and so on.[48] The history of these committees has yet to be written but the Dutch example reveals that, especially from the nineteenth century, and perhaps earlier, experts were sent to Cuba, Brazil, or Ceylon to study agricultural and labour-management techniques. Sometimes, this movement even resulted in a kind of transcontinental debate. In 1885, for example, the expert Van Delden Laërne published a long report on Brazilian coffee cultures, in which he also discussed the problems of slave labour in these cultures. This provoked Brazilian reactions (especially from émigrés in Paris) and a response by the Dutchman.[49]

What all this suggests is that labour-management techniques should not be studied in geographical isolation but as parts of an ongoing stream of constantly revised, adapted, and extended knowledge systems.[50]

In sum, modern labour management has many roots. There is no doubt that the 'disciplinary revolution' in European monasteries in the fifteenth and sixteenth centuries played a role, as did the 'military revolution' of the seventeenth century. But, in the future, we should also take into account the 'disciplinary revolution' in the colonial world. It is likely that different practices influenced each other.[51]

It seems obvious that slave plantations and other institutions based on coercion have been important sources of inspiration for modern labour management. It was not only eighteenth-century factory discipline that was anticipated in the colonies but also, for example, aspects of Scientific Management. In the 1830s, the former slave John Brown recounted in an interview:

> My old master ... would pick out two or more of the strongest [hands], and excite them to race at hoeing or picking ... He would stand with his watch in his hand, observing their movements, whilst

they hoed or picked ... Whatever [the winner] did, within a given time, would be multiplied by a certain rule, for the day's work, and every man's task would be staked out accordingly.[52]

Contemporaries in the nineteenth century frequently observed the similarities between some industrial production systems and slave plantations. In his *Journal of a Tour in Scotland in 1819*, Robert Southey criticized Robert Owen's New Lanark cotton mills in Scotland and their treatment of the workers as 'human machines':

> Owen in reality deceives himself. He is part-owner and sole Director of a large establishment, differing more in accidents than in essence from a plantation: the persons under him happen to be white, and are at liberty by law to quit his service, but while they remain in it they are as much under his absolute management as so many negro-slaves.[53]

Elsewhere, one planter based in the US South hinted at the factory-like nature of the plantation, writing in 1833 that the 'plantation might be considered as a piece of machinery' whose successful operation required that 'all of its parts should be uniform and exact, and the impelling force regular and steady'.[54]

Against this backdrop, the blind spot of those studying the history of labour management is remarkable. In 1973, Michel Foucault lectured in Rio de Janeiro on 'Truth and Juridical Forms'. In a critical analysis of the three aspects of 'panopticism' (supervision, control, and correction) he emphasized, as he had done in *Discipline and Punish*, the common deep structures of the prison, the factory, the psychiatric hospital, the barracks, and such forth. By way of illustration, he described a factory employing four hundred female workers in the Rhône area in the early 1840s. The women, who slept together in a dormitory:

> ... had to get up every morning at 5 o'clock; at 5:50 they had to have finished washing and dressing, made their bed, and had their coffee; at 6 the compulsory work began, lasting until 8:15 in the evening, with a one-hour break for lunch; at 8:15, dinner and group prayer; retirement to the dormitories was at 9 o'clock on the hour ... The residents received no wages but, rather, a payment, a lump sum set at 40–80 francs per year, which was given to them only upon leaving.[55]

The strong similarities between this industrial setting and the earlier coerced labour forms in the colonies are striking. Erving Goffman was justified when, before Foucault, he observed that, in some total institutions, 'a kind of slavery' existed.[56] But neither Foucault nor Goffman thought of drawing a parallel with plantations – which is especially remarkable in the case of Foucault, since he was lecturing in the very Latin American country that had been the last to abolish slavery, in 1888. Such a huge blindspot can remain undetected for a long time. But once we have stepped outside the grid, there is no way back.

## Notes

1. Tucker, *Instructions for Travellers*, 38.
2. Ferguson, *An Essay on the History of Civil Society*, 280, 285.
3. Marx, *Capital*, I, 550.
4. James, *The Black Jacobins*, 66.
5. Taylor, *Principles of Scientific Management*, 40.
6. Gramsci, *Prison Notebooks*, II, 200 (Notebook 4, § 49).
7. Street, 'Mechanizing the cotton harvest', 13.
8. Ferguson, *An Essay on the History of Civil Society*, 280.
9. See, for example, Wren's influential book *The History of Management Thought*.
10. Pollard, *Genesis of Modern Management*, 6–7.
11. Pathbreaking was Rusche & Kirchheimer, *Punishment and Social Structure*.
12. Foucault, *Discipline and Punish*, 221.
13. For example, Melossi & Pavarini, *Prison and the Factory*, or Treiber & Steinert, *Fabrikation des zuverlässigen Menschen*.
14. Chandler, *Visible Hand*, 65–6.
15. Support for my contention comes from Cooke, 'Denial of slavery', a very stimulating essay focusing on a part of the Global North (the United States).
16. Marx, *Capital*, I, 1026.
17. Marx, *Capital*, I, 1026–7.
18. Marx, *Capital*, I, 1034–5.
19. Sombart, *Der moderne Kapitalismus*, 830–2.
20. Beckles & Downes, 'Economics of transition', 227.
21. Dunn, *Sugar and Slaves*, 96.
22. Dunn, *Sugar and Slaves*, 189–90.
23. Fogel, *Without Consent or Contract*, 26.
24. Burawoy & Wright, 'Coercion and consent', 81–2.
25. Tilly & Tilly, *Work Under Capitalism*, 74.
26. Fenoaltea, 'Slavery and supervision', 639–40. Severe physical punishments can, in addition, have the economic disadvantage that workers become temporarily or permanently unable to work.
27. Gray, *History of Agriculture*, I, 556; Fogel & Engerman, *Time on the Cross*, I, 204 (including quote); Toman, 'Gang system'. Further reflections in Morgan, 'Task and gang systems'.
28. Although there was probably a *tendency* toward total domination and control in unfree labour, there likely always remained a marginal manoeuvring space for coerced labourers.
29. For the trajectory of the North American 'plantation revolution', see Berlin, *Generations of Captivity*, ch. 2.
30. Olmstedt, *Cotton Kingdom*, 452. Gradually, many slave plantations in several parts of the Americas made the uniform slave gang the backbone of their agricultural labour process. In the nineteenth century, many plantations in the US used three kinds of work gangs, of which the so-called 'great gang' was the most important. 'It was under the head driver. Composed of the ablest men and women, it sometimes numbered as many as a hundred … The Negroes worked in one or more parallel lines or rows. The head driver, his assistant, and perhaps a "bookkeeper" visited each row and saw that the work was done well. An animating folk song,

started by one of the Negroes, was sung by the gang, and was encouraged as a stimulus to labor and a relief to its monotony. Such a song, sometimes composed by the African, was sung as a solo, the gang joining in the chorus.' Pitman, 'Organization of slave labor', 599–600.

31  Coclanis, 'How the Low Country was taken to task', 61.
32  Macintyre, *Concise History of Australia*, 35 and 43.
33  Robbins, 'Governor Macquarie's job descriptions', 5.
34  Robbins, 'Governor Macquarie's job descriptions', 7 (quote), 10, and 13 (quote).
35  See, for example, Gilbreth, *Psychology of Management*.
36  Rottenburg, 'Social and public experiments', 434.
37  Blackburn, *Making of New World Slavery*, 565. Compare Michael Craton's remark: 'A hitherto unnoticed transition – awaiting a full etymological investigation – was the way in which the transference described in this paper [the rise of the modern slave-based plantation] were accompanied by the narrowing down of the very word "plantation" in the English Language – from being simply a synonym for overseas colonisation of all types, coined in Ireland under the Tudors, to meaning only that extremely profitable, and therefore preferred, type of colonial exploitation here defined and described as the classic plantation model.' Craton, *Empire, Enslavement and Freedom*, 30–1.
38  *Barnhart Dictionary of Etymology*, 802.
39  Esch & Roediger, 'One symptom of originality', 9.
40  Williams, *Capitalism and Slavery*, ch. 4.
41  'Everybody in eighteenth-century England was interested in farming. Even the distinctly urban minority was acquainted with farms, fields, and trees, and since farming became more profitable as the century progressed, interest in it grew greater.' Fussell, 'Farming writers', 1.
42  See, for example, Starobin, *Industrial Slavery*, or Whitman, 'Industrial slavery'.
43  Naturally, there have been other mechanisms than the ones discussed here. Jacobs, *Merchant in Asia*, 48, mentions the case of the son of a sugar planter from Guadeloupe who, during the late-eighteenth century, came as a military man to Ceylon and was requested by the Dutch governor to found sugar plantations on the island.
44  See, for example, Darrac & van Schendel, *Global Blue*.
45  Kiernan, *Lords of Human Kind*, 79.
46  Tinker, *New System of Slavery*, 177.
47  Peebles, *Plantation Tamils of Ceylon*, 55.
48  For an interesting case study, see, for example, Lobdell, '"Repression is not a policy"'.
49  An English version of the report was published as van Delden Laërne, *Brazil and Java*. Reactions in *Revue commerciale, financière et maritime* [Rio de Janeiro] 73 (21 June–5 July 1885); *La Liberté* [Paris] 7 July 1885; and *Le Brésil* [Paris] 94 (23 July 1885). Van Delden Laërne responded in his 'La culture du café au Brésil'.
50  The *North–South diffusion* is probably documented best. In numerous cases in both the past and the present, engineers and skilled workers were transferred to colonial industries. The Bengal jute industry, for example, or other textile industries in the Global South made extensive use of such experts. This, of course, makes a lot of sense. As Nathan Rosenberg correctly observed: 'Where the transfer of technology involved places geographically distant from one another, the reliance upon the migration of trained personnel (at least temporarily) was very strong.' Rosenberg, *Perspectives on Technology*, 154.
51  According to Blackburn, *Making of New World Slavery*, 335, labour management on plantations echoed 'not only shipboard life but also the related revolution in seventeenth-century military training and tactics associated with Maurits of Nassau'.
52  Brown, *Slave Life in Georgia*, 145, 160. Compare also some observations in Aufhauser, 'Slavery and scientific management'.
53  Southey, *Journal*, 263–4. In this context, the attempts of a Mississippi planter to transplant Owen's practices to a slave plantation become understandable. See Hayek et al., 'Ending the denial of slavery'.
54  NN, 'On the management of slaves', 286; quoted in Smith, 'Time, slavery and plantation capitalism', 151.
55  Foucault, 'Truth and juridical forms', 73–4.
56  Goffman, 'Characteristics of total institutions', 10.

# 11
# The abolition of the slave trade and slavery: intended and unintended consequences

## The Act for the Abolition of the Slave Trade

Operating with slave labour, the first Atlantic plantation complex, built up from the sixteenth century, began to disintegrate in the eighteenth century.[1] Several factors contributed to its collapse. In 1738, for economic reasons, the Dutch West Indies Company decided not to take any more slaves to Suriname.[2] Sierra Leone was founded in 1787, providing a sanctuary for free blacks from England and North America, later joined by Caribbean Maroons and other 'troublemakers' in the American slave societies. In 1791, a great slave rebellion broke out in Saint-Domingue, which horrified slaveholders and inspired many slaves worldwide.[3] And, in 1803, Denmark became the first European nation to outlaw the slave trade.[4]

Soon afterward, the British Act for the Abolition of the Slave Trade received Royal Assent on 25 March 1807. It was an exceptionally significant event. From 1 May 1807 onward, the Act prohibited all British citizens from participating in the purchase, sale, or transfer of African slaves – with the exception of ships that had left Britain before that date and delivered slaves in the West Indies up to 1 March 1808.[5] What the precise motivations were for this Act remains the subject of passionate controversy,[6] but it definitely made the whole of the Atlantic slave trade illegal for all British subjects, and, in that sense, it represents a genuine milestone in the international history of human rights.

The Act and its consequences deserve critical scientific attention from scholars. After all, it represented the first significant attempt by a Great Power to exert *global* influence over the development of human rights, and, relatedly, labour conditions worldwide. How that happened, and the consequences it had for many millions of working people on different continents, is exceptionally relevant both for our understanding of global labour relations and in view of later attempts by the ILO as well as allied institutions to promote labour standards across the world.

To enforce abolition, more and more state interventions proved necessary, for which the juridical basis was often very unclear or nonexistent. Those interventions, moreover, took place in circumstances about which there was, in truth, a lack of reliable and timely information, often leading them to fail or to produce the opposite effect to that intended. Not infrequently, the stubborn promotion of the humanitarian policy ran into conflict with other Great Power interests at stake. In turn, it meant that the lofty principles proclaimed by legislators were regularly overruled by military, political, and economic interests – with the result that what was actually done differed significantly from what was officially claimed. It follows that detailed knowledge of international political developments, international law, and changing commercial circumstances is also indispensable to understanding changes in the world of work after the abolition of the slave trade. Historians confront great analytical challenges in that respect.

It is widely accepted that the policies of the Great Powers affected the internal relations of other countries. Yet, rarely have historians reflected systematically on the reality that the politics of the Great Powers could also strongly and directly influence *labour relations* in different parts of the world. Among labour historians, this insight surprisingly occurs much less often than one might expect, in a 'globalizing' world. Historical research about the British Act and its consequences has, in fact, not yet been truly global in scope. First, until recently, most scholars focused primarily on developments in the (North) Atlantic region, considering the Atlantic 'as a "world" unto itself'.[7] What happened in the Southern part of the Atlantic region, in East Africa, the Middle East, and South and Southeast Asia was often not included in their portrayals.[8] Second, many publications on this topic focus on only one region, without paying serious attention to interregional and transcontinental entanglements.

The Act for the Abolition of the Slave Trade was the crowning moment of a 20-year campaign by the abolitionists, who formed what may well have been the first international 'social movement'. The Committee for the Abolition of the Slave Trade, founded in 1787, 'created the characteristic forms of the modern pressure group, public meetings, petitions and reports in the growing newspaper press'.[9] Already in the first months after its foundation, the Committee decided that, in its campaigning in the years to come, it would not target *slave labour*, as such, but only the *slave trade*. Later, Thomas Clarkson, one of the co-founders of the Committee, summarized clearly the arguments behind this decision. Two considerations, he said, were of overriding importance. First, it was assumed that, after the abolition of the slave trade, slaves' living standards would improve:

> For, the planters and others being unable to procure more slaves from the coast of Africa, it would follow directly, whenever this great event should take place, that they must treat those better, whom they might then have. They must render marriage honourable among them. They must establish the union of one man with one wife. They must give the pregnant woman more indulgencies. They must pay more attention to the rearing of their offspring. They must work and punish the adults with less rigour.[10]

Second:

> … [the committee] would not incur the objection that they were meddling with the property of the planters, and letting loose an irritated race of beings, who, in consequence of all the vices and infirmities, which a state of slavery entails upon those who undergo it, were unfit for their freedom. By asking the government of the country to do this, and this only, they were asking for that, which it had an indisputable right to do; namely, to regulate or abolish any of its branches of commerce; whereas it was doubtful, whether it could interfere with the management of the internal affairs of the colonies, or whether this was not wholly the province of the legislatures established there.[11]

From the outset, a step-by-step approach was envisaged by the abolitionists. While the campaign was directed, in the first instance, against the slave trade, its ultimate goal was to be the abolition of slave labour as such.

## The campaign

From the outset, British politicians realized that, if the British state were the only one to outlaw the slave trade, it would have little effect. The other European slave-trading nations would simply take over the British share of the trade, meaning that, ultimately, Britain would merely be helping its competitors economically, to its own disadvantage. Therefore, it was essential to convince France, Spain, Portugal, the Netherlands, and other major slave-trading nations to cease their trading as well. The negotiations to achieve this objective were protracted, featuring complex trade-offs. Tactics such as offering enticements were attempted, for instance in 1814, by offering France a West Indian Island or a sum of money in exchange for immediate abolition, or offering Spain large subsidies, provided that it agreed to restrict its slave trade to the area South of the equator and abolish the trade completely within five years.[12]

No significant decline in the slave trade occurred in the Atlantic region after 1807–8, and that is putting it mildly. Admittedly, the volume of the trade was temporarily reduced upon the impact of the Napoleonic Wars (1803–15) but, afterward, it revived. During the period 1801–10, an estimated 683,000 slaves were transported across the Atlantic Ocean; in the period 1811–20, the number decreased to 599,600; but, between 1821 and 1830, it increased again to 694,400.[13] At the same time, all sorts of reports reached Britain suggesting that the treatment of slaves in the Americas was getting worse. In the 1820s, veteran abolitionists published critical surveys intended to prove that slave mortality was extremely high, that slave families were living under very difficult conditions, and that the Christian faith itself was being damaged. Particularly in the West Indies, the exploitation of the remaining slaves appeared to be alarming. The price of cane sugar and coffee decreased from the mid-1820s, which led the planters to endeavour to maintain their profit margins by raising total output. As a result, the slaves' quality of life became even worse.[14]

Despite its initial difficulties, the campaign against slavery continued rigorously in the years that followed and, gradually, gained momentum. In 1839, Pope Gregory XVI published his apostolic letter *In Supremo*, in which he declared the slave trade 'in Negroes and all other men' from that point onward to be sinful, although slaves who had already been sold or who were born in the New World should not be released, provided that they were treated mercifully.[15] Slowly but surely, more and more countries joined the British campaign.

The campaign against the slave trade eventually proved largely successful, especially in the northern half of the Atlantic Ocean. During the period 1841–50, the number of slaves traded across the Atlantic amounted to 435,300, but, by 1851–60, the figure had dwindled to 179,100; and between 1861 and 1867, it was reduced even further, to 52,600.[16] That success obviously had repercussions, both in the Americas and in Africa.

In the Americas, the declining transatlantic supply of new slaves meant that slaveholders were forced to find alternative sources of labour, which, incidentally, were not always mutually exclusive. First, the slaveholders could improve the quality of their slaves' lives, meaning that they brought up (more) children, lived longer – and could be exploited for longer. Indeed, just as the British abolitionists had hoped, the evidence suggests that, in many cases, slaves were treated better. In many regions where slave labour was common, the native slave populations began to experience endogenous growth (though not in the two most important slave societies, Brazil and Cuba).[17] An unanticipated aspect of this change was that, in some cases, deliberate slave 'breeding' was probably practised, especially in the American border-states. Slave breeding, popularized in novels, is difficult for the historian to prove, especially in the more distant past, but there are indications that such a practice, including in 'human stud houses', really did occur.[18]

Second, it was still permitted for slaves to be bought and sold within nations. When the cross-border slave trade declined, the domestic slave trade within the Americas seems to have grown. In Cuba, the US, and Brazil, slaves were transferred from declining to growing branches of industry. In the US, a significant slave trade between the Lower and the Upper South developed. The more that settlers moved to the South West to grow cotton and sugar, the more the flow of slaves increased. A comparable tendency can be observed in the history of Cuba and Brazil.[19] As regards the inter-provincial slave trade in Brazil, Robert Conrad states that this 'maintained many of the practical and brutal characteristics of the African trade'.[20] Third, workers from other parts of the world, ranging from 'free' Europeans to Asian 'coolies', could be imported. I will say more about this variant later.

In Africa, there were several (mostly unexpected) consequences of the decline in the slave trade. First, in reality, 'the end of the slave trade ... did not *cause* the rise of "legitimate trade". This happened simultaneously and independently; and the slave trade within Africa continued to flourish long after the export trade had ended'.[21] In some cases, the transition to cash-crop production (such as palm oil, peanuts, or rubber) provided an independent income for people of slave origin, but, in other cases, slaves who could no longer be sold to European traders were used instead to produce the cash crops.[22] In Cameroon, for example, the internal demand for slaves actually increased because the production of palm oil and palm seeds was extraordinarily labour-intensive.[23] Similar situations developed in many other parts of West Africa.[24] At the Bight of Biafra, there is evidence that the trade in slaves increased right up to the

1830s, corresponding to the growth of the palm-oil business. During the last decades of the nineteenth century, the growing European demand for ivory was accompanied in parts of Southern Africa by 'an increase in the slave trade both for hunters and soldiers and human porterage'.[25] As late as 1900, at least a million and perhaps even as many as 2.5 million slaves lived in the Sokoto Caliphate, in what is now Northern Nigeria. This figure compares with approximately 4 million slaves in the US in 1860.[26]

Second, although the anti-slavery campaign did reduce the transatlantic slave trade further – its total volume during the nineteenth century is estimated at about 42 per cent of the trade in the eighteenth century – the trade in slaves within Africa itself, and from Africa to Europe and Asia, not only remained intact but increased, albeit in different geographic settings.[27] On the African west coast, the locations of the slave export shifted. For instance, from Senegambia up to and including the Bight of Benin and Biafra, slave exports declined but continued to flourish in the Congo and the Angolan regions, while Mozambique became even more important as a source of slave exports. Typically, even in the colony of Sierra Leone – Britain's most important African bastion in the fight against slave trading – the coastal slave traffic carried on as before because the demand for slaves from inland areas continued and even grew.[28]

The slave trade in the Southern Hemisphere remained fairly intact for quite some time, while new demand for slaves emerged in Europe and Asia. In the Ottoman Empire, for example, the demand for African slaves increased during the nineteenth century, in part because the Russian occupation of Georgia and the Caucasus caused stagnation in the transport of slaves from those areas, and because the opening of the Suez Canal made transportation from Africa much easier.[29] Parallel to these geographic shifts, the centre of gravity of the slave trade also changed location. Zanzibar remained a hub until the twentieth century, while, in the East African kingdom of Buganda, for example, 'the slave trade reached its height from the late 1870s onwards'.[30]

In addition to the transatlantic routes, there were three other great trading routes, the trans-Saharan trade, the Indian Ocean trade, and the trade from Ethiopia across the Red Sea (Table 11.1).

Third, it seems that, especially in the Western part of Africa, slaves became also objects of 'conspicuous consumption'. Especially after 1850, rulers in Yorubaland, the Congo, and elsewhere expressed their political authority by accumulating slaves as prestige objects.[31] These kinds of 'luxury slaves' were sometimes sacrificed at funerals – it had been an old tradition but, previously, there had been fewer victims of it. The number,

**Table 11.1** Slave exports from Africa, 1400–1900.

|  | 1400–1900 | 1800–1900 |
|---|---|---|
| Transatlantic | 10,308,213 (65.8 %) | 3,466,000 (61.9 %) |
| Trans-Saharan | 3,124,435 (19.9 %) | 1,200,000 (21.4 %) |
| Red Sea | 1,305,404 (8.3 %) | 492,000 (8.8 %) |
| Indian Ocean | 939,504 (6.0 %) | 442,000 (7.9 %) |
| **Total** | 15,677,556 (100 %) | 5,600,000 (100 %) |

Sources: for 1400–1900: Nunn, 'Long-term effects', Table II; for 1800–1900: Lovejoy, *Transformations in Slavery*, Table 7.1.

sex, and age of slaves killed at funerals depended on the wealth, influence, and wishes of their masters, their relations, and their social expectations.[32] Such ritual killings had the social effect of disciplining the other slaves by fear, particularly those engaged in plantation labour and similar work. As a result of diminishing exports, the number of slaves available within Africa had increased. The sheer number of them was actually a threat to their masters at the time, especially after several slave rebellions occurred in the Futa Jalon, the Niger Delta, and among the Yoruba.[33] King Kwaku Dua I (1833–67) explicitly justified the sacrifice of slaves to a missionary: 'If I were to abolish human sacrifices, I should deprive myself of one of the most effectual means of keeping the people in subjection'.[34]

The European abolitionists at that time were unaware of the full extent of all these effects. Nevertheless, it was certainly obvious to them that the measures taken so far were insufficient to fully achieve their aim. Therefore, feeling obliged to promote additional strategies, they developed two further approaches. One response was to expand the campaign to include East Africa and the Indian Ocean. Already since the capture of Mauritius in 1810, the British had attempted to curb the slave trade in the region but, for a long time, they had little success. The most important slave trade centres were the port city of Kilwa and the island of Zanzibar, both belonging to the Empire of Seyyid Said, the Imam of Muscat. The number of slaves exported from the region grew from roughly 6,500 in 1834 to between 13,000 and 15,000 in the 1840s.[35] Several agreements with Seyyid Said remained ineffective, but 1845 seemed to mark a turning point, when the sultan agreed to prohibit the slave trade within his empire, permitting the British Navy to seize and condemn any slavers found in any seas as if they were British ships. Yet again, however, that agreement existed mainly on paper.

The Arab slave trade encountered serious problems only when Britain consolidated its rule in the Sudan and East Africa at the end of the nineteenth century. In 1873, the Sultan of Zanzibar was forced to abolish his entire domestic coastal slave trade immediately; to close down all public slave markets; and to render all transit slave trade impossible. Similar treaties were concluded with Egypt in 1877, the Ottoman Empire in 1880, and Persia in 1882.[36] But even then, the campaign was not over because the measures taken did not show a lasting effect. The Anglo–Egyptian Convention of 1877, for instance, seemed to signal a significant change because the Khedive, Ismail Pasha, was forced to appoint a British subject, Charles Gordon, as Governor-General of the Sudan; and Gordon immediately began to suppress the slave trade. In 1879 Gordon's troops defeated an alliance of slave traders, after which the trade reduced for a while. But just a few years later, the trade began to recover because the local elite had no interest in total abolition.[37] The success of the campaign against slavery became clearly visible only at the beginning of the twentieth century.

When, in 1909, serious steps were taken at last in Zanzibar to put a stop to the slave trade as a whole, the local British consul, General Basil Cave, retrospected:

> Very little advance could be made towards closing the sources from which raw slaves were supplied so long as Mohammedan influence was still paramount on the Coast, and the slave-dealers could count on the active co-operation of the Arab authorities, and it was not until the 'partition of Africa' had taken definite shape that a death-blow could be struck at this inhuman traffic. The first step in this direction was the incorporation of the Imperial British East Africa Company in 1888, which was quickly followed by the transfer of a large portion of the Zanzibar mainland dominions to the German Government, by the establishment of a British Protectorate in Uganda, and by the extension of European administration throughout the central regions of the African Continent. With these forces at work the Slave Trade was doomed, and in a very few years it had altogether ceased to exist.[38]

A second response in the anti-slavery campaign was to move the stage of the struggle from the Atlantic Ocean to mainland Africa. If they could not succeed in wiping out the slave trade by taking action on the high seas, then they would have to go ashore and attempt to intervene directly – preferably, in a peaceful manner (with political persuasion and treaties), but if necessary by brute force. Local rulers were put under severe pressure; they were forced to sign treaties and accept heavy sanctions if they broke the agreements.

In the 1840s, more and more agreements were made with local rulers that included sanctions in addition to material incentives. For instance, the Treaty with the Kings and Chiefs of Bonny, signed in 1844, stated that the leaders of Bonny (on the Bight of Biafra) agreed that Great Britain could stamp out the slave trade by force and carry out 'severe acts of displeasure' against them and their subjects if evidence was found that the export of slaves had not stopped completely and the slave pens had not been burnt.[39] Acting on these kinds of unequal treaties, the British did, indeed, use force, as happened, for example, in 1840, when Commander Denman signed an agreement with the Chiefs of the River Gallinas and destroyed the property of the Spanish slave merchant there, rescuing and liberating the human chattels.[40]

In the second half of the nineteenth century, a welter of treaties and Christian missions brought more and more African lands under direct British control. It was not so much that the work of these missions was a direct, deliberate instrument for colonialization as such,[41] but, rather, that, in many regions, the missionaries gained influence among the native populations, which could then easily turn into political control by European officials and magistrates.[42] Concurrently, however, the British concluded that, in the battle against the slave trade, they could not rely simply on treaties with the chiefs because the latter kept breaking the agreements – which meant that enforcement had to be pursued with policing expeditions.

In the course of several military campaigns, the British became convinced that the straightforward subjection of the local population would be a more effective method. Such a conclusion was also encouraged by the turbulent economic growth in Britain itself, coupled with constantly increasing demand for African raw materials (palm oil, minerals, foodstuffs, tobacco, and such like). There was a growing desire among British enterprises to control the production of raw materials locally, and that meant penetrating, subordinating, and exploiting the African hinterlands more and more.[43]

In summary, *coercion* (the enforcement of anti-slavery treaties), *commitment* (missionary work), and *compensation* (legitimate trade) all helped to advance the colonial subjection of Africa, resulting in a decline in the slave trade.

## The abolition of slavery

The dwindling of the slave trade did not, however, mean that slave labour necessarily reduced everywhere; in reality, the effects of the campaign remained very unevenly distributed. From the 1820s, a modernized plantation complex with 'second slavery' developed in some parts of the New World, especially in Cuba and the American South.[44] This development, as well as other influences retarding the campaign, meant that this trade lasted much longer than the abolitionists had initially envisaged. Many of them soon became convinced that the main tactics agreed upon in 1787 had not worked well enough. In their opinion, it was now necessary to go a step further and work on the gradual abolition of slavery *as such*.[45]

From 1823 onward, they set a new campaign in motion that appeared to be widely supported by the British public. Various factors contributed to the passage of an Act for the Abolition of Slavery in 1833; and, from 1 August 1834 onward, slave labour was prohibited in the West Indies, Cape of Good Hope, and Mauritius. Another factor working in this direction was that West Indian agriculture had slumped; sugar could be obtained easily from other parts of the world; and the Jamaican slave revolt of Christmas 1831 had made a great impression on the public. The attempt to abolish slavery *as such* marked the beginning of a new phase in the struggle. People no longer directed their efforts towards the symptoms but at the disease itself.

The campaign rapidly developed its own dynamics. It spread to other parts of the British Empire and it gained support from abolitionists in other countries, which became evident, for example, during the World Anti-Slavery Convention (London 1840), in which a few American and French abolitionists also took part.[46] The Act of 1833 excluded the territories of the East India Company from its scope, but, in 1843, the Council of India and the Governor-General of India also prohibited slavery.

The success of British abolitionism owed much to the broad social base, the continuity, and the persistence of the movement from 1787 until the 1840s and even later. Other colonial powers in Europe simply did not enjoy such a long-lasting social movement. It is true that, in France, for example, slavery was abolished for a second time in 1848 (the first attempt was in 1793–4) but the French movement evolved with serious interruptions from the founding of the Société des Amis des Noirs in 1788 until the second French slave emancipation in 1848. For nearly two-thirds of this epoch of 60 years, there was no abolitionist movement in France. And, in most other European countries, the movement remained rather weak.[47] Nevertheless, the second half of the nineteenth century did witness a series of legislative acts to abolish slavery, ranging from the Dutch colonies (1863) and the US (1865), to Cuba (1886) and

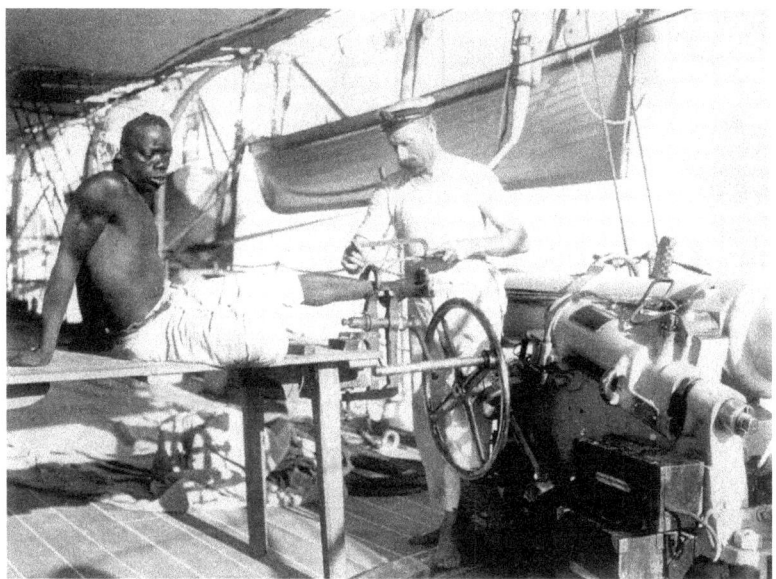

**Figure 11.1** Sailor removing the manacle from a newly freed slave. The African featured in the image and five others escaped in a canoe from a slave-trading village on the coast on hearing that a Royal Navy ship was in the area. In his report dated 15 October 1907, Commander Litchfield of *HMS Sphinx* wrote that the ship received 'six fugitives' on a cruise off the Batineh Coast, Oman between 10 and 14 October. One of the fugitives had been manacled for three years and had escaped with his leg irons still on. Image published by courtesy of the National Museum of the Royal Navy, Portsmouth, UK.

Madagascar (1897). It was only well into the twentieth century that slavery was abolished almost everywhere in the world – at least legally but not necessarily in practice (Figure 11.1).

In some countries, abolition did not occur so abruptly as in the British, French, or Dutch colonies. In Brazil, where the slave emancipations in the British, Portuguese, and French empires, the Russian abolition of serfdom in 1861, and the American Civil War had exerted a background influence on attitudes, the emancipation process was much more protracted. After the importation of slaves had been halted in 1851, the power of the slaveholders was reduced further; in 1865, the Emperor prohibited whipping and all cruel punishment; in 1869, a law was enacted that prohibited the public auctioning of slaves and the separation of married couples, as well as the separation of their children under the age of fifteen; and, in 1871, the Rio Branco Law stipulated that, with immediate effect, the children of women slaves 'shall be considered free'.[48] Therewith the end of slavery in Brazil was in sight, at least in the longer term. Finally, in 1888, slavery was outlawed completely.[49]

When slavery was formally abolished throughout much of the British Empire on 1 August 1834, the slaveholders received cash compensation, and all slaves aged six years and older were redesignated as 'apprentices' who would have to work for their former owners for several further years. The planters were obliged to provide their workers with 'Food, Clothing, Lodging, Medicine, Medical Attendance and [other such] Maintenance and Allowances'.[50] In exchange, the apprentices were compelled to perform 'forty-five Hours *per* Week' of unpaid labour for their former owners. This system was adopted by several other countries, the last one being Cuba, in 1886. The official intention was to prevent any abrupt, disorderly change to new socioeconomic relations:

> Theoretically, apprenticeship offered important strategic advantages to the European establishment. It afforded missionaries additional time to mould the thinking of the apprentices, to encourage habits of industry, to build churches, and to establish social patterns that would induce freedmen to remain in settled estate villages when the system ended. It allowed time for the orderly preparation of a legal system to supersede discarded slave codes. It provided sufficient time for the establishment of colonial banking institutions that could meet the needs of a free plantation economy, and it offered the Treasury an opportunity to rectify serious monetary problems and supply the colonists with enough coinage to pay the wages of free workers. Moreover, apprenticeship gave the planters a brief period before the onset of full freedom to introduce new equipment, to experiment with new techniques, and to revise methods of labour movement.[51]

In practice, apprenticeship meant mainly that the slaves subsidized their own emancipation, as some abolitionists recognized already early on.[52] After the abolition of slavery – and, where applicable, the end of apprenticeship – many slaves wanted to leave the sites (plantations, mines, etc.) where they had previously worked; they sought alternative employment and often preferred to become peasant proprietors.[53] Although the demand for plantation products usually continued, a crisis situation could nevertheless emerge, with three possible outcomes: the plantations collapsed because the slaves departed without alternative labour being available; more and more arable land was then offered for sale, and a new peasantry settled on it; the plantations reorganized the production process, introduced new technology, and in this way succeeded in reducing their labour requirements; or the plantations found a way to attract labour at a lower cost than in a completely 'free' labour market.[54]

Given these three possible outcomes, it was obvious that the planters and the government authorities that typically supported them sought to *restrict* alternative employment opportunities for former slaves as much as possible. Whether they succeeded depended greatly on the extent to which former slaves were able to acquire unused agricultural land. In some parts of the Caribbean (such as Jamaica, Trinidad, and British Guiana), this was feasible. But, elsewhere, for example in the small, densely populated islands of Barbados, Antigua, or St. Kitts, insufficient free land was available and the former slaves were forced either to emigrate or continue working on the plantations.[55] Indeed, in some instances – such as in the case of the French islands Martinique and Guadeloupe after 1848 – the planters and authorities exercised financial pressure:

> The ex-slaves incurred expenses unknown to the slave. Food, medical bills, clothing, rents – all wholly or partly supplied by the plantation before. The plantocracy and the administration increased these expenses even more in the attempt to create an artificial need for money wages so that the blacks would be forced to work on the plantations. Subsistence farming alone, the blacks quickly realized, could not meet these expenses.[56]

## Alternative labour relations

In the South of the US, no alternative employment opportunities were created for slaves after 1865, as a deliberate policy. During the Civil War, the Northern soldiers had spread the idea that the lands owned by those who had fought against the North would be confiscated and distributed among former slaves. As Zeichner explains, '[f]reedmen expecting land hesitated to return to the plantation system of farming, either on a wage basis or on shares, and as a result, many refused to make contracts for the resumption of activities on the plantations'.[57] Towards 1867, it became very clear to the ex-slaves that nothing would come of the promises and that they would not receive their 'forty acres and a mule'. Yet there was no point in migrating to the North either, because an alternative demand for the labour of the ex-slaves was not forthcoming there – among other reasons, because of the massive inflow of unskilled European workers during the last half of the nineteenth century.[58] The planters, for their part, faced an intractable problem. Many of them would have preferred to recruit Asian coolies or European immigrants rather than ex-slaves, but that turned out to be difficult. At the same time, partly because of the lack of development of bank capital in the American South, they had rather little cash on hand.[59]

And so, just as in parts of the British West Indies,[60] a system of share-cropping was introduced that, in many respects, continued the fundamental social relations existing before the Civil War. 'With misgivings and distaste, landowners began about 1867 to give freedmen a share of the crop made by them in lieu of wages'.[61] Share-cropping was thus a new way to bind the former slaves to the planters:

> The cropper … is hired just before the spring plowing season to grow a crop of cotton or tobacco on a number of acres corresponding to the size of his family. That is, the more prospective pickers there are in the family, the larger the number of acres. The owner gives close supervision to everything that is done, and he wants nothing grown except what he can sell. If the tenant takes time to keep a garden he does so at the neglect of his major interest, and furthermore, he deprives the owner of the privilege of selling him additional groceries. At the end of the season the whole crop is taken by the landlord, who assesses its value, deducts what the cropper owes from his share, and pays for the remainder, if any. The shares in general are in thirds, one for labor, another for land, and the last for draft animals, implements, seed, fertilizer, and other farming necessities.[62]

In part, however, the abolition of the slave trade and slave labour only occurred formally but not in reality; traders and employers sought ways to evade the new laws. In so doing, they were not infrequently offered a helping hand from the government authorities, who tolerated a 'broad' interpretation of anti-slavery legislation and sometimes provided for it. One method commonly used was that of the 'pseudo-contract', signed by the worker under duress. In such a contract, the worker agreed to commit himself 'voluntarily' to working for an employer for a limited or indefinite time, under conditions where there was no other realistic option.[63] This construction had already been tried early on by the French; they referred to de facto slaves as *engagés à temps*; officially, these workers signed a contract out of their own free will for fourteen years (!), but, in practice, their situation was little different from ordinary slavery.[64]

The British journalist Henry Nevinson described how the system worked, after a voyage through the Portuguese colony of Angola in 1905. He discovered that the slave trade was still secretly going on in this region, decades after it had officially been abolished. Deep in the hinterlands of Southern Africa, slaves were caught and forced to walk hundreds of miles to the coast until they arrived at Katumbella; there, 'the slaves were rested, sorted out, dressed, and then taken on over the fifteen miles to Benguela, usually disguised as ordinary carriers'. On Benguela's main street:

> ... there is a government office where the official representative of the 'Central Committee of Labor and Emigration for the Islands' (having its headquarters in Lisbon) sits in state, and under due forms of law receives the natives, who enter one door as slaves and go out of another as *serviçaes*. Everything is correct. The native, who has usually been torn from his home far in the interior, perhaps as much as eight hundred miles away, and already sold twice, is asked by an interpreter if it is his wish to go to San Thomé, or to undertake some other form of service to a new master. Of course he answers, 'Yes'. It is quite unnecessary to suppose, as most people suppose, that the interpreter always asks such questions as, 'Do you like to fish?' or, 'Will you have a drink?' though one of the best scholars in the languages of the interior has himself heard those questions asked at an official inspection of *serviçaes* on board ship. It would be unnecessary for the interpreter to invent such questions. If he asked, 'Is it your wish to go to hell?' the *serviçal* would say 'yes' just the same. In fact, throughout this part of Africa the name of San Thomé is becoming identical with hell, and when a man has been brought hundreds of miles from his home by an unknown road and through long tracts of 'hungry country' – when also he knows that if he did get back he would probably be sold again or killed, – what else can he answer but 'yes'? Under similar circumstances the Archbishop of Canterbury would answer the same. The *serviçal* says 'yes', and so sanctions the contract for his labor. The decencies of law and order are respected.[65]

Pseudo-contracts were also regularly used for the exploitation of native peoples in settler colonies like the US and Australia.[66]

Closely related to this kind of enslavement was *debt bondage*, a form of unfreedom often combined with share-cropping. The jurist Tobias

Wolff described the system operated in the post-Civil War American South as follows:

> ... in the wake of the Civil War, Southern industrial interests strove to devise employment schemes that would reproduce the reality of slave labor even in the absence of the formal institution. Thus arose the system of peonage. Peonage was a system of forced labor that depended upon the indebtedness of a worker, rather than an actual property right in a slave, as the means of compelling work. A prospective employer would offer a laborer a 'loan' or 'advance' on his wages, typically as a condition of employment, and then use the newly created debt to compel the worker to remain on the job for as long as the employer wished. As the system of slavery looked to the law to enforce the property rights of the owner, so peonage pressed the law into service to enforce the property rights of the creditor, compelling service from the worker in payment of the debt. The juridical category was different – the property right in a human being, now forbidden, was replaced with the generally accepted right of a creditor to enforce a debt – but the result was largely the same. The coercive power of the State was used to compel labor from poor (and usually black) workers, on threat of imprisonment.[67]

Unlike a slave, the peon could not be sold. But the creditor could assign or sell the peon's debt to a third party. This form of bondage continued to exist in the US even in the twentieth century.[68] Debt peonage occurred, and still occurs, in many places in the world. In British India, for example, the prohibition of slavery in 1843 paved the way for hereditary debt bondage. Instead of the old multidimensional dependence, a unidimensional dependence was created, based on an apparent contractual credit relationship. In other words, 'servitude had not disappeared; it had only become formally monetized'.[69]

Not only private employers used this method. The case of the Netherlands illustrates this fact. From the 1830s, the Dutch colonial army in the Netherlands Indies recruited soldiers in West Africa (Ghana). To evade the British prohibition of the slave trade (and, later, slave labour), the freedom of the West African slaves was purchased by the Dutch from their owners, after which the ex-slaves had to 'repay' the sum by serving as soldiers in the Indonesian archipelago. In total, some 3,000 African men ended up in the Dutch East Indies under this scheme.[70]

A further method for replacing slavery with another form of coercion was *indentured labour*. This way of recruiting and exploiting workers was, of course, of a much older vintage – in some parts of the Americas, indentured labour had existed before the large-scale introduction of slavery.[71] Already at the beginning of the nineteenth century, there were experiments with this system, for example in 1806, when just under two hundred Chinese were transported to Trinidad, and in 1810, when a few hundred Chinese were brought to Brazil. But large increases occurred only from the 1830s. According to an arrangement between the French and Indian authorities in 1827, the first *engagés à temps* arrived in La Réunion from the beginning of the 1830s; these were indentured labourers, usually with a contract of three to five years, who worked side-by-side with the slaves still on the island at the time and who could renew their contract after it ended. If they did not wish to do so, they had to leave the island. In this way 'a system for the rotation of labourers' emerged between India and Réunion.[72]

In the British Empire, the migration of indentured labourers began in earnest from 1834, the year in which the apprenticeship period for former slaves started in the West Indies. In subsequent decades, many hundreds of thousands of labourers from Asia and Oceania were transported to other parts of the world. The most important regions of origin were British India and China. Estimates of the migration of coolies from India, not only to other parts of the British Empire but also to French and Dutch colonies, are available (see Table 11.2).

Table 11.2 Major colonies importing Indian indentured labour, 1834–1921.

|  | Period of migration | Number of migrants |
|---|---|---|
| Mauritius | 1834–1900 | 453,063 |
| British Guiana | 1838–1916 | 238,909 |
| Malaya | 1844–1910 | 250,000 |
| Trinidad | 1845–1916 | 143,939 |
| Jamaica | 1845–1913 | 36,412 |
| Grenada | 1856–1885 | 3,200 |
| St. Lucia | 1858–1895 | 4,350 |
| Natal | 1860–1911 | 152,184 |
| St. Kitts | 1860–1861 | 337 |
| St. Vincents | 1860–1880 | 2,472 |
| Réunion | 1861–1883 | 26,507 |
| Surinam | 1873–1916 | 34,304 |
| Fiji | 1879–1916 | 60,965 |
| East Africa | 1896–1921 | 39,282 |
| Seychelles | 1904–1916 | 6,315 |

Source: Lal, *Girmitiyas*.

But much less is known about the numbers of Chinese labourers who migrated under indenture schemes.[73] It is not unreasonable to suppose that, in the period 1800–1925, indentured migration involved some two to three million Chinese (Figure 11.2). One should add that, in both India and China, indentured labourers were only one part of the total outflow of emigrants.[74]

After the large-scale international migration of indentured labourers came to a halt in the 1920s, the phenomenon nevertheless continued to exist. Already during the nineteenth century, the practice had been, as it were, 'exported' to areas where no chattel slavery previously existed. There, workers were no longer imported from overseas destinations but arrived from areas closer by. Well into the twentieth century, young men were recruited in Papua New Guinea to work in the gold mines, with a system that Hubert Murray, a colonial governor, described at the time as 'really rather like slavery'.[75] Even in the 1920s and 30s, tens of thousands of contract labourers worked on the rubber plantations in Cochinchina (French Indochina), who originated from places including Annam and Laos.[76] And, on the tea plantations in Assam and Darjeeling, hundreds of thousands of labourers lived under indenture at that time.[77] These new workers often seemed to be 'free' but were not so in reality. About the Tamils from India, who, in the second half of the nineteenth century, worked on plantations in Ceylon, the historian Patrick Peebles comments: 'Despite the planters' repeated insistence that workers were free to leave even when they were needed most to work, the image of the plantation laborer as a semi-slave persists'.[78]

Another alternative method was the *labour-tax system*, in which farmers were forced to work part of their time or part of their land for the colonizer, ostensibly to pay their tax levy. A well-known variant was introduced by the Dutch during the 1830s in Java, the so-called Cultivation System (*Cultuurstelsel*), which forced the native population to use 20 per cent of their land to grow coffee, indigo, tea, and sugar. The crops had to be delivered to the colonial government. As Clifford Geertz remarked: 'The Javanese cane worker remained a peasant at the same time that he became a coolie … He had one foot in the rice terrace and the other in the mill'.[79] The introduction of the Cultivation System should be seen in its global context, in that it:

> … developed in the context of early nineteenth-century experiments with the plantation system in Asia when British and French Caribbean islands were declining as the primary base for tropical production aimed at the European market. The System

**Figure 11.2** 'Importing Chinese labourers to work in the gold mines of South Africa in 1904'. Illustration from *Le Petit Journal*, 1904 (colour litho). © Archives Charmet/Bridgeman Images.

was meant to provide an answer to the almost insurmountable problem of labour recruitment, confronting planters in South and Southeast Asia.[80]

Numerically less important was *convict labour*. This mode of exploitation obviously had already existed for centuries. But it now gained a new lease of life. Road-gangs in nineteenth-century India, 'agricultural penitentiaries' in French North Africa and Italian Tripolitania, convict labour in the De Beers Mining Company in Kimberley – the so-called *shibalo* system through which Mozambican men worked in the mines in South Africa, Rhodesia, and the Congo until the 1940s – are all proof of this resurgance.[81] In the US South, the leasing-out of state convicts became a mass phenomenon after the emancipation of the slaves (Figure 11.3):

> The old and new elites of the South remained interested to an equal extent in keeping up this forced labour, both to supply workers for the plantations, but also to build and maintain infrastructure. To achieve this, the threshold for arrests were lowered (the so-called

**Figure 11.3** 'The chain gang, Thomasville, Georgia'. Black convicts forced to work, c. 1884–91. Photograph by Joseph John Kirkbride. Library of Congress, LC-USZ6-1848. https://www.loc.gov/item/00652806/.

Pig Laws) and prison terms extended. Since the private users of the prisoners' labour power did not own the prisoners, their interest in maintaining the exploited prisoners was even less than in the case of slaves. Work conditions were accordingly brutal. An intended side effect was the disciplining of the black population and free workers. In case of protests, the latter had to fear losing their workplace to a prisoner.[82]

After World War II, the number of convicts in the US declined considerably, until the 1970s. Thereafter, the number of inmates exploded, from approximately 200,000 in 1975 to 1.9 million in 2022.[83] In addition, as of 2022, there are another 822,000 people on parole and 2.9 million people on probation. Loïc Wacquant explains this astonishing growth through the structural decline of the ghettos – 'ethnoracial prisons' – since the 1960s.[84] Indeed, both the US (since the 1970s) and the People's Republic of China (since the 1950s) have built huge prison–industrial complexes through which industries can employ inmates:

> In a broad sense, P. R. C. and U. S. federal prison-labor laws are surprisingly similar. Both nations have laws requiring rather than simply permitting prisoners to work. Moreover, the laws of each nation predicate this requirement principally on the desirability of providing an opportunity for prisoners to reform themselves through their own prison-labor.[85]

The last method to be mentioned by which slavery was replaced by another form of coercion was the immigration of *free labour*. The supply of 'free' migrants from Europe increased significantly in the nineteenth century, due to dislocations caused by industrialization processes, the emergence of steam shipping, and the growing exploitation of frontier regions in the Americas.

The different labour systems obviously did not exclude each other; they could be complementary, and they often merged or metamorphosed fluidly into each other. Some employers, like Brazilian coffee planters, occasionally combined them; and, naturally, employers often resorted to trial-and-error experimentation to determine which approach was most profitable.[86] On the whole, the abolition of slavery led to a broad spectrum of labour relations, varying from complete physical coercion to pure ('free') dependence on wages for a living.[87] It is a great challenge for future research to demonstrate the real determinants that led to the different combinations of these labour-supply systems.

However, the formal abolition of slavery did not just result in all kinds of alternative labour relations and modes of exploitation. There were also other consequences. Here, I will mention two that were historically significant. First, the profitability of Caribbean large-scale agriculture declined, which stimulated a transfer of production to Asia.[88] From the 1830s, many planters moved to Ceylon, and although they rapidly began to grow cash crops other than sugarcane in the new environment, they nevertheless applied the same management techniques that they had used in the Americas.

Second, another unanticipated consequence became visible in South Africa. In 1828, the Dutch-speaking white settlers in the Cape Colony had been very disturbed by Ordinance No. 50, which gave the native Khoi the same rights as themselves. And the announcement in 1834 that slavery would be abolished and that ex-slaves would also fall under Ordinance No. 50 worried them even more. The Boers became convinced that the government was out to undermine the socioeconomic and cultural foundations of their society. The plan to secede from the colonial government won popularity, and, from 1836, it resulted in the mass migration to the East and North-East, better known as the Great Trek:

> The trekkers left the colony in protest against the ungodly equality implied in the 50th Ordinance and the general attitude of the British authorities, and determined to establish a society in which 'proper relations' between master and servant would be preserved.[89]

## Coda

What had begun as a mainly British initiative gained support from other European states within a few decades: 'by the second half of the nineteenth century, anti-slavery was more a hallmark of European civilization than just a peculiarly British preoccupation'.[90] Just as in Britain itself, the earlier participation in the slave trade was played down on the Continent. During the African conferences in Berlin (1884–5) and Brussels (1890), it was evident at last that all the important Western powers had reviewed their thinking on the slave trade and now wanted to give a high priority to banning human trafficking.[91]

Sometimes, another factor played a role in the new consensus. As the colonial territories in Africa and Asia expanded, the slave trade of competitors became a nuisance, which the metropolitan powers sought to eradicate for reasons other than humanitarian ones. A case in point is the Sulu Sultanate – located at the boundary of what are now Indonesia and the Philippines – which, from the second half of the eighteenth century, operated human trafficking in many parts of Southeast Asia, both in the West (the Dutch East Indies, Malaya, etc.) and in the East (the Philippines). It has been estimated that, in the period 1770–1870, the Sulu Sultanate trafficked between 200,000 and 300,000 people, with the trade reaching its peak in 1836–48.

In the end, the colonial powers affected by Sulu slave raids in their sphere of influence – Britain, the Netherlands, and Spain – began to coordinate their battle against the Sultanate. The Dutch and English entered into a 'joint venture' to protect the coasts of Borneo, Java, and Sumatra in 1862; during the trafficking season, they stationed steam-powered gunboats at various points along the usual route of Sulu raids. Together with Spanish interventions in the Sulu Sea, this strategy had markedly reduced the action radius of the Sulu raiders by 1875, although human trafficking persisted in Northern Borneo until the 1890s.[92]

The success of the campaign against the slave trade and slavery had major side-effects that no one could have foreseen in 1807 or in 1833 – in particular, the conquest of very large parts of the African continent by Britain and other powers. To be sure, it is likely that, even without the campaign against the slave trade, Africa would have been colonized anyway.[93] But the way in which this colonization took place (and could be legitimized by Britain and other European powers) was, to a large extent, determined by the anti-slavery campaign. The General Act adopted in July 1890 by the Brussels Conference for the repression of the slave trade cloaked the entire conquest of Africa in a 'humanitarian' guise by presenting European rule and capitalist enterprise, including the employment of freed slaves, as *anti-slavery* measures. Thus, the ideology of the anti-slavery movement became part-and-parcel of the European mission to 'civilize' Africa.[94] At the same time, there were at least two fundamental ambivalences of policy.

On the one hand, Britain and other colonial powers abhorred slavery; but, on the other, they needed coerced labour because it was cheaper and easier to discipline. That is why, until the very end of their empires, they rarely hesitated to use physical force to put people to work. On the Gold Coast (Ghana) in the first half of the twentieth century, 'the colonial state adopted ad hoc measures to satisfy the dictates of the antislavery societies, while at the same time exploiting female and child forced labor'.[95] In French West Africa, the peak of coercive labour mobilization occurred from 1920 to 1936.[96] In Southeast Asia, '[t]o the end of the colonial period, there was little real evidence of a transition to a system of free wage labour'.[97] Slavery was replaced by all kinds of other forms of forced labour.[98]

The policy ambivalences became extreme in the suppression of the Mau Mau rebellion of 1952–60 in Kenya, when the British actually built a huge system of concentration camps with forced labour – a situation that led Kenya's Minister for Defence, Jake Cusack, to comment in 1954: 'We are *slave traders* and the employment of our slaves are, in this instance, by the Public Works Department'.[99]

Of course, it is quite valid to argue that the British 'determination to blockade the West African slave factories of its European rivals and to interdict their slave ships seamlessly linked Enlightenment human rights discourse to the project of securing the British navy's maritime sovereignty and the British economy's global hegemony'.[100] But it is far too simplistic to think that there ever was, or could be, a complete congruence between commercial interests and humanitarian politics. There wasn't. Only if we keep in mind the tensions and conflicts between the two can we explain why traditions of forced labour and slavery persisted in the industrialized countries even after the close of the colonial era. The National Socialist regime in Germany and the Stalinist regime in the Soviet Union featured unfree labour in many varieties, of which some were hardly distinguishable from classic slavery.[101] Nowadays, the prison–industrial complexes in the US, China, and elsewhere provide examples of large-scale systems of commodity-production with forced labour.[102] Pure chattel slavery has been reduced to a relatively marginal phenomenon, but human trafficking and unfree labour continue to exist on an alarmingly large scale.[103]

## Notes

1 Curtin, *Rise and Fall of the Plantation Complex*.
2 Jungman, 'Waarom stopte de WIC de slavenhandel'.
3 Geggus, *Impact of the Haitian Revolution*.
4 Green-Pedersen, 'The economic considerations'; Hopkins, 'The Danish ban on the Atlantic slave trade'; Gøbel, *Det danske slavehandelsforbud*.
5 The text of the Act for the Abolition of the Slave Trade is published in Marcel van der Linden (ed.), *Humanitarian Intervention and Changing Labor Relations*, 46–54.
6 See also Chapter 2.
7 Allen, 'Suppressing a nefarious traffic', 873.
8 Exceptions prove the rule, of course. See, for example, Kelly, *Britain and the Persian Gulf*, ch. 10 and 13, or Graham, *Great Britain in the Indian Ocean*, ch. 2, 3 and 5.
9 Morris, 'Clubs, societies, and associations', 409; Tilly, *Popular Contention in Great Britain*, 173, 199. Morgan (*Slavery and the British Empire*, 157) estimates 'that between 1787 and 1792 petitions against the slave trade were signed by 1.5 million out of 12 million people in Britain (almost one-sixth of the total population)'. The literature on the movement's history is enormous. Important early studies were Klingberg, *Anti-Slavery Movement in England*, and

Coupland, *British Anti-Slavery Movement*. Recent contributions include D'Anjou, *Social Movements and Cultural Change*; Brown, *Moral Capital*; and Hochschild's excellent *Bury the Chains*.
10  Clarkson, *History*, I, 284–5.
11  Clarkson, *History*, I, 286–7.
12  Nelson, 'Slave trade', 195–6.
13  Lovejoy, *Transformations in Slavery*, 146.
14  Blackburn, *Overthrow of Colonial Slavery*, 421, 428.
15  Priesching, 'Verurteilung der Sklaverei'; Quinns, 'Three cheers for the abolitionist pope!'.
16  Lovejoy, *Transformations in Slavery*, 146.
17  Klein, *Atlantic Slave Trade*, 194.
18  Moes, 'Absorption of capital in slave labor'; Conrad & Meyer, 'Economics of slavery'; Sutch, 'Breeding of slaves'; Lowenthal & Clarke, 'Slave-breeding in Barbuda'; Wilson, 'People as crops'. Conrad (*Destruction of Brazilian Slavery*, 31–3) discusses the Brazilian debate about slave 'breeding' but claims that 'Brazilian slaveowners were "conscious" slave breeders only rarely' (32). Even in systematic studies of the reproduction of slaves, attention is hardly ever given to this phenomenon (see, for example, Gautier, 'Traite et politiques démographiques esclavagistes'). However, there are strong indications that, in several places in the world, slaveholders bred slaves when they were no longer able to buy any or there were not enough. This happened, for example, in Ethiopia, even at the end of the 1920s, where the prices for slaves, due to decreasing supplies, had risen to incredible heights (see Edwards, 'Slavery, the slave trade and the economic reorganization').
19  NN, 'Slave trade', 92; Miller, 'Note on the significance of the interstate slave trade'; Klein, 'Internal slave trade', 567; Klein, *Atlantic Slave Trade*, 194; Conrad, *Destruction of Brazilian Slavery*, 47–69; Toplin, *Abolition of Slavery*, 10–12, 89–92; Johnson, *Chattel Principle*.
20  Conrad, *Destruction of Brazilian Slavery*, 50.
21  Curtin, 'Abolition of the slave trade from Senegambia', 96.
22  Hopkins, *Economic History of West Africa*; Austin, 'Cash crops and freedom'; Klein, 'Slavery, the slave trade, and legitimate commerce'; Korieh, 'The nineteenth century commercial transition'; Law, 'Historiography of the commercial transition'; Law, *From Slavery to 'Legitimate' Commerce*. The income earned through legitimate trade could also be used to purchase slaves for non-commercial purposes. In parts of south-central Africa, 'the slave and ivory trades developed together as predominantly male ivory hunters desired slaves, often women. With ivory destined for international markets, the Chokwe purchased female slaves from Ovimbundu caravans that reached the interior and had previously supplied slaves for the Atlantic trade'. Gordon, 'Abolition of the slave trade', 920.
23  Wirz, *Vom Sklavenhandel zum kolonialen Handel*, 63.
24  See, for example, Lynn, *Commerce and Economic Change*, 52; Wariboko, 'Lineage slavery at New Calabar'.
25  Marks, 'Southern Africa', 414.
26  Lovejoy, 'Plantations'; Lovejoy, 'Characteristics of plantations'; Lovejoy, 'Slavery in the Sokoto Caliphate'; Lovejoy & Hogendorn, *Slow Death for Slavery*, 1.
27  Lovejoy, *Transformations in Slavery*, 142.
28  Howard, 'Nineteenth-century coastal slave trading'.
29  Moore-Harell, 'Economic and political aspects of the slave trade in Ethiopia', 410–11.
30  Reid, *Political Power*, 161.
31  Graham, 'Slave trade, depopulation and human sacrifice'; Johnston, *Of God and Maxim Guns*, 14; Kiernan, *Lords of Human Kind*, 215.
32  Ojo, 'Slavery and human sacrifice', 386.
33  Collins & Burns, *History of Sub-Saharan Africa*, 211.
34  Collins & Burns, *History of Sub-Saharan Africa*, quoting Freeman, *Journal of Various Visits*, 164.
35  Iliffe, *Modern History of Tanganyika*, 42.
36  Wilson, 'Some principal aspects of British efforts', 520–1; Toledano, *Ottoman Slave Trade*; Clarence-Smith, *Islam and the Abolition of Slavery*.
37  Moore-Harell, 'Slave trade in the Sudan'; Moore-Harell, 'Economic and political aspects of the slave trade in Ethiopia', 417–20.
38  Cave, 'The end of slavery in Zanzibar', 21.
39  Wilson, 'Some principal aspects of British efforts', 515.
40  Wilson, 'Some principal aspects of British efforts', 514.

41 See, for example, Porter, 'Religion and empire'.
42 Reinsch, *Colonial Government*, 45.
43 Wylie, 'Slave trade in nineteenth century Temneland', 215.
44 Tomich, '"Second slavery"'.
45 On the campaign during the period 1807–23, see Wesley, 'Neglected period of emancipation'. Additional information in Martin, 'Some international aspects of the anti-slavery movement'.
46 Maynard, 'The world's Anti-Slavery Convention'.
47 Drescher's *Capitalism and Antislavery* is an attempt at comparative historiography. See also Pétré-Grenouilleau, *Les traites négrières*, 253–378. For the developments in the Netherlands, see Oostindie, *Fifty Years Later*; Siwpersad, *Nederlandse regering*; Willemsen, *Dagen van gejuich en gejubel*. There is evidently room for further research here; more attention could be paid, for instance, to the interactions with slave protests overseas.
48 An English translation of the law is available in Conrad, *Destruction of Brazilian Slavery*, 305–9.
49 Conrad, *Destruction of Brazilian Slavery*; Toplin, *Abolition of Slavery*.
50 'An Act for the Abolition of Slavery throughout the British Colonies ...', 3° & 4° Gulielmi IV, cap. LXXIII. About the economic aspects, see Engerman, 'Pricing freedom'. Additional background information in Burns, *Emancipation and Apprenticeship*. The fact that the bondage of ex-slaves in the first years after abolition was called 'Apprenticeship' is no coincidence. The legal status of apprenticeship derives, of course, from the European guild system. Apprenticeship as an unfree form of labour continued to exist, however, long after the guilds had been abolished; it has been characterized as a kind of 'industrial serfdom'. McKinlay, 'From industrial serf to wage-labourer'; also Steinberg, 'Unfree labor'.
51 Green, *British Slave Emancipation*, 130.
52 Davis, *Slavery and Human Progress*, 205; Green, *British Slave Emancipation*, 129–61.
53 About the mood among former slaves in the British Caribbean, see Marshall, '"We be wise to many more things"'. Hall ('Flight from the estates reconsidered', 24) argues that, in the British West Indies: 'The movement of the ex-slaves from the estates in the immediate post-emancipation years was not a flight from the horrors of slavery. It was a protest against the inequities of early "freedom".' About similar tendencies in the French West Indies, see Butel, *Histoire des Antilles françaises*, 384–6, 390–4.
54 Mandle, *Patterns of Caribbean Development*, 41–3.
55 Courtenay, *Plantation Agriculture*, 27.
56 Renard, 'Labour relations in Martinique and Guadeloupe', 81.
57 Zeichner, 'Transition from slave to free agricultural labor', 23–4.
58 Evans Jr., 'Some notes on coerced labor'.
59 Ransom & Sutch, *One Kind of Freedom*.
60 Marshall, 'Metayage in the sugar industry'.
61 Taylor, 'Post-bellum southern rental contracts', 121. Taylor provides verbatim texts for such contracts.
62 Shannon, *Farmer's Last Frontier*, 88. For an overview of historians' debates on these developments, see Schweninger, 'Black economic reconstruction'.
63 The contract as a metaphor for freedom and as a form of unfreedom is analyzed by Stanley, *From Bondage to Contract*, and Steinfeld, *Coercion, Contract, and Free Labor*.
64 '... they left Africa as slaves and consequently, from an African perspective, must be included in the volume of slave exports in the nineteenth century'. Lovejoy, *Transformations in Slavery*, 151. For a detailed analysis, see Renault, *Libération des esclaves*. Also compare Zuccarelli, 'Régime des engagés à temps au Senegal'.
65 Nevinson, 'The slave-trade of to-day', 670, 672. See also Umbelino, 'Emigration ou déportation'.
66 See, for example, Finkelman, 'Evading the ordinance'; Magliari, 'Free soil, unfree labor'; Martinez, 'When wages were clothes'.
67 Wolff, 'Thirteenth Amendment', 981–2.
68 Goluboff ('Thirteenth Amendment', 1661) mentions 'the common practice among farmers and employers of selling the debt of their employees to one another'. See also Jones, *The Dispossessed*, 107.
69 Pouchepadass, 'After slavery', 29–30.
70 Verhoog, 'De werving van Westafrikanen'; van Kessel, *Zwarte Hollanders*.

71  See, for example, Bean & Thomas, 'Adoption of slave labor'; Galenson, 'White servitude'; Beckles & Downes, 'Economics of transition'. To what degree indentured labour and slavery differed is a matter of debate. In some cases, the recruitment, transport, and labour relations of coolies resembled the situation of slaves, but a general characterization of it as *A New System of Slavery* (the title of Hugh Tinker's well-known book) seems unwarranted because there were, in reality, great variations within the system. See also Shepherd, 'The "Other Middle Passage?"'.
72  Ho, 'La transition de l'esclavage au salariat', 152–5. Compare Rivaltz Quenette, 'De l'esclavage à l'engagisme', 58–70.
73  Figures for the Chinese in the West Indies are provided in Roberts & Byrne, 'Summary statistics'.
74  For the Indian migration as a whole, see Lal, *Encyclopedia of the Indian Diaspora*, and for the Chinese migration, Pan, *Encyclopedia of the Chinese Overseas*. Much has been written about indentured labour. Some important works include: Campbell, *Chinese Coolie Emigration*; Chen, *Chinese Migrations*; Christophe, 'Tamil migration cycle'; Kaur, *Wage Labour in Southeast Asia*; Look Lai, *Indentured Labor, Caribbean Sugar*; Look Lai, *Chinese in the West Indies*; Northrup, *Indentured Labor*; Metcalf, *Imperial Connections*, 136–64; Saunders, *Indentured Labour*; Schmidt, 'Les migrations de main-d'oeuvre'; Tinker, *New System of Slavery*; Wang, *China and the Chinese Overseas*.
75  Fitzpatrick, '"Really rather like slavery"'.
76  Brocheux, 'Le prolétariat des plantations d'hévéas', 60. See also Murray, '"White Gold" or "White Blood?"'.
77  Behal & Mohapatra, 'Tea and money'; Gupta, 'From peasants and tribesmen to plantation workers'.
78  Peebles, *Plantation Tamils*, 54.
79  Geertz, *Agricultural Involution*, 89; compare, for example, Emmer, 'Ideology of free labor', 211–18.
80  Bosma, 'The Cultivation System', 278.
81  De Vito & Lichtenstein, 'Writing a global history', 294–301.
82  Scherrer & Shah, 'Political economy of prison labour', 32–48. See also De Vito & Lichtenstein, 'Writing a global history'; Lichtenstein, *Twice the Work of Free Labor*; Mancini, *One Dies, Get Another*; Oshinsky, *Worse Than Slavery*.
83  Prison Policy Initiative, 'Mass incarceration'.
84  Wacquant, 'From slavery to mass incarceration'.
85  Cowen, 'One nation's "gulag"', 203.
86  See, for example, Starobin, *Industrial Slavery in the Old South*; Hall & Stolcke, 'Introduction of free labour'; Whitman, 'Industrial slavery at the margin'; Wagner, *Deutsche als Ersatz für Sklaven*; Mattos, *Escravizados e livres*.
87  See also Kloosterboer's pioneering work *Involuntary Labour*.
88  Kiernan, *Lords of Human Kind*, 79.
89  Omer-Cooper, 'Colonial South Africa', 368.
90  Quirk & Richardson, 'Anti-slavery', 68.
91  The developments between 1884 and 1890 have been carefully reconstructed in Miers, *Britain and the Ending of the Slave Trade*, 169–314.
92  Warren, *Sulu Zone*, 197, 208.
93  It is probably no coincidence that colonial expansion by Britain, France, and other countries increased to the extent that British hegemony weakened. During the late-nineteenth century, the core of the world-system became 'multicentric' and unstable, and this led to protectionism and expanding colonialism. According to Bergesen & Schoenberg ('Long waves of colonial expansion and contraction', 239), colonialism is, in this sense, 'an extra-economic mechanism for resetting the basic core-periphery division of labor in times of disorder and stress'.
94  Roberts & Miers, 'End of slavery in Africa', 16–17. An English version of the Brussels 'General Act for the Repression of African Slave Trade' is published in Miers, *Britain and the Ending of the Slave Trade*, 346–63.
95  Akurang-Parry, '"The loads are heavier than usual"', 36.
96  Fall, *Le travail forcé*.
97  Elson, 'International commerce, the state and society', 171.
98  See also Maul, *Menschenrechte*, 35–88; Banton, 'The "taint of slavery"'; Stone, 'The Foreign Office and Forced Labour'.
99  Elkins, *Britain's Gulag*, 130. Emphasis in the original.

100 Baucom, *Specters of the Atlantic*, 193. Mason ('Keeping up appearances', 831) argues that '[t]he desire to occupy the moral high ground helped motivate the British government to put its power and prestige behind securing abolition. Alongside whatever strictly humanitarian motives may have been involved, the benefits of leading the charge included mollifying powerful abolitionist lobbying groups at home and sanctifying the expanding British Empire'.
101 The critical historiography of national socialism is much more developed than the critical historiography of the USSR. For a summary of unfree labour under the Nazi regime, see Roth, 'Unfree labour in the area under German hegemony'; and, for an overview of the Gulag, see Gregory & Lazarev, *Economics of Forced Labor*; Applebaum, *Gulag*; and Khlevniuk, *History of the Gulag*. For attempts at comparative analysis, see Van der Linden, 'Forced labour', and Buggeln, 'Were concentration camp prisoners slaves?'. In a remarkable essay, Jürgen Zimmerer has suggested that, when it annexed Eastern Europe, the Nazi regime used techniques of exploitation and oppression that had been learnt in the German colonies before World War I. The transmission mechanisms by which the knowledge of such techniques was transferred to Europe are nevertheless insufficiently explained. See Zimmerer, 'Geburt des "Ostlandes"'.
102 Wacquant, 'From slavery to mass incarceration'.
103 See the publications of the Anti-Slavery Society and the US Department of State's *2021 Trafficking in Persons Report*.

# 12
# The ILO, 1919–2019: an appraisal

> The source almost always disapproves of the river's course.
> 
> Jean Cocteau[1]

The International Labour Organisation (ILO) held its inaugural conference in Washington, DC, in October–November 1919. Since then, the organization has experienced a turbulent history, including important successes and painful failures. The questions this chapter addresses are straightforward. How might we appraise the ILO's record over the last century? What are the results and future prospects of its efforts? Is the organization truly inconsequential, a '90-pound weakling', a 'toothless tiger', as critics have argued?[2] But these questions are difficult to answer – not only because of the variegated history of the ILO, rife with ongoing controversies, but also because the literature on the subject is overwhelming.

I will argue that the first half-century of the ILO consisted of 'fat years', in which regulating the global labour market achieved limited but clear progress, and that the second half-century was a time of 'lean years', when the ILO accomplished less. Following a brief review of the origins and early history of the organization, I will illustrate this by showing how the relative attainments from the period until around 1970 were subsequently weakened. Unless it manages to reinvent itself in the near future, the ILO is now in danger of further marginalization. This chapter consists of three parts: prehistory and founding; a stylized account of the history of the past century; and an appraisal.

## Prehistory and founding

In 1919, the ILO was founded following a long-term trend and a series of major, isolated events, or, as Fernand Braudel would put it, a combination of *longue durée* and *événements*. The long-term trend derived from the organization of the emerging global capitalism in national states. In 1788, the French–Swiss Jacques Necker (1732–1804) had noted that working conditions in competing countries were interdependent, thereby enabling a race to the bottom:

> The kingdom that in its barbaric ambition, abolishes the day of rest established by the laws of religion, is likely to procure an advantage, if it aligns with such a change; if, however, all rulers follow this example, the old proportions that presently determine the respective advantages of the different trading nations shall remain unaltered.[3]

This problem soon became acute when, in Britain, the prohibition of the slave trade received Royal Assent in 1807, and the danger loomed that other countries would profit from this economically (Chapter 11). The British abolitionist campaign inspired the coordination of social and labour legislation internationally. In 1838–9, the liberal economist Jérôme Blanqui argued, for example, that improvements in working conditions in internationally competitive industries could endure only if such improvements were introduced simultaneously:

> ... by all the industrial peoples facing external competition ... to date, treaties have come about between powers committed to killing; why not make one today to preserve their lives and appease them? – This idea would at least be new and might, on that basis, perhaps succeed: it is worth a try![4]

Daniel Legrand, a Swiss industrialist and philanthropist (1783–1859), had a major role in preparing this argument. In a great many letters to ministers and other high-ranking officials, he mentioned the example of the abolitionists and urged using the same internationally coordinated approach to end abuses in the factories. In 1845, Legrand wrote to French Minister of Foreign Affairs François Guizot: 'The negotiations conducted between the governments of France and England to end the trade in blacks [the slave trade] offer new evidence of the promising results that may be forthcoming from agreements between powers in the greater interests of humanity.'[5] The state of the working class, observed Legrand, was 'a disgrace to our civilization, in the same manner as that of the slaves of the colonies' and should likewise be improved.

Ongoing capital accumulation in Europe and North America heightened the need to coordinate social legislation. In 1881 a breakthrough appeared on the horizon, when the Swiss Federal Government asked other

European governments whether they would participate in an international convention on factory labour.[6] Various congresses on the protection of workers followed, yielding important results, including the establishment of the International Association for Labour Legislation in Basle in 1900 and several international conferences on working conditions, unemployment, and related matters.[7]

This trend towards international coordination accelerated dramatically, due to World War I, which, from 1916, led to an enormous surge in labour protests and culminated in revolutionary situations in East and Central Europe, as well as the Bolshevik seizure of power. These events shocked the established powers and, in many places, led to a 'Red Scare' – a widespread fear that communist rebellions in the West were imminent. During the peace negotiations in Paris in early 1919, Europe was still experiencing pre-revolutionary upheavals.[8]

The gradually expanding pursuit of internationally coordinated social legislation and the recent fear of the Bolshevik threat converged in the Versailles Treaty of 28 June 1919. The treaty noted the existing 'injustice, hardship, and privation' suffered by 'large numbers of people'.[9] These conditions were producing 'unrest so great that the peace and harmony of the world are imperilled' and should urgently be improved by the regulation of working hours and labour supply, adequate living wages, and so on. At the same time, such ameliorating measures clearly could not be meaningfully implemented by individual states independently of one another, since 'the failure of any nation to adopt humane conditions of labour is an obstacle in the way of other nations which desire to improve the conditions in their own countries'.

As a consequence, the ILO was set up in 1919 to raise labour standards around the world.[10] There are at least two different ways in which this event can be conceptualized. One possibility is to interpret it as a Gramscian 'passive revolution', that is, as a result of attempts of the established order to disarm antagonistic forces by partly incorporating their methods and goals, up to the point where even representatives of the antagonist are absorbed.[11] The other possibility is to follow Karl Polányi and assert that the ILO was established as an instrument to re-embed the economy in society and was part of the second phase of what he was to call the Great Transformation. According to Polányi: 'The League of Nations itself had been supplemented by the International Labour Office partly in order to equalize conditions of competition among the nations so that trade might be liberated without danger to standards of living.'[12]

## How the ILO operates: some essentials

The ILO was originally set up mainly as a mechanism for shaping regulated national labour markets. The most important means to this end were (and remain) the *binding Conventions and non-binding Recommendations* on national labour practices covering industrial relations, employment policy, and labour-based social security. A country that ratifies a Convention agrees to implement it and allows such implementation to be supervised. The country also accepts that negligence may lead to a proper protest procedure – which, in fact, has occurred very rarely. Conventions and Recommendations are decided by the delegations of the affiliated countries over the course of several weeks at the annual International Labour Conference.

Three important qualifications are in order here. First, the national delegations have a tripartite composition: each country may send one delegate for the 'workers', one for the 'employers', and two from the government. The structure of the ILO is therefore 'based on an ideology of non-antagonistic class relations and on bureaucratized structures of representation and control'.[13] Albert Thomas, the first Director-General of the Organization (Figure 12.1), defended this corporatism by saying that

**Figure 12.1** French socialist reformer Albert Thomas (1878–1932), 1910. Thomas was the first Minister of Armament for the French Third Republic during World War I. Following the Treaty of Versailles, he became the first Director-General of the International Labour Office, a position he held until his death in 1932. https://commons.wikimedia.org/wiki/File:Albert_Thomas_LCCN2014700210.tif.

the governments were the captains of the ILO, the workers were the engine, and 'the employers should serve as the brake, even though this brake often operated counter to the wishes of the conductor'.[14]

Second, only *organized* workers and employers are represented. The moderate secular trade unions consistently dominated the workers' delegations. The International Federation of Trade Unions (IFTU) had been a significant force ever since the ILO was established. In the 1920s, the IFTU accepted that the Christian unions were represented as well but only in a subordinate capacity. Even in 1954, when the communist World Federation of Trade Unions joined, national members of the International Confederation of Free Trade Unions (ICFTU), as the successor of the IFTU, remained dominant on behalf of the workers. The same has held true since 2006 for the International Trade Union Confederation (ITUC) that resulted from the merger between the ICFTU and the Christian World Confederation of Labour. Only a fraction of the world's working class is therefore represented in the ILO.

Third, the ILO has virtually no sanctions to impose when countries fail to observe the conventions they ratify. 'The conference was given a legislative role but not the power to impose its legislative enactments.'[15]

The International Labour Office is the permanent secretariat of the ILO, a rigidly hierarchical multinational bureaucracy based in Geneva for most of the past century. Within this hierarchy, the role of Director-General has always been absolutely crucial. Robert Cox and Harold Jacobson called the ILO a 'limited monarchy':

> The model has certain analogies with monarchies of fifteenth-century Europe. In these monarchies the king is the central, most powerful figure, but his power has limits. He must retain support among the barons, for he has not the power to crush them. He can strengthen his own position by enlarging his own court. Courtiers are dependent on him for favor; but he must always be watchful of courtly intrigue, or the ambitions of courtiers to become barons.[16]

The history of the ILO and its Office is therefore typically classified in periods according to the successive Directors-General.[17]

The ILO has always been part of a larger umbrella organization – initially, the League of Nations (1920–45) and, thereafter, the United Nations. The organization is based on the idea that the world comprises nation-states. At the time the United Nations was established, it was assumed that capital mainly circulated inside national borders and subsequently competed on the world market – an idea that has, of course, become obsolete, with the rise of multinational corporations and globalization.

## A brief overview of the ILO during the last century

### Years of relative prosperity: 1919-69

During the first twenty years of its existence, the ILO was mainly a European organization. Relations with the US were strained from the outset. Although US-based Samuel Gompers had chaired the commission that prepared the establishment of the ILO, and although the first ILO conference was held in Washington, DC, the US opted not to join the new organization, out of its mistrust of the League of Nations. Only the pressure of the Great Depression led to entry and full participation, beginning in 1934.[18]

The anti-Bolshevik tendency of the ILO, moreover, made for animosity between the ILO and the USSR in the early period. The first congress of the Red International of Labour Unions (Profintern) in 1921 appealed for 'a determined and merciless fight' against the ILO, while its Constitution mentioned 'a decisive battle against the International Bureau of Labor attached to the League of Nations and against the Amsterdam IFTU which by their program and tactics are but the bulwark of the world bourgeoisie'.[19] This dynamic seemed to change briefly from 1934, once Stalin had consolidated his power. *Realpolitik* came to prevail, and the USSR sought allies in the battle against Nazi Germany, which had left the ILO that same year.[20] In 1939, this alliance ceased when, following its invasion of Finland, the USSR was expelled from the League of Nations and, automatically, from the ILO as well.[21]

It was only in 1954, after Stalin had died, that the USSR rejoined the ILO; and it remained there until its disintegration in 1991. The Soviet Union, however, like the other communist satellite-states, was always the exception in the ILO fold because its state-and-society model was entirely incompatible with the tripartite consultation structure. Soviet trade unions were merely transmission conduits for the government, which, moreover, was by far the country's largest employer; the Gulag Archipelago and the corresponding mass forced labour that existed until the end of the 1950s were, of course, diametrically opposed to the principles of the ILO.

Europe's dominance was universally visible within the ILO during the interwar years. Although, in 1930, half of the 51 member states were outside Europe, a majority of the Governing Body was made up of Europeans.[22] In the first twenty years of its existence, the organization had two Directors-General: one French (Albert Thomas, 1919–32) and the other British (Harold Butler, 1932–8). Despite repeated requests from Indian delegates, only one corresponding office was established in Asia (Tokyo, in 1923), 'since the heavy expenditure for a central office at Geneva and correspondents' offices in Europe left only a limited sum available for work in the Orient'.[23]

Because of the preponderance of the colonial powers, the ILO pursued two lines of action from the outset. On the one hand, labour standards in the industrialized countries were to be aligned, while, on the other, working conditions in the more 'backward' countries, including the colonies, were to be improved.[24] The founding declaration from 1919 stated:

> The Members undertake that Conventions which they have ratified ... shall be applied to the non-metropolitan territories for whose international relations they are responsible ... except where ... the Convention is inapplicable owing to the local conditions or subject to such modifications as may be necessary to adapt the Convention to local conditions.[25]

This approach – whether intentionally or unintentionally – complicated operations on the global market for the colonies and, therefore, locked them into the existing international division of labour. David Morse, the US Director-General who, after World War II, had a defining influence on the organization, stated explicitly in 1957: 'to put it bluntly, an implicit purpose of the early ILO was to prevent any country, and particularly the less industrialized countries, from entering into international trade competition on the basis of cheap labor standards'.[26]

## Conventions and recommendations

The ILO was a vibrant organization at first. At the three General Conferences from 1919 to 1921, 'in the first flush of enthusiasm and under the pressure of world upheaval', no fewer than 16 Draft Conventions were composed. The Workers' Delegates of the IFTU were the driving force behind these efforts. They often received strong support from the Government Delegates, who were convinced that concessions had to be made to labour to avert the danger of social revolutions.²⁷ The 8-hour day or 48-hour week adopted during the first Conference in 1919 was a source of international inspiration.²⁸

Once the danger of revolution seemed less imminent and many countries had lapsed into an economic depression, this dynamism ground to a halt. A later ILO text relates that the 'early zeal was quickly toned down because some governments felt there were too many Conventions, the budget too high and the reports too critical'.²⁹ After 1921, the focus shifted to ratifying the previously adopted Conventions, propaganda, and research.³⁰ From 1922, the Christian trade unions were represented as a minority in the Workers' Delegations. The organization was streamlined and its bureaucracy grew.

From 1923–4, the organization began to stabilize. Interest in research and information-provision as policy tools continued to grow. From 1923, International Conferences of Labor Statisticians were held.³¹ In addition, Albert Thomas periodically wrote a report for the Governing Body. While, at first, this was a general update on the International Labour Office's operations, it evolved into a continuously expanding international, social-political yearbook.³² From 1935, the technical sections were published separately as a *Yearbook of Labour Statistics*, 'which was launched in response to unemployment and poverty in industrialized countries, and … took a lead in disseminating on family budget surveys, setting living standards for employees. These were precursor statistics that were to preoccupy agencies over fifty years later'.³³ The International Trade Secretariats of the trade unions, in particular, made intensive use of the material that became available as a result.³⁴

New Draft Conventions often applied only to narrow segments of the labour force, such as maritime labour. As explained by the political scientist Ernst Haas, the ILO leadership was 'compelled to follow the path of least resistance, that is, to draft Conventions on very specialized topics appealing to a well-defined portion of the clientele in the major industrial nations. In short, subgoals soon became dominant over the general program'.³⁵ In conjunction with this retreat, from 1924, the necessity of a collusion of capital and labour was increasingly emphasized. The Eleventh Session of the International Labour Conference, for example, adopted a resolution, stating that 'a policy of active collaboration between employers and employed, such as exists in certain countries, has resulted both in an improvement in the level of real wages and working conditions, and also in greater and more economical production'.³⁶

## Colonial labour standards

Although the ILO comprised all major colonial powers (Britain, France, the Netherlands, Belgium, and Portugal), the organization showed virtually no interest in the colonial world until about 1926. Only after Albert Thomas had journeyed to some of the colonies and returned horrified at the unfree working relations and inferior working conditions did interest in colonial territories increase. Abolishing forced-labour recruitment soon became a core theme for the ILO. After three years of intensive consultation, the organization presented a first draft of a convention against forced labour in 1929.[37] However, in the course of implementing this Convention, conflicting interests came into play. Countries without colonies (such as Germany) adopting positions of principle faced colonial powers that opposed forced labour mainly for the sake of appearances. This latter group of countries actually obstructed implementation of the Convention, despite supporting it officially.

The obstruction started as early as 1929, when the ILO distributed a 'Forced Labour Questionnaire' to be completed by the colonial authorities and intended to ascertain the extent of forced labour in the colonies. The information derived from this survey was of very little use because the authorities had no interest in providing honest answers. Some powers also attempted to delay ratification of the Convention because they understood that their colonial economies could not operate without forced labour. The United Kingdom and the Netherlands ratified the Convention in 1931, France in 1937, Belgium in 1944, and Portugal only in 1956. Archival research also reveals that, from 1929, the colonial powers – despite competing against one another – endeavoured to devise a common strategy with respect to the ILO. Their shared objective was not to abolish forced labour but to conceal it. The case of the Belgian Congo illustrates this point: here, forced labour in agriculture was simply renamed, from *travail obligatoire* to *travail éducatif*.[38] Similar cosmetic measures were taken in other colonies.[39]

## 'Philadelphia' and the effort to expand the scope of responsibilities

Following the outbreak of World War II in 1939 and the German occupation of Belgium and the Netherlands, an attack on Switzerland could not be ruled out, and the ILO's headquarters were at risk. The organization decided to relocate to Canada, and a small section of the bureaucratic apparatus duly set up shop at McGill University in Montreal.

The war plunged the ILO into a crisis: 'Whereas war strengthens national organizations, giving them an increased sense of responsibility and a greater cohesion, it produces exactly the opposite effects on an international organization'.[40] Europe, the ILO's traditional political basis, lost most of its influence while the US rose to global power. Adapting to this new balance of power, the organization's social priorities began to shift from 'the protection of the working population and the distribution of wealth towards development and free trade as a promise for a better life globally'.[41] Building on this reorientation, Director-General Edward Phelan claimed that, after the war, the organization should be allocated a greater role and should be involved in all reconstruction operations. This idea was recorded in what was known as the Philadelphia Declaration at the 26th International Labour Conference in 1944. This document – sometimes regarded as the 'second establishment' of the ILO – in addition to strongly emphasizing human rights, indicated the need for international economic planning:

> Confident that the fuller and broader utilization of the world's productive resources necessary for the achievement of the objectives set forth in this Declaration can be secured by effective international and national action, including measures to expand production and consumption, to avoid severe economic fluctuations, to promote the economic and social advancement of the less developed regions of the world, to assure greater stability in world prices of primary products, and to promote a high and steady volume of international trade, the Conference pledges the full cooperation of the International Labour Organization with such international bodies as may be entrusted with a share of the responsibility for this great task and for the promotion of the health, education and well-being of all peoples.[42]

Norman Dufty rightly noted that, had the Philadelphia Declaration been taken literally by those who voted for it, 'the ILO would have developed into the master agency among the specialized international bodies'.[43] This objective went unfulfilled, however. With the establishment of the United Nations, all specialized agencies, including the ILO, were rendered subordinate to the Economic and Social Council.[44] Even the proposal to make the ILO the main international agency to manage international migration failed. Instead, in 1951, a new institution was formed that later became the International Migration Organization.[45]

Although the ambitions of the ILO thus proved impossible to realize, the organization easily adapted to the postwar economic and political constellations. The corporatist structure of the ILO beautifully matched the Fordist compromise in the Global North, which focused on boosting labour productivity, leading to higher profit margins for corporate industry and higher wages for employees.[46] The organization embraced the logic of this compromise and also accepted its gendered aspects, such as the breadwinner model, in which the male breadwinner was expected to earn a wage enabling him to support a housewife and some children. This was clear, for example, from Convention 102 on 'Minimum Standards of Social Security', adopted in 1952. A 'wife' was defined as 'a wife who is maintained by her husband'; those left behind by a deceased employee were described as 'the wives and the children of breadwinners'; and the standard beneficiary of protective measures in cases of sickness, unemployment, incapacity of work, or invalidity was defined as a 'Man with wife and two children'.[47] Gender-biases like this had been visible in ILO's policies since its founding.[48]

## US dominance, decolonization, and 'technical assistance'

Two major changes exercised a strong influence on the ILO's postwar policies. One was the collapse of the colonial empires during the first three decades after 1945, in parallel with the political independence of most Asian and African countries. The other was the new hegemony of the US, manifested in the partial victory march of the Fordist compromise in the advanced capitalist countries. The combination of the two transformations shaped much of the ILO's activities, resulting in new priorities.

From 1948 to 1970, the organization had an American Director-General, David A. Morse. Under his aegis, policy underwent major revisions to accommodate American preferences, with sweeping consequences. Unlike many European countries, the US had never had great faith in the Conventions or their ratification. One possible reason for this reticence was suggested in the 1950s by Walter H. Judd, a member of the House of Representatives for Minnesota:

> [Many] countries in the world have the habit of trying to raise standards or change practices by beginning with edicts from the government, from the top down, whereas our pattern is basically through negotiation, collective bargaining, and various processes beginning at the bottom ... in general our Government comes along and passes, for example, a fair labor standards act as a sort of official formalization of a position that has been gradually developed, shall

I say, democratically? And ... therefore, the ILO members, by and large, are more inclined to adopt the pattern of solving problems by passing standards and conventions and resolutions at the top, than we are; is that not a fact?[49]

The US had ample incentive to displace the focus of the ILO from Conventions and Recommendations to other activities. As Ernest Wilkins, US Assistant Secretary for International Affairs, remarked in 1956: 'The United States has, with some success, sought to shift the emphasis of ILO activities away from the traditional standards development work, to more practical operational programs, practical research and technical work on specific problems (safety, control of dust, increasing productivity, and the like), and dissemination of information'.[50]

As a result, practical policy support from governments became far more important for the ILO than in the past – especially in the former colonies and other countries of the Global South. The organization had, of course, been cautiously expanding its scope of responsibilities since as early as the 1930s, when ILO specialists in Cuba, Venezuela, and Bolivia had helped draft labour legislation as a way of 'selling' the organization's expertise.[51] After 1945, despite initial resistance on the part of trade unions and employers, this trend became far more forceful. In 1949, an ILO Field Office for Asia was set up in Bangalore, soon to be followed by similar offices in São Paulo (1950) and Istanbul (1952). 'Technical' activities in the Global South received a boost when, in December 1949, the Economic Cooperation Administration – the US organization administering the Marshall Plan – offered the ILO one million US dollars to carry out an operational programme. Although 'Morse had the greatest difficulty persuading the Officers that the Governing Body should accept this sum',[52] in the end, he succeeded: the money was used to set up 15 projects. Through these and other initiatives, hundreds of persons were moved to other countries for periods of training abroad, under the Technical Assistance fellowship procedure.[53]

The more important technical assistance became, the more elaborate the non-European network of the ILO also became. In the 1960s and 70s, over 30 branch offices were established, from Abuja to Tokyo. In 1964, an International Training Centre was founded in Turin, Italy, with the support of the Italian Government, and was soon followed by regional training centres covering Asia and the Pacific, Africa, and Latin America.[54]

The increasing emphasis on technical assistance programmes in the Global South went hand-in-hand with a growing interest in agricultural issues. But the ILO model of labour relations remained that of Western

Europe.⁵⁵ Still, the balance of power shifted within the ILO because the extra-budgetary funds from bodies promoting development aid became more important for the organization. In 1950, just 14 per cent of the funding had been extra-budgetary; by 1958, the share had increased to 34 per cent; and, by 1967, it accounted for 55 per cent.⁵⁶ In 1975, Bert Seidman, an officer at the American Federation of Labor and Congress of Industrial Organizations, noted that 'the bulk of ILO resources' went to 'technical assistance programs ("technical cooperation") in fields such as vocational training, workers' education, cooperative development, social security, labour administration (development of effective labour departments), management development, and assistance to employer organizations'.⁵⁷ As a consequence of this trend, the Director-General relied less on the membership dues from the participating states, and third-parties acquired greater influence over the policy of the ILO.

The symbolic peak of the ILO was achieved in 1969, when it was awarded the Nobel Peace Prize in recognition of its 50th anniversary. Aase Lionæs, the Nobel Committee chairwoman, stated:

> As we look at the world around us today, we must admit that many of the aims that the ILO set itself have been achieved in many parts of the industrialized world. Working earnestly and untiringly, the ILO has succeeded in introducing reforms that have removed the most flagrant injustices in a great many countries, particularly in Europe. By means of a levering of income and a progressive policy of social welfare, the ILO has played its part in these countries in bridging the gap between rich and poor.⁵⁸

## The soul-searching years: 1970–2019

Almost immediately after this commendation from the Nobel Committee, at least two serious problems became visible. First, the balances of power shifted in advanced capitalism. The period until c. 1970 was, as stated earlier, the time of 'Fordist compromise', in which the wage share (the tranche of national income allocated to wages) remained fairly stable, and rising labour productivity coincided with increasing wages and almost universal employment. Unemployment rates reached extraordinarily low levels in the early 1960s, thus stimulating the recruitment of women and migrant workers.

From the late 1960s, the *trente glorieuses* came to an end. As predicted by economist Michał Kalecki during World War II, full-employment capitalism did, indeed, reflect increased power among the working classes, and capital had to answer this challenge. The average profit rate began to fall again, and economic growth declined. An ideological shift occurred 'from expansionary demand-side policies to anti-labour supply-side policies, and contradictory demand policies'.[59] As a result, the labour share declined from the 1980s in several countries at different paces.[60] The declining labour share revealed that economic growth did not generate more employment. In the Global South, the number of precarious jobs rose continuously – a trend that soon manifested in the new concept of the 'informal sector'.[61] The number of workers with precarious labour relations grew, as they derived no benefit from traditional forms of collective bargaining. Moreover, land reform became an acute problem in the poor countries, and the worrying trend towards de-skilling (and less unionized) labour increased in many industries.

Second, criticism of the ILO mounted in the US. In 1971, the journal *Foreign Affairs* reported that the ILO had 'lost its relevance to domestic policy in the Western countries' and had 'come to the end of its usefulness'.[62] From 1970, the increasing influence of the Soviet Union and the Palestine–Israel conflict led the US to suspend its dues-payments for a while; and, in 1975, it cancelled its membership of the organization altogether – a decision that became effective in 1977 and was reversed again by 1980.[63] In addition to impacting on the prestige of the ILO, the action by the US came as a serious financial blow because the US covered one-quarter of the regular budget. According to former ILO programme director Guy Standing, the rift between the US and the ILO had a 'bigger underlying reason': the increasing influence of supply-side economics, in general, and its ruthless application since 1973 by the Chilean dictatorship of General Augusto Pinochet, in particular. The US supported Pinochet but the ILO 'was constitutionally obliged to take up the labour abuses that were taking place in Chile, as the country's previous governments had ratified major ILO Conventions'.[64] From the perspective of the US Government, the ILO was an outmoded organization emphasizing demand-side policies – and an obstacle to economic progress.

In the context of these two major challenges, the ILO once again attempted to return to the offensive by launching an ambitious plan that was remotely reminiscent of Edward Phelan's ambitious designs from 1941–4. It was the World Employment Programme (WEP), which Director-General Morse had already announced upon accepting the Nobel Peace Prize and which was intended to carry on from the first United Nations Development Decade (1961–70). The programme was to focus on working with the national authorities in Latin America, Asia, and Africa to formulate plans to provide the labour force with vocational training and employment. The next step would be for the ILO and other international organizations to work with the governments concerned to introduce agrarian reforms, public works, and the like. Technical assistance would thus become far more comprehensive and would be raised to a higher level of sophistication.[65] According to program leader Louis Emmerij from the Netherlands, the WEP was an outcome of the insight that economic growth did not automatically lead to more and better jobs – or, in other words, that the Fordist compromise no longer worked.[66]

The WEP transformed the ILO, in part, into a development agency, although this 'whim' was relatively short-lived. While the programme officially remained in operation into the 1980s, it had lost its momentum by around 1976–7 and, ultimately, was a miserable failure. Its demise made it clear that not even technical assistance could sustain the ILO anymore.

In the years that followed, attempts were made to restore the dynamics of the organization. For some time, two concepts that were 'discovered' in the early 1970s in the context of the WEP – the 'informal sector' and 'basic needs' – were emphasized. Even so, from the 1970s and definitely from the 1980s, the ILO lost much of its intellectual impact. The organization was unable to compete theoretically or materially with rising competition from other organizations that were better aligned with the neoliberal offensive – especially the World Bank, the International Monetary Fund (IMF), and the Organization for Economic Cooperation and Development (OECD).

These three bodies and related institutions aimed, within what was known as the Washington Consensus, to bring about 'deregulation', especially of the labour markets. While this did not mean fewer rules, these rules more clearly benefited employers. Since the 1970s, the Structural Adjustment Programmes of the World Bank had visibly provided the context for dismantling regulations protecting employees. Pension plans were threatened as well. For decades, the ILO had been governments' most important advisor on pension plans. But, from 1994, this changed, when the World Bank published *Averting the Old Age Crisis*, which advocated pension privatization. Supporters of the Bank included the US Agency for International Development, the Inter-American Development Bank, and the OECD. The response from the ILO – the report *Social Security Pensions* – appeared six years late.[67] By then, the pension privatization trend had gained considerable influence. This arose, in part, thanks to the World Bank's financial strength:

> Primarily, the ILO lacked the resources to oppose the World Bank successfully worldwide. The World Bank publication and conference budget was far higher than that of the ILO and, as a result, the ILO was unable to get its ideas in front of policy-makers with the speed of the World Bank.[68]

Research has demonstrated that the respective programmes of the World Bank, IMF, and similar institutions have negatively impacted workers' rights. They undermine collective labour laws; their loans are associated with lower rates of unionization and with lower wages in manufacturing industries and the public sector; there is also a negative correlation between IMF and World Bank programmes and government respect for workers' rights.[69] Why did the ILO not resist the neoliberal offensive more forcefully? First, the World Bank, IMF, and related institutions were financially stronger than the ILO.[70] They had more experts, who, in many cases, were also more intellectually renowned.[71] And, what is more, neoliberal thinking also gained influence among ILO staff. Sometimes, policy papers argued that social-security contributions could be disincentives to work; and the *Social Security Pensions* report was ambiguous about labour market 'flexibility'. As one observer wrote: 'These developments in the ILO are astonishing, considering that a contrary principle is laid down in the ILO Constitution, prescribing that labor should not be treated as a commodity'.[72] The World Bank and the IMF had far greater financial means than the ILO:

> The [World] Bank finances more education programs than UNESCO, more health programs than WHO, spends more on HIV/AIDS than any other international agency, and it has the potential to finance more workplace-oriented or labour programmes than the ILO. The IMF, too, spends more on poverty reduction than the ILO or any other specialized agency.[73]

The ILO also relied, in part, on the ample funds of the World Bank for its technical assistance projects.

The debate at the World Trade Organization (WTO) on social clauses in trade agreements further increased the danger of marginalization for the ILO. When the US and France proposed, in 1996, that the WTO incorporate a social clause to link labour standards to trade liberalization, parties such as the Association of South East Asian Nations objected, because they regarded the measure as protectionist.[74] This controversy instigated debate within the ILO as well. To mitigate the tensions within the organization between employers, unions, states, and NGOs, the ILO presented a Declaration on Fundamental Principles and Rights at Work and its Follow-up (1998) and stressed that 'labour standards should not be used for protectionist trade purposes'. The essence of the Declaration is captured in the following sentence:

> [The ILO] Declares that all Members, even if they have not ratified the Conventions in question, have an obligation, arising from the very fact of membership in the Organization, to respect, to promote and to realize, in good faith and in accordance with the Constitution, the principles concerning the fundamental rights which are the subject of those Conventions, namely: (a) freedom of association and the effective recognition of the right to collective bargaining; (b) the elimination of all forms of forced or compulsory labour; (c) the effective abolition of child labour; and (d) the elimination of discrimination in respect of employment and occupation.[75]

This declaration was an effort to reposition the ILO in international dynamics.[76] But it was a problematic endeavour. First, it replaced hard law with soft law: 'Unlike its hard counterpart, soft law has no binding power and only expresses broad goals or political commitments or principles of an inspirational nature'.[77] Second, it implicitly devalued all non-core Conventions. Third, it tended to undermine the power of existing labour organizations. By emphasizing *free* instead of *powerful* trade unions, 'many labour regulations that limit union fragmentation and that increase union bargaining power are considered to be violations of freedom of association. In practice this has meant that the ILO makes policy recommendations that encourage union competition and that discourage centralized collective bargaining'.[78] And, fourth, it only related to civil and common law: the eight core Conventions articulate '"negative" rights, not substantive progressive rights that could be used to forge a new model of work and social policy'.[79] International law scholar Philip Alston therefore spoke of a 'revolutionary transformation' that would culminate in a 'new normative hierarchy' in which 'principles' would replace rights as a central force, rendering a 'gradual downgrading of the role of the ILO's traditional "enforcement" mechanisms' highly likely.[80] Soon afterward, the Declaration was supplemented by a new organizing framework for ILO activities – the 'Decent Work' concept that incoming

Chilean Director-General Juan Somavía introduced in 1999. He described the concept as providing 'opportunities for women and men to obtain decent and productive work in conditions of freedom, equity, security and human dignity'.[81]

Both innovations have been frequent subjects of debate since then. The Decent Work concept was important, as it implied a reorientation. No longer would the ILO focus primarily on 'established' labour groups. In addition to waged workers in formal enterprises, also unprotected workers, homeworkers, and the self-employed would henceforth be taken into account. Decent work was, therefore, as Leah Vosko put it, 'a metaphor in identifying the dire need to improve the conditions of all people, waged and unwaged, working in the formal or informal economy'.[82] In defending the interests of all these different types of workers, the Core Conventions served as guiding 'principles'. Countries with a lot of informal labour thus avoided having to enforce labour standards that were originally intended for formal employment.[83] Both the Declaration of 1998 and the Decent Work campaign from 1999 onward made clear that the original principles of the organization were reconsidered.

The 2000s thus far have been devoted mainly to an ongoing reorientation of the ILO. In 2008, the Governing Body adopted an additional Declaration, this one entitled Social Justice for a Fair Globalization. In his preface, Director-General Juan Somavía hailed the new text as a 'landmark' – the third fundamental document, after the Philadelphia Declaration of 1944 and the Declaration on Fundamental Principles and Rights at Work of 1998, 'a renewed statement of faith in the ILO'. This formulation was, of course, meaningful, as such a renewed statement appears to have been necessary. The new declaration formulated four mutually supportive strategic objectives promoting: employment; social security and labour protection; social dialogue and tripartism; and freedom of association and collective bargaining.[84] All these points may be perceived as underpinning the pursuit of Decent Work. In 2011, the adoption of Convention No. 189 on Decent Work for Domestic Workers was a historic milestone in this respect, as it was the first time that employees who had previously remained in the margins were directly addressed.[85]

After the Englishman Guy Ryder was elected Director-General in 2012, the effort to re-profile the ILO was reinforced by a major reform process, which was intended to enable the organization to 'maximize its impact and overall influence'. According to Ryder, this was indispensable if the ILO was to be more effective for 'the weakest and most disadvantaged, for those in poverty, without work, without opportunity, prospects or hope, for those suffering denial of fundamental rights and freedoms'.[86] These objectives are important and appealing, but will the ILO be able to achieve them?

## On balance: an appraisal

The ILO faces grave difficulties. Its original core mission – designing, accepting, and implementing international labour standards – remains largely unaccomplished. After getting off to a flying start during the early years after its establishment, the organization has lost momentum in this field. Many conventions were restricted to segments of the working class, and many were eventually revoked. Moreover, interest in formulating additional Conventions, after resurging in the 1930s–40s and the 1970s, has declined continuously (Table 12.1).

The second difficulty in this respect is that the ratification of conventions has been most unsatisfactory. While there are now 190 ILO conventions, no single country has ratified them all.[87] The third problem is enforcement: what if governments merely ratify conventions pro forma and do not implement them in practice or do so only in part? The ILO has no independent labour inspectorate and must therefore rely on trade unions, (I)NGOs, and national labour inspectorates – where these exist – pertaining to the official mechanisms controlled by the respective national governments.[88] Finally, sanctions are the fourth problem. As noted earlier,

Table 12.1  Adoption of ILO Conventions by decade, 1919–2019.

| Year | Number of Conventions adopted | Average per year |
| --- | --- | --- |
| 1919 | 6 | 6 |
| 1920–9 | 22 | 2.2 |
| 1930–9 | 39 | 3.9 |
| 1940–9 | 31 | 3.1 |
| 1950–9 | 16 | 1.6 |
| 1960–9 | 16 | 1.6 |
| 1970–9 | 23 | 2.3 |
| 1980–9 | 16 | 1.6 |
| 1990–9 | 13 | 1.3 |
| 2000–9 | 6 | 0.6 |
| 2010–19 | 2 | 0.2 |

Data sourced from ILO Information System on International Labour Standards. https://www.ilo.org/dyn/normlex/en.

the ILO has hardly any means to impose sanctions on governments that fail to implement ratified conventions or that do so insufficiently. It cannot hold leaders to account, issue fines, or declare trade embargoes. The only possible option available to the ILO is to request assistance from other actors that *can* impose sanctions: 'governments can raise tariffs and deny investment guarantees, and unions and NGOs can organize consumer boycotts'.[89] This option is realistic only if a country commits very serious violations and, moreover, wields little economic or political power. One rare example is the intervention by the ILO in Myanmar, where violations of the Conventions on Forced Labour and Freedom of Association were widespread.[90]

Still, ILO standards may be conducive to policymaking in two ways: they provide 'a script or model that actors can draw upon to design policy', and they may legitimate the policies of governments and unions.[91] Examples abound of such influences, especially – but not exclusively – in advanced capitalist countries.[92] In some cases, unratified ILO conventions have nonetheless motivated welfare provisions. This seems to have been especially commonplace in less-developed countries.[93]

Technical assistance, the second field where the ILO operates, has had some impact in several developing countries, mainly through advice on setting-up social security systems.[94] One problem has been that the ILO approach was heavily inspired by examples in the advanced capitalist countries and was therefore often difficult to use in practice. The ILO long neglected informal and unwaged labour.[95] Welfare policies based on salaried urban workers, for example, are poorly suited to countries where the labour force consists mostly of agricultural workers and the self-employed. In large parts of Europe, social security is financed by contributions from workers and employers alike and is based on the salary of the worker. However: 'The self-employed worker in Latin America cannot afford to pay the employer's contribution, and low-income agricultural workers who tend to be migratory and change employers frequently are difficult to identify'.[96]

As noted, an additional effect of the strong interest in technical assistance has been that the ILO has become partially dependent on external funding sources and, therefore, cannot operate entirely autonomously. The biennial budget of the organization still has a large extra-budgetary component. In 2006–7, the ratio was roughly as follows (in US$ millions): budgetary 443.9 and extra-budgetary 306.0; for 2016–17, the distribution was: budgetary 640.5 and extra-budgetary 410.0.[97]

Statistics and information provision comprise the third core business of the ILO and are the least problematic areas. Scholar of law

Anne Trebilcock has rightly noted that ILO reports are useful instruments for legislators and in legal procedures, and that ILO databases such as NORMLEX, and information from the Gender, Equality and Diversity Branch, can 'provide ammunition for arguments'.[98] The statistical material produced by the ILO, despite the potential criticism about some sections, is of exceptional value for scholarship and politics.[99]

Overall, the ILO, as a response to '1917', has certainly achieved positive effects for groups of workers on different continents – although those effects are often more ambiguous and less dazzling than many believe. The ILO's sphere of interest has gradually expanded; at first, it focused on industry and mines but, later, successively included agricultural, informal and domestic labour in its activities. Women's work now receives more attention than before, although women are still often seen as a category that does not exist independently of men.[100]

The organization appears to be at a crossroads.[101] Even from the point of view of corporatism itself, the present tripartite structure has outlived itself. As a recent ILO publication points out, there are at least two major weaknesses. Tripartism in its current form necessarily represents 'the formal economy rather than the huge – and growing – informal economy, especially in developing nations'. And, in addition, 'with membership of trade unions shrinking in many industrialized states, the representativeness of these organizations even in the formal sector is often questioned'.[102]

Either the ILO manages to develop some clout and promote labour standards more forcefully as a supranational authority, or it will increasingly be reduced to an information and advice service. But, to wield that clout, the organization would have to acquire the means to impose sanctions, and its internal decision making procedure would have to change, to allow for greater influence of workers' delegates, in general, and of non-union and self-employed workers, in particular. Within the organization, the awareness of being in transition is manifest:

> In contrast to the post-Second World War era, national unions, women's groups and a variety of NGOs are receiving a genuine hearing, particularly on issues related to marginalized workers, in the corridors of the International Labour Office and in the ILO's official platform, albeit alongside the still louder voices of dominant actors.[103]

Whether the 'dominant actors' will cede their dominance is highly questionable. As Robert Cox, former director of the International Institute for Labour Studies (the ILO research institute), noted in the late 1970s: 'Some conjunction of radical forces in core and periphery would be the condition necessary for an effective challenge to or reversal of existing world social power relations. Just to spell out this possibility is to realize how remote it is.'[104]

## Notes

1. 'La source désapprouve presque toujours l'itinéraire du fleuve.' Cocteau, *Romans, Poésies, Œuvres diverses*, 430.
2. Helfer, 'Monitoring compliance', 194.
3. Necker, *De l'importance des opinions religieuses*, 245–6.
4. Blanqui, *Cours d'économie industrielle*, 120–1.
5. Legrand, *Appel*, 4.
6. Delevigne, 'Pre-war history', 20.
7. Still useful is the reconstruction of this development in Follows, *Antecedents*. The German chancellor Bismarck played an important role in the prehistory of the International Association for Labour Legislation. Inviting Britain to attend a conference on labour standards in Berlin in 1890, he wrote to Prime Minister Lord Salisbury: 'The competition of nations in the trade of the world, and the community of interests proceeding therefrom, makes it impossible to create successful institutions for the benefit of working men of our country without curtailing that country's power of competing with other countries. Such institutions can only be established on a basis adopted in common in all countries concerned.' Quoted in Potter, 'Movement for international labour legislation', 353.
8. Shotwell, 'International Labor Organization', 22.
9. Versailles Treaty, Part XIII, Section 1, Preamble (and quotes in the rest of this paragraph).
10. There are quite a few good recent studies on aspects of the ILO's founding, including Ruotsila, '"The great charter for the liberty of the workingman"'; Tosstorff, 'International trade-union movement'; Van Daele, '"Engineering social peace"'; McKillen, 'Integrating labor'; McKillen, 'Beyond Gompers'; Cobble, 'Other ILO founders'.
11. Gramsci, *Selections from the Prison Notebooks*, 110.
12. Polányi, *Great Transformation*, 27–8.
13. Cox, 'Labor and hegemony', 389, note; Cox, 'Pour une étude prospective'.
14. Schaper, *Albert Thomas*, 245–6.
15. Burge, 'Some aspects of administration', 22.
16. Cox & Jacobsen, 'Anatomy of influence', 429.
17. The Directors-General are: Albert Thomas (1919–32, France); Harold Butler (1932–8, UK); John G. Winant (1939–41, US); Edward Phelan (1941–8, Ireland); David A. Morse (1948–70, US); C. Wilfred Jenks (1970–3, UK); Francis Blanchard (1974–89, France); Michel Hansenne (1989–99, Belgium); Juan Somavía (1999–2012, Chile); Guy Rider (2012–2022, UK); and Gilbert F. Houngbo (as of 2022, Togo). Except for Somavia and Houngbo, all the DGs have come from Western Europe and the United States.
18. Tipton, *Participation of the United States*; Ostrower, 'The American decision to join'.
19. Tosstorff, *The Red International of Labour Unions*; NN, 'Constitution of the Red International of Labor Unions', § II, 4.
20. Some background information can be found in Tosstorff, *Wilhelm Leuschner*. Italy, the other major European fascist power, left the ILO in 1938. See Allio, *Organizzazione Internazionale del Lavoro* – an informative but analytically weak study – and Gallo, 'Dictatorship and international organizations'. During the period 1941–4, the Nazis published their own journal as an alternative to the ILO's *International Labour Review*: the *Neue internationale Rundschau der Arbeit*.
21. Windmuller, 'Soviet employers in the ILO'.
22. Kott, 'Constructing a European social model', 176.
23. Wagner, 'International Labor Organization', 7.
24. Burge, 'Some aspects of administration', 27.

25  ILO Constitution. Article 35.1.
26  Morse, 'International Labor Organization', 33. Morse's statement is confirmed by the Briton George Nicoll Barnes, one of the ILO's founding fathers, who, much earlier, had already admitted that 'our motives were not altogether humanitarian ... We were specially concerned in Eastern labour conditions being raised to a higher level because European standards were in jeopardy by the products of the East being brought into competition with the Western world. If, in short, Eastern conditions remained low, the old industrial world would be faced with only two alternatives – either to accept a lower standard of life or lose the Eastern market'. Barnes, *History of the International Labour Office*, 45–7.
27  Lorwin, *Labor and Internationalism*, 489.
28  On the eight-hour working day, see Cross, 'Les trois huits'; Heerma van Voss, 'International Federation of Trade Unions', esp. 521–31; Hidalgo-Weber, 'Les Britanniques et la Convention'.
29  https://web.archive.org/web/20160117000539/http://www.ilo.org/global/about-the-ilo/history/lang--en/index.htm (the quoted text does not appear on this page at the time of publication in 2023, hence the link to an earlier version in which it does). See also Burge, 'Some aspects of administration', 22.
30  After ten years, only seven countries had ratified the Convention on the eight-hour working day.
31  World Peace Foundation, *Industry, Governments and Labor*, 84–9. Reports on the various statistical conferences since 1923 can be found at http://www.ilo.org/global/statistics-and-databases/meetings-and-events/international-conference-of-labour-statisticians/lang--en/index.htm.
32  Schaper, *Albert Thomas*, 235.
33  Standing, 'ILO: An agency for globalization?', 357.
34  Cheyney, 'Character and accessibility'.
35  Haas, *Beyond the Nation-State*, 147. According to Haas, the exceptions were Conventions 11 and 29 (which were general), while Conventions 1, 5, 10, 14, and 33 on maximum hours and protection of young workers were phrased in such a general way that they 'approach[ed] the aims of the ideology' (also, 146).
36  The context for this resolution appears in Johnston, 'International Labor Office'.
37  On this Convention, see Miers, *Slavery in the Twentieth Century*, 134–51.
38  Seibert, *In die globale Wirtschaft gezwungen*, 179–90.
39  See, for example, Keese, 'Slow abolition within the colonial mind', and the essays in the special issue on 'Developmentalism, labor, and the slow death of slavery in twentieth century Africa' in *International Labor and Working-Class History* 92 (2017). On Portugal, one contemporary observer wrote: 'The new Colonial Statute, promulgated on July 8, declares that "the State may not compel the natives to work, except on public works of general concern to the community, or on work which will be profitable to the natives themselves, or in execution of a judicial sentence of a penal character, or for the fulfilment of fiscal liabilities." The exceptions may seem more important than the general principle. But the change is radical from the previous Portuguese hair-splitting between forced labour, compulsory labour and the obligation to labour.' Benson, 'African labour in 1930', 147.
40  ILO, *Edward Phelan and the ILO*, 283–4.
41  Kott, 'Fighting the war', 375.
42  Declaration concerning the aims and purposes of the International Labour Organisation: https://tinyurl.com/2ruc65h3.
43  Dufty, 'Organizational growth', 481–2.
44  Fried, 'Relations'.
45  Rodgers et al., *ILO and the Quest for Social Justice*, 27, 77–82. Already before World War II, the ILO had been involved in migration issues, especially in Europe: see Rosental, 'Géopolitique et Etat-providence'. On ILO activities in the field of migration since the 1970s, see Böhning, 'ILO'.
46  Already in 1946, an observer spoke about 'the ILO-New Deal prescription', writing: 'Of recent years the influence of the ILO has been increasingly directed to spreading the doctrine of full employment that has of late become very popular, in the United States.' Van Sickle, 'International Labor Office', 362.
47  Social Security (Minimum Standards) Convention, 1952 (No. 102): https://tinyurl.com/msjrtt8d. I quote here Articles 1 (c), 61, and 67. The breadwinner model was a historically specific articulation of the idea of the 'living wage' that had been advanced by the ILO since its foundation. See the interesting analysis in Reynaud, *International Labour Organization*.
48  See, for example, the nuanced analysis in Zimmermann, 'Globalizing gendered labour policy'.
49  NN, 'International Labor Organization'. In *Hearings*, 83.

50  NN, 'International Labor Organization'. In *Hearings*, 65.
51  Blelloch, 'Latin America'; Jensen, 'From Geneva to the Americas'; Pernet, 'Developing nutritional standards'.
52  Alcock, *History*, 219. Compare James R. Fuchs's interview with David A. Morse from 1977: http://www.trumanlibrary.org/oralhist/morse3.htm. 'FUCHS: When you began to redirect the ILO from setting standards into technical cooperation did you meet resistance? MORSE: I met resistance from many people in the labor movement to start with and from employers. Not from the governments. The labor movement was afraid at the start although a little later they became great supporters of it. But you had to be educated to it. They'd been accustomed to the ILO fixing world social policies, world standards, laws, legislation – laws that could be adopted by different countries on the elimination of diseases and certain other hazards – in mines for example; or relative health hazards or laws to set up social security systems. Now the employers generally didn't want to go beyond legislation to start with, because they felt that this might activate the labor movement too much into getting into the picture nationally, because to make technical cooperation work you've got to get workers and employers to cooperate together with governments. They were rather resistant to that. It was really an educational job that had to be done on them to get them to recognize the need for change, and this was done.'
53  Phelan, 'Human welfare and the ILO', 31.
54  A helpful analysis of the ILO's organizational changes is available in Ghebali, *Organisation Internationale du Travail*.
55  Strang & Chang, 'International Labor Organization', 241.
56  Cox, 'Limited monarchy', 106.
57  Seidman, 'ILO accomplishments', 38.
58  The Nobel Peace Prize 1969.
59  Bowles & Boyer, 'Wage-led employment regime', 212.
60  ILO & OECD, *Labour Share in G20 Economies*, with graphs for the years 1897 (for France), 1856 (for Britain), and 1899 (for the US), all on p. 15; Karabarbounis & Neiman, 'Global decline of the labor share' (for the period after 1975). See also Kristal, 'Good times, bad times'; Stockhammer, *Why Have Wages Shares Fallen?*; and Smith, *Imperialism*, 145–55.
61  Benanav, 'End of unemployment?'.
62  NN, 'International labor in crisis', 521 and 529.
63  Secretary of State Henry Kissinger signed the letter of notice, but industrial relations expert John Dunlop had drafted the text. Kaufman, 'Reflections on six decades', 341.
64  Standing, 'The ILO', 360–1.
65  ILO Acceptance Speech.
66  Saith, 'Reflections', 1168. Compare the notes published by Dharam Ghai, the head of the WEP's research wing, in 'The world employment programme at ILO'.
67  Gillion et al., *Social Security Pensions*.
68  Orenstein, 'Pension privatization', 285.
69  See, for example, Vreeland, 'Effect of IMF programs on labor'; Cammack, 'Attacking the poor'; Martin & Brady, 'Workers of the less developed world unite?'; Abouharb & Cingranelli, *Structural Adjustment*; Nooruddin & Vreeland, 'Effect of IMF programs'; Anner & Caraway, 'International institutions'; Blanton, Blanton & Peksen, 'Impact of IMF and World Bank programs'. See also Wade, 'Showdown at the World Bank'. On aspects of the OECD policy, see Leimgruber, 'Embattled standard-bearer'.
70  Currently, the ILO's annual budget is about one-third that of the IMF, and less than one-sixth of the World Bank budget.
71  The ILO had previously comprised great thinkers, such as Robert W. Cox, the director of a think tank affiliated with the organization, the International Institute for Labour Studies (1965–71). Precisely because such independent-minded intellectuals were difficult to discipline, they encountered obstruction the moment they became too outspoken.
72  Maier-Rigaud, *Global Pension Policies*, 237. The author is referring to the Philadelphia Declaration of 1944; its first point reads: 'labour is not a commodity'.
73  Hagen, *Policy Dialogue*, 10.
74  Newland, 'Workers of the world, now what?'. For a historical perspective on trade agreements and labour standards, see Charnovitz, 'Influence of International Labour Standards'. Even though the reproach about protectionism is certainly valid, the South-Asian activist Rohini Hensman rightly emphasized: 'Trade unionists who are genuinely fighting for workers' rights as well as NGOs fighting for children's rights feel that the social clause proposal, even in its present form, can help in their struggles.' Hensman, 'World trade and workers' rights', 1250.

75  ILO Declaration on Fundamental Principles and Rights at Work, http://www.ilo.org/declaration/info/publications/WCMS_467653/lang--en/index.htm, 7. Eight Conventions are now officially fundamental for the ILO: 1) Forced Labour Convention, 1930 (No. 29); 2) Freedom of Association and Protection of the Right to Organize Convention, 1948 (No. 87); 3) Right to Organize and Collective Bargaining Convention, 1949 (No. 98); 4) Equal Remuneration Convention, 1951 (No. 100); 5) Discrimination (Employment and Occupation) Convention, 1958 (No. 111); 6) Abolition of Forced Labour Convention, 1957 (No. 105); 7) Minimum Age Convention, 1973 (No. 138); 8) Worst Forms of Child Labour Convention, 1999 (No. 182).
76  Vosko, '"Decent work"', 22.
77  Baccaro & Mele, 'Pathology of path dependency?', 200.
78  Caraway, 'Freedom of association', 211.
79  Standing, 'International Labour Organization', 313.
80  Alston, '"Core Labour Standards"'. Alston's article provoked a debate: Langille, 'Core labour rights'; Maupain, 'Revitalization not retreat'; Alston, 'Facing up to the complexities'. For a defence of ILO's soft-law approach in the context of globalization, see Posthuma & Rossi, 'Coordinated governance'. See also comparative reflections in Blanpain & Colucci, *Globalisation of Labour Standards*.
81  'ILO and today's global challenges (Part 2: 1999–), inception of the Decent Work Agenda'. https://www.ilo.org/legacy/english/lib/century/index6.htm.
82  Vosko, '"Decent work"', 26.
83  'In developing and less developed countries, the informal sector makes up a large share of the overall economy, and of overall work possibilities for the labor force. National legislation regularly exempts such informal businesses from coverage, rendering labor standards unenforceable for a high proportion of workers. Moreover, even when the labor law formally applies, the practicalities of enforcement against marginal employers or in cases of formal self-employment or micro-business are likely to make the legal rights a dead letter. In areas such as social security, the extreme fragmentation of the working world in and of itself poses an important barrier to extension of coverage of basic social insurance schemes to many workers.' Weiss, 'Ruminations on the past', 79.
84  'ILO Declaration on Social Justice for a Fair Globalization', http://www.ilo.org/global/about-the-ilo/mission-and-objectives/WCMS_371208/lang--en/index.htm.
85  Albin & Mantouvalou, 'ILO Convention on Domestic Workers'; Blackett, 'Decent Work for Domestic Workers Convention'; Boris & Fish, '"Slaves no more"'.
86  '2016 vision statement of ILO's Director-General Guy Ryder', http://www.ilo.org/global/about-the-ilo/how-the-ilo-works/ilo-director-general/WCMS_477719/lang--en/index.htm.
87  Note that several Conventions have been revoked over time. The number of ratified Conventions *in force* is presently 80 for Brazil, 67 for The Netherlands, 66 for Sweden, and 12 for the US. Ernst Haas calculated the 'coverage' of labour standards for 1960 by counting the actual ratifications and stating them as a percentage of possible ratifications for all member states. He concluded that international labour conventions did *not* tend to equalize conditions of competition among industrialized countries as well as among developing and mature economies. 'Differences in coverage between mature and underdeveloped countries are obvious. What is more important, however, is the highly uneven incidence of conventions in specific fields among the countries most concerned in terms of their economic structure.' Haas, 'System and process', 334.
88  Back in 1933, the political scientist Francis Wilson wrote: 'The present machinery of enforcement has no doubt been pushed to its constitutional limit. The next step is probably the adoption of a strong convention on factory inspection which will enable the Office to secure complete information on the administration of national labor laws. Such a convention would supplement, of course, the present recommendations on factory inspection. The meetings of factory inspectors which have been held for some years during the Labor Conference must be developed and stabilized, but before national factory inspection can become a regular part of the machinery for supervising the enforcement of conventions, the states must become thoroughly accustomed to having their voluntarily assumed international social obligations examined each year in the Conference.' Wilson, 'Enforcement', 101. There have been quite a few cases in which ratified conventions had little or no impact. A clear example is China, a co-founder of the ILO in 1919. Here: 'Measured by the effect of its draft conventions in improving labor conditions, the I.L.O.'s influence has been negligible' during the interwar years. Wagner, 'International Labor Organization', 16.
89  Douglas, Ferguson & Klett, 'Effective confluence of forces', 276.

90  See NN, 'ILO: Resolution on the widespread use of forced labour', and http://www.ilo.org/yangon/country/lang--en/index.htm. A recent study argued that, in the case of labour-standards violations, 'the unions and NGOs provide the "eyes and ears", the ILO provides the "brains", and US trade legislation provides the "teeth"'. Douglas, Ferguson & Klett, 'Effective confluence of forces', 273. The authors do not ask themselves how standards can be maintained within the US or in other powerful countries. Some more general considerations are offered in Landy, 'Influence of international labour standards', 555–604, and in Haas, *Beyond the Nation-State*.
91  Strang & Chang, 'International Labor Organization', 242–3.
92  See, for example, Valticos, 'Influence'; Berenstein, 'Influence'; Cook, 'ILO and Japanese politics, II'; Cashiell, 'Influence'; Hanami, 'Influence'; Lagergren, 'Influence'; Landau, 'Influence'.
93  Kanappan, 'Impact'; Menon, 'Influence'; Abdeljaouad, 'Influence'; Shah, 'Impact'.
94  See, for example, NN, 'Social Security'.
95  Cox, 'Labor and hegemony'; Whitworth, *Feminism*; Prugl, *Global Construction of Gender*; Vosko, *Temporary Work*.
96  Mesa-Lago, *Ascent to Bankruptcy*, 13.
97  ILO, *Programme and Budget 2006–07*, Table 3, 23; *Programme and Budget 2016–17*, Table 2, 5.
98  Trebilcock, 'Using ILO sources', 268.
99  For some critical observations, see Wobbe & Renard, 'Category of "family workers"', and Wobbe, 'Der überlokale Wandel'.
100 Whitworth, 'Gender', 404; Lotherington & Flemman, 'Negotiating gender'. Within the ILO's bureaucracy, women have always been under-represented, though the situation is gradually improving. For an older analysis of the problem, see Lubin & Winslow, *Social Justice for Women*.
101 Hughes and Haworth contrast different views on the ILO's prospects in their *International Labour Organization*, 95–103.
102 Rodgers et al., *ILO*, 17. The problem of tripartism was already brought up in 1991 by Matthias Stiefel, at that time an ILO staff member, in a paper entitled 'Democratization, participation and the search for a new polity: The ILO and tripartism in a changing environment'. This text was never published. A slightly different perspective is developed in Hagen, *International Labour Organization*, 14–39.
103 Vosko, '"Decent work"', 24.
104 Cox, 'Labor and hegemony', 424.

# 13
# How some workers benefit from the exploitation of other workers

> Subtly they had been bribed, but effectively: Were they not lordly whites and should they not share in the spoils of rape? High wages in the United States and England might be the skillfully manipulated result of slavery in Africa and of peonage in Asia.
>
> W. E. B. Du Bois, 'The souls of white folk'[1]

## The challenge

Genuine international solidarity – solidarity that has visible positive effects – has often proved difficult to achieve. There have been some magnificent examples of workers' solidarity across borders during the last two centuries – for example, when the First International organized cross-national support for strikers in the 1860s, or when dockers protested against *apartheid* by boycotting South African cargo worldwide in the 1980s. But often, all too often, international solidarity remains fragile, conditional, or fails to be realized in practice, no matter how lofty rhetorics may be. The collapse of the Second International in 1914 was the most spectacular and tragic failure, of course. But the twentieth century has witnessed many other tragedies, including the refusal of many metropolitan trade-union movements and Labour parties to give genuine support to the anti-colonial struggles in Africa and Asia after World War II.

*Why* is working-class internationalism so difficult to achieve? Why could workers so often be seduced by jingoism and xenophobia? Why do Northern workers frequently behave indifferently towards the misery of workers in the Global South? Socialists have been discussing these questions for a long time, across the world. Often, these discussions are framed in moral or even moralistic terms (such as Christian notions of universal charity). A materialist approach, however, demands that we address at least the following issues: i) the dynamics of global capitalism and its ramifications for the emancipation of the world's working class; ii) the relationship between this capitalist dynamic and changing moralities; iii) the fear, among slightly 'privileged' workers, of deteriorating living conditions; and iv) the necessary conditions for organizing countervailing power and a radical counter-culture. The issue is as important as it is complex; and its analysis can only proceed step by step.

## A preliminary exploration

The present chapter will reflect on just one specific thesis, which concerns the *differences in wealth* between segments of the world's working class. Wage-earners in the Global North can buy T-shirts cheaply because their real wages are much higher than the real wages of labourers in the Global South who produce these garments. What is more, this may apply as well to indispensable achievements in the living standards of the Northern working class, such as all household appliances and electronic communication and media devices. In that sense, workers in the North benefit from and rely on the exploitation of workers in the South. This is what I would like to call a *relational inequality* within the world's working class: some workers are much better off than they were in the past *because* other workers, who may also be better off than they were in the past, are vastly lagging behind in living standards and, thence, in absolute terms, are worse off than their Northern brothers and sisters.

The idea of such a relational inequality is already old, and it has consistently been articulated by socialists. Lenin put forward such an idea in 1907, in the context of discussions about colonial policy, although it seems he did not regard it necessarily as a durable, structural feature at that time:

> Marx frequently quoted a very significant saying of Sismondi's. The proletarians of the ancient world, this saying runs, lived at the expense of society; modern society lives at the expense of the proletarians … Only the proletarian class, which maintains the whole of society, can bring about the social revolution. However, as a result of the extensive colonial policy, the European proletarian *partly* finds himself in a position where it is *not* his labour, but the labour of the practically enslaved natives in the colonies, that maintains the whole of society. The British bourgeoisie, for example, derives more profit

from the many millions of the population of India and other colonies than from the British workers. In certain countries this provides the material and economic basis for infecting the proletariat with colonial chauvinism. Of course, this may be only a temporary phenomenon, but the evil must nonetheless be clearly realised and its causes understood in order to be able to rally the proletariat of all countries for the struggle against such opportunism. This struggle is bound to be victorious, since the 'privileged' nations are a diminishing fraction of the capitalist nations.[2]

At the end of World War I, Nikolai Bukharin made this idea more explicit in his book *Imperialism and World Economy* (1918), in which he wrote:

> The colonial policy yields a colossal income to the great powers, *i.e.*, to their ruling classes, to the 'state capitalist trust'. This is why the bourgeoisie pursues a colonial policy. This being the case, there is a possibility for raising the workers' wages at the expense of the exploited colonial savages and conquered peoples'.[3]

Similar ideas continued to be suggested in later decades as well. Reporting on the Asian Socialist Conference held in Rangoon in 1953, Su Lin Lewis tells of:

> ... a story recounted by Indonesian socialist Hamid Algadri in his memoirs about one of the British Labour Delegation waking him up in his hotel room late at night to find out why the Asian Socialists were refusing to unite with the Socialist International. Algadri, confused, had told him he was not the right person to ask, but that he was inclined to agree with the resolution, based on the great differences in wages, rights, and living standards between the British and Indonesian laborer. When the European socialist outlined plans for providing aid to 'underdeveloped areas', Algadri asked why, realistically, would British workers want to give up part of their hard-earned rights and income to help socialists in Asia, and that in comparison to the Asian laborer, the European laborer was a 'capitalist' from the viewpoint of income and salary. After a moment of silence, the European acknowledged that he was beginning to understand the Asian Socialist position and left.[4]

The first attempt to systematically theorize relational inequality was a hefty volume, *Imperialismus*, published by the Rosa Luxemburg follower

Fritz Sternberg in 1926, arguing that the prosperity of the metropolitan working classes was financed through colonial exploitation.[5] Sternberg's work was never translated into English and, therefore, made little impact in English-speaking circles. But, exiled in 1940s New York, Sternberg repeated his argument in his book *The Coming Crisis* (1947). This led to an interesting critique from the influential mainstream economist Abba Lerner in the journal *Social Research*:

> An ordinary economist might think that the growth of real wages of workers in capitalist countries could be connected with the growth of productivity as capitalism developed ... It would be possible to raise the living standard of the workers by the simple device of producing more, so that they (and the capitalists too, of course) have had more. It would not be so essential to find nonexistent markets abroad.[6]

I suspect that there is truth in the arguments of both antagonists (colonial exploitation versus an endogenous increase in productivity). Differential labour productivities have certainly contributed significantly to the divergence between North and South. But it can also not be denied that at least some of this global inequality *is* relational. The approach represented by Lerner has had many followers, and a lot of research has been done on diverging productivities. The approach represented by Sternberg, however, has been much neglected by scholars – although it has popped up time and again, such as in the writings of Arghiri Emmanuel and, more recently, Zak Cope, Ulrich Brand, and Markus Wissen.[7] Here, I would like to explore the possibility of testing Sternberg's idea.

Workers can benefit from the exploitation of other workers, either directly or indirectly, which may entice them to consciously or unconsciously give priority to their sectional interests over general class interests. *Direct* benefits can take two forms: either individual working-class families employ other workers at a wage-level far below their own wage-level (as was the case with the white South African workers employing black houseboys around 1900) or Northern working-class organizations employ Southern workers, as in the case of British consumer cooperatives that owned plantations for cash crops in West Africa and Ceylon. All such direct benefits seem to have remained rather marginal. *Indirect* benefits, however, appear to have been much more important. I see a number of possible varieties of indirect benefits, but there may be more:

a) *Importing of cheap commodities from the South*. This could include the importation of consumer goods in the North from

the South (consumed by workers in the North) that are produced in the South for wages that are lower than the wages workers would have earned in the North if they had produced the same or equivalent goods. (Child labour plays a role here as well, of course.)
b) *Buying of cheap services in the South*. This could include Northern workers enjoying services (such as tourism and prostitution) in the South where workers earn less than workers in the North would earn if they were to provide the same services. The same goes for outsourced call centres, and so on.
c) *Exporting of commodities* (consumer goods, machines, etc.) from the North to the South – because the South cannot produce these commodities or cannot produce them cheaply enough, which creates additional job opportunities in the North. Examples include complicated integrated structures such as airplanes or, as in shipbuilding, rough manufacturing such as ship hulls that are produced in the South, whilst the final production happens in the North.
d) *Transport*. The import and export of cheap commodities, tourism in low-wage locations, and so on, may lead to additional job opportunities in logistics for workers from the North (railway personnel, sailors, dockers, truck drivers, and so forth).
e) *Financial services*. All these economic activities (*a, b, c, d*) may lead to banking and insurance activities and, therefore, to increased employment for Northern workers in the financial sector.

In short, workers in the North may probably mainly benefit from the exploitation of workers in the South in two ways: they (1) enjoy more purchasing power (cheap commodities and services) and/or (2) have more or better jobs. *Indirect* profiting seems to be the real issue here.[8]

In what follows, I will focus on two main periods: the first international division of labour (1830s–1940s) and the era of Fordism and post-Fordism (1940s to the present).

## The first international division of labour, 1830s–1940s

From around 1750 to 1950, capitalist industrialization was largely limited to the North Atlantic region and large parts of the Global South tendentially de-industrialized. Patrick O'Brien has estimated that 'the share of world industrial output emanating from production located within third-world economies declined from around 70 per cent,

1750–1800, down into the 10 percent range, ca. 1950'.[9] In the South, agriculture shifted increasingly from subsistence to commodity-production; it supplied especially tropical and subtropical cash crops and South American meat, while the North now provided manufactured goods.

This first international division of labour occurred in a global market that may be characterized as *semi-capitalist*. As Ken Tarbuck noted: 'Many of the recipients of the capitalist commodities produced in Britain (and increasingly in Western Europe and America) did not have capitalist economies. More particularly, the commodities which were imported into the capitalist countries were, by and large, still produced in a non-capitalist manner'.[10]

From the 1870s, this development culminated in the first stage of globalization. Harry Magdoff has noted that, during the final decades of the nineteenth century, a new global pattern of economic relations emerged, with three distinctive traits:

> (1) the number of commodities entering international trade on a large scale multiplied greatly, (2) competition between many widely separated regions of the world first appeared or grew more intense, and (3) the standard of living of workers and the profitability of industry in European nations came to depend on maintenance of overseas supplies, while the standard of living of the producers of raw materials came to depend on market fluctuations occurring sometimes on the other side of the world.[11]

During the interwar years, global growth slowed, world trade declined, and autarkic tendencies arose in the Global South. Moreover, the problems of the capitalist world economy seemed to worsen as a result of the establishment of the Soviet Union after 1917 and the extension of 'real existing socialism' to Eastern Europe and China, for example, following World War II. These developments had two main consequences: capitalist enterprise ceased to be possible in a considerable part of the world; and, for several decades, a concrete alternative to capitalism seemed to have come about: the centrally planned economy.[12]

## Consumer goods and services

It was within this context that the 'economic parity across major regions of the world around 1800 … was replaced for the most part by growing regional disparities'.[13] Where colonialism could strengthen its hold on local populations, the situation of these populations deteriorated. As the Indian economist Utsa Patnaik correctly observes, there was 'a surge in exports from plantations and from peasant agriculture, but always at the expense of falling foodgrains output and availability for colonized populations, reducing their nutritional standard and even leading to the extreme outcome of famine'. Patnaik therefore argues that there is an 'inverse relation between primary exports and domestic food grains availability'. The reason for this is simple, she explains: 'There is a limited supply of tropical lands and if heavy external demands are made on its productive capacity while insufficient investment is put in, then history demonstrates that the satisfaction of domestic needs is not possible and local populations are plunged into undernutrition and poverty'. Thus emerges 'a *global asymmetry of primary productive capacities relative to demands on them*'.[14]

The other side of the coin was the development of effective demand in the metropoles. During the nineteenth century, tropical consumer goods increasingly changed from luxury commodities to commodities consumed by working-class families as well. The underlying reason for this shift was probably the increase in real wages: the more technologically advanced the metropolitan production of consumer goods became, the cheaper these goods and the higher the level of real wages. The growing purchasing power of working-class families resulted *directly* in an increased demand for tropical products, since these were new, different, exotic, and thus highly appealing.[15] And it led *indirectly* to increased demand for tropical products as soon as the supply of equivalent products from temperate climate zones proved to become insufficient, given the growing consumer interest. For example: 'During the late decades of the 19th century the European demand for edible fats began to outrun mid-latitude supplies, and the coconut began its rise as an item of export agriculture in the Asiatic tropics'.[16] Something similar seems to have happened in the case of West African palm oil that was used for soap, candles, and so on. In any case, from the late-nineteenth century onward, tropical products increasingly featured in the consumption habits of low- and middle-income groups.

It is likely that Northern working-class consumption of (sub-)tropical textiles, such as cotton, increased. But it is very difficult to substantiate this hypothesis empirically. Studies of family budgets almost always give figures for 'clothing', without further specification. And the historians writing on class-specific dressing habits mainly focus on the period up to 1800 or 1850.[17]

The (slowly) growing consumption of tropical goods in the North (also by wage-earners) and increasing exploitation of workers and peasants in the South had a very positive effect on the Northern economies. In the Dutch case, Buelens and Frankema observe that:

> The extraordinary profitability of the 'cultivation system' introduced by the Dutch on Java in the 1830s, contributed substantially to the economic development of the metropole. At its peak, in the 1850s, the forced cultivation of sugar, tea, indigo and coffee by Javanese peasants contributed an estimated 52 % to Dutch central tax revenues and an estimated 4 % to Dutch GDP. The net surplus on the Indonesian balance of payments was used to service high levels of Dutch state debt, to finance Dutch infrastructural investments and to subsidize the less 'productive' Dutch colonies in the West Indies ... We find that returns to FDI [foreign direct investment] in the Netherlands Indies during 1919–28 were impressive (14.3 %), almost 3 percentage points higher than the world average. During 1929–38 the tides turned, with an average annual rate of return of -2.8 % compared to a world average of 2.2 %. Compared to the general rate of return on the Amsterdam stock exchange, the returns to colonial FDI were considerably higher: 2.1 % for the period 1920–39 versus 5.4 % for our sample 1919–38. However, returns to FDI in the Netherlands Indies were subject to a higher degree of volatility and became worthless after 1940. We will argue that high returns to colonial FDI in tropical agriculture were underpinned by repressive colonial labor policies and cheap access to land, but also may have partly reflected a higher risk-premium.[18]

## Employment

The uneven global development created jobs in 'de metropoles' as well, for instance in the textile industries and in shipping. The British Fair Trade League, founded in 1881, received enthusiastic support from British cotton operatives: 'The Lancashire – and what is less often appreciated, the Scottish – textile industry did export large quantities of goods of all kinds all over Africa'. Therefore, 'The English working-man did not necessarily mistake his own interest in this. If goods could not be sold, men could not be employed ... Their support for imperialism, which Engels noted, may well not have been, as Lenin supposed, simply the result of clever deception by the bourgeoisie'.[19]

Charles Guillaume Cramer, a leading social-democratic expert on colonial affairs, made the following reflection at the so-called 'Colonial Congress' of the Dutch Labour Party (SDAP) in 1930:

> What are at present the existing interests of the Dutch working class in the colonial question? The colonial wage sources can be split up as follows:
>
> 1. Drainage: the outflow of profits made by land reclamation and the exploitation of the Indonesian worker. The profits from this source for the Netherlands can be estimated at on average 400 million guilders per year. Naturally, this profit creates employment; capitalized at 10 per cent, it amounts to 17 per cent of the national capital.
> 2. Market for Dutch industry. In 1920 the total value of exports was 1700 million guilders, of which 14 per cent went to Indonesia. In 1927 these figures were 1900 million guilders and 7.2 per cent. In 1922 the textile industry exported 67.1 per cent of its total production to Indonesia. In 1928 this figure had decreased to 55.9 per cent ...
> 3. Market for personal labour power. According to Van Gelderen (*Socialistische Gids* 1921, p. 99) 43,500 Europeans have leading positions in Indonesia. This is the 'upper layer'. The number of people originating directly from the Netherlands is roughly 40,000.
>
> For an estimate of what an immediate severance of the colonial ties would mean for the Dutch workers, the speaker consulted our competent fellow party member Dr Tinbergen; he calculated, globally of course, a loss of employment for 150,000 Dutch workers – that is, about 10 per cent of the total number.[20]

## The era of Fordism and post-Fordism, from the 1940s to the present

With the rise of the *second division of labour*, industrialization got under way in the South. This trend was, of course, considerably strengthened when, from the 1980s–90s, the People's Republic of China started to evolve into an emerging capitalist superpower. The new international division of labour has extended all over the world, resulting in accelerated 'globalization'. As a consequence, the world's working class has been growing and changing rapidly. Seemingly contradictory trends have been observed in labour settings: on the one hand, transcontinental connections have been intensified, making the world appear increasingly homogeneous – which is the well-known 'globalization'; and, on the other hand, fragmentation and heterogenization are ongoing as well.

While 'globalization' has greatly boosted industrialization in the Global South, the jobs that are created are largely unskilled, substandard, and increasingly – especially in the Global South – performed by women. The ITUC notes:

> Eighty per cent of world trade and 60% of global production is now captured by the supply chains of multinational companies. The majority of supply chain workers are trapped in insecure and often unsafe jobs with poverty wages and long hours. Informal work, forced overtime and slavery are also found in the mix. A recent ITUC report shows that 50 of the world's largest companies directly employ just 6% of the workers in their supply chains – the remaining 94% are part of the hidden workforce of global production.[21]

Within global supply chains, core firms and intermediaries earn by far the most, and producers in developing countries make considerably less. The Samsung Galaxy S7 mobile phone, which retailed at 809 US dollars in 2016, illustrates this point: 'Costs for components like the touchscreen were 249.55 US dollars, manufacturing costs were not more than 10 US dollars and, hence, total factory costs not more than 260 US dollars'.[22]

## Goods and services

Within this context of increasing global connectedness, the role played by Southern goods and services in the consumption patterns of Northern workers is likely to have grown significantly. Let me give three examples. First: mass motorization, which began in the 1920s in the US and spread to the other advanced capitalist countries, especially after World War II. The enormous diffusion of cars implied, among many other things, a significant growth in rubber consumption, in particular for tyres.[23] The miserable labour conditions on the tropical plantations where this rubber was (and is) produced are well-known.[24] Second: the mobile phone, the global diffusion of which has been nothing less than explosive. The number of mobile phone contracts in operation increased from 23,500 in 1980 to 2.7 billion in 2019.[25] And, as is common knowledge, the rare metals used to make cell phones are frequently mined under horrendous circumstances. Cobalt and coltan, for example, are often extracted in Sub-Saharan Africa by children and violently oppressed workers.[26] Third: the increase in tourism. Worldwide, tourism has grown phenomenally, from 25 million arrivals (overnight visitors) in 1950 to 808 million in 2005, and 1.4 billion in 2018.[27]

## Employment

Due, in part, to the second globalization, industrial jobs dropped sharply in the North, although there was little or no decline in industrial output there. More and more products are assembled from parts manufactured in different countries and even on different continents. Currently, at least one-quarter of all employees worldwide pertains to global supply chains.

\*\*\*

It appears, then, that workers in the North structurally benefit from the exploitation of workers in the South through cheap commodities and services, and additional job opportunities.

The *provision of goods and services* produced in the South for the North seems to cover three domains: 1) consumer goods and services for the Northern elites; 2) raw materials and intermediary goods for Northern manufacturing and so on; and 3) consumer goods and services for the Northern working classes and other subordinate groups. Historically, South–North transfers began with the first domain (expensive spices and textiles), later followed by the other two. Of particular interest is the third domain (plus the second in as much as it produces goods for the third). The primary questions seem to be: when did a significant share of Northern working-class consumption begin to consist of Southern goods and services? And how did this share develop over time? A third question would then be: to what extent did the Northern working classes, as consumers, profit over time from the exploitation of the Southern working classes? When attempting to answer this third question, it would also be important to ask to what extent 'the provision of a mass of very cheap wage goods produced under conditions of super-exploitation in the global south facilitates intensified wage repression and exploitation (including super-exploitation) across the global north'.[28]

*Job creation* in the North, enabled by exploitation in the South, may take place in manufacturing, services, etc., as exemplified by Tinbergen's calculations of the 1930s. The fourth question is: when did a significant share of Northern working-class jobs begin to depend on the exploitation of Southern workers and how did this share develop over time? And a final question would be: to what degree did the extent and quality of Southern working-class employment depend on trade with the North?

These are simple, empirical questions but they are hard to answer. My very preliminary analysis suggests that the years after World War II witnessed the real take-off of relational inequality, but my reconstruction is, of course, overly impressionistic.[29] For more solid answers, we would need detailed knowledge of the long-term development of Northern working-class consumption patterns – through family-budget reconstructions and other methods. And we would need to know a lot more about transcontinental commodity chains – chains that, over the course of time, have become much more numerous and complicated[30] – and then combine this knowledge with the already extensive (but still imperfect) knowledge of the employment and working conditions of the working classes across the globe.[31]

The political implications of this *problématique* are huge. Indeed, they may lead to a serious reconsideration of the limits and possibilities of working-class internationalism.

## Notes

1. Du Bois, *Writings*, 935.
2. Lenin, 'International Socialist Congress in Stuttgart', 77.
3. Bukharin, *Imperialism and World Economy*, 164.
4. Lewis, 'Asian Socialism', 70. A similar point is made in Lohia, *Third Camp*, 6–7.
5. Sternberg, *Imperialismus*.
6. Lerner, [review], 125–9.
7. Emmanuel, *Unequal Exchange*; Cope, *Divided World Divided Class*; Cope, *Wealth of (Some) Nations*; Brand & Wissen, *Limits to Capitalist Nature*; Brand & Wissen, *Imperial Mode of Living*.
8. There is, of course, an additional factor contributing to relational inequality: the income of Northern states that is based on colonial/imperialist exploitation and that is partly used for social provisions, such as good education, healthcare, and so on. I leave this element aside for the moment.
9. O'Brien, 'Industrialization', 309. O'Brien means 'manufacturing' when he writes 'industry'.
10. Tarbuck, 'Marxism in the New Age'.
11. Magdoff, *Age of Imperialism*, 32.
12. The competition between the capitalist and the Soviet communist systems and the rapid growth of the Soviet economy were presumably conducive to the rise of the welfare states in North Atlantic capitalism into the 1950s. This threat was, however, relatively short-lived. The Soviet Union was a distinctive social formation without endogenous dynamics, and its stagnation and downfall were inevitable.
13. Alam, 'Global disparities since 1800', 52–3.
14. Patnaik, *Republic of Hunger*, 2–3.
15. Schoeller, *Die offene Schere im Welthandel*, 31.
16. Spencer & Horvath, 'How does an agricultural region originate?', 83.
17. See, for example, Riello & Parthasarathi, *Spinning World*, or Lemire, *Global Trade*.
18. Buelens & Frankema, 'Colonial adventures in tropical agriculture', 198–9.
19. Chamberlain, 'Imperialism and social reform', 159–60.

20 *Verslag van het koloniaal congres*, 13–14. 'Dr Tinbergen' was the economist Jan Tinbergen (1903–94), co-recipient of the first Nobel Prize for Economic Sciences in 1969. The reasons for the Dutch Social Democratic (and Communist) opposition to Indonesian independence are explored in Ferares, *De revolutie die verboden werd*.
21 ITUC, Supply Chains Resources Hub, https://www.ituc-csi.org/supply-chains-resources-hub. This hidden workforce thus concerns about 116 million workers.
22 Herr & Scherrer, 'Trade, global value chains and working conditions', 2–3. See also Dedrick, Kraemer & Linden, 'Who profits from innovation', but that work does not start at the beginning of the supply chain (mining coltan in the Democratic Republic of Congo, etc.), so that the chain studied connects only East Asia with the US.
23 Naturally, the diffusion process was uneven. Australia and Britain were faster, Germany was slower. See Barker, 'The international history of motor transport', 6.
24 See, for example, Tu, *Red Earth*; Ramasamy, 'Labour control and labour resistance'; Hochschild, *King Leopold's Ghost*; and Slocomb, *Colons and Coolies*.
25 Comer & Wikle, 'The worldwide diffusion of the cellular telephone'; Techjury, '67+ revealing smartphone statistics for 2023'.
26 For example, *Child Labour in Mining*; 'Tech giants sued over child deaths in DRC cobalt mining', *Financial Times*, 16 December 2019 (on Apple, Google, Microsoft, Dell, and Tesla).
27 United Nations World Tourism Organization, *World Tourism Barometer*.
28 Selwyn, 'Poverty chains and global capitalism', 78. Compare Araghi, 'Food regimes'; and Hammer, Plugor, Nolan & Clark, *A New Industry*.
29 It may, however, not be coincidental that debates about the 'imperial mode of living' took off in this period. See, for example, Brand & Wissen, *The Limits to Capitalist Nature*.
30 The technical complexities of transcontinental chain analysis are impressive: 'In this context, it is well known that international trade statistics fail to offer a good picture of trade integration and the global division of labour. They cannot answer the question "who produces for whom?" To illustrate the point, let us take an example extracted from Benhamou (2005) … The firm Burberry sends perfume bottles from France to Shanghai to be decorated with a Scottish pattern before bringing them back to be sold on the French market. Standard trade statistics suggest that France is exporting perfume bottles to China and China is exporting perfume bottles to France. Yet France does not export anything for Chinese consumption, as the perfume bottles are consumed in France. China simply exports decoration for French consumption. Suppose the pigments used for the decoration of the perfume bottles are imported by China from Japan. This Japan-China trade flow does not mean that China consumes Japanese products, as the final consumer is in France. Unravelling these long supply chains is impossible using simply trade statistics.' Daudin, Rifflart & Schweisguth, 'Who produces for whom', 1404. The reference is to Benhamou, *Le grand Bazar mondial*.
31 Here, too, we should be aware of contradictory effects, such as social improvements effected by some multinational corporations in the South. In Central America, banana-producing multinationals like United Fruit provided hospitals and field dispensaries that, in 1930, were serving 200,000 employees and nationals. Palmer, 'The banana in Caribbean trade', 271.

# Part IV
**Conflicts**

# 14
# Walking fish: how conservative behaviour generates and processes radical change

There is a well-known quotation from the philosopher and cultural critic Walter Benjamin (1892–1940), which he wrote just before he died: 'Marx says that revolutions are the locomotive of world history. But perhaps it is quite otherwise. Perhaps revolutions are an attempt by the passengers on this train – namely, the human race – to activate the emergency brake'.[1] The message from Benjamin may seem somewhat paradoxical: revolutions might be attempts to force a standstill. I aim to argue that Benjamin's statement conceals a deeper logic, and I will substantiate my assertion by going back to prehistory. Unlikely though it may seem, palaeontology – the study of early lifeforms and fossils – may offer the answers we seek.

Crossopterygians are a group of primitive, lobe-finned, bony fishes. They first appeared on Earth about 416 million years ago, at the beginning of the Devonian Period, and became all but extinct a long time ago, except for two or perhaps three species of so-called coelacanths or *Latimeria*. For many years, the coelacanths were believed to be extinct as well, until, in 1938, the trawler Captain Hendrick Goosen caught a live specimen near the South African coast (Figure 14.1). Since this first discovery, almost 200 coelacanths have been found in the Comoros, Kenya, Tanzania, Mozambique, Madagascar, Indonesia, and of course South Africa. They live at depths of 150 to 200 metres and cannot survive near the surface. But they have been filmed under water and appear to use their fins strangely, paddling with them alternately, *as if walking*.

Crossopterygians are considered to be the ancestors of all amphibians and other vertebrate animals living on land. In the 1930s, the famous palaeontologist Alfred Sherwood Romer (1894–1973) argued that crossopterygians were the historical bridge between fish in the sea and

**Figure 14.1** Postcard commemorating the discovery of the coelacanth by Marjorie Courtenay-Latimer in December 1938, when she discovered a strange fish among the catch of Captain Goosen's trawler. She made a rough sketch and sent it to Prof. J. L. B. Smith, an ichthyologist at Rhodes University, who identified the fish as a coelacanth and named it *Latimeria chalumnae* in her honour. After this first specimen, despite trawler searches and issuing a reward leaflet, no further 'uglyfish' were caught until 1952. Source: South African Institute for Aquatic Biology, public domain, https://bit.ly/3ryaQR9.

vertebrate animals on land. Romer wondered why amphibians and other animals previously living under the sea had switched to terra firma. Why would fish have become amphibians, and why had they developed limbs and become land dwellers?:

> Not to breathe air, for that could be done by merely coming to the surface of the pool. Not because they were driven out in search of food, for they were fish-eating types for which there was little food to be had on land. Not to escape enemies, for they were among the largest animals of the streams and pools of that day.[2]

No, Romer found a different and, I believe, more convincing reason: 'The development of limbs and the consequent ability to live on land seems, paradoxically, to have been an adaptation for remaining in the water, and true land life seems to have been, so to speak, only the result of a happy accident'. If the water dried up and did not soon return, the fish were helpless and inevitably died. But, if they became amphibian and developed land limbs, they could crawl out of the shrunken pool, walk up or down the stream bed or over land, and reach another pool where they might resume their aquatic existence. Romer concluded: 'Land limbs were developed to reach the water, not to leave it'.[3]

This explanation was a kind of Copernican revolution in palaeontology. The astronomer Copernicus once demonstrated that the sun did not revolve around the earth but, conversely, that the earth revolved around the sun. Romer used a similar rationale to reverse our mindset. In addition to explaining convincingly why fish had left the water, he argued that this radical transformation had been inspired by a conservative impulse. *Change had been caused by the very attempt to resist it.*

In 1964, the anthropologists Charles Hocket and Robert Ascher rediscovered this idea and called it *Romer's Rule*: innovations may render possible 'the maintenance of a traditional way of life in the face of changed circumstances'.[4] Soon, the rule was applied to human societies. For example, Conrad Kottak, another anthropologist, held that people 'usually wish to *change just enough to maintain what they have*. Although people do want certain changes, their motives to modify their behavior derive from their traditional culture and minor concerns of everyday existence'.[5] Unlike intellectuals, planners, or strategic thinkers, most people are driven not by abstract motives (such as 'revolution' or 'innovation') but by conservative desires. On aggregate, most people seek to avoid serious risks and endeavour to make do.[6]

## Romer's Rule in history

Careful observers will notice countless examples of Romer's Rule in social and economic history. The voyages of discovery by Columbus, Da Gama, and others, for example, were responses to the reduced access to the Levant. As a consequence of the rising influence of Islamic power in the Middle East and North Africa, overland trade routes to Asia were blocked. Explorers tried sailing around Africa or searching for a Western route to Asia in the hope of finding different ways of reaching India. They resorted to new means in the hope of restoring the old situation.

Romer's Rule surfaces continually in the history of social movements as well. E. P. Thompson, possibly the most important founder of modern labour history and author of the renowned work *The Making of the English Working Class* (1963), concluded that, in eighteenth-century England, 'a rebellious traditional culture' prevailed among the lower classes: resistance to the advancing capitalist economy, which the plebeian masses perceived as 'exploitation, or the expropriation of customary use-rights, or the violent disruption of valued patterns of work and leisure'. Accordingly, plebeian culture was rebellious – but 'rebellious in defence of custom'.[7] Such observations have also been made with respect to other European countries in this era.[8]

George Rudé, who was a contemporary of Thompson and, in my view, the greatest historian of riots and popular protest in Britain and France, made a similar argument. He believed that rebellious peasants and artisans 'tended to prefer the "devil they knew" to the one they did not'. They wanted 'to be "backward" rather than "forward"-looking in the sense that they were more inclined to demand the restoration of rights that were lost or were threatened with expropriation than change or reform'.[9] In *Captain Swing*, a study Rudé published in 1969 with Eric Hobsbawm about violent uprisings among agricultural workers in Southeast England in 1830, the authors submit that 'the labourers and their sympathizers did not normally want a disruption of the old society, but a restoration of their rights within it'.[10] People rebelled because they hoped to block disconcerting innovations.

Romer's Rule also sheds a different light on later developments. As a witness for the defence, I call upon the historian, sociologist, and criminologist Frank Tannenbaum (1893–1969). Tannenbaum had an intriguing life-course. He was born in the Habsburg Empire and emigrated to the US when he was about 12. There, he became very active for the new radical trade union, the Industrial Workers of the World (IWW). Charged with instigating a riot, Tannenbaum was sentenced to a year's imprisonment in 1914; and, following his release, he immediately reconnected with the IWW. Yet, he seized the opportunity he was offered by a philanthropist to study at university, completed his PhD, and even went on to become a professor at the prestigious Columbia University. Tannenbaum therefore knew from personal experience what a radical and even a revolutionary trade union was. But this same experience also led him to a remarkably idiosyncratic analysis.

His book, *A Philosophy of Labor*, starts with the provocative sentence: 'Trade unionism is the conservative movement of our time. It is the counterrevolution.' Conceivably, Tannenbaum could have been evolving into a union-buster here. But nothing was further from the truth. He did not mean to condemn trade unions. Rather, he believed they arose from conservative motives. The Industrial Revolution had destroyed the traditional ways of life in the countryside:

> The peasant who had been reared in the intimacy of a small village, where customary values prescribed for every act between the cradle and the grave and where each man played a role in a drama known to all, now found himself isolated and bewildered in a city crowded with strangers and indifferent to a common rule. The symbolic universe that had patterned the ways of men across the ages in village, manor, or guild had disappeared.

Once they were in the city, the workers had to fend for themselves. They had become completely dependent upon wages:

> If they lose their jobs they lose every resource, except for the relief supplied by the various forms of social security. Such dependence of the mass of the people upon others for *all* of their income is something new in the world. *For our generation, the substance of life is in another man's hands.*

Tannenbaum believed that the role of trade unions had to be considered from this perspective:

> In terms of the individual, the union returns to the worker his 'society'. It gives him a fellowship, a part in a drama that he can understand, and life takes on meaning once again because he shares a value system common to others. Institutionally the trade-union movement is an unconscious effort to harness the drift of our time and reorganize it around the cohesive identity that men working together always achieve ... The trade-union movement is an unconscious rebellion against the atomization of industrial society.[11]

Basically, in the words of Michael Merrill, 'trade unions restored social connections that the imposition of a labor market had undone'.[12]

## The Red Queen in reverse

You will likely know of that wonderful book from 1871, *Through the Looking Glass, and What Alice Found There* by Lewis Carroll. In this story, Alice meets the Red Queen. Racing along continuously, the Queen tells

Alice that she should not expect to 'get anywhere' by running. Inhabitants of Looking Glass Land were obliged to run as fast as they could just to stay where they were: '*here*, you see, it takes all the running *you* can do, to keep in the same place. If you want to get somewhere else, you must run at least twice as fast as that!' Romer's Rule may be interpreted as a case of the Red Queen effect, an evolutionary principle formulated in 1973 by the biologist Leigh Van Valen. According to Van Valen, in an evolutionary system, continuous development is needed simply to remain fit relative to the systems with which the person or entity is co-evolving.[13] In daily life, we encounter the Red Queen effect all the time, for example when we keep having to master new technologies (smartphones, apps, and such like) because we would otherwise fall behind.

But what happens if the Red Queen effect reverses direction? In other words, what if the surroundings start moving more slowly than the people who are present there? What if we suddenly have far more opportunities than in the past? Examples abound. Consider, for example, people who become rich overnight. Conservatism often turns out to be a powerful driving force there as well. Let me provide a single historical example. In 1879, the German economist Alphons Thun was travelling across the Rhineland and reported that the income of the families of local textile workers was up sharply. Even though they could now afford better, they continued to drink the same weak coffee and ate the same potatoes and the same bread they always had. As a consequence, they obviously had more money left and spent that on weekends indulging in binges or occasionally going to an opera.[14]

Many people who win a fortune in the lottery at first have no idea what to do with all that money. Like the textile workers and their families from the Rhineland, they usually combine old habits with exorbitant excesses. Sociological research has revealed that the adjustment requires about a year.[15]

## Cognitive conservatism

In 1291, on his journey from China back to Italy, Marco Polo was stuck on Sumatra for five months waiting for the monsoon winds to change course so that he could sail westward. On Sumatra, he saw enormous animals that were so unfamiliar to him that they seemed like the mythical unicorn, except that, whereas unicorns were appealing and elegant, these animals were not:

> They have the hair of a buffalo and feet like an elephant's. They have a single large, black horn in the middle of the forehead … They have

a head like a wild boar's and always carry it stooped towards the ground. They spend their time by preference wallowing in mud and slime. They are very ugly brutes to look at. They are not at all such as we describe them when we relate that they let themselves be captured by virgins ...[16]

Marco Polo uses several *analogies* here ('hair of a buffalo', 'feet like an elephant's', 'head like a wild boar's') but, because of the single horn in the middle of the forehead, he regarded the rhinoceroses mainly as unicorns, those animals he knew from myths and legends – except that they appeared as monsters here. Acknowledging what is truly new as such often takes us a long time. The platypus was another such case. Was it fake? A kind of duck? A type of mole? Over 80 years passed after the animal was discovered before science accepted that this was a previously unknown species (Figure 14.2). In his *Kant and the Platypus: Essays on Language and Cognition*, Umberto Eco rightly noted: 'Often, when faced with an unknown phenomenon, we react by approximation: we seek that scrap of content, already present in our encyclopedia, which for better or worse seems to account for the new fact'.[17] This pattern is common in

**Figure 14.2** 'Duck-billed platypus', engraving, 1809. George Shaw (1751–1813). After Europeans first encountered platypuses in 1797, several specimens arrived in Britain and Europe, prompting taxonomic description and anatomical studies. George Shaw, keeper of the natural history collections at the British Museum, which were later to form the Natural History Museum, accepted the platypus as a real animal. In 1799, he was the first to scientifically describe it, assigning it the species name *Platypus anatinus*, meaning flat-footed duck. Source: New York Public Library Digital Collections, public domain, https://on.nypl.org/3EkUrqI.

many contexts. The first passenger trains, for example, were simply separate but connected coaches without horses: locomotives replaced draught animals but everything else remained as it had been.

Precisely because of the difficulty of coming to terms with the unexpected, those taking part in social protests may be completely astonished at the consequences of their own actions. The Russian Revolution, for example, was, for many peasants and workers, an unanticipated and unintended consequence of their collective actions. Maurice Merleau-Ponty captures this nicely in *Phénoménologie de la perception*: 'it is doubtful', he writes:

> ... whether the Russian peasants of 1917 expressly envisaged revolution and the transfer of property. Revolution arises day by day from the concatenation of less remote and more remote ends. It is not necessary that each member of the proletariat should think of himself as such, in the sense that a Marxist theoretician gives to the word. It is sufficient that the journeyman or the farmer should feel that he is on the march toward a certain crossroads, to which the road trodden by the town labourers also leads. Both find their journey's end in revolution, which would perhaps have terrified them had it been described and represented to them in advance.[18]

In other words, Walter Benjamin's paradox of the revolutionary emergency brake reflects great historical insight.

Of course, Romer's Rule and the Red Queen effect are ephemeral. After an adjustment period (which may be very protracted), people usually grow accustomed to the radical change they have brought about or are experiencing.

## Causal mechanisms

Based on my arguments thus far, I would like to conclude with two observations. First, different disciplines can learn from one another. Even palaeontology and biology can inspire historians and social scientists. Second, a *mechanismic approach* can be useful. As social scientists, we should abandon our quest to identify general transhistorical patterns and should instead concentrate on reconstructing social mechanisms. As Alfred Cobban observed more than 50 years ago:

> In practice, general social laws turn out to be one of three things. If they are not dogmatic assertions about the course of history, they

are either platitudes, or else, to be made to fit the facts, they have to be subjected to more and more qualifications until in the end they are applicable only to a single case.[19]

Both social-scientific and social-historical progress is more likely to be forthcoming from growing knowledge of causal mechanisms than from devising increasingly general theories. Statements based on Romer's Rule, for example, lack predictive value. Nobody can predict whether fish will learn to walk. Only in hindsight, *ex post facto*, can one say with certainty whether the Rule applied. Romer's Rule might more accurately be called a mechanism in Jon Elster's sense. Elster defines a mechanism as a frequently occurring and easily recognizable causal pattern that is triggered under generally unknown conditions or with indeterminate consequences.[20] Unlike an overarching law, a mechanism does not say 'if A, then always B' but 'if A, then sometimes B' or 'if A, then often B'.

Causal mechanisms may recur over time. The greater the accuracy and detail in the description, the more precisely we can determine whether a mechanism is likely to recur and whether history is repeating itself in this very limited sense. Participants in social movements know this; in some situations, they recognize causal mechanisms that occurred previously. Romer's Rule and the Red Queen effect may both be regarded as examples of such mechanisms.

## Notes

1. Benjamin, 'Paralipomena', 402.
2. Romer, *Man and the Vertebrates*, 47–8.
3. Romer, *Man and the Vertebrates*, 52–3.
4. Hockett & Ascher, 'Human revolution', 137.
5. Kottak, 'Culture and "economic development"', 724. Italics in the original.
6. Rothstein, 'Broaching a cultural logic', 367. Rothstein also quotes the psychologist Stephen Kaplan: 'selection pressures in early humans favored acquiring new information about one's environment while not straying too far from the known'. Kaplan, 'Environmental preference', 585.
7. Thompson, 'Eighteenth-century English society', 154.
8. 'The impression could come about that the peasants were struggling against historical progress when they resisted the expropriation of their land and the growing exploitation related to the development of production for the large market. As is well known, in their struggles with the estate owners, they often demanded a return to old conditions and the restoration of old rights. However, by fighting for a reduction of taxes, the release from corvée, the abolition of serfdom, and better ownership rights, they shook up the very basis of feudalism. Thereby, they struggled against the economic and political domination of the nobility vis-à-vis the bourgeoisie. They stood up for a different path of development of capitalism in the agricultural sector … '. Nichtweiss, *Bauernlegen in Mecklenburg*, 48.
9. Rudé, *Ideology and Popular Protest*, 25.
10. Hobsbawm & Rudé, *Captain Swing*, 61.
11. Tannenbaum, *Philosophy of Labor*, 3–4, 7–11 (and preceding quotes). Italics in the original.
12. Merrill, 'Even conservative unions', 126.

13 Van Valen, 'New evolutionary law'.
14 Thun, *Industrie am Niederrhein*, I, 68.
15 Abrahamson, 'Sudden wealth'.
16 Polo, *Travels of Marco Polo*, 253.
17 Eco, *Kant and the Platypus*, 57. I borrowed the unicorn and platypus examples from this magisterial book.
18 Merlau-Ponty, *Phenomenology of Perception*, 517.
19 Cobban, *Social Interpretation*, 13–14.
20 Elster, *Alchemies of the Mind*.

# 15
# Mass exits: who, why, how?

> If my soldiers began to think, not one would remain in the ranks.
> Frederick the Great

Desertion derives from the Late Latin verb *desertare*, meaning to abandon, to leave, or to forsake. The verb denotes all manner of connections severed. In most cases, its use is intended to mean 'the wilful abandonment of an employment or duty, in violation of legal or moral obligation; *esp.* such abandonment of the military or naval service'.[1] Desertion in this sense has existed for thousands of years. One such reference appears on the island of Rhodes, where, in around 900 BCE, a code stipulated: 'mariners who, without sufficient reason, quit their service during the period of their engagement, shall be severely punished'.[2] Desertion is not restricted to the 'West'. In India, for example, desertions were an ongoing problem in the army of the East India Company.[3] And, regarding the millenarian Taiping Rebellion in China (1850–64), it has been written:

> The clarion call of the Taiping way of life resonated with imperial rank and file troops, many of whom were peasants themselves, and the Qings experienced, in the early years of the conflict, massive waves of desertion. Thousands upon thousands of soldiers crossed the lines at night to throw in their lot with the Son of Heaven.[4]

In this chapter, I will focus mainly on mass desertion. Mass desertion can be molecular or coordinated. Molecular desertion consists of escape attempts by individuals or small groups, although such efforts may become so numerous that, taken together, they become a mass phenomenon. In coordinated desertion, dozens or hundreds of people try to escape together as a group. Historically, molecular mass desertion has occurred far more frequently than coordinated desertion, but historians are not always able to distinguish between the two types in practice because the precise motives of the runaways are often unknown.[5]

## Who?

Deserters are, by definition, in 'violation of legal or moral obligation'.[6] Their flight or escape is therefore always an act of serious disobedience. *Mass desertion* assumes a high concentration of people in similar situations, detained under more or less the same conditions, with some deciding that they have had enough.

Examples from history reveal at least six such social groups that have resorted to mass desertion on occasion. Many – but not all – groups of runaways may be counted among the general working class.[7] Desertion by the first of the six groups – soldiers and navy personnel – has been a longstanding problem for armies around the world. This practice has, in some cases, cost these armies large swathes of their personnel and severely weakened them. During the Seven Years' War from 1756–63 (the actual 'first world war'), at least 300,000 soldiers deserted the different armies.[8] Following the introduction of the *levée en masse* as an almost universal military service during the French Revolution, tens of thousands tried to evade conscription.[9] In the first year of the Great War of 1914–18, half a million men ran away from the Czarist army.[10]

Sailors on merchant fleets, the second group, were similarly known for their 'mobility'. In the eighteenth century, desertion by sailors was 'one of the most chronic and severe problems faced by the merchant capitalists of the shipping industry' in the North Atlantic and elsewhere.[11]

Slaves are the third major group. The best-known example is the escape by a few dozen gladiators from their 'school', which resulted in the Spartacus Rebellion (73–71 BCE). About 70,000 slaves ended up joining. Another important case was the revolt in 869 of the *Zanj*, the East African slaves forced to work in the salt marshes in South Iraq. Just south of Basra, they founded a new, expansive city called al-Mokhtára ('the elect city') with elaborate defence measures, which was home to a population of 50,000 or more. Only after 14 years were these rebels defeated.[12] The best-known case from the modern age is probably the 'Negro Republic' of Palmares (Brazil, 1605–94), where between ten and twenty thousand *marrons* lived.[13] Such large-scale *marronages* continued to occur into the early-twentieth century:

> On the eve of the 1905 agricultural season the slaves of Banamba, a Maraka town in the Middle Niger valley, began to leave their masters ... Within a year of the original departures from Banamba the events had been repeated in hundreds of other locations. By 1908 the wave of departures had swept through the Middle

Niger valley. Elsewhere in the Western Sudan the movement continued for years.

When the commander of Bamako asked some of the first refugees why they had fled, they replied 'that they had no animosity to their masters. They simply wanted to return [home]'.[14]

Peasants, the fourth group, fled *en masse* in some cases as well. In the seventeenth and eighteenth centuries, Russian serfs regularly 'voted with their feet'. Peter Kolchin illustrates this by mentioning the thousands of subjects who, in the 1730s, abandoned their lord, the wealthy nobleman Prince A. M. Cherkasskii:

> [E]ntire villages typically migrated *en masse*, leaving and settling together in new surroundings ... The decision to flee was thus a communal not an individual one, and flight resulted in the reconstitution rather than the destruction of familial and communal ties ... 86.8 percent of the fugitives went in groups to previously selected villages, where advance parties had already prepared for their arrival, sometimes even buying land from nearby pomeshchiki [noble landowners]. Most often, however, they settled on previously unused land, where they established new communities in which they passed as state peasants. Village leaders ... usually organized the flight and continued to fulfill their traditional functions in the newly established communities.[15]

Similar exits occurred around the same time in East and North Germany, especially in Holstein, Mecklenburg, and New Western Pomerania. Thanks to the absence of a strong central authority, the large landowners were able to establish such despotic control that they could sell their serfs like cattle. Motivated, in part, by this practice, around the mid-eighteenth century, thousands of peasants moved away without authorization to Astrakhan in Russia or to Prussia under Frederick II, who, after the Seven Years' War, hoped to draw settlers to Prussian Pomerania.[16] Somewhat later, massive numbers of poor peasants fled *inter alia* in South and Southeast Asia.[17]

Indentured labourers are the fifth group. Everywhere in the world, coolies and other contract workers have absconded over the centuries. In the early decades of the twentieth century in Assam (East India), however, such forms of desertion took on mass proportions. One particularly noteworthy example has become known as the Chargola Exodus. In May 1921, indentured labourers on the tea plantations in the

Chargola Valley staged a strike for higher wages, but the managers rejected their demands. As a result, increasing numbers of men and women left the plantation permanently; ultimately, about 200,000 people departed:

> [The coolies] resolved to go back to their home districts, chanting victory cries to Mahatma Gandhi and claiming to have served under his orders. Having started from one or two gardens, by the middle of June, the entire Chargola Valley looked deserted, with two gardens reported to have 'lost' virtually their entire labour force, and on an average, most gardens had suffered losses of around thirty to sixty percent. The coolies of Chargola Valley marched right through Karimganj, the subdivisional headquarters, continuing their onward journey either by train or on foot, and also by steamer they made their way back to their home districts.[18]

The sixth and final group comprises convicts and inmates of concentration camps. When inmates were not yet contained in separate, closely guarded buildings but had to perform forced labour outdoors or in mines, desertions were commonplace. Even the subsequent measures of forming chain gangs and imposing mass incarceration did not put an end to the escapes. Although the greatest resistance came from *inside* prisons, and riots were common, inmates sometimes succeeded – possibly helped by outsiders – in escaping. In a more recent jail break in 2011, about seven hundred Egyptian prisoners reclaimed their freedom.[19] In some instances, groups even escaped from Nazi concentration camps, for example the 300 Jewish inmates of the extermination camp at Sobibor, who broke out successfully in 1943.[20]

All these groups were subject to a power beyond their control and were forced to live, and often work, under what were frequently highly authoritarian conditions.

## Why?

Generally, desertions rely both on the subjective willingness of the potential deserters and on the material opportunity. Subjective willingness to run away involves a combination of two criteria: issues and triggers. Issues are longstanding sources of discontent among employees. Triggers are specific incidents that crystallize into feelings of displeasure.

Discontent may result from many causes. In most cases, historians can ascertain them only when the deserters in question were caught and a written record of their interrogation is available. Three types of issues surface regularly in such sources.[21] The first type of issue concerns social and labour relations – for example, relating to bad food, harsh discipline, racial discrimination, or overdue pay. Second is the fear or horror of the future course of anticipated events, such as fear of imminent punishment or an upcoming battle. Other reasons include the refusal to fight a certain group out of a sense of loyalty towards this 'adversary'. Such sentiments figured, for example, during the German Peasant War in 1525: many mercenaries were originally peasants themselves and, moreover, were dependent on the peasants for handouts in what was known as the *Gartzeit* (the period between mercenary contracts).[22] Third, temptations or obligations elsewhere might come into play. Sons of farmers often disappeared at harvest time to help out on the farm back home. Mercenaries might be lured into switching sides by higher rates of pay from the adversary. During the California Gold Rush in the 1850s, so many sailors wanted to try their luck that '[v]essels travelling to California were unable to maintain predictable schedules due to the high incidence of crew desertion'.[23]

Such considerations could give rise to desertion if a certain event made 'the fat hit the fire'. Triggers came in many different manifestations. Consider the Sepoy Mutiny in India (1857), in which festering discontent instigated a social explosion when a new type of rifle was introduced. The powder for these rifles came in Minié cartridges wrapped in greased-paper that the soldiers had to tear open with their teeth. The grease used on the cartridges was rumoured to contain cow or pig fat, rendering them offensive to both Hindus and Muslims. This example shows that triggers were often embedded in religious or ideological discourse.[24]

Desertion was not a decision to be taken lightly. If caught trying to escape, deserters faced severe punishments, ranging from flogging to execution. And what prospects did successful deserters face? Their decisions are certain to have been impacted by anxiety, indignation, doubt, and hope. In many cases, discontent is likely to have been fairly widespread, since all groups mentioned here were exploited and/or severely oppressed.[25]

But discontent alone is, of course, insufficient to instigate any type of collective action; opportunities and resources matter as well. Can aspiring escapees deliberate with each other? Do they have contacts outside? Do they have inspiring leaders with a viable plan? If all these conditions have been met, then an exit is possible even under severely repressive conditions.

Those considering desertion always allow their emotions and interests to guide their decisions.[26] Theoretically, after all, aside from exit, two alternatives are available. These are voice, which means expressing discontent by attempting to improve the organization 'from within' (from the army unit, ship, plantation, and so on); or acquiescence, which means accepting an unsatisfactory situation and leaving things as they are.[27] Examining under which conditions soldiers, peasants, slaves, and others opt for voice or exit is, of course, immensely important for our topic.

How these two options relate to one another is more complicated than might appear on the surface. First, voice and exit are not always mutually exclusive. Voice may be a first step. Only when that proves ineffective will people resort to exit, as the second step. The reverse obviously does not happen: whoever has left the organization can no longer protest from within. And there is more. There is also the 'noisy exit', combining defection and protest. The threat of exit may strengthen voice,[28] although, in extremely authoritarian organizations, any type of voice will be punished as severely as desertion.

Sometimes, collective actions are at the interface of exit and voice, if exit is used as leverage in negotiations. Consider, for example, the illegal *uitgangen* (protests) that Dutch textile workers organized from the fourteenth century onward. They followed a typical pattern. The workers would leave the city in which labour relations were unacceptable and travel to another city, in order to renegotiate from there. The exit of the fullers of Leiden in 1478, heading for the city of Gouda, has been well documented: 'Although the distance between Leiden and Gouda was no more than twenty kilometres, negotiations also then took place by letter. The first letter of the fullers contained a list of thirty-four demands. After three months of negotiations, the fullers returned to Leiden'.[29]

Occasionally, voice may also serve to enable an exit.[30] The best-known example is probably the exodus of the Jews from Egypt – albeit this is an event that has never been proven to have actually taken place. The Egyptians, according to the Old Testament, 'made the people of Israel serve with rigor, and made their lives bitter with hard service, in mortar and brick, and in all kinds of work in the field; in all their work they made them serve with rigor'. The people of Israel 'groaned under their bondage, and cried out for help'. Moses, who had killed a cruel Egyptian before, decided to lead the Exodus and tried to convince the Pharaoh to let the Jews go. But the Pharaoh was hard-hearted, increasing the workload by telling the taskmasters:

> You shall no longer give the people straw to make bricks, as heretofore; let them go and gather straw for themselves. But the

number of bricks which they made heretofore you shall lay upon them, you shall by no means lessen it; for they are idle; therefore they cry, 'Let us go and offer sacrifice to our God'. Let heavier work be laid upon the men that they may labor at it and pay no regard to lying words.

Only after Yahweh had cast many plagues on Egypt (the River Nile turned into blood; frogs, gnats, and locusts afflicted the land; and all first-born animals and sons died) did the Pharaoh give in and were the Jews able to leave the house of bondage.[31] In this story, the exit is prepared by negotiations and reciprocal punishments. Exit coincided with voice.

The 'costs' of voice and exit are the second important factor. Voice always has a price, if only because organizing collective protest requires time and effort at the very least. Anybody who resists may face severe punishments, meted out not only to her or him but also to those around them. Nor is exit entirely without cost.[32] Whoever deserts confronts the prospect of persecution, torture, and death.

Seeking to 'curtail costs', deserters frequently chose not to escape entirely on their own. 'Whether one fled with a relative, wife, neighbor, slave, or other soldiers, departing with a person whom the deserter trusted was a key consideration. Having a running-mate encouraged desertion because soldiers benefited from the companionship, shared resources, and advice offered by accomplices in an enterprise of considerable risk'.[33]

Loyalty is the third factor that 'holds exit at bay and activates voice'.[34] When the 'members' feel a strong sense of loyalty, they tend to be very willing to try hard to make the 'voice' option work. Loyalty is undermined when people are recruited through coercion. This is obviously the case with chattel slaves but it may hold true for army units as well. Because Frederick William I of Prussia (early-eighteenth century) prized tall soldiers in particular, many of his elite troops were enlisted through coercion or were misled, leading to a high propensity to desert.[35]

The loyalty of 'subalterns' towards one another could be another factor. Studies on different armies have revealed that soldiers hardly ever went into battle exclusively on ideological grounds but usually for very different reasons. During World War II, for example, the German soldier 'fought for the reasons that men have always fought; because he felt himself a member of a well-integrated, well-led team whose structure, administration, and functioning were perceived to be, on the whole … equitable and just'.[36]

That the fleeing peasants often left in groups or even with entire villages similarly reflects this type of loyalty, which appears to have two potential outcomes: as long as 'acquiescence' or even voice prevails in a group, such loyalty will ensure that most people participate. The reverse holds true as well: once the tipping-point has been reached and a substantial tranche opts to desert, this may instigate a general departure. One very revealing practice of the *marrons* in Suriname was that, after they had deserted, they identified themselves by their plantation of origin. The slaves who had fled the plantation run by the widow of Johan (Dyan) Bosseliers called themselves *Misidyan*. Those who had escaped from the L'Espinasse family were called *Pinasi-lo* (lo = clan), and the *Dikan* came from the Nessenkamp plantation of the De Camp family.[37] *Marrons* from different plantations might become very suspicious of one another, sometimes resulting in armed conflicts. Mass desertions were thus promoted by local, ethnic, or racial homogeneity.[38]

## How?

Adopting an instrumental perspective on desertion yields three distinct elements: preparation for the escape, the escape itself, and the subsequent course of events. Regarding the first element, some information about abortive collective escapes is available from reports or court records. Still, we know fairly little about how such exits were organized.[39] Escapees attempting a coordinated mass exit may be assumed to have had 'a rudimentary organization and acknowledged leaders when they planned and carried out their escape'.[40] Even under highly repressive conditions, escapes or uprisings could be organized in some cases. On Barbados, male slaves managed to keep a conspiracy so secret for three years that even their own wives were unaware of it.[41]

In some cases, desertion was not difficult. In eighteenth-century Suriname, for instance, nearly all plantations backed onto the jungle, which facilitated exit:

> Slaves had reasonable freedom of movement. Every plantation had tracts of land that were not used to cultivate market crops; slaves could plant their own small fields, provision grounds (*goon*) to raise edible crops. Some of these provision grounds were even in the 'forest' behind the plantations. Slaves would hunt in these jungles, and they caught fish in the swamps. The slaves also had small dugout canoes, in which they paddled through creeks and swamps. The Bakaa, their white masters, owners, and foremen never went along on these journeys, so that the slaves knew considerably

more than their masters about the geographic state of this terrain. *Slaves usually had little difficulty slipping away from the plantation unnoticed.*[42]

When desertion became a serious problem for the 'incumbent rulers', however, they would resort to countermeasures. For thousands of years, escapes by convicts, slaves, and others have been complicated by giving them a *stigma* – the ancient Greek term for the lasting mutilation of potential runaways (Figure 15.1).

> In fact, branding, tattooing and incising the skin are traceable about as far back as one can trace things in the ancient Near East: brands and tattoos could function as signs of captivity and enslavement, record the name of the slave's owner, or warn the unwary observer (e.g., '[This is a] runaway! Arrest!'); they were apparently placed on the hands, wrists, and (perhaps less frequently) on the face or forehead.[43]

In the South of the US, their skin colour made escaped slaves easily identifiable.[44] The introduction of uniforms for soldiers (from the seventeenth century) and prison garb (from the nineteenth century) also served as a stigma that facilitated the identification of runaways. Prisoners in Czarist Russia and in the Stalinist Soviet Union could not escape their camps because they were located in desolate, isolated areas.[45] And the British-Indian prisoners on the Andaman islands were told that, should they try to escape, they risked death at the hands of the hostile tribal population in the surrounding forest.[46]

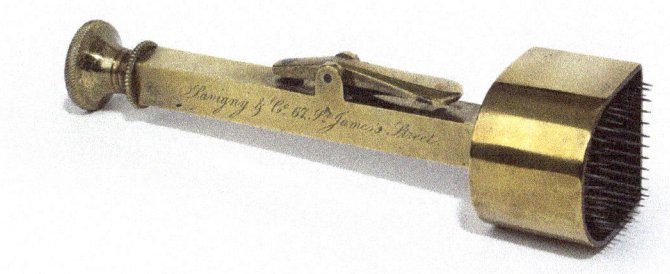

**Figure 15.1** Brass and steel instrument used for tattooing the initial 'D' for 'deserter' on the face or armpit. c. 1850. © National Army Museum/Bridgeman Images.

All kinds of other precautions against escape were taken as well. Troops were stationed on peninsulas, sentries were posted along possible escape routes, or passes were issued, so that any soldier or slave far away from the army camp or plantation might be asked to present identification.[47] Several of these actions prompted resourceful counter-measures: 'deserters learned to leave in bands and so to force their passage by violence against the guards',[48] passes were forged, and so on.

The actual escape – usually at night – was often highly ingenious. Myriad methods were used. A study about the American Civil War reports, for example:

> The tactics followed by the soldiers to effect their escape are fairly obvious: passage from the picket line or rifle-pit to the enemy's line; dropping out from the column at the fords and ferries and while on the march; taking advantage of gaps and passes while traversing rough country, or of the presence of swamps in the vicinity of the camp or station; slipping away at railroad stations or even jumping from a moving train; failure to return from hospitals or from furloughs; use of stolen or forged passes; escape under the confusion of attacks or captures by the enemy; and escape in civilian clothes through the connivance of friends and relatives.[49]

The days, months, and years after the escape were an entirely different matter. Runaways faced two immediate problems: how to avoid being recaptured, and how to obtain adequate provisions.[50] They basically had three options to 'solve' these problems: blend in with the locals, find a hiding place, or attempt to travel far away, to a place where different authorities were in control or where no central authority existed. The first option was the easiest for runaways whose appearance did not draw attention (thanks to their complexion or the absence of tattoos or other markings) and who had formed small groups. Sometimes, the escapees found shelter with friends or relatives; and, in times of labour scarcity, employers would even agree to hire escapees.[51] In some cases, deserters managed to settle among friendly indigenous groups.[52] This latter alternative is somewhat similar to the second option of disappearing from public view by hiding in an impenetrable area – a jungle, swamp, or rugged mountain range. The Great Dismal Swamp in North Carolina and Virginia, where, between 1630 and 1865, many thousands of disenfranchised Native Americans and *marrons* lived, was well-known.[53]

When runaways collectively settled somewhere in a new place, their logistical problems were obviously quite extensive. There was a constant

**Figure 15.2** Maroon village by the Cottica river near Moengo, Suriname. Photograph: C. R. Singh. Courtesy of Allard Pierson, Universiteit van Amsterdam (ref. VAR0266).

danger of punitive expeditions by their former rulers. Yet, the fugitives were forced to build their settlements in inhospitable areas (Figure 15.2) precisely because these were difficult for such expeditions to access. The more rugged the terrain, the more spartan everyday life became. *Marrons* on the Caribbean island of St Thomas who, in the eighteenth century, retreated to virtually inaccessible caves along the coast 'went naked and subsisted on fish, fruit, small game such as land turtles, or stolen provender'.[54] Confined in surroundings that were not suitable for self-subsistence, the inhabitants of such concealed settlements were often forced to resort to plundering and looting in the 'established' outside world, which, in turn, of course, prompted punitive expeditions and persecution.

The final option was departure to a remote place, where the rulers one had escaped had no direct influence. Where runaways had a place of origin that was accessible by available means of transportation, they could, following their escape, collectively seek to return there. Most deserters from the West African Banamba exodus had been enslaved only a short time before:

> This meant that many of the slaves knew another home, and even those born to slavery knew where they had originated. The slaves of the Banamba plantations formed a relatively homogeneous group,

since most of them came from Samory's conquests. Thus, the capacity for cooperation was undoubtedly greater than in plantations of diverse origins.[55]

The coolies of the Chargola Valley in Assam, who downed tools during their Exodus, stayed in touch with their regions of origin as well. In other cases, returning to the former place of residence is not an option, either because it is too far away or because no social or emotional ties exist anymore. In that event, a new domicile must be found. Those who escaped might attempt to sail to a safer area. Or they could be forced to reach another country on foot. An impressive example of this practice was the Underground Railroad, which guided escaped slaves from the South of the US to Canada.

Of course, deserters were recaptured in some cases. More often than not, they would be severely punished. But there were exceptions. Especially when the escaped persons were indispensable because of their special skills, or because they were difficult to replace for other reasons, they could expect some mercy. With mercenaries, for example, it was 'far cheaper to extend mercy to a soldier than it was to execute the offender, locate, enlist, train, cloth[e], and pay a further enlistment bounty to a recruit'.[56] The situation was similar with some slaves.

## Avoiding the stings

Desertion by oppressed and exploited groups appears to reflect a certain logic. Still more importantly, no matter how oppressed and humiliated people may be, they keep trying to 'walk with dignity'. Elias Canetti argued that commands always leave behind a painful sting in the persons forced to carry them out. However:

> Only commands which have been carried out leave their sting lodged in the obeyer. Commands which have been evaded need not be stored; the 'free' man is not the man who rids himself of commands after he has received them, but the man who knows how to evade them in the first place … there is no man who does not turn against a command imposed on him from the outside; in this case everyone speaks of pressure and reserves the right of vengeance or rebellion.[57]

# Notes

1. Murray, *New English Dictionary*, 241.
2. Clee, 'Desertion', 650.
3. See, for example, Dutta, 'Disciplining the Madras Army'; Peers, 'Sepoys, soldiers and the lash'.
4. Cummins, *War Chronicles*, 95.
5. Handler, 'Slave revolts and conspiracies', 12; Kaiser, 'Ausreißer und Meuterer', 51.
6. Murray, *New English Dictionary*, 241.
7. According to this interpretation, mercenaries also pertain to the working class, as do convict labourers. See Lichtenstein & De Vito, 'Writing a global history'; Zürcher, *Fighting for a Living*.
8. Agostini, '"Deserted His Majesty's Service"', 960.
9. See, for example, Bertaud, *Révolution Armée*, ch. 5, and Forrest, *Conscripts and Deserters*.
10. Sanborn, *Drafting the Russian Nation*, 33.
11. Rediker, *Between the Devil and the Deep Blue Sea*, 100; De Vliegher, 'Desertie bij Oostendse Oost-Indiëvaarders'.
12. Nöldeke, 'Servile war in the east', 165, 167.
13. Anderson, 'Quilimbo of Palmares'.
14. Roberts & Klein, 'Banamba slave exodus', quotes at 375 and 388.
15. Kolchin, *Unfree Labor*, 279.
16. Nichtweiss, *Bauernlegen in Mecklenburg*, 136–8.
17. Chowdhury-Zilly, *Vagrant Peasant*; Adas, 'From footdragging to flight', esp. 72–8.
18. Varma, 'Chargola exodus', 34. On the context, see also Varma, 'Producing tea coolies?' and Behal, *One Hundred Years of Servitude*.
19. Reflections on the nature of recent prison riots appear in Useem & Kimball, 'Theory of prison riots', and Useem & Reisig, 'Collective action in prisons'. For an eighteenth-century example of a prison rebellion, see Truter, 'Robben Island rebellion'.
20. Rashke, *Escape from Sobibor*.
21. Rose, 'Anatomy of mutiny'.
22. Baumann, 'Protest und Verweigerung', 41.
23. Dutka, 'New York discovers gold!', 319.
24. Taylor, *Companion to the 'Indian Mutiny'*; Ward, *Our Bones are Scattered*.
25. Skocpol (*States and Social Revolutions*, 115) explains, for example: 'By definition, peasants are primary agricultural cultivators who must … bear the burden of varying combinations of taxes, rents, corvée, usurious interest rates, and discriminatory prices. *Peasants always have grounds for rebellion* against landlords, state agents, and merchants who exploit them. What is at issue is not so much the objective potential for revolts on grounds of justifiable grievances. It is rather the degree to which grievances that are always at least implicitly present can be collectively perceived and acted upon.' [My italics]
26. I do not mean to suggest that such decisions result from careful calculations in all cases. In some, for example, alcohol abuse led to reckless acts. See, for example, the case of the Cape desertion of 1727 in Penn, 'Great escapes', 176–84.
27. Hirschman, *Exit, Voice, and Loyalty*. Hirschman defines voice as: 'any attempt at all to change, rather than to escape from, an objectionable state of affairs, whether through individual or collective petition to the management directly in charge, through appeal to a higher authority with the intention of forcing a change in management, or through various types of actions and protests, including those that are meant to mobilize public opinion' (p. 30). Acquiescence is also labelled 'apathy' or 'toleration' in the literature. See, for example, Bajoit, 'Exit, voice, loyalty … and apathy'; Hoffmann, 'Exit and voice'.
28. Hirschman, *Exit, Voice, and Loyalty*, 37, 82.
29. Dekker, 'Labour conflicts'.
30. 'Through boycott, exit is actually consummated rather than just threatened; but it is undertaken for the specific and explicit purpose of achieving a change of policy on the part of the boycotted organization and it is therefore a true hybrid of the two mechanisms.' Hirschman, *Exit, Voice, and Loyalty*, 86.
31. May & Metzger, *New Oxford Annotated Bible* (including preceding quotes), 68–70, 72, 75–9, 82–3.
32. Hirschman, '*Exit, Voice, and Loyalty*': Further reflections, 439–40.

33 Agostini, '"Deserted His Majesty's Service"', 969.
34 Hirschman, *Exit, Voice, and Loyalty*, 78.
35 Fann, 'Peacetime attrition', 326.
36 Van Creveld, *Fighting Power*, 163–4. Of course, we must not overlook the fact that ideology came into play here as well. Not necessarily the Nazi ideology as such but the conviction that one was fighting for 'a good cause' against the 'diabolical' adversary. Bartov, 'Daily life and motivation'.
37 Wong, 'Hoofdenverkiezing', 311–14.
38 For an excellent study on this subject, see Bearman, 'Desertion as localism'.
39 But, see Kamp & van Rossum, *Desertion in the Early Modern World*.
40 Schuler, 'Ethnic slave rebellions', 380.
41 Handler, 'Slave revolts and conspiracies', 15.
42 Thoden van Velzen & Hoogbergen, *Een zwarte vrijstaat in Suriname*, 1 (my italics).
43 Robinson, 'Neck-sealing in early Islam', 407; Jones, 'Stigma'.
44 Kolchin, *Unfree Labor*, 16.
45 In Stalinist labour camps, there was an occasional practice known as 'internal desertion'. There was a secret fraternity of convicted criminals (mainly pickpockets) called *vory-v-zakone*, the members of which consistently refused to work. And, although such behaviour was ordinarily punished by camp authorities and Soviet courts, the 'authorities generally avoided direct confrontation with the *vory*'. Varese, 'Society of the *Vory-v-zakone*', 518. I owe this reference to Zhanna Popova.
46 Pandya, 'Sacrifice and escape'.
47 In eighteenth-century Prussia, deserted soldiers were hunted very intensively. Any civilian was entitled to ask a passing soldier to present his pass. If a soldier had run away, the garrison would shoot a canon, informing peasants from the surrounding villages that they should assemble units immediately to search the undergrowth and other impenetrable places. Peasants were also required to occupy bridges, dams, and pathways for a while. Sikora, 'Das 18. Jahrhundert', 86 and 97.
48 Lonn, *Desertion*, 40.
49 Lonn, *Desertion*, 38.
50 Roberts & Klein, 'Banamba slave exodus', 382.
51 Agostini, '"Deserted His Majesty's Service"', 972–3.
52 Gaspar, 'Runaways', 4.
53 Sayers, Burke & Henry, 'Political economy of exile'.
54 Hall, 'Maritime maroons', 483.
55 Roberts & Klein, 'Banamba slave exodus', 379.
56 Agostini, '"Deserted His Majesty's Service"', 967.
57 Canetti, *Crowds & Power*, 58 and 306 (quotation).

# 16
# Workers and revolutions: a historical paradox

The concept of 'revolution', which derives from astrology and astronomy, became more widely known after Copernicus published *De revolutionibus orbium coelestium* in 1543, in which he described both the rotation of the planets around the sun and that of the Earth around its axis as 'revolutions'. In the three centuries that followed, huge social changes were increasingly described as revolutions.[1] Often, such changes encompassed all aspects of life and were supposed to lead to a better future.[2] The term 'social revolution' can probably be attributed to a book entitled *Considérations sur la révolution sociale*, published by the Comte de Ferrand in 1794.[3] In this period, revolution was regarded mainly as a conflict between the aristocracy and the increasingly class-conscious bourgeoisie.[4]

Between 1831 and 1848, German intellectuals comparing recent developments in different parts of Western Europe then discovered that the working classes could figure in revolutions as well. In 1842, the economist Lorenz von Stein published a book on *The Socialism and Communism of Contemporary France*, in which he argued that the rising industrial society either made workers obstinate and malicious or transformed them into dull instruments and servile subordinates. He considered personal and hereditary property to be the root cause of this decline of the working classes, since it resulted in the dominant power of some and the unfreedom of others. However, a proletarian revolution was not inexorable. Von Stein proposed a reformist political strategy in which the state should guide the redistribution of economic resources so as to prevent class polarization.[5]

In late 1843 or early 1844, Karl Marx characterized the proletariat as:

> ... a class with *radical chains*, a class *in* civil society which is not a class *of* civil society, an estate which is the dissolution of all estates,

> a sphere which has a universal character by its universal suffering and claims no *particular right* because no *particular wrong*, but *wrong generally*, is perpetrated against it.[6]

The proletariat, he continued, was the 'all-round antithesis' to existing society, which is 'the *complete loss* of man and hence can win itself only through the *complete re-winning* of man'. Gradually, the nature of this proletarian self-emancipation became clearer to Marx. In a fragment from 1845–6, written jointly with Friedrich Engels, he asserted that the abolition of bourgeois society would require the collective appropriation of all productive forces. This could be effected only through:

> ... a revolution, in which, on the one hand, the power of the earlier mode of production and intercourse and social organisation is overthrown, and, on the other hand, there develops the universal character and the energy of the proletariat, which are required to accomplish the appropriation, and the proletariat moreover rids itself of everything that still clings to it from its previous position in society'.[7]

Moses Hess – the philosopher who, together with Karl Marx, Friedrich Engels, and others, had worked on *The German Ideology* – wrote in 1847 about the 'Consequences of a Revolution of the Proletariat'.[8] Engels noted in *Principles of Communism*, published that same year: 'In all probability, the proletarian revolution will transform existing society gradually and will be able to abolish private property only when the means of production are available in sufficient quantity'.[9]

The discovery of radical labour struggles, of course, related directly to its growing visibility in the three most important countries in Western Europe. Between 1831 and 1834, the uprising by silk workers in Lyon had instigated a general strike unique for that era, as well as two very bloody confrontations with the authorities.[10] In England, the proletarian Chartist movement for political reform had an enormous impact from 1838.[11] And, in 1844, the rebellion of weavers in Peterswaldau and Langenbielau (Silesia) revealed that, in Germany, the working class was starting to awaken as well.[12]

## The Marx–Hess–Engels hypothesis

Marx, Hess, Engels, and others believed that the rise of capitalism would yield continuous expansion of the working class in the decades ahead.

Labour would therefore become ever more important in future revolutions, which would soon result in the subversion of capitalist relations. This view seemed to find resounding confirmation in the revolutions of 1848–9 in France, Central Europe, and so on, which explicitly shifted the focus to the working class as an emergent – albeit not yet dominant – vector in the social and political field of forces.[13] Was this perception accurate?

In answering this question, I shall apply the broad concept of the working class as elaborated in global labour history in recent years (Chapter 2). In this perception, the history of capitalist labour must encompass all forms of physically or economically coerced commodification of labour-power. This includes wage labourers, slaves, sharecroppers, convict labourers, and so on, plus all labour that creates such commodified labour or regenerates it – that is, parental labour, household labour, care labour, and subsistence labour. This broad description enables us to acknowledge the role of housewives (for example, as instigators of the February Revolution in Russia in 1917), as well as the actions of cottage labourers or chattel slaves.

The rise of the working class according to this broad perception, of course, largely paralleled the rise of capitalism. After all, capitalism is merely a progressively self-reinforcing commodification of consumer goods, natural resources, means of production, and labour-power. Labour-power commodification became widespread early on in certain urban industries, such as in porcelain production in the Chinese city of Jingdezhen, where several hundred thousand workers were employed during the Qing Dynasty (Figure 16.1).[14] Only a small share of this industry was capitalist because most production was not for the market but for the imperial household. Still, many conflicts arose here as well:

> ... disputes, which sometimes led to death, ... broke out between workers and kiln owners on the issue of working conditions and wages. The town therefore was often in riot. Indeed, the local gazetteer of Fuliang County attests to this last characteristic, saying that 'all kinds of people from across the country were taking refuge in Jingdezhen. One intrigue would cause the whole town to react. This town is difficult to govern'.[15]

Labour concentrations in European textile cities in Flanders and Italy were more clearly capitalist from the fourteenth century. From the seventeenth century, relatively large proletarian concentrations also existed in the Caribbean, where entire islands were based on slave labour.

**Figure 16.1** Late handcrafted Jingdezhen porcelain production: glaze pouring workshop, depicted on one of 17 handcrafted porcelain plaques, datable to the late-nineteenth–early-twentieth century. Photographer: Thomas M. Mueller © Shirley Maloney Mueller/Thomas M. Mueller, with permission.

The formation of proletarian concentrations was conducive to rebellious sentiment. John Millar, one of the leading intellectuals of the Scottish Enlightenment, observed the consequences of economic growth towards the end of the eighteenth century:

> As the advancement of commerce and manufactures in Britain has produced a state of property highly favourable to liberty, so it has contributed to collect and arrange the inhabitants in a manner which enables them, with great facility, to combine in asserting their privileges … Villages are enlarged into towns; and these are often swelled into populous cities. In all those places of resort, there arise large bands of labourers or artificers, who by following the same employment, and by constant intercourse, are enabled, with great rapidity, to communicate all their sentiments and passions. Among these there spring up leaders, who give a tone and direction to their companions … In this situation, a great proportion of the people are easily aroused by every popular discontent, and can unite with no less facility in demanding a redress of grievances. The least ground of complaint, in a town, becomes the occasion of a riot; and the flames of sedition spreading from one city to another, are blown up into a general insurrection.[16]

The first radical proletarian uprisings remained local, as the capitalist concentrations were also local. Nevertheless, such rebellions could acquire a revolutionary logic. Tuscany in the late-fourteenth century was a case in point. In those days, Florence was a very important city with large textile manufactories, ruled by the aristocracy and the *popolo grasso* (the 'fat people' – wealthy merchants and bankers). The city had a population of about 55,000. There were 21 guilds, with a total male membership of 4,000 to 5,000. The other working-age males – about 10,000 or 11,000 souls – were not organized; they belonged to the lower strata of the working class, with the wool carders (the unskilled *ciompi*) as the bottom tier.

Political tensions existed in the region between factions of the elite, and a large share of the working population became increasingly dissatisfied over taxes, debt, and irregular employment. The 'unorganized' (the *popolo minuto*) were strictly prohibited from convening their own gatherings or forming organizations. Still, over the course of June–July 1378, they did convene secret meetings, where workers took ritual oaths to support each other as long as they lived, in the struggle against anyone who intended to harm them. The resulting underground network was to be decisive in the subsequent course of events.

On 21 July, a crowd of about 7,000 workers and guildsmen from all guilds (except the elitist wool guild, which was, in fact, an employers' organization) marched to the city palace, the Bargello. While some of the insurgents destroyed the records of investigations and convictions of workers on the lower floors, others hung the flag of the blacksmith's guild from the tower – this flag depicted tongs, intentionally symbolizing violence. The flags of all guilds (except the wool guild) were suspended from a lower floor. The message was clear: the revolution was the work of the community as a whole.

Three new guilds were formed for all those not yet organized, thereby ensuring that the entire working population was represented on the city council. During the weeks that followed, the new administration took forceful measures. For the next two years, nobody was to be imprisoned for indebtedness, the flour tax was abolished, and the price of salt reduced. To stabilize employment, the industry as a whole was required to produce at least 2,000 wool cloths (*panni*) a month, 'whether they wanted to or not, or suffer great penalties'. In addition, needy families were to receive a bushel of grain per capita, and money was to be provided to those in need who resided within a three-mile radius of the city limits.

These measures were less effective than envisaged, however, because employers undermined them at every opportunity. The *ciompi*, in particular, urged a tougher approach and sustained a campaign of ongoing criticism. Thus, when, on 31 August, a large crowd of *ciompi* gathered on the Piazza della Signoria, representatives of the other guilds violently chased them from the city. The other two guilds founded around the same time, those of dyers and doublet-makers, continued to exist and for a few more years formed a Government of the Minor Guilds. Their rule ended on 19 January 1382, when the soldiers of the wool guild and patricians toppled the administration.[17]

The revolt in Florence may certainly be qualified as an attempt at a proletarian revolution. Still, other cases of rebellious workers are known, and in at least one other instance they achieved lasting change. This example concerns the slave uprising on Saint-Domingue between 1791 and 1804. The island was among the most profitable colonies in the world and comprised a great many lucrative sugarcane plantations, based on slave labour. Of the total population (about 640,000), nearly 570,000 were enslaved. The other inhabitants were white people and free blacks. Inspired by the French Revolution, many slaves staged an uprising. They drove out the plantation owners and withstood French and British invasions. Their uprising was, as Peter Linebaugh and Marcus Rediker aptly described it, 'the first successful workers' revolt in modern history'.[18]

In both Florence and Saint-Domingue, these were true social revolutions driven by large numbers of workers – wage workers in the former, enslaved labourers in the latter. The revolution in Florence was defeated; the one in Saint-Domingue prevailed, despite very lengthy and strong opposition by foreign potentates. Social revolutions are understood here as historical situations in which (i) fundamental contrasts exist between social classes that (ii) lead to a revolt by subordinate classes aimed at seizing political and economic power to (iii) achieve drastic change in social relations. This description does not necessarily mean that a successful change leads the subordinate classes to be the main beneficiaries of such change. Alvin Gouldner even argued that this process followed a general pattern to the contrary:

> The *Communist Manifesto* had held that the history of all hitherto existing society was the history of class struggles: freeman and slave, patrician and plebian, lord and serf, guildmaster and journeyman, and, then, bourgeoisie and proletariat. In this series, however, there was one unspoken regularity: the slaves did not succeed the masters, the plebians did not vanquish the patricians,

the serfs did not overthrow the lords, and the journeymen did not triumph over the guildmasters. *The lowliest class never came to power.*[19]

This argument seems overly adamant. In Saint-Domingue, for instance, the slaves did achieve abolition, although admittedly they did not fully seize societal control. Nonetheless, Gouldner's position contains some truth. Moreover, revolutions ordinarily follow a complicated course. There is hardly ever a clear-cut situation where two classes (such as aristocracy and bourgeoisie) diametrically oppose one another in closed ranks. There will always be more than two classes, and, ordinarily, (temporary) multi-class blocs arise. In addition, classes are dynamic relationships, and oppositions will also exist *within* separate classes. A section of the struggling classes will consistently stay outside the conflict. Revolution may even come about 'from above', in that part of the elite wants radical change – such as in Japan during the Meiji Restauration from 1868.[20]

## Workers as auxiliaries

The relentless capitalist expansion never led to proletarian concentrations that were as dense nationally as they had become in smaller settings in Florence or Saint-Domingue. Large local proletarian uprisings continued to occur until well into the twentieth century, for example in France (Paris, 1871), China (Shanghai, 1927), Argentina (Cordoba, 1969), and Pakistan (Karachi, 1972).[21]

Our knowledge of the social aspects of revolutions has increased considerably in recent decades. For a long time, historians paid little attention to the lowest classes or greatly relativized their role. Even in 1972, Lawrence Stone argued with respect to the English Revolution that: 'the labouring poor, both rural and urban, played no part whatever in the Revolution except as cannon-fodder'.[22] And very recently, Boris Mironov defended a similar argument about the Russian Revolution of 1917.[23] However, the work of scholars such as Gregor Benton, Norah Carlin, Daniel Guérin, Dirk Hoerder, Erich Kuttner, Brian Manning, Alexander Rabinowitch, and many others has demonstrated that such views are untenable. Let us consider some major revolutions.

The Peasants' Wars in Central Europe in 1524–6 were, as the name indicates, waged by rebellious agriculturalists but were, on occasion, supported by the miners in the Erz Mountains, Bohemia, North Tyrol, and elsewhere:

> Influenced by the revolutionary peasant movement, sections of the miner class sporadically joined forces with the peasants in many places, with the former supporting the latter in most cases. Nowhere – except perhaps in the special case of Salzburg – did a broad alliance come about, where the mutual aid societies or the entire community of the miners, respectively, express solidarity or engaged in joint actions with the peasants in a place or mining region'.[24]

Elsewhere, the Dutch Revolt against Spanish rule (1566–1609) started as a revolutionary movement, in which workers, mainly from the textile industry, played a major part. Despite their very strident disposition, their influence remained limited. Erich Kuttner, who was the first to study this revolution from a social-historical perspective, observed:

> ... true class-consciousness is rare among the masses. They tend to submit to any leadership from above: the aristocracy or the wealthy bourgeoisie. Still, the class instinct is penetrating the masses in a purely elementary sense, primitive communist slogans ... surface, and we constantly observe an unfathomable hatred of the poor for the rich, without the poor having been indoctrinated about the class struggle. Back in the sixteenth century, only the material power of the authorities withheld the masses from murdering and pillaging the wealthy, whom they regard as 'bloodsuckers' – as the moment such power diminishes, that passionate longing consistently resurfaces. Based on this example, we may conclude that class hatred considerably predates its discovery by scholars or even its propagation by political parties.[25]

In the run-up to the English Revolution of 1642–60 the popular classes figured prominently, both the 'middling sort', consisting of the social groups ranging 'from the larger farmers (called "yeomen") and the substantial tradesmen to the mass of land-holding peasants (called "husbandmen") and self-employed craftsmen', as well as the 'poorer sort' (wage-labourers and paupers):[26]

> Popular disorders in 1640–42 were heterogeneous in causes and aims, sometimes they united the 'middling sort' with the 'poorer sort', sometimes they involved only the 'poorer sort'. These disorders

ushered in the civil war because they influenced many nobles and gentlemen to rally to the king's cause. But the popular support which enabled parliament to fight and win the civil war came from amongst the 'middling sort'.[27]

At no point, however, does an independent workers' movement appear to have crystallized; the craftsmen and peasants were in charge. 'Many of those who took part in the revolt of 1640–42, in the New Model Army during the war and in radical movements later, were indeed independent small producers'.[28] Moreover, the radical ideas of the Levellers, Diggers, and Ranters 'failed to gel with popular grievances and experiences'.[29]

The American Revolution of 1765–83 was, in some respects, comparable to the earlier Dutch Revolt, as it was a relatively decentralized process, occurring mainly in the cities on the East coast and varying depending on the place. Gary B. Nash nevertheless noted that:

> ... the American Revolution could not have unfolded when or in the manner it did without the self-conscious action of urban laboring people – both those at the bottom and those in the middle – who became convinced that they must create power where none had existed before or else watch their position deteriorate, both in absolute terms and relative to that of others. Thus, the history of the Revolution is in part the history of popular collective action and the puncturing of the gentry's claim that their rule was legitimized by custom, law, and divine will. Ordinary people sometimes violently took over power and the procedures of the constituted authorities.[30]

Notwithstanding, no social revolution occurred in America in the 1770s.

Daniel Guérin observed that, during the French Revolution of 1789–99, it was the proletarian *bras nus* who, by marching to Versailles on 5 October 1789, had forced the Assembly to adopt the Declaration of the Rights of Man, which would probably not have happened without such an intervention. Nor would the expropriation without compensation of feudal dues on 10 August 1792 have come about without pressure from the masses. More generally, however:

> Whenever the course of the revolution intensifies one finds the bourgeois equivocating, or stopping half-way, and each time it is the pressure from the *bras nus* that forces them to push the bourgeois revolution to its conclusion. Even insofar as it was a bourgeois revolution, bringing the bourgeoisie to power in the end rather than

the proletariat, the French revolution was a mass revolution ... But this revolution was not a revolution in which the masses worked on behalf of the bourgeoisie without realising it. It was also, to a certain degree, a revolution that the masses were making for themselves and nobody else ... They rose up in the hope that it would alleviate their poverty and misery and throw off an age-old yoke, not just that of the feudal lords, the clergy and the agents of royalist absolutism, but the yoke of the bourgeoisie as well.[31]

Basically, in the bourgeois revolutions of the sixteenth–eighteenth centuries, the role of the working class gradually became more visible and, at some moments, even substantial but was never decisive for the outcome.

The same holds true for the Mexican Revolution of 1910–20. It was driven mainly by peasant communities, who were supported by disaffected urban intellectuals. Many workers embraced this cause as well, such as the cowboys of the northern cattle ranches, labourers on sugar plantations, and trade unions. Their role remained subordinate, however, partly because of their relatively small number. 'Some of [the working class's] struggles were important and its class organization moved forward, but its policy and leadership did not attain independence of the state and the leading bourgeois tendencies of the revolution.'[32]

## Workers centre-stage

During the twentieth century, workers started to figure more prominently in revolutions. At the same time, the complexity of proletarian action became more manifest:

> Because class conflict is experienced as uneven, discontinuous, and partial, its organisational expressions normally reflect this. The working class is sectionalised and fragmented. One section is fighting while others are not. Workers are opposing the symptoms rather than the root causes of exploitation and oppression. The overall level of conflict – measured, say in the pattern of strikes – rises and falls in intensity and extent. Particular kinds of organisation, with definite kinds of politics, are erected to express this contradictory pattern of consciousness and struggle.[33]

Even in the 'new' proletarian type of revolutions, however, workers were never the *sole* drivers of the revolutionary process. The best-known case of a change often described as 'proletarian' was the Russian Revolution of October 1917. This revolution was, in fact, a combination of three factors: the struggle of the workers, the struggle of the peasants, and the struggle of the oppressed nationalities. The industrial working class was not very large – possibly two million people in 1917 – but its strike movements achieved an enormous impact; in Trotsky's words, they became 'the battering ram which the awakening nation directs against the walls of absolutism'.[34] At the same time, the proletariat could never have brought about the downfall of the Tsarist Regime on its own. The very position of the working class as a minority of the nation suggests that 'it could not have given its struggle a sufficient scope – certainly not enough to take its place at the head of the state – if it had not found a mighty support in the thick of the people. Such a support was guaranteed to it by the agrarian problem'.[35]

Nonetheless, the action by the workers had such an immense impact that the October Revolution became *the* prototype of a 'proletarian revolution'. As Georges Haupt observed:

> Those were the years of the radicalization of Europe, coming after the First World War. There was a tremendous anticapitalist, antibourgeois feeling. People were looking for a social force able to bring about the revolution, and that social force was going to be the proletariat … If one looks at the cultural history of the Soviet Union in the years 1918–1924, one discovers a fantastically interesting phenomenon. Everyone would like to be a worker. This is the mode in the Soviet Union. Everyone wears working clothes. The reference group is the working class, which is the center of the whole self-understanding of the revolution in the future society.[36]

The October Revolution of 1917 ushered in a series of upheavals in which workers played an essential role. Their actions brought about the demise of the *anciens régimes* because they immobilized key industries. During the Bolivian Revolution of 1952, the peasants were initially passive, whereas the action by the tin miners proved decisive: they defeated the demoralized armed forces and opened the door to massive economic and social changes:

> The tin magnates, who had created a state within a state, *un superestado*, manipulating Bolivian presidents and legislators at will, lost their lucrative mines and power. The Army, which had largely functioned as an instrument of suppression and political

manipulation, and as protector of the established social order, was abolished. The Indians, who comprised an overwhelming majority of the population of Bolivia, gained for the first time full civil and political rights. The MNR [Revolutionary Nationalist Movement] instituted a radical program of land reform through which the Indian won property rights. The educational system was re-organized along more democratic lines.[37]

Yet, despite their crucial role, the workers did not achieve a lasting victory. The MNR accommodated only some of their demands, and, after the military coup in 1964, their unions and parties were destroyed in violent clashes.[38]

The course of events in the Cuban Revolution of 1953–9 was entirely different. Fidel Castro's so-called 26th of July Movement (also known as M-26-7) was a de-classed populist movement, with Castro initially supporting the left wing of the *Partido Ortodoxo* (Orthodox Party), the liberal–bourgeois opposition. The struggle of his *guerilleros* (possibly amounting to one thousand members at its peak) was supported by spontaneous popular uprisings and strikes, with broad participation by parts of the vast labour movement (sugar workers, railway workers) between August 1957 and January 1959. As a social force, the working class contributed substantially to the victory. Politically, however, it remained an appendage of Castro's initially liberal policy. The first government formed by Castro was therefore still liberal-bourgeois. It was only during the next two years that the regime radicalized.[39]

In the Iranian Revolution of 1978–9, workers were not pivotal. Until mid-1978, the main operators were 'students and intellectuals, the urban poor, and the modern and traditional middle classes' that agitated against the regime of the Shah.[40] Proletarian resistance increased only later on. The participation of the oil workers from the autumn was decisive: they deactivated the most important source of state income, and the battle soon ended. In January 1979, the Shah fled the country.[41]

The Polish Revolution of 1980–1 was largely driven by proletarian rebelliousness. The revolt began in the middle of 1980 as a wave of strikes, soon spreading throughout much of the country and reaching its peak in mid-August in the port cities of Gdansk, Gdynia, and Szczecin. With support from the Workers' Defence Committee (KOR), it evolved into a national counterweight organization (Solidarność), gradually bringing about the start of 'dual power'; many farmers supported the protest as well. The power and authority of the state visibly declined. Only in December 1981 did the situation change, when 'order' was restored via a military coup; Solidarność was suspended and martial law introduced.[42]

Looking back on the developments over the past five centuries reveals that, from 1917, workers figured more prominently in national revolutions than they had previously. Still, their role was never as great as the Marx–Hess–Engels hypothesis would have led us to believe. Nowhere did a revolution culminate in a stable society that revolved around the interests of workers. Admittedly, the 'lowliest class' – contrary to what Gouldner argued – sometimes did rise to power (Russia), but it never managed to retain this power for long.

## Two complications

The analysis becomes still more complicated. The first complication is that, even in the twentieth century, there were revolutions in which workers remained entirely subordinate. These uprisings were led by communist parties that believed in the Stalinist two-stage theory – that, first, a bourgeois–democratic change was necessary and, then, a socialist (proletarian) change. The most important example of this process was the Chinese Revolution of 1927–49. In 1927, the Kuomintang nationalist party had achieved a crushing defeat of the labour movement in Shanghai and suppressed it through mass terror. A few years later, the Japanese occupation forces dismantled part of the Chinese industry, thereby reducing the numbers of the working class. These developments turned the Chinese Communist Party progressively from a proletarian into a military organization of peasants demanding massive agricultural reform. They built an expanding territorial counterforce that ultimately defeated the Kuomintang and established a state. Workers were completely ignored as social forces. When the People's Liberation Army entered the cities, they urged workers not to strike or demonstrate. The following eight points formed the basis of their propaganda:

1) People's lives and property will be protected. Keep order and don't listen to rumors. Looting and killing are strictly forbidden.
2) Chinese individual commercial and industrial property will be protected. Private factories, banks, godowns [warehouses], etc., will not be touched and can continue operating.
3) Bureaucratic capital, including factories, shops, banks, godowns, railways, post offices, telephone and telegraph installations, power plants, etc., will be taken over by the Liberation Army, although private shares will be respected. Those working in these organizations should work peacefully

and wait for the takeover. Rewards will be given to those who protect property and documents; those who strike or who destroy will be punished. Those wishing to continue serving will be employed.

4) Schools, hospitals, and public institutions will be protected. Students, teachers and all workers should protect their records. Anyone with ability to work will be employed.

5) Except for a few major war criminals and notorious reactionaries, all Kuomintang officials, police and *Pao-Chia* workers of the Provincial, Municipal, and *Hsien* Governments will be pardoned, if they do not offer armed resistance. They should protect their records. Anyone with ability to work will be employed.

6) As soon as a city is liberated, displaced soldiers should report immediately to the new garrison headquarters, the police bureau, or army authorities. Anyone surrendering his weapons will not be questioned. Those who hide will be punished.

7) The lives and property of all foreigners will be protected. They must obey the laws of the Liberation Army and Democratic Government. No espionage or illegal actions will be allowed. No war criminals should be sheltered. They will be subject to military or civilian trial for violations.

8) People in general should protect all public property and keep order.[43]

Only after 1949 did the social and political importance of the working class start to grow again.[44]

In several respects, the revolution in Vietnam in August 1945 was a harbinger of the Chinese Revolution. In the years following its establishment in 1930, the Indochinese Communist Party had given extensive consideration to workers and their struggle; but, over the course of the 1930s, interest had shifted towards mobilizing peasants. At the party's Eighth Conference in May 1941, it definitively changed course:

> It considered that 'the preparation for insurrection is the central responsibility of our Party in the present period'. It called for a 'national liberation revolution' and temporary postponement of the class struggle … On May 19, 1941, at the conclusion of the conference, the Alliance for Vietnamese Independence (*Viet nam Doc lap Dong minh Hoi*), or the Viet Minh Front, was created. It was the organizational expression of the united front proposed by the Resolution of the Conference.[45]

The coup that took place three months later focused on reforming land ownership, rather than on the liberation of wage labour.

The second complication is that the revolutions of the twentieth century all took place in pre-industrial or industrializing countries, and never in fully developed capitalist societies. Some may consider this a coincidence; but the systematic non-manifestation of working-class revolutions from the bottom-up under developed capitalism suggests a structural reason. Although the working class (in the broad sense described) became very large over the course of the twentieth century, under the advanced conditions, it never again behaved so radically anywhere as in Russia in 1917 or in Bolivia in 1952. As an indication to the contrary, consider the events in France in May–June 1968. Research reveals that the revolutionary students were vastly different from the considerably less revolutionary workers:

> Ironically enough, Maoists, Trotskyites, and *Les Temps Modernes* have rather uncritically accepted PCF [French Communist Party] claims to represent the working class. They assumed that the party controlled the workers and could have made revolution. It is doubtful, though, that even a revolutionary PCF would have been able to convince wage earners to take power … Wage earners might have desired to limit the 'arbitrary' authority of supervisory personnel and to slow down production rhythms, but little evidence exists to suggest that workers wanted to take over their factories. Instead, they demanded higher pay (especially for lower-paid personnel), a further reduction of work time, total (and not half) payment for days lost to strikes, a nominal recuperation of strike time, and—for the activists—a union presence in the factory.[46]

Another symptom of the non-manifestation of revolutions in advanced capitalist societies seems to be the fact, noted by Perry Anderson, that counter-institutions of dual power have never arisen in consolidated parliamentary democracies: 'all the examples of soviets or councils so far have emerged out of disintegrating autocracies (Russia, Hungary, Austria), defeated military regimes (Germany), ascendant or overturned fascist states (Spain, Portugal)'.[47]

## The paradox and its possible explanation

The latter complication gives rise to a paradox: the 'purest' proletarian revolutions – those with absolute dominance by the proletariat – occurred early on in capitalism. In advanced capitalism, however, under circumstances that, according to the Marx–Hess–Engels hypothesis, are supposed to be the most conducive to a proletarian revolution, they do not take place. How is this possible? A convincing answer will require much additional research and I can merely speculate about it here. I suspect that three factors come into play: the transition dip, deflection, and incorporation.

## The transition dip

The 'transition dip' idea elaborates on the work of Charles Tilly and Adam Przeworski. Tilly asserts that states in advanced capitalist countries function very differently from those in the less advanced ones.[48] In Europe and North America, well into the nineteenth century (as in many less-developed capitalist countries nowadays), states were not clearly visible to ordinary people, and the occasions where they did manifest their presence tended to be decidedly unpleasant. In those 'pre-advanced' days, states usually maintained a system of *indirect* rule. They hardly ever intervened in the lives of ordinary people directly but, instead, had relatively autonomous local representatives. On the rare occasions that states did penetrate everyday lives, their main purpose was to *take* (money, goods, people) and almost never to *give*. In these circumstances, workers hoping to halt deteriorating conditions or even to improve their fates did not think first (if at all) of the state. Under 'pre-advanced' conditions, groups of workers therefore primarily devised alternatives without a significant role for the state. In the North Atlantic region, trade unions, journeymen's associations, and the like were transnational *avant la lettre* and, in many cases, coordinated operations across national borders. Alternative concepts were based on autonomous cooperatives and on anarchist and liberal experiments.[49] For 'pre-advanced' populations, the social revolution idea often exuded a broad appeal as well, as the state tended to be regarded as a hostile military and tax-collecting apparatus that had to be eliminated.

This stage ended – at least in the North Atlantic region – during the extended nineteenth century as a consequence of the Napoleonic wars and their aftermath. The immense citizens' armies of post-revolutionary France and of many other countries that followed the French example, as well as the rise of relatively comprehensive tax systems, made for qualitatively stronger state interference in everyday social relations. This change coincided with the transition to *direct* rule, in which the central government started to intervene far more directly in the lives of the population than it had in the past. Direct rule, in turn, led to a rapid expansion of the purview of involvement. Non-military state expenditures increased exponentially. States 'began to monitor industrial conflict and working conditions, install and regulate national systems of education, organize aid to the poor and disabled, build and maintain communication lines, impose tariffs for the benefit of home industries'.[50] Somewhat parallel to this process, systems of surveillance were devised to block the emergence of forms of protest and resistance that might threaten states and their clients.

As states began to demand more from their subjects and became more closely involved with them, their subjects started to expect something in return. Modern citizenship, which in the past had sometimes existed at the municipal level, became a national phenomenon concurrent with the rise of direct rule. Precisely during this stage, as 'subjects' became 'citizens', national trade unions and other national labour organizations gradually consolidated. No longer in a position to ignore the state and no longer interested in immediately destroying it, they sought primarily to influence or even conquer it (possibly with the intention of destroying it at a later stage):

> In the process, organized claimants including workers and capitalists found themselves embedding their rights and privileges in the state. Establishing the right to strike, for example, not only defined a number of previously common worker actions (such as attacks on nonstrikers and scabs) as illegal, but also made the state the prime adjudicator of that right.[51]

This, in essence, meant an enormous increase 'in the importance of the [collectively useful] functions, and therefore of the functioning, of public administration in the daily life of the people'.[52] A revolution would therefore completely disrupt daily life. And the changed role of the state considerably drove up the 'costs' of attempts to overthrow capitalist society.[53] As Adam Przeworski remarked:

> Suppose that socialism is potentially superior to capitalism at any moment of capitalist development (or at least after some threshold, if one believes that conditions must be 'ripe') but that immediate steps toward socialism leave workers worse off than they would have been had they advanced along the capitalist path ... Between the capitalist path and the socialist one there is a valley that must be traversed if workers move at any time toward socialism. If such

conditions indeed exist and if workers are interested in a continual improvement of their material welfare, then this descent will not be undertaken or, if it is undertaken, will not be completed by workers under democratic conditions. At any time workers would thus face a choice between climbing upward toward the best situation they could obtain under capitalism and a temporary deterioration of their conditions on the road to socialism.[54]

The period of direct rule may thus have attenuated any revolutionary influences in the working class and stimulated the rise of movements that aimed to achieve reforms via the state – as a prelude to social revolution or as a cumulative strategy of small steps.

It seems likely that this observation depends on long periods of improving living standards and a stable state-apparatus. The transition dip (Figure 16.2) would probably lose much of its relevance if states were to fall into crisis (such as in a war) and/or if the material conditions of the population were to deteriorate seriously.

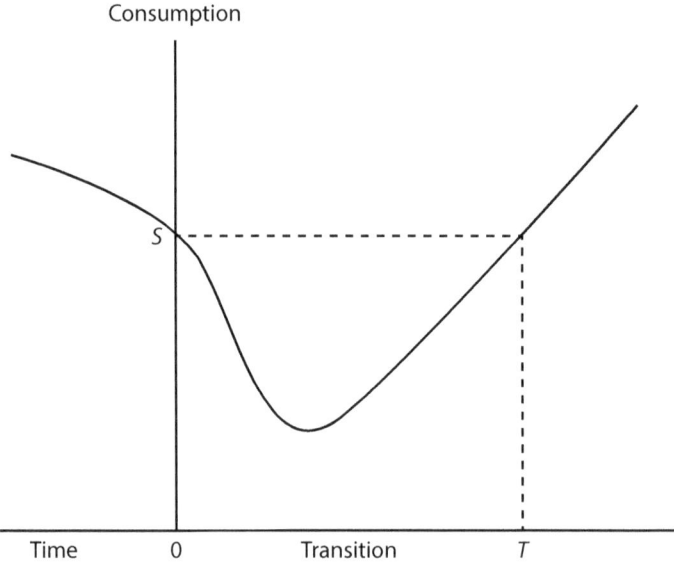

**Figure 16.2** The 'transition dip'. Source: Przeworski, *Capitalism and Social Democracy*, p. 177. At any given time, workers face a choice between climbing upwards towards the best situation they can obtain under capitalism vs. a temporary deterioration of their conditions on the road to socialism – even if socialism is potentially superior to capitalism.

## Deflection

I would describe the second possible factor as 'deflection'. By this, I mean that the state – even in the stage of direct rule – is not regarded as playing a major part in causing social, economic, political, or cultural injustice. There are at least three probable causes. First, under capitalism, the economic sphere becomes separated from the political sphere. Class conflicts are therefore initially situated at work sites, and are thus local and particularistic:

> In this respect, the organization of capitalist production itself resists the working class unity which capitalism is supposed to encourage. On the one hand, the nature of the capitalist economy—its national, even supra-national, character, the interdependence of its constituent parts, the homogenization of work produced by the capitalist labour-process—makes both necessary and possible a working class consciousness and class organization on a mass scale. This is the aspect of capitalism's effects on class-consciousness that Marxist theory has so often emphasized. On the other hand, the development of this consciousness and this organization must take place against the centrifugal force of capitalist production and its 'privatization' of political issues.[55]

Even very militant workers' struggles may become detracted from their *political* and *general* character.

Second, many intermediary institutions and organizations emerge; and, to some extent, they perform the functions of the state, although they do not pertain to the state or otherwise qualify as 'semi-state' apparatuses. These would include what Louis Althusser described as 'ideological' state apparatuses, such as schools, the family, religious institutions, and the mass media.[56] They also include public transport, NGOs, and other non-profit organizations.[57] Third, racist, sexist, and nationalist influences may further undermine working-class unity and combativity.[58]

## Incorporation

The third possible factor I propose is incorporation. The Marx–Hess–Engels hypothesis underestimated capitalism's ability to incorporate the proletariat. Marx, as we have seen, considered the proletariat as 'a class *in* civil society which is not a class *of* civil society'.[59] Gradually, however, the proletariat *has* become a part of civil society. At least two influences probably played a role in this process, starting with the political incorporation of the proletariat, partly also resulting from the efforts of labour movements. In the British case, Bert Moorhouse has argued that:

> ... the majority of the ruling class believed that incorporation was necessary to bind the masses to the prevailing system but also wanted such integration to be constrained and channeled so that, though institutional forms might change, and could be promoted as having changed, the differential distribution of power in society would remain unaltered.[60]

The second influence facilitating proletarians' integration into civil society was their incorporation as consumers. It is true that Marx, in his *Grundrisse*, drew our attention to the capitalist's attempts to spur the workers 'on to consumption, to endow his commodities with new attractions, to talk the workers into feeling new needs, etc.', but nowhere does he evince the idea that he understood the huge implications of the proletariat's golden chains.[61] Consumption's seductive power culminated in the relations of production and consumption (sometimes called 'Fordist') whereby working-class families not only produce and reproduce labour-power to be hired-out but also operate simultaneously as units of individualized mass consumption, purchasing many of the consumer goods they produce within a system that permits capital to expand and workers' material standards of living to improve. The ideology of consumerism made them (partly) consumption-driven. As Richard Wolff wrote on the US:

> They had to define themselves as above all 'consumers' who willingly suffered the 'disutility' of labor to acquire the 'utilities' embodied in consumption ... The advertising that pervades every aspect of life relentlessly popularizes this interpellation ... The 'manipulation' of the masses entailed in such consumerism was possible because it 'latched onto' something real enough in workers' lives: the need for a compensation, rationale, and justification for ... their alienated and exhausting labor.[62]

The combined effect of the transition dip, deflection, and incorporation probably explains why revolutions have not occurred in advanced capitalist countries. Deflection and incorporation were considerably less important in the so-called 'socialist' societies of Eastern Europe. This may explain why revolutions in which workers were sometimes pivotal *did* occur there; there was no separation of the political and the economic spheres, and intermediary institutions and organizations were mostly absent, as were political incorporation and the possibilities for consumerism.

All in all, 'workers' revolutions' are much more complicated than is often assumed. One gets the impression that Karl Marx, Moses Hess, and Friedrich Engels – impressed by the West European workers' revolts of the 1830s and 40s – first proclaimed the wage-labouring class to be the revolutionary subject on philosophical grounds, and then collected arguments that were partly of an ad-hoc nature.[63] The outcome was a theory of the working class that has been partly refuted by historical experience. The Marx–Hess–Engels hypothesis clearly did not anticipate the seductive and deceptive powers of advanced capitalism. My own exploration of these powers remains highly speculative, and, in my defence, I can only share the insight of Pierre Bourdieu that 'an obvious fault is better than a hidden error'.[64]

## Notes

1. The first transition identified as a 'revolution' was probably the upheaval in the North German town of Emden in 1595. See van Lengen, *Die 'Emder Revolution'*.
2. Koselleck et al., 'Revolution', 655.
3. Ferrand, *Considérations*.
4. See, for example, Miliband, 'Barnave'.
5. von Stein, *Socialismus und Communismus*; Singelmann & Singelmann, 'Lorenz von Stein'.
6. *MECW*, Vol. 3, 186; translation corrected.
7. *MECW*, Vol. 5, 88.
8. Hess, 'Consequences of a revolution'.
9. *MECW*, Vol. 6, 684 (§ 17).
10. Rudé, *Révoltes des canuts*; Moissonnier, *Révolte des canuts*. The best monograph in English is that of Bezucha, *Lyon Uprising of 1834*.
11. The literature about the Chartists is vast. See, for example, Thompson, *Chartists*, or Chase, *Chartism*. Marx and Engels were in contact with a few Chartist leaders. See, for example, Cadogan, 'Harney and Engels', and Collins & Abramsky, *Karl Marx*.
12. Kroneberg & Schloesser, *Weber-Revolte 1844*; von Hodenberg, *Aufstand der Weber*.
13. Extensive information appears in the journal *La révolution de 1848*, published in France since 1904 and later renamed *Revue d'histoire du XIXe siècle*. Studies focusing explicitly on the role of the workers in 1848 include Gossez, *Ouvriers de Paris*, I; Meriggi, *L'invenzione della classe operaia*; Noyes, *Organization and Revolution*; Pech, 'Czech working class in 1848'; Mérei, 'Mouvement ouvrier en Hongrie'; Tønnesson, 'Popular protest and organization'. See also 'Encyclopedia of 1848 Revolutions' (online).
14. See the eyewitness reports from the Jesuit Francis d'Entrecolles, written between 1712 and 1722. He noted, for example: 'The establishments of some of the larger tradesmen occupy a vast area and contain an enormous number of workers. It is generally said that there are more than a million souls here and that ten thousand loads of rice and a thousand pigs are consumed

daily. It is over a league long on the banks of a beautiful river and not a heap of houses as you might imagine; the streets are as straight as a bowstring and intersect at regular intervals. All the land is occupied and the houses are too close and the streets too narrow.' Quoted in Michael Dillon, 'A history of the porcelain industry in Jingdezhen', 47.
15 Hsu, 'Social and economic factors', 146.
16 Millar, 'The advancement of manufacture, commerce, and the arts', 337–9.
17 This description is based on a compilation of data from: NN, 'Diario dello Squittinatore'; Doren, *Florentiner Wollentuchindustrie*, 241–2; Trexler, 'Follow the flag'; Cohn, *Lust for Liberty*, 59–62; and Najemy, *History of Florence*, 160–5.
18 Linebaugh & Rediker, *The Many-Headed Hydra*, 319. While much has been written about the slave rebellion of Saint-Domingue, the best book on the event remains that of James, *Black Jacobins*.
19 Gouldner, *Future of Intellectuals*, 93. This seems to relate, in part, to the thesis of Alex Callinicos that bourgeois revolutions need not be achieved by the bourgeoisie: 'Bourgeois revolutions should not be conceived as revolutions which are made consciously by capitalists, but as revolutions which promote capitalism. The emphasis should not be placed on the class which makes the bourgeois revolution, but on the implications of such a revolution – for the class that benefits from it. More particularly, a bourgeois revolution is a political transformation, a change in state power, which is a condition for large scale capital accumulation and the establishment of the bourgeoisie as dominant class. This definition therefore requires a political change with definite consequences. It does not say anything about the social forces which carry through the revolution.' Callinicos, 'Bourgeois revolutions', 124.
20 Trimberger, 'State power and modes of production'; Allinson & Anievas, 'Uneven and combined development'; Cohen, 'Historical sociology's puzzle'.
21 See, for example, Gould, 'Trade cohesion'; Brennan, *Cordobazo*; Ali, 'Strength of the street'.
22 Stone, *Causes of the English Revolution*, 145.
23 Mironov, 'Cannon fodder'.
24 Laube, 'Problem des Bündnisses', 105–6; Laube, 'Aufstand der Schwazer Bergarbeiter'.
25 Kuttner, *Hongerjaar 1566*, 425. Kuttner's work was inspired by an essay by the Marxist de Wolff, 'Het proletariaat'.
26 Manning, 'Introduction', 7–8. Also Holstun, *Ehud's Dagger*. For a different perspective, see Underdown, *Revel, Riot and Rebellion*.
27 Manning, 'Introduction', 25.
28 Carlin, 'Marxism and the English Civil War', 114.
29 Walter, 'English people', 180.
30 Nash, *Urban Crucible*, 383–4; see also Hoerder, *Crowd Action*.
31 Guérin, 'Preface', 2–3. Guérin's book was originally published in French in 1946. Works elaborating on this premise but without admitting it explicitly are Soboul, *Sans-culottes*, and Cobb, *Armées révolutionnaires*. Compare Guérin, 'D'une nouvelle interprétation'.
32 Gilly, *Mexican Revolution*, 329. See also Anderson, 'Mexican workers', at 112: 'Working or fighting, the Mexican proletariat were not engaged in an "anti-capitalist revolution", as some maintain, though they certainly would have identified the foreign and domestic industrialists as their enemies. Rather, they viewed the struggle from the perspective of Mexican patriots, fighting the conservative, ultramontane forces gathering anew, this time under the banner of "Progress and Order".'
33 Barker, 'Perspectives', 221.
34 Trotsky, *History of the Russian* Revolution, II, 24.
35 Trotsky, *History of the Russian Revolution*, II, 32.
36 Haupt, 'In what sense', 32–3.
37 Arnade, 'Bolivia's social revolution', 341–2.
38 Lora, *Historia del movimiento obrero boliviano*, esp. Vol. 4, covering the period 1933–52; a summary is to be found in Lora's *History of the Bolivian Labour Movement*.
39 Opinions vary on the relative importance of the labour movement in the Cuban Revolution. Cushion (*Hidden History*) argues that workers carried more weight, in contrast to, for example, Farber, *Origins of the Cuban Revolution*.
40 Poya, 'Iran 1979', 139.
41 Jafari, 'Oil, labour and revolution'.
42 Barker & Weber, *Solidarność*; Laba, *Roots of Solidarity*.
43 Barnett, *China on the Eve*, 327–8.

44 As the Sinologist Andrew Walder has observed: 'It is commonly remarked, and with obvious justification, that the working class did not make the Chinese revolution. An equally justified remark is rarely heard: that the revolution, on the contrary, has made the Chinese working class.' Walder, 'Remaking of the Chinese working class', 4.
45 Khanh, 'Vietnamese August Revolution', 772–3.
46 Seidman, *Imaginary Revolution*, 197.
47 Anderson, *Arguments*, 196.
48 See also the discussion of Tilly's vast oeuvre in van der Linden, 'Charles Tilly's historical sociology'.
49 Perhaps views oblivious to the state depend on (1) workers' suffrage and (2) the relative size of the working class. As suffrage becomes less favourable and the working class proportionately smaller, the working class becomes politically powerless. It may choose either (i) to ignore the state or (ii) to try to 'conquer' the state, by (a) struggling to expand suffrage and/or (b) expanding the working class (such as socialist diatribes against contraceptives). Presumably, the transition from (i) to (iia) and/or (iib) would require a certain threshold value. Below this threshold value, the working class does not consider conquering the state as feasible; above it, this objective becomes more realistic. This threshold is obviously not absolute but depends, in part, on reports from abroad (have workers managed to influence or conquer the state elsewhere, and, if so, how did they go about this?).
50 Tilly, *Coercion, Capital, and European States*, 115.
51 Tilly, 'Futures of European states', 711.
52 Löwenthal, 'The "Missing revolution" in industrial societies'.
53 Eduard Bernstein wrote, after the failed German revolution of 1918–19: 'the more varied the internal structure, the more developed the division of labour and the cooperation of its organs, the greater the risk of serious damage to their possibilities for life if an attempt is made to radically transform their form and content in a short time with the use of violent means'. Bernstein, *Die deutsche Revolution*, 172. The same point was made somewhat later by the anarchist Gerhard Wartenberg (Gerhard, 'Unsere Staatsauffassung') – a reference I owe to Dieter Nelles.
54 Przeworski, *Capitalism and Social Democracy*, 176–7.
55 Wood, 'Separation', 93.
56 Althusser, *Reproduction of Capitalism*.
57 Brand et al., *Nichtregierungsorganisationen*. This deflection results, in part, from the activities of the working classes. Sanford Jacoby, for example, has argued that trade-union opposition to managerial discretionary power has furthered the bureaucratization of American industrial firms. Jacoby, *Employing Bureaucracy*. While an important achievement, at the same time it made the essential power relations still harder to discern.
58 On the interconnectedness of these discriminatory practices, see Brah, 'Re-framing Europe'.
59 *MECW*, Vol. 3, 186.
60 Moorhouse, 'Political incorporation', 346.
61 *MECW*, Vol. 28, 217; Lebowitz, *Following Marx*, 308.
62 Wolff, 'Ideological state apparatuses', 230–1. See also Haug, *Critique of Commodity Aesthetics*.
63 I explore this more fully in 'Proletariat'.
64 Bourdieu, *On the State*, 82.

# 17
# 1968: the enigma of simultaneity

When we understand '1968' as a code for the rebellious period between approximately 1966 and 1975, then we also understand that it was not only about an international wave of student rebellions but also of important forms of workers' struggles. Sometimes, these expressions of protest worked together, and sometimes they didn't. The most well-known example of a coalition of workers and students is what happened in Paris in May and June of 1968. The students there were able to weaken state power with their rebellion, which, in turn, initiated the biggest wave of strikes in the history of France. In Argentina, radicalization took place more or less at the same time within universities and factories. The climax was reached with the workers' uprising in Cordoba in May of 1969. In Italy, in the 'Hot Fall' of 1969, a coalition between workers and students was formed. And, in 1974–5, the protests against Burma's Ne Win government were carried out by a coalition of workers and students.[1] Furthermore, in various parts of the world, there was a whole array of mass protests, in which workers and students articulated their discontent without significant support from each other. The large uprising in Karachi in 1972, in which part of the city became a liberated zone, was an overwhelmingly proletarian matter (beforehand, from October 1968 to March 1969, there had been powerful student protests), whereas the suppression of the military coup in Thailand in 1974 largely resulted from the resistance of the students.[2]

Of course, workers' and student protests both had long prior histories. Radical workers' resistance can, when defined narrowly, boast hundreds of years of prior history and has appeared in different forms: from Luddism in England, Anatolia, Brazil, and South China to experiments with workers' councils in Petersburg, the Ruhr region, and Tehran. Rebellious students have participated in anticolonial struggles in India as well as in overthrowing regimes in Cuba (1933, 1959), Guatemala (1944), Venezuela (1958), and Bolivia (1964). In '1968', both of these traditions reached their climax, whereby, sometimes, they interacted more and sometimes less.

Naturally, the question that involuntarily poses itself is: where there *was* synchrony, how can it be explained? In this chapter, I cannot give an exhaustive answer to this question. At most, I will offer food for thought for a very necessary further discussion.[3] I see five logical possibilities. First, it may be a coincidence, as, according to the motto of Leonardo Sciascia, the only things that are certain in this world are coincidences. Second, the *Zeitgeist* may have changed in an unexplainable way. Third, we can look for the cause in structural causes, such as the shifts in the world economy, that trigger specific changes at the same time in multiple countries. Fourth, 'external' events – like the Cuban Revolution, the Chinese Cultural Revolution, the Prague Spring, the Vietnamese Tet Offensive, or the very violent suppression of the Mexican student protests of 1968 (Figure 17.1) – may have served as sources of inspiration on a number of continents. Fifth, it is possible that contacts between movements in different countries encouraged synchrony. The first option seems very unlikely to me. The second is intellectually unsatisfactory. I would like to propose looking at the other three explanations first. I suspect that, when combined, they can help us to understand '1968' on a world scale.

But, first, let us look at the large structural changes that can possibly offer part of the explanation. Without a doubt, the impetuous growth of

**Figure 17.1** M8 Greyhounds (armoured vehicles) at the Zócalo (main square) of Mexico City, 28 August 1968. Photographer: Cel·lí. Public domain, https://bit.ly/3rDT8vz.

Table 17.1 Average per capita gross national product in different world regions (in international dollars, 1990) for a total of 56 countries, 1950–73.

| | 1950 | 1973 | Growth (%) |
|---|---|---|---|
| Western Europe (12 countries) | 5,513 | 11,694 | 212 |
| Settler colonies (Australia, Canada, New Zealand, USA) | 8,083 | 12,828 | 171 |
| Southern Europe (Greece, Ireland [!], Portugal, Spain, Turkey) | 2,259 | 6,770 | 300 |
| Eastern Europe (seven countries) | 2,235 | 5,289 | 236 |
| Latin America (seven countries) | 3,478 | 5,017 | 144 |
| Asia (11 countries) | 863 | 2,442 | 282 |
| Africa (10 countries) | 893 | 1,332 | 149 |

Source: Maddison, *Monitoring the World Economy*, pp. 23–4.

the world economy after 1945 – and especially since around 1950 – influenced worldwide developments. This growth did not only take place in the 'core' of the world system. It also appeared on the periphery (Table 17.1).

Large parts of the capitalist world underwent a process of expansion, and parts of the formerly underdeveloped world gained certain 'modern' capitalist traits. This did not do away with the fundamental differences between the core and the periphery. However, it did lead industrial working classes to emerge in other parts of the world, as well as trade unions and other labour organizations to develop.

A significant aspect of this growth, which culminated in a worldwide economic recession in 1973–4, was that it began to stagnate towards the end of the 1960s. Historical experience teaches us that the final phases of long growth periods are often accompanied by more intensive class struggle. Ernesto Screpanti suggested that three large international strike waves took place on a world scale in the years 1869–75, 1910–20, and 1968–74, all of which came at the end of long periods of economic growth. He explains this phenomenon as follows: 'the tension provoked by growth will be suppressed but accumulated for a long time; it will then break out periodically either as a direct consequence of strong compression, as in a Diesel engine, or in response to an external spark, as in a normal combustion engine'.[4]

A second structural factor is related in part, but not completely, to the process of capital accumulation – to be precise, to the expansion of mass education in general and, specifically, to higher (tertiary) education.

**Table 17.2** Average participation of relevant age groups in primary, secondary, and tertiary education, 1950–70.

|  | 1950 (%) | 1960 (%) | 1970 (%) | Number of countries |
|---|---|---|---|---|
| **Primary education** | | | | |
| All countries | 58 | 71 | 83 | 117 |
| Richer countries | 90 | 98 | 102 | 51 |
| Poorer countries | 37 | 53 | 72 | 56 |
| **Secondary education** | | | | |
| All countries | 12.7 | 21.5 | 30.5 | 102 |
| Richer countries | 21.3 | 35.8 | 46.4 | 49 |
| Poorer countries | 5.3 | 9.4 | 17 | 46 |
| **Tertiary education** | | | | |
| All countries | 1.4 | 2.8 | 5.3 | 109 |
| Richer countries | 2.6 | 5.2 | 9.2 | 46 |
| Poorer countries | 0.6 | 1.2 | 2.6 | 55 |

Source: Meyer, Ramirez, Rubinson & Boli-Bennett, 'The world educational revolution', 244.

Primary education was already almost universal in the core countries of the world system around 1870. After 1945, it expanded relatively evenly and at a faster rate across the globe.[5] In the wake of this trend, the relative number of students and school students increased throughout the world – even reaching the poorest countries (Table 17.2).

This expansion of education is so general that every explanation based on factors such as economic growth or 'social modernization' can be considered refuted. 'Higher-educational enrollment rates increased many times in countries that varied greatly in economic resources or modernization.'[6] Whatever the reason(s) may be, the expansion of higher education certainly must have had an influence on the emergence of the student protests that spread throughout large parts of the world during the 1960s and 1970s. Solely the fact that there were so many students must have had, as Victor Kiernan phrased it, a 'transformative influence': 'Youth feels able to act on its own because it has a mass basis of its own. Young people now felt capable to act themselves, as they had their own mass base.'[7] Thereby, and also as a result of the impetuous growth of the economy, which sometimes led to a considerable rise in purchasing power, an autonomous youth culture with its own musical and visual language developed for the first time in history.

Wherever the number of students grew – especially of those not from an elite background – a 'trade union consciousness' grew as well.

In many places, this, in turn, led to the establishment of organizations that represented students' interests. The French students, who proclaimed that they were 'young intellectual workers' in 1946 and, as a consequence, founded the Union nationale des étudiants de France (UNEF), started quite early on, when one considers the international context. However, their example was followed by many, including in the Global South.[8] 'Because the university system is an import from the West, the idea of student unions and student organizations was imported along with it.'[9]

The process of decolonization, as it developed after World War II and especially in the early 1960s, constitutes a third structural factor (Table 17.3).[10]

The struggle for independence, especially in Asia and Africa, announced a new era of autonomy; it now seemed possible to overcome societal injustice on a global level. Precisely because so many countries managed to achieve independence in the first decades after World War II, attempts coming from the metropolises to maintain colonial and neocolonial domination were met with outrage – first and foremost,

Table 17.3  Formal independence of colonies, 1946–70.

| Period | Countries | Number of Countries |
| --- | --- | --- |
| 1946–50 | Jordan, Lebanon, Syria, India, Pakistan, Ceylon, Burma, Israel, Indonesia | 9 |
| 1951–55 | Libya, Cambodia, Laos, Vietnam | 4 |
| 1956–60 | Morocco, Sudan, Tunisia, Malaya, Ghana, Guinea, Cyprus, Cameroon, Central African Republic, Chad, Kongo-Brazzaville, Kongo-Leopoldville, Dahomey, Gabon, Ivory Coast, Republic of Malagasy, Mali, Mauritania, Niger, Nigeria, Senegal, Somalia, Togo, [Upper Volta] | 24 |
| 1961–65 | Kuwait, Sierra Leone, Tanganyika, Burundi, Algeria, Rwanda, Uganda, Jamaica, Trinidad and Tobago, Malaysia, Kenya, Zanzibar, Malta, Malawi, Zambia, Gambia, Maldives | 17 |
| 1966–70 | Botswana, Lesotho, Barbados, Guyana, South Yemen, Equatorial Guinea, Swaziland, Mauritius, Fiji, Tonga | 10 |

Source: Abernethy, *Dynamics of Global Dominance*, pp. 140–1.

of course, the US intervention in Vietnam but also the so-called 'Congo crisis' and the premeditated murder of Patrice Lumumba (1961) that was supported by the CIA; the counterrevolutionary efforts of the US, in Brazil or Guyana, for instance; and the attempts of the Portuguese colonizers to maintain power in Angola, Guinea Bissau, and Mozambique.[11]

Alongside all these structural influences, 'external' events also inspired workers and students, as they seemed to show that very different forms of politics were possible than those that had been assumed to be natural. The Cuban Revolution from 1959 to 1960 was very influential, especially in Latin America and the Caribbean, but also in other parts of the world. In Cuba, a group of revolutionaries (partly operating against the will of the Communist Party) had been able to overthrow a dictatorial system. They sought to establish a new, radically democratic society. *Fidelismo* gained supporters at universities from Chile to Mexico and became the 'hope of all non-privileged [people]' in Latin America.[12] Seemingly everywhere, there was much sympathy for the island that had been able to remove itself from the shackles of the western superpower in such a bold way. The Cuban Government also disseminated its ideas proactively, not solely via the news agency *Prensa Latina* but also with the efforts of Che Guevara to create 'many Vietnams'.[13]

The Chinese Great Cultural Revolution (1966–9), which was actually not much more than a youth movement with terrorist tendencies that had been manipulated by a faction within the party, was influential on a global scale. Many were willing to believe the official rhetoric, according to which the nature of the struggle was anti-bureaucratic and was meant to save China from post-revolutionary solidification, which was what had led the Soviet Union, among others, to degenerate. In addition, Maoist trends developed in many countries. Sometimes, Maoist parties were established in a strict sense. Mostly, however, loosely organized, spontaneous movements came about.[14] In 1968, the 'year of marvels', two influential events took place. First, the 'Prague Spring', which seemed to be leading to 'socialism with a human face' – until the Warsaw Pact sent tanks in August of the same year. Second, a number of months later, the Tet Offensive of the National Liberation Front and North Vietnamese troops led to serious losses among the US troops in South Vietnam.

The last factor that needs to be analysed is how movements and organizations learned from each other. During the 1960s, both on the periphery and in the metropolises of the world system, parts of the working classes became conscious of the fact that the 'new international division of labour' was leading to deindustrialization in countries with high wages and industrialization in the 'third world'.[15] More or less at the same time as this trend, multinational corporations were quickly becoming more important. The economic cycles in different countries around the world synchronized increasingly, thereby no longer weakening each other but, on the contrary, strengthening each other.[16] Against this backdrop, the exchange of information among the rank-and-file of the workers' groups increased steadily. Worldwide committees were founded in multinational corporations, which (usually unsuccessfully) organized the cross-border representation of interests.[17] For the first time, trade-union actions were organized and carried out in multiple countries at the same time, such as in 1969, during the conflict between the International Federation of Chemical and General Workers' Unions (ICF) and the multinational glass corporation Saint-Gobain, and in 1972 when struggles took place contemporaneously against Akzo/Enka Glanzstoff in the Netherlands (Breda) and West Germany (Wuppertal).[18]

The communication between radical students in the North Atlantic region became even more well-known than these important manifestations of international workers' solidarity. Types of actions such as *teach-ins* spread from the US to Western Europe while leading activists got in touch with each other and led strategic debates. These examples also spread beyond the wealthy West. In South Africa, for example, where black students were relegated to separate universities under apartheid, the Civil Rights Movement in the US as well as the student protests in the northern hemisphere served as radical inspirations.[19] The students from the Global South that studied in the metropolises played a special role. They often took up radical ideas and translated them into the context of their country of origin. Bahru Zewde, for instance, showed how Ethiopian students in Europe and North America took up revolutionary ideas, which gave them a theoretical advantage and a different point of view from those who didn't study abroad, which triggered substantial political conflicts in the Ethiopian movement.[20]

The interplay between the three originally delineated factors can more or less explain why so many students' and workers' protests took place on different continents at the end of the 1960s and the beginning of the 1970s. However, this rough outline immediately leads to numerous further questions. First, it remains unclear why, regardless of the global character of resistance, there are some countries in which *no* protests of particular importance arose. An answer to this question would probably have to refer to aspects such as insufficient 'resources' able to take advantage of the protests, extensive state repression, and weak integration of the national society into the world system.

Second, the political tendency of the student protests requires a more precise explanation. The fact that the workers' protests had a leftist orientation was not very surprising. However, against the backdrop of the earlier right-wing, even fascist, protests at universities, the leftist orientation of the student protests was remarkable. The growing number of students may have played a role.[21] But perhaps the most important question is under which circumstances coalitions between students and workers were possible and under which circumstances they were not.

Multiple elements appear to be important in order to answer the last question. Although the number of students was rather large in most countries around 1970 (Table 17.2), the working class had not yet become extensive everywhere. And, in the case that such a working class existed, it didn't always have access to developed means of communication and organizational structures. This was especially true in a number of African and Asian countries, in which the workers' movements were only just emerging. Kalman Silvert's observation that the political activities of students were the most effective in countries in which the institutional infrastructure was weak and potentially more powerful groups were not organized can be noted in this context.[22] The social background of the student population was most probably important. Josef Silverstein concluded from a comparison of student protests in Thailand, Burma/Myanmar, Malaysia, and Singapore that the social composition of the student body had a large influence when it came to the issues that the student movement dealt with:

> Where the majority of students are drawn from urban areas and come from the upper levels of society, protest is likely to be over educational and job issues; where students are drawn from the poorer levels of society (and especially from the rural areas), they are likely to favor involvement in issues which support social and economic change.[23]

In other words, to the extent to which students are of 'lower' descent, they will be more likely to take up issues that are important for workers. And, ultimately, the structure of the workers' organizations also seems to have an influence. Presumably, very strongly and hierarchically structured trade unions act less sympathetically towards a collaboration with students than weak and less hierarchical organizations do.[24]

# Notes

1. Overviews can be found in Gilcher-Holthey, *'Die Phantasie an die Macht'*; Joffrin, *Mai 68*; Seidman, *Imaginary Revolution*; Balvé & Balvé, *'69 huelga politica de masas*; Brennan & Gordillo, 'Working class'; Pizzorno, *Lotte operaie e sindacato, 1968–1972*; Tarrow, *Democracy and Disorder*; and Silverstein, 'Students in Southeast Asian politics'.
2. Ali, 'Strength of the street'; Heinze, 'Ten days in October'; and Ingavata, *Students as Agents of Social Change*.
3. There are a number of international comparative studies regarding the history of the protests but these are limited to the North Atlantic area: Ortoleva, *Movimenti del '68*; Gilcher-Holthey, *68-er Bewegung*; and Horn, *Spirit of '68*. Katsiaficas, *Imagination of the New Left: A global analysis of 1968*, does not fulfill what is promised in the subtitle.
4. Screpanti, 'Long cycles in strike activity', 110. More in-depth information on this topic can be found in Screpanti, *Onde lunghi*.
5. Coombs, *World Educational Crisis*; Meyer, Ramirez & Soysal, 'World expansion of mass education'.
6. Ramirez & Meyer, 'Comparative education', 379.
7. Kiernan, 'Notes on the intelligentsia', 70.
8. Morder, *Naissance d'un syndicalisme étudiant*; Moore & Hochschild, 'Student unions in North African politics'. An interesting analysis of the Dutch case can be found in Lammers, 'Student unionism in the Netherlands'.
9. Silverstein, 'Students in Southeast Asian politics', 210.
10. For a more precise analysis of the pattern of decolonization and for its explanation, see Boswell, 'Colonial empires'; Strang, 'From dependency to sovereignty'; and Strang, 'Global patterns of decolonization'.
11. As far as I can tell, the analysis of the influences has not advanced much. One of the exceptions that confirms the rule is Juchler's *Studentenbewegungen*.
12. Goldenberg, *Lateinamerika*, 444.
13. See, for example, Elbaum, *Revolution in the Air*; Spencer, 'Impact of the Cuban Revolution'.
14. For an initial orientation, see the introductory literature by Alexander, *International Maoism*; and Alexander, *Maoism in the Developed World*.
15. The classical literature on this topic includes Fröbel, Heinrichs & Kreye, *New International Division of Labour*; and Fröbel, Heinrichs & Kreye, *Umbruch in der Weltwirtschaft*.
16. Jones, 'Multinationals'; MacEwan, 'Interdependence and instability'.
17. For a brilliant analysis, see Hildebrandt, Olle & Schoeller, 'National unterschiedliche Produktionsbedingungen'.
18. Northrup & Rowan, 'Multinational bargaining approaches'; Håkansson, *Standing up to a Multinational Giant*; Hoffmann & Langwieler, *Noch sind wir da!*; Benschop & Kee, *Bedrijfsbezetting van de Enka-Breda*.
19. Gwala, 'State control', 176; Franklin, 'Patterns of student activism'.
20. Zewde, *A History of Modern Ethiopia 1855–1991*, 225; Zewde, '1969 – Ethiopia's 1968'.
21. This is what Eric Hobsbawm assumes in *Age of Extremes*, 299–301.
22. Silvert, 'The university student'.
23. Silverstein, 'Students in Southeast Asian politics', 207. By the way, Silverstein also says that student protests, in which children of the elite stand out, are usually treated more gently than protests of lower-class children: 'Firm and harsh action by government against university students creates a problem for government in most developing areas. Generally, the students are the sons and daughters of the rulers and the bureaucracy who one day will be coopted into the elite' (205).
24. I have established this more extensively in *Transnational Labour History*, 127–30.

# Epilogue: global labour history and the crisis of workers' movements

> Boldness is the beginning of action; chance determines the end.
> Democritus

## The paradox

One of the great paradoxes of the current era is that the world's working class continues to grow, while, at the same time, many labour movements are experiencing a crisis. The percentage of pure wage dependents ('employees') rose between 1991 and 2019 from 44 to 53 per cent of the global labour force.[1] In that sense, we see an ongoing proletarianization that has progressed the most in the advanced capitalist countries. It is estimated that, in developed economies, wage-earners represent around 90 per cent of total employment. In developing and emerging economies, employees may, however, represent as little as 30 per cent or less of total employment.[2] The actual world's working class is, of course, considerably more numerous than the number of employees; in any case, contributing family members and most of the unemployed should be added to this figure, as well as an unknown share of the own-account workers that, in fact, consists of false self-employed – that is, those who are formally self-employed but actually have only one or two main clients and are therefore directly dependent on them. Those performing domestic subsistence labour (largely women) and thereby enabling employees and others to offer their labour capacity on the labour market are also part of the working class.

Paralleling this trend, ever greater numbers of workers worldwide maintain direct economic contacts with one another, even though many are probably unaware of this. Goods manufactured in one country are increasingly assembled from components produced in other countries, which, in turn, contain subcomponents made in still other countries. This process – also known as 'slicing up' or 'unbundling' supply chains – started at about the same time in North America and East Asia in the 1960s–70s, followed somewhat later by Europe.[3] As a result, a growing share of employees has become part of global supply chains. The ILO's *World Economic and Social Outlook 2015* report estimated that:

> ... in 40 countries representing 85 per cent of world gross domestic product and covering approximately two-thirds of the global labour force, the number of global supply chain-related jobs increased by 157 million or 53 per cent between 1995 and 2013, resulting in a total of 453 million global supply chain-related jobs in 2013.[4]

A final factor intensifying economic connections between workers from different parts of the world is migration. The proportion of international migrants in the world population increased from 2.8 per cent to 3.5 per cent between 2000 and 2020.[5] According to a study by the World Bank, the proportion of world migration attributable to South–North migration rose from 16 per cent to 37 per cent between 1960 and 2000. At the same time, the share of North–North, North–South, and South–South migrations declined. Moreover, migrants – increasingly, women – 'widen their destination choices ... For example, migrants from East Asia and Pacific who once migrated elsewhere within the region now constitute sizable communities across the world. An increasing number of Africans make their homes in Europe and the United States'.[6]

The absolute and relative growth of the global working class and its increasing interconnectedness might suggest that the world labour movement is growing stronger. Nothing could be further from the truth. Traditional labour movements are in trouble almost everywhere.[7] They have been severely enfeebled by the political and economic changes of the last forty years. Their core consists of three forms of social movement organizations: cooperatives, trade unions, and workers' parties. All three organizational types are currently in decline, though this is an uneven development with vast differences between countries and regions.

Since the 1940s or 50s, the consumer cooperatives, like all businesses under capitalism, were increasingly forced to centralize and to concentrate capital, due to improved transportation facilities and new retail forms. This trend manifested itself partly in the declining number of cooperatives and also in the increasing membership strength per cooperative unit.[8] Often, the average age of members rose, as elderly members remained loyal to their cooperatives, and younger ones failed to materialize.

Independent mass trade unions had their origin in the nineteenth century and continue to exist today in large parts of the world – although there are also major regions where they have almost no influence. The most striking example of a fast-growing capitalist economy without independent trade unions is the People's Republic of China. It hosts the world's largest workers' organization, the All-China Federation of Trade Unions (ACFTU) with more than 300 million members; but, rather than being an independent union, it is a transmission belt for the Chinese Communist Party.[9]

In most countries *with* independent workers' organizations, union density (union members as a percentage of the total labour force) generally has been declining. On a global scale, union density is almost insignificant. Independent trade unions organize only a small percentage of their target group worldwide, and the majority of them live in the relatively wealthy North Atlantic region. By far the most important global umbrella organization is the ITUC, founded in 2006 as a merger of two older organizations, the secular reform-oriented ICFTU and the Christian World Confederation of Labour. In 2014, the ITUC estimated that about 200 million workers worldwide belonged to trade unions (excluding those of China's), and that 176 million of these were organized in the ITUC.[10] The ITUC also estimated that the total global workforce in 2014 was roughly 2.9 billion (of whom 1.2 billion were active in the informal economy). Therefore, global union density amounted to no more than 7 per cent (200 million as a percentage of 2.9 billion).[11] Since then, unions in most parts of the world have continued to lose members, so that global union density may, as of 2023, be approaching 6 per cent!

Labour, Social Democratic, and Communist parties are generally considered to be political representatives of the working class. The oldest parties, the Social Democrats and Labour, are not doing very well electorally. Table 18.1 indicates that, of the 18 parties listed, 13 reached their apex before 1990, while Spain, Portugal, and Brazil did so later (early twenty-first century). Only Canada's social democratic party has been faring relatively well during the last decade.

Communist parties in non-communist countries are the second major political form. The large majority of them was born or grew significantly in three waves: during the five years from mid-1918 to 1923, in the aftermath of the October Revolution; in the 1930s, as a response to the economic depression; and during and immediately after World War II. Some parties still have a rather solid, albeit often small, base, such

Table 18.1 Average parliamentary electoral results of Social Democratic and Labour Parties, 1920–2019.

| | 1920s | 1930s | 1940s | 1950s | 1960s | 1970s | 1980s | 1990s | 2000s | 2010s |
|---|---|---|---|---|---|---|---|---|---|---|
| Australia | 45.2 | 32.4 | 46.5 | 46.3 | 45.1 | 45.4 | 47.0 | 40.8 | 39.2 | 34.9 |
| Austria | 39.3 | 41.1 | 41.7 | 43.3 | 50.0 | 45.4 | 47.6 | 37.3 | 33.7 | 25.0 |
| Belgium | 36.7 | 33.1 | 30.7 | 35.9 | 31.0 | 26.6 | 28.0 | 23.2 | 24.0 | 13.9 |
| Brazil | – | – | – | – | – | – | – | 12.1 | 16.8 | 15.4 |
| Canada | – | – | – | – | 15.4 | 17.1 | 19.7 | 9.0 | 15.0 | 22.1 |
| Denmark | 34.5 | 43.9 | 39.1 | 40.2 | 39.1 | 33.6 | 30.9 | 36.0 | 26.8 | 25.7 |
| Finland | 27.4 | 37.5 | 25.7 | 25.3 | 23.4 | 24.5 | 25.4 | 24.4 | 23.0 | 17.8 |
| France | 19.1 | 20.2 | 20.9 | 15.1 | 15.9 | 21.0 | 35.3 | 34.6 | 38.8 | 18.4 |
| Germany | 29.3 | 21.2 | 29.2 | 30.3# | 39.4# | 44.2# | 39.4# | 36.9 | 31.9 | 23.1 |
| Italy | 24.7 | – | 20.7 | 13.5 | 13.8 | 9.7 | 12.9 | 7.9* | – | 22.1** |
| Netherlands | 22.0 | 21.7 | 27.0 | 30.7 | 25.8 | 28.6 | 31.0 | 26.5 | 21.2 | 16.7 |
| NZ | 25.7 | 45.4 | 48.7 | 46.1 | 43.2 | 42.8 | 43.3 | 34.2‡ | 38.8‡ | 29.8‡ |
| Norway | 25.5 | 38.0 | 43.4 | 47.5 | 45.5 | 38.8 | 27.4 | 36.0 | 30.8 | 29.1 |
| Portugal | – | – | – | – | – | 35.2 | 27.6 | 39.0 | 39.8 | 32.7 |
| Spain | – | 23.1 | – | – | – | 30.4 | 44.1 | 38.2 | 40.2 | 25.4 |
| Sweden | 36.0 | 43.8 | 48.8 | 45.6 | 48.4 | 43.7 | 44.5 | 39.8 | 37.5 | 30.0 |
| Switzerland | 25.5 | 27.5 | 27.4 | 26.5 | 25.1 | 24.1 | 20.7 | 20.9 | 21.4 | 18.1 |
| UK | 37.7 | 34.4 | 49.7 | 46.3 | 46.1 | 39.1 | 29.2 | 38.7 | 38.0 | 32.9 |

Source: Author.

Notes:
* Party disbanded in November 1994.
** Result for the 'new' Democratic Party.
# Figures between 1950 and 1990 refer to West Germany.
‡ In 1993, the first-past-the-post electoral system was replaced by a mixed–member proportional voting system.

as those in Portugal, Spain, and Greece. These parties all developed under right-wing dictatorships and are characterized by their intransigence. Similarly, the South African Communist Party seems still to have a significant influence on the African National Congress's politics. But, for most parties, the high point was in the 1940s. Now, many Communist parties are having a hard time. In quite a few countries, they have been dissolved following electoral decline, internal rifts, or bankruptcy. This has been the case, for example, in Britain (dissolved 1991), Italy (disbanded 1991), Finland (bankrupt 1992), and Brazil (internal coup and split 1992). Other parties have gone through mergers, such as in Mexico (founding of the Unified Socialist Party, 1981), Denmark (formation of the Red-Green Alliance, 1989), and the Netherlands (founding of the Green Left Party in 1989). Even the CPI-M (the Communist Party of India–Marxist) in West Bengal, which received a majority of the votes in a whole series of elections from the 1970s until 2011, has now been reduced to a minor player because of widespread resistance to its violent neoliberal policies.

All in all, the foregoing seems to suggest three things: on a world scale, consumer cooperatives have either not been doing well or they have morphed into retail industries without members democratically controlling the business. Trade unions are not only a weak force but their power is also decreasing; and, in many countries, trade unions have lost their allies, the workers' parties – either because these parties have disappeared or because they have adopted a variant of neoliberalism. As a consequence, INGOs and NGOs have partly shouldered activities that traditionally would have been the responsibility of the international trade union movement, such as the struggle to regulate and abolish child labour. The downturn of labour movements seems to be almost all-pervading.

## A great cycle

This crisis appears to mark the end of a long cycle. Following a prelude that began in the fourteenth century, countless efforts at self-organization and political articulation of labour interests have been observed from the eighteenth century, peaking *inter alia* with the revolutions in Haiti, Russia, and Bolivia and the rise of powerful labour organizations in parts of the Americas, Europe, Southern Africa, East Asia, and the western Pacific. Of course, this advance has not consisted exclusively of successes, and the defeats may even have outnumbered the victories. For a long time, however, the general trend seemed to be one of improvement: 'tomorrow the International will be the human race'.

The different efforts, however, mainly appear to be at an impasse – in some cases, stagnating very rapidly and in others more gradually. Anarchism among workers and small farmers thrived between roughly 1860 and 1940, reaching its heyday globally in the decades preceding World War I. The significant lifespan of revolutionary syndicalism, viewed globally, was between 1900 and 1940. Consumer cooperatives controlled by their members emerged in the first half of the nineteenth century and then declined from the 1950s. During the early decades of the twentieth century, the breakthrough of the trade-union movement began, climaxing in the 1950s–80s. 'Real socialist' attempts in the Soviet Union, Eastern Europe, China, and Southeast Asia ultimately led to capitalist societies. Many of the communist parties in other countries have disappeared, and most social-democratic and Labour parties have veered off their political course.

At the same time, the labour movements in the South, on average, remained considerably weaker than their Northern counterparts. While pockets of trade-union power admittedly emerged, union density was generally rather low and is in decline. In the case of countries with relatively powerful unions, the density declined, for instance in Brazil, from 28.3 to 16.6 between 2000 and 2013, and in India from 13.8 in 2004 to 9.8 in 2012 – keeping in mind that such figures ordinarily reflect only the formal sector and that the informal sector is much larger by comparison (in India, about 8 versus 92 per cent). And, as far as workers' parties are concerned, the situation in the South is grimmer still. Eric Hobsbawm noted that, since World War II, 'hardly any such parties have emerged out of the working classes, notably in the so-called "Third World"'.[12] The exception proving the rule was the Brazilian Workers' Party, launched in 1980; at its peak in 2014, it received nearly 17 per cent of the votes cast.[13]

Critical analysis of this great cycle – specifically in combination with the continuously growing global working class – is a challenge of enormous scholarly and political interest, especially because, in many countries, the decline coincides with a revival of the radical right, which presents itself as an alternative to the traditional workers' organizations.[14] The perspective offered by global labour history appears perfectly suited to this task. The worldwide simultaneity of the crisis in the movements suggests that the cause lies not primarily in the errors of organizational leadership, but that more general factors have been decisive. A convincing explanation is probably discernible only if we examine the long-term development of global capitalism, possibly revolving around two questions:

- How can we explain the (uneven) rise, heyday, and relative decline of the labour movements in the Global North (the advanced capitalist countries) in the years 1860–1980?
- Why did the spread of capitalism to the Global South after World War II largely result in different types of labour movements than in the Global North?

These questions are, of course, very schematic and insufficiently nuanced. Indisputably, the movements in the North still achieve occasional victories; and, in some fields, the movements in the South followed the same logic of development as in the North. Still, differences between North and South remain evident. Every historical comparison is, to some degree, based on simplifications. Almost continuously we face 'overdetermined' complex phenomena, in which independent variables outnumber instances. As a consequence, there may be several explanations for a phenomenon, and this opens the door to controversies that cannot be settled by research.[15]

I suspect that diachronic comparisons may offer preliminary clues. This idea is perhaps best illustrated by two examples: mass migration and underemployment; and the return of merchant capital.

## Mass migration and underemployment

The consolidation of the labour movement was made possible, in part, by the enormous migration wave from Europe to the Americas and other parts of the world in the long nineteenth century. Mass migration reduced the relative overpopulation in Europe. As a result, the total population in all 14 of its countries grew by approximately 93 million between c. 1850 and c. 1910, while, in the same period, over one-third of this figure – about 32 million people – emigrated. This probably served as a safety valve. Fritz Sternberg has already suggested that European mass emigration 'opened up an important channel through which the European reserve armies could pour away, and it diminished social antagonisms'.[16] And Albert Hirschman suspected that '[t]he history of Europe in the nineteenth century would probably have been either far more turbulent or far more repressive and the trend towards representative government much more halting, had it not been possible for millions of people to emigrate towards the United States and elsewhere'.[17]

A different situation prevailed in the Global South. Many people migrated from China and British India during the same period, although in numbers representing a far smaller share of their respective populations. Moreover, Asian and European migration flows remained separate. As a result, 'the metropolis could use the labour reserves located in the periphery for its systemic *economic* stability even while achieving a degree of *social* stability within its own frontiers'.[18]

During the rise of the second international division of labour after 1945, the situation in the Global South did not change in that respect. India illustrates this point. In 1951, the country had 361 million inhabitants; and in 2011, it had 1,211 million: 850 million more. Relieving the labour-market pressure in equal measure to the corresponding reduction in Western Europe would have required net emigration of over 280 million people. Although total figures over the entire period are unavailable, the actual number of Indian emigrants must have been considerably lower during those 60 years: in 2010, the diaspora was 21.7 million and the number of Indian emigrants 11.0 million, yielding a total of 32.7 million Indians abroad.[19] In short, the early industrializers had proportionately fewer people to absorb.

Understandably, therefore, underemployment became widespread, especially in Africa, Asia, and Latin America. Gallup, the American management consulting company, has shared some interesting observations about this. Its global surveys reveal that, in 2014 and 2016, 32 per cent of residents aged 23 to 65 across 155 countries had so-called 'good jobs' – meaning that they worked at least 30 hours per week for an employer. Gallup believes that a large share of all other workers – half of the self-employed and people who work part-time but want full-time work – should be added to the unemployment figures, which would yield a total of roughly 33 per cent currently unemployed or underemployed.[20]

Under these circumstances, many tried-and-tested methods from the first stage of the labour movement proved ineffective. Decades ago, Adolf Sturmthal observed, with respect to the Global South:

> Effective unions have rarely if ever been organized by 'non-committed' workers, i.e., casual workers who change jobs frequently, return periodically to their native village, and have no specific industrial skill, even of a very simple kind. In most (though by no means all) newly industrializing countries, large excess supplies of common labor are available for nonagricultural work. Not only are

unskilled workers rarely capable of forming unions of their own under such conditions; if they succeed in doing so, their unions have little or no bargaining power.[21]

Collective bargaining thus became exceptionally difficult when workers constantly changed employers and were sometimes also forced to earn their living through self-employment. For a genuine collective-bargaining system to work, there are preconditions that are not found in many countries, including 'a legal and political system permitting the existence and functioning of reasonably free labor organizations' and the requirement that 'unions be more or less stable, reasonably well organized, and fairly evenly matched with the employers in bargaining strength'.[22] This also complicated the establishment of large workers' parties.

## The return of merchant capital

This uneven development was further complicated by major changes relating to capital. Trends that had been clearly visible before World War I were interrupted for over half a century and are starting to reappear. 'The entire period from 1929 until the 1970s constitutes a significant divergence from the trends unleashed by the industrial and transportation revolution of the nineteenth century. The post-1970s period returned the world to nineteenth-century trends and their associated financial turbulence'.[23]

One aspect I would like to highlight here is the return of merchant capital. I am referring to three processes. The first is the rise of retailers with unprecedented power, such as Amazon, eBay, IKEA, Aldi, and Walmart – the largest private employer in the world, accounting for 2.2 million employees. According to Vamsi Vakulabharana:

> ... most of the retail giant corporations that are now dominant emerged in the late 1950s and 1960s ... and consolidated themselves in the 1970s or later. Initially, these firms were family establishments and then by the 1970s, as capital had become footloose due to the profitability crisis, they went public and started raising capital from the stock markets and interest-bearing capital. As they grew in size, and as workers began to face the dismantling of various welfare-related institutions that led to declines in real wages, there was need for a new market for cheap consumer goods sourced from across the globe for (especially American working class) consumers at relatively low prices.[24]

Second, the putting-out systems are returning with new methods and are sometimes investing vast sums of money. In 1996, for example, Volkswagen (VW) opened a new branch in the Brazilian municipality of Resende, which it called 'the factory of the future'. Every day, 4,500 people produce 240 trucks and buses. What makes *Volkswagen Caminhões e Ônibus* special is that VW itself does next to nothing in Resende. The corporation owns the buildings, provides the equipment, and checks the quality of the final output. But the actual work of construction or assembly of subcontracted parts is being done by labourers hired by six contractors who are combined in a so-called Modular Consortium. We were already familiar with this type of 'arm's-length outsourcing' from the garment and shoe industry, but it is also becoming increasingly commonplace in very different sectors, such as in aircraft manufacturing (Boeing).[25] The main difference compared to many putting-out systems in the nineteenth century and earlier is that, nowadays, in some cases, the core enterprise provides not only circulating capital (raw materials, etc.) but also fixed capital in the form of buildings and machines.

Finally, the third trend is the well-known financialization – the increasing power of the financial sector (in Marx's terms: mercantile money and interest-bearing capital). The economic power of banks and insurance companies has increased enormously, and the short-term interests of shareholders often weigh more heavily than the long-term interests of enterprises, let alone care and respect for the workforce. A recent Dutch study of 698 West European publicly traded companies revealed that only 139 of them – 20 per cent – applied more than solely financial success indicators.[26]

Naturally, all these developments articulate important shifts in global capitalism. The growing influence of merchant and money capital has changed the balance of power within the capitalist class. Productive (industrial) capital is often no longer dominant and has become subordinate. The power of trade unions, where they are allowed to operate, is weakened by this development, since they are often much stronger in the productive than in the mercantile and financial sectors. In addition, there is the aforementioned transnationalization of labour processes. As a consequence, transport (logistics) has grown explosively as well.

## A second cycle?

The above remarks are merely initial suggestions that point to areas for further research. The 'great cycle' needs to be studied in depth as a cohesive unit to discover what the results and prospects of labour movements are. Why could certain results be achieved, and others not? Why did certain failures and defeats happen? Obtaining such insights is not an antiquarian exercise. If a second great cycle emerges, historical research might help avert mistakes. Such research may build on the provisional results of the global labour history project.

A second 'great cycle' is by no means inconceivable. This may be assumed for several reasons. Class conflicts will not diminish, and workers all over the world will continue to feel the ever-present need for effective organizations and forms of struggle. Even the influence of right-wing movements that has grown among the world's working class is an indirect and somewhat perverse indication to this effect. Many poor people are drawn into such movements, in all their variants – from the Pentecostalist movements of Latin America and Sub-Saharan Africa, to Salafism in North Africa, the Middle East, and Central Asia. Historian Sabyasachi Bhattacharya called this trend the 'vernacularization of labour politics'; it gives rise to 'solidarity of people with a common cause which may be social or cultural or sometimes regressively religious; the solidarity thus obtained can be and is used to pursue an agenda that runs parallel with or replaces the trade unions' agenda'.[27]

Ongoing efforts at self-organization are emerging everywhere. In India, on 8 and 9 January 2019, 150 million workers across the country went on strike for a list of demands including a national minimum wage, universal food security, and equal pay for equal work. In China, the labour shortages that began to emerge from 2004 led to a rapid growth of workers' protests, which have 'not only increased in number but have shifted focus from a reactive response to labour rights violations towards more proactive demands for higher wages and improved working conditions'.[28] The Chinese Academy of Social Sciences reported that there were more than 60,000 so-called 'mass incidents' (popular protests conducted by waged workers *and* others, such as peasants and the quasi-religious group Falun Gong) in 2006 and over 80,000 in 2007 (the specific breakdown of 'mass incidents' were not released by the authorities). Since then, official figures on 'mass incidents' have no longer been published but experts believe the number has further increased.[29] Since the beginning of the economic crisis of 2008, more than 30 national strikes occurred in Greece, while Spain and Portugal saw several general strikes, including bi- and multi-national ones. The dramatic overthrowing of the Mubarak dictatorship in Egypt in 2011 could not have happened without the labour movement's strong support. And, in South Africa, massive and often violent strikes follow one another rapidly. There is, therefore, a lot of militancy, but this is not matched by the strength of labour organizations. Conceivably, other structures – kinship networks, local communities, social movements, and other types of associations – will increasingly manifest as alternatives to unions.[30]

And finally, there are also explicit signs of a renewal. Organizing drives for previously unorganized workers in hospitals and the care sector, in general, have been increasing in recent years. The rise of the International Domestic Workers Network since 2009, including its campaign resulting in ILO Convention 189 on Decent Work for Domestic Workers (2011), has been an inspiration for many (see also Chapter 12). Strikes of incarcerated workers in the US reveal that new segments of the working class are beginning to be mobilized. In many countries, trade unions are attempting to open up to 'informal' and 'illegal' workers. Quite spectacular is India's New Trade Union Initiative, founded in 2006, which recognizes the importance of both paid and unpaid women's work; attempts to organize not only the 'formal' sector but also contract workers, casual workers, household workers, the self-employed, and the urban and rural poor; and endeavours to restructure collective-bargaining frameworks accordingly.

There is, however, an important obstacle to the renewal of labour movements, which makes successes difficult to effectuate: since the 1970s, national states have lost much of their sovereignty, but this loss of power has not been compensated by supranational authorities. We live in a transitional period in which many challenges can *no longer* be dealt with by national authorities, and *not yet* (if ever) by supranational (or world) authorities:

> In the contemporary global world there is no equivalent of the nation state at the world level that could implement fiscal and welfare policies, anti-trust controls, labor and environmental laws aimed at regulating markets and at correcting market failures. Nor is there a world independent judiciary which can control and sanction illegal behavior. Nor is there a democratic polity at the world level …[31]

This helps to explain the 'negative' attitude of many social movements that say 'no' to certain developments and have no positive alternative, because this would require a world authority. Nevertheless, transnational action focused on states is even possible in these adverse circumstances – either by pressing national governments to coordinate policies across borders or by exemplary local activities that can inspire movements in other parts of the world.

A new labour movement will have to develop an internationalist approach that is based on cross-border solidarity, even under these challenging conditions. It can partly find its foundations in the old labour movements, but these will have to change considerably.

## Notes

1. ILO WESO Data Finder.
2. ILO, 'Who is an employee?'.
3. Baldwin & Venables, 'Spiders and snakes', 245–6.
4. This was equal to one-quarter of the employees of those 40 countries. ILO, *World Employment and Social Outlook 2015*. Estimates of the employment in global supply chains are difficult to obtain, however, as information given in national statistics is often incomplete. On job losses due to the Covid-19 pandemics, see ILO, *World Employment and Social Outlook 2021*, 89–90.
5. International Organization for Migration, *World Migration Report 2020*.
6. Özden et al., 'Where on earth is everybody?', 15–16.
7. See also van der Linden, 'The crisis of the world's old labour movements'.
8. Hilson, Neunsinger & Patmore, *Global History of Consumer Co-operation*.
9. Most of the numerous labour conflicts in the People's Republic take place not with the support of the ACFTU. Bai, 'Role of the All China Federation of Trade Unions'.
10. This calculation is probably misleading. A significant, but unknown, part of the union membership consists of pensioners. It is therefore likely that the number of employed or employable members is lower.
11. ITUC, *Building Workers' Power*, 8.
12. Hobsbawm, *Worlds of Labour*, 60.
13. French, *Brazilian Workers' ABC*; Keck, *Workers' Party and Democratization*.
14. Van der Linden, 'Workers and the radical right'; Mosimann, Rennwald & Zimmermann, 'Radical right'.
15. López, 'Theory choice', 279–81.
16. Sternberg, *Capitalism and Socialism on Trial*, 62.
17. Hirschman, '*Exit, Voice, and Loyalty*', 442.
18. Patnaik & Patnaik, *Theory of Imperialism*, 56.
19. Tumbe, *India Moving*. I owe this reference to K. P. Kannan.
20. Gallup, *State of the Global Workplace*, 18; Clifton, 'Real global unemployment is 33%, not 6%'.
21. Sturmthal, 'Industrial relations strategies', 10.
22. Sturmthal, 'Industrial relations strategies', 9.
23. Schwartz, *States versus Markets*, 181.
24. Vakulabharana, 'Merchant capital', 112. See also Lichtenstein, 'Return of merchant capitalism'.
25. 'Boeing's 737 Max software outsourced to $9-an-hour engineers'.
26. Duurzaam Ondernemen, 'Maatschappelijk verantwoord ondernemen' [Survey among CEOs of European companies: Shareholder value over stakeholder value].
27. Bhattacharya, 'Introduction', 2.
28. China Labour Bulletin, *A Decade of Change*, 5.
29. China Labour Bulletin, *A Decade of Change*, 9; China Labour Bulletin, *Searching for the Union*.
30. Jörg Nowak's recent comparative study of mass strikes in India and Brazil reveals, for example, that numerous labour conflicts develop in the absence of trade unions. See his *Mass Strikes and Social Movements*.
31. Martinelli, 'From world system to world society?', 247.

# References

Note: Entries with same authorship are ordered alphabetically by title. Solo-authored works precede collaborative works. Collaborative works ordered by first author name, then second, third etc. All URLs correct as of January 2023.

A Mining Expert [Boris P. Torgasheff]. 'The contract system in Chinese mining', *The People's Tribune: An organ of national-revolutionary thought and opinion* 1 (1932): 152–8.
Abdeljaouad, Amor. 'The influence of international labour conventions on Tunisian legislation', *International Labour Review* 91 (1965): 191–209.
Abernethy, David B. *The Dynamics of Global Dominance: European overseas empires 1415–1980*. New Haven, CT and London: Yale University Press, 2000.
Abouharb, M. Rodwan and David L. Cingranelli. *Structural Adjustment and Human Rights*. Cambridge: Cambridge University Press, 2007.
Abrahamson, Mark. 'Sudden wealth, gratification and attainment: Durkheim's anomie of affluence reconsidered', *American Sociological Review* 45 (1980): 49–57.
Abramovitz, Moses. 'Economics of growth'. In *A Survey of Contemporary Economics*. Vol. II, edited by Bernard F. Haley, 132–78. Homewood, IL: Richard D. Irwin, Inc., for the American Economic Association, 1952.
Acemoglu, Daron and Alexander Wolitzky. 'The economics of labor coercion', *Econometrica* 79 (2011): 555–600.
Acheson, James M. 'Household organization and budget structures in a Purepecha pueblo', *American Ethnologist* 23 (1996): 331–51.
Adas, Michael. 'From footdragging to flight: The evasive history of peasant avoidance protest in South and South-east Asia', *Journal of Peasant Studies* 13 (1986): 64–86.
Agier, Michel, Jean Copans and Alain Morice (eds). *Classes ouvrières d'Afrique noire*. Paris: Karthala/Orstom, 1987.
Agostini, Thomas. '"Deserted His Majesty's Service": Military runaways, the British-American press, and the problem of desertion during the Seven Years' War', *Journal of Social History* 40 (2007): 957–85.
Ahuja, Ravi. 'A freedom still enmeshed in servitude: The unruly "Lascars" of the *SS City of Manila* or, a micro-history of the "free labour" problem'. In *Working Lives and Worker Militancy: The politics of labour in colonial India*, edited by Ravi Ahuja, 97–133. New Delhi: Tulika, 2013.
Akurang-Parry, Kwabena O. '"The loads are heavier than usual": Forced labor by women and children in the Central Province, Gold Coast (Colonial Ghana), ca. 1900–1940', *African Economic History* 30 (2002): 31–51.
Alam, M. Shahid. 'Global disparities since 1800: Trends and regional patterns', *Journal of World-Systems Research* 12 (2006): 37–59.
Albin, Einat and Virginia Mantouvalou. 'The ILO Convention on Domestic Workers: From the shadows to the light', *Industrial Law Journal* 41 (2012): 67–78.
Alcock, Anthony E. *History of the International Labour Organization*. New York: Octagon Books, 1971.
Alexander, Robert J. *International Maoism in the Developing World*. Westport, CT: Praeger, 1999.
Alexander, Robert J. *Maoism in the Developed World*. Westport, CT: Praeger, 2001.
Ali, Kamran Asdar. 'The strength of the street meets the strength of the state: The 1972 labor struggle in Karachi', *International Journal of Middle East Studies* 37 (2005): 83–107.
Allen, Joe. 'Studying logistics', *Jacobin* (2015). https://jacobin.com/2015/02/logistics-industry-organizing-labor/.

Allen, Richard B. 'Suppressing a nefarious traffic: Britain and the abolition of slave trading in India and the Western Indian Ocean, 1770–1830', *The William and Mary Quarterly*, Third Series, 66 (2009): 873–94.
Allen, Victor L. 'The meaning of the working class in Africa', *Journal of Modern African Studies* 10 (1972): 169–89.
Allinson, Jamie C. and Alexander Anievas. 'The uneven and combined development of the Meiji Restoration: A passive revolutionary road to capitalist modernity', *Capital and Class* 34 (2010): 469–90.
Allio, Renata. *L'Organizzazione Internazionale del Lavoro e il sindacalismo fascista*. Bologna: Il Mulino, 1973.
Alston, Philip. '"Core Labour Standards" and the transformation of the international labour rights regime', *European Journal of International Law* 15 (2004): 457–521.
Alston, Philip. 'Facing up to the complexities of the ILO's Core Labour Standards agenda', *European Journal of International Law* 16 (2005): 467–80.
Altena, Bert. *'Een broeinest der anarchie': Arbeiders, arbeidersbeweging en maatschappelijke ontwikkeling, Vlissingen 1875–1929 (1940)*. Two volumes. Haarlem: Thesis, 1989.
Altena, Bert. 'The Dutch Social Democratic Workers' Party in the Province of Zeeland, 1898–1920', *Tijdschrift voor Sociale Geschiedenis* 18 (1992): 389–403.
Althusser, Louis. *On the Reproduction of Capitalism: Ideology and ideological state apparatuses*. London: Verso, 2014 [1970].
Amin, Shahid and Marcel van der Linden (eds). *'Peripheral' Labour? Studies in the history of partial proletarianization*. Cambridge: Cambridge University Press, 1996.
Amiti, Mary and Lisa Cameron. 'Economic geography and wages', *Review of Economics and Statistics* 89 (2007): 15–29.
Anderson, Clare (ed.). *A Global History of Convicts and Penal Colonies*. London: Bloomsbury Academic, 2018.
Anderson, Perry. *Arguments within English Marxism*. London: Verso, 1980.
Anderson, Perry. *Lineages of the Absolutist State*. London: New Left Books, 1974.
Anderson, Robert N. 'The Quilimbo of Palmares: A new overview of a maroon state in seventeenth-century Brazil', *Journal of Latin American Studies* 28 (1996): 545–66.
Anderson, Rodney D. 'Mexican workers and the politics of revolution, 1906–1911', *Hispanic American Historical Review* 54 (1974): 94–113.
Andrees, Beate and Patrick Belser (eds). *Forced Labor: Coercion and exploitation in the private economy*. Boulder, CO: Lynne Rienner, 2009.
Anner, Mark and Teri Caraway. 'International institutions and workers' rights: Between labor standards and market flexibility', *Studies in Comparative International Development* 4 (2010): 151–69.
Anti-Slavery International. 'What is modern slavery?' https://www.antislavery.org/slavery-today/modern-slavery/.
Applebaum, Anne. *Gulag: A history*. New York: Doubleday, 2003.
Araghi, Farshad. 'Food regimes and the production of value: Some methodological issues', *Journal of Peasant Studies* 30 (2003): 41–70.
Architecture Lobby. 'San Precario: Prayers from architectural workers'. https://architecture-lobby.org/project/san-Precario/.
Arestis, Philip, Georgios Chortareas, Evangelia Desli and Theodore Pelagidis. 'Trade flows revisited: Further evidence on globalisation', *Cambridge Journal of Economics* 36 (2012): 481–93.
Aristotle. *Politeia*. In *The Complete Works of Aristotle: The revised Oxford translation*, edited by Jonathan Barnes. Vol. II. Princeton: Princeton University Press, 1984.
Arnade, Charles W. 'Bolivia's social revolution, 1952–1959: A discussion of sources', *Journal of Inter-American Studies* 1 (1959): 341–52.
Arrighi, Giovanni. 'Marxist century, American century: The making and remaking of the World Labour Movement', *New Left Review* 179 (1) (1990): 29–63.
Arrighi, Giovanni. 'Workers of the world at century's end', *Review* [Fernand Braudel Center] 19 (1996): 335–51.
Arrighi, Giovanni. *Adam Smith in Beijing: Lineages of the twenty-first century*. London and New York: Verso, 2007.
Arrighi, Giovanni, Beverly J. Silver and Benjamin D. Brewer. 'Industrial convergence, globalization, and the persistence of the North–South divide', *Studies in Comparative International Development* 38 (2003): 3–31.

Aspers, Patrik. 'Markets, sociology of'. In *International Encyclopedia of Economic Sociology*, edited by Jens Beckert and Milan Zafirovski, 427–32. London: Routledge, 2005.

Audring, Gert. 'Zur sozialen Stellung der Hirten in archaischer Zeit'. In *Antike Abhängigkeitsformen in den griechischen Gebieten ohne Polisstruktur und den römischen Provinzen*, edited by Heinz Kreißig and Friedmar Kühnert, 12–19. Berlin: Akademie-Verlag, 1985.

Aufhauser, R. Keith. 'Slavery and scientific management', *Journal of Economic History* 33 (1973): 811–24.

Austen, Ralph A. and Woodruff D. Smith. 'Images of Africa and British slave-trade abolition: The transition to an imperialist ideology, 1787–1807', *African Historical Studies* 2 (1969): 69–83.

Austin, Gareth. 'Cash crops and freedom: Export agriculture and the decline of slavery in colonial West Africa', *International Review of Social History* 54 (2009): 1–37.

Austin, Gareth. 'The return of capitalism as a concept'. In *Capitalism: The reemergence of a historical concept*, edited by Jürgen Kocka and Marcel van der Linden, 207–34. London: Bloomsbury, 2016.

Baccaro, Lucio and Valentina Mele. 'Pathology of path dependency? The ILO and the challenge of new governance', *Industrial and Labor Relations Review* 65 (2012): 195–224.

Backhaus, Wilhelm. *Marx, Engels und die Sklaverei: Zur ökonomischen Problematik der Unfreiheit*. Düsseldorf: Schwann, 1974.

Bai, Ruixue. 'The role of the All China Federation of Trade Unions: Implications for workers today'. In *China's Rise: Strength and fragility*, edited by Au Loong-Yu with contributions from Bai Ruixue, Bruno Jetin and Pierre Rousset, 199–224. London: Merlin Press, 2012.

Bairoch, Paul. *Victoires et déboires III: Histoire économique et sociale du monde du XVIe siècle à nos jours*. Paris: Gallimard, 1997.

Bajoit, Guy. 'Exit, voice, loyalty … and apathy: Les réactions individuelles au mécontentement', *Revue française de sociologie* 29 (1988): 325–45.

Bakke, E. Wight. *The Unemployed Man: A social study*. London: Nisbet and Co., 1935.

Baldwin, Richard and Anthony J. Venables. 'Spiders and snakes: Offshoring and agglomeration in the global economy', *Journal of International Economics* 90 (2013): 245–54.

Balvé, Beba C. and Beatriz Balvé. *El '69 huelga politica de masas: Rosarioza, cordobazo, rosarioza*. Buenos Aires: Contrapunto, 1989.

Banaji, Jairus. *A Brief History of Commercial Capitalism*. Chicago: Haymarket, 2020.

Banton, Mandy. 'The "taint of slavery": The Colonial Office and the regulation of free labour'. In *Slavery, Diplomacy and Empire: Britain and the Suppression of the Slave Trade, 1807–1975*, edited by Keith Hamilton and Patrick Salmon, 143–64. Brighton: Sussex Academic Press, 2009.

Barbier, Edward B. *Scarcity and Frontiers: How economies have developed through natural resource exploitation*. Cambridge: Cambridge University Press, 2011.

Bardhan, Pranab K. 'Labor-tying in a poor agrarian economy: A theoretical and empirical analysis', *Quarterly Journal of Economics* 98 (1983): 501–14.

Barker, Colin (ed.). *Revolutionary Rehearsals*. London: Bookmarks, 1987.

Barker, Colin. 'Perspectives'. In *Revolutionary Rehearsals*, edited by Colin Barker, 217–45. London: Bookmarks, 1987.

Barker, Colin and Kara Weber. *Solidarność: From Gdansk to military repression*. London: International Socialism, 1982.

Barker, Geoffrey Russell. *Some Problems of Incentives and Labour Productivity in Soviet Industry*. Oxford: Blackwell, 1956.

Barker, T. C. 'The international history of motor transport', *Journal of Contemporary History* 20 (1985): 3–19.

Barnes, George N. *History of the International Labour Office*. London: Williams and Norgate, 1926.

Barnett, Arthur Doak. *China on the Eve of Communist Takeover*. New York: Praeger, 1963.

*Barnhart Dictionary of Etymology* (n.p.: H. H. Wilson, 1988).

Barragán Romano, Rossana. 'La geografía diferencial de los derechos: Entre la regulación del trabajo forzado en los países coloniales y la disociación entre trabajadores e indígenas en los Andes (1920–1954)'. In *Una historia regional de la OIT: Aportes sobre regulación y legislación del trabajo latinoamericano*, edited by Laura Caruso and Andrés Stagnate, 25–64. La Plata: Universidad Nacional de La Plata, 2017.

Barragán Romano, Rossana. *Potosí Global: Viajando con sus primeras imágenes, 1550–1650*. La Paz: Plural, 2019.

Barragán Romano, Rossana (ed.). *Trabajos y trabajadores en América Latina, siglos XVI–XXI*. La Paz: Centro de Investigaciones Sociales, 2019.

Barrett, James R. *Work and Community in the Jungle: Chicago's packinghouse workers 1894–1922*. Urbana and Chicago: University of Illinois Press, 1987.

Bartha, Eszter. *Alienating Labour: Workers on the road from socialism to capitalism in East Germany and Hungary*. New York and Oxford: Berghahn, 2013.

Bartov, Omer. 'Daily life and motivation in war: The *Wehrmacht* in the Soviet Union', *Journal of Strategic Studies* 12 (1989): 200–14.

Basu, Arnab K. and Nancy H. Chau. 'Exploitation of child labor and the dynamics of debt bondage', *Journal of Economic Growth* 9 (2004): 209–38.

Baucom, Ian. *Specters of the Atlantic: Finance capital, slavery, and the philosophy of history*. Durham, NC: Duke University Press, 2005.

Baumann, Reinhart. 'Protest und Verweigerung in der Zeit der klassischen Sölnerheere'. In *Armeen und ihre Deserteure: Vernachlässigte Kapitel einer Militärgeschichte der Neuzeit*, edited by Ulrich Bröckling and Michael Sikora, 16–48. Göttingen: Vandenhoeck & Ruprecht, 1998.

Bayles, Michael D. 'A concept of coercion'. In *Coercion*, edited by J. Roland Pennock and John W. Chapman, 16–29. Chicago: Aldine-Atherton, 1972.

Bean, Richard and Robert Thomas. 'The adoption of slave labor in British America'. In *The Uncommon Market: Essays in the economic history of the Atlantic slave trade*, edited by Henry A. Gemery and Jan S. Hogendorn, 377–98. New York: Academic Press, 1979.

Bearman, Peter S. 'Desertion as localism: Army unit solidarity and group norms in the U.S. Civil War', *Social Forces* 70 (1991): 321–42.

Beckert, Sven. *Empire of Cotton: A global history*. New York: Alfred A. Knopf, 2014.

Beckert, Sven. 'The new history of capitalism'. In *Capitalism: The reemergence of a historical concept*, edited by Jürgen Kocka and Marcel van der Linden, 235–49. London: Bloomsbury, 2016.

Beckles, Hilary M. and Andrew Downes. 'The economics of transition to the black labor system in Barbados, 1630–1680', *Journal of Interdisciplinary History* 18 (1987): 225–47.

Bedoya, Eduardo, Alvaro Bedoya and Patrick Belser. 'Debt bondage and ethnic discrimination in Latin America'. In *Forced Labor: Coercion and exploitation in the private economy*, edited by Beate Andrees and Patrick Belser, 35–50. Boulder, CO: Lynne Rienner, 2009.

Behal, Rana P. *One Hundred Years of Servitude: Political economy of tea plantations in colonial Assam*. New Delhi: Tulika, 2014.

Behal, Rana, Alice Mah and Babacar Fall (eds). *Rethinking Work: Global historical and sociological perspectives*. New Delhi: Tulika, 2011.

Behal, Rana P. and Prabhu P. Mohapatra. '"Tea and money versus human life": The rise and fall of the indenture system in the Assam tea plantations, 1840–1908', *Journal of Peasant Studies* 19 (1992): 142–72.

Bellucci, Stefano and Andreas Eckert (eds). *General Labour History of Africa: Workers, employers and governments, 20th–21st centuries*. Woodbridge: James Currey, 2019.

Benanav, Aaron. 'Landscapes of labour', *New Left Review* Second series, 61 (2010): 222–32.

Benanav, Aaron. 'The origins of informality: The ILO at the limit of the concept of unemployment', *Journal of Globul History* 14 (2019): 107–25.

Bender, Donald R. 'A refinement of the concept of household: families, co-residence, and domestic functions', *American Anthropologist* 69 (1967): 493–504.

Benenson, Harold. 'The community and family bases of U.S. working class protest, 1880–1920: A critique of the "skill degradation" and "ecological" perspectives', *Research in Social Movements, Conflicts and Change* 8 (1985): 109–32.

Benería, Lourdes. 'Shifting the risk: New employment patterns, informalization, and women's work', *International Journal of Politics, Culture, and Society* 15 (2001): 27–53.

Benhamou, Laurence. *Le grand Bazar mondial: La folie aventure de ces produits apparemment 'bien de chez nous'*. Paris: Bourin, 2005.

Benjamin, Walter. 'Paralipomena to "On the Concept of History"'. In *Walter Benjamin: Selected writings*. Vol. 4: *1938–1940*, edited by Howard Eiland and Michael W. Jennings, 401–11. Cambridge, MA: Harvard University Press, 2003.

Benschop, Albert and Ton Kee. *De bedrijfsbezetting van de Enka-Breda: De vakbonden en een multinational*. Nijmegen: SUN, 1974.

Bensimon, Fabrice, Quentin Deluermoz and Jeanne Moisand (eds). *'Arise Ye Wretched of the Earth': The First International in a global perspective*. Leiden and Boston: Brill, 2018.

Benson, John. *The Penny Capitalists: A study of nineteenth-century working class entrepreneurs*. Dublin: Gill and Macmillan, 1983.

Benson, Susan Porter. 'Living on the margin: Working-class marriages and family survival strategies in the United States, 1919–1941'. In *The Sex of Things: Gender and consumption in historical perspective*, edited by Victoria de Grazia, with Ellen Furlough, 212–43. Berkeley: University of California Press, 1996.

Benson, W. 'African labour in 1930', *Journal of the Royal African Society* 30 (1931): 142–7.

Benston, Margaret. 'Political economy of women's liberation', *Monthly Review* 21 (1969): 13–27.

Benveniste, Emile. *Le Vocabulaire des institutions indo-européennes*. Vol. I. Paris: Minuit, 1968.

Berenstein, Alexandre. 'The influence of international labour conventions on Swiss legislation', *International Labour Review* 77 (1958): 495–518.

Berger, Johannes. 'Warum arbeiten die Arbeiter? Neomarxistische und neodurkheimianische Erklärungen', *Zeitschrift für Soziologie* 24 (1995): 407–21.

Bergesen, Albert and Ronald Schoenberg. 'Long waves of colonial expansion and contraction, 1415–1969'. In *Studies of the Modern World-System*, edited by Albert Bergesen, 231–77. New York: Academic Press, 1980.

Berkhout, A. H. 'De rentabiliteit van eene kina-onderneming in verband met hare exploitatie', *Tijdschrift voor Nijverheid in Nederlandsch Indië* 35 (1887): 593–626.

Berlin, Ira. *Generations of Captivity: A history of African-American slaves*. Cambridge, MA: The Belknap Press of Harvard University Press, 2003.

Bernstein, Eduard. *Die deutsche Revolution, ihr Ursprung, ihr Verlauf und ihr Werk*. Vol. I: *Geschichte der Entstehung und ersten Arbeitsperiode der deutschen Republik*. Berlin: Verlag Gesellschaft und Erziehung, 1921.

Bertaud, Jean-Paul. *La révolution armée: Les soldats-citoyens et la Révolution Française*. Paris: Robert Laffond, 1979.

Bezís-Selfa, John. 'A tale of two ironworks: Slavery, free labor, work, and resistance in the early republic', *The William and Mary Quarterly* 56 (1979): 677–700.

Bezucha, Robert J. *The Lyon Uprising of 1834: Social and political conflict in the early July Monarchy*. Cambridge, MA: Harvard University Press, 1974.

Bhagat, R. B. and S. Mohanty. 'Emerging pattern of urbanization and the contribution of migration in urban growth in India', *Asian Population Studies* 5 (2009): 5–20.

Bhaskar, Roy. *The Possibility of Naturalism*. Brighton: Harvester Press, 1979.

Bhattacharya, Sabyasachi. 'Introduction'. In *The Vernacularization of Labour Politics*, edited by Sabyasachi Bhattacharya and Rana P. Behal, 1–21. New Delhi: Tulika, 2016.

Binger, Louis G. *Du Niger au Golfe du Guinée par le pays de Kong et le Mossi*. Paris: Librairie Hachette, 1892.

Birkbeck, Chris. 'Self-employed proletarians in an informal factory: The case of Cali's garbage dump', *World Development* 6 (1978): 1173–85.

Blackburn, Robin. *The Making of New World Slavery*. London and New York: Verso, 1997.

Blackburn, Robin. *The Overthrow of Colonial Slavery 1776–1848*. London and New York: Verso, 1988.

Blackett, Adelle. 'The Decent Work for Domestic Workers Convention and Recommendation, 2011', *American Journal of International Law* 106 (2012): 778–94.

Blackmon, Douglas A. *Slavery by Another Name: The re-enslavement of Black Americans from the Civil War to World War II*. New York: Doubleday, 2008.

Blanpain, Roger and Michele Colucci (eds). *The Globalisation of Labour Standards: The soft law track* [*Bulletin of Comparative Labour Relations*, No. 52]. Dordrecht: Kluwer, 2004.

Blanqui, [Jerôme]. *Cours d'économie industrielle*. 2nd edition, ed. A. Blaise. Paris: Librairie scientifique et industrielle, 1839.

Blanton, Robert G., Shannon Lindsey Blanton and Dursun Peksen. 'The impact of IMF and World Bank programs on labor rights', *Political Research Quarterly* 68 (2015): 324–6.

Blelloch, D. H. 'Latin America and the international labour standards', *International Labour Review* 43 (1941): 377–400.

Bodemann, Y. Michal. 'Relations of production and class rule: The hidden basis of patron-clientage'. In *Households and the World-Economy*, edited by Joan Smith, Immanuel Wallerstein and Hans-Dieter Evers, 198–220. Beverly Hills, CA: Sage, 1984.

Böhning, W. R. 'The ILO and contemporary international economic migration', *International Migration Review* 10 (1976): 147–56.

Bohstedt, John. 'Gender, household and community politics: Women in English riots 1790–1810', *Past and Present* 120 (1988): 88–122.

Bolt, Christine. 'The anti-slavery origins of concern for American Indians'. In *Anti-Slavery, Religion and Reform: Essays in memory of Roger Anstey*, edited by Christine Bolt and Seymour Drescher, 233–53. Hamden, CT: Archon, 1980.

Bonacich, Edna. 'The past, present, and future of split labor market theory', *Research in Race and Ethnic Relations* 1 (1979): 17–64.

Bonn Center for the Study of Slavery and Dependency. https://www.dependency.uni-bonn.de/en.

Boomgaard, Peter. 'Labour, land, and capital markets in early modern Southeast Asia from the fifteenth to the nineteenth century', *Continuity and Change* 24 (2009): 55–78.

Boomgaard, Peter and Ian Brown. 'Introduction'. In *Weathering the Storm: The economies of Southeast Asia in the 1930s depression*, edited by Peter Boomgaard and Ian Brown, 1–19. Leiden: KITLV Press, 2000.

Boris, Eileen and Jennifer N. Fish. '"Slaves no more": Making global labor standards for domestic workers', *Feminist Studies* 40 (2014): 411–43.

Boris, Eileen, Dorothea Hoehtker and Susan Zimmermann (eds). *Women's ILO: Transnational networks, global labour standards and gender equity, 1919 to present*. Leiden and Boston: Brill, 2018.

Bosanquet, Helen. 'The burden of small debts', *Economic Journal* 6 (1896): 212–25.

Bosma, Ulbe. 'The Cultivation System (1830–1870) and its private entrepreneurs on colonial Java', *Journal of Southeast Asian Studies* 38 (2007): 275–91.

Bosma, Ulbe. *The Making of a Periphery: How island Southeast Asia became a mass exporter of labor*. New York: Columbia University Press, 2019.

Bosma, Ulbe. *The Sugar Plantation in India and Indonesia: Industrial production, 1770–2010*. Cambridge: Cambridge University Press, 2013.

Bosma, Ulbe, Gijs Kessler and Leo Lucassen (eds). *Migration and Membership Regimes in Global and Historical Perspective: An introduction*. Leiden and Boston: Brill, 2013.

Boswell, Terry. 'Colonial empires and the capitalist world-economy: A time series analysis of colonization, 1640–1960', *American Sociological Review* 54 (1989): 180–96.

Bourdieu, Pierre. *Algeria 1960*. Trans. Richard Nice. Cambridge: Cambridge University Press, and Paris: Editions de la Maison des Sciences de l'Homme, 1979.

Bourdieu, Pierre. *On the State: Lectures at the Collège de France, 1989–1992*. Ed. Patrick Champagne, Remi Lenoir, Franck Poupeau and Marie-Christine Riviere. Trans. David Fernbach. Cambridge: Polity Press, 2014.

Bouton, Cynthia A. 'Gendered behavior in subsistence riots: The Flour War of 1775', *Journal of Social History* 23 (1990): 735–54.

Bowles, Samuel and Robert Boyer. 'A wage-led employment regime: Income distribution, labour discipline, and aggregate demand in welfare capitalism'. In *The Golden Age of Capitalism: Reinterpreting the postwar experience*, edited by Stephen A. Marglin and Juliet B. Schor, 187–217. Oxford: Clarendon Press, 1990.

Bracke, Maud Anne. 'Between the transnational and the local: Mapping the trajectories and contexts of the Wages for Housework campaign in 1970s Italian feminism', *Women's History Review* 22 (2013): 625–42.

Bradbury, Bettina. 'Pigs, cows, and boarders: Non-wage forms of survival among Montreal families, 1861–91', *Labour/Le Travailleur* 14 (1984): 9–46.

Brah, Avtar. 'Re-framing Europe: En-gendered racisms, ethnicities and nationalisms in contemporary Western Europe', *Feminist Review* 45 (1993): 9–29.

Brand, Donald D. 'The origin and early distribution of New World cultivated plants', *Agricultural History* 13 (1939): 109–17.

Brand, Ulrich and Markus Wissen. *The Imperial Mode of Living: Everyday life and the ecological crisis of capitalism*. Trans. Zachary King. London and New York: Verso, 2021.

Brand, Ulrich and Markus Wissen. *The Limits to Capitalist Nature: Theorizing and overcoming the imperial mode of living*. London and New York: Rowman & Littlefield International, 2018.

Brand, Ulrich, Alex Demirovic and Christoph Görg (eds). *Nichtregierungsorganisationen in der Transformation des Staates*. Münster: Das Westfälische Dampfboot, 2003.

Brandon, Pepijn. '"With the Name Changed, the Story Applies to You!": Connections between slavery and "free" labor in the writings of Marx'. In *The Life Work of a Labor Historian: Essays in honor of Marcel van der Linden*, edited by Ulbe Bosma and Karin Hofmeester, 47–70. Leiden and Boston: Brill, 2018.

Brass, Tom. 'Immobilised workers, footloose theory', *Journal of Peasant Studies* 24 (1997): 337–58.

Brass, Tom. *Towards a Comparative Political Economy of Unfree Labour*. London: Frank Cass, 1999.

Braudel, Fernand. *Civilization and Capitalism, 15th–18th Century*. Vol. I: *The structures of everyday life*. Trans. Siân Reynolds. Berkeley: University of California Press, 1992.
Braudel, Fernand. *Civilization and Capitalism, 15th–18th Century*. Vol. II: *The wheels of commerce*. Trans. Siân Reynolds. Berkeley: University of California Press, 1992.
Braun, Adolf. *Die Gewerkschaften, ihre Entwicklung und Kämpfe: Eine Sammlung von Abhandlungen*. Nuremberg: Fränkische Verlagsanstalt, 1914.
Brecht, Bertolt. 'Fragen eines lesenden Arbeiters' (Questions from a Worker who Reads). Trans. M. Hamburger. In *Bertolt Brecht: Poems 1913–1956*. New York and London: Methuen, 1976.
Breman, Jan. 'De strijd voor maatschappelijke gelijkheid in India'. In *Uit de Zevende: Vijftig jaar politieke en sociaal-culturele wetenschappen aan de Universiteit van Amsterdam*, edited by Anne Gevers, 395–409. Amsterdam: Amsterdam University Press, 1998.
Breman, Jan. 'Dualistic labour system? A critique of the "informal sector" concept'. In *Wage Hunters and Gatherers: Search for work in the urban and rural economy of South Gujarat*, by Jan Breman, 3–45. Delhi: Oxford University Press, 1994.
Breman, Jan. 'Over oriëntalistiek en occidentalistiek', *De Gids* 154 (1991): 501–4.
Breman, Jan. 'Primitive racism in a colonial setting'. In *Imperial Monkey Business: Racial supremacy in social Darwinist theory and colonial practice*, edited by Jan Breman, 89–121. Amsterdam: VU University Press, 1990.
Breman, Jan. 'The study of industrial labour in post-colonial India – The Informal Sector: A concluding review'. In *The Worlds of Indian Industrial Labour*, edited by Jonathan P. Parry, Jan Breman and Karin Kapadia, 407–31. New Delhi: Sage Publications, 1999.
Breman, Jan. 'The Village on Java and the early colonial state', *Journal of Peasant Studies* 9 (1982): 189–240.
Breman, Jan. *Footloose Labour: Working in India's informal economy*. Cambridge: Cambridge University Press, 1996.
Breman, Jan. *Labour Bondage in West India: From past to present*. New Delhi: Oxford University Press, 2007.
Breman, Jan. *Mobilizing Labour for the Global Coffee Market: Profits from an unfree work regime in colonial Java*. Amsterdam: Amsterdam University Press, 2015.
Breman, Jan. *Of Peasants, Migrants and Paupers: Rural labour circulation and capitalist production in West India*. Delhi: Oxford University Press, 1985.
Breman, Jan. *Patronage and Exploitation: Changing agrarian relations in South Gujarat, India*. Berkeley: University of California Press, 1974.
Breman, Jan. *Taming the Coolie Beast: Plantation society and the colonial order in Southeast Asia*. Delhi: Oxford University Press, 1989.
Breman, Jan. *Wage Hunters and Gatherers: Search for work in the urban and rural economy of South Gujarat*. Delhi: Oxford University Press, 1994.
Breman, Jan, Arvind Das and Ravi Agarwal. *Down and Out: Labouring under global capitalism*. New Delhi: Oxford University Press and Amsterdam: Amsterdam University Press, 2000.
Breman, Jan, Kevan Harris, Ching Kwan Lee and Marcel van der Linden (eds). *The Social Question in the Twenty-First Century: A global view*. Berkeley: University of California Press, 2019.
Brennan, James P. and Monica B. Gordillo. 'Working class protest, popular revolt, and urban insurrection in Argentina: The 1969 Cordobazo', *Journal of Social History* 27 (1994): 477–98.
Brennan, James P. and Mónica R. Gordillo. *Cordoba rebelde: El cordobazo, el clasismo y la movilización social*. Buenos Aires: De la Campana, 2008.
Brenner, Robert. 'The origins of capitalist development: A critique of neo-Smithian Marxism', *New Left Review*, First series, 104 (1977): 25–92.
Brentano, Lujo. *On the History and Development of Gilds, and the Origin of Trade Unions*. London: Trübner & Co., 1870.
Breschi, Marco, Matteo Manfredini and Alessio Fornasin. 'Demographic responses to short-term stress in a 19th century Tuscan population: The case of household out-migration', *Demographic Research* 25 (2011): 491–512.
Briefs, Goetz. 'Das gewerbliche Proletariat'. In *Grundriss der Sozialökonomik*, Part IX, 142–240. Tübingen: J. C. B. Mohr, 1926.
Brocheux, Pierre. 'Le prolétariat des plantations d'hévéas au Vietnam méridional: Aspects sociaux et politiques (1927–1937)', *Le Mouvement Social* 90 (1975): 55–86.
Brock, Ditmar. *Der schwierige Weg in die Moderne: Umwälzungen in der Lebensführung der deutschen Arbeiter zwischen 1850 und 1980*. Frankfurt am Main and New York: Campus, 1991.

Bröckling, Ulrich and Michael Sikora (eds). *Armeen und ihre Deserteure: Vernachlässigte Kapitel einer Militärgeschichte der Neuzeit*. Göttingen: Vandenhoeck & Ruprecht, 1998.

Brockway, Lucile H. *Science and Colonial Expansion: The role of the British Royal Botanic Gardens*. New York: Academic Press, 1979.

Brower, Daniel R. 'Labor violence in Russia in the late nineteenth century', *Slavic Review* 41 (1982): 417–31.

Brown, Christopher L. *Moral Capital: Foundations of British abolitionism*. Chapel Hill: University of North Carolina Press, 2006.

Brown, Ian. *Economic Change in South-East Asia, c. 1830–1980*. Kuala Lumpur: Oxford University Press, 1997.

Brown, John. *Slave Life in Georgia: A narrative of the life, sufferings and escape of John Brown, a fugitive slave*. Edited by F. N. Boney. Savanna: Beehive Press, 1972 [1855].

Bruce, Judith. 'Homes divided', *World Development* 17 (1989): 979–91.

Bruegel, Martin. '"Un sacrifice de plus à demander au soldat": L'armée et l'introduction de la boîte de conserve dans l'alimentation française, 1872–1920', *Revue historique* 294 (1995): 259–84.

Bruegel, Martin. 'Du temps annuel au temps quotidien: La conserve appertisée à la conquête du marché, 1810–1920', *Revue d'histoire moderne et contemporaine* 44 (1997): 40–67.

Brüggemeier, Franz and Lutz Niethammer. 'Schlafgänger, Schnapskasinos und schwerindustrielle Kolonie: Aspekte der Arbeiterwohnungsfrage im Ruhrgebiet vor dem ersten Weltkrieg'. In *Fabrik, Familie, Feierabend: Beiträge zur Sozialgeschichte des Alltags im Industriezeitalter*, edited by Jürgen Reulecke and Wolfhard Weber, 153–74. Wuppertal: Peter Hammer Verlag, 1978.

Brunt, P. A. *Italian Manpower, 225 B.C.–A.D. 14*. Oxford: Clarendon Press, 1971.

Buelens, Frans and Ewoud Frankema. 'Colonial adventures in tropical agriculture: New estimates of returns to investment in the Netherlands Indies, 1919–1938', *Cliometrica* 10 (2016): 197–224.

Buggeln, Marc. 'Were concentration camp prisoners slaves? The possibilities and limits of comparative history and global historical perspectives', *International Review of Social History* 53 (2008): 101–29.

Bukharin, Nikolai. *Imperialism and World Economy*. Introduction by Lenin. London: The Merlin Press, 1972.

Burawoy, Michael. *Manufacturing Consent: Changes in the labor process under monopoly capitalism*. Chicago: University of Chicago Press, 1979.

Burawoy, Michael and Erik Olin Wright. 'Coercion and consent in contested exchange'. In *Interrogating Inequality: Essays on class analysis, socialism and Marxism*, edited by Erik Olin Wright, 72–87. London and New York: Verso, 1994.

Burge, M. R. K. 'Some aspects of administration in the International Labour Office', *Public Administration* 23 (1945): 21–31.

Busch, Lawrence and Carolyn Sachs. 'The agricultural sciences and the modern world system'. In *Science and Agricultural Development*, edited by Lawrence Busch, 131–56. Totowa, NJ: Allanheld, Osmun, 1981.

Butel, Paul. *Histoire des Antilles françaises, XVIIe–XXe siècle*. Paris: Perrin, 2007.

Cabedoce, Béatrice. 'Jardins ouvriers et banlieue: Le bonheur au Jardin?'. In *Les Premiers banlieusards: Aux Origines des banlieues de Paris 1860–1940*, edited by Alain Faure, 249–79. Paris: Créaphis, 1991.

Cadogan, Peter. 'Harney and Engels', *International Review of Social History* 10 (1965): 66–104.

Cairnes, John E. *Some Leading Principles of Political Economy Newly Expounded*. London: Macmillan, 1874.

Callinicos, Alex. 'Bourgeois revolutions and historical materialism', *International Socialism* 2 (1989): 113–71.

Callinicos, Alex. *Making History: Agency, structure, and change in social theory*. Cambridge: Polity Press, 1989.

Cameron, Ardis. 'Bread and roses revisited: Women's culture and working-class activism in the Lawrence Strike of 1912'. In *Women, Work and Protest: A century of US women's labor history*, edited by Ruth Milkman, 42–61. Boston: Routledge & Kegan Paul, 1985.

Cameron, Meribeth E. 'The periodization of Chinese history', *Pacific Historical Review* 15 (1946): 171–7.

Cammack, Paul. 'Attacking the poor', *New Left Review*, Second series, 13 (2002): 125–34.

Campbell, Gwyn and Persia Crawford. *Chinese Coolie Emigration to Countries within the British Empire*. London: Frank Cass, 1971.

Canetti, Elias. *Crowds and Power*. Trans. Carol Stewart. New York: Viking Press, 1963.
Caraway, Teri L. 'Freedom of association: Battering ram or Trojan horse?', *Review of International Political Economy* 13 (2006): 210–32.
Card, Claudia. 'Genocide and social death', *Hypatia* 18 (2003): 63–79.
Carew, Anthony. *American Labour's Cold War Abroad: From deep freeze to détente, 1945–1970*. Edmonton, AB: AU Press, 2018.
Carlin, Norah. 'Marxism and the English Civil War', *International Socialism Journal* 2 (1980–1): 106–28.
Carlyle, Thomas. *Chartism*. London: James Fraser, 1840.
Carney, Judith A. and Richard Nicholas Rosomoff. *In the Shadow of Slavery: Africa's botanical legacy in the Atlantic world*. Berkeley: University of California Press, 2009.
Carothers, Thomas and Richard Youngs. *The Complexities of Global Protests*. New York: Carnegie Endowment for International Peace, 2015.
Cashiell, Maurice. 'The influence on Irish law and practice of international labor standards', *International Labour Review* 106 (1972): 47–74.
Cassis, Youssef. 'Economic and financial crises'. In *Capitalism: The reemergence of a historical concept*, edited by Jürgen Kocka and Marcel van der Linden, 13–31. London: Bloomsbury, 2016.
Casson, Mark and John S. Lee. 'The origin and development of markets: A business history perspective', *Business History Review* 85 (2011): 9–37.
Cave, Basil S. 'The end of slavery in Zanzibar and British East Africa', *Journal of the Royal African Society* 9 (1909): 20–33.
Chamberlain, M. E. 'Imperialism and social reform'. In *British Imperialism in the Nineteenth Century*, edited by C. C. Eldridge, 148–67. London and Basingstoke: Macmillan, 1984.
Chandavarkar, Rajnarayan. 'The decline and fall of the jobber system in the Bombay cotton textile industry, 1870–1955', *Modern Asian Studies* 42 (2008): 117–210.
Chandler, Alfred D. *The Visible Hand: The managerial revolution in American business*. Cambridge, MA and London: The Belknap Press of Harvard University Press, 1977.
Chang, Jen-Hu. 'Global distribution of net radiation according to a new formula', *Annals of the Association of American Geographers* 60 (1970): 340–51.
Chang, Jen-Hu. 'Potential photosynthesis and crop productivity', *Annals of the Association of American Geographers* 60 (1970): 92–101.
Chang, Jen-Hu. 'Tropical agriculture: crop diversity and crop yields', *Economic Geography* 53 (1977): 241–54.
Charnovitz, Steve. 'The influence of international labour standards on the world trading regime: A historical overview', *International Labour Review* 126 (1987): 565–84.
Chase, Malcolm. *Chartism: A new history*. Manchester: Manchester University Press, 2007.
Chen, Ta. *Chinese Migrations, with Special Reference to Labor Conditions*. Washington, DC: Government Printing Office, 1923.
Chesneaux, Jean, *Le mouvement ouvrier en Chine de 1919 à 1927*. Paris: Mouton, 1962.
Cheyney, Alice S. 'The character and accessibility of office research materials', *Annals of the American Academy of Political and Social Science* 166 (1933): 114–18.
CHIA (Collaborative for Historical Information and Analysis). http://www.chia.pitt.edu/.
China Labour Bulletin. *A Decade of Change: The workers' movement in China 2000–2010*. Research Report, March 2012. https://tinyurl.com/dy39phvj.
China Labour Bulletin. *Searching for the Union: The workers' movement in China 2011–13*. Research Report, February 2014. https://tinyurl.com/5dr4mfzx.
Chinese contractarbeiders in Suriname 1858–1874. National Archives of the Netherlands. https://www.nationaalarchief.nl/onderzoeken/zoekhulpen/chinese-contractarbeiders-in-suriname-1858-1874.
Chomsky, Aviva. *Linked Labor Histories: New England, Colombia, and the making of a global working class*. Durham, NC: Duke University Press, 2008.
Chowdhury-Zilly, Aditee Nag. *The Vagrant Peasant: Agrarian distress and desertion in Bengal, 1770 to 1830*. Wiesbaden: Franz Steiner Verlag, 1982.
Christophe, Guilmoto. 'The Tamil migration cycle, 1830–1950', *Economic and Political Weekly*, 16–23 January (1993): 112–20.
Ciriacy-Wantrup, Siegfried von. 'Resource conservation and economic stability', *Quarterly Journal of Economics* 60 (1946): 412–52.
Ciscel, David H. and Barbara Ellen Smith. 'The impact of supply chain management on labor standards: The transition to incessant work', *Journal of Economic Issues* 39 (2005): 429–37.

Clapham, Sir John. *A Concise Economic History of Modern Britain from the Earliest Times to 1750*. Cambridge: Cambridge University Press, 1951.

Clarence-Smith, William Gervase. *Islam and the Abolition of Slavery*. London: Hurst & Co., 2006.

Clarkson, Thomas. *The History of the Rise, Progress and Accomplishment of the Abolition of the African Slave Trade by the British Parliament*. Two volumes. London: Longman, Hurst, Rees and Orme, 1808.

Clawson, Mary Ann. *Constructing Brotherhood: Class, gender, and fraternalism*. Princeton: Princeton University Press, 1989.

Clee, Charles R. 'Desertion and the freedom of the seaman', *International Labour Review* 13 (1926): 649–72, 808–49.

Clifton, Jon. 'Real global unemployment is 33%, not 6%', *Gallup Blog*, 1 May 2018. https://news.gallup.com/opinion/gallup/233459/billion-worldwide-looking-great-jobs.aspx.

Clio-Infra. https://clio-infra.eu/.

Cobb, Richard. *Les armées révolutionnaires: Instrument de la terreur dans les départements, Avril 1793–Floréal An II*. Two volumes. Paris: Mouton, 1961, 1963.

Cobban, Alfred. *The Social Interpretation of the French Revolution*. Cambridge: Cambridge University Press, 1964.

Cobble, Dorothy Sue. 'The other ILO founders: 1919 and its legacies'. In *Women's ILO*, edited by Eileen Boris, Dorothea Hoehtker and Susan Zimmermann, 27–49.

Coclanis, Peter A. 'How the Low Country was taken to task: Slave-labor organization in coastal South Carolina and Georgia'. In *Slavery, Secession, and Southern History*, edited by Robert Louis Paquette and Louis A. Ferleger, 59–78. Charlottesville: University Press of Virginia, 2000.

Cocteau, Jean. *Romans, Poésies, Œuvres diverses*. Paris: La Pochothèque, 1995.

Cohen, G. A. 'The structure of proletarian unfreedom', *Philosophy and Public Affairs* 12 (1983): 3–33.

Cohen, Jeffrey H. 'Migration, remittances, and household strategies', *Annual Review of Anthropology* 40 (2011): 103–14.

Cohen, Mark. 'Historical sociology's puzzle of the missing transitions: A case study of early modern Japan', *American Sociological Review* 80 (2015): 603–25.

Cohen, Robin. 'Resistance and hidden forms of consciousness amongst African workers', *Review of African Political Economy* 7 (1980): 8–22; reprinted in Robin Cohen, *Contested Domains: Debates in international labour studies*, 91–109. London: Zed Books, 1991.

Cohen, Robin, Peter C. W. Gutkind and Phyllis Brazier (eds). *Peasants and Proletarians: The struggles of third world workers*. New York: Monthly Review Press, 1979.

Cohn, Samuel Kline. *Lust for Liberty: The politics of social revolt in medieval Europe, 1200–1425*. Cambridge, MA: Harvard University Press, 2006.

Cole, Anna Marie. 'Twenty years on: Feminism's "three body problem"', *Women's History Review* 22 (2013): 559–75.

Collier, Paul. 'The importance of belonging', *International Politics and Society*, 21 November 2017. http://www.ips-journal.eu/in-focus/they-dont-care-about-us/article/show/the-importance-of-belonging-2416/.

Collins, Henry and Chimen Abramsky. *Karl Marx and the British Labour Movement*. London: Macmillan, 1965.

Collins, Robert O. and Burns, James M. *A History of Sub-Saharan Africa*. Cambridge: Cambridge University Press, 2007.

Comer, Jonathan C. and Thomas A. Wikle. 'The worldwide diffusion of the cellular telephone, 1995–2005', *The Professional Geographer* 60 (2008): 252–69.

Commodities of Empire (British Academy research project). https://commoditiesofempire.org.uk/.

Conell, Carol and Samuel Cohn. 'Learning from other people's actions: Environmental variation and diffusion in French coal mining strikes, 1890–1935', *American Journal of Sociology* 101 (1995): 366–403.

Conrad, Alfred H. and John R. Meyer. 'The economics of slavery in the ante-bellum South', *Journal of Political Economy* 66 (1958): 95–130.

Conrad, Robert E. *The Destruction of Brazilian Slavery, 1850–1888*. Berkeley: University of California Press, 1972.

Cook, Alice H. 'The ILO and Japanese politics, II: Gain or loss for labor?', *Industrial and Labor Relations Review* 22 (1969): 375–98.

Cook, Alice H., Val R. Lorwin and Arlene Kaplan Daniels. *The Most Difficult Revolution: Women and trade unions*. Ithaca, NY: Cornell University Press, 1992.

Cooke, Bill. 'The denial of slavery in management studies', *Journal of Management Studies* 40 (2003): 1895–1918.

Coombs, P. H. *The World Educational Crisis: A systems analysis*. London: Oxford University Press, 1968.

Cooper, Frederick. *From Slaves to Squatters: Plantation labour and agriculture in Zanzibar and coastal Kenya, 1890–1925*. New Haven, CT and London: Yale University Press, 1980.

Cope, Zak. *Divided World, Divided Class: Global political economy and the stratification of labour under capitalism*. Montreal: Kersplebedeb, 2012.

Cope, Zak. *The Wealth of (Some) Nations*. London: Pluto Press, 2019.

Coupland, Reginald. *Wilberforce: A narrative*. Oxford: Clarendon Press, 1923.

Courtenay, Philip Percy. *Plantation Agriculture*. London: G. Bell & Sons, 1965.

Cowen, Jonathan M. 'One nation's "gulag" is another nation's "factory within a fence": Prison-labor in the People's Republic of China and the United States of America', *Pacific Basin Law Journal* 12 (1993): 190–236.

Cowie, Jefferson. *Capital Moves: RCA's Seventy-year quest for cheap labor*. Ithaca, NY: Cornell University Press, 1999.

Cox, Oliver. *Caste, Class, and Race: A study in social dynamics*. New York: Monthly Review Press, 1959.

Cox, Robert W. 'Labor and hegemony: A reply', *International Organization* 34 (1980): 159–76.

Cox, Robert W. 'Labor and hegemony', *International Organization* 31 (1977): 385–424.

Cox, Robert W. 'Limited monarchy'. In *Anatomy of Influence: Decision making in international organization*, edited by Robert W. Cox and Harold K. Jacobsen, 102–38. New Haven, CT: Yale University Press, 1974.

Cox, Robert W. 'Pour une étude prospective des relations de production', *Sociologie du Travail* 20 (1977): 113–37.

Cox, Robert W. and Harold K. Jacobsen. 'The anatomy of influence'. In *Anatomy of Influence: Decision making in international organization*, edited by Robert W. Cox and Harold K. Jacobsen, 371–436. New Haven, CT: Yale University Press, 1974.

Craton, Michael. *Empire, Enslavement and Freedom in the Caribbean*. Kingston: Ian Randle, 1997.

Craton, Michael. *Testing the Chains: Resistance to slavery in the British West Indies*. Ithaca, NY: Cornell University Press, 1982.

Crenshaw, Kimberlé. 'Demarginalizing the intersection of race and sex: A black feminist critique of antidiscrimination doctrine', *University of Chicago Legal Forum* 1 (1989): 139–68.

Crosby, Alfred. *Ecological Imperialism: The biological expansion of Europe, 900–1900*. Cambridge: Cambridge University Press, 1986.

Crosby, Alfred. *Germs, Seeds, and Animals: Studies in ecological history*. Armonk, NY: M. E. Sharpe, 1994.

Crosby, Alfred. *The Columbian Exchange: Biological and cultural consequences of 1492*. Westport, CT: Greenwood Press, 1973.

Crosby, Alfred. *The Measure of Reality: Quantification and Western society, 1250–1600*. Cambridge: Cambridge University Press, 1997.

Cross, Gary. 'Les trois huits: Labor movements, international reform, and the origins of the eight hour day, 1919–1924', *French Historical Studies* 14 (1985): 240–68.

Crouch, Colin. *Trade Unions: The logic of collective action*. London: Fontana, 1982.

Cucu, Alina-Sandra. *Planning Labour: Time and the foundations of industrial socialism in Romania*. New York and Oxford: Berghahn, 2019.

Cumbler, J. T. 'Transatlantic working-class institutions', *Journal of Historical Geography* 6 (1980): 275–90.

Cummins, Joseph. *The War Chronicles: From flintlocks to machine guns*. Beverly, MA: Fair Winds Press, 2009.

Curthoys, Ann. 'The three body problem: Feminism and chaos theory', *Hecate* 17 (1991): 14–21.

Curtin, Philip D. 'The abolition of the slave trade from Senegambia'. In *The Abolition of the Atlantic Slave Trade: Origins and effects in Europe, Africa, and the Americas*, edited by David Eltis and James Walvin, 83–97. Madison: University of Wisconsin Press, 1981.

Curtin, Philip D. *The Rise and Fall of the Plantation Complex: Essays in Atlantic history*. Cambridge: Cambridge University Press, 1990.

Cushion, Steve. *A Hidden History of the Cuban Revolution: How the working class shaped the guerrillas' victory*. New York: Monthly Review Press, 2016.
D'Anjou, Leo. *Social Movements and Cultural Change: The first abolition campaign revisited*. New York: Aldine De Gruyter, 1996.
Darrac, Pierre-Paul and Willem van Schendel. *Global Blue: Indigo and espionage in colonial Bengal*. Dhaka: University Press, 2006.
Dasgupta, Partha. *An Inquiry into Well-Being and Destitution*. Oxford: Clarendon Press, 1993.
Daudin, Guillaume, Christine Rifflart and Danielle Schweisguth. 'Who produces for whom in the world economy?', *Canadian Journal of Economics/Revue canadienne d'économie* 44 (2011): 1403–37.
Davies, Sam, Colin J. Davis, David de Vries, Lex Heerma van Voss, Lidewij Hesselink and Klaus Weinhauer. (eds). *Dock Workers: International explorations in comparative labour history, 1790–1970*. Two volumes. Aldershot: Ashgate, 2000.
Davin, Anna. 'Working or helping? London working-class children in the domestic economy'. In *Households and the World-Economy*, edited by Joan Smith, Immanuel Wallerstein and Hans-Dieter Evers, 215–32. Beverly Hills, CA: Sage, 1984.
Davis, David Brion. *Slavery and Human Progress*. New York and Oxford: Oxford University Press, 1984.
Davis, Mike. *Late Victorian Holocausts: El Niño famines and the making of the Third World*. London and New York: Verso, 2001.
Day, John. *Money and Finance in the Age of Merchant Capitalism*. Oxford: Blackwell, 1999.
De Belder, Jos. 'Het arbeiderssparen 1850–1890'. In *De Belgische spaarbanken: Geschiedenis, recht, economische funktie en instellingen*, edited by August Van Put, 91–119. Tielt: Lannoo, 1986.
De Board, Robert. *The Psychoanalysis of Organizations*. London: Tavistock, 1978.
De Haan, Arjan. 'Migration as family strategy: Rural-urban labor migration in India during the twentieth century', *The History of the Family* 2 (1997): 481–505.
De Roever, Arend. *De jacht op sandelhout: De VOC en de tweedeling van Timor in de zeventiende eeuw*. Zutphen: Walburg Pers, 2002.
De Sainte Croix, Geoffrey E. M. 'Karl Marx and the history of classical antiquity', *Arethusa* 8 (1975): 7–41.
De Sainte Croix, Geoffrey E. M. *The Class Struggle in the Ancient Greek World: From the archaic age to the Arab conquests*. London: Duckworth, 1981.
De Vito, Christian and Alex Lichtenstein. *Global Convict Labor*. Leiden and Boston: Brill, 2015.
De Vliegher, Ruth. 'Desertie bij Oostendse Oost-Indiëvaarders'. In *Orbis in Orbem: Liber amicorum John Everaert*, edited by Jan Parmentier and Sander Spanoghe, 171–85. Ghent: Academia Press, 2001.
De Vries, Jan. 'The labour market'. In *The Dutch Economy in the Golden Age: Nine studies*, edited by Karel Davids and Leo Noordegraaf, 55–78. Amsterdam: NEHA, 1993.
De Wolff, Sam. 'Het proletariaat in de beginjaren van den strijd tegen Spanje', *De Nieuwe Tijd* 9 (1906): 378–88.
Dean, Warren. 'The green wave of coffee: Beginnings of tropical agricultural research in Brazil (1885–1900)', *Hispanic American Historical Review* 69 (1989): 91–115.
Dean, Warren. *Brazil and the Struggle for Rubber: A study in environmental history*. Cambridge: Cambridge University Press, 1987.
Dedrick, Jason, Kenneth L. Kraemer and Greg Linden. 'Who profits from innovation in global value chains? A study of the iPod and Notebook PCs', *Industrial and Corporate Change* 19 (2010): 81–116.
Dekker, Rudolf. 'Labour conflicts and working-class culture in early modern Holland', *International Review of Social History* 35 (1990): 377–420.
Delevigne, Sir Malcolm. 'The pre-war history of international labor legislation'. In *The Origins of the International Labor Organization*. Vol. I, edited by James T. Shotwell, 19–54. New York: Columbia University Press, 1934.
Denzer, Jörg. *Die Konquista der Augsburger Welser-Gesellschaft in Südamerika 1528–1556*. Munich: C. H. Beck, 2005.
Deutsch, Jan-Georg. *Emancipation without Abolition in German East Africa c. 1884–1914*. Oxford: Oxford University Press, 2006.
Devos, Isabelle. 'Te jong om te sterven: De levenskansen van meisjes in België omstreeks 1900', *Tijdschrift voor Sociale Geschiedenis* 26 (2000): 55–75.

Dillon, Michael. 'A history of the porcelain industry in Jingdezhen' (PhD thesis, University of Leeds, 1976).
Ditchfield, Peter Hampson. *Old English Customs, Extant at the present time: An account of local observances*. London: Methuen, 1896.
Ditton, Jason. 'Perks, pilferage, and the fiddle: The historical structure of invisible wages', *Theory and Society* 4 (1977): 39–71.
Ditton, Jason. *Part-Time Crime: An ethnography of fiddling and pilferage*. London: Macmillan, 1977.
Domar, Evsey D. 'The causes of slavery and serfdom: A hypothesis', *Journal of Economic History* 30 (1970): 18–32.
Donkin, R. A. *Between East and West: The Moluccas and the traffic in spices up to the arrival of Europeans*. Philadelphia, PA: American Philosophical Society, 2003.
Doren, Alfred. *Die Florentiner Wollentuchindustrie vom vierzehnten bis zum sechzehnten Jahrhundert: Ein Beitrag zur Geschichte des modernen Kapitalismus*. Stuttgart: J. G. Cotta'sche Buchhandlung Nachf., 1901.
Dorn, Franz. 'Selbstverknechtung – Selbstversklavung durch Vertrag?'. In *Sklaverei und Zwangsarbeit zwischen Akzeptanz und Widerstand*, edited by Elisabeth Herrmann-Otto, 94–117. Hildesheim: Georg Olms Verlag, 2011.
Douglas, Mary and Aaron Wildawsky. *Risk and Culture: An essay on the selection of technological and environmental dangers*. Berkeley: University of California Press, 1982.
Douglas, William A., John-Paul Ferguson and Erin Klett. 'An effective confluence of forces in support of workers' rights: ILO standards, US trade laws, unions, and NGOs', *Human Rights Quarterly* 26 (2004): 273–99.
Douwes Dekker, Eduard (Multatuli). *Max Havelaar, of de koffijveilingen der Nederlandsche Handel-Maatschappij*. Amsterdam: De Ruyter, 1860. English translation: *Multatuli, Max Havelaar, or, The Coffee Auctions of a Dutch Trading Company*. Trans. with notes by Roy Edwards. Harmondsworth: Penguin, 1987.
Dovring, Folke. 'Bondage, tenure and progress: Reflections on the economics of forced labor', *Comparative Studies in Society and History* 7 (1965): 309–23.
Drescher, Seymour. *Capitalism and Antislavery: British mobilisation in comparative perspective*. London: Macmillan, 1986.
D'Sena, Peter. 'Perquisites and casual labour on the London wharfside in the eighteenth century', *London Journal* 14 (1989): 130–47.
Du Bois, W. E. B. 'The souls of white folk'. In W. E. B. Du Bois, *Writings*. New York: The Library of America, 1986 [1920].
Duby, Georges. 'L'histoire des systèmes de valeurs', *History and Theory* 11 (1972): 15–25.
Dufty, Norman F. 'Organizational growth and goal structure: The case of the ILO', *International Organization* 26 (1972): 479–98.
Dunn, Richard S. *Sugar and Slaves: The rise of the planter class in the English West Indies, 1624–1713*. Chapel Hill: University of North Carolina Press, 1972.
Durkheim, Emile. [review of Ferdinand Tönnies, *Gemeinschaft und Gesellschaft*], *Revue philosophique de la France et de l'étranger* 37 (1889): 416–22.
Durkheim, Emile. *De la division de travail: Étude sur l'organisation des sociétés supérieures*. Paris: Alcan, 1893.
Dutka, Barry L. 'New York discovers gold! In California', *California History* 63 (1984): 313–19.
Dutta, Manas. 'Disciplining the Madras Army during the early years of the English East India Company's dominance in South India', *Socialnių makslų studijos/Societal Studies* 4 (2012): 887–99.
Duurzaam Ondernemen. 'Maatschappelijk verantwoord ondernemen. Onderzoek onder CEO's Europese bedrijven: Shareholder value boven stakeholder value'. https://www.duurzaam-ondernemen.nl/onderzoek-onder-ceos-europese-bedrijven-shareholder-value-boven-stakeholder-value/.
Earle, Carville. *Geographical Inquiry and American Historical Problems*. Stanford, CA: Stanford University Press, 1992.
Eckert, Andreas (ed.). *Global Histories of Work*. Berlin: Walter de Gruyter, 2016.
Eco, Umberto. *Kant and the Platypus: Essays on language and cognition*. Trans. Alastair McEwen. New York: Harcourt Brace & Company, 2000.
Economist Intelligence Unit. 'Rebels without a cause: What the upsurge in protest movements means for global politics'. EIU, 2013. http://www.eiu.com/ProtestUpsurge.
Edwards, Jon R. 'Slavery, the slave trade and the economic reorganization of Ethiopia 1916–1935', *African Economic History* 11 (1982): 3–14.

Ehmer, Josef. 'Wohnen ohne eigene Wohnung: Zur sozialen Stellung von Untermietern und Bettgehern'. In *Wohnen im Wandel: Beiträge zur Geschichte des Alltags in der bürgerlichen Gesellschaft*, edited by Lutz Niethammer, 132–50. Wuppertal: Peter Hammer Verlag, 1979.

Ehrenberg, Ronald G. and Robert S. Smith. *Modern Labor Economics: Theory and public policy*. Fourth edition. New York: HarperCollins, 1991.

Ehrenreich, Barbara and Hochschild Arlie Russell (eds). *Global Woman: Nannies, maids and sex workers in the new economy*. New York: Metropolitan Books, 2003.

Ehrenreich, Nancy. 'Subordination and symbiosis: Mechanisms of mutual support between subordinating systems', *UMKC Law Review* 71 (2002): 251–323.

Eickhof, Norbert. *Eine Theorie der Gewerkschaftsentwicklung*. Tübingen: J. C. B. Mohr (Paul Siebeck), 1973.

Eisenberg, Christiane. *Frühe Arbeiterbewegung und Genossenschaften: Theorie und Praxis der Produktivgenossenschaften in der deutschen Sozialdemokratie und den Gewerkschaften der 1860er/1870er Jahre*. Bonn: Verlag Neue Gesellschaft, 1985.

Elbaum, Max. *Revolution in the Air: Sixties radicals turn to Lenin, Mao and Che*. London and New York: Verso, 2002.

Elias, Norbert. *The Civilizing Process: Sociogenetic and psychogenetic investigations*. Oxford: Blackwell, 2000.

Elkins, Caroline. *Britain's Gulag: The brutal end of empire in Kenya*. London: Pimlico, 2005.

Elson, Robert E. 'International commerce, the state and society: Economic and social change'. In *The Cambridge History of Southeast Asia*. Vol. III: *From c. 1800 to the 1930s*, edited by Nicholas Tarling, 127–91. Cambridge: Cambridge University Press, 1999.

Elster, Jon. *Alchemies of the Mind: Rationality and the emotions*. Cambridge: Cambridge University Press, 1999.

Elster, Jon. *Making Sense of Marx*. Cambridge: Cambridge University Press, 1985.

Elwert, Georg. 'Conflicts inside and outside the household: A West African case study'. In *Households and the World-Economy*, edited by Joan Smith, Immanuel Wallerstein and Hans-Dieter Evers, 272–96. Beverly Hills, CA: Sage, 1984.

Ely, Richard T. *The Labor Movement in America*. New York: Thomas Y. Crowell & Co., 1886.

Emmanuel, Arghiri. *Unequal Exchange: A study of the imperialism of trade*. Trans. Brian Pearce. New York and London: Monthly Review Press, 1972.

Emmer, Pieter C. 'The ideology of free labor and Dutch colonial policy'. In *Fifty Years Later: Antislavery, capitalism and modernity in the Dutch orbit*, edited by Gert Oostindie, 207–22. Leiden: KITLV Press, 1995.

*Encyclopedia of 1848 Revolutions*. https://www.ohio.edu/chastain/index.htm.

Engels, Friedrich. 'The housing question', *MECW*, Vol. 23, 317–91.

Engerman, Stanley L. 'Pricing freedom: Evaluating the costs of emancipation and of manumission'. In *Working Slavery, Pricing Freedom: Perspectives from the Caribbean, Africa and the African diaspora*, edited by Verene Shepherd, 273–302. Kingston: Ian Randle Publishers, 2002.

Engerman, Stanley L. 'Slavery, freedom, and Sen'. In *Buying Freedom: The ethics and economics of slave redemption*, edited by Kwame Anthony Appiah and Martin Bunzl, 77–107. Princeton: Princeton University Press, 2007.

Engerman, Stanley L. 'Some considerations relating to property rights in man', *Journal of Economic History* 33 (1973): 43–65.

Epstein, S. R. *Freedom and Growth: The rise of states and markets in Europe, 1300–1750*. London and New York: Routledge, 2000.

Esch, Elizabeth and David Roediger. 'One symptom of originality: Race and the management of labour in the history of the United States', *Historical Materialism* 17 (2009): 3–43.

Esper, Thomas. 'The condition of the serf workers in Russia's metallurgical industry, 1800–1861', *Journal of Modern History* 50 (1978): 660–79.

ESTA (Exploring Slave Trade in Asia) (online resource). https://iisg.amsterdam/en/research/projects/slave-trade-asia.

European Commission. *Precarious Employment in Europe: A comparative study of labour market related risks in flexible economies*. Brussels: European Commission, 2004.

European Labour History Network. https://socialhistoryportal.org/elhn.

Evans Jr., Robert. 'Some notes on coerced labor', *Journal of Economic History* 30 (1970): 861–6.

Evenson, Robert E. and Douglas Gollin. 'Assessing the impact of the Green Revolution, 1960 to 2000', *Science* 300 (2003): 758–62.

Evers, Hans-Dieter. 'Schattenwirtschaft, Subsistenzproduktion und informeller Sektor'. In *Soziologie wirtschaftlichen Handelns*, edited by Klaus Heinemann, 353–66. Opladen: Westdeutscher Verlag, 1987.
Expertus [pseudonym]. 'Negroes and the slave trade', *The Times*, 21 November 1857, 8–9.
Fall, Babacar. *Le travail au Sénégal au XXe siècle*. Paris: Karthala, 2011.
Fall, Babacar. *Le travail forcé en Afrique Occidentale Française (1900–1945)*. Paris: Karthala, 1993.
Fang Zhuofen, Hu Tiewen, Jian Rui and Fang Xing. 'Capitalism during the early and middle Qing (2)'. In *Chinese Capitalism, 1522–1840*, edited by Xu Dixin and Wu Chengming, 249–371. New York: St. Martin's Press, 2000.
Fann, Willerd R. 'Peacetime attrition in the army of Frederick William I, 1713–1740', *Central European History* 11 (1978): 323–34.
Fanon, Frantz. *The Wretched of the Earth*. Trans. Constance Farrington. Harmondsworth: Penguin, 1967.
Farber, Samuel. *The Origins of the Cuban Revolution Reconsidered*. Chapel Hill: University of North Carolina Press, 2006.
Faure, Alain. 'Classe malpropre, classe dangereuse? Quelques remarques à propos des chiffoniers parisiens au XIXe siècle et de leurs cités', *Recherches* 29 (1977): 79–102.
Faye, Valy. *Économie arachidière et dynamiques du peuplement au Sénégal: Kaffrine et le Saloum oriental de 1891 à 1960*. Paris: Karthala, 2016.
Fayissa, Bichaka, Christian Nsiah and Badassa Tadasse. 'The impact of tourism on economic growth and development in Africa', *Tourism Economics* 14 (2007): 807–18.
Feldman, Gerald D. and Klaus Tenfelde (eds). *Workers, Owners and Politics in Coal Mining: An international comparison of industrial relations*. New York: Berg, 1990.
Fenoaltea, Stefano. 'Slavery and supervision in comparative perspective: A model', *Journal of Economic History* 44 (1984): 635–68.
Ferares, Maurice. *De revolutie die verboden werd: Indonesië, 1945–1949*. Amsterdam: Uitgeverij Abigador, 2014.
Ferguson, Adam. *An Essay on the History of Civil Society*. Edinburgh: A. Kincaid & J. Bell, 1767.
Ferrand, Antoine François Claude Comte de. *Considérations sur la révolution sociale*. London: n.p., 1794.
Filtzer, Donald A. *Soviet Workers and De-Stalinization: The consolidation of the modern system of Soviet production relations, 1953–1964*. Cambridge: Cambridge University Press, 1992.
Filtzer, Donald A. *Soviet Workers and Late Stalinism: Labour and the restoration of the Stalinist system after World War II*. Cambridge: Cambridge University Press, 2002.
Filtzer, Donald A. *Soviet Workers and Stalinist Industrialization: The formation of modern Soviet production relations, 1928–1941*. London and Dover, NH: Pluto Press, 1986.
Filtzer, Donald A. *Soviet Workers and the Collapse of Perestroika: The Soviet labour process and Gorbachev's reforms, 1985–1991*. Cambridge: Cambridge University Press, 1992.
Filtzer, Donald, Wendy Z. Goldman, Gijs Kessler and Simon Pirani. (eds). *A Dream Deferred: New studies in Russian and Soviet labour history*. New York: Peter Lang, 2008.
Fink, Leon (ed.). *Workers across the Americas: The transnational turn in labor history*. New York: Oxford University Press, 2011.
Fink, Leon. *Sweatshops at Sea: Merchant seamen in the world's first globalized industry, from 1812 to the present*. Chapel Hill: University of North Carolina Press, 2011.
Finkelman, Paul. 'Evading the ordinance: The persistence of bondage in Indiana and Illinois', *Journal of the Early Republic* 9 (1989): 21–51.
Finkelman, Paul. 'Regulating the African slave trade', *Civil War History* 54 (2008): 379–405.
Finlay, Mark R. 'The German agricultural experiment stations and the beginnings of American agricultural research', *Agricultural History* 62 (1988): 41–50.
Finley, M. I. 'Between slavery and freedom', *Comparative Studies in Society and History* 6 (1964): 233–49.
Finley, Moses. *Ancient Slavery and Modern Ideology*. New York: Viking Press, 1980.
Fitzpatrick, Peter. '"Really rather like slavery": Law and labour in the colonial economy of Papua New Guinea'. In *Essays in the Political Economy of Australian Capitalism*, edited by Edward L. Wheelwright and Ken Buckley, 108–18. Sydney: ANZ Press, 1978.
Fogel, Robert W. *Without Consent or Contract: The rise and fall of American slavery*. New York: Norton, 1989.
Fogel, Robert W. and Stanley L. Engerman. *Time on the Cross: The economics of American negro slavery*. Two volumes. New York and London: Norton, 1989.

Follows, John W. *Antecedents of the International Labour Organization*. Oxford: Clarendon Press, 1951.
Ford, Martin. 'The political economy of taxation in Liberia, *ca.* 1830–1930', *Research in Economic Anthropology* 16 (1995): 397–419.
Forrest, Alan. *Conscripts and Deserters: The army and French society during the revolution and empire*. Oxford: Oxford University Press, 1989.
Fosberg, F. R. 'Cinchona plantation in the New World', *Economic Botany* 1 (1947): 330–3.
Foucault, Michel. *Discipline and Punish: The birth of the prison*. Trans. Alan Sheridan. Harmondsworth: Penguin, 1977.
Foucault, Michel. 'Truth and juridical forms'. In Michel Foucault, *Power*, edited by James D. Faubion 1–89. New York: The New Press, 2000.
Franke, Gunther. *Nutzpflanzen der Tropen und Subtropen*. Vol. I. Leipzig: S. Hirzel Verlag, 1980.
Franklin, V. P. 'Patterns of student activism at historically black universities in the United States and South Africa, 1960–1977', *Journal of African American History* 88 (2003): 204–17.
Freeman, Jo. 'The origins of the women's liberation movement', *American Journal of Sociology* 78 (1973): 792–811.
Freeman, Joshua B. *Behemoth: A history of the factory and the making of the modern world*. New York and London: W. W. Norton, 2018.
Freeman, Otis W. 'Economic geography of the Hawaiian islands', *Economic Geography* 5 (1929): 260–76.
Freeman, Richard. 'What really ails Europe (and America): The doubling of the global workforce', *The Globalist*, 5 March 2010. https://www.theglobalist.com/what-really-ails-europe-and-america-the-doubling-of-the-global-workforce/.
French, John D. *The Brazilian Workers' ABC: Class conflict and alliances in modern São Paulo*. Chapel Hill: University of North Carolina Press, 1992.
Freud, Sigmund. *A General Introduction to Psychoanalysis*. Trans. G. Stanley Hall. New York: Horace Liveright, 1920.
Freund, William. 'Theft and social protest among the tin miners of Northern Nigeria', *Radical History Review* 26 (1982): 68–86.
Fridenson, Patrick. 'Is there a return of capitalism in business history?'. In *Capitalism: The reemergence of a historical concept*, edited by Jürgen Kocka and Marcel van der Linden, 107–31. London: Bloomsbury, 2016.
Friebel, Guido and Sergei Guriev. 'Attaching workers through in-kind payments: Theory and evidence from Russia', *World Bank Economic Review* 19 (2005): 175–202.
Fried, J. H. E. 'Relations between the United Nations and the International Labor Organization', *American Political Science Review* 41 (1947): 963–77.
Friedman, Debra. 'Toward a theory of union emergence and demise'. In *Social Institutions: Their emergence, maintenance and effects*, edited by Michael Hechter, Karl-Dieter Opp and Reinhard Wippler, 291–306. Berlin and New York: Walter de Gruyter, 1990.
Friedman, Debra. 'Why workers strike: Individual decisions and structural constraints'. In *The Microfoundations of Macrosociology*, edited by Michael Hechter, 250–83. Philadelphia: Temple University Press, 1983.
Friedman, Kathie. 'Households as income-pooling units'. In *Households and the World-Economy*, edited by Joan Smith, Immanuel Wallerstein and Hans-Dieter Evers, 37–55. Beverly Hills, CA: Sage, 1984.
Fröbel, Folker, Jürgen Heinrichs and Otto Kreye, *The New International Division of Labour: Structural unemployment in industrialised countries and industrialisation in developing countries*. Cambridge: Cambridge University Press, 1982.
Fröbel, Folker, Jürgen Heinrichs and Otto Kreye. *Umbruch in der Weltwirtschaft: Die globale Strategie: Verbilligung der Arbeitskraft/ Flexibilisierung der Arbeit/ Neue Technologien*. Reinbek: Rowohlt, 1986.
Fuchs, James R. Oral history interview with David A. Morse (3 August 1977). Online. http://www.trumanlibrary.org/oralhist/morse3.htm.
Führer, Karl Christian. 'Das Kreditinstitut der kleinen Leute: Zur Bedeutung der Pfandleihe im deutschen Kaiserreich', *Bankhistorisches Archiv* 18 (1992): 3–21.
Fuks, Alexander. 'κολωνός μισθιος: Labour exchange in classical Athens', *Eranos* 49 (1951): 171–3.
Furåker, Bengt. *Sociological Perspectives on Labor Markets*. Houndmills and New York: Palgrave Macmillan, 2005.
Füredi, Frank. *The Soviet Union Demystified: A materialist analysis*. London: Junius, 1986.
Furedy, C. 'Survival strategies of the urban poor: Scavenging and recuperation in Calcutta', *GeoJournal* 8 (1984): 129–36.

Fussell, George E. 'The farming writers of eighteenth-century England', *Agricultural History* 21 (1947): 1–8.
Gabaccia, Donna R. and Dirk Hoerder (eds). *Connecting Seas and Connected Ocean Rims: Indian, Atlantic, and Pacific Oceans and China Seas migrations from the 1830s to the 1930s*. Leiden and Boston: Brill, 2011.
Gailus, Manfred. *Straße und Brot: Sozialer Protest in den deutschen Staaten unter besonderer Berücksichtigung Preußens, 1847–1849*. Göttingen: Vandenhoeck & Ruprecht, 1990.
Galenson, David. 'White servitude and the growth of black slavery in colonial America', *Journal of Economic History* 41 (1981): 39–47.
Galenson, David. *White Servitude in Colonial America: An economic analysis*. Cambridge: Cambridge University Press, 1981.
Gallo, Stefano. 'Dictatorship and international organizations: The ILO as a "test ground" for fascism'. In *Globalizing Social Rights: The International Labour Organization and beyond*, edited by Sandrine Kott and Joëlle Droux, 153–71. New York: Palgrave Macmillan, 2013.
Gallup. *State of the Global Workplace*. New York: Gallup Press, 2017.
Gambetta, Diego (ed.). *Trust: Making and breaking cooperative relations*. New York: Basil Blackwell, 1988.
Gardner, Leigh. *Taxing Colonial Africa: The political economy of British imperialism*. Oxford: Oxford University Press, 2012.
Gaspar, David Barry. 'Runaways in seventeenth-century Antigua', *Boletín de Estudios Latinoamericanos y del Caribe* 26 (1979): 3–13.
Gaud, William S. 'The Green Revolution: Accomplishments and apprehensions'. Speech given before the Society for International Development, Washington DC, 8 March 1968. Reprinted online in *AgBioWorldArchives*. www.agbioworld.org/biotech-info/topics/borlaug/borlaug-green.html.
Gautier, Ariette. 'Traite et politiques démographiques esclavagistes', *Population* 41 (1986): 1005–24.
Geertz, Clifford. *Agricultural Involution: The processes of ecological change in Indonesia*. Berkeley: University of California Press, 1963.
Geggus, David P. (ed.). *The Impact of the Haitian Revolution in the Atlantic World*. Columbia: University of South Carolina, 2001.
Genovese, Eugene D. and Elizabeth Fox-Genovese. *Fruits of Merchant Capital: Slavery and bourgeois property in the rise and expansion of capitalism*. Oxford: Oxford University Press, 1983.
Gerber, James and Lei Guang (eds). *Agriculture and Rural Connections in the Pacific, 1500–1900*. Aldershot: Ashgate, 2006.
Gerhard, H. W. (Gerhard Wartenberg). 'Unsere Staatsauffassung', *Die Internationale: Zeitschrift für die revolutionäre Arbeiterbewegung, Gesellschaftskritik und sozialistischen Neuaufbau* 4 (1931): 128–31.
Gernet, Jacques. *Le monde chinois*. Third revised edition. Paris: Armand Colin, 1990.
Ghai, Dharam. *The World Employment Programme at ILO*. Geneva: ILO, 2009. https://ilo.primo.exlibrisgroup.com/permalink/41ILO_INST/1jaulmn/alma994450533402676.
Ghebali, Victor-Yves. *L'Organisation Internationale du Travail (OIT)*. Geneva: Georg, 1987.
Gidron, Noam and Peter A. Hall. 'The politics of social status: Economic and cultural roots of the populist Right', *British Journal of Sociology* 68 (2017, Supplement 1): S57–S84.
Gier, Jaclyn J. and Laurie Mercier (eds). *Mining Women: Gender in the development of a global industry, 1670 to 2005*. New York: Palgrave Macmillan, 2006.
Gilbreth, Lilian. *The Psychology of Management: The function of the mind in determining, teaching and installing methods of least waste*. New York: Sturgis & Walton, 1914.
Gilcher-Holthey, Ingrid. *'Die Phantasie an die Macht': Mai 68 in Frankreich*. Frankfurt am Main: Suhrkamp, 1995.
Gilcher-Holthey, Ingrid. *Die 68-er Bewegung: Deutschland – Westeuropa – USA*. Munich: Beck, 2001.
Gillion, Colin, John Turner, Clive Bailey and Denis Latulippe (eds). *Social Security Pensions: Development and reform*. Geneva: ILO, 2000. https://www.ilo.org/secsoc/information-resources/publications-and-tools/books-and-reports/WCMS_SECSOC_7776/lang--en/index.htm.
Gilly, Adolfo. *The Mexican Revolution*. Trans. Patrick Camiller. London: Verso, 1983.
Glassman, Jonathan. 'The bondsman's new clothes: The contradictory consciousness of slave resistance on the Swahili coast', *Journal of African History* 32 (1991): 277–312.

Global Hub Labour Conflicts (International Institute of Social History). https://datasets.iisg. amsterdam/dataverse/labourconflicts.

Gøbel, Erik. *Det danske slavehandelsforbud 1792: Studier og kilder til forhistorien, forordningen og følgerne*. Odense: Syddansk Universitetsforlag, 2008.

Goffman, Erving. 'On the characteristics of total institutions'. In Erving Goffman, *Asylums: Essays on the social situation of mental patients and other inmates*, 1–124. New York: Anchor Books, 1961.

Goldenberg, Boris. *Lateinamerika und die kubanische Revolution*. Cologne: Kiepenheuer und Witsch, 1963.

Goldfarb, Stephen J. 'An inquiry into the politics of the prohibition of the international slave trade', *Agricultural History* 68 (1994): 20–34.

Golombek, Lisa. 'Timurid potters abroad', *Oriente Moderno*, New Series, 15 (1996): 577–86.

Goluboff, Risa L. 'The Thirteenth Amendment and the lost origins of civil rights', *Duke Law Journal* 50 (2001): 1609–85.

Goodrich, Carter L. *The Frontier of Control: A study in British workshop politics*. New York: Harcourt, Brace and Howe, 1920.

Gorr, Michael. 'Toward a theory of coercion', *Canadian Journal of Philosophy* 16 (1986): 383–405.

Gossez, Rémi. *Les ouvriers de Paris*. Vol. 1: *L'organisation, 1848–1851*. La Roche-sur-Yon: Imprimerie Centrale de l'Ouest, 1968.

Gould, Roger V. 'Trade cohesion, class unity, and urban insurrection: Artisanal activism in the Paris Commune', *American Journal of Sociology* 98 (1993): 721–54.

Gouldner, Alvin W. *The Future of Intellectuals and the Rise of the New Class*. London and Basingstoke: Macmillan, 1979.

Graham, Gerald S. *Great Britain in the Indian Ocean: A study of maritime enterprise 1810–1850*. Oxford: Clarendon Press, 1967.

Graham, J. C. 'The French connection in the early history of canning', *Journal of the Royal Society of Medicine* 74 (1981): 374–81.

Graham, James D. 'The slave trade, depopulation and human sacrifice in Benin history', *Cahiers d'études africaines* 5 (1965): 317–34.

Gramsci, Antonio. *Prison Notebooks*. Vol. II. Edited and translated by Joseph A. Buttigieg. New York: Columbia University Press, 2011.

Gramsci, Antonio. *Selections from the Prison Notebooks*. Edited and translated by Quintin Hoare and Geoffrey Nowell Smith. London: Lawrence and Wishart, 1971.

Granovetter, Mark. 'The strength of weak ties', *American Journal of Sociology* 78 (1973): 1360–80.

Granovetter, Mark. *Getting a Job: A study of contacts and careers*. Chicago: University of Chicago Press, 1995.

Gras, Norman S. B. 'What is capitalism in the light of history?', *Bulletin of the Business Historical Society* 21 (1947): 79–120.

Gray, Lewis C. *History of Agriculture in the Southern United States to 1860*. Two volumes. New York: Peter Smith, 1941.

Green, Anna. 'Spelling, go-slows, gliding away and theft: Informal control over work on the New Zealand waterfront, 1915–1951', *Labour History* 63 (1992): 100–14.

Green, Erik. 'The economics of slavery in the eighteenth-century Cape Colony: Revising the Nieboer-Domar hypothesis', *International Review of Social History* 59 (2014): 39–70.

Green, William A. *British Slave Emancipation: The sugar colonies and the great experiment 1830–1865*. Oxford: Clarendon Press, 1976.

Green, William A. 'Periodization in European and world history', *Journal of World History* 3 (1992): 13–53.

Green-Pedersen, Svend E. 'Slave demography in the Danish West Indies and the abolition of the Danish slave trade'. In *The Abolition of the Atlantic Slave Trade: Origins and effects in Europe, Africa, and the Americas*, edited by David Eltis and James Walvin, 231–57. Madison: University of Wisconsin Press, 1981.

Gregory, Paul R. and Valery Lazarev (eds). *The Economics of Forced Labor: The Soviet gulag*. Stanford, CA: Hoover Institution Press, 2003.

Greiff, Mats. '"Marching through the streets singing and shouting": Industrial struggle and trade unions among female linen workers in Belfast and Lurgan, 1872–1910', *Saothar* 22 (1997): 29–44.

Griaule, Marcel. 'Labour in Abyssinia', *International Labour Review* 23 (1931): 181–202.

Grigg, David B. *The Agricultural Systems of the World: An evolutionary approach*. Cambridge: Cambridge University Press, 1992.

Grigg, David B. 'The world's agricultural labour force 1800–1970', *Geography* 60 (1975): 194–202.
Grigg, David B. 'Trends in the World's Agricultural Population', *Geography* 56 (1971): 320–4.
Grossmann, Henryk. *Das Akkumulations- und Zusammenbruchsgesetz des kapitalistischen Systems*. Leipzig: Hirschfeld, 1929.
Grüttner, Michael. 'Working-class crime and the labour movement: Pilfering in the Hamburg docks, 1888–1923'. In *The German Working Class 1888–1933: The politics of everyday life*, edited by Richard J. Evans, 54–79. London and Totowa, NJ: Croom Helm and Barnes & Noble, 1982.
Guérin, Daniel. 'D'une nouvelle interprétation de la Révolution française', *Annales: Histoire, Sciences Sociales* 20 (1965): 84–94.
Guérin, Daniel. 'Preface to the English edition'. In Daniel Guérin, *Class Struggle in the First French Republic: Bourgeois and bras nus 1793–1795*, 1–20. Trans. Ian Patterson. London: Pluto Press, 1973.
Gueye, Omar. *Mai 1968 au Sénégal: Senghor face aux étudiants et au mouvement syndical*. Paris: Karthala, 2017.
Gupta, Ranajit Das. 'From peasants and tribesmen to plantation workers: Colonial capitalism, reproduction of labour power and proletarianisation in North East India, 1850s to 1947', *Economic and Political Weekly* 21 (1986): PE2–PE10.
Gutkind, Peter C. W., Robin Cohen and Jean Copans (eds). *African Labor History*. Beverly Hills, CA: Sage, 1978.
Gutmann, Matthew C. 'Rituals of resistance: A critique of the theory of everyday forms of resistance', *Latin American Perspectives* 20 (1993): 74–92.
Gwala, Nkosinathi. 'State control, student politics and the crisis in black universities'. In *Popular Struggle in South Africa*, edited by William Cobbett and Robin Cohen, 163–82. London: James Currey, 1988.
Haarer, A. E. *Modern Coffee Production*. London: Leonard Hill, 1923.
Haas, Ernst B. 'System and process in the International Labor Organization: A statistical afterthought', *World Politics* 14 (1962): 322–52.
Haas, Ernst B. *Beyond the Nation-State: Functionalism and international organization*. Stanford, CA: Stanford University Press, 1964.
Habib, Irfan. 'Forms of class struggle in Mughal India'. In Habib, *Essays in Indian History*, 233–58.
Habib, Irfan. *Essays in Indian History: Towards a Marxist perception*. New Delhi: Tulika, 1995.
Habib, Irfan. *The Indian Economy, 1858–1914*. New Delhi: Tulika, 2007.
Hagemann, Karen. 'Frauenprotest und Männerdemonstrationen? Zum geschlechtsspezifischen Aktionsverhalten im großstädtischen Arbeitermilieu der Weimarer Republik'. In *Massenmedium Straße: Zur Kulturgeschichte der Demonstration*, edited by Bernd Jürgen Warneken, 202–30. Frankfurt am Main and New York: Campus, 1991.
Hagen, Karin. *Policy Dialogue between the International Labour Organization and the International Financial Institutions: The search for convergence*. Geneva: Friedrich-Ebert-Stiftung, 2003.
Hagen, Katherine A. *The International Labour Organization: Can it deliver the social dimension of globalization?* Geneva: Friedrich-Ebert-Stiftung, 2003.
Haggis, Alec W. J. 'Fundamental errors in the early history of Cinchona', *Bulletin of the History of Medicine* 10 (1941): 417–59 and 568–92.
Håkansson, Fredrik. *Standing up to a Multinational Giant: The Saint-Gobain World Council and the American window glass workers' strike in the American Saint-Gobain Corporation in 1969*. Växjö: Linnaeus University Press, 2011.
Hall, Douglas. 'The flight from the estates reconsidered: The British West Indies, 1838–1842', *Journal of Caribbean History* 10–11 (1978): 7–24. Reprinted in *Caribbean Freedom: Economy and society from emancipation to the present: A student reader*, edited by Hilary M. Beckles and Verene Shepherd, 55–63. Kingston: Ian Randle, 1993.
Hall, Michael and Verena Stolcke. 'The introduction of free labour on São Paulo coffee plantations', *Journal of Peasant Studies* 10 (1983): 170–200.
Hall, N. A. T. 'Maritime maroons: "Grand marronage" from the Danish West Indies', *William and Mary Quarterly*, Third Series, 42 (1985): 476–98.
Hammer, Nikolaus, Réka Plugor, Peter Nolan and Ian Clark. *A New Industry on a Skewed Playing Field: Supply chain relations and working conditions in UK garment manufacturing*. Leicester: University of Leicester, 2015.
Hammond, John L. Le Breton and Barbara Hammond. *The Skilled Labourer 1760–1832*. London: Longmans, Green and Co., 1919.

Hammond, John L. Le Breton and Barbara Hammond. *The Town Labourer, 1760–1832: The new civilisation*. London: Longmans, Green and Co., 1917.

Hammond, John L. Le Breton and Barbara Hammond. *The Village Labourer, 1760–1832: A study in the government of England before the Reform Bill*. London: Longmans, Green and Co., 1911.

Hammurabi. *Code of Hammurabi*. Trans. L. W. King (1915), 15. http://www.general-intelligence.com/library/hr.pdf.

Hanami, Tadashi. 'The influence of ILO standards on law and practice in Japan', *International Labour Review* 120 (1981): 765–79.

Handler, Jerome S. 'Slave revolts and conspiracies in seventeenth-century Barbados', *Nieuwe West-Indische Gids/New West Indian Guide* 56 (1982): 5–42.

Hareven, Tamara K. 'A complex relationship: Family strategies and the processes of economic and social change'. In *Beyond the Marketplace: Rethinking economy and society*, edited by Roger Friedland and A. F. Robertson, 215–44. New York: Aldine de Gruyter, 1990.

Hareven, Tamara. *Family Time and Industrial Time: The relationship between the family and work in a New England industrial community*. Cambridge: Cambridge University Press, 1982.

Harris, Donald J. 'The circuit of capital and the "labour problem" in capitalist development', *Social and Economic Studies* 37 (1988): 15–31.

Harris, William V. 'Towards a study of the Roman slave trade', *Memoirs of the American Academy in Rome* 36 (1980): 117–40.

Haug, Wolfgang Fritz. *Critique of Commodity Aesthetics: Appearance, sexuality, and advertising in capitalist society*. Trans. Robert Bock. Minneapolis: University of Minnesota Press, 1986.

Haupt, Georges. 'In what sense and to what degree was the Russian Revolution a proletarian revolution?', *Review* [Fernand Braudel Center] 3 (1979): 21–33.

Hay, Douglas and Paul Craven (eds). *Masters, Servants, and Magistrates in Britain and the Empire, 1562–1955*. Chapel Hill: University of North Carolina Press, 2004.

Hayek, Mario, Milorad M. Novicevic, John H. Humphreys and Nicole Jones. 'Ending the denial of slavery in management history: Paternalistic leadership of Joseph Emory Davis', *Journal of Management History* 16 (2010): 367–79.

Haymond, John A. *Soldiers: A global history of the fighting man, 1800–1945*. Lanham, MD: Stackpole Books, 2019.

Headrick, Daniel R. 'Technological change'. In *The Earth as Transformed by Human Action: Global and regional changes in the biosphere over the past 300 years*, edited by B. L. Turner, William C. Clark, Robert W. Kates, John F. Richards, Jessica T. Mathews and William B. Meyer, 55–67. Cambridge: Cambridge University Press, 1990.

Headrick, Daniel R. *The Tools of Empire: Technology and European imperialism in the nineteenth century*. New York and Oxford: Oxford University Press, 1981.

Hechter, Michael. *Principles of Group Solidarity*. Berkeley: University of California Press, 1987.

Hedström, Peter. 'Contagious collectivities: On the spatial diffusion of Swedish trade unions, 1890–1940', *American Journal of Sociology* 99 (1994): 1157–79.

Heerma van Voss, Lex. 'The International Federation of Trade Unions and the attempt to maintain the eight-hour working day (1919–1929)'. In *Internationalism in the Labour Movement, 1870–1940*, edited by Frits L. van Holthoon and Marcel van der Linden, 518–42. Leiden and Boston: Brill, 1988.

Heerma van Voss, Lex, Els Hiemstra-Kuperus and Elise van Nederveen Meerkerk (eds). *The Ashgate Companion to the History of Textile Workers, 1650–2000*. Farnham: Ashgate, 2010.

Hegel, Georg Wilhelm Friedrich. *Wissenschaft der Logik*. Frankfurt am Main: Suhrkamp, 1986.

Heinze, Ruth-Inge. 'Ten days in October – students vs. the military: An account of the student uprising in Thailand', *Asian Survey* 14 (1974): 491–508.

Helfer, Laurence R. 'Monitoring compliance with unratified treaties: The ILO experience', *Law and Contemporary Problems* 71 (2008): 193–217.

Hellie, Richard. *Slavery in Russia, 1450–1725*. Chicago: University of Chicago Press, 1982.

Hensman, Rohini. 'World trade and workers' rights: To link or not to link?', *Economic and Political Weekly* 35 (2000): 1247–54.

Herod, Andrew. 'Labor as an agent of globalization and as a global agent'. In *Spaces of Globalization: Reasserting the power of the local*, edited by Kevin R. Cox, 167–200. New York: The Guilford Press, 1997.

Herodotus. *History*. Translated from the ancient Greek by George Rawlinson. Vol. II. New York: Tandy-Thomas, [1909].

Herr, Hansjörg and Christoph Scherrer. 'Trade, global value chains and working conditions'. In *Who Benefits from Trade? Findings on the link between trade and labour standards in the garment, footwear and electronics industries in Bangladesh, Cambodia, Pakistan, and Vietnam*, 1–8. Bonn: Friedrich-Ebert-Stiftung, 2017.

Hershey, David. 'Doctor Ward's accidental terrarium', *American Biology Teacher* 58 (1996): 276–81.

Hess, Moses. 'Consequences of a revolution of the proletariat'. In Moses Hess, *The Holy History of Mankind and Other Writings*, edited by Shlomo Avineri, 128–35. Cambridge: Cambridge University Press, 2004.

Hicks, John R. *A Theory of Economic History*. London: Oxford University Press, 1969.

Hidalgo-Weber, Olga. 'Les Britanniques et la Convention de l'Organisation internationale du travail sur la journée de 8 heures (1919–1932)', *Traverse: Zeitschrift für Geschichte/Revue d'histoire* 20 (2013): 28–43.

Hildebrandt, Eckart, Werner Olle and Wolfgang Schoeller. 'National unterschiedliche Produktionsbedingungen als Schranke einer gewerkschaftlichen Internationalisierung', *Prokla* 24 (1976): 27–57.

Hill, Arthur W. 'The history and functions of botanic gardens', *Annals of the Missouri Botanical Garden* 2 (1915): 185–240.

Hill, Christopher. 'Pottage for freeborn Englishmen: Attitudes to wage labour in the sixteenth and seventeenth centuries'. In *Socialism, Capitalism and Economic Growth: Essays presented to Maurice Dobb*, edited by C. H. Feinstein, 338–50. Cambridge: Cambridge University Press, 1967.

Hilson, Mary, Silke Neunsinger and Greg Patmore (eds). *A Global History of Consumer Co-operation since 1850: Movements and businesses*. Leiden and Boston: Brill, 2017.

Hindostanen in Suriname. National Archives of the Netherlands. https://www.nationaalarchief.nl/onderzoeken/zoekhulpen/hindostanen-in-suriname#collapse-8684.

Hirschman, Albert O. '*Exit, Voice, and Loyalty*: Further reflections and a survey of recent contributions', *The Milbank Memorial Fund Quarterly* 58 (1980): 430–53.

Hirschman, Albert O. *Exit, Voice, and Loyalty: Responses to decline in firms, organizations, and states*. Cambridge, MA: Harvard University Press, 1970.

Hirst, Paul, Grahame Thompson and Simon Bromley. *Globalization in Question*. Third edition. London: Polity Press, 2009.

History of Labour Relations (Global Collaboratory on the History of Labour Relations, 1500–2000). https://datasets.iisg.amsterdam/dataverse/labourrelations.

Ho, Hai-Quang. 'La transition de l'esclavage au salariat à La Réunion (1828–1853)'. In *L'économie de l'esclavage colonial*, edited by Fred Célimène and André Legris, 151–81. Paris: CNRS Editions, 2002.

Hobsbawm, Eric J. *Age of Extremes: The short twentieth century, 1914–1991*. London: Michael Joseph, 1994.

Hobsbawm, Eric J. *Labouring Men: Studies in the history of labour*. London: Weidenfeld & Nicolson, 1964.

Hobsbawm, Eric J. *Worlds of Labour: Further studies in the history of labour*. London: Weidenfeld & Nicolson, 1984.

Hobsbawm, Eric J. and George Rudé. *Captain Swing*. London: Lawrence and Wishart, 1969.

Hochschild, Adam. *King Leopold's Ghost: A story of greed, terror, and heroism in colonial Africa*. London: Pan, 2002.

Hochschild, Adam. *Bury the Chains: Prophets and rebels in the fight to free an empire's slaves*. Boston: Houghton Mifflin, 2005.

Hochstetter, Franz. *Die wirtschaftlichen und politischen Motive für die Abschaffung des britischen Sklavenhandels im Jahre 1806/1807*. Staats- und sozialwissenschaftliche Forschungen, Vol. 25 Part 1, 1906.

Hockett, Charles F. and Robert Ascher. 'The human revolution', *Current Anthropology* 5 (1964): 135–68.

Hodenberg, Christina von. *Aufstand der Weber: Die Revolte von 1844 und ihr Aufstieg zum Mythos*. Bonn: Dietz, 1997.

Hoerder, Dirk. *Crowd Action in Revolutionary Massachusetts 1765–1780*. New York: Academic Press, 1977.

Hoerder, Dirk. *Cultures in Contact: World migrations in the second millennium*. Durham, NC: Duke University Press, 2002.

Hoerder, Dirk and Amarjit Kaur (eds). *Proletarian and Gendered Mass Migrations: A global perspective on continuities and discontinuities from the 19th to the 21st centuries*. Leiden: Brill, 2013.

Hoerder, Dirk, Elise van Nederveen Meerkerk and Silke Neunsinger (eds). *Towards a Global History of Domestic and Caregiving Workers*. Leiden and Boston: Brill, 2015.

Hoffmann, Elizabeth A. 'Exit and voice: Organizational loyalty and dispute resolution strategies', *Social Forces* 84 (2006): 2313–30.

Hoffmann, Pierre and Albert Langwieler. *Noch sind wir da! Arbeiter im multinationalen Konzern – Der Erfolg des ersten internationalen Solidaritätsstreiks in Westeuropa*. Reinbek: Rowohlt, 1974.

Hofmeester, Karin and Christine Moll-Murata (eds). *The Joy and Pain of Work: Global attitudes and valuations, 1500–1650*. Cambridge: Cambridge University Press, 2012.

Hofmeester, Karin and Elise van Nederveen Meerkerk. 'Family, demography and labour relations', *The History of The Family* 22 (2017): 3–102.

Hofmeester, Karin and Jan Lucassen. 'Shifting labor relations in the Ottoman Empire and Turkey 1500–2000', *International Labor and Working-Class History* 97 (2020): 6–80.

Hofmeester, Karin and Marcel van der Linden (eds). *Handbook Global History of Work*. Berlin: Walter de Gruyter, 2018.

Hofmeester, Karin and Pim de Zwart (eds). *Colonialism, Institutional Change and Shifts in Global Labour Relations*. Amsterdam: Amsterdam University Press, 2018.

Hofmeester, Karin. 'Diamonds from mine to finger: Doing global labour history by way of a luxury commodity'. In *The Global History of Work: Critical readings*. Vol. II: *Work sites*, edited by Marcel van der Linden, 135–53. London: Bloomsbury Academic, 2019.

Hofmeester, Karin. 'Labour relations: Introductory remarks'. In Hofmeester and van der Linden, *Handbook Global History of Work*, edited by Karin Hofmeester and Marcel van der Linden, 317–27. Berlin: Walter de Gruyter, 2018.

Hofmeester, Karin, Gijs Kessler and Christine Moll-Murata (eds). *Conquerors, Employers and Arbiters: States and shifts in labour relations, 1500–2000*. Cambridge: Cambridge University Press, 2016.

Hofmeester, Karin, Jan Lucasssen and Filipa Ribeiro da Silva (eds). 'Labour relations in Sub-Saharan Africa', special section of *History in Africa* 41 (2014): 249–306.

Hohfeld, Wesley Newcomb. *Fundamental Legal Conceptions as Applied in Judicial Reasoning*. New Haven, CT: Yale University Press, 1919; reprinted Westport, CT: Greenwood Press, 1978.

Holstun, James. *Ehud's Dagger: Class struggle in the English Revolution*. London: Verso, 2000.

Homans, George C. 'Rational-choice theory and behavioral psychology'. In *Structures of Power and Constraint: Papers in honor of Peter M. Blau*, edited by Craig Calhoun, Marshall W. Meyer and W. Richard Scott, 77–89. Cambridge: Cambridge University Press, 1990.

Honig, Emily. 'Burning incense, pledging sisterhood: Communities of women workers in the Shanghai cotton mills, 1919–1949', *Signs* 10 (1985): 700–14.

Honoré, Anthony M. 'Ownership'. In *Oxford Essays in Jurisprudence: A collaborative work*, edited by Anthony Gordon Guest, 107–47. Oxford: Clarendon Press, 1961.

Hoover, Greg A. 'Supplemental family income sources: Ethnic differences in nineteenth-century industrial America', *Social Science History* 9 (1985): 293–306.

Hopkins, Anthony G. *An Economic History of West Africa*. London: Longman, 1973.

Hopkins, Daniel P. 'The Danish ban on the Atlantic slave trade and Denmark's African colonial ambitions, 1787–1807', *Itinerario* 25 (2001): 154–84.

Horn, Gerd-Rainer. *The Spirit of '68: Rebellion in Western Europe and North America, 1956–1976*. Oxford: Oxford University Press, 2007.

Howard, Allen M. 'Nineteenth-century coastal slave trading and the British abolition campaign in Sierra Leone', *Slavery and Abolition* 27 (2006): 23–49.

Howell, Jude. 'Household coping strategies in Kyrgyzstan', *Development in Practice* 5 (1995): 361–4.

Hsu, Wen-Chin. 'Social and economic factors in the Chinese porcelain industry in Jingdezhen during the late Ming and early Ching period, ca. 1620–1683', *Journal of the Royal Asiatic Society of Great Britain and Ireland* 1 (1988): 135–59.

Hübner, Peter, Christoph Klessmann and Klaus Tenfelde (eds). *Arbeiter im Staatssozialismus: Ideologischer Anspruch und soziale Wirklichkeit*. Cologne: Böhlau, 2005.

Hübner, Peter and Klaus Tenfelde (eds). *Arbeiter in der SBZ-DDR*. Essen: Klartext Verlag, 1999.

Hufton, Olwen. 'Women in revolution, 1789–1796', *Past and Present* 53 (1971): 90–108.

Hughes, Steve and Nigel Haworth. *The International Labour Organization (ILO): Coming in from the cold*. London: Routledge, 2010.

Hugill, Peter J. *World Trade since 1431: Geography, technology, and capitalism*. Baltimore, MD: Johns Hopkins University Press, 1993.

Humboldt, Alexander von. *Essai politique sur la Royaume de la Nouvelle-Espagne*. Vol. III. Paris: F. Schoell, 1811.

Humboldt, Alexander von. *Reise auf dem Río Magdalena, durch die Anden und Mexico, Teil II: Übersetzung, Anmerkungen, Register*. Edited and translated by Margot Faak. Berlin: Akademie-Verlag, 1986.

Humboldt, Alexander von. *The Island of Cuba*. Translated from the Spanish with Notes and a Preliminary Essay by J. S. Thrasher. New York: Derby & Jackson, 1856.

Humphries, Jane. 'Class struggle and the persistence of the working class family', *Cambridge Journal of Economics* 1 (1977): 242–58.

Ihonvbere, Julius O. 'Resistance and hidden forms of protest amongst the petroleum proletariat in Nigeria'. In *Midnight Oil: Work, energy, war, 1973–1992*, edited by Midnight Notes Collective, 91–105. Brooklyn: Autonomedia, 1992.

Iliffe, John. *A Modern History of Tanganyika*. Cambridge: Cambridge University Press, 1979.

ILO. *Child Labour in Mining and Global Supply Chains*. Geneva: ILO, 2019. https://www.ilo.org/wcmsp5/groups/public/---asia/---ro-bangkok/---ilo-manila/documents/publication/wcms_720743.pdf.

ILO. *Edward Phelan and the ILO: The life and views of an international social actor*. Geneva: ILO, 2009. https://labordoc.ilo.org/permalink/41ILO_INST/8s7mv9/alma994312973402676.

ILO. *Programme and Budget for the Biennium 2006–07*. Geneva: ILO, 2005. https://www.ilo.org/pls/prdutf8/finapps.dochandle?p_file=36.

ILO. *Programme and Budget for the Biennium 2016–17*. Geneva: ILO, 2015. https://www.ilo.org/wcmsp5/groups/public/---ed_mas/---program/documents/genericdocument/wcms_565220.pdf.

ILO. *Sectoral Studies on Decent Work in Global Supply Chains: Comparative analysis of good practices by multinational enterprises in promoting decent work in global supply chains*. Geneva: ILO, 2016. https://www.ilo.org/sector/Resources/publications/WCMS_467295/lang--en/index.htm.

ILO. 'Who is an employee?' (n.d.) https://www.ilo.org/global/topics/wages/minimum-wages/beneficiaries/WCMS_436463/lang--en/index.htm.

ILO. *World Employment and Social Outlook 2015: The changing nature of jobs*. Geneva: ILO, 2015. https://www.ilo.org/global/research/global-reports/weso/2015/lang--en/index.htm.

ILO. *World Employment and Social Outlook: Trends 2018*. Geneva: ILO, 2018. https://www.ilo.org/global/research/global-reports/weso/2018/lang--en/index.htm.

ILO and OECD. *The Labour Share in G20 Economies: Report prepared for the G20 Employment Working Group, Antalya, Turkey, 26–27 February 2015*. https://www.oecd.org/g20/topics/employment-and-social-policy/The-Labour-Share-in-G20-Economies.pdf.

ILO WESO Data Finder. https://www.ilo.org/wesodata.

ILOSTAT. https://ilostat.ilo.org/.

Imle, Ernest P. 'Hevea rubber: Past and future', *Economic Botany* 32 (1978): 264–77.

Ingavata, Chaichana. 'Students as agents of social change: A case of the Thai student movement during the years 1973–1976: A critical political analysis', (PhD thesis, Florida State University, 1981).

International Association Strikes and Social Conflicts. https://iassc-net.org/.

International Organization for Migration. *World Migration Report 2020*. https://www.un-ilibrary.org/migration/world-migration-report-2020_b1710e30-en.

ITUC. *Building Workers' Power: Congress statement*. Berlin, 2014. https://www.ituc-csi.org/IMG/pdf/ituc-3co-e-5-congressstatement-en-210x297-01-140819.pdf.

Itzigsohn, Jose. 'Migrant remittances, labor markets, and household strategies: A comparative analysis of low-income household strategies in the Caribbean Basin', *Social Forces* 74 (1995): 633–55.

Ivleva, Tatiana. 'Peasants into soldiers: Recruitment and military mobility in the early Roman Empire'. In *Migration and Mobility in the Early Roman Empire*, edited by Luuk de Ligt and Laurens E. Tacoma, 158–75. Leiden and Boston: Brill, 2016.

Jackson, Wes. 'Toward a unifying concept for an ecological agriculture'. In *Agricultural Ecosystems: Unifying concepts*, edited by Richard Lowrance, Benjamin R. Stinner and Garfield J. House, 209–21. New York: John Wiley & Sons, 1984.

Jacobs, Els M. *Merchant in Asia: The trade of the Dutch East India Company in the eighteenth century*. Leiden: CNWS Publications, 2006.

Jacoby, Sanford M. *Employing Bureaucracy: Managers, unions, and the transformation of work in American industry, 1900–1945*. New York: Columbia University Press, 1985.

Jafari, Peyman. 'Oil, labour and revolution in Iran: A social history of labour in the Iranian oil industry, 1973–1983' (PhD thesis, Leiden University, 2018).

Jaganathan, N. Vijay. *Informal Markets in Developing Countries*. New York and Oxford: Oxford University Press, 1987.

James, C. L. R. *Spheres of Existence*. London: Alison & Busby, 1980.

James, C. L. R. *The Black Jacobins: Toussaint L'Ouverture and the San Domingo Revolution*. New York: The Dial Press, 1938.

James, Harold. 'Finance capitalism'. In *Capitalism: The reemergence of a historical concept*, edited by Jürgen Kocka and Marcel van der Linden, 133–63. London: Bloomsbury, 2016.

James, Paul. 'Forms of abstract "community": From tribe and kingdom to nation and state', *Philosophy of the Social Sciences* 22 (1992): 313–36.

James, Selma. *Sex, Race and Class: The perspective of winning: A selection of writings, 1952–2011*. Oakland, CA: PM Press, 2012.

James, William R. 'Subsistence, survival and capitalist agriculture: Aspects of the mode of production among a Colombian proletariat', *Latin American Perspectives* 2 (1975): 84–95.

Janssens, Angélique. 'The rise and decline of the male breadwinner family? An overview of the debate', *International Review of Social History* 42 (1997) Supplement: 1–23.

Jas, Nathalie. *Au carrefour de la chimie et de l'agriculture: Les sciences agronomiques en France et en Allemagne, 1840–1914*. Paris: Ed. des Archives contemporaines, 2001.

Jasper, James M. 'The emotions of protest: Affective and reactive emotions in and around social movements', *Sociological Forum* 13 (1998): 397–424.

Jaumain, Serge. 'Contribution à l'histoire comparée: Les colporteurs belges et québécois au XIXe siècle', *Histoire sociale/Social History* 39 (1987): 49–77.

Javaanse contractarbeiders in Suriname 1890–1930. National Archives of the Netherlands. https://www.nationaalarchief.nl/onderzoeken/zoekhulpen/javaanse-contractarbeiders-in-suriname-1890-1930.

Jenkins, Virginia Scott. *Bananas: An American history*. London and Washington, DC: Smithsonian Institution Press, 2000.

Jensen, Jill. 'From Geneva to the Americas: International Labor Organization and inter-American social security standards, 1936–1948', *International Labor and Working-Class History* 80 (2011): 215–40.

Jessop, Bob. 'What follows Fordism? On the periodization of capitalism and its regulation'. In *Phases of Capitalist Development: Booms, crises and globalizations*, edited by Robert Albritton, 282–99. Basingstoke: Palgrave Macmillan, 2002.

Joffrin, Laurent. *Mai 68: Histoire des événements*. Paris: Seuil, 1998.

John, Michael. '"Kultur der Armut" in Wien 1890–1923: Zur Bedeutung von Solidarstrukturen, Nachbarschaft und Protest', *Zeitgeschichte* 20 (1993): 158–86.

Johnson, Paul. *Saving and Spending: The working-class economy in Britain 1870–1939*. Oxford: Clarendon Press, 1985.

Johnson, Walter (ed.). *The Chattel Principle: Internal slave trades in the Americas*. New Haven, CT: Yale University Press, 2004.

Johnston, G. A. 'The International Labor Office and industrial relations', *Annals of the American Academy of Political and Social Science* 166 (1933): 75–9.

Johnston, Geoffrey. *Of God and Maxim Guns: Presbyterianism in Nigeria, 1846–1966*. Waterloo, Ontario: Wilfrid Laurier University Press, 1988.

Jonasson, Olof. *Kaffet och kaffeländer*. Stockholm: Kooperativa Förbundets Press, 1932.

Jonasson, Olof. 'Natural conditions for coffee culture', *Economic Geography* 9 (1933): 356–67.

Jonasson, Olof. 'The potential areas of coffee-growing and their relation to the settlement of the white man', *Geografiska Annaler* 40 (1958): 89–100.

Jones, C. P. 'Stigma: Tattooing and branding in Graeco-Roman antiquity', *Journal of Roman Studies* 77 (1987): 139–55.

Jones, Gareth Stedman. *Outcast London: A Study in the relationship between classes in Victorian society*. Fourth edition. London: Verso, 2013.

Jones, Geoffrey. 'Multinationals from the 1930s to the 1980s'. In *Leviathans: Multinational corporations and the new global history*, edited by Alfred D. Chandler, Jr. and Bruce Mazlish, 81–103. Cambridge: Cambridge University Press, 2005.

Jones, Jacquelin. *The Dispossessed: America's underclasses from the Civil War to the present*. New York: Basic Books, 1992.

Jordheim, Helge. 'Against periodization: Koselleck's theory of multiple temporalities', *History and Theory* 51 (2012): 151–71.

Joseph, Suad. 'Working-class women's networks in a sectarian state: A political paradox', *American Ethnologist* 10 (1983): 1–22.

Joshi, Chitra. 'Dak roads, Dak runners, and the reordering of communication networks', *International Review of Social History* 57 (2012): 169–89.

Joyce, Patrick. *Work, Society and Politics: The culture of the factory in Victorian England*. Brighton: Harvester Press, 1980.

Juchler, Ingo. *Die Studentenbewegungen in den Vereinigten Staaten und der Bundesrepublik Deutschland in den sechziger Jahren: Eine Untersuchung hinsichtlich ihrer Beeinflussung durch Befreiungsbewegungen und -Theorien aus der Dritten Welt*. Berlin: Duncker & Humblot, 1996.

Jungman, Alex. 'Waarom stopte de WIC de slavenhandel op Suriname in 1738?', *OSO: Tijdschrift voor surinamistiek en het Caraïbisch gebied* 27 (2008): 252–65.

Kaiser, Michael. 'Ausreißer und Meuterer im Dreißigjährigen Krieg'. In *Armeen und ihre Deserteure: Vernachlässigte Kapitel einer Militärgeschichte der Neuzeit*, edited by Ulrich Bröckling and Michael Sikora, 49–71. Göttingen: Vandenhoeck & Ruprecht, 1998.

Kalecki, Michal. 'Political aspects of full employment', *Political Quarterly* 14 (1943): 322–30.

Kalleberg, Arne L. 'Precarious work, insecure workers: Employment relations in transition', *American Sociological Review* 74 (2009): 1–22.

Kamp, Jeannette and Matthias van Rossum (eds). *Desertion in the Early Modern World: A comparative history*. London: Bloomsbury Academic, 2016.

Kanappan, S. 'The impact of the I.L.O. in labour legislation and policy in India'. In *Labour Management and Economic Growth: Proceedings*, edited by Robert L. Aronson and John P. Windmuller, 175–90. New York: Institute of International Industrial and Labor Relations, 1954.

Kapil, R. N. and A. K. Bhatnagar. 'Portuguese contributions to Indian botany', *Isis* 67 (1976): 449–52.

Kaplan, Stephen. 'Environmental preference in a knowledge-seeking, knowledge-using organism'. In *The Adapted Mind: Evolutionary psychology and the generation of culture*, edited by Jerome H. Barkow, Leda Cosmides and John Tooby, 581–98. New York: Oxford University Press, 1992.

Kaplan, Steven. 'Les corporations, les "faux ouvriers" et le faubourg Saint-Antoine au XVIIIe siècle', *Annales: Histoire, Sciences Sociales* 43 (1988): 353–78.

Kapsos, Steven. *World and Regional Trends in Labour Force Participation: Methodologies and key results*. Geneva: International Labor Organization, 2007.

Karabarbounis, Loukas and Brent Neiman. 'The global decline of the labor share', *Quarterly Journal of Economics* 129 (2014): 61–103.

Kasmir, Sharryn and August Carbonella (eds). *Blood and Fire: Toward a global anthropology of labor*. New York and Oxford: Berghahn, 2014.

Katsiaficas, George. *The Imagination of the New Left: A global analysis of 1968*. Boston: South End Press, 1987.

Kaufman, Bruce. 'Reflections on six decades in industrial relations: An interview with John Dunlop', *Industrial and Labor Relations Review* 55 (2002): 324–48.

Kaur, Amarjit. *Wage Labour in Southeast Asia since 1840: Globalisation, the international division of labour and labour transformations*. Houndmills and New York: Palgrave Macmillan, 2004.

Keck, Margaret E. *The Workers' Party and Democratization in Brazil*. New Haven, CT: Yale University Press, 1992.

Keddie, Nikki R. *Modern Iran: Roots and results of revolution*. New Haven, CT: Yale University Press, 2003.

Keese, Alexander. 'Slow abolition within the colonial mind: British and French debates about "vagrancy", "African laziness", and forced labour in west central and south central Africa, 1945–1965', *International Review of Social History* 59 (2014): 377–407.

Keiser, Thorsten. 'Between status and contract? Coercion in contractual labour relationships in Germany from the 16th to the 20th century', *Rechtsgeschichte/Legal History* 21 (2013): 32–47.

Keiser, Thorsten. *Vertragszwang und Vertragsfreiheit im Recht der Arbeit von der Frühen Neuzeit bis in die Moderne*. Frankfurt am Main: Vittorio Klostermann, 2013.

Kelly, J. B. *Britain and the Persian Gulf 1795–1880*. Oxford: Clarendon Press, 1968.

Kessel, Ineke van. *Zwarte Hollanders: Afrikaanse soldaten in Nederlands-Indië*. Amsterdam: KIT Publishers, 2005.

Kessler, Gijs and Jan Lucassen. 'Labour relations, efficiency and the great divergence: Comparing pre-industrial brick-making across Eurasia, 1500–2000'. In *Technology, Skills and the*

Pre-Modern Economy in the East and the West, edited by Maarten Prak and Jan Luiten van Zanden, 259–322. Leiden and Boston: Brill, 2013.

Khaldûn, Ibn. *The Muqaddimah: An introduction to history*. Trans. Franz Rosenthal. Two volumes. London: Routledge & Kegan Paul, 1958.

Khanh, Huynh Kim. 'The Vietnamese August Revolution reinterpreted', *Journal of Asian Studies* 30 (1971): 761–82.

Khlevniuk, Oleg V. *The History of the Gulag: From collectivization to the Great Terror*. New Haven, CT and London: Yale University Press, 2004.

Kiernan, V. G. *Lords of Human Kind: European attitudes to the outside world in the Imperial Age*. Revised Edition. Harmondsworth: Penguin, 1972.

Kiernan, V. G. 'Notes on the intelligentsia', *Socialist Register 1969*, 55–84. https://socialistregister.com/index.php/srv/article/view/5280/2181.

King, Samuel T. 'Lenin's theory of imperialism today: The global divide between monopoly and non-monopoly capital' (PhD thesis, Victoria University, 2018).

Kirk, Neville. 'Transnational labor history: Promise and perils'. In *Workers across the Americas: The transnational turn in labor history*, edited by Leon Fink, 18–22. New York: Oxford University Press, 2011.

Kish, Matthew. 'The cost breakdown of a $100 pair of sneakers', *Portland Business Journal* (19 December 2014). https://www.bizjournals.com/portland/blog/threads_and_laces/2014/12/the-cost-breakdown-of-a-100-pair-of-sneakers.html.

Klein, Herbert S. 'The internal slave trade in nineteenth-century Brazil: A study of slave importations into Rio de Janeiro in 1852', *Hispanic American Historical Review* 51 (1971): 567–85.

Klein, Herbert S. *The Atlantic Slave Trade*. Cambridge: Cambridge University Press, 1999.

Klingberg, Frank J. *The Anti-Slavery Movement in England: A study in English humanitarianism*. New Haven, CT: Yale University Press, 1926.

Kloosterboer, Wilhelmina. *Involuntary Labor since the Abolition of Slavery: A survey of compulsory labor throughout the world*. Leiden: E. J. Brill, 1960.

Knight, Alan. 'Debt bondage in Latin America'. In *Slavery and Other Forms of Unfree Labour*, edited by Léonie Archer, 102–17. London: Routledge, 1988.

Knowles, Paulden F. 'New crop establishment', *Economic Botany* 14 (1960): 263–75.

Kocka, Jürgen. 'Problems of working-class formation in Germany: The early years, 1800–1875'. In *Working Class Formation: Nineteenth-century patterns in Western Europe and the United States*, edited by Ira Katznelson and Aristide R. Zolberg, 279–351. Princeton: Princeton University Press, 1986.

Kocka, Jürgen. *Capitalism: A short history*. Princeton: Princeton University Press, 2016.

Kocka, Jürgen and Marcel van der Linden (eds). *Capitalism: The reemergence of a historical concept*. London: Bloomsbury Academic, 2016.

Kofman, Eleonore and Parvati Raghuram. 'Gender and global labour migrations: Incorporating skilled workers', *Antipode* 38 (2006): 282–303.

Kolchin, Peter. *Unfree Labor: American slavery and Russian serfdom*. Cambridge, MA: The Belknap Press of Harvard University Press, 1987.

Komlosy, Andrea. *Work: The last 1,000 years*. Trans. Loren Balhorn and Jacob K. Watson. London and New York: Verso, 2017.

Komlosy, Andrea. 'Work and labour relations'. In *Capitalism: The reemergence of a historical concept*, edited by Jürgen Kocka and Marcel van der Linden, 33–69. London: Bloomsbury, 2016.

Komlosy, Andrea and Goran Musić (eds). *Commodity Chains and Labor Relations*. Leiden and Boston: Brill, 2021.

Kondratieff, Nikolai D. 'Die langen Wellen der Konjunktur', *Archiv für Sozialwissenschaft und Sozialpolitik* 56 (1926): 573–609. English translation in *The Works of Nikolai D: Kondratiev*. Four volumes. Edited by Natalia Makasheva, Warren J. Samuels and Vincent Barnett. Vol. I. London: Pickering & Chatto, 1998.

Korieh, Chima J. 'The nineteenth century commercial transition in West Africa: The case of the Biafra Hinterland', *Canadian Journal of African Studies* 34 (2000): 588–615.

Korovkin, Michael A. 'Exploitation, cooperation, collusion: An enquiry into patronage', *Archives Européennes de Sociologie* 29 (1988): 105–26.

Koselleck, Reinhart. 'Revolution: Rebellion, Aufruhr, Bürgerkrieg'. In *Geschichtliche Grundbegriffe: Historisches Lexikon zur politisch-sozialen Sprache in Deutschland*. Vol. 5, edited by Otto Brunner, Werner Conze and Reinhart Koselleck, 653–788. Stuttgart: Klett-Cotta, 1984.

Kott, Sandrine. 'Constructing a European social model: The fight for social insurance in the interwar period'. In Van Daele et al., *ILO Histories*, 173–95.
Kott, Sandrine. 'Fighting the war or preparing for peace? The ILO during the Second World War', *Journal of Modern European History* 12 (2014): 359–76.
Kott, Sandrine and Joëlle Droux (eds). *Globalizing Social Rights: The International Labour Organization and beyond*. New York: Palgrave Macmillan, 2013.
Kottak, Conrad Phillip. 'Culture and "economic development"', *American Anthropologist* 92 (1990): 723–31.
Kristal, Tali. 'Good times, bad times: Postwar labor's share of national income in capitalist democracies', *American Sociological Review* 75 (2010): 729–63.
Krohn, Wolfgang and Wolf Schäfer. 'Ursprung und Struktur der Agrikulturchemie'. In *Starnberger Studien 1: Die gesellschaftliche Orientierung des wissenschaftlichen Fortschritts*, edited by Gernot Böhme and Sigrid Meuschel 23–68. Frankfurt am Main: Suhrkamp, 1978.
Kroneberg, Lutz and Rolf Schloesser. *Weber-Revolte 1844: Der schlesische Weberaufstand im Spiegel der zeitgenössischen Publizistik und Literatur*. Cologne: C. W. Leske, 1979.
Krugman, Paul R. 'Growing world trade: Causes and consequences', *Brookings Papers on Economic Activity* 26 (1995): 327–77.
Kuczynski, Thomas. 'What is sold on the labour market?'. In *Beyond Marx: Confronting labour history and the concept of labour with the global labour relations of the 21st century*, edited by Marcel van der Linden and Karl Heinz Roth, 305–18. Leiden and Boston: Brill, 2013.
Kumar, Dharma K. *Land and Caste in South India: Agricultural labour in the Madras presidency during the nineteenth century*. Cambridge: Cambridge University Press, 1965.
Kurnitzky, Horst. *Der heilige Markt: Kulturhistorische Anmerkungen*. Frankfurt am Main: Suhrkamp, 1994.
Kuttner, Erich. *Het Hongerjaar 1566*. Amsterdam: Amsterdamsche Boek- en Courantmaatschappij, 1949.
Kuznets, Simon. *Seasonal Variations in Industry and Trade*. New York: National Bureau of Economic Research, 1933.
Laba, Roman. *The Roots of Solidarity: A political sociology of Poland's working class democratization*. Princeton: Princeton University Press, 1991.
Lachs, Manfred. 'Slavery: The past and the present'. In *Humanitarian Law of Armed Conflict: Challenges ahead: Essays in honour of Frits Kalshoven*, edited by Astrid J. M. Delissen and Gerard J. Tanja, 613–25. Dordrecht: Martinus Nijhoff Publishers, 1991.
Lagergren, Stina. 'The influence of ILO standards on Swedish law and practice', *International Labour Review* 125 (1986): 305–28.
Lal, Brij V. *Girmitiyas: The origins of the Fiji Indians*. Canberra: Journal of Pacific History Monograph, 1983.
Lal, Brij V. (ed.). *The Encyclopedia of the Indian Diaspora*. Singapore: Editions Didier Millet, 2006.
Lal, Brij V. 'The indenture system'. In *The Encyclopedia of the Indian Diaspora*, edited by Brij V. Lal, 48–53. Singapore: Editions Didier Millet, 2006.
Lammers, Cornelis J. 'Student unionism in the Netherlands: An application of a social class model', *American Sociological Review* 36 (1971): 250–63.
Landau, C. E. 'The influence of ILO standards on Australian labour law and practice', *International Labour Review* 126 (1987): 669–90.
Landy, E. A. 'The influence of international labour standards: Possibilities and performance', *International Labour Review* 101 (1970): 555–604.
Langille, Brian A. 'Core labour rights: The true story (reply to Alston)', *European Journal of International Law* 16 (2005): 409–37.
Lara, Silvia Hunold. 'Escradivão, cidadania e história do trabalho no Brasil', *Projeto História* 16 (1998): 25–38.
Larson, Barbara K. 'The rural marketing system of Egypt over the last three hundred years', *Comparative Studies in Society and History* 27 (1985): 494–530.
Lash, Scott and John Urry. *The End of Organized Capitalism*. Cambridge: Polity Press, 1987.
Laslett, Peter. 'The family as a knot of individual interests'. In *Households: Comparative and historical studies of the domestic group*, edited by R. M. Netting, R. R. Wilk and E. J. Arnould, 353–79. Berkeley: University of California Press, 1984.
Laube, Adolf. 'Der Aufstand der Schwazer Bergarbeiter 1525 und ihre Haltung im Tiroler Bauernkrieg: Mit einem Quellenanhang', *Jahrbuch für Geschichte des Feudalismus* 2 (1978): 225–58.

Laube, Adolf. 'Zum Problem des Bündnisses von Bergarbeitern und Bauern im deutschen Bauernkrieg'. In *Der Bauer im Klassenkampf: Studien zur Geschichte des deutschen Bauernkrieges und der bäuerlichen Klassenkämpfe im Spätfeudalismus*, edited by Gerhard Heitz, Adolf Laube, Max Steinmetz and Günter Vogler, 83–110. Berlin: Akademie-Verlag, 1975.

Laum, Bernhard. *Heiliges Geld*. Tübingen: J. C. B. Mohr (Paul Siebeck), 1924.

Law, Robin (ed.). *From Slavery to 'Legitimate' Commerce: The commercial transition in nineteenth century West Africa*. Cambridge: Cambridge University Press, 1995.

Law, Robin. 'The historiography of the commercial transition in nineteenth-century West Africa'. In *African Historiography: Essays in honour of Jacob Ade Ajayi*, edited by Toyin Falola, 91–115. London: Harlow, 1993.

Lebowitz, Michael A. *Following Marx: Method, critique and crisis*. Leiden and Boston: Brill, 2009.

Lee, M. R. 'Plants against malaria. Part 1: Cinchona or the Peruvian bark', *Journal of the Royal College of Physicians of Edinburgh* 32 (2002): 189–96.

Lefèvre, Wolfgang. *Zum historischen Charakter und zur historischen Funktion der Methode bürgerlicher Soziologie*. Frankfurt am Main: Suhrkamp, 1971.

Legrand, Daniel. *Appel respectueux d'un industriel de la vallée des Vosges, illustrée par le vénérable Oberlin, adressé aux gouvernements de la France, de l'Angleterre, de la Prusse, des autres états de l'Allemagne et de la Suisse; dans le but de provoquer des lois particulières et une loi internationale, destinées à protéger la classe ouvrière contre le travail précoce et excessif*. Strasbourg: Imprimerie de veuve Berger-Levrault, 1848.

Leimgruber, Mathieu. 'The embattled standard-bearer of social insurance and its challenger: The ILO, the OECD and the "crisis of the welfare state", 1975–1985'. In *Globalizing Social Rights: The International Labour Organization and beyond*, edited by Sandrine Kott and Joëlle Droux, 293–309. New York: Palgrave Macmillan, 2013.

Lekas, Padelis. *Marx on Classical Antiquity: Problems of historical methodology*. New York: Wheatsheaf Books, 1988.

Lemire, Beverly. *Global Trade and the Transformation of Consumer Cultures: The material world remade, c. 1500–1820*. Cambridge: Cambridge University Press, 2018.

Lengen, Hajo van (ed.). *Die 'Emder Revolution' von 1595*. Aurich: Ostfriesische Landschaft, 1995.

Lenin. 'The International Socialist Congress in Stuttgart', *Lenin Collected Works*. Vol. 13. Moscow: Progress, 1972: 75–81.

Leong, Priscilla. 'Understanding the seafarer global labour market in the context of a seafarer "shortage"' (PhD thesis, School of Social Sciences, Cardiff University 2012).

Lerner, Abba. 'Review of Fritz Sternberg, The Coming Crisis. New York: John Day, 1947', *Social Research* 15 (1948): 125–9.

Leupp, Gary P. *Servants, Shophands, and Laborers in the Cities of Tokugawa Japan*. Princeton: Princeton University Press, 1992.

Levasseur, Emile. *Histoire des classes ouvrières en France depuis la conquête de Jules César jusqu'à la Révolution*. Two volumes. Paris: Guillaumin, 1859.

Levy, Oscar (ed.). *Complete Works of Friedrich Nietzsche: The first complete and authorised translation*. Vol. 10. Trans. Thomas Common. New York: Macmillan, 1924.

Lewis, Mark E. *Sanctioned Violence in Early China*. Albany, NY: SUNY Press, 1990.

Lewis, Su Lin. 'Asian socialism and the forgotten architects of post-colonial freedom, 1952–1956', *Journal of World History* 30 (2019): 55–88.

Lewis, W. Arthur. 'The export stimulus'. In *Tropical Development, 1880–1913: Studies in economic progress*, edited by W. Arthur Lewis, 13–45. London: George Allen & Unwin, 1970.

Lewis, W. Arthur. *The Evolution of the International Economic Order*. Princeton: Princeton University Press, 1978.

Lichtenstein, Alex. *Twice the Work of Free Labor: The political economy of convict labor in the New South*. London and New York: Verso, 1996.

Lichtenstein, Alex and Christian De Vito. 'Writing a global history of convict labour', *International Review of Social History* 58 (2013): 285–325.

Lichtenstein, Nelson. 'The return of merchant capitalism', *International Labor and Working-Class History* 81 (2012): 8–27.

Lieten, Kristoffel and Elise van Nederveen Meerkerk (eds). *Child Labour's Global Past, 1650–2000*. Bern: Peter Lang, 2011.

Linebaugh, Peter. *The London Hanged: Crime and civil society in the eighteenth century*. Harmondsworth: Penguin, 1993.
Linebaugh, Peter and Marcus Rediker. *The Many-Headed Hydra: Sailors, slaves, commoners, and the hidden history of the revolutionary Atlantic*. Boston: Beacon Press, 2000.
Lionæs, Aase. Presentation speech, Nobel Peace Prize 1969. https://www.nobelprize.org/nobel_prizes/peace/laureates/1969/press.html.
Lipp, Carola. 'Frauenspezifische Partizipation an Hungerunruhen des 19. Jahrhunderts'. In *Der Kampf um das tägliche Brot: Nahrungsmangel, Versorgungspolitik und Protest 1770–1990*, edited by Manfred Gailus and Heinrich Volkmann, 200–13. Opladen: Westdeutscher Verlag, 1994.
Lobdell, Richard A. '"Repression is not a policy": Sydney Olivier on the West Indies and Africa'. In *West Indies Accounts: Essays on the history of the British Caribbean and the Atlantic Economy in honour of Richard Sheridan*, edited by Roderick A. McDonald, 343–54. Kingston: University of the West Indies Press, 1996.
Lohia, Ram Manohar. *The Third Camp in World Affairs*. Bombay: Praja Socialist Party, 1950.
Lonn, Ella. *Desertion during the Civil War*. New York: The Century Co., 1928.
Look Lai, Walton. *Indentured Labor, Caribbean Sugar: Chinese and Indian migrants to the British West Indies, 1838–1918*. Baltimore, MD: Johns Hopkins University Press, 1993.
Look Lai, Walton. *The Chinese in the West Indies 1806–1950: A documentary history*. Kingston: University of the West Indies Press, 1998.
López, Juan J. 'Theory choice in comparative social inquiry', *Polity* 25 (1992): 267–82.
Lora, Guillermo. *A History of the Bolivian Labour Movement, 1848–1971*. Edited and Abridged by Laurence Whitehead. Trans. Christine Whitehead. Cambridge: Cambridge University Press, 1977.
Lora, Guillermo. *Historia del movimiento obrero boliviano*. Four volumes. La Paz and Cochabamba: Editorial Los Amigos del Libro, 1967–80.
Lorwin, Lewis L. *Labor and Internationalism*. New York: Macmillan, 1929.
Lotherington, Ann Thérèse and Anne Britt Flemman. 'Negotiating gender: The case of the International Labour Organization'. In *Gender and Change in Developing Countries*, edited by Kristi Anne Stolen and Mariken Vaa, 273–307. Oslo: Norwegian University Press, 1991.
Lourens, Piet and Jan Lucassen. *Arbeitswanderung und berufliche Spezialisierung: Die lippischen Ziegler im 18. und 19. Jahrhundert*. Osnabrück: Universitätsverlag Rasch, 1999.
Lovejoy, Paul E. 'Slavery in the Sokoto Caliphate'. In *The Ideology of Slavery in Africa*, edited by Paul E. Lovejoy, 11–38. Beverly Hills, CA: Sage, 1981.
Lovejoy, Paul E. 'The characteristics of plantations in the nineteenth-century Sokoto Caliphate (Islamic West Africa)', *American Historical Review* 84 (1979): 1267–92.
Lovejoy, Paul E. 'Plantations in the economy of the Sokoto Caliphate', *Journal of African History* 19 (1978): 341–68.
Lovejoy, Paul E. *Transformations in Slavery: A history of slavery in Africa*. Second edition. Cambridge: Cambridge University Press, 2000.
Lovejoy, Paul E. and Jan S. Hogendorn. *Slow Death of Slavery: The course of abolition in Northern Nigeria, 1897–1936*, Cambridge: Cambridge University Press, 1993.
Lowenthal, David and Colin G. Clarke. 'Slave-breeding in Barbuda: The past of a Negro myth', *Annals of the New York Academy of Sciences* 292 (1977): 510–35.
Löwenthal, Richard. 'The "missing revolution" in industrial societies: Comparative reflections on a German problem'. In *Germany in the Age of Total War*, edited by Volker R. Berghahn and Martin Kitchen, 240–60. London: Croom Helm, 1981.
Lubin, Carol Riegelman and Anne Winslow. *Social Justice for Women: The International Labor Organization and women*. Durham, NC: Duke University Press, 1990.
Lucassen, Jan (ed.). *Global Labour History: A state of the art*. Bern: Peter Lang, 2008.
Lucassen, Jan. 'A multinational and its labor force: The Dutch East India Company, 1595–1795', *International Labor and Working-Class History* 66 (2004): 12–39.
Lucassen, Jan. 'Wage labour'. In *Handbook Global History of Work*, edited by Karin Hofmeester and Marcel van der Linden, 395–409. Berlin: Walter de Gruyter, 2018.
Lucassen, Jan. *The Story of Work: A new history of humankind*. New Haven, CT: Yale University Press, 2021.
Lucassen, Jan and Leo Lucassen (eds). *Globalising Migration History: The Eurasian experience*. Leiden and Boston: Brill, 2014.
Lucassen, Jan and Leo Lucassen. 'The mobility transition revisited, 1500–1900: What the case of Europe can offer to global history', *Journal of Global History* 4 (2009): 347–77.

Lucassen, Jan, Leo Lucassen and Patrick Manning (eds). *Migration History in World History: Multidisciplinary approaches*. Leiden and Boston: Brill, 2010.
Luxemburg, Rosa. 'Frauenwahlrecht und Klassenkampf'. In *Frauenwahlrecht*, edited by Clara Zetkin, 8–10. Stuttgart: Clare Zetkin, 1912.
Lynn, Martin. *Commerce and Economic Change in West Africa: The palm oil trade in the nineteenth century*. Cambridge: Cambridge University Press, 1997.
MacEwan, Arthur. 'Interdependence and instability: Do the levels of output in the advanced capitalist countries increasingly move up and down together?', *Review of Radical Political Economy* 16 (1984): 57–79.
MacEwan, Arthur. 'What's "new" about the "new international economy"?', *Socialist Review* 21 (1991): 111–31.
Macintyre, Stuart. *A Concise History of Australia*. Third Edition. Cambridge: Cambridge University Press, 2009.
MacLennan, Carol A. 'Foundations of sugar's power: Early Maui plantations, 1840–1860', *Hawaiian Journal of History* 29 (1995): 33–56.
MacLeod, William Christie. 'Some aspects of primitive chattel slavery', *Social Forces* 4 (1925): 137–41.
Maddison, Angus. *Monitoring the World Economy 1820–1992*. Paris: OECD Development Centre, 1995.
Magdoff, Harry. *The Age of Imperialism: The economics of U.S. foreign policy*. New York: Monthly Review Press, 1969.
Magliari, Michael. 'Free soil, unfree labor: Cave Johnson Couts and the binding of Indian workers in California, 1850–1867', *Pacific Historical Review* 73 (2004): 349–89.
Maier-Rigaud, Remi. *Global Pension Policies: Programs, frames and paradigms of the World Bank and the International Labour Organization*. Berlin: Duncker & Humblot, 2009.
Maine, Henry. *Ancient Law*. London: John Murray, 1861.
Mancini, Matthew J. *One Dies, Get Another: Convict leasing in the American South, 1866–1928*. Columbia: University of South Carolina Press, 1996.
Mandel, Ernest. 'Introduction'. In *Fifty Years of World Revolution 1917–1967: An international symposium*, edited by Ernest Mandel, 11–34. New York: Merit Publishers, 1968.
Mandle, Jay R. *Patterns of Caribbean Development: An interpretative essay on economic change*. New York: Gordon & Breach, 1982.
Manning, Brian. 'Introduction to the Second Edition'. In Brian Manning, *The English People and the English Revolution*, 7–47. Second edition. London: Bookmarks, 1991.
Mark-Lawson, Jane and Anne Witz. 'From "family labour" to "family wage"? The case of women's labour in nineteenth-century coalmining', *Social History* 13 (1988): 151–74.
Marks, Shula. 'Southern Africa, 1867–1886'. In *The Cambridge History of Africa*. Vol. 6: *From 1870 to 1905*, edited by Roland Olivier and G. N. Anderson, 359–421. Cambridge: Cambridge University Press, 1985.
Marques, Leonardo. 'Digital history of the Transatlantic slave trade: An interview with David Eltis', *Tempo* 25 (2019): 520–7.
Mars, Gerald. 'Dock pilferage: A case study in occupational theft'. In *Deviance and Social Control*, edited by Paul Rock and Mary McIntosh, 209–28. London: Routledge, 1974.
Marshall, William. *The Rural Economy of the Midland Counties, Including the Management of Livestock in Leicestershire and Its Environs: Together with minutes on agriculture and planting in the district of the Midland station*. Second Edition. Vol. II. London: G. Nicol, 1796.
Marshall, Woodville K. 'Metayage in the sugar industry of the British Windward Islands, 1838–65', *Jamaican Historical Review* 5 (1965): 28–55.
Marshall, Woodville K. '"We be wise to many more things": Black hopes and expectations of emancipation'. In *Caribbean Freedom: Economy and society from emancipation to the present: A student reader*, edited by Hilary McD. Beckles and Verene Shepherd, 12–20. Kingston: Ian Randle, 1993.
Martin, Cheryl English. *Governance and Society in Colonial Mexico: Chihuahua in the eighteenth century*. Stanford, CA: Stanford University Press, 1996.
Martin, John. *An Account of the Natives of the Tonga Islands, in the South Pacific Ocean: With an original grammar and vocabulary of their language, compiled and arranged from the extensive communications of Mr. William Mariner*. Two volumes. London: John Murray, 1817.
Martin, Nathan D. and David Brady. 'Workers of the less developed world unite? A multi-level analysis of unionization in less developed countries', *American Sociological Review* 72 (2007): 562–84.

Martin, Thomas P. 'Some international aspects of the anti-slavery movement, 1818–1823', *Journal of Economic and Business History* 1 (1928–9): 137–48.
Martinelli, Alberto. 'From world system to world society?', *Journal of World-Systems Research* 11 (2005): 241–60.
Martinez, Julia. 'When wages were clothes: Dressing down Aboriginal workers in Australia's Northern Territory', *International Review of Social History* 52 (2007): 271–86.
Martinez, Julia T. and Adrian H. Vickers. *The Pearl Frontier: Indonesian labor and indigenous encounters in Australia's Northern Trading Network*. Honolulu: University of Hawaii Press, 2015.
Martínez, Julia, Claire Lowrie, Frances Steel and Victoria Haskins. *Colonialism and Male Domestic Service across the Asia Pacific*. London: Bloomsbury Academic, 2019.
Maruani, Margaret and Anne Borzeix. *Le temps des chemises: La grève qu'elles gardent au cœur*. Paris: Syros, 1982.
Marx, Karl. 'Contribution to the critique of Hegel's philosophy of law [1843–1844]', *MECW*, Vol. 3, 3–129. London: Lawrence and Wishart, 1975.
Marx, Karl. *Capital*. Vol. I. Trans. Ben Fowkes. Harmondsworth: Penguin, 1976.
Marx, Karl. *Capital*. Vol. III. Trans. David Fernbach. Harmondsworth: Penguin, 1981.
Marx, Karl. *Grundrisse. Foundations of the critique of political economy (rough draft)*. Trans. Martin Nicolaus. Harmondsworth: Penguin, 1973.
Marx, Karl and Friedrich Engels. 'Manifesto of the Communist Party' (1848). In Karl Marx, *The Revolutions of 1848*, edited, with introduction, by David Fernbach, 67–98. Harmondsworth: Penguin, 1973.
Marx, Karl and Friedrich Engels. 'The German ideology', *MECW*, Vol. 5, 88. London: Lawrence and Wishart, 1975.
Mason, Matthew. 'Keeping up appearances: The international politics of slave trade abolition in the nineteenth-century Atlantic world', *The William and Mary Quarterly*, Third Series, 66 (2009): 809–32.
Mason, Michael. 'Working on the railway: Forced labor in Northern Nigeria, 1907–1912'. In *African Labor History*, edited by Peter C. W. Gutkind, Robin Cohen and Jean Copans, 56–79. London and Beverly Hills, CA: Sage, 1978.
Mathias, Regine. 'Japan in the seventeenth century: Labour relations and work ethics'. In *The Joy and Pain of Work: Global Attitudes and Valuations, 1500–1650*, edited by Karin Hofmeester and Christine Moll-Murata, 217–43. Cambridge: Cambridge University Press, 2011.
Mattos, Marcelo Badaró. *Escravizados e livres: Experiências comuns na formação da classe trabalhadora carioca*. Rio de Janeiro: Bom Texto, 2008. English translation: *Laborers and Enslaved Workers: Experiences in common in the making of Rio de Janeiro's working class, 1850–1920*. New York and Oxford: Berghahn, 1917.
Mattos, Marcelo Badaró, Filipa Ribeiro da Silva, Paulo Matos, Raquel Varela and Sónia Ferreira (eds). *Relações laborais em Portugal e no mundo lusófono: História e demografía*. Lisbon: Edições Colibri, 2014.
Mattos, Marcelo Badaró, Paulo Terra and Raquel Varela (eds). *Historia das relações de trabalho: Brasil e Portugal em perspectiva global*. Rio de Janeiro: Consequência Editora, 2017.
Maul, Daniel. *Human Rights, Development and Decolonization: The International Labour Organization, 1940–1970*. New York: Palgrave Macmillan, 2011.
Maul, Daniel. *The International Labour Organization: 100 years of global social policy*. Berlin: De Gruyter Oldenbourg, 2020.
Maume, David J. and R. Gregory Dunaway. 'Determinants of the prevalence of mother-only families', *Research in Social Stratification and Mobility* 8 (1989): 313–27.
Maupain, Francis. 'Revitalization not retreat: The real potential of the 1998 ILO Declaration for the Universal Protection of Workers' Rights', *European Journal of International Law* 16 (2005): 439–65.
May, Herbert G. and Bruce M. Metzger (eds). *The New Oxford Annotated Bible with Apocrypha*. New York: Oxford University Press, 1977.
Mayer-Mali, Theo. *Locatio conductio: Eine Untersuchung zum klassischen römischen Recht*. Vienna and Munich: Herold, 1956.
Maynard, Douglas H. 'The world's Anti-Slavery Convention of 1840', *The Mississippi Valley Historical Review* 47 (1960): 452–71.
Mbodj, Mohammed. 'The abolition of slavery in Senegal, 1820–1890: Crisis or the rise of a new entrepreneurial class?'. In *Breaking the Chains: Slavery, bondage, and emancipation in*

*modern Africa and Asia*, edited by Martin A. Klein, 197–213. Madison: University of Wisconsin Press, 1993.
McCulloch, John Ramsay. *The Principles of Political Economy: With a sketch of the rise and progress of the science*. Edinburgh: William and Charles Tait, 1825.
McConnell, Campbell R., Stanley L. Brue and David A. Macpherson. *Contemporary Labor Economics*. Eleventh Edition. New York: McGraw-Hill, 2017.
McGuire, Randall H., Joan Smith and William G. Martin. 'Patterns of household structures and the world-economy', *Review* [Fernand Braudel Center] 10 (1986): 75–97.
McKeown, Adam. 'Global migration, 1846–1940', *Journal of World History* 15 (2004): 155–89.
McKeown, Adam. *Melancholy Order: Asian migration and the globalization of borders*. New York: Columbia University Press, 2008.
McKeown, Adam. 'World migration in the age of industrial globalization, 1840–1940'. In *The Global History of Work: Critical readings*. Vol. III: *Labor markets*, edited by Marcel van der Linden, 3–16. London: Bloomsbury Academic, 2019.
McKillen, Elizabeth. 'Beyond Gompers: The American Federation of Labor, the creation of the ILO, and U.S. labor dissent'. In Van Daele et al., *ILO Histories*, 41–66.
McKillen, Elizabeth. 'Integrating labor into the narrative of Wilsonian internationalism: A literature review', *Diplomatic History* 34 (2010): 643–62.
McKinlay, Alan. 'From industrial serf to wage-labourer: The 1937 apprentice revolt in Britain', *International Review of Social History* 31 (1986): 1–18.
McQuarrie, Michael. 'The revolt of the rust belt: Place and politics in the age of anger', *British Journal of Sociology* 68 (2017, Supplement 1): S120–S152.
*MECW*: Karl Marx and Frederick Engels, *Collected Writings*. 49 volumes. Moscow: Progress, 1974–2001.
Meillassoux, Claude. *Maidens, Meal and Money: Capitalism and the domestic community*. Cambridge: Cambridge University Press, 1981.
Melossi, Dario and Massimo Pavarini. *The Prison and the Factory: Origins of the penitentiary system*. Trans. Glynis Cousin. London and Basingstoke: Macmillan, 1981.
Mendelsohn, I. 'Free artisans and slaves in Mesopotamia', *Bulletin of the American Schools of Oriental Research* 89 (1943): 25–9.
Menon, Vadakke K. R. 'The influence of international labour conventions on Indian labour legislation', *International Labour Review* 73 (1956): 551–71.
Mérei, Gyula. 'Le mouvement ouvrier en Hongrie pendant la révolution de 1848', *Le Mouvement Social* 50 (1965): 71–80.
Meriggi, Maria Grazia. *L'invenzione della classe operaia: Conflitti di lavoro, organizzazione del lavoro e della società in Francia intorno al 1848*. Milan: FrancoAngeli, 2002.
Merleau-Ponty, Maurice. *Signes*. Paris: Gallimard, 1960.
Merleau-Ponty, Maurice. *Phenomenology of Perception*. Trans. Colin Smith. London and New York: Routledge, 2004.
Merrill, Michael. 'Even conservative unions have revolutionary effects: Frank Tannenbaum on the labor movement', *International Labor and Working-Class History* 77 (2010): 115–33.
Mesa-Lago, Carmelo. *Ascent to Bankruptcy: Financing social security in Latin America*. Pittsburgh, PA: University of Pittsburgh Press, 1989.
Mészáros, István. *Beyond Capital: Towards a theory of transition*. London: Merlin Press, 1995.
Metcalf, Thomas R. *Imperial Connections: India in the Indian Ocean arena, 1860–1920*. Berkeley: University of California Press, 2007.
Meyer, John W., Francisco O. Ramirez, Richard Rubinson and John Boli-Bennett. 'The world educational revolution, 1950–1970', *Sociology of Education* 50 (1977): 242–58.
Meyer, John W., Francisco O. Ramirez and Yasemin Nuhoglu Soysal. 'World expansion of mass education, 1870–1980', *Sociology of Education* 65 (1992): 128–49.
Middleton, Chris. 'The familiar fate of the *famulae*: Gender divisions in the history of wage labour'. In *On Work: Historical, comparative and theoretical approaches*, edited by R. E. Pahl, 21–47. Oxford: Blackwell, 1988.
Middleton, Christopher. 'The sexual division of labour in feudal England', *New Left Review* First Series, 113–14 (1979): 147–68.
Miers, Suzanne. *Britain and the Ending of the Slave Trade*. London: Longman, 1975.
Miers, Suzanne. *Slavery in the Twentieth Century: The evolution of a global problem*. New York: AltaMira Press, 2003.

Migration Data Portal. https://www.migrationdataportal.org/.
Miliband, Ralph. 'Barnave: A case of bourgeois class consciousness'. In *Aspects of History and Class Consciousness*, edited by István Mészáros, 22–48. London: Routledge and Kegan Paul, 1971.
Millar, John. 'The advancement of manufacture, commerce, and the arts, since the reign of William III and the tendency of this advancement to diffuse a spirit of liberty and independence', [c. 1800]. In *John Millar of Glasgow, 1735–1801*, edited by William C. Lehmann, 326–39. Cambridge: Cambridge University Press, 1960.
Miller, Joseph C. *Way of Death: Merchant capitalism and the Angolan slave trade, 1730–1830*. London: James Currey, 1988.
Miller, William L. 'A note on the significance of the interstate slave trade of the ante bellum south', *Journal of Political Economy* 73 (1965): 181–7.
Mills, C. Wright. *The Sociological Imagination*. New York: Oxford University Press, 1959.
Mintz, Sidney W. *Sweetness and Power: The place of sugar in modern history*. New York: Viking, 1985.
Mintz, Sidney W. and Eric R. Wolf. 'An analysis of ritual co-parenthood (compadrazgo)', *Southwestern Journal of Anthropology* 6 (1950): 341–68.
Mironov, Boris. 'Cannon fodder for the revolution: The Russian proletariat in 1917', *Kritika: Explorations in Russian and Eurasian History* 18 (2017): 351–70.
Mitchell, Robert D. 'American origins and regional institutions: The seventeenth-century Chesapeake', *Annals of the Association of American Geographers* 73 (1983): 404–20.
Mitterauer, Michael. *Familie und Arbeitsteilung: Historischvergleichende Studien*. Vienna: Böhlau Verlag, 1992.
Moch, Leslie Page and Rachel G. Fuchs. 'Getting along: Poor women's networks in nineteenth-century Paris', *French Historical Studies* 18 (1993): 34–49.
Modell, John and Tamara Hareven. 'Urbanization and the malleable household: An examination of boarding and lodging in American families', *Journal of Marriage and the Family* 35 (1973): 467–79.
Moes, John E. 'The absorption of capital in slave labor in the ante-bellum south and economic growth', *American Journal of Economics and Sociology* 20 (1961): 535–41.
Moissonnier, Maurice. *La révolte des canuts, Lyon, novembre 1831*. Paris: Ed. Sociales Messidor, 1958.
Moll-Murata, Christine. 'Work ethics and work valuations in a period of commercialization: Ming China, 1500–1644'. In *The Joy and Pain of Work: Global attitudes and valuations, 1500–1650*, edited by Karin Hofmeester and Christine Moll-Murata, 165–95. Cambridge: Cambridge University Press, 2011.
Moore Jr., Barrington. *Injustice: The social bases of obedience and revolt*. White Plains, NY: M. E. Sharpe, 1978.
Moore, Clement H. and Arlie R. Hochschild. 'Student unions in North African politics', *Daedalus: Journal of the American Academy of Arts and Sciences* 97 (1968): 21–50.
Moore-Harell, Alice. 'Economic and political aspects of the slave trade in Ethiopia and the Sudan in the second half of the nineteenth century', *International Journal of African Historical Studies* 32 (1999): 407–21.
Moore-Harell, Alice. 'Slave trade in the Sudan in the nineteenth century and its suppression in the years 1877–80', *Middle Eastern Studies* 34 (1998): 113–28.
Moorhouse, H. F. 'The political incorporation of the British working class: An interpretation', *Sociology* 7 (1973): 341–59.
Morder, Robi (ed.). *Naissance d'un syndicalisme étudiant: 1946 – La Charte de Grenoble*. Paris: Edition Syllepse, 2006.
Morgan, Philip D. 'Task and gang systems: The organization of labor on New World plantations'. In *Work and Labor in Early America*, edited by Stephen Innes, 189–220. Chapel Hill: University of North Carolina Press, 1988.
Morris, John. 'Slaves and serfs', *Modern Quarterly* 3 (1948): 42–62.
Morris, R. J. 'Clubs, societies, and associations'. In *The Cambridge Social History of Britain, 1750–1950*. Vol. 3, edited by F. M. L. Thompson, 395–443. Cambridge: Cambridge University Press, 1990.
Morse, David A. 'The International Labor Organization in a changing world', *Annals of the American Academy of Political and Social Science* 310 (1957): 31–8.

Morse, David A. Acceptance speech by David A. Morse, Director-General, on the occasion of the award of the Nobel Peace Prize, Oslo, 10 December 1969. https://www.nobelprize.org/nobel_prizes/peace/laureates/1969/labour-acceptance.html.

Mosimann, Nadja, Line Rennwald and Adrian Zimmermann. 'The radical Right, the Labour movement and the competition for the workers' vote', *Economic and Industrial Democracy* 40 (2019): 65–90.

Moulier Boutang, Yann. *De l'esclavage au salariat: Économie historique du salariat bridé*. Paris: PUF, 1998.

Mueller, Shirley M. 'Plaques portraying late porcelain production in Jingdezhen', *Collections* 18 (2022): 343–61. Plaque 9.

Mukhtyar, Gatoolal C. *Life and Labour in a South Gujarat Village*. Calcutta: Longmans, Green and Co., 1930.

Muldrew, Craig. 'Atlantic world 1760–1820: Economic impact'. In *The Oxford Handbook of the Atlantic World c. 1450–c. 1850*, edited by Nicholas Canny and Philip Morgan, 618–33. Oxford: Oxford University Press, 2011.

Munck, Ronaldo. *Rethinking Global Labour after Neoliberalism*. Newcastle upon Tyne: Agenda Publishing, 2018.

Munslow, Barry and Henry Finch (eds). *Proletarianisation in the Third World*. London: Croom Helm, 1984.

Murray, James A. H. (ed.). *A New English Dictionary on Historical Principles; Founded Mainly on the Materials Collected by The Philological Society*. Volume III. Oxford: Clarendon Press, 1897.

Murray, Martin J. '"White gold" or "white blood"? The rubber plantations of colonial Indochina, 1910–40', *Journal of Peasant Studies* 19 (1992): 41–67.

Mysyk, Avis. 'Land, labor, and indigenous response: Huaquechula (Mexico), 1521–1633', *Colonial Latin American Review* 24 (2015): 336–55.

Nagata, Mary Louise. *Labour Contracts and Labour Relations in Early Modern Central Japan*. London: RoutledgeCurzon, 2005.

Najemy, John M. *A History of Florence 1200–1575*. Oxford: Blackwell, 2008.

Nash, Gary B. *The Urban Crucible: Social change, political consciousness, and the origins of the American Revolution*. Cambridge, MA: Harvard University Press, 1979.

Necker, Jacques. *De l'importance des opinions religieuses*. London: n.p., 1788.

Nelson, Bernard H. 'The slave trade as a factor in British foreign policy, 1815–1862', *Journal of Negro History* 27 (1942): 192–209.

Nevinson, Henry W. 'The slave-trade of to-day (III)', *Harper's Monthly Magazine* 111/665 (1905): 668–76.

Newland, Kathleen. 'Workers of the world, now what?', *Foreign Policy* 114 (1999): 52–65.

Nichtweiss, Johannes. *Das Bauernlegen in Mecklenburg: Eine Untersuchung zur Geschichte der Bauernschaft und der zweiten Leibeigenschaft in Mecklenburg bis zum Beginn des 19. Jahrhunderts*. Berlin: Rütten und Loening, 1954.

Nietzsche, Friedrich. *On the Genealogy of Morals* [1887]. Trans. Walter Kaufmann and R. J. Hollingdale. In Friedrich Nietzsche, *On the Genealogy of Morals* and *Ecce Homo*, edited by Walter Kaufman. New York: Vintage Books, 1989.

NN (no name). 'Cinchona cultivation in India: Its past, present and future', *Journal of the Asiatic Society* 3 (1962): 63–80.

NN. 'Constitution of the Red International of Labor Unions, as of 2nd World Congress, November 1922', *Labor Herald Library* 6. Chicago: Trade Union Educational League, 1923.

NN. 'Diario dello Squittinatore'. In Giuseppe Odoardo Corazzini, *I ciompi – cronache e documenti: Con notizie intorno alla vita di Michele di Lando*, 19–92. Florence: G. C. Sansoni, 1887.

NN. 'ILO: Resolution on the Widespread Use of Forced Labour in Myanmar', *International Legal Materials* 38 (1999): 1215–16.

NN. 'International Labor Organization'. In *Hearings before the Subcommittee on International Organizations and Movements of the Committee on Foreign Affairs, House of Representatives*, 84th Congress, Second Session, 61–122. Washington, DC: United States Government Printing Office, 1956.

NN. 'International labor in crisis', *Foreign Affairs* 49 (1971): 519–32.

NN. 'Manufacture of quinine in India', *Bulletin of Miscellaneous Information: Royal Gardens, Kew*, 1888, No. 18, 139–44.

NN. 'On the management of slaves', *Southern Agriculturalist* 6 (1833): 281–7.

NN. 'Quinine synthesized', *The Science News-Letter* 45, 20 (13 May 1944): 307.

NN. 'Slave trade, the American', *Dictionary of American History*, Second Edition, Vol. V, 91–3. New York: Charles Scribner's Sons, 1946.
NN. 'Social Security and I.L.O. technical cooperation in Libya', *International Labour Review* 91 (1965): 292–320.
NN. 'Stations (proef-)'. In *Encyclopaedie van Nederlandsch-Indië* (second printing), Vol. 4, edited by D. G. Stibbe, 94–103. The Hague: Martinus Nijhoff and Leiden: Brill, 1921.
Nöldeke, Theodor. 'A servile war in the East'. In *Sketches from Eastern History*, trans. John Sutherland Black, edited by Theodor Nöldeke, 146–75. London and Edinburgh: Adam and Charles Black, 1892.
Nooruddin, Irfan and James Vreeland. 'The effect of IMF programs on public wages and salaries'. In *Global Governance, Poverty, and Inequality*, edited by Rorden Wilkinson and Jennifer Clapp, 90–111. London: Routledge, 2010.
NORMLEX. https://www.ilo.org/dyn/normlex/en/f?p=NORMLEXPUB.
North, Douglass C. 'Markets and other allocative systems in history: The challenge of Karl Polanyi', *Journal of European Economic History* 6 (1977): 703–16.
Northrup, David. *Indentured Labor in the Age of Imperialism, 1834–1922*. Cambridge: Cambridge University Press, 1995.
Northrup, Herbert R. and Richard L. Rowan. 'Multinational bargaining approaches in the Western European glass industry', *Industrial and Labor Relations Review* 30 (1976): 32–46.
Nosow, Sigmund. 'Toward a theory of the labor market', *Social Forces* 33 (1955): 218–24.
Nowak, Jörg. *Mass Strikes and Social Movements in Brazil and India: Popular mobilisation in the long depression*. Cham: Palgrave Macmillan, 2019.
Noyes, P. H. *Organization and Revolution: Working-class associations in the German revolutions 1848–1849*. Princeton: Princeton University Press, 1966.
Nun, José. 'Sobrepopulación relativa, ejercito industrial de reserva y masa marginal', *Revista Latino-Americano de Sociología* 5 (1969): 178–236.
Nun, José. 'The end of work and the "marginal mass" thesis', *Latin American Perspectives* 27 (2000): 6–32.
Nunn, Nathan. 'The long-term effects of Africa's slave trades', *Quarterly Journal of Economics* 123 (2008): 139–76.
O'Brien, Patrick Karl. 'Industrialization'. In *The Oxford Handbook of World History*, edited by Jerry H. Bentley, 304–24. Oxford: Oxford University Press, 2011.
OECD. *International Trade and Core Labour Standards*. Paris: OECD, 2000.
Oesch, Daniel. 'Explaining workers' support for right-wing populist parties in Western Europe: Evidence from Austria, Belgium, France, Norway, and Switzerland', *International Political Science Review* 29 (2008): 349–73.
Offe, Claus and Helmut Wiesenthal. 'Two logics of collective action', *Political Power and Social Theory* 1 (1980): 67–115; reprinted in Offe, *Disorganized Capitalism: Contemporary transformations of work and politics*. Cambridge: Polity Press, 1985: 170–220, 334–40.
Ojo, Olatunji. 'Slavery and human sacrifice in Yorubaland: Ondo, c. 1870–94', *Journal of African History* 46 (2005): 379–404.
Okeke, Philomena E. 'Female wage earners and separate resource structures in post oil boom Nigeria', *Dialectical Anthropology* 22 (1997): 373–87.
Olmstedt, Frederick Law. *The Cotton Kingdom: A traveller's observations on cotton and slavery in the American slave states 1853–1861* (1861). Edited with an Introduction by Arthur M. Schlesinger. New York: Knopf, 1953.
Omer-Cooper, J. D. 'Colonial South Africa and its frontiers'. In *The Cambridge History of Africa*. Vol. 5: *From c. 1750 to c. 1870*, edited by John E. Flint, 353–92. Cambridge: Cambridge University Press, 1976.
Oostindie, Gert (ed.). *Fifty Years Later: Anti-slavery, capitalism and modernity in the Dutch orbit*. Leiden: KITLV Press, 1995.
Oppenheimer, Franz. *Die soziale Frage und der Sozialismus: Eine kritische Auseinandersetzung mit der marxistischen Theorie*. Jena: G. Fischer, 1912.
Orenstein, Mitchell A. 'Pension privatization: The transnational campaign'. In *Globalizing Social Rights: The International Labour Organization and beyond*, edited by Sandrine Kott and Joëlle Droux, 280–92. New York: Palgrave Macmillan, 2013.
Ortiz, Isabel, Sara Burke, Mohamed Berrada and Hernán Cortés. *World Protests 2006–2013*. New York: Initiative for Dialogue Policy and Friedrich-Ebert-Stiftung, 2013.

Ortmayr, Norbert. 'Kulturpflanzen: Transfers und Ausbreitungsprozesse im 18. Jahrhundert'. In *Vom Weltgeist beseelt: Globalgeschichte 1700–1815*, edited by Margarete Grandner and Andrea Komlosy, 73–99. Vienna: Promedia, 2004.

Ortoleva, Peppino. *I movimenti del '68 in Europa e in America*. Rome: Riuniti, 1998.

Osawa, Mari. 'The vicious cycle of the "male breadwinner" model of livelihood security', *Voices from Japan* 16 (2006): 1–5.

Oshinsky, David M. *Worse Than Slavery: Parchman Farm and the ordeal of Jim Crow Justice*. New York: Free Press, 1996.

Osterhammel, Jürgen. *Colonialism: A theoretical overview*. Trans. Shelley L. Frisch. Princeton: Markus Wiener, 1997.

Ostrower, Gary B. 'The American decision to join the International Labor Organization', *Labor History* 16 (1975): 495–504.

Oxaal, Ivar. *Black Intellectuals Come to Power: The rise of Creole nationalism in Trinidad and Tobago*. Cambridge, MA: Schenkman Publishing Company, 1968.

Özden, Çağlar, Christopher R. Parsons, Maurice Schiff and Terrie L. Walmsley. 'Where on earth is everybody? The evolution of global bilateral migration 1960–2000', *The World Bank Economic Review* 25 (2011): 12–56.

Palmer, David. 'Foreign forced labor at Mitsubishi's Nagasaki and Hiroshima shipyards: Big business, militarized government, and the absence of shipbuilding workers' rights in World War II Japan'. In *On Coerced Labor: Work and compulsion after chattel slavery*, edited by Marcel van der Linden and Magaly Rodríguez García, 159–84. Leiden: Brill, 2016.

Palmer, Jesse T. 'The banana in Caribbean trade', *Economic Geography* 8 (1932): 262–73.

Pamuk, Şevket. 'Changes in factor markets in the Ottoman Empire, 1500–1800', *Continuity and Change* 24 (2009): 107–36.

Pan, Lynn (ed.). *The Encyclopedia of the Chinese Overseas*. Richmond, Surrey: Curzon, 1999.

Pan, Lynn. 'Patterns of migration'. In *The Encyclopedia of the Chinese Overseas*, edited by Lynn Pan, 60–3. Richmond, Surrey: Curzon, 1999.

Pandya, Vishvajit. 'Sacrifice and escape as counter-hegemonic rituals: A structural essay on an aspect of Andamanese history', *Social Analysis* 41 (1997): 66–98.

Papathanassiou, Maria. *Zwischen Arbeit, Spiel und Schule: Die ökonomische Funktion der Kinder ärmerer Schichten in Österreich 1880–1939*. Vienna and Munich: Verlag für Geschichte und Politik and R. Oldenbourg Verlag, 1999.

Paris, Rainer and Wolfgang Sofsky. 'Drohungen: Über eine Methode der Interaktionsmacht', *Kölner Zeitschrift für Soziologie und Sozialpsychologie* 39 (1987): 15–39.

Parmer, J. Norman. *Colonial Labor Policy and Administration: A history of labor in the rubber plantation industry in Malaya, c. 1910–1941*. Locust Valley, NY: Published for the Association for Asian Studies by J. J. Augustin, 1960.

Parnaby, Andrew. 'Indigenous labor in mid-nineteenth-century British North America: The Mi'kmaq of Cape Breton and Squamish of British Columbia in comparative perspective'. In *Workers across the Americas: The transnational turn in labor history*, edited by Leon Fink, 109–35. New York: Oxford University Press, 2011.

Passow, Richard. *'Kapitalismus': Eine begrifflich-terminologische Studie*. Jena: Verlag von Gustav Fischer, 1918.

Patnaik, Prabhat. 'The labour market under capitalism', *Social Scientist* 34 (2006): 9–20.

Patnaik, Utsa. *The Republic of Hunger and Other Essays*. Gurgaon: Three Essays Collective, 2007.

Patnaik, Utsa and Prabhat Patnaik. *A Theory of Imperialism*. New Delhi: Tulika, 2016.

Patterson, Orlando. 'The structural origins of slavery: A critique of the Nieboer-Domar hypothesis from a comparative perspective', *Annals of the New York Academy of Science* 292 (1977): 12–34.

Patterson, Orlando. *Freedom in the Making of Western Culture*. New York: Basic Books, 1991.

Patterson, Orlando. *Slavery and Social Death: A comparative study*. Cambridge, MA: Harvard University Press, 1982.

Pech, Stanley Z. 'The Czech working class in 1848', *Canadian Slavonic Papers* 9 (1967): 60–73.

Peebles, Patrick. *The Plantation Tamils of Ceylon*. Leicester: Leicester University Press, 2001.

Peemans, Jean-Philippe. 'Capital accumulation in the Congo under colonialism: The role of the state'. In *Colonialism in Africa, 1870–1960*. Vol. 4: *The Economics of Colonialism*, edited by Peter Duignan and L. H. Gann, 165–212. Cambridge: Cambridge University Press, 1975.

Peers, Douglas M. 'Sepoys, soldiers and the lash: Race, caste and army discipline in India, 1820–50', *Journal of Imperial and Commonwealth History* 23 (1995): 211–47.

Peloso, Vincent C. *Peasants on Plantations: Subaltern strategies of labor and resistance in the Pisco Valley, Peru*. Durham, NC: Duke University Press, 1999.
Penn, Nigel. 'Great escapes: Deserting soldiers during Noodt's Cape governorship, 1727–1729', *South African Historical Journal* 59 (2007): 171–203.
Perkins, Dwight H. *Agricultural Development in China 1368–1968*. Edinburgh: Edinburgh University Press, 1969.
Pernet, Corinne A. 'Developing nutritional standards and food policy: Latin American reformers between the ILO, the League of Nations Health Organization, and the Pan-American Sanitary Bureau'. In *Globalizing Social Rights: The International Labour Organization and beyond*, edited by Sandrine Kott and Joëlle Droux, 249–61. New York: Palgrave Macmillan, 2013.
Perrot, Michelle. *Les ouvriers en grève: France 1871–1890*. Two volumes. Paris and The Hague: Mouton, 1974.
Pestoff, Victor A. *Between Markets and Politics: Co-operatives in Sweden*. Frankfurt am Main: Campus and Boulder, CO: Westview, 1991.
Peterson, Jean Treloggen. 'Interhousehold exchange and the public economy in three Highland Philippine communities', *Research in Economic Anthropology* 11 (1989): 123–42.
Petras, James and Maurice Zeitlin. 'Miners and agrarian radicalism', *American Sociological Review* 32 (1967): 578–86.
Pétré-Grenouilleau, Olivier. *Les traites négrières: Essai d'histoire globale*. Paris: Gallimard, 2004.
Pfau-Effinger, Birgit. 'Socio-historical paths of the male breadwinner model. An explanation of cross-national differences', *British Journal of Sociology* 55 (2004): 377–99.
Phelan, Craig. 'Editorial introduction', *Labor History* 45 (2004): 3–7.
Phelan, Craig (ed.). *Trade Unionism since 1945: Towards a global history*. Oxford: Peter Lang, 2009.
Phelan, V. C. 'Human welfare and the ILO', *International Journal* 9 (1954): 24–33.
Pierenkemper, Toni. 'Der Auf- und Ausbau eines "Normalarbeitsverhältnisses" in Deutschland im 19. und 20. Jahrhundert'. In *Geschichte der Arbeitsmärkte: Erträge der 22. Arbeitstagung der Gesellschaft für Sozial- und Wirtschaftsgeschichte 11. bis 14. April 2007 in Wien*, edited by Rolf Walter, 77–112. Stuttgart: Franz Steiner Verlag, 2009.
Piketty, Thomas. *Capital in the Twenty-First Century*. Cambridge, MA: Harvard University Press, 2014.
Pingali, Prabhu L. 'Green Revolution: Impacts, limits, and the path ahead', *Proceedings of the National Academy of Sciences of the United States of America (PNAS)* 109 (31 July 2012): 12302–8.
Pirenne, Henri. 'The stages in the social history of capitalism', *American Historical Review* 19 (1914): 494–515.
Pitman, Frank Wesley. 'The organization of slave labor', *Journal of Negro History* 11 (1926): 595–605.
Pizzorno, Alessandro (ed.). *Lotte operaie e sindacato, 1968–1972*. Six volumes. Bologna: Il Mulino, 1974–8.
Polányi, Karl. *The Great Transformation: The political and economic origins of our time*. Boston: Beacon Press, 2001.
Pollard, Sidney. *The Genesis of Modern Management: A study of the Industrial Revolution in Great Britain*. London: Edward Arnold, 1965.
Polo, Marco. *The Travels of Marco Polo*. Translated and with an introduction by Ronald Latham. London: Penguin, 1958.
Popenoe, Wilson. 'Cinchona cultivation in Guatemala', *Economic Botany* 3 (1949): 150–7.
Popovic, Alexandre. 'al-Mukhtara', *Encyclopedia of Islam: New Edition*. Vol. VII, 526. Leiden and Boston: Brill, 1993.
Popovic, Alexandre. *The Revolt of African Slaves in Iraq, in the 3rd/9th Century*. Trans. Léon King. Princeton: Markus Wiener Publishers, 1999.
Porter, Andrew. 'Religion and empire: British expansion in the long nineteenth century, 1780–1914', *Journal of Imperial and Commonwealth History* 20 (1993): 370–90.
Porter, Philip W. 'A note on cotton and climate: A colonial conundrum'. In *Cotton, Colonialism, and Social History in Sub-Saharan Africa*, edited by Allen Isaacman and Richard Roberts, 43–9. London: James Currey, 1995.
Posthuma, Anne and Arianna Rossi. 'Coordinated governance in global value chains: Supranational dynamics and the role of the International Labour Organization', *New Political Economy* 22 (2017): 186–202.
Potter, D. Shena. 'The movement for international labour legislation', *The Economic Journal* 20 (1910): 347–57.
Potts, Lydia. *The World Labour Market: A history of migration*. London: Pluto Press, 1990.

Pouchepadass, Jacques. 'After slavery: Unfree rural labour in post-1843 Eastern India'. In *India's Unfree Workforce: Of bondage old and new*, edited by Jan Breman, Isabelle Guérin and Aseem Prakash, 21–43. New Delhi: Oxford University Press, 2009.
Poya, Maryam. 'Iran 1979: Long live revolution! ... Long live Islam?', In *Revolutionary Rehearsals*, edited by Colin Barker, 123–68. London: Bookmarks, 1987.
Preisendörfer, Peter. 'Vertrauen als soziologische Kategorie: Möglichkeiten und Grenzen einer entscheidungstheoretischen Fundierung des Vertrauenskonzepts', *Zeitschrift für Soziologie* 24 (1995): 263–72.
Priesching, Nicole. 'Die Verurteilung der Sklaverei unter Gregor XVI., im Jahr 1839', *Saeculum* 59 (2008): 143–62.
Prison Policy Initiative. 'Mass incarceration: The whole pie 2022'. https://www.prisonpolicy.org/reports/pie2022.html.
Probert, Alan. 'Bartolomé de Medina: The patio process and the sixteenth century silver crisis', *Journal of the West* 8 (1969): 90–124.
Prugl, Elisabeth. *The Global Construction of Gender: Home-based work in the political economy of the 20th century*. New York: Columbia University Press, 1999.
Pruns, Herbert. *Europäische Zuckerwirtschaft*. Vol. I: *Europa auf der Suche nach Zucker in einheimischen Kulturpflanzen*. Berlin: Albert Bartens, 2004.
Przeworski, Adam. *Capitalism and Social Democracy*. Cambridge: Cambridge University Press, 1985.
Przeworski, Adam and John Sprague. *Paper Stones: A history of electoral socialism*. Chicago: University of Chicago Press, 1986.
Pulleyblank, E. G. 'The origins and nature of chattel slavery in China', *Journal of the Economic and Social History of the Orient* 1 (1958): 185–220.
Puls, Detlev. '"Ein im ganzen gutartiger Streik": Bemerkungen zu Alltagserfahrungen und Protestverhalten der oberschlesischen Bergarbeiter am Ende des 19. Jahrhunderts'. In *Wahrnehmungsformen und Protestverhalten: Studien zur Lage der Unterschichten im 18. und 19. Jahrhundert*, edited by Detlev Puls, 175–227. Frankfurt am Main: Suhrkamp, 1979.
Qi, Shi and Fang Zhuofen. 'Capitalism in agriculture in the early and middle Qing dynasty'. In *Chinese Capitalism, 1522–1840*, edited by Xu Dixin and Wu Chengming, 113–62. Houndmills: Palgrave Macmillan, 2000.
Quataert, Jean H. 'Combining agrarian and industrial livelihood: Rural households in the Saxon Oberlausitz in the nineteenth century', *Journal of Family History* 10 (1985): 145–62.
Quijano Obregón, Anibal. 'The marginal pole of the economy and the marginalised labour force', *Economy and Society* 3 (1974): 393–428.
Quinns, John E. 'Three cheers for the abolitionist pope! American reactions to Gregory XVI's condemnation of the slave trade, 1840–1860', *Catholic Historical Review* 90 (2004): 67–93.
Quirk, Joel and David Richardson. 'Anti-slavery, European identity and international society: A macro-historical perspective', *Journal of Modern European History* 7 (2009): 68–92.
Rabeherifara, Jean-Claude. 'Réseaux sociaux et familiaux: Détournement du salarial?'. In *Classes ouvrières d'Afrique noire*, edited by Michel Agier, Jean Copans and Alain Morice, 183–213. Paris: Kathala/ORSTOM, 1987.
Radforth, Ian. *Bushworkers and Bosses: Logging in Northern Ontario, 1900–1980*. Toronto: Toronto University Press, 1987.
Ramasamy, P. 'Labour control and labour resistance in the plantations of Malaya', *Journal of Peasant Studies* 19 (1992): 87–105.
Ramirez, Francisco O. and John W. Meyer. 'Comparative education: The social construction of the modern world system', *Annual Review of Sociology* 6 (1980): 369–99.
Randall, Adrian J. 'Peculiar perquisites and pernicious practices: Embezzlement in the West of England woollen industry, c. 1750–1840', *International Review of Social History* 35 (1990): 193–219.
Ransom, Roger L. and Richard Sutch. *One Kind of Freedom: The economic consequences of emancipation*. Cambridge: Cambridge University Press, 1977.
Rao, J. Mohan. 'Agrarian power and unfree labour', *Journal of Peasant Studies* 26 (1999): 242–62.
Rashke, Richard. *Escape from Sobibor*. Reading: Sphere Books, 1983.
Rawski, Evelyn Sakakida. *Agricultural Change and the Peasant Economy of South China*. Cambridge, MA: Harvard University Press, 1972.
re: work (IGK Work and Human Life Cycle in Global History). https://rework.hu-berlin.de/news.html.

Red Latinoamericana y del Caribe de Trabajo y Trabajador@s (REDLATT). https://redlatt.org/inicio.

Rediker, Marcus. *Between the Devil and the Deep Blue Sea: Merchant seamen, pirates, and the Anglo-American maritime world, 1700–1750*. Cambridge: Cambridge University Press, 1987.

Rediker, Marcus, Titas Chakraborty and Matthias van Rossum (eds). *A Global History of Runaways: Workers, mobility, and capitalism 1600–1850*. Berkeley: University of California Press, 2019.

Reichardt, Tobias. 'Marx über die Gesellschaft der klassischen Antike', *Beiträge zur Marx-Engels-Forschung*, New Series, 2004, 194–222.

Reid, Richard. *Political Power in Pre-Colonial Buganda: Economy, society and warfare in the nineteenth century*. Oxford: James Currey, 2002.

Reinsch, Paul S. *Colonial Government: An introduction to the study of colonial institutions*. New York: Macmillan, 1916.

Reis, João José. '"The Revolution of the *Ganhadores*": Urban labour, ethnicity and the African strike of 1857 in Bahia, Brazil', *Journal of Latin American Studies* 29 (1997): 355–93.

Renard, Rosamunde. 'Labour relations in Martinique and Guadeloupe, 1848–1870'. In *Caribbean Freedom: Society and economy from emancipation to the present*, edited by Hilary Beckles and Verene Shepherd, 80–92. Kingston: Ian Randle, 1993.

Renault, François. *Libération des esclaves et nouvelle servitude: Les rachats de captifs africains pour le compte des colonies françaises après l'abolition de l'esclavage*. Abidjan: Nouvelles Éditions Africaines, 1976.

Reynaud, Emmanuel. *The International Labour Organization and the Living Wage: A historical perspective*. Conditions of Work and Employment Series No. 90. Geneva: ILO, 2017. https://labordoc.ilo.org/permalink/41ILO_INST/1s2ok2m/alma994967590602676.

Richards, John F. *The Unending Frontier: An environmental history of the early modern world*. Berkeley: University of California Press, 2003.

Riello, Giorgio and Prasannan Parthasarathi (eds). *The Spinning World: A global history of cotton textiles, 1200–1850*. Oxford: Oxford University Press, 2009.

Riseman, Noah. 'Australian [mis]treatment of indigenous labour in World War II Papua and New Guinea', *Labour History* 98 (2010): 163–82.

Rivaltz Quenette, L. 'De l'esclavage à l'engagisme, les motivations réelles'. In *Slavery in the South West Indian Ocean*, edited by U. Bissoondoyal and S. B. C. Servansing, 45–73. Moka, Mauritius: Mahatma Gandhi Institute, 1989.

Robbins, Bill. 'Governor Macquarie's job descriptions and the bureaucratic control of the convict labour process', *Labour History* [Australia] 96 (2009): 1–18.

Robbins, Stephen P. *Organizational Behavior: Concepts, controversies, applications*. Seventh edition. Englewood Cliffs, NJ: Prentice Hall, 1996.

Roberts, Clayton. *The Logic of Historical Explanation*. University Park: Pennsylvania State University Press, 1996.

Roberts, David Andrew. 'The "knotted hands that set us high": Labour history and the study of convict Australia', *Labour History* [Australia] 100 (2011): 33–50.

Roberts, G. W. and J. Byrne. 'Summary statistics on indenture and associated migration affecting the West Indies, 1834–1918', *Population Studies* 20 (1966): 125–34.

Roberts, Richard and Martin A. Klein. 'The Banamba slave exodus of 1905 and the decline of slavery in the Western Sudan', *Journal of African History* 21 (1980): 375–94.

Roberts, Richard and Suzanne Miers. 'The end of slavery in Africa'. In *The End of Slavery in Africa*, edited by Suzanne Miers and Richard Roberts, 3–68. Madison: University of Wisconsin Press, 1988.

Robertson, James A. 'Some notes on the transfer by Spain of plants and animals to its colonies overseas', *The James Sprunt Historical Studies* 19 (1927): 7–21.

Robinson, Chase F. 'Neck-sealing in early Islam', *Journal of the Economic and Social History of the Orient* 48 (2005): 401–41.

Robison, Peter. 'Boeing's 737 Max software outsourced to $9-an-hour engineers'. Bloomberg online. 28 June 2019. https://www.bloomberg.com/news/articles/2019-06-28/boeing-s-737-max-software-outsourced-to-9-an-hour-engineers.

Rodgers, Gerry, Lee Swepston, Eddy Lee and Jasmien van Daele. *The ILO and the Quest for Social Justice, 1919–2009*. Geneva: ILO, 2009.

Rodrigues, José Honório. 'The influence of Africa on Brazil and of Brazil on Africa', *Journal of African History* 3 (1962): 49–67.

Rodríguez García, Magaly. *Liberal Workers of the World, Unite? The ICFTU and the defence of labour liberalism in Europe and Latin America, 1949–1969*. Oxford: Peter Lang, 2010.
Rodríguez García, Magaly, Lex Heerma van Voss and Elise van Nederveen Meerkerk (eds). *Selling Sex in the City: A global history of prostitution, 1600s–2000s*. Leiden and Boston: Brill, 2017.
Rodrik, Dani. 'Premature deindustrialization', *Journal of Economic Growth* 21 (2016): 1–33.
Romer, Alfred Sherwood. *Man and the Vertebrates*. Chicago: University of Chicago Press, 1933.
Rose, Elihu. 'The anatomy of mutiny', *Armed Forces and Society* 8 (1982): 561–74.
Roseberry, William. 'Introduction'. In *Coffee, Society, and Power in Latin America*, edited by William Roseberry, Lowell Gudmundson and Mario Samper Kutschbach, 1–37. Baltimore, MD: Johns Hopkins University Press, 1995.
Rosenbaum, Heidi. *Proletarische Familien: Arbeiterfamilien und Arbeiterväter im frühen 20. Jahrhundert zwischen traditioneller, sozialdemokratischer und kleinbürgerlicher Orientierung*. Frankfurt am Main: Suhrkamp, 1992.
Rosenberg, Nathan. 'Economic experiments', *Industrial and Corporate Change* 1 (1992): 181–203.
Rosenberg, Nathan. *Perspectives on Technology*. Cambridge: Cambridge University Press, 1976.
Rosental, Paul-André. 'Géopolitique et Etat-providence: Le BIT et la politique mondiale des migrations dans l'entre-deux-guerres', *Annales HSS* 61 (2006): 99–134.
Ross, Ellen. 'Survival networks: Women's neighbourhood sharing in London before World War I', *History Workshop Journal* 15 (1983): 4–27.
Rostovtzeff, Michael I. *The Social and Economic History of the Hellenistic World*. Two volumes. Oxford: Clarendon Press, 1941.
Roth, Karl Heinz. 'Unfree labour in the area under German hegemony, 1930–1945: Some historical and methodological questions'. In *Free and Unfree Labour: The debate continues*, edited by Tom Brass and Marcel van der Linden, 127–43. Bern: Peter Lang, 1997.
Rothstein, Eric. 'Broaching a cultural logic of modernity', *Modern Language Quarterly* 61 (2000): 359–94.
Rottenburg, Richard. 'Social and public experiments and new figurations of science and politics in postcolonial Africa', *Postcolonial Studies* 12 (2009): 423–40.
Roy, Tirthankar. 'Factor markets and the narrative of economic change in India, 1750–1950', *Continuity and Change* 24 (2009): 137–67.
Rude, Fernand. *Les révoltes des canuts, novembre 1831–avril 1834*. Paris: Maspero, 1982.
Rudé, George. *Ideology and Popular Protest*. Chapel Hill: University of North Carolina Press, 1980.
Ruotsila, Markku. '"The great charter for the liberty of the workingman": Labour, liberals and the creation of the ILO', *Labour History Review* 67 (2002): 29–47.
Rusche, Georg and Otto Kirchheimer. *Punishment and Social Structure*. New York: Columbia University Press, 1939.
Sahlins, Marshall. *Stone Age Economics*. New York: Aldine, 1972.
Saith, Ashwani. 'Reflections: Interview with Louis Emmerij', *Development and Change* 36 (2005): 1163–76.
Sakamoto, Leonardo. '"Slave labor" in Brazil'. In *Forced Labor: Coercion and exploitation in the private economy*, edited by Beate Andrees and Patrick Belser, 15–33. Boulder, CO: Lynne Rienner, 2009.
Samkoff, Aneta. 'From Central Asia to Anatolia: The transmission of the black-line technique and the development of pre-Ottoman tilework', *Anatolian Studies* 64 (2014): 199–215.
Sanborn, Joshua A. *Drafting the Russian Nation: Military conscription, total war, and mass politics, 1905–1925*. DeKalb: Northern Illinois University Press, 2003.
Sandbrook, Richard and Robin Cohen (eds). *The Development of an African Working Class: Studies in class formation and action*. Toronto: University of Toronto Press, 1975.
Sanjek, Roger. 'The organization of households in Adabraka: Toward a wider comparative perspective', *Comparative Studies in Society and History* 24 (1982): 57–103.
Santiago-Valles, Kelvin. 'Coercion and concrete labor within historical capitalism: Reexamining intersectionality theory'. In *The World-System as Unit of Analysis: Past contributions and future advances*, edited by Roberto Patricio Korzeniewicz, 17–26. New York and London: Routledge, 2018.
Sarkar, Sumit. *Writing Social History*. New Delhi: Oxford University Press, 1997.
Sauer, Jonathan D. *Historical Geography of Crop Plants*. Boston: CRC Press, 1993.
Saunders, Kay (ed.). *Indentured Labour in the British Empire, 1834–1920*. London: Croom Helm, 1984.

Sayers, Daniel O., P. Brendan Burke and Aaron M. Henry. 'The political economy of exile in the Great Dismal Swamp', *International Journal of Historical Archaeology* 11 (2007): 60–97.
Schaper, Bertus W. *Albert Thomas: Trente ans de réformisme social*. Assen: Van Gorcum, 1959.
Schechter, Patricia A. 'Free and slave labor in the Old South: The Tredegar ironworkers' strike of 1847', *Labor History* 35 (1994): 165–86.
Scherrer, Christoph and Anil Shah. 'The political economy of prison labour: From penal welfarism to the penal state', *Global Labour Journal* 8 (2017): 32–48.
Schiel, Tilman and Georg Stauth. 'Unterentwicklung und Subsistenzproduktion', *Peripherie* 5–6 (1981): 122–43.
Schiller, Friedrich. 'What is, and to what end do we study, universal history?', In *Friedrich Schiller, Poet of Freedom*. Vol. II. Trans. Caroline Stephan and Robert Trout, edited by Christina Huth, Marianna Wertz and Ronald Kokina, 253–72. New York: New Benjamin Franklin House, 1988.
Schmidt, Nelly. 'Les migrations de main-d'oeuvre dans la politique coloniale française aux Caraïbes pendant la seconde moitié du XIXe siècle', *Le Mouvement Social* 151 (1990): 11–37.
Schoeller, Wolfgang. *Die offene Schere im Welthandel: Und wie sie zu schließen ist*. Heilbronn: Distel Verlag, 2005.
Schoenberger, Erica. 'The origins of the market economy: State power, territorial control, and modes of war fighting', *Comparative Studies in Society and History* 50 (2008): 663–91.
Schuler, Monica. 'Akan slave rebellions in the British Caribbean', *Savacou* 1 (1970). Reprinted in *Caribbean Slave Society and Economy: A student reader*, edited by Hilary Beckles and Verene Shepherd, 373–86. Kingston and London: Ian Randle, 1991.
Schuler, Monica. 'Ethnic slave rebellions in the Caribbean and the Guianas', *Journal of Social History* 3 (1970): 374–85.
Schulz, Günther. '"Der konnte freilich ganz anders sparen als ich": Untersuchungen zum Sparverhalten industrieller Arbeiter im 19. Jahrhundert'. In *Arbeiterexistenz im 19. Jahrhundert. Lebensstandard und Lebensgestaltung deutscher Arbeiter und Handwerker*, edited by Werner Conze and Ulrich Engelhardt, 487–515. Stuttgart: Klett-Cotta, 1981.
Schumpeter, Joseph. 'Social classes in an ethnically homogeneous environment' (1927). Reprinted in *Imperialism and Social Classes*, edited by Joseph Schumpeter, 101–79. Oxford: Basil Blackwell, 1951.
Schüren, Ute. 'Reconceptualizing the post-peasantry: Household strategies in Mexican Ejidos', *European Review of Latin American and Caribbean Studies / Revista Europea de Estudios Latinoamericanos y del Caribe* 75 (2003): 47–63.
Schwander, Hanna and Philip Manow. *It's Not the Economy, Stupid! Explaining the electoral success of the German right-wing populist AfD*. Center for Comparative and International Studies, Working Paper No. 94. Zürich: ETH Zürich/University of Zürich, 2017.
Schweninger, Loren. 'Black economic reconstruction in the South'. In *The Facts of Reconstruction: Essays in honor of John Hope Franklin*, edited by Eric Anderson and Alfred A. Moss, Jr., 167–88. Baton Rouge: Louisiana State University Press, 1991.
Scipes, Kim. 'Building global labor solidarity today: Learning from the KMU of the Philippines', *Class, Race and Corporate Power* 2 (2014), Article 2.
Scott, Alan. 'Irrational choice? On freedom, coercion and the labour contract', *Capital and Class* 64 (1998): 119–30.
Scott, James C. *The Moral Economy of the Peasant: Rebellion and subsistence in Southeast Asia*. New Haven, CT: Yale University Press, 1976.
Scott, James C. *Weapons of the Weak: Everyday forms of peasant resistance*. New Haven, CT: Yale University Press, 1985.
Scott, Joan Wallach. *The Glassworkers of Carmaux: French craftsmen and political action in a nineteenth-century city*. Cambridge, MA: Harvard University Press, 1974.
Scott, Peter M. and James Walker. 'Working-class household consumption smoothing in interwar Britain', *Journal of Economic History* 72 (2012): 797–825.
Screpanti, Ernesto. 'Long cycles in strike activity: An empirical investigation', *British Journal of Industrial Relations* 25 (1987): 99–124.
Screpanti, Ernesto. *Onde lunghi del conflitto di clase*. Milan: Puntorosso, 1994.
Seibert, Julia. *In die globale Wirtschaft gezwungen: Arbeit und kolonialer Kapitalismus im Kongo (1885–1960)*. Frankfurt am Main: Campus, 2016.
Seidman, Bert. 'ILO accomplishments: Organized labor's view', *Monthly Labor Review* 98 (1975): 37–9.

Seidman, Michael. *The Imaginary Revolution: Parisian students and workers in 1968*. New York and Oxford: Berghahn, 2004.
Selwyn, Ben. 'Poverty chains and global capitalism', *Competition and Change* 23 (2019): 71–97.
Selznick, Philip. *Law, Society and Industrial Justice*. New York: Russell Sage Foundation, 1969.
Servet, Jean-Marie. *Nomismata: Etat et origines de la monnaie*. Lyon: Presses Universitaires de Lyon, 1984.
Shah, Bahadar. 'Impact of ILO conventions on labour laws in Pakistan', *Pakistan Horizon* 48 (1995): 81–93.
Shannon, Fred A. *The Farmer's Last Frontier: Agriculture, 1860–1897*. New York: Harper & Row, 1945.
Shepherd, Verene A. 'The "other middle passage?": Nineteenth-century bonded labour migration and the legacy of the slavery debate in the British-colonised Caribbean'. In *Working Slavery, Pricing Freedom: Perspectives from the Caribbean, Africa and the African diaspora*, edited by Verene A. Shepherd, 343–76. Kingston: Ian Randle, 2002.
Sheridan, Richard. *The Development of Plantations to 1750: An era of West Indian prosperity 1750–1775*. Barbados: Caribbean Universities Press, 1970.
Shiva, Vandana. 'The Green Revolution in the Punjab', *The Ecologist* 21 (1991): 57–60.
Shlomowitz, Ralph. 'Plantations and smallholdings: Comparative perspectives from the world cotton and sugar cane economies, 1865–1939', *Agricultural History* 58 (1984): 1–16.
Shotwell, James T. 'The International Labor Organization as an alternative to violent revolution', *Annals of the American Academy of Political and Social Science* 166 (1933): 18–25.
Sicular, Daniel T. 'Pockets of peasants in Indonesian cities: The case of scavengers', *World Development* 19 (1991): 137–61.
Siefert, Marsha (ed.). *Labor in State Socialist Europe, 1945–1989: Contributions to a history of work*. Budapest: Central European University Press, 2020.
Siegel, Bernard. 'Some methodological considerations for a comparative study of slavery', *American Anthropologist* 47 (1945): 357–92.
Sierra Alvarez, José. *El obrero soñado: Ensayo sobre el paternalismo industrial (Asturias 1860–1917)*. Madrid: Siglo Veintiuno, 1990.
Sikora, Michael. 'Das 18. Jahrhundert: Die Zeit der Deserteure'. In *Armeen und ihre Deserteure: Vernachlässigte Kapitel einer Militärgeschichte der Neuzeit*, edited by Ulrich Bröckling and Michael Sikora, 86–111. Göttingen: Vandenhoeck & Ruprecht, 1998.
Silver, Allan. 'Friendship in commercial society: Eighteenth-century social theory and modern sociology', *American Journal of Sociology* 95 (1990): 1474–504.
Silver, Beverly J., *Forces of Labor: Workers' Movements and Globalization since 1870*. Cambridge: Cambridge University Press, 2003.
Silver, Beverly J., Giovanni Arrighi and Melvyn Dubofsky (eds). 'Labor unrest in the world-economy, 1870–1990', special issue of *Review* [Fernand Braudel Center] 18 (1995): 1–206.
Silverstein, Josef. 'Students in Southeast Asian politics', *Pacific Affairs* 49 (1976): 189–212.
Silvert, Kalman. 'The university student' In *Continuity and Change in Latin America*, edited by John J. Johnson, 206–22. Stanford, CA: Stanford University Press, 1964.
Simon, Herbert A. 'A formal theory of the employment relationship', *Econometrica* 19 (1951): 293–305.
Simpson, Ida Harper and Elizabeth Mutran. 'Women's social consciousness: Sex or worker identity', *Research in the Sociology of Work* 1 (1981): 335–50.
Singeling, Mascha. *Rural Livelihoods, Resources and Coping with Crisis in Indonesia: A comparative study*. Amsterdam: Amsterdam University Press, 2008.
Singelmann, Joachim and Peter Singelmann. 'Lorenz von Stein and the paradigmatic bifurcation of social theory in the nineteenth century', *British Journal of Sociology* 37 (1986): 431–52.
Sinha, Nitin and Nitin Varma (eds). *Servants' Pasts*. Vol. 2: *18th–20th centuries*. New Delhi: Orient Blackswan, 2019.
Sinha, Nitin, Nitin Varma and Pankaj Jha (eds). *Servants' Pasts*. Vol. 1: *16th–18th centuries*. New Delhi: Orient Blackswan, 2019.
Siwpersad, Jozef. *De Nederlandse regering en de afschaffing van de Surinaamse slavernij (1833–1863)*. Groningen and Castricum: Bouma's Boekhuis and Bert Hagen, 1979.
Skinner, G. William. 'Marketing and social structure in rural China (Part I)', *Journal of Asian Studies* 24 (1964): 3–43.

Skocpol, Theda. *States and Social Revolutions: A comparative analysis of France, Russia, and China*. Cambridge: Cambridge University Press, 1979.
SlaveVoyages. https://www.slavevoyages.org/.
Slocomb, Margaret. *Colons and Coolies: The development of Cambodia's rubber plantations*. Bangkok: White Lotus, 2007.
Slucki, David. *The International Jewish Labor Bund after 1945: Toward a global history*. New Brunswick, NJ: Rutgers University Press, 2012.
Smallwood, Scott and David Glenn. 'Editor of "Labor History" quits, and dozens join him; Oxford Press hires editor from Princeton', *The Chronicle of Higher Education*, 4 July 2003.
Smith, Adam. *The Wealth of Nations*, Books I–III, edited by Andrew Skinner. Harmondsworth: Penguin, 1999.
Smith, Adam. *The Wealth of Nations*, Books IV–V, edited by Andrew Skinner. Harmondsworth: Penguin, 1999.
Smith, Joan and Immanuel Wallerstein. 'Households as an institution of the world-economy'. In Joan Smith and Immanuel Wallerstein (eds), *Creating and Transforming Households: The constraints of the world-economy*, 3–23. Cambridge: Cambridge University Press, 1992.
Smith, Joan, Immanuel Wallerstein and Hans-Dieter Evers (eds). *Households and the World-Economy*. Beverly Hills, CA: Sage, 1984.
Smith, John. *Imperialism in the Twenty-First Century*. New York: Monthly Review Press, 2016.
Smith, Mark M. 'Time, slavery and plantation capitalism in the ante-bellum American South', *Past and Present* 150 (1996): 142–68.
Snow, David A., Louis A. Zurcher, Jr. and Sheldon Ekland-Olson. 'Social networks and social movements: A microstructural approach to differential recruitment', *American Sociological Review* 45 (1980): 787–801.
Soboul, Albert. *Les Sans-culottes parisiens en l'an II: Mouvement populaire et gouvernement révolutionnaire, 2 juin 1793–9*. Paris: Librairie Clavreuil, 1958.
Social History Portal: Global Labour History Network. https://socialhistoryportal.org/glhn.
Sombart, Werner. *Der moderne Kapitalismus: Historisch-systematische Darstellung des gesamteuropäischen Wirtschaftslebens von seinen Anfängen bis zur Gegenwart*. Third edition. Vol. II Part 1. Munich: Duncker & Humblot, 1919.
Southall, Humphrey. 'Mobility, the artisan community and popular politics in early nineteenth-century England'. In *Urbanising Britain: Essays on class and community in the nineteenth century*, edited by Gerry Kearns and Charles W. J. Withers, 103–53. Cambridge: Cambridge University Press, 1991.
Southey, Robert. *Journal of a Tour in Scotland in 1819*. London: John Murray, 1929.
*Sozialgeschichtliche Kommunismusforschung*. Special issue of *Bohemia: A Journal of History and Civilisation in East Central Europe*, 42 (2001).
Spencer, David. 'The impact of the Cuban Revolution on Latin American student politics'. In *Student Politics in Latin America*, edited by David Spencer, 91–5. Madison, WI: United States National Student Association, 1965.
Spencer, Joseph E. and Ronald J. Horvath. 'How does an agricultural region originate?', *Annals of the Association of American Geographers* 53 (1963): 74–92.
Standing, Guy. 'The ILO: An agency for globalization?', *Development and Change* 39 (2008): 355–84.
Standing, Guy. 'The International Labour Organization', *New Political Economy* 15 (2010): 307–18.
Stanley, Amy Dru. *From Bondage to Contract: Wage labor, marriage, and the market in the age of slave emancipation*. Cambridge: Cambridge University Press, 1998.
Stanziani, Alessandro (ed.). *Le travail contraint en Asie et en Europe: XVII–XXe siècles*. Paris: Éditions de la Maison des sciences de l'homme, 2010.
Stanziani, Alessandro. *Bâtisseurs d'empires: Russie, Chine et Inde à la croisée des mondes, XVe–XIXe siècle*. Paris: Raisons d'Agir, 2012.
Stanziani, Alessandro. *Bondage: Labor and rights in Eurasia from the sixteenth to the early twentieth centuries*. New York and Oxford: Berghahn, 2014.
Stanziani, Alessandro. *Labour, Coercion, and Economic Growth in Eurasia, 17th–20th Centuries*. Leiden and Boston: Brill, 2013.
Starobin, Robert S. *Industrial Slavery in the Old South*. New York: Oxford University Press, 1970.
Stearns, Peter N. 'Stages of consumerism: Recent work on the issues of periodization', *Journal of Modern History* 69 (1997): 102–17.

Steffen, Charles G. 'The pre-industrial iron worker: Northampton iron works, 1780–1820', *Labor History* 20 (1979): 89–110.
Stein, Lorenz von. *Der Socialismus und Communismus des heutigen Frankreichs: Ein Beitrag zur Zeitgeschichte.* Leipzig: Wigand, 1842.
Steinberg, Mark W. *Moral Communities: The culture of class relations in the Russian printing industry, 1867–1907.* Berkeley: University of California Press, 1992.
Steinberg, Marc W. 'Unfree labor, apprenticeship, and the rise of the Victorian Hull fishing industry: An example of the importance of law and the local state in British economic change', *International Review of Social History* 51 (2006): 243–76.
Steinfeld, Robert J. *Coercion, Contract, and Free Labor in the Nineteenth Century.* Cambridge: Cambridge University Press, 2001.
Steinfeld, Robert J. *The Invention of Free Labor: The employment relation in English and American law and culture, 1350–1870.* Chapel Hill: University of North Carolina Press, 1991.
Sternberg, Fritz. *Capitalism and Socialism on Trial.* Trans. Edward Fitzgerald. London: Victor Gollancz, 1951.
Sternberg, Fritz. *Der Imperialismus.* Berlin: Malik-Verlag, 1926.
Stetson, Sarah P. 'The traffic in seeds and plants from England's colonies in North America', *Agricultural History* 23 (1949): 45–56.
Stevenson, John. *Popular Disturbances in England, 1700–1832.* Second Edition. Harlow: Longman, 1992.
Stewart-McDougall, Mary Lynn. *The Artisan Republic: Revolution, reaction, and resistance in Lyon, 1848–1851.* Kingston and Montreal: McGill-Queen's University Press, 1984.
Stiglitz, Joseph E. 'Principal and agent (II)'. In *The New Palgrave: A dictionary of economics.* Vol. 3, edited by John Eatwell, Murray Milgate and Peter Newman, 966–71. London: Macmillan, 1987.
Stockhammer, Engelbert. *Why Have Wages Shares Fallen? A panel analysis of the determinants of functional income distribution.* Geneva: ILO, 2013.
Stolcke, Verena and Michael M. Hall. 'The introduction of free labour on Sao Paulo's coffee plantations', *Journal of Peasant Studies* 10 (1983): 170–200.
Stone, Glyn. 'The Foreign Office and forced labour in Portuguese West Africa, 1894–1914'. In *Slavery, Diplomacy and Empire: Britain and the suppression of the slave trade, 1807–1975*, edited by Keith Hamilton and Patrick Salmon, 165–95. Brighton: Sussex Academic Press, 2009.
Stone, Lawrence. *The Causes of the English Revolution, 1529–1642.* New York: Harper & Row, 1972.
Strabo. *The Geography of Strabo.* With an English Translation by Horace Leonard Jones. Vol. VI. Cambridge, MA: Harvard University Press and London: William Heinemann, 1950).
Strang, David. 'From dependency to sovereignty: An event history analysis of decolonization 1870–1987', *American Sociological Review* 55 (1990): 846–60.
Strang, David. 'Global patterns of decolonization, 1500–1987', *International Studies Quarterly* 35 (1991): 429–54.
Strang, David and Patricia Mei Yin Chang. 'The International Labor Organization and the welfare state: Institutional effects on national welfare spending, 1960–80', *International Organization* 47 (1993): 235–62.
Strecker, Mark. *Shanghaiing Sailors: A maritime history of forced labor, 1849–1915.* Jefferson, NC: McFarland & Company, 2014.
Streeck, Wolfgang. 'How will capitalism end?', *New Left Review* Second Series 87 (2014): 35–64.
Streeck, Wolfgang. *Buying Time: The delayed crises of democratic capitalism.* London: Verso, 2014.
Street, James H. 'Mechanizing the cotton harvest', *Agricultural History* 31 (1957): 12–22.
Stromquist, Shelton. *Claiming the City: A global history of workers' fight for municipal socialism.* London and New York: Verso, 2023.
Sturmthal, Adolf. 'Industrial relations strategies'. In *The International Labor Movement in Transition*, edited by Adolf Sturmthal and James G. Scoville, 1–33. Urbana: University of Illinois Press, 1973.
Sturmthal, Adolf. 'Unions and economic development', *Economic Development and Cultural Change* 8 (1960): 199–205.
Supply Chains Resources Hub. https://www.ituc-csi.org/supply-chains-resources-hub.
Sutch, Richard. 'The breeding of slaves for sale and the westward expansion of slavery, 1850–1860'. In *Race and Slavery in the Western Hemisphere: Quantitative studies*, edited by Stanley L. Engerman and Eugene D. Genovese, 173–210. Princeton: Princeton University Press, 1975.

Szekely-Lulofs, Madelon H. *Rubber: Roman uit Deli*. Amsterdam: Elsevier, 1931.
Tannenbaum, Frank. *A Philosophy of Labor*. New York: Alfred A. Knopf, 1951.
Tarbuck, Kenneth. 'Marxism in the New Age: Towards the twenty-first century', *New Interventions* 3 (1992) [Part 3.1] (Unpaged).
Tarì, Marcello and Ilaria Vanni. 'On the life and deeds of San Precario, Patron Saint of Precarious Workers and Lives', *The Fibreculture Journal* 5 (2005), 1–33. http://hdl.handle.net/10453/3295.
Tarrow, Sidney. *Democracy and Disorder: Protest and politics in Italy, 1965–1975*. Oxford: Clarendon Press, 1989.
Tarus, Isaac. 'Peasants, money and markets: A century of taxation in Kenya and its global roots'. In *Globalization and Its Discontents, Revisited*, edited by Jomo Kwame Sundaram and Khoo Khay Jin, 84–100. New Delhi: Tulika Books, 2003.
Tawney, Richard Henry. 'Preface to 1937'. In R. H. Tawney, *Religion and the Rise of Capitalism: A historical study*, vii–viii. Harmondsworth: Penguin, 1937.
Taylor, Frederick W. *Principles of Scientific Management*. New York: Harper, 1911.
Taylor, Marcus and Sébastien Rioux. *Global Labour Studies*. Cambridge and Medford, MA: Polity, 2018.
Taylor, Norman. *Cinchona in Java: The story of quinine*. New York: Greenberg, 1945.
Taylor, P. J. O. (ed.). *A Companion to the 'Indian Mutiny' of 1857*. Oxford: Oxford University Press, 1995.
Taylor, Rosser H. 'Post-bellum southern rental contracts', *Agricultural History* 17 (1943): 121–8.
Taylor, Stan. 'Parkin's theory of working class conservatism: Two hypotheses investigated', *Sociological Review* 26 (1978): 827–42.
Tax, Sol. *Penny Capitalism: A Guatemalan Indian economy*. Washington, DC: Smithsonian Institution, 1953.
Tebbutt, Melanie. *Making Ends Meet: Pawnbroking and working-class credit*. New York: St. Martin's Press, 1983.
Techjury. '67+ revealing Smartphone statistics for 2023'. https://techjury.net/stats-about/smartphone-usage/.
Tedesco, Paulo. '"The missing factor": Economy and labor in late Roman North Africa (400–600 CE)', *Journal of Late Antiquity* 11 (2018): 396–431.
Temin, Peter. *The Roman Market Economy*. Princeton: Princeton University Press, 2013.
Testart, Alain. *L'esclave, la dette et le pouvoir: Etudes de sociologie comparative*. Paris: Errance, 2001.
Teuteberg, Hans-Jürgen. 'Zur Geschichte der Kühlkost und des Tiefgefrierens', *Zeitschrift für Unternehmensgeschichte* 36 (1991): 139–55.
Tevera, D. S. 'Dump scavenging in Gaborone, Botswana: Anachronism or refuge occupation of the poor?', *Geografiska Annaler: Series B, Human Geography* 76 (1994): 21–32.
Theobald, Robin. 'On the survival of patronage in developed societies', *Archives Européennes de Sociologie* 33 (1992): 183–91.
Theobald, Robin. 'The decline of patron–client relations in developed societies', *Archives Européennes de Sociologie* 24 (1983): 136–47.
Thiemer-Sachse, Ursula. 'Marktwesen und Fernhandel bei den Azteken am Vorabend der spanischen Eroberung Mexikos', *Das Altertum* 35 (1989): 241–8.
Thoden van Velzen, H. U. E. and Wim Hoogbergen. *Een zwarte vrijstaat in Suriname: De Okaanse samenleving in de 18ᵉ eeuw*. Leiden: KITLV, 2011.
Thompson, Dorothy. *The Chartists: Popular politics in the industrial revolution*. London: Temple Smith, 1984.
Thompson, Edward P. 'Eighteenth-century English society: Class struggle without class?', *Social History* 3 (1978): 133–65.
Thompson, Edward P. *The Making of the English Working Class*. London: Victor Gollancz, 1963.
Thorner, Daniel and Alice Thorner. *Land and Labour in India*. London: Asia Publishing House, 1962.
Thun, Alphons. *Die Industrie am Niederrhein und ihre Arbeiter*. Vol. I. Leipzig: Duncker & Humblot, 1879.
Ticktin, Hillel. *Origins of the Crisis in the U.S.S.R.: Essays on the political economy of a disintegrating system*. Armonk, NY: Sharp, 1992.
Tidbury, G. E. *The Clove Tree*. London: Crosby Lockwood & Son, 1949.
Tierney, Kathleen J. 'Toward a critical sociology of risk', *Sociological Forum* 14 (1999): 215–42.
Tilly, Charles. 'Demographic origins of the European proletariat'. In *Proletarianization and Family History*, edited by David Levine, 1–85. Orlando, FL: Academic Press, 1984.

Tilly, Charles. 'Futures of European states', *Social Research* 59 (1992): 705–17.
Tilly, Charles. 'Getting it together in Burgundy, 1675–1975', *Theory and Society* 4 (1977): 479–504.
Tilly, Charles. *Coercion, Capital, and European States, AD 990–1990*. Cambridge, MA and Oxford: Blackwell, 1990.
Tilly, Charles. *Popular Contention in Great Britain, 1758–1834*. London and Boulder, CO: Paradigm Press, 2005.
Tilly, Chris and Charles Tilly. *Work under Capitalism*. Boulder, CO: Westview Press, 1998.
Tilly, Louise and Charles Tilly (eds). *Class Conflict and Collective Action*. Beverly Hills, CA: Sage, 1981.
Tinker, Hugh. *A New System of Slavery: The export of Indian labour overseas, 1830–1920*. London and New York: Oxford University Press, 1974.
Tipton, John B. *Participation of the United States in the International Labor Organization*. Champaign, IL: Institute of Labor and Industrial Relations, 1959.
Toledano, Ehud R. *The Ottoman Slave Trade and Its Suppression, 1840–1890*. Princeton: Princeton University Press, 1982.
Toman, J. T. 'The gang system and comparative advantage', *Explorations in Economic History* 42 (2005): 310–23.
Tomich, Dale W. 'The "second slavery": Bonded labor and the transformations of the nineteenth-century world economy'. In *Rethinking the Nineteenth Century: Contradictions and movement*, edited by Francisco O. Ramírez, 103–17. Westport, CO: Greenwood Press, 1988.
Tønnesson, Kåre. 'Popular protest and organization: The Thrane movement in pre-industrial Norway, 1849–55', *Scandinavian Journal of History* 13 (1988): 121–39.
Tönnies, Ferdinand. *Gemeinschaft und Gesellschaft: Abhandlung des Communismus und des Socialismus als empirischer Culturformen*. Leipzig: Fues, 1887.
Toplin, Robert Brent. *The Abolition of Slavery in Brazil*. New York: Atheneum, 1992.
Tosstorff, Reiner. 'The International Trade-Union Movement and the founding of the International Labour Organization', *International Review of Social History* 50 (2005): 399–433.
Tosstorff, Reiner. *The Red International of Labour Unions (RILU) 1920–1937*. Leiden and Boston: Brill, 2016.
Tosstorff, Reiner. *Wilhelm Leuschner gegen Robert Ley: Ablehnung der Nazi-Diktatur durch die Internationale Arbeitskonferenz 1933 in Genf*. Frankfurt am Main: VAS, 2007.
Tran, Tu Binh. *Red Earth: A Vietnamese memoir of life on a colonial rubber plantation*. Athens, OH: Ohio University Centre for International Studies, 1985.
Traugott, Mark. 'Barricades as repertoire: Continuities and discontinuities in the history of French contention', *Social Science History* 17 (1993): 309–23.
Trebilcock, Anne. 'Using ILO sources to vindicate women's economic rights', *Proceedings of the Annual Meeting (American Society of International Law)* 108 (2014): 265–9.
Treiber, Hubert and Heinz Steinert. *Die Fabrikation des zuverlässigen Menschen: Über die 'Wahlverwandtschaft' von Kloster- und Fabrikdisziplin*. Munich: Heinz Moos, 1980; second edition Münster: Westfälisches Dampfboot, 2005.
Tremblay, Diane-Gabrielle. 'From casual work to economic security: The paradoxical case of self-employment', *Social Indicators Research* 88 (2008): 115–30.
Trexler, Richard C. 'Follow the flag: The Ciompi Revolt seen from the streets'. In Richard C. Trexler, *Power and Dependence in Renaissance Florence*. Vol. 3: *The Workers of Renaissance Florence*, 30–60. Binghamton, NY: Medieval and Renaissance Texts & Studies, 1993.
Trimberger, Ellen Kay. 'State power and modes of production: Implications of the Japanese transition to capitalism', *The Insurgent Sociologist* 7 (1977): 85–98.
Trotsky, Leon. *The History of the Russian Revolution*. Trans. Max Eastman. New York: Simon and Schuster, 1932. Vol. 2.
Truter, Paul. 'The Robben Island Rebellion of 1751: A study of convict experience at the Cape of Good Hope', *Kronos* 31 (2005): 34–49.
Ts'ao, Yung-ho. 'Pepper trade in East Asia', *T'oung Pao* 68 (1982): 221–47.
Tucker, Josiah. *Instructions for Travellers*. Dublin: William Watson, 1758.
Tumbe, Chinmay. *India Moving: A history of migration*. New Delhi: Penguin India, 2019.
Turner, H. A. *Trade Union Growth, Structure and Policy*. London: George Allen & Unwin, 1962.
Umbelino, Natalia. 'Emigration ou déportation entre deux océans? Les travailleurs sous contrat (*servicaes*) de l'Afrique Portugaise (1908–1922)'. In *Eclats d'Empire du Brésil à Macao*, edited by Ernestine Carreira and Idelette Muzart-Fonseca dos Santos, 173–200. Paris: Maisonneuve & Larose, 2000.

Underdown, David. *Revel, Riot and Rebellion: Popular politics and culture in England, 1603–1660*. Oxford: Oxford University Press, 1987.
United Nations. Supplementary Convention on the Abolition of Slavery, the Slave Trade, and Institutions and Practices Similar to Slavery (entered into force April 30, 1957), 226 U.N.T.S. 3. https://treaties.un.org/doc/Treaties/1957/04/19570430%2001-00%20AM/Ch_XVIII_4p.pdf.
United Nations World Tourism Organization (UNTWO). *World Tourism Barometer* 2019. https://www.e-unwto.org/doi/epdf/10.18111/wtobarometereng.2019.17.1.4.
United States Department of State. *2021 Trafficking in Persons Report*. https://www.state.gov/reports/2021-trafficking-in-persons-report.
Useem, Bert and Michael D. Reisig. 'Collective action in prisons: Protests, disturbances, and riots', *Criminology* 37 (1999): 735–59.
Useem, Bert and Peter A. Kimball. 'A theory of prison riots', *Theory and Society* 16 (1987): 87–122.
Uselding, Paul J. 'Peddling in the antebellum economy: Precursor of mass-marketing or a start in life?', *American Journal of Economics and Sociology* 34 (1975): 55–66.
Valticos, Nicolas. 'The influence of international labour conventions on Greek legislation', *International Labour Review* 71 (1955): 593–614.
Van Bavel, Bas J. P. 'Markets for land, labor, and capital in Northern Italy and the Low Countries, twelfth to seventeenth centuries', *Journal of Interdisciplinary History* 41 (2011): 503–31.
Van Creveld, Martin. *Fighting Power: German and US Army performance, 1939–1945*. Westport, CT: Greenwood Press, 1982.
Van Daele, Jasmien. '"Engineering social peace": Networks, ideas, and the founding of the International Labour Organization', *International Review of Social History* 50 (2005): 435–66.
Van Daele, Jasmien, Magaly Rodriguez Garcia, Geert van Goethem and Marcel van der Linden (eds). *ILO Histories: Essays on the International Labor Organization and its impact in the world during the twentieth century*. Bern: Peter Lang, 2010.
Van Delden Laërne, C. F. *Brazil and Java: Report on coffee-culture in America, Asia and Africa, to H.E. the Minister of the Colonies*. London: W. H. Allen & Co., 1885.
Van Delden Laërne, C. F. 'La culture du café au Brésil', *Bijdragen tot de Taal-, Land- en Volkenkunde van Nederlandsch-Indië* 35 (1886): 246–56.
Van der Linden, Marcel (ed.). *Humanitarian Intervention and Changing Labor Relations: The long-term consequences of the abolition of the slave trade*. Leiden and Boston: Brill, 2011.
Van der Linden, Marcel (ed.). *The Global History of Work: Critical readings*. Four volumes. London: Bloomsbury, 2019.
Van der Linden, Marcel (ed.). *The International Confederation of Free Trade Unions*. Bern: Peter Lang, 2000.
Van der Linden, Marcel (ed.). *Was war die Sowjetunion? Kritische Beiträge zum real existierenden Sozialismus*.Vienna: Promedia, 2007.
Van der Linden, Marcel. 'Charles Tilly's historical sociology', *International Review of Social History* 54 (2009): 237–74.
Van der Linden, Marcel. 'Forced labour and non-capitalist industrialization: The case of Stalinism (c. 1929–c. 1956)'. In *Free and Unfree Labour: The debate continues*, edited by Tom Brass and Marcel van der Linden, 351–62. Bern: Peter Lang, 1997.
Van der Linden, Marcel. 'Notes from an outsider'. In *'Those Emblems of Hell'? European sailors and the maritime labour market, 1570–1870*, edited by Paul C. van Royen, Jaap R. Bruijn and Jan Lucassen, 349–62. St. John's, NL: International Maritime Economic History Association, 1997.
Van der Linden, Marcel. 'Old workers' movements and "new political economy"', *Traverse: Zeitschrift für Geschichte/Revue d'histoire* 4 (1997): 128–43.
Van der Linden, Marcel. 'Proletariat'. In *The Marx Revival: Key concepts and new critical interpretations*, edited by Marcello Musto, 70–91. Cambridge: Cambridge University Press, 2020.
Van der Linden, Marcel. 'The crisis of the world's old labour movements'. In *Labour and Transnational Action in Times of Crisis*, edited by Andreas Bieler, Roland Erne, Darragh Golden, Idar Helle, Knut Kjeldstadli, Tiago Matos and Sabina Stan, 29–40. London: Rowman & Littlefield, 2015.
Van der Linden, Marcel. 'Workers and the radical right', *International Labor and Working-Class History* 93 (2018): 74–8.

Van der Linden, Marcel. 'Zur Logik einer Nicht-Entscheidung: Der Wiener Kongress und der Sklavenhandel'. In *Der Wiener Kongress: Die Erfindung Europas*, edited by Thomas Just, Wolfgang Maderthaner and Helene Maimann, 354–73. Vienna: Gerold Verlag, 2014.

Van der Linden, Marcel. *Transnational Labour History: Explorations*. Aldershot: Ashgate, 2003.

Van der Linden, Marcel. *Western Marxism and the Soviet Union: A survey of critical theories and debates since 1917*. Leiden and Boston: Brill, 2007.

Van der Linden, Marcel. *Workers of the World: Essays toward a global labor history*. Leiden and Boston: Brill, 2008.

Van der Linden, Marcel and Jan Lucassen. *Prolegomena for a Global Labour History*. Amsterdam: IISH, 1999.

Van der Linden, Marcel and Magaly Rodríguez García (eds). *On Coerced Labor: Work and compulsion after chattel slavery*. Leiden: Brill, 2016.

Van der Velden, Sjaak. 'Strikes, lockouts, and informal resistance'. In *Handbook Global History of Work*, edited by Karin Hofmeester and Marcel van der Linden, 521–50. Berlin: Walter de Gruyter, 2018.

Van der Velden, Sjaak. *Striking Numbers: New approaches to strike research*. Amsterdam: IISH, 2012.

Van der Walt, Lucien and Steven Hirsch (eds). *Anarchism and Syndicalism in the Colonial and Postcolonial World, 1870–1940: The praxis of national liberation, internationalism, and social revolution*. Leiden and Boston: Brill, 2010.

Van Goethem, Geert. *The Amsterdam International: The world of the International Federation of Trade Unions (IFTU), 1913–1945*. Burlington, VT: Ashgate, 2006.

Van Nederveen Meerkerk, Elise. *Women, Work and Colonialism in the Netherlands and Java: Comparisons, contrasts and connections, 1830–1940*. London: Palgrave Macmillan, 2019.

Van Rossum, Matthias. 'Changing tides: Maritime labour relations in Europe and Asia'. In *Colonialism, Institutional Change and Shifts in Global Labour Relations*, edited by Karin Hofmeester and Pim de Zwart, 239–64. Amsterdam: Amsterdam University Press, 2018.

Van Sickle, J. V. 'The International Labor Office: An appraisal', *Southern Economic Journal* 12 (1946): 357–64.

Van Valen, Leigh. 'A new evolutionary law', *Evolutionary Theory* 1 (1973): 1–30.

Van Zanden, Jan Luiten. *The Rise and Decline of Holland's Economy: Merchant capitalism and the labour market*. Manchester: Manchester University Press, 1993.

Van Zanden, Jan Luiten, Joerg Baten, Marco Mira d'Ercole, Auke Rijpma, Conal Smith and Marcel Timmer (eds). *How Was Life? Global well-being since 1820*. Paris: OECD, 2014.

Varela, Raquel, Hugh Murphy and Marcel van der Linden (eds). *Shipbuilding and Ship Repair Workers around the World: Case studies 1950–2010*. Amsterdam: Amsterdam University Press, 2017.

Varese, Federico. 'The society of the *Vory-v-zakone*, 1930s–1950s', *Cahiers du monde russe* 39 (1998): 515–38.

Varma, Nitin. *Coolies of Capitalism: Assam tea and the making of coolie labour*. Berlin and Boston: De Gruyter Oldenbourg, 2016.

Varma, Nitin. 'Chargola exodus and collective action in the colonial tea plantations of Assam'. In *The Global History of Work: Critical readings*. Vol. IV: *Collective Action*, edited by Marcel van der Linden, 95–117. London: Bloomsbury Academic, 2019.

Vellenga, Dorothy Dee. 'Women, households, and food commodity chains in Southern Ghana', *Review* [Fernand Braudel Center] 8 (1994–5): 293–318.

Verhoog, J. 'De werving van Westafrikanen voor het Nederlands-Indische Leger, 1831–1872', *Mededelingen van de Sectie Militaire Geschiedenis Landmachtstaf* 12 (1989): 5–26.

*Verslag van het koloniaal congres der Sociaal-Democratische Arbeiderspartij in Nederland, gehouden op zaterdag 11 en zondag 12 januari 1930 te Utrecht*. Amsterdam: N. V. De Arbeiderspers, 1930.

Vicziany, Marika. 'Imperialism, botany and statistics in early nineteenth-century India: The surveys of Francis Buchanan (1762–1829)', *Modern Asian Studies* 20 (1986): 625–60.

Voon Phin Keong. *Western Rubber Planting Enterprise in Southeast Asia, 1876–1921*. Kuala Lumpur: Penerbit Universiti Malaya, 1976.

Vosko, Leah F. '"Decent work": The shifting role of the ILO and the struggle for global justice', *Global Social Policy* 2 (2002): 19–46.

Vosko, Leah F. *Temporary Work: The gendered rise of a precarious employment relationship*. Toronto: University of Toronto Press, 2000.

Vosko, Leah F., Martha MacDonald and Iain Campbell (eds). *Gender and the Contours of Precarious Employment*. New York: Routledge, 2009.

Vreeland, James. 'The effect of IMF programs on labor', *World Development* 30 (2002): 121–39.
Vries, Peer. *Escaping Poverty: The origins of modern economic growth*. Vienna: Vienna University Press, 2013.
Vriese, W. H. de. *De Kina-boom uit Zuid-Amerika overgebragt naar Java onder de regering van Koning Willem III*. The Hague: C. W. Mieling, 1855.
Wacquant, Loïc. 'From slavery to mass incarceration: Rethinking the "race question" in the US', *New Left Review* Second Series 13 (2002): 41–60.
Wade, Robert. 'Showdown at the World Bank', *New Left Review* Second Series 7 (2001): 124–37.
Wagner, Augusta. 'The International Labor Organization and the regulation of labor conditions in China', *The Yenching Journal of Social Studies* 2 (1939): 1–38.
Wagner, Reinhardt W. *Deutsche als Ersatz für Sklaven: Arbeitsmigranten aus Deutschland in der brasilianischen Provinz São Paulo 1847–1914*. Frankfurt am Main: Vervuert, 1995.
Wakefield, Edward G. *A View of the Art of Colonization, with Present Reference to the British Empire: In letters between a statesman and a colonist*. London: John Parker, 1849.
Walder, Andrew G. 'The remaking of the Chinese working class, 1949–1981', *Modern China* 10 (1984): 3–48.
Walk Free Foundation. *The Global Slavery Index 2014*. https://reporterbrasil.org.br/wp-content/uploads/2014/11/GlobalSlavery_2014_LR-FINAL.pdf.
Wallerstein, Immanuel. 'Capitalism as an essential concept to understand modernity'. In *Capitalism: The reemergence of a historical concept*, edited by Jürgen Kocka and Marcel van der Linden, 187–204. London: Bloomsbury, 2016.
Wallerstein, Immanuel. 'Dependence in an interdependent world: The limited possibilities of transformation within the capitalist world economy', *African Studies Review* 17 (1974): 1–27.
Wallerstein, Immanuel. *Historical Capitalism*. London and New York: Verso, 1983.
Walter, John. 'The English people and the English Revolution revisited', *History Workshop Journal* 61 (2006): 171–82.
Wang, Gungwu. *China and the Chinese Overseas*. Singapore: Times Academic Press, 1991.
Ward, Andrew. *Our Bones are Scattered: The Cawnpore Massacres and the Indian Mutiny of 1857*. London: John Murray, 1996.
Wareing, John. *Indentured Migration and the Servant Trade from London to America, 1618–1718*. Oxford: Oxford University Press, 2017.
Wariboko, Waibinte. 'Lineage slavery at New Calabar, Eastern Niger Delta, 1850–1950: A reassessment'. In *Working Slavery, Pricing Freedom: Perspectives from the Caribbean, Africa and the African diaspora*, edited by Verene A. Shepherd, 69–90. Kingston: Ian Randle, 2002.
Warren, James Francis. *The Sulu Zone 1768–1898: The dynamics of external trade, slavery, and ethnicity in the transformation of a Southeast Asian maritime state*. Singapore: Singapore University Press, 1981.
Waters Jr., Robert Anthony and Geert Van Goethem (eds). *American Labor's Global Ambassadors: The international history of the AFL–CIO during the Cold War*. New York: Palgrave Macmillan, 2013.
Watson, Andrew M. *Agricultural Innovation in the Early Islamic World*. Cambridge: Cambridge University Press, 1983.
Watson, James L. 'Chattel slavery in Chinese peasant society: A comparative analysis', *Ethnology* 15 (1976): 361–75.
Watts, Ian. 'Linkages between industrial radicalism and the domestic role among working women', *Sociological Review* 28 (1980): 55–74.
Weatherford, Jack. *Genghis Khan and the Making of the Modern World*. New York: Three Rivers Press, 2004.
Weatherhead Initiative on Global History. https://wigh.wcfia.harvard.edu/.
Weber, Max. 'Developmental tendencies in the situation of East Elbian labourers' (1894). In *Reading Weber*, edited by Keith Tribe, 177–205. London: Routledge, 1989.
Weber, Max. 'Die "Objektivität" sozialwissenschaftlicher und sozialpolitischer Erkenntnis' (1904). In Max Weber, *Gesammelte Aufsätze zur Wissenschaftslehre*, 146–214. Tübingen: J. C. B. Mohr (Paul Siebeck), 1988.
Weber, Max. *Die protestantische Ethik und der Geist des Kapitalismus*. In Max Weber, *Gesammelte Aufsätze zur Religionssoziologie*. Vol. I, Ninth edition. Tübingen: Mohr Siebeck, 1988: 17–206.
Weber, Max. *Parlament und Regierung im neugeordneten Deutschland*. Second edition. Berlin: Duncker & Humblot, 2011.
Weber, Max. *Wirtschaft und Gesellschaft*. Tübingen: J. C. B. Mohr (Paul Siebeck), 1922.

Weber, Wilhelm and Theo Mayer-Maly. 'Studie zur spätmittelalterlichen Arbeitsmarkt- und Wirtschaftsordnung', *Jahrbücher für Nationalökonomie und Statistik* 166 (1954): 358–89.

Weddell, M. H. A. *Histoire naturelle de Quinquinas ou Monographie du Genre Cinchona suivie d'une description du genre Cascarilla et de quelques autres plantes de la même tribu*. Paris: Victor Masson, 1846.

Weinberg, Marina and Pablo H. Mercolli. 'Sweet death: Indigenous labour exploitation in the San Martín de Tabacal Sugar Mill, Salta, Argentina', *Cultural Studies* 31 (2017): 70–92.

Weinstein, Barbara. 'The persistence of pre-capitalist relations of production in a tropical export economy: The Amazon rubber trade, 1850–1920'. In *Proletarians and Protest: Studies in class formation*, edited by Michael P. Hanagan and Charles Stephenson, 55–76. Westport, CT: Greenwood Press, 1986.

Weiss, Holger. *Framing a Radical African Atlantic: African American agency, West African intellectuals and the International Trade Union Committee of Negro Workers*. Leiden and Boston: Brill, 2014.

Weiss, Marley S. 'Ruminations on the past, present and future of international labor standards: Empowering law in the brave new economic world', *The Good Society* 16 (2007): 73–81.

Wellcome, Henry S. 'The Cinchona forests of South America', *The Scientific Monthly* 71 (1950): 205–8. [Originally published in *Popular Science Monthly* 17 (1880): 507]

Wellman, Barry, Peter J. Carrington and Alan Hall. 'Networks as personal communities'. In *Social Structures: A network approach*, edited by Barry Wellman and S. D. Berkowitz, 130–84. Cambridge: Cambridge University Press, 1988.

Wendt, Reinhardt. 'Globalisierung von Pflanzen und neue Nahrungsgewohnheiten: Zur Funktion botanischer Gärten bei der Erschließung natürlicher Ressourcen der Überseeischen Welt'. In *Überseegeschichte: Beiträge der jüngeren Forschung: Festschrift anläßlich der Gründung der Forschungsstiftung für vergleichende europäische Überseegeschichte 1999 in Bamberg*, edited by Thomas Beck, Horst Gründer, Horst Pietschmann and Roderich Ptak, 206–20. Stuttgart: Franz Steiner Verlag, 1999.

Wengel, Jan ter and Alfred Kleinknecht. 'The myth of economic globalisation', *Cambridge Journal of Economics* 22 (1998): 637–47.

Wesley, Charles H. 'The neglected period of emancipation in Great Britain 1807–1823', *Journal of Negro History* 17 (1932): 156–79.

Whitman, T. Stephen. 'Industrial slavery at the margin: The Maryland Chemical Works', *Journal of Southern History* 59 (1993): 31–62.

Whitworth, Sandra. 'Gender, international relations and the case of the ILO', *Review of International Studies* 20 (1994): 389–405.

Whitworth, Sandra. *Feminism and International Relations*. New York: St. Martin's Press, 1994.

Wickham, Chris. *Framing the Early Middle Ages: Europe and the Mediterranean, 400–800*. Oxford: Oxford University Press, 2005.

Wickham, Henry A. *On the Plantation, Cultivation, and Curing of Pará Indian Rubber (Hevea brasiliensis) with an Account of its Introduction from the West to the Eastern Tropics*. London: K. Paul, Trench, Trübner & Co., 1908.

Wilk, Richard. 'Inside the economic institution: Modeling budget structures'. In *Anthropology and Institutional Economics*, edited by James M. Acheson, 365–90. Lanham, MD: University Press of America, 1994.

Willemsen, Glenn. *Dagen van gejuich en gejubel: Viering en herdenking van de afschaffing van de slavernij in Nederland, Suriname en de Nederlandse Antillen*. The Hague and Amsterdam: Amrit/Ninsee, 2006.

Williams, David M. 'Abolition and the re-deployment of the slave fleet, 1807–11', *Journal of Transport History* 2 (1973): 103–15.

Williams, Donovan. 'Clemens Robert Markham and the introduction of the Cinchona tree into British India, 1861', *The Geographical Journal* 128 (1962): 431–42.

Williams, Eric. *Capitalism and Slavery*. Chapel Hill: University of North Carolina Press, 1944.

Wilson, Evelyn L. 'People as crops', *University of Toledo Law Review* 40 (2009): 695–709.

Wilson, Francis G. 'The enforcement of international labor standards', *Annals of the American Academy of Political and Social Science* 166 (1933): 95–101.

Wilson, Howard Hazen. 'Some principal aspects of British efforts to crush the African slave trade, 1807–1829', *American Journal of International Law* 44 (1950): 505–26.

Windmuller, John P. 'Soviet employers in the ILO: The Experience of the 1930s', *International Review of Social History* 6 (1961): 353–74.

Winkler, Heinrich August (ed.). *Organisierter Kapitalismus: Voraussetzungen und Anfänge.* Göttingen: Vandenhoeck & Ruprecht, 1974.

Wirz, Albert. *Vom Sklavenhandel zum kolonialen Handel: Wirtschaftsräume und Wirtschaftsformen in Kamerun vor 1914.* Zurich: Atlantis Verlag, 1972.

Wobbe, Theresa. 'Der internationale Wandel statistischer Repräsentationen der Arbeitswelt: Vom nationalen Zensus um 1900 zur internationalen Vergleichbarkeit in der International Labour Organization (ILO), 1882–1938'. In *Kulturgeschichte der Statistik*, edited by Stefan Haas, Michael Schneider and Nicolas Bilo, 149–67. Stuttgart: Steiner, 2019.

Wobbe, Theresa and Léa Renard. 'The category of "family workers" in International Labour Organization statistics (1930s–1980s): A contribution to the study of globalized gendered boundaries between household and market', *Journal of Global History* 12 (2017): 340–60.

Wolf, Diane L. 'Daughters, decisions and domination: An empirical and conceptual critique of household strategies', *Development and Change* 21 (1990): 43–74.

Wolf, Diane L. *Factory Daughters: Gender, household dynamics, and rural industrialization in Java.* Berkeley: University of California Press, 1992.

Wolff, Richard D. 'Ideological state apparatuses, consumerism, and U.S. capitalism: Lessons for the Left', *Rethinking Marxism* 17 (2005): 223–35.

Wolff, Tobias Barrington. 'The Thirteenth Amendment and slavery in the global economy', *Columbia Law Review* 102 (2002): 973–1050.

Wong, Diane. 'The limits of using the household as a unit of analysis'. In *Households and the World-Economy*, edited by Joan Smith, Immanuel Wallerstein and Hans-Dieter Evers, 56–63. Beverly Hills, CA: Sage, 1984.

Wong, E. 'Hoofdenverkiezing, stamverdeeling en stamverspreiding der boschnegers van Suriname in de 18$^e$ en 19$^e$ eeuw', *Bijdragen tot de Taal-, Land- en Volkenkunde* 97 (1938): 295–362.

Wood, Ellen Meiksins. 'From opportunity to imperative: The history of the market', *Monthly Review* 46 (1994): 14–40.

Wood, Ellen Meiksins. 'The separation of the economic and the political in capitalism', *New Left Review* First Series 127 (1981): 66–95.

Woodford-Berger, Prudence. 'Women in houses: The organization of residence and work in rural Ghana', *Antropologiska Studier* 30–1 (1981): 3–35.

Woodward, Alison E. and Håkon Leiulfsrud. 'Masculine/feminine organization: Class versus gender in Swedish unions'. In *Organization Theory and Class Analysis: New approaches and new issues*, edited by Stewart R. Clegg, 407–25. Berlin and New York: Walter de Gruyter, 1990.

World Bank. *Averting the Old Age Crisis: Policies to protect the old and promote growth.* Oxford: Oxford University Press, 1994.

World History Center. https://www.worldhistory.pitt.edu/.

World Peace Foundation. *Industry, Governments and Labor: Record of the International Labor Organization*, 1919–1928. Boston: World Peace Foundation, 1928.

Worsley, Peter. 'Frantz Fanon and the "Lumpenproletariat"', *Socialist Register* 9 (1972): 193–230.

Woytinsky, Wladimir S. and Emma S. Woytinsky. *World Commerce and Governments: Trends and outlook.* New York: The Twentieth Century Fund, 1955.

Wren, Daniel R. *The History of Management Thought.* Fifth Edition. Hoboken, NJ: Wiley, 2005.

Wright, Tim. '"A Method of Evading Management": Contract labor in Chinese coal mines before 1937', *Comparative Studies in Society and History* 23 (1981): 656–78.

Wylie, Kenneth C. 'The slave trade in nineteenth century Temneland and the British sphere of influence', *African Studies Review* 16 (1973): 203–17.

Yaganisako, Sylvia Junko. 'Explicating residence: A cultural analysis of changing households among Japanese-Americans'. In *Households: Comparative and historical studies of the domestic group*, edited by Robert M. Netting, Richard R. Wilk and Eric J. Arnould, 330–52. Berkeley: University of California Press, 1984.

Yaganisako, Sylvia Junko. 'Family and household: The analysis of domestic groups', *Annual Review of Anthropology* 8 (1979): 161–205.

Yi, Kei-Mu. 'Can vertical specialization explain the growth of world trade?', *Journal of Political Economy* 111 (2003): 52–102.

Young, Arthur. *Political Essays Concerning the Present State of the British Empire.* London: Strahan and Cadell, 1772.

Youngs, Richard. 'What are the meanings behind the worldwide rise in protest?', *Open Democracy*, 2 October 2017. https://www.opendemocracy.net/en/multiple-meanings-global-protest/.

Yudelman, Montague. 'The transfer of agricultural techniques'. In *Colonialism in Africa, 1870–1960*. Vol. 4: *The Economics of Colonialism*, edited by Peter Duignan and L. H. Gann, 329–59. Cambridge: Cambridge University Press, 1969.

Zeichner, Oscar. 'The transition from slave to free agricultural labor in the Southern States', *Agricultural History* 13 (1939): 22–32.

Zelnick-Abramovitz, Rachel. *Not Wholly Free: The concept of manumission and the status of manumitted slaves in the Ancient Greek world*. Leiden: Brill, 2005.

Zeuske, Michael. *Handbuch Geschichte der Sklaverei: Eine Globalgeschichte von den Anfängen bis zur Gegenwart*. Berlin: Walter de Gruyter, 2013.

Zewde, Bahru. '1969 – Ethiopia's 1968'. In *The Routledge Handbook of the Global Sixties: Between protest and nation-building*, edited by Chen Jian, Martin Klimke, Masha Kirasirova, Mary Nolan, Marilyn Young and Joanna Waley-Cohen, 356–66. London: Routledge, 2018.

Zewde, Bahru. *A History of Modern Ethiopia 1855–1991*. Second edition. Oxford: James Currey, 2001.

Zimmerer, Jürgen. 'Die Geburt des "Ostlandes" aus dem Geiste des Kolonialismus: Die nationalsozialistische Eroberungs- und Beherrschungspolitik in (post-)kolonialer Perspektive', *Sozial.Geschichte: Zeitschrift für historische Analyse des 20. und 21. Jahrhunderts* 19 (2009): 10–43.

Zimmermann, Susan. 'Globalizing gendered labour policy: International labour standards and the Global South, 1919–1947'. In Boris, Hoehtker and Zimmermann, *Women's ILO*, 227–54.

Zingales, Luigi. 'Who is responsible for a declining labor share of output? Michael Porter'. *Promarket* (16 November 2016). https://www.promarket.org/2016/11/16/responsible-declining-labor-share-output-michael-porter/.

Zuccarelli, François. 'Le régime des engagés à temps au Sénégal (1817–1848)', *Cahiers d'études africaines* 2 (1962): 420–61.

Zürcher, Erik-Jan (ed.). *Fighting for a Living: A comparative study of military labour, 1500–2000*. Amsterdam: Amsterdam University Press, 2014.

Zwahr, Hartmut. *Zur Konstituierung des Proletariats als Klasse: Strukturuntersuchungen über das Leipziger Proletariat während der industriellen Revolution*. Berlin: Akademie-Verlag, 1978.

# Index

References to figures are in *italics*; references to notes are indicated by n.

abduction 91–2, 95
abolition of the slave trade 13, 85–6, 100, 197–201, 210–12, 218
   1807 Act 189–91
   alternative labour 201–6, *207*, 208–10
   campaign 191–7
abstract accumulation 58–9
Acemoglu, Daron 104–5
Act for the Abolition of Slavery (1833) 198
Act for the Abolition of the Slave Trade (1807) 13, 189–91
Africa 5, 9, 136–7, 231
   abolition of the slave trade 190, 193–7
   agriculture 168
   anti-colonialism 243
   Caribbean 38
   coerced labour 91–3
   colonization 211–12
   convict labour 208
   crops 151, 152, 153, 154, 163
   debt peonage 204
   decolonization 310–11
   migration 316
   subsistence labour 74
   unemployment 35
   workers' movements 313
   *see also* individual countries
agriculture 8, 13, 50
   coerced labour 105, 106, 134
   commodities 248
   food grains 249
   household labour 113
   in India 43, 46–7
   labour markets 138–9
   labour-tax system 206, 208
   migrants 184–5
   research stations 168
   slave labour 130–1
   *see also* cash–crop transfers; peasantry; plantations; sharecropping
Albert, Michel: *Capitalisme contre capitalisme* 66
Algeria 23
Allen, Vic 74
Alston, Philip 233
Althusser, Louis 301
American Civil War 76, 100, 201, 278
American Federation of Labor 3
American Revolution 291

amphibians 259–61
anarchist movements 7, 320
Anatolia 133, 306
ancient Greece 21, 26, 34, 42n33, 58
   coerced labour 86
   desertion 269, 270
   labour markets 125
   slavery 130–1, 132
Anderson, Perry 297
Anglo–Egyptian Convention (1877) 196
Angola 154, 203, 311
anti-colonialism 243
Anti-Slavery International (ASI) 85
anti-slavery *see* abolition
apartheid 243, 312
Appert, Nicolas 167
apprenticeships 200
Argentina 142, 289, 306
aristocracy 49, 135–6, 183, 283, 287, 289, 290
Aristotle 128
   *Politeia* 86–7
artisanal labour 32, 71, 73, 74, 79, 262
   early history 130
Ascher, Robert 261
Asia 5, 8, 223, 231, 264–5
   abolition of the slave trade 190
   anti-colonialism 243
   crops 152, 154
   decolonization 310–11
   slavery 10, 194
   Sulu Sultanate 211
   unemployment 35
   workers' movements 313
   *see also* individual countries
Assyria 131
astronomy 261, 283
Austin, Gareth 68
Australia 13, 144, 181–2, 203, 208
auxiliaries 289–92
Aztecs 58, 159

Babylonia 131
Bairoch, Paul 35
Bakke, E. Wight 108n31
Barbados 40, 178–81
Barker, Geoffrey Russell 98–9
Basu, Arnab 105
Beckert, Sven 8, 62
Belgian Congo 45, 93–4, 225, 311

Belgium 142, 225
Benjamin, Walter 259, 266
Benston, Margaret 37, 39
Benton, Gregor 289
Bhattacharya, Sabyasachi 325
Bible, the 125, 274–5
birth 90–1
Bismarck, Otto von 238n7
Blackburn, Robin 183
Blanqui, Jérôme 218
Bodemann, Y. Michal 117
Bolivia 23, 228, 307
  Revolution 293–4, 297
bonded labour 8, 45, 47, 74, 134–5
Bonn Center for Dependency and Slavery Studies 2
Bonny 197
Bosma, Ulbe 8
botanical gardens 152, 155, 158–60, 172n27
Boulvware, Samuel 111
Bourdieu, Pierre 120, 303
bourgeoisie 283, 284, 289, 290, 291–2, 304n19
Brand, Ulrich 246
Brass, Tom 90
Braudel, Fernand 217
  *The Wheels of Commerce* 61
Brazil 74, 76, 88, 228, 324
  abolition of the slave trade 193, 199–200
  agriculture 168
  coerced labour 95
  communism 319
  crops 154
  indentured labour 205
  Italian immigrants 131
  labour management 185
  'modern slavery' 84
  'Negro Republic' of Palmares 270
  trade unions 320
  uprisings 306
  and USA 311
breadwinners 34, 70, 227
Breman, Jan 11, 43–52, 100–1
Brentano, Lujo: *On the History and Development of Gilds, and the Origin of Trade Unions* 4
brickmakers 7
Briefs, Götz 31
Britain *see* Great Britain
British India *see* India
broad labour 3, 4
Brock, Ditmar 120
Brown, John 185–6
Bukharin, Nikolai: *Imperialism and World Economy* 245
Burma *see* Myanmar
business organization 163–5
Butler, Harold 223

*Cahiers de doléances* (petitions) 34
Cairnes, John E. 142
Callinicos, Alex 103–4
Canada 1, 3
Canetti, Elias 280
canning processes 167

capitalism 3, 5, 11–12, 44, 57–61
  alternatives 248
  definitions 61–4
  expansion 308
  labour management 175, 177
  labour markets 142–3, 146
  patterns and trends 66–8
  periods and types 64–6
  plantations 27–8
  precarious labour 36
  relational inequality 244, 246
  revolution 14, 297–8
  slavery 30, 31–2, 38, 39–40
  socialism 299–300
  work relationships 79–80
  working classes 76–9, 229–30, 284–7, 301
  *see also* merchant capitalism
caregiving workers 7, 326
Caribbean 13, 31, 38, 184, 285
  abolition 85–6, 191, 192, 198, 201
  cash–crop transfers 157–8
  *see also* individual countries; plantations
Carlin, Norah 289
Carlyle, Thomas 59
Carroll, Lewis: *Through the Looking Glass, and What Alice Found There* 263–4
cash payment 59
cash-crop transfers 13, 151–8, 163–5, 193
  growing and harvesting 161–3
  labour 165–6
  seeds and seedlings 158–61
  transportation and sale 166–8, 170–1
Cassis, Youssef 67
Castro, Fidel 294
casual labour *see* precarious labour
causal mechanisms 266–7
Cave, Gen Basil 196
Ceylon 21, 156, 158, 206, 210
  planters 184, 185
chain gangs 208–9
Chainworkers of Milan 32–3
Chandler, Alfred: *The Visible Hand* 176–7
change 259–66
Chargola Exodus 271–2, 280
Chartist movement 284
chattel slaves *see* slavery
Chau, Nancy 105
cheap foreign labour 7
Chesneaux, Jean: *Le mouvement ouvrier en Chine de 1919 à 1927* 46
child labour 7, 105, 319
children 90–1, 112–13
Chile 230, 311
China 58, 62, 135, 175
  agriculture 130
  capitalism 251
  coerced labour 89, 96
  communism 295–6
  convict labour 209, 212
  crops 151–2, 153–4, 155
  Cultural Revolution 307, 311
  globalization 255n30
  indentured labour 137, 205–6, *207*
  labour markets 138, 143
  migration 322
  military markets 132

INDEX 381

porcelain production 285, *286*
socialism 248
Taiping Rebellion 269
trade unions 317
uprisings 289, 306, 325
Chinchona, Countess 22, 23
Chomsky, Aviva 7
*Cinchona* tree 22–6, 161
cinnamon production 10–11, 21–2
citizenship 299
Civil Rights Movement 312
Clarkson, Thomas 191
class *see* aristocracy; bourgeoisie; working classes
Clio Infra 9
clove trees 163
Cobban, Alfred 266–7
Coclanis, Peter 181
coconuts 151, 165, 249
*Code of Hammurabi* 89, 108n18
coelacanths 259, *260*
coerced labour 7, 8, 11, 12, 13, 102–3, 134
   conceptual clarification 85–8
   definition 84–5
   employers 109n39
   entry 88–96
   exit 99–102
   ILO 225
   labour extraction 96–9
   multicausality 103–7
   quinine 24–8
coffee production 29n17, 157, 162, 164, 166
   Ceylon 184
   ecology 163
   expansion 170, 171
cognition 264–6
Collaborative for World-Historical Information 9
collective action 14, 71, 103–4, 113–14, 117–18; *see also* mass desertion; strikes
colonialism 5, 8, 40, 45–6
   abolition of the slave trade 210–11
   Africa 211–12
   coerced labour 93–4
   ILO 225
   indentured labour 205–6
   labour management 182, 183, 184–5
   labour markets 135–6, 143, 144–5
   local populations 249
   quinine 22–3, 26
   relational inequality 244–6
   working classes 48
   *see also* anti-colonialism; decolonization; Dutch East Indies; forced labour
Columbian Exchange 153, 154
commitment 97, 98–9
Committee for the Abolition of the Slave Trade 190–1
commodified labour 11–12, 31, 37, 39–40, 62–3
commodities 8, 73, 76–8, 115, 127–9
   semi-capitalism 248
   *see also* commodified labour; supply chains
Commons, John 4

communism 38, 46, 219, 221, 222
   China 295–6
   parties 317, 319, 320
   Vietnam 296–7
community pressure 92–3
commuters 50–1
*compadrazgo* (fictitious parenthood) 117
compensation 97, 98, 200
competition 63, 64
concentration camps 96, 212, 272
conditional exit 101, 108n15
Conermann, Stephan 2
Congo *see* Belgian Congo
Conrad, Robert 193
conservatism 264–6
constrained choice 87
consumer goods 249–50, 302
contract labourers 6, 10, 74, 80, 206; *see also* indentured labour
convict labourers 7, 13, 181–2, 208–9, 272, 277
coolies *see* contract labourers; indentured labour
cooperatives 3, 8, 14, 165, 316–17
Cope, Zak 246
Copernicus, Nicolaus 261
   *De revolutionibus orbium coelestium* 283
Cottenham, Green 95
cotton production 8, 40, 151, 154, 250
   abolition 193
   consumer goods 249
Courten, Sir William 40
Cowie, Jefferson 7
Cox, Oliver Cromwell 38, 40
Cox, Robert 221, 237–8
Cramer, Charles Guillaume 251
credit 63, 106
Crenshaw, Kimberlé 75
crops *see* cash–crop transfers
crossopterygians 259–60
Cuba 185, 193, 198, 200, 228, 306
   Revolution 294, 307, 311
Cumbler, J. T. 141
Curthoys, Ann 75
Cusack, Jake 212

Dafert, Franz Wilhelm 168
Das Gupta, Ranajit: *Labour and Working Class in Eastern India* 46
De Vries, Jan 134
death 101
debt peonage 7, 12, 103, 203–4
   child labour 105
   coerced labour 90, 95–6
Decent Work concept 233–4
Declaration on Fundamental Principles and Rights at Work 233, 234
decolonization 5, 310–11
deflection 301, 303
Denmark 189, 319
desertion 269–80
diamond mining 8
direct rule 298–300
direct wages 98
discipline 176, 181, 185

Ditchfield, Peter 139
dockers 46, 125, 132, 243, 247
Domar, Evsey: 'The causes of slavery and serfdom' 104
domestic workers 7, 326
Dovring, Folke 105
Dufty, Norman 226
Durkheim, Emile: *De la division du travail* 60
Dutch East India Company 141
Dutch East Indies 23, 45, 168, 251
  Bogor Botanical Garden *159*
  Cultivation System 165
  debt peonage 204
  *see also* Java
Dutch Revolt 290, 291
Dutch West Indies Company 189

Eastern Europe 7, 248
Eckert, Andreas 2
Eco, Umberto: *Kant and the Platypus* 265
ecology 13, 163
economics 308
  centrally planned 248–9
  coerced labour 104–5
  crises 65–6, 67, 69n38
  international links 315–16
  *see also* capitalism; labour markets
Ecuador 23
education 60, 308–9; *see also* universities
Egypt 58, 175, 196, 274–5, 325
Elias, Norbert 63
Elster, Joe 267
Eltis, David 137
Ely, Richard T.: *The Labor Movement in America* 4
Emmanuel, Arghiri 246
Emmerij, Louis 231
employers 70, 73, 220–1
  coerced labour 99–101, 105–6, 109n39
  indentured labour 136
  labour markets 144, 145, 146
  pseudo-contracts 202–3
employment 33–4, 250–1, 253; *see also* employers; underemployment; unemployment
*engagés à temps* 202, 205
Engels, Friedrich 303
  *Manifesto of the Communist Party* 59
  *Principles of Communism* 284
Engerman, Stanley 105, 107
England 135, 139, *140*, 284, 306
  migration 141, 142
  Revolution 289, 290–1
Epstein, Stephan 143
escape *see* desertion
Esch, Elizabeth 183
Esping-Anderson, Gøsta: *The Three Worlds of Welfare Capitalism* 66
Ethiopia 90–1, 312
Eurocentrism 4–5
Europe *see* individual countries
European Labour History Network 2
exchange 127–9
exit *see* desertion
expenditure 114–15

exploitation 246–7, 250, 252–4
explorers 261

factories 175, 176, 184, 185, 186, 219
Fair Trade League 250
families 11, 12, 33–4, 45–8, 59–60, 70–1
  households 111–13, 116–17
  strategies 118–21
  subsistence labour 72–4
Fanon, Frantz: *The Wretched of the Earth* 48, 49
feminism 12–13, 40
Ferguson, Adam 175
Ferrand, Comte de: *Considérations sur la révolution sociale* 283
financialization 324
Fink, Leon 1
Finland 319
Finley, Moses 86
First International 8, 243
first international division of labour 248
First World War *see* World War I
flax production 151
Fogel, Robert 179
Foner, Philip 4
food *see* cash–crop transfers
food riots 114, 121
forced labour *see* coerced labour
Fordism 227, 229, 231, 247, 302
Foucault, Michel 176, 186, 187
France 3, 5, 135, 225
  abolition of the slave trade 192, 198, 202
  globalization 255n30
  indentured labour 205
  labour management 176
  quinine 23
  and the state 298
  strikes 284
  trade 232–3
  uprisings 289, 297, 310
  *see also* French Revolution
Frederick II of Prussia, King 271
Frederick William I of Prussia, King 275
free choice 94
'free' wage labour 94, 103
French Revolution 270, 288, 291–2
Fridenson, Patrick 66
Furåker, Bengt 126

gang system *179*, 180–1, 187n30
*ganhadores* (slaves-for-hire) 74, 88
Geertz, Clifford 206, 208
gender *see* men; women
*General Labour History of Africa* (Bellucci/Eckert) 9
Germany 117, 121, 133, 176
  bonded labour 135
  desertions 271, 273
  revolution 283, 284, 305n53
  uprisings 306
  *see also* Nazi Germany
Gilbreth, Frank and Lillian 13, 182
Global Collaboratory on the History of Labour Relations, 1500–2000 9–10
global economic crises 65–6
global labour history 1–10
Global Labour History Network 2

Global South *see* South, the
globalization 13, 67, 145–6, 248
    crops 155–8, 170–1
    labour movements 319–21
    supply chains 255n30
    working classes 251–3
Goffman, Erving 186–7
Gompers, Samuel 222
goods and services 252–3
Goosen, Hendrick 259
Gordon, Charles 196
Gouldner, Alvin 288–9
Gramsci, Antonio 175
Gras, Norman 61
Great Britain 5, 176, 183–4, 225, 319
    abolition of the slave trade 13, 189, 191–2, 197, 198, 218
    Kenya 212
    peasant rebellions 262
    quinine 23
    sugar 31
    Sulu Sultanate 211
    *see also* England
Great Powers 189–90
Greece 319, 325; *see also* ancient Greece
greed 64, 69n32
Green Revolution 168, 170, 173n63
Gregory XVI, Pope: *In Supremo* 192
Guatemala 306
Guérin, Daniel 289, 291–2
Guevara, Che 311
Guinea Bissau 311
Guizot, François 218
Gujarat 11, 45, 46–7, 50, 51, 100–1
Guyana 311

Haarer, A. E.: *Modern Coffee Production* 162
Haas, Ernst 224
Habsburg Empire 100
Haiti 73, 101, 106, 184, 189, 288, 289
    sugarcane *164*
Hammond, John and Barbara 4
Hareven, Tamara 116, 120
Harris, William 132
Hasskarl, Julius C. 23
Haupt, Georges 293
Hawai'i 161, 167
Herodotus 26
    *Histories* 21
Hess, Moses 284, 303
Hicks, John 139
Hilferding, Rudolf 66
hiring fairs 139, *140*
hiring-out 88
Hirschman, Albert 321
Hobsbawm, Eric 4, 262, 320
Hocket, Charles 261
Hoerder, Dirk 289
Hofmeester, Karin 8, 9–10
household labour 11, 36–8, 39, 47–8, 227
    Aristotle 86–7
    budgets 122n27
    principles 111–16
    strategies 116–21
human rights 189–90
Humboldt, Alexander von 24, 25, 172n28

Ibn Khaldûn 58–9
ideology 106
ILO *see* International Labour Organization
impediment 100–1
imperialism *see* colonialism
income *see* wage workers
incorporation 301–3
indentured labour 10, 74
    abolition 204–6, *207*
    capitalism 62
    desertion 271–2
    labour markets 136, 137–8
India 62, 182, 228
    abolition of the slave trade 198
    agriculture 43
    coerced labour 96, 134
    communism 319
    convict labour 208
    crops 152, *153*, 157
    debt peonage 204
    desertions 269, 271–2, 273, 280
    indentured labour 137–8, 205–6
    jute 141–2
    migration 184–5, 322
    prison camps 277
    quinine 23
    slavery 133
    strikes 325
    sugar 31
    trade unions 320, 326
    uprisings 306
    *see also* Gujarat
indigenous labour 7, 23–8
indigo production 40, 161
indirect benefits 246–7
indirect wages 98
Indonesia 5, 8, 152; *see also* Java
Industrial Revolution 79, 143, 155, 175, 263
Industrial Workers of the World (IWW) 262
industrialization 247–8, 251–2
informal sector 49–50
insecurity *see* precarious labour
intermediaries 96, 142
International Association for Labour Legislation 219
International Association Strikes and Social Conflicts 2
International Confederation of Free Trade Unions (ICFTU) 221, 317
International Federation of Trade Unions (IFTU) 221, 222
International Institute of Social History (IISH) 2
*International Labor and Working Class History* (journal) 1
International Labour Office 221
International Labour Organization (ILO) 8, 9, 13–14, 217–19, 235–8
    coerced labour 84, 85, 100, 106
    Conventions and Recommendations 223–4, 241n87–8
    operations 220–2
    Philadelphia Declaration 225–7
    prosperity 222–3

soul-searching 229–35
standards 190
technical assistance 228–9
and USA 227–8
International Monetary Fund (IMF) 231, 232
international pressure 106
*International Review of Social History* (journal) 1
International Trade Union Confederation (ITUC) 221, 317
intersectionality 75
invisible wages 98
Iran 294, 306
Iraq 133, 270
Islam 152, 159
Italy 32–3, 131, 142, 287–8, 306, 319

Jacobson, Harold 221
Jamaica 198
James, C. L. R. 38, 40
    *The Black Jacobins: Toussaint L'Ouverture and the San Domingo Revolution* 30–2
James, Harold 63
James, Selma 39
    *The Power of Women and the Subversion of the Community* 37
Japan 23, 35, 295
    coerced labour 89, 92, *93*
    colonialism 135
    crops 152–3
    revolution 289
    slavery 132, 133, 134
Java 8, 23, 26–7, 29n17, 158
    Cultivation System 206, 208, 250
Jesuits 22, 23
Jews 274–5
Judd, Walter H. 227–8
jute 141–2

Kalecki, Michał 229
Kalleberg, Arne 145
Keiser, Thorsten 135
Kenya 212
Khubilai Khan 152
Kiernan, Victor 309
kinship 92–3, 116–17
Kirk, Neville 7
Knowles, P. F. 161
Kolchin, Peter 271
Komlosy, Andrea 9, 65
Korea 92, *93*, 132, 152–3
Kottak, Conrad 261
Kumar, Dharma 46
Kuttner, Erich 289, 290

*Labor: Studies in Working-Class History* (journal) 1
Laborie, P. J.: *Coffee Planter of Saint Domingo* 185
labour camps 87
labour extraction 96–9
labour history *see* global labour history
labour management 175–8
    circulation of knowledge 182–7
    direct supervision 178–81
    standardization 181–2

labour markets 11, 13, 125–7, 146–7
    concepts 127–9
    early history 129–35
    expansion 144–6
    integration 143–4
    segmentation 142–3
    transcontinental 135–42
Labour parties 317–18
labour processes 10–11, 43–5, 62–3, 220
    cinnamon 21–2
    colonies 45–6
    quinine 23–8
labour supply 105–6
labour-tax system 206, 208
labouring poor *see* working classes
Latin America 1, 5, 35, 192–3, 231
    crops 151, 153
    *see also* individual countries
League of Nations 84, 219, 221, 222
legislation 106
Legrand, Daniel 218
Lenin, Vladimir 30, 244–5
Lerner, Abba 246
Levasseur, Emile 3
Lewis, Su Lin 245
liberalism 4
Liebig, Justus von 168
Linebaugh, Peter 73
    *The Many-Headed Hydra* 7
Locke, John 89
longshoremen 7
Lora, Guillermo: *Historia del movimento obrero boliviano* 46
loyalty 275–6
Lucassen, Jan 8, 9, 125–6
Lucassen, Leo 8
Luddism 306
lumpenproletariat 48, 49, 70, 74
Lumumba, Patrice 311
Luxemburg, Rosa 36–7, 245

McCulloch, John Ramsay 64
MacEwan, Arthur 140
McKeown, Adam 8
MacLennan, Carol 161
Macquarie, Lachlan 181–2
Madagascar 199
Magdoff, Harry 248
Magellan Exchange 153, 154
mail runners 7
Maine, Sir Henry: *Ancient Law* 59–60
malaria 22–3, 25
Malaya 46, 158, 184
Malaysia 313
management *see* labour management
Mandel, Ernest 67
Manning, Brian 289
Manning, Patrick 9
Maoism 311
maritime labour 141, 144–5
markets 58, 125–6, 132, 139, *140*
*marronage* 270–1, 276, 279
Marshall, William 139
Marx, Karl 5, 12, 43, 44, 303
    capitalism 31, 39, 41n32, 62, 63
    commodities 127, 128

labour management 177
*Manifesto of the Communist Party* 59
pioneers 162
production 27
proletariat 73, 283–4, 301–2
slavery 32, 82n2, 86
surplus population 35
wage workers 76–9, 83n28, 83n34
mass desertion 269–80
Mau Mau rebellion 212
Mauritius 195, 198
mechanisms 266–7
medicine 22, 25, 151–2, 155, 157
men 34, 70, 115–16, 227
mercenaries 130, 132, 138, 140, 273, 280
merchant capitalism 66, 323–4
Merleau-Ponty, Maurice 120
 *Phénoménologie de la perception* 266
Merrill, Michael 263
Mészáros, István 146
Mexico 7, 58, 292, 307, 311, 319
Middle East 21, 66, 125–6, 136, 152, 261, 190
migrants 5, 8, 10, 50–1, 80, 209, 316
 Brazil 131
 England 141, 142
 families 112, 116
 indentured labour 136, 137–8
 mass movement 321–3
 planters 184–5
military service 7, 38, 71, 90, 130
 desertion 269, 270, 275, 277–8, 280, 282n47
 markets 132–3
Millar, John 286
miners 7, 8, 80, 133, 206, *207*
 revolution 290
Mironov, Boris 289
mobile phones 252–3
'modern slavery' 84–5
molecular desertion 269
money 63, 64, 69n32, 127–8
monopoly mechanism 63
Montesquieu 89
Moore, Barrington 96
Moorhouse, Bert 302
morality 243–4
Morse, David 223, 227, 228
motorization 252
Mozambique *91*, 194, 208, 311
Murray, Hubert 206
Myanmar 236, 306, 313

Napoleonic wars 298
narrow labour 3, 4
Nash, Gary B. 291
nation-states 4, 5, 64, 143, 221
nationalism 4
Nazi Germany 96, 212, 216n101, 222
Necker, Jacques 218
neoliberalism 145
Netherlands 5, 8, 185, 225, 319
 abolition of the slave trade 192, 198
 labour markets 134, 135
 quinine 23, 26
 Sulu Sultanate 211

textile workers 274
*see also* Dutch East Indies
Nevinson, Henry 203
New Lanark 186
Nietzsche, Friedrich:
 *Gay Science* 60
 *On the Genealogy of Morals* 15
Nigeria 5
non-governmental organizations (NGOs) 84–5, 319
North Africa 134
North, the 35–6, 144–5, 183–4, 249–50, 227
 cash-crop transfers 156, 158, 166–71
 exploitation 243, 244, 246–7, 253–4
 *see also* United States of America
Nosow, Sigmund 146
Nun, José 35

O'Brien, Patrick 247
October Revolution *see* Russia
Olmstedt, Frederick M. 180–1
Oppenheimer, Franz 78
Organization for Economic Cooperation and Development (OECD) 231
organized capitalism 66
Ortelius, Abraham: *Théâtre de l'Universe* 157
Osterhammel, Jürgen 135
Ottoman Empire 133, 194, 196
overseeing 179–80, 183
Owen, Robert 186

Padmore, George 38, 40
Pakistan 289, 306
palaeontology 259–61
Palestine–Israel conflict 230
palm oil 193–4, 249
Pan-Africanism 5, 7
Panama Canal 167
panopticism 186
pantometry 60
Papua New Guinea 206
Paris uprising (1968) 14
Parmer, J. Norman: *Colonial Labor Policy and Administration* 46
Passow, Richard 57
Patnaik, Utsa 249
patriarchy 34, 58, 86–7
patronage 47, 117
Patterson, Orlando 89, 105
peasantry 28, 34, 37, 48, 72–3, 117, 130
 change 263
 child labour 105
 crops 165
 desertion 271, 273, 275–6
 impediments 100
 markets 58
 Marx 86
 rebellion 262, 281n25
 revolution 292, 293–4
 Russian Revolution 266
 subsistence 94
Peasants' Wars 289–90
Peebles, Patrick 185, 206
pensions 231–2
peonage *see* debt peonage
pepper 152–3, 157

personal communities 117, 123n43
Peru 22, 23–4, 26–7
Peterson, Jean 117
petty bourgeoisie 49
Petty, William 155, 182
Phelan, Craig 1, 2
Phelan, Edward 226, 230
Philadelphia Declaration 226, 234
Philippines 8, 117
physical compulsion 87, 96, 108n15
Piketty, Thomas 67
Pinochet, Augusto 230
Pirenne, Henri 61–2
plantations 29n17, 50, 79, 202, 210
   abolition of slavery 200–1
   cash-crop transfers 157–8
   desertion 271–2, 276–7
   exploitation 246
   indentured labour 137, 138, 206
   labour management 183–4, 185–6, 187
   migrants 184–5
   quinine 26–8
   strikes 80–1
   sugar 13, 31, 40
plants (industrial complexes) 183
Plassey, Battle of 31
Polányi, Karl 219
Polish Revolution 294
politics 3–4, 30–1, 317–19
Polo, Marco 264–5
Portugal 135, 153–4, 192, 225, 311, 325
poverty 89–90
Prague Spring 307, 311
Pre-Columbian empires 90, 135
Precario, San 32–3, 36, 39, 40
precarious labour 11, 34–6, 40–1, 50, 130
   growth 230
   labour markets 145–6
   San Precario 32–3
prisons 176, 186, 212; *see also* convict labourers
profit 11, 31, 37, 38, 59, 61–3
proletariat 43–4, 48, 73, 134–5, 302
   revolution 283–4, 292–3, 297–8
property rights 63, 64, 68n24, 127–8
prostitution 7
protests *see* uprisings
Przeworski, Adam 298, 299–300
pseudo-contracts 202–3

Quataert, Jean 39
Quesnay, François 155
Quijano, Aníbal 35
quinine production 10–11, 22–8

Rabinowitch, Alexander 289
race 38, 106, 144, 312; *see also* slavery
radicalism 262–3, 283–9
Radio Corporation of America 7
Rawski, Evelyn Sakakida 130
're: work – Work and Human Life Cycle in Global History' 2
real subsumption 177–82
rebellion 262, 269, 306–13

Red International of Labour Unions (Profintern) 222
Red Queen effect 263–4, 266, 267
Rediker, Marcus 73
   *The Many-Headed Hydra* 7
REDLATT network 2
relational inequality 244–6
religion 58; *see also* Islam
resistance 7, 8, 14, 80–2, 106, 117–18
retail corporations 323
*REVLATT* (journal) 2
revolutions 3, 14, 259, 289–95, 303
   Bolshevik 219, 266
   bourgeoisie 304n19
   China 295–6
   desertion 270
   Haiti 73, 101, 106, 184, 189
   Italy 287–8
   Jamaica 198
   Vietnam 296–7
   working classes 283–5
   *see also* anarchist movements; rebellion
Rhodesia 46
Roediger, David 183
Roman Empire 125, 131, 132, 133
Romer, Alfred Sherwood 259–61
Romer's Rule 14, 261–4, 266, 267
Rosenbaum, Heidi 117
Rosenberg, Nathan 162
Rostovtzeff, Michael 62
Rousseau, Jean-Jacques 89
rubber production 28n15, 46, 158, 184
   transportation 151, 154, 161, 252
Rudé, George 262
runaways 7, 269–80
rural areas *see* agriculture
Russia 89–90, 96, 194, 306
   Revolution 266, 289, 293, 297
   serfs 100, 271
   *see also* Soviet Union
Ryder, Guy 234

Said, Seyyid, Imam of Muscat 195
sailors 7, 141, 270, 273
Saint-Domingue *see* Haiti
sanctions 235–6
sandalwood 152
Santiago-Valles, Kelvin 75
Schiller, Friedrich 155
Schoenberger, Erica 132
Schumpeter, Joseph 47
Sciascia, Leonardo 307
Scientific Management 176, 185
Screpanti, Ernesto 308
seasonal variations 105
Second International 243
seeds and seedlings 158–61, 168, 172n28
Seidman, Bert 229
self-employment 49–50, 70, 73
self-sale 88–90
selling 88–9
Selznik, Philip 99
semi-capitalism 248

INDEX    **387**

serfs 24, 28, 37, 62, 74
    desertion 271
    emancipation 100
    strikes 80
Seven Years' War 270
sexism 106
sharecropping 12, 72–3, 80, 202
Shen Nung, Emperor 151–2
shipbuilders 7
Sierra Leone 189, 194
Silverstein, Josef 313
Singapore 313
slavery 6, 7, 10, 11, 12, 74, 79–80, 87
    Barbados 178–81
    capitalism 30, 31–2, 38, 39–40, 62, 65
    conspicuous consumption 194–5
    desertion 270–1, 276–80
    exchange 129
    families 111
    labour management 176–7, 183–4, 185–6, 187, 191
    labour markets 130–2, 133, 136–7, 139–40, 141
    Marx 76–9
    resistance 117–18
    strikes 80–1
    see also abolition; coerced labour; Haiti; 'modern slavery'
Smith, Adam 44, 62, 104, 127, 155
Social Democrat parties 317–18
social security 34
socialism 4, 7, 248, 299–300
    relational inequality 245, 246
society 58–60
soldiers 7
soldiers see military service
solidarity 243
Somavía, Juan 234
Sombart, Werner 60–1, 177
Songjong, King 152–3
South, the 1, 5, 14–15, 28, 40, 175, 183–7
    cash-crop transfers 156, 158, 160–1, 168
    exploitation 243, 244, 246–7, 253–4
    ILO 228, 230
    industrialization 247–8, 251–2
    labour markets 144–5
    migration 322
    underemployment 35, 36
    working classes 73
South Africa 8, 80, *207*, 208, 210
    apartheid 243
    Communist Party 319
    exploitation 246
    strikes 325–6
    student uprisings 312
Southey, Robert: *Journal of a Tour in Scotland* 186
South–North transfer 183–4
South–South transfer 184–7
Soviet Union 7, 98–9, 212, 222, 230, 248
    economics 254n12
    labour camps 277, 282n45
Spain 135, 153–4, 192, 211, 290, 325
spices 154, 155, 156, 157, 167, 253
Stalin, Joseph 222

Standard Employment Relationship 33–4, 35–6, 40
Standing, Guy 230
Stanziani, Alessandro 7–8
states 298–302
Stein, Lorenz von: *The Socialism and Communism of Contemporary France* 283
Sternberg, Fritz 245–6, 321
Stetson, Sarah 160
stigma 277
Stone, Lawrence 289
Strabo 132
strikes 3, 5, 80–2, 308, 325–6
    households 120
    solidarity 243
students 306–7, 309–10, 311, 312–13
Sturmthal, Adolf 322–3
sub-proletariat 49
subaltern households 12–13
subsistence labour 37, 40, 73–4, 129–30
Sudan 195–6
Suez Canal 167, 194
sugar production 13, 31, 40, 76, 166
    abolition of slavery 192, 193, 198
    Barbados 178–81
    business organization 163–5
    Hawai'i 161
    medicinal uses 157
    migrants 184
Sulu Sultanate 211
supervision 106
supply chains 8, 252, 253, 315–16
Suriname 10, 189, 276–7, *279*
Switzerland 218–19
Sydney 181–2
syndicalist movements 7

Tannenbaum, Frank 262–3
Tarbuck, Ken 248
*Taufpaten* (godparents) 117
Tawney, R. H.: *Religion and the Rise of Capitalism* 57
taxametrization 60–1
taxation 93–4
Taylor, Frederick Winslow 175
tea production 138, 184, 206, 271–2, 280
teach-ins 312
Temin, Peter 125
textile workers 7, 46, 115, 120, 141, 250–1
    cotton 183, 249
    Germany 264
    India 96
    Italy 285, 287
    Netherlands 274, 290
Thailand 306, 313
Thomas, Albert 220–1, 223, 224
Thompson, E. P. 71, 261–2
    *The Making of the English Working Class* 4
Thorner, Daniel and Alice 46
Thun, Alphons 264
Tilly, Charles 134, 298
time 60–1, 98, 175, 177
tobacco production 40

Tönnies, Ferdinand: *Gemeinschaft und Gesellschaft* 60
tourism 247, 253
trade 21–2, 57–9, 229, 232–3, 255n30
   slaves 191, 192, 193–7
   *see also* cash–crop transfers
trade unions 3, 4, 8, 14, 49
   colonialism 243
   decline 317, 320
   ILO 221, 222, 224, 233
   internationalism 312
   radicalism 262–3
   the state 299
   students 309–10
Trades Union Congress (TUC) 3
training 175
transcontinental labour markets 135–42
transition dip 298–300
transport 140–1, 166–7, 252, 266
Trebilcock, Anne 237
Trinidad 30
tropical goods 249–50
Trotsky, Leon 293
Trotskyism 46
Turkey 228

unconditional exit 101, 108n15
underemployment 14, 35, 321–3
Underground Railroad 280
unemployment 35, 229
unfree labour *see* bonded labour; child labour; coerced labour; convict labour; debt peonage; indentured labour; slavery
United Nations 10, 84, 221, 226, 230
United States of America (USA) 1, 5, 7, 176, 184
   abolition of the slave trade 192–3
   abolition of slavery 198, 201–2
   California Gold Rush 273
   Chinese immigrants 144
   Civil Rights Movement 312
   coerced labour 95
   colonies 136
   consumerism 302
   convict labour 208–9, 212
   debt bondage 204
   decolonization 311
   ILO 222, 223, 227–8, 230
   labour markets 131–2
   migrants 141, 142
   pseudo-contracts 203
   quinine 23
   slavery 76, 80, 180–1
   strikes 326
   trade 232–3
   unemployment 35
   *see also* American Civil War; American Revolution
universities 2; *see also* students
uprisings 5, 14, 306–13
urban areas 50
USSR *see* Soviet Union

Vakulabharana, Vamsi 323
Van Nederveen Meerkerk, Elise 8
Van Onselen, Charles: *Chibaro* 46

Van Rossum, Matthias 141, 144–5
Van Valen, Leigh 264
Van Zanden, Jan Luiten 9
Venezuela 228, 306
Versailles Treaty (1919) 219
Vietnam 5, 296–7, 307, 311
voice 274–6, 281n27
Volkswagen (VW) 324
Vosko, Leah 234

Wacquant, Loïc 209
wage fund 3–4
wage workers 7, 11, 13, 130
   capitalism 31–2
   definition 70–1
   exploitation 246–7
   formation 71–2
   households 114–15
   ILO 220–1
   labour markets 138–41
   Marx 76–9
   peripheral 72–3, 74
   socialization 108n31
   Standard Employment 33–4, 35–6
   strikes 80–2
Wakefield, Edward 104
Walk Free Foundation 84–5
Wallerstein, Immanuel 5, 9, 62, 63, 66, 155
war 107; *see also* American Civil War; World War I; World War II
Ward, Nathaniel 160–1
Webb, Beatrice and Sidney 4
Weber, Max 5, 31, 43, 44, 62, 64
Weddell, Hugh 23, 24–5
welfare states 67, 144, 236
Wellcome, Henry 25
West Indies *see* Caribbean
Wickham, Chris 130
Wickham, Henry A. 158
Wilkins, Ernest 228
Williams, Eric 40
   *Capitalism and Slavery* 30–2, 183
Willoughby, Francis 40
Wissen, Markus 246
Wolff, Richard 302
Wolff, Tobias 203–4
Wolitzky, Alexander 105
women 8, 34, 142–3, 227, 252
   household labour 11, 36–8, 39, 115–16
   India 326
   kinship 123n43
   *see also* feminism
workers *see* wage workers; working classes
workers' parties 3, 14
workers' rights 34, 232, 233–4
working classes 3, 4, 5–6, 7, 45, 48–9
   '1968' uprisings 306, 313
   China 295–6
   consumer goods 249
   definition 70–1
   exploitation 246–7, 253–4
   feminism 12–13
   globalization 251–3
   increased power 229–30

international solidarity 243–4, 311–12
peripheral 72–5
rebellious culture 261–2
relational inequality 244–6
revolution 14, 283–95, 297–8
Standard Employment 34
the state 298–302, 305n49
strike action 325–6
supply chains 315–16
World Anti-Slavery Convention (1840) 198
World Bank 231–2
World Employment Programme (WEP) 230–1
World Federation of Trade Unions 221
World Trade Organization (WTO) 232–3
World War I 219, 270
World War II 225–6, 275

xenophobia 144

Zanzibar 163, 194, 195–6
Zewde, Bahru 312

Ingram Content Group UK Ltd.
Milton Keynes UK
UKHW022052150523
421784UK00003B/19